Exploring Art

GLENCOE
Macmillan/McGraw-Hill

Understanding Art

Picture the perfect art course:

STUDENT EDITIONS

Exploring Art

Media Intensive The media experience energizes students to discover how artists are inspired and why they choose a particular medium of expression. From drawing and painting to architecture, graphic design and photography, chapters interweave studio production with narrative lessons on the elements and principles of art, techniques, art history and criticism. This curriculum yields a first-hand appreciation for artists' skills as well as the basis to evaluate the art itself.

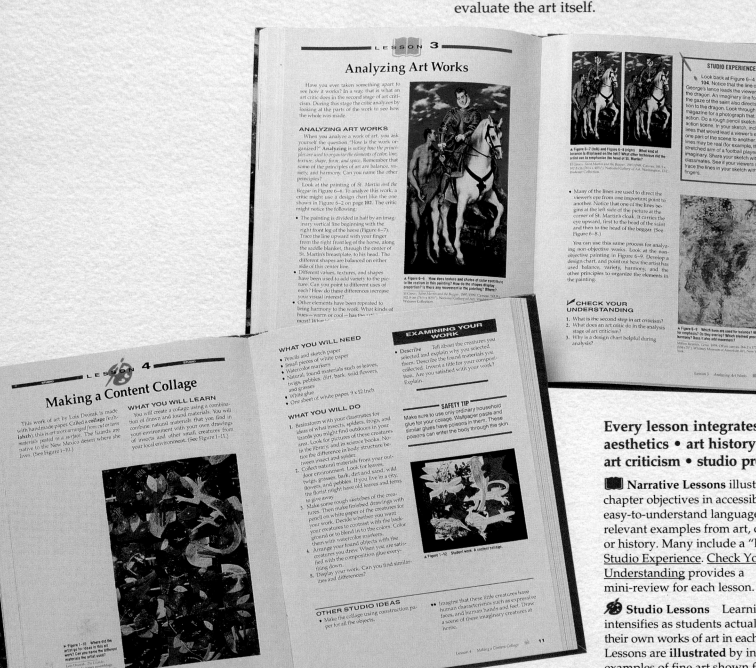

Every lesson integrates:
aesthetics • art history
art criticism • studio production

Narrative Lessons illustrate chapter objectives in accessible, easy-to-understand language, using relevant examples from art, daily life or history. Many include a "hands-on" Studio Experience. Check Your Understanding provides a mini-review for each lesson.

Studio Lessons Learning intensifies as students actually create their own works of art in each medium. Lessons are **illustrated** by intriguing examples of fine art shown full frame and in detail. Features: Examining Your Work (applied art criticism), Other Studio Ideas, Safety Tips.

Whether your focus is hands-on . . .

Understanding Art

Art & Culture From earliest time to the contemporary, this student text blends art history with the religious, political, geographical, and social events which make each culture's art unique. Traditions of Western Europe are augmented by those of China, Japan, India and Africa. Each narrative lesson includes a studio experience to heighten understanding. And studio lessons build active involvement while balancing aesthetic and critical values.

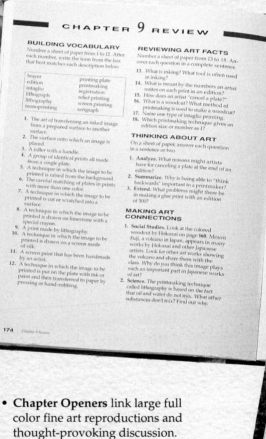

- **Chapter Openers** link large full color fine art reproductions and thought-provoking discussion. This interactive format engages students' thinking and provides activities to reinforce each chapter's primary goal.

- **Chapter Reviews** include Building Vocabulary, Reviewing Art Facts, Thinking About Art, Making Art Connections, and Looking At The Details.

- **50-page handbook** (uniquely developed to support each text) enriches learning with Artist Profiles, Career Spotlights, Studio Extensions and Technique Tips.

- **Features ethnic, women and minority artists.**

- **Representative student work** builds interest, motivation and confidence.

. . . . . . *or discussion* . . . .

TEACHER'S WRAPAROUND EDITION

The first middle school/ junior high art textbooks to offer a Teacher's Wraparound Edition.
Sized-down Student Text pages surrounded by teaching materials save you time and effort while enhancing every lesson.

LESSON 6

Creating Visual Movement

LESSON PLAN
(pages 92–93)

Objectives
After completing this lesson, students will be able to:
- Create construction paper designs that express visual movement.
- Describe their own designs.

Supplies
- Small pieces of construction paper; red, yellow, orange, blue, green, and violet.
- Sports magazines or other magazines from which students can cut action figures; scissors; fine-tip markers; sheets of cool-colored construction paper, 12 x 18 inches (30 x 46 cm); sheets of warm-colored construction paper, 9 x 12 inches (23 x 30 cm); pencils; erasers; glue; envelopes, 9 1/2 x 4 inches (24 x 10 cm).
- Reproductions of Marcel Duchamp's *Nude Descending a Staircase*, Umberto Boccioni's *Dynamism of a Cyclist*, and/or Giacomo Balla's *Dynamism of a Dog on a Leash*; sheets of drawing paper; colored pencils.

TRB Resource
- 5-5 *Expressing Movement*, (studio)

TEACHING THE LESSON

Getting Started

Motivator. Begin by having students form small groups, and give each group six small pieces or scraps of construction paper in these colors: red, yellow, orange, blue, green, violet. Ask students in each group to categorize the colors: warm and cool. Then let them experiment with different combinations of warm and cool colors.

Vocabulary. Help students review the definitions of *movement* and *rhythm*. (Refer them to pages 90 and 91 if necessary.) Then let volunteers suggest several specific techniques for creating movement and rhythm in works of art.

LESSON 6 STUDIO · STUDIO

Creating Visual Movement

This painting by Jacob Lawrence has a strong sense of visual movement. The artist has used several special effects to create the feeling that the soldiers are surging forward. (See Figure 5–15.) First he used diagonal lines to form arrow-like movement to the right. Notice how the guns and hats slant down to the right, while the bodies of the soldiers slant up to the right. Second, he has repeated lines and shapes to create a visual rhythm that makes your eye move through the painting from left to right. The repetition of the waving vertical grasses balances the strong movement. This helps to rest the viewers' eyes.

WHAT YOU WILL LEARN

You will create a construction paper design using repeated silhouettes of one action figure. You will use visual rhythm to create a sense of visual movement. Use a cool color for the background and warm colors for the figures.

WHAT YOU WILL NEED

- One whole action figure cut from a magazine (sports magazines are good sources)
- Scissors and fine-tip marker
- One sheet of cool-colored construction paper, 12 x 18 inch (30 x 46 cm)
- Several sheets of warm-colored construction paper, 9 x 12 inch (23 x 30 cm)
- Pencil, eraser, and glue
- Envelope to hold cutouts, 9 1/2 x 4 inch (24 x 10 cm)

► Figure 5–15 What are the elements used in repetition? How do they also provide harmony?

Jacob Lawrence, *Toussaint L'Overture Series*, 1938. Tempera on paper, 46.4 x 61.6 cm (18¼ x 24¼"). Fisk University.

92   Lesson 6   *Creating Visual Movement*

WHAT YOU WILL DO

1. Look through magazines and newspapers to find a whole body of an action figure. Be sure the figure is complete with both hands and feet.
2. Using a fine-tip marker, outline the figure. Then carefully cut out the figure by cutting along the outline. You will use this figure for the motif of your design.
3. Select a sheet of cool-colored construction paper. This will be used for your background. Select several sheets of smaller pieces of warm-colored construction paper. These will be used for the figures. (See Figure 5–16.)
4. Place the magazine cutout figure on a piece of construction paper and trace around it. Conserve paper by arranging the tracing on one side of the paper and using the other half for another cutout. Cut out five, seven, or nine figures or silhouettes. Keep them in the envelope until you are ready to use them.
5. Experiment with several arrangements of the silhouettes on the background. You may want to include the original magazine cutout to create a center of interest. The figures may overlap. When you have an arrangement that shows visual movement, glue it to the background piece of construction paper.
6. Display your design. Compare the designs with those of your classmates, and look for different rhythmic beats. Which designs have a strong sense of movement?

EXAMINING YOUR WORK

- **Describe** Identify the action figure you selected. Did you cut it out carefully? What colors did you choose for the background? What colors did you choose for the cutout figures? Tell why, or why not, you chose to use the magazine cutout. Explain what kind of rhythm you created and how you achieved a feeling of visual movement.

▲ Figure 5–16 Student work. An action figure.

OTHER STUDIO IDEAS

- Do the visual movement problem above, but use complementary colors for the color scheme.
- Create a rhythmic design, using geometric shapes, that has a strong sense of movement. Use cool colors for the shapes and a warm color for the background.

Lesson 6   *Creating Visual Movement*   93

Developing Concepts

Exploring Aesthetics. Let students work in groups to discuss their responses to Lawrence's painting shown in Figure 5-15. How does this work make you feel? What aspects of the work evoke that response? How do you account for different responses among group members?

Understanding Art History. Let students use historical almanacs or other reference works to research the social and political climate during the time Jacob Lawrence painted *Toussaint L'Overture Series*. Then help them discuss how that climate may have influenced Lawrence's work.

Following Up

Closure. Let students work in small groups to discuss their designs, following the instructions in "Examining Your Work." After the group discussion, have each student write a short description of the rhythm and movement in his or her work (following the final step in the "Examining Your Work" instructions).

Evaluation. Review students' construction paper designs, listen to their contributions to group discussions, and read their descriptions of their work.

Reteaching. Work with small groups of students. Ask them to browse through this text (or other books with reproductions of art works). Have each group member identify and share several works that show the use of movement and rhythm.

Enrichment. Show students reproductions of Marcel Duchamp's *Nude Descending a Staircase*, Umberto Boccioni's *Dynamism of a Cyclist*, and/or Giacomo Balla's *Dynamism of a Dog on a Leash*. All these works show human figures in motion, using repetition, overlapping, and/or extensions of natural boundaries. Guide students in discussing and analyzing the movement in each painting. Then ask a volunteer to model a motion (such as walking or jumping rope); have the other students draw the movement of the model, using the techniques they have discussed.

Background Information

Jacob Lawrence (United States, born 1917) is an African American painter who first became famous during the Harlem Renaissance of the 1920s and 1930s.

Lawrence produced graphic images of urban life. As a Social Realist, he has used his art as a means of expressing his social values. Major themes in his work include violence and injustice. The uprootedness of African Americans is the subject of a series of paintings entitled *The Migration of the Negro* (1940–41). There are 60 individual works in this series.

A prolific artist, Lawrence has completed series of paintings on several different themes, including *War*, *Coast Guard*, *Sanitarium*, and *Life in Harlem*.

Cooperative Learning

Divide students into groups of three. Tell them the object of this lesson will be to create visual movement by showing the arc a ball takes when thrown through the air. Distribute a 9 x 12 (23 x 30 cm) piece of colored construction paper and a 12 x 18 (30 x 46 cm) piece of plain paper to each group. One student will draw 10 circles decreasing in size from about 3 inches (8 cm) to about 1 inch (2.5 cm). The second student will cut out the circles, starting with the smallest. The third will draw a curved line on the large piece of plain paper. The line will start in the lower left corner, travel up to the top middle of the page, and drop down toward the right center. The third student will arrange the circles, placing the smallest at the end of the line and ending with the largest circle at the lower left corner where the line began. The circles can be adjusted for best position and then glued down. Let students display work and compare. Ask it using different tints of the color would have helped to make the ball disappear into the distance.

92   93   93

Side panels provide daily lesson plans:

On Chapter Pages you'll find <u>Chapter Scan</u> (helps you allocate time), and <u>Using the Chapter Opener</u> (artist's background for opening works of art, with suggestions for introducing, examining, and discussing).

<u>Answers to the Chapter Review</u> and <u>Using the Chapter Detail</u> are page-specific, <u>Building Self-Esteem</u> enhances each student's artistic and personal development, and <u>Evaluation Techniques</u> monitor progress and success.

Lesson Pages give you <u>Lesson Objectives</u>, <u>Teacher's Resource Binder Resources</u>, a daily <u>Motivator</u> that sparks interest in lesson content, plus defined <u>Vocabulary</u> and exercises.

<u>Exploring Aesthetics</u> encourages discussion and thinking skills, and <u>Art Criticism</u> relates to the text's art or activity. <u>Art History</u> activities build interest in research. <u>Appreciating Cultural Diversity</u> helps you develop a sensitive multicultural art program.

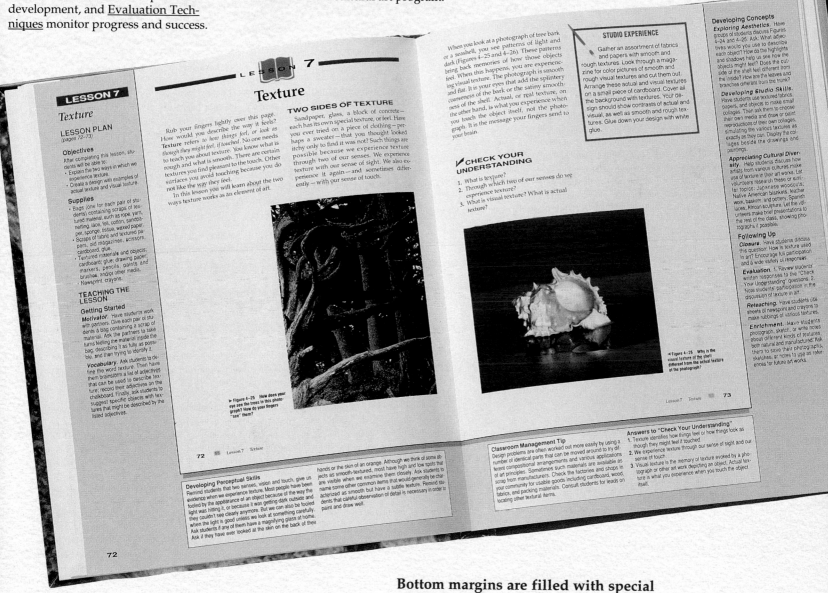

Bottom margins are filled with special studio emphasis and annotations:

<u>Background Information</u> on artists' lives and art styles plus media techniques are strategically placed to correlate to text.

You'll also find <u>Classroom Management Tips</u> from other classroom art teachers, <u>Cooperative Learning</u>, a <u>Cross-reference to Handbook</u> and <u>Answers to Review Questions.</u>

TEACHER'S RESOURCE BINDER

For the first time, an art course offers a Teacher's Resource Binder— separate for each text. Tabbed to correspond to chapters, there's a wealth of supplementary handouts, teaching strategies and resource materials to complement the skill level, time framework and interest level of your class:

- **Reproducible masters** Planned for each lesson, these provide supplementary material for your students.

- **Cooperative Learning Activities** Each has been selected to promote teamwork, cooperation and responsibility.

- **Aesthetics/Art Criticism** As aestheticians and art critics, students explore, theorize and apply principles to practical situations.

- **Art History** Activity sheets relate to each chapter.

- **Studio Lessons** Additional lessons supplement or replace those in texts. Field-tested by classroom teachers and selected to reinforce and extend chapter contents.

- **Appreciating Cultural Diversity** In the ideal setting of the art classroom, students celebrate their ethnicity and gain understanding for global views.

- **Evaluation Techniques** A reproducible objective testing program is provided for each chapter.

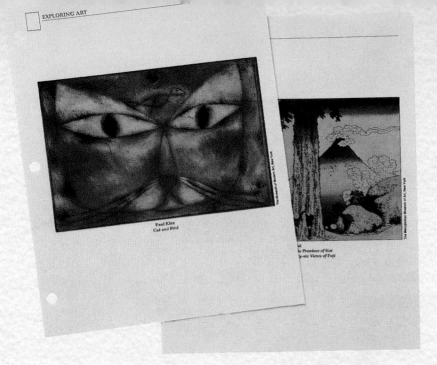

OVERHEAD COLOR TRANSPARENCIES

- Two color transparencies for each chapter

- Transparencies project large enough for detail examination

- Accompanied by Instructor's Guide

FINE ART PRINTS

- 20 masterworks for each text; no duplications from the textbook

- 22-1/2" x 28-1/2", the largest practical classroom size

- Printed on sturdy self-supporting stock

- Laminated to resist wear and tear

- Reinforced corner holes

- Presented in a handsome and durable portfolio

- Top quality fine art pieces differ from text

- Includes an extensive Instructor's Guide and Resource Book

. . . . . so you have more time for the art!

PROGRAM COMPONENTS

Exploring Art

STUDENT TEXT	0-02-662281-5
TEACHER'S WRAPAROUND EDITION	0-02-662282-3
TEACHER'S RESOURCE BINDER	0-02-662283-1
FINE ART PRINTS	0-02-662284-X
OVERHEAD COLOR TRANSPARENCIES	0-02-662293-9

Understanding Art

STUDENT TEXT	0-02-662286-6
TEACHER'S WRAPAROUND EDITION	0-02-662287-4
TEACHER'S RESOURCE BINDER	0-02-662288-2
FINE ART PRINTS	0-02-662289-0
OVERHEAD COLOR TRANSPARENCIES	0-02-662294-7

GLENCOE
Macmillan/McGraw-Hill
936 Eastwind Drive • Westerville, Ohio 43081

1. NORTHEAST REGION
GLENCOE
17 Riverside Drive
Nashua, NH 03062
603-880-4701

2. MID-ATLANTIC REGION
GLENCOE
Princeton-Hightstown Road
P.O. Box 409
Hightstown, NJ 08520
609-426-7356

3. ATLANTIC-SOUTHEAST REGION
GLENCOE
Brookside Park
One Harbison Way, Suite 101
Columbia, SC 29212
803-732-2365

4. SOUTHEAST REGION
GLENCOE
6510 Jimmy Carter Boulevard
Norcross, GA 30071
404-446-7493

5. MID-AMERICA REGION
GLENCOE
4635 Hilton Corporate Drive
Columbus, OH 43232
614-759-6600

6. MID-CONTINENT REGION
GLENCOE
846 East Algonquin Road
Schaumburg, IL 60173
708-397-8448

7. SOUTHWEST REGION
GLENCOE
320 Westway Pl., Suite 550
Arlington, TX 76018
817-784-2100

8. TEXAS REGION
GLENCOE
320 Westway Pl., Suite 550
Arlington, TX 76018
817-784-2100

9. WESTERN REGION
GLENCOE
610 E. 42nd St. #102
Boise, ID 83714
208-378-4002
Includes Alaska

10. CALIFORNIA REGION
GLENCOE
15319 Chatsworth Street
Mission Hills, CA 91345
818-898-1391

FOR CANADIAN ORDERS
Maxwell Macmillan Canada
1200 Eglinton Ave., East, Suite 200
Don Mills, Ontario M3C 3NI
Telephone: 416-449-6030
Telex: 069.59372
Telefax: 416-449-0068

FOR HAWAII
Donald Hosaka, Rep.
Macmillan/McGraw-Hill International
1613 Kanalui Street
Honolulu, HI 96816
Telephone: 808-734-6971
Telefax: 808-735-4590

FOR ALL OVERSEAS K-12 SCHOOLS
Macmillan/McGraw-Hill International
866 Third Avenue
New York, NY 10022-6299
Telephone: 212-702-3276
Telex: 225925 MACM UR
Telefax: 212-605-9377

Understanding Art

Rosalind Ragans, Ph.D.
Associate Professor Emerita
Georgia Southern University

Jane Rhoades, Ph.D
Teacher Educator
Georgia Southern University

GLENCOE
Macmillan/McGraw-Hill

Lake Forest, Illinois   Columbus, Ohio   Mission Hills, California   Peoria, Illinois

Send all inquiries to:
Glencoe Division, Macmillan/McGraw-Hill
15319 Chatsworth Street
P.O. Box 9609
Mission Hills, California 91346-9609

ISBN 0-02-662286-6 Student Text
ISBN 0-02-662287-4 Teacher's Wraparound Edition

2 3 4 5 6 7 8 9   95 94 93 92

CONTENTS

CONTRIBUTORS

Jill Ciccone-Corey
Art Teacher
Monmouth Regional High School
Tenton Falls, New Jersey

Pat Gullett
Art Teacher
Morton East Intermediate School
Highland Park, Illinois

Josephine Julianna Jones
Art Teacher
Booker T. Washington High School
for the Performing Arts
Dallas, Texas

Jennifer Lawler
Art Consultant
Lenexa, Kansas

Diane Mark-Walker
Art Consultant
Los Angeles, California

Johanna Stout
Art Teacher
New Caney High School
New Caney, Texas

Introduction

The experience of watching students involved in the process of exploring, understanding, and producing works of art is exciting and professionally rewarding. Today's art classroom fosters this instructional climate by providing a place where students can express artistic talent and develop creative thinking; a forum where students are encouraged to ask questions and challenged to find answers to their questions; an environment that encourages students to think, to learn, and to create.

Understanding Art has been designed to meet the needs of today's art classroom and to address in a systematic and integrated fashion the major goals of art education. These goals include:

- The development, expression, and evaluation of ideas and processes;
- The ability to produce, read, and interpret visual symbols;
- The assimilation of information needed to recognize and understand the artistic achievements and expectations of various societies.

By achieving these goals students gain an awareness and sensitivity to the humanmade and natural environment and develop the skills to become visually literate.

The *Understanding Art* program has been written and designed specifically for middle school/junior high students. Its motivational appeal and high-interest, interactive approach stems from the philosophy that *all* students benefit from a well-planned and sequentially articulated art program. *Understanding Art* is based on the belief that a quality art program allows for discovery and creative problem solving, and in the process, cultivates learners who are able to make positive contributions to society.

Teaching with Understanding Art

Understanding Art is a middle school/junior high textbook written collaboratively by Dr. Rosalind Ragans and Dr. Gene Mittler. Both of these experienced art specialists, teachers, and writers recognized the need for developing a quality middle school/junior high textbook program based on an integrated approach of aesthetics, art criticism, art history, and studio production. Throughout the development of the textbook, material was reviewed and field tested in classrooms across the United States by middle school/junior high teachers. These combined efforts bring you an innovative art program that both students and teachers will find meaningful and rewarding.

Understanding Art is based on the assumption that the following features are an essential part of an effective art program.

- **Program articulation and flexibility.** A quality art education program provides students with experiences that are sequentially planned, building on previous art concepts and skills. At the same time the program must fit the configuration and topic emphases of the middle school/junior high program, which vary from school district to school district. *Understanding Art* meets these needs. The program builds sequentially on content giving students experiences in the various aspects of an art program. Its short, self-contained lessons, which are appropriate for 45-minute class periods, have built-in flexibility allowing the teacher to adapt the content to a 6-week, 9-week, 18-week, or 36-week course.
- **Visual perception and creative problem solving.** *Understanding Art* is a visually oriented program, incorporating reproductions of

masters' works and other art works so that students can develop an appreciation and understanding for various artists, works of art, and artistic styles. Each illustration in the text is discussed and explored within the narrative and studio lessons. After examining the works of art, students explore concepts related to these works and apply specific techniques in the hands-on Studio Experiences and Studio Lessons. The art production segments allow for personal expression, encourage discovery, and promote creative problem solving.

- **Integration of aesthetics, art criticism, art history, and studio production.** *Understanding Art* successfully weaves aesthetics, art criticism, art history, and studio production throughout the narrative and studio lessons and the correlated program components. Each lesson discusses works of art from aesthetic viewpoints and provides teaching strategies that deal with the steps of art criticism and art history. In each narrative lesson a Studio Experience is included to provide hands-on application of the material. In each studio lesson, students are encouraged to critique their works of art. This assists the teacher in providing a unified program that meets today's curriculum direction in art education.
- **Appreciation of cultural diversity.** *Understanding Art* addresses a variety of cultural and ethnic groups. This attention to cultural diversity is represented in works of art, teaching strategies, and curriculum content.

Understanding Art consists of the following components:

- **Student Text.** The 352-page book introduces students to a solid art program, laying the foundation for lifelong art appreciation and art production skills.
- **Teacher's Wraparound Edition.** This edition provides a complete teaching program, including lesson plans, teaching suggestions, classroom management tips, and supplemental information—conveniently wrapped around the outside column of a reduced student page. A 48-page Teacher's Manual is included in the wraparound edition, which is designed to assist the teacher in setting up his or her classroom and listing effective teaching techniques.

- **Teacher's Resource Binder.** This separate component includes reproducible masters, handouts, and student activity sheets, which emphasize aesthetics and art criticism, art history, evaluation techniques, cooperative learning, and appreciation for cultural diversity. Also included are additional studio lessons and teacher-ready overhead color transparencies.
- **Overhead Color Transparencies.** Ready-to-use color transparencies are an effective way to introduce and reinforce concepts. This separate package of overhead color transparencies can be used to extend the lessons and develop higher-level thinking skills as students compare, analyze, and evaluate works of art.

The Student Text

Understanding Art offers a broad range of visual art experiences based on art works and art styles of various cultures and times in history. The concepts of aesthetics, art criticism, art history, and art production are applied and reinforced throughout the program.

After students are introduced to the elements and principles of art, students learn about art criticism and art history. Next they explore the art produced from the earliest times and then follow various art styles in chronological order. The text is augmented with chapters pertaining to art of China, Japan, India, Africa, and Native America. Studio lessons appear throughout the text and as a model for each studio lesson a work of a master is included. Each studio lesson also involves creating works of art using a range of art media and techniques. Exemplary age-appropriate student art work is displayed in the text to be used as a source of inspiration and motivation.

The structure of the textbook provides for flexibility to accommodate the varied configuration of the middle school/junior high program. By consulting the pacing chart and the scope and sequence chart, the teacher can tailor a course that is appropriate for his or her specific teaching methods and the local, state, and national art education framework.

Organization of the Text

The text is divided into 17 chapters. Chapters 1 and 2 introduce students to the elements and principles of art and the media of art. In Chapter 3 students learn about different aesthetic views and the steps of art criticism and art history. In Chapter 4 students learn about art of the earliest times. After covering art of China, India, Japan, Mesoamerica, and Africa, students follow the progression of Western European art in chronological order. Chapters 16 and 17 cover art of the twentieth century.

Chapters

Understanding Art is divided into chapters, which are further divided into self-contained narrative or studio lessons. In each chapter the following recurring learning aids and textbook features are integrated:

- **Chapter Opener.** Each chapter begins with a two-page spread that includes:
  - **Full-color reproduction of a work of art** to provide visual motivation for the student.
  - **Chapter learning objectives** to help students identify the behavioral goals of the chapter.
  - **Vocabulary terms** to help students develop an art vocabulary, enabling them to understand and participate in class discussion.
  - **Artists You Will Meet** to introduce students to the artists whose art works appear within the chapter.
- **Chapter Review.** The two-page chapter review includes:
  - **Building Vocabulary** to check comprehension of vocabulary terms.
  - **Reviewing Art Facts** to help teachers monitor the recall and comprehension of the material.
  - **Thinking About Art** to provide exercises involving higher-level thinking skills.
  - **Making Art Connections** to suggest other interdisciplinary activities.
  - **Looking at the Details** to enable students to apply the information that they have learned in the chapter to a segment of the work of art that appears on the chapter opener.

Lessons

Each chapter is divided into self-contained lessons. There are two types of lessons: narrative and studio. Both types of lessons use a work of art as point of departure for explanation of content and studio production. The narrative lessons present art concepts and help increase cognitive learning. The studio lessons provide manipulative experiences that build on previous studio exercises and give students the opportunity to use various media and techniques.

Features found in the lessons include:

- **Studio Experience.** A studio experience in each narrative lesson provides immediate hands-on application of the content.
- **Check Your Understanding.** Comprehension questions enable the teacher to quickly assess students' understanding of the narrative lessons.
- **Examining Your Work.** This section guides students in applying the process of art criticism to their own works of art.
- **Safety Tip.** Where appropriate, a note alerts students to take precautions when dealing with certain items, such as utility knives, paints, and glues.

Handbook

A 40-page handbook, which appears at the end of the Student Text provides resource and reference information for students.

- **Technique Tips.** Step-by-step procedures or techniques that pertain to drawing, printmaking, painting, sculpting, and other production skills are presented and illustrated.
- **Artist Profiles.** This handy reference material gives students additional information about the lives of artists. The section can be used as a separate art history unit or used in the context of the Student Text and presented as the artist's work is presented in the text.
- **Career Spotlights.** The purpose of the career spotlights is to acquaint students with a variety of career opportunities within the field of art. This section can be covered as a separate unit or assigned as extra credit.
- **Additional Studios.** Additional studio lessons provide enrichment and extension. These

optional studio activities are designed for cooperative learning and/or the creatively gifted student.

Other Features

- **Student Art Work.** Exemplary student art work of middle school/junior high students is displayed within the studio lessons.
- **Artists and Their Works.** All artists and the names of their works are previewed on the chapter opening page. A comprehensive listing of all artists and the titles of their art works and page references appears in the section, Artists and Their Works.
- **Glossary.** Every vocabulary term (identified in boldface type) is listed and defined in the Glossary. Where needed, a pronunciation guide is also provided. Page references assist students in locating where key words are introduced and defined in context within the text.
- **Index.** A comprehensive index is provided as a study aid and to assist students in finding particular topics.

The Teacher's Wraparound Edition

Understanding Art is the first middle school/junior high art textbook program that offers a Teacher's Wraparound Edition. The Teacher's Wraparound Edition differs from the Student Text in the following ways: (1) material from the Student Text is reproduced in a slightly smaller size to allow more room for the teaching material, which fills the side and bottom columns; (2) a 48-page Teacher's Manual (the section you are reading now) is bound into the book.

Teacher's Manual

To assist in course planning and to increase teacher effectiveness, a Teacher's Manual is included in the Teacher's Wraparound Edition. This manual explains the program components and how to use them. Other parts of the Teacher's Manual include:

- **A Pacing Chart** to help you decide how much time to spend on each lesson.
- **A Scope and Sequence Chart** to help you identify topics and where they appear in each chapter and lesson.
- **A Teaching Methods Manual** to help articulate the criteria of a quality art education program,

explain how to teach students with varying ability levels, and suggest ways to create a positive classroom environment. This mini-manual also discusses classroom organizational and management techniques.

Lesson Plans

In the Teacher's Wraparound Edition the lesson plans fill the outside column of the Student Text page. The consistent, easy-to-follow lesson plans give the teacher a variety of teaching strategies to motivate students, to introduce, teach, and reinforce concepts, and to provide enrichment and extension ideas.

Chapter Pages

On the two-page spreads that begin and end each chapter, these elements are provided:

- **Chapter Scan.** In the left column a listing of the lesson titles that appear in the chapter is provided. The quick scan enables you to see the scope of the chapter at a glance and helps decide how much time to spend on each lesson.
- **Using the Chapter Opener.** This information helps the teacher effectively use the chapter opening work of art. Background information about the artist is given along with suggestions for introducing, examining, and discussing the art work.
- **Answers to the Chapter Review and to Looking at the Details.** Answers to all questions are provided on the same page as the questions themselves.
- **Building Self-Esteem.** At the beginning of each chapter a teaching strategy is provided to build students' self-esteem and to show students the relationship between art and self-esteem. In using some of the self-esteem strategies, it is suggested that the art teacher invite the school counselor into the classroom to team teach the lesson. An effective team teaching program may be developed between the counselor and the art teacher; thus providing the strongest possible experience for the students, in terms of both their personal and artistic development.
- **Evaluation Techniques.** At the end of each chapter there are at least three evaluation techniques that help to monitor students' progress and evaluate students' success with the material.

Lesson Pages

On the various lesson pages these elements are provided:

- **Lesson Objectives.** Student objectives for the lesson are provided.
- **Supplies.** A listing of supplies that the teacher will need for implementing the art production experiences and for following the lesson plan are listed.
- **Teacher's Resource Binder.** This is a list of student handouts and activities from the Teacher's Resource Binder that are correlated to the chapter and lesson.
- **Motivator.** This short motivational teaching strategy is designed to spark students' interest in the content of the lesson.
- **Vocabulary.** The vocabulary is identified in boldface type within the lesson and defined in italics. To help students grasp concepts, a vocabulary exercise is given in the lesson plan.
- **Exploring Aesthetics.** This teaching strategy is based on the aesthetic viewpoints presented in the text. These types of activities lend themselves well to classroom discussion and help students develop critical thinking skills.
- **Using Art Criticism.** This type of activity challenges students to apply the steps of art criticism to the work of art that appears within the text or to a related activity.
- **Understanding Art History.** These teaching activities provide additional information for the students in relationship to art history. Many of the art history activities develop research and language art skills.
- **Developing Studio Skills.** This section offers a variety of activities that help students develop and practice art production skills.
- **Appreciating Cultural Diversity.** To help the teacher develop a sensitive multicultural art program, various multicultural teaching strategies are provided.
- **Closure.** Suggestions for bringing closure to the instructional period are presented.
- **Evaluation.** An objective testing program is included in the Teacher's Resource Binder.

Other evaluation methods are listed at the end of each chapter.

- **Reteaching/Enrichment.** These activities are suggested so that the teacher has easily accessible teaching suggestions to meet the needs of all students. The enrichment strategy can be used to keep gifted students challenged and make it possible for the instructor to spend time with students who need more instructional time.

Annotations

Annotations appear at the bottom of the pages. These include: Background Information, Note, Handbook Cross-Reference, Classroom Management Tip, Cooperative Learning, Developing Perceptual Skills, and Answers to "Check Your Understanding."

- **Background Information.** Background information about an artist, art style, medium, and technique is listed so that you have supplemental information at your fingertips.
- **Note.** This annotation is directed to the teacher as a reminder of where important concepts are presented in the program, or as a reminder of information that you may wish to share with students.
- **Handbook Cross-Reference.** Bound into the student text is a 40-page handbook that lists Technique Tips, Artist Profiles, Career Spotlights, and Additional Studios. This handy resource manual is cross-referenced in the bottom-page annotations.
- **Classroom Management Tips.** These helpful suggestions have been written by classroom art teachers as ideas that might help organize or manage an art classroom.
- **Cooperative Learning.** Teaching strategies that encourage teamwork and cooperative interaction among all levels of students are provided.
- **Developing Perceptual Skills.** Suggestions for improving perceptual skills and enhancing students' observational skills are provided.
- **Answers to "Check Your Understanding."** Answers to the factual recall questions are provided on the same page as the questions.

The Teacher's Resource Binder

A separate *Understanding Art* Teacher's Resource Binder is designed to provide you with a correlated supplemental resource for *Understanding Art*. The purpose of the Teacher's Resource Binder is to provide a wealth of additional handouts, teaching strategies, and resource material designed for more effective teaching. You can choose the materials that complement the skill level, time framework, and interest level of your class. Most of its pages are designed to be reproduced for classroom use. The Teacher's Resource Binder is organized into chapters. The following types of teaching materials have been provided for each chapter:

- **Reproducible Master.** Reproducible masters have been planned for each lesson to provide supplementary material for your students. They can be used to create an overhead transparency master, which visually introduces or reinforces information, or they can be used as black-line masters and distributed as handouts to students.
- **Cooperative Learning Activities.** Cooperative learning activities have been developed to promote teamwork, cooperation, and responsibility. They require students to work in small groups or teams of three or four. Each team member is responsible not only for his or her own learning but also for the learning of the other team members. Students assist and help each other master skills, solve problems, and find creative solutions. In this type of learning environment students are encouraged to share ideas, interpret material, and cooperate to help each other learn. Working in small groups gives all students the opportunity to experience success. In addition, the active participation of the students and the group creates a positive, stimulating classroom environment.

- **Aesthetics/Art Criticism.** These student worksheets are designed to make the teaching and application of aesthetics and art criticism meaningful and enjoyable to middle school/junior high students. As aestheticians and art critics, they explore, theorize, and apply the principles learned in the text to practical situations.
- **Art History.** Every chapter contains an activity sheet pertaining to art history. *Understanding Art* takes a chronological approach to the introduction of art beginning with art of earliest times and progressing to contemporary art. The activity sheets in the Teacher's Resource Binder reinforce and extend the information.
- **Studio.** The Teacher's Resource Binder offers a variety of studio activities that help students develop and practice art production skills. These activities can be used in place of or in addition to the studio lessons in the Student Text. Each lesson has been field tested by classroom teachers and selected for its ability to reinforce and extend chapter content.
- **Appreciating Cultural Diversity.** Worksheets are presented for each chapter to help students celebrate their cultural diversity and understand various global views.
- **Evaluation Techniques.** To help teachers measure students' performance and attest to accountability, a reproducible objective testing program is provided for each chapter.

Overhead Color Transparency Packet

The ready-to-use overhead color transparency packet is provided as a way to introduce, reinforce, or extend the chapter. The package contains 34 full-color overhead transparencies along with a 32-page instructional manual to assist the teacher in guiding discussion.

Recognizing the Importance of a Quality Art Program

Young people learn about the visual arts outside of school through their family and friends, through the mass media, and perhaps even by teaching themselves. Sometimes the information learned this way is valuable, but it should not be relied upon to always give correct and adequate information about art. Our schools are the most available and most effective place for giving students the opportunity to learn about the visual arts.

Benefits of a Quality Art Program

A quality art education program taught by a qualified art specialist benefits every adolescent student. If art educators teach their subject matter in a systematic, coherent, and meaningful fashion, students will acquire knowledge about art that will benefit them throughout their life. Such a program promotes growth in many areas. Some of these areas are noted below.

- **Art Teaches Effective Communication.** In order for students to become visually literate, they need to understand that the visual symbols developed by artists and designers transmit information that cannot be disclosed through other modes of communication. Adolescent students should be encouraged to learn visual literacy by looking, understanding, talking, writing, and, of course, creating images. Through a quality art education program, students should be able to discuss and create images—images that convey knowledge, create new knowledge, reveal opinions and shape opinions, disclose the depths of human emotion, and impart the most profound values.
- **Art Teaches Creativity.** All people possess creative intelligence. When a quality art program is implemented, creativity in all students is nurtured and stimulated. Through an art program, students learn to solve prob-

lems creatively. Every time a student creates an art work, he or she has to make creative decisions. Research has shown that experiences in art are ideal for cultivating, exercising, and stimulating the imagination and for developing creative problem-solving abilities.
- **Art Teaches About Civilizations.** Through a quality art program, students develop a sensitivity and understanding of the history of humankind. For many periods in history it is only through visual remains or material culture that a societies' culture can be pieced together. A study of art history reveals varied world views, concepts, symbols, styles, feelings, and perceptions. Experiences that adolescent students have with these art objects from the past teach them respect for others, challenge their minds, and stimulate not only the intellect but also the imagination.
- **Art Teaches Critical Thinking.** A quality art program encourages a variety of critical thinking skills. Students are asked to identify and recall information; to organize select facts and ideas; to use particular facts, rules, and principles; to be able to figure out component parts or to classify; to combine ideas and form a new whole; and to make critical judgments and develop their own opinions.
- **Art Teaches Perceptual Sensitivity and Aesthetic Awareness.** As a result of a quality art program, students develop a keen sense of awareness and an appreciation for beauty. Art experiences help cultivate an aesthetic sensitivity and respect for the natural and humanmade environment. Art classes are the only place in the school curriculum where students learn about what constitutes quality design—about harmony, order, organizations, and specific design qualities (such as balance, movement, and unity).

- **Art Teaches Personal Expression.** Art is an effective way to express emotions. The adolescent years are often filled with emotional turmoil—frustrations, tensions, and irritations. Art experiences permit the expression of ideas, feelings, and perceptions in a healthy, socially acceptable way. Although art educators are not trained art therapists, they understand that art experiences help adolescents release emotions in a positive way. Through their art, students sometimes begin to discover their own identity and build self-esteem. Personal expression is encouraged and the result is often a statement in visual form that is both inventive and filled with personal meaning.

- **Art Teaches the Value of Work.** Through a quality art program, students learn the meaning and joy of work. Working to the best of one's ability is a noble expression of the human spirit. Students learn the satisfaction and excitement that comes from developing their art skills and craftsmanship when they have successfully completed an art production project.

Planning the Course

To implement a quality art education program there is no standard formula or format that will work for every program. The content of the lessons in *Understanding Art* draws upon the fundamental disciplines that contribute to the understanding and making of art—art production or studio art, art criticism, aesthetics, and art history. Goals and objectives will be developed by the professional art teacher and will depend upon the interests, ability levels, learning styles, and instructional time allotted for the individual program.

To assist with the planning and development of individual courses, a Pacing Chart, Scope and Sequence Chart, and overall suggestions are included in this section. These are only intended as suggested guidelines. Individual teachers will need to make necessary adjustments and modifications as required by their local, state, and national curriculum guidelines, and by the ability level and learning styles of their students.

Pacing Chart

		6 wk	9 wk	18 wk	36 wk
Total Days		**30 days**	**45 days**	**90 days**	**180 days**
Chapter 1	*The Language of Art*				
Lesson 1	The Elements of Art	1 day	1 day	1 day	2 days
Lesson 2	Using the Elements of Art	1 day	1 day	1 day	2 days
Lesson 3	The Principles of Art	1 day	1 day	1 day	2 days
Lesson 4	Using the Principles of Art	1 day	1 day	1 day	2 days
	Total	4 days	4 days	4 days	8 days
Chapter 2	*The Media of Art*				
Lesson 1	Drawing, Painting, and Printmaking	1 day	1 day	1 day	2 days
Lesson 2	Creating Mixed Media Art	1 day	1 day	1 day	2 days
Lesson 3	Sculpture, Architecture, and Crafts Media	1 day	1 day	1 day	2 days
Lesson 4	Creating an Environmental Design		1 day	1 day	2 days
	Total	3 days	4 days	4 days	8 days

	Total Days	6 wk 30 days	9 wk 45 days	18 wk 90 days	36 wk 180 days
Chapter 3	***Art Criticism, Aesthetics, and Art History***				
Lesson 1	Art Criticism and Aesthetics	1 day	1 day	1 day	3 days
Lesson 2	Painting an Expressive Scene	1 day	1 day	1 day	2 days
Lesson 3	Art History	1 day	1 day	1 day	3 days
Lesson 4	Painting in the Cubist Style	1 day	1 day	1 day	2 days
	Total	4 days	4 days	4 days	10 days
Chapter 4	***Art of Earliest Times***				
Lesson 1	Prehistoric Art	1 day	1 day	1 day	2 days
Lesson 2	Painting Using Earth Pigments			1 day	2 days
Lesson 3	Art of Ancient Egypt	1 day	1 day	1 day	2 days
Lesson 4	Ancient China, India, and Mesopotamia		1 day	1 day	2 days
Lesson 5	Creating a Picture Story	1 day	1 day	1 day	2 days
	Total	3 days	4 days	5 days	10 days
Chapter 5	***Art of the Far East***				
Lesson 1	The Art of China	1 day	1 day	1 day	2 days
Lesson 2	Making a Scroll		1 day	1 day	2 days
Lesson 3	The Art of Japan	1 day	1 day	1 day	2 days
Lesson 4	Creating a Time Capsule			2 days	3 days
	Total	2 days	3 days	5 days	9 days
Chapter 6	***The Art of Pre-Columbian America***				
Lesson 1	Art of Mesoamerica	1 day	1 day	1 day	2 days
Lesson 2	Making a Clay Urn			2 days	3 days
Lesson 3	Art of the Andes		1 day	1 day	2 days
Lesson 4	Making a Stylized Motif	1 day	1 day	1 day	2 days
	Total	2 days	3 days	5 days	9 days

	Total Days	6 wk 30 days	9 wk 45 days	18 wk 90 days	36 wk 180 days
Chapter 7 **Art of Greece and Rome**					
Lesson 1 Art of Ancient Greece		1 day	1 day	1 day	2 days
Lesson 2 Making a Painting for a Greek Vase			1 day	1 day	2 days
Lesson 3 Art of Ancient Rome		1 day	1 day	1 day	2 days
Lesson 4 Making a Model of a Roman Triumphal Arch		_____	_____	2 days	3 days
Total		2 days	3 days	5 days	9 days
Chapter 8 *Art of India and Islam*					
Lesson 1 Art of India		1/2 day	1/2 day	1 day	2 days
Lesson 2 Making a Tempera Batik			1 day	2 days	2 days
Lesson 3 Art of Islam		1/2 day	1/2 day	1 day	2 days
Lesson 4 Making a Collage in the Islamic Style		_____	_____	1 day	2 days
Total		1 day	2 days	5 days	8 days
Chapter 9 *Art of Africa*					
Lesson 1 The Figure Sculptures of Africa		1 day	1 day	1 day	2 days
Lesson 2 Abstract Self-Portrait Cutout			1 day	1 day	2 days
Lesson 3 The Masks of Africa				1 day	2 days
Lesson 4 Making a Mood Mask Relief		_____	_____	2 days	2 days
Total		1 day	2 days	5 days	8 days
Chapter 10 *Art of the Middle Ages*					
Lesson 1 Art of the Romanesque Period		1 day	1 day	1 day	2 days
Lesson 2 Romanesque Castle Relief				2 days	2 days
Lesson 3 Art of the Gothic Period		1 day	1 day	1 day	2 days
Lesson 4 Making a Gothic Gargoyle		_____	_____	1 day	2 days
Total		2 days	2 days	5 days	8 days

	Total Days	6 wk 30 days	9 wk 45 days	18 wk 90 days	36 wk 180 days
Chapter 11 *Art of the Renaissance*					
Lesson 1 Art of Italian Renaissance		1 day	1 day	1 day	3 days
Lesson 2 Drawing a Still Life			1 day	1 day	2 days
Lesson 3 Art of the Northern Renaissance			1 day	1 day	3 days
Lesson 4 Designing a Visual Symbol		____	____	2 days	2 days
Total		1 day	3 days	5 days	10 days
Chapter 12 *European Art of the 1600s and 1700s*					
Lesson 1 Art of the 1600s		1 day	1 day	1 day	3 days
Lesson 2 Drawing Expressive Hands				1 day	2 days
Lesson 3 Art of the 1700s			1 day	1 day	3 days
Lesson 4 Constructing a Rococo Shoe		____	____	2 days	2 days
Total		1 day	2 days	5 days	10 days
Chapter 13 *Native American Art*					
Lesson 1 Native American Art of the Past		1 day	1 day	1 day	3 days
Lesson 2 Making a Round Weaving				3 days	3 days
Lesson 3 Native American Art Today				1 day	3 days
Lesson 4 Inuit-Style Print		____	____	1 day	2 days
Total		1 day	1 day	6 days	11 days
Chapter 14 *European Art of the 1800s*					
Lesson 1 Neoclassic and Romantic Art			1 day	1 day	3 days
Lesson 2 Designing a Neoclassic Stage Set				1 day	2 days
Lesson 3 European Art—Late 1800s		1 day	1 day	1 day	3 days
Lesson 4 Painting an Impressionist Landscape		____	____	1 day	1 day
Total		1 day	2 days	4 days	9 days

		Total Days	6 wk 30 days	9 wk 45 days	18 wk 90 days	36 wk 180 days
Chapter 15	***European Art of the Late Nineteenth Century***					
Lesson 1	Art of the Post-Impressionists		1 day	1 day	1 day	3 days
Lesson 2	Painting in the Style of Post-Impressionists				1 day	2 days
Lesson 3	American Painting in the Late 1800s		1 day	1 day	1 day	3 days
Lesson 4	Making an Expressive Watercolor Painting				1 day	2 days
	Total		2 days	2 days	4 days	10 days
Chapter 16	***Art of the Early Twentieth Century***					
Lesson 1	Art of the Early Twentieth Century in Europe		1 day	1 day	1 day	3 days
Lesson 2	Making a Cubist Chalk Drawing				1 day	2 days
Lesson 3	Art of the Early Twentieth Century in America		1 day	1 day	1 day	3 days
Lesson 4	Making a Print of a Figure in Action				1 day	2 days
	Total		2 days	2 days	4 days	10 days
Chapter 17	***Art of Today***					
Lesson 1	European Art Today		1 day	1 day	1 day	3 days
Lesson 2	Painting in the Surrealist Style		1 day	1 day	1 day	2 days
Lesson 3	American Art Today				1 day	3 days
Lesson 4	Making a Hard-Edge Op Art Work				1 day	2 days
Lesson 5	Art of the Next Frontier				1 day	2 days
	Total		2 days	2 days	5 days	12 days
Handbook						
	Total				10 days	22 days

Scope and Sequence Chart

	Chapter 1 *The Language of Art*	Chapter 2 *The Media of Art*
Elements and Principles of Art	• Introducing the **elements of art** (L1) • Defining **color** (L1) • Hue, value, intensity (L1) • Color schemes (L1) • Defining **line** (L1) • Line quality vs. line variation (L1) • Defining **shape** and **form** (L1) • Defining **space** (L1) • Defining **texture** (L1) • Defining non-objective art (L2) • Introducing **principles of art** (L3) • Defining **balance** (L3) • Defining **harmony** (L3) • Defining **emphasis** (L3) • Defining **proportion** (L3) • Defining **movement** (L3) • Defining **rhythm** (L3) • Defining **unity** (L3)	• Use of line in printmaking (L1) • Movement in sculptural design (L3) • Blending of values in lithography (L1) • Using elements and principles in mixed-media design (L2) • Visual unity in playgrounds (L4)
Aesthetics/ Art Criticism	• Examining Your Work (L2, L4) • Effect of lines (L1) • Interpreting Lindner's *Rock-Rock* (L3)	• Examining Your Work (L2, L4) • Seeing difference in media (L1)
Art History	• Van Gogh: movement (L3) • Demuth: simple images (L4) • Harnett: realistic scenes (L1) • Chagall: use of color (L1) • Hartigan: non-objective art (L2) • Renoir: creating mood (L3)	• Cassatt: pastels (L1) • Cézanne: pencil and watercolor (L1) • Marin: watercolor (L1) • Frankenthaler: acrylic (L1) • Bishop: aquatint (L1) • Aubin: mix media (L2) • Hoxie: sculpture (L3) • Eberle: bronze (L3) • Gaudi: architecture (L3) • Early crafts (L3)
Media and Techniques	• Drawing media (L2) • Painting media (L4)	• Defining **medium of art** (L1) • Describing **drawing** (L1) • Describing **painting** (L1) • Kinds of paint media, oil paint, tempera, watercolor, acrylic (L1) • Defining **printmaking** (L1) • Edition defined (L1) • Printmaking methods, relief, intaglio, lithography, screen printing (L1) • **Sculpture** defined (L3) • Freestanding vs. relief (L3) • Methods of sculpture, carving, casting, modeling, assembly (L3) • Defining **architecture** (L3) • Describing **crafts** (L3) • Pottery, weaving, glassblowing (L3)
Studio Production	• Designing non-objective art (L2) • Using principles of art in design (L4)	• Creating a mixed-media design (L2) • Creating a playground design (L4)
Safety	• Checking paint labels (L4) • AP and CP vs. HL (L4)	
Artists	• Münter, Harnett, Chagall (L1) • Hartigan (L2) • Lindner, Renoir, van Gogh (L3) • Demuth (L4)	• Escher, Cassatt, Cézanne, Frankenthaler, Bishop, Marin (L1) • Aubin (L2) • Hoxie, Eberle, Gaudi, Natzler, Miró (L3)

	Chapter 3 *Art Criticism, Aesthetics, & Art History*	**Chapter 4** *Art of Earliest Times*
Elements and Principles of Art	• Describing the elements of art in a work (L1) • Using elements and principles in Cubist style painting (L4)	• Ancient vase: use of balance and harmony (L1) • Creating shapes for hieroglyphics (L3) • Egyptian style: no depth of space (L5) • Using proportion in Egyptian pictures (L5)
Aesthetics/ Art Criticism	• Defining **art criticism** (L1) • Steps in art criticism (L1) • Subject, composition, and content defined (L1) • Aesthetic view defined (L1) • Types of aesthetic view (L1) • Examining Your Work (L2, L4)	• Examining Your Work (L2, L5) • Examining old stone age crafts (L1)
Art History	• Defining **art history** (L3) • Steps art historians use (L3) • **Cubism** defined (L3)	• Culture defined (L1) • Understanding **Old Stone Age** life (L1) • Describing cave paintings (L1) • Understanding **New Stone Age** life (L1) • Describing crafts and architecture (L1) • Megalith defined (L1) • Stonehenge (L1) • Post and lintel system (L1) • **Ancient Egyptian** life (L3) • Pharaoh defined (L3) • Understanding Egyptian architecture (L3) • Describing Egyptian sculpture (L3) • Stele defined (L3) • Interpreting Egyptian painting (L3) • Explaining hieroglyphics (L3) • Art of **China, India,** and **Mesopotamia** (L4) • Introducing Chinese history (L4) • Describing Chinese sculpture and crafts (L4) • Introducing ancient Indian culture (L4) • Urban planning defined (L4) • Mohenjo-Daro described (L4) • Understanding Mesopotamian culture (L4) • Describing Sumerian writing, sculpture and architecture (L4)
Media and Techniques	• Tempera paint (L2) • Tempera paint (L4)	• Natural objects (L1) • Natural pigments (L2) • Pencil, paper (L3) • Watercolors (L5)
Studio Production	• Extending an expressive painting (L2) • Creating a Cubist painting (L4)	• Finding an image in a natural form (L1) • Creating an earth pigment painting (L2) • Designing a hieroglyphic system (L3) • Creating a picture story (L5)
Safety		
Artists	• Rouault, Brooks, Steen, Van Ness (L1) • Hopper (L2, L3) • Picasso (L4)	• Artists of ancient Egypt, Europe (L1, L2) • China, India, Mesopotamia (L5)

Scope and Sequence Chart

	Chapter 5 *Art of the Far East*	**Chapter 6** *Art of Pre-Columbian America*
Elements and Principles of Art	• Observing line, form and texture (L1) • Blue pigment in vases (L1) • Chinese use of space (L2) • **Ukiyo-e**: strong lines and flat areas of color (L3)	• Observing balance in a headdress (L1) • Mayan architecture: using balance (L1) • Using formal balance and repeating patterns (L2) • Using shapes in weaving (L3) • Using elements and principles in designing a motif (L4)
Aesthetics/ Art Criticism	• Examining Your Work (L2, L4) • Describing an art work (L1) • Chinese art and mood (L1)	• Examining Your Work (L2, L4) • Comparing pottery (L3)
Art History	• Early **Chinese** inventions (L1) • Introducing **Han dynasty** (L1) • **Buddhist** influence on art (L1) • Scroll defined (L1) • **T'ang dynasty** (L1) • **Sung dynasty** (L1) • Porcelain of **Ming dynasty** (L1) • Introducing **Japanese** culture (L3) • Korean influence on Japanese religion and art (L3) • Clay objects of **Jomon** culture (L3) • Pagoda defined (L3) • Introducing **Yamato-e** painting (L3) • Screen defined (L3) • Introducing **Ukiyo-e** pictures (L3) • Woodblock printing defined (L3) • Describing **Kabuki** theater (L3) • **Nō** drama defined (L3)	• Pre-Columbian defined (L1) • Early Mexican cultures (L1) • Map of Mexican cultures (L1) • **Olmec** artifacts (L1) • **West Mexican** effigy (L1) • Genre defined (L1) • **Mayan** accomplishments (L1) • **Aztec** architecture (L1) • Funerary defined (L2) • Motif defined (L2) • Art development in the **Andes** (L3) • Map of Andean cultures (L3) • Describing **Chavín** culture and crafts (L3) • **Tiahuanaco** culture (L3) • Monolith defined (L3) • **Incan** culture (L3)
Media and Techniques	• Natural object, paper, brush, ink (L1) • Scroll paper, pencil, watercolor markers (L2) • Acrylics, headband material (L3) • Clay supplies, scissors, fabric (L4)	• Clay and modeling (L2) • Sketch paper, white paper, construction paper, glue, scissors (L4)
Studio Production	• Drawing with brush, ink (L1) • Making a scroll (L2) • Designing a pattern (L3) • Creating a time capsule (L4)	• Making a clay urn (L2) • Making a stylized motif (L4)
Safety	• Choosing waterbased markers (L2)	
Artists	• Meng-fu (L2) • Kiyotada (L3)	• Artists of ancient cultures: Olmec, Maya, Aztec (L1) • Chavín, Moche, Tiahuanaco, Inca (L3)

Scope and Sequence Chart

	Chapter 7 *Art of Greece and Rome*	Chapter 8 *Art of India and Islam*
Elements and Principles of Art	• Shapes of Greek vases (L1) • Pantheon: source of light (L3) • Triumphal arch: using balance (L4) • Creating sense of movement (L2) • Using elements in architecture (L4)	• Examining an Islamic painting (L4) • Hindu sculpture: using balance (L1) • Using movement in batik (L2) • Weaving: using balance (L5)
Aesthetics/ Art Criticism	• Examining Your Work (L2, L4) • Greeks: lifelike sculpture (L1) • Greek amphora: aesthetic views (L2) • Using realistic figures (L2) • Romans: lifelike sculpture (L3) • Interpreting and judging architecture (L4)	• Examining Your Work (L2, L4) • Interpreting Hindu sculpture (L2) • Interpreting Indian sculpture (L1)
Art History	• Introducing **Greek** culture (L1) • Locating the Aegean Sea (L1) • The importance of Athens (L1) • Describing Greek **architecture** (L1) • Describing Greek **sculpture** (L1) • Frieze defined (L1) • Describing Greek **painting** (L1) • Amphora defined (L1) • Introducing **Roman** culture (L3) • Describing Roman **architecture** (L3) • Inventing concrete (L3) • Describing the Pantheon (L3) • Inventing rounded arches (L3) • Roman aqueducts (L3) • Triumphal arch (L3) • Describing Roman **sculpture** (L3)	• Introducing **Hinduism** (L1) • Defining **stupas** (L1) • Map of India (L1) • Describing Hindu temples (L1) • Explaining a **Buddha** sculpture (L1) • Describing the Hindu **tree of life** (L1) • Introducing **Shiva** (L2) • Defining **batik** (L1) • Introducing **Islam** (L3) • Map of the lands of Islam (L3) • **Muhammad** (L3) • **Calligraphy** (L3) • Defining **Arabesque** (L3) • Building **mosques** (L3) • Describing mihrabs and minarets (L3)
Media and Techniques	• Paper, scissors (L1) • Paper and black tempera (L2) • Paper, pencil (L3) • Cereal box, construction paper (L4)	• Fine-tipped markers and drawing (L1) • Tempera, ink and printmaking (L2) • Yarn and weaving (L3) • Collage (L4)
Studio Production	• Symmetrical vase (L1) • Painting a design for a vase (L2) • Designing a triumphal arch (L3) • Making a model of an arch (L4)	• Creating a tree of life (L1) • Making a tempera Batik (L1) • Making a Persian weaving (L3) • Making an Islamic collage (L4)
Safety	• Using safe paints (L2) • Handling cutting tools (L4)	• Using an apron to avoid ink stains (L2)
Artists	• Myron, Phidias (L1)	• Nadu (L2) • Musawwir (L4) • Sultan Muhammed (L1)

Scope and Sequence Chart

	Chapter 9 *Art of Africa*	Chapter 10 *Art of the Middle Ages*
Elements and Principles of Art	• Showing mood with texture and composition (L1) • Bronze sculpture: texture and pattern (L1) • Masks: made for movement (L3) • Masks: using line (L4) • African sculpture: using shape and form (L2) • Using elements in headpiece (L3) • Using line and shape in a mask (L4)	• Using line in church architecture (L1) • Giotto: use of emphasis (L3) • Using elements of art in illumination (L1) • Using elements of art to design castle (L2) • Gargoyles: using texture (L4)
Aesthetics/ Art Criticism	• Examining Your Work (L2, L4) • Interpreting sculpture (L1) • Defining abstract (L1) • Describing **carved wood figures** (L1) • Describing **cast bronze figures** (L1) • Spiritual meaning of sculptures (L2) • African sculpture: abstract (L2) • Interpreting face masks (L3)	• Examining Your Work (L2, L4) • Interpreting church sculpture (L1) • Interpreting church art (L1) • Understanding stained glass (L3) • Giotto: lifelike painting (L3) • Gargoyle: imaginary proportion (L4)
Art History	• Introducing **African** cultures (L1) • **Map** of African cultures (L1) • Describing the **face mask**, headpiece, and shoulder mask (L3) • Introducing **Tyi Wara** (L3)	• **Middle Ages** (L1) • Describing the fall of the Roman Empire (L1) • Influence of **Christianity** in the Middle Ages (L1) • **Romanesque** and **Gothic** (L1) • Describing Romanesque sculpture and painting (L1) • Defining **illumination** (L1) • Introducing **Gothic** times (L3) • Describing **cathedrals** (L3) • Defining the **pointed arch** (L3) • Defining the **flying buttress** (L3) • Describing Gothic painting and **crafts** (L3) • Gargoyle defined (L4)
Media and Techniques	• Pencil, paper, and drawing (L1) • Pencil, paper, scissors, tempera, brushes, gloss, cardboard (L2) • Cardboard, material, stapler, tempera (L5) • Papier-mâché (L4)	• Oil pastels and drawing (L1) • Pencil, paper, cardboard, and assembling (L2) • Pencil, paper, black construction paper, chalk, tissue paper, scissors, glue (L3) • Clay supplies and modeling (L4)
Studio Production	• Drawing a self image (L1) • Making an abstract cut-out (L2) • Designing a mask (L3) • Making a papier-mâché mask (L4)	• Creating an illumination (L1) • Designing a castle (L2) • Making a rose window design (L3) • Making a Gothic gargoyle (L4)
Safety	• Avoiding unsafe paste (L4)	
Artists	• African artists of Nigeria, West Africa, Ivory Coast, Guinea (L3)	• Giotto (L3) • Artists of Early Spain, France (L1) • Italy, Spain (L2) • Italy, France (L3) • France (L4)

Scope and Sequence Chart

	Chapter 11 *Art of the Renaissance*	**Chapter 12** *European Art of the 1600s and 1700s*
Elements and Principles of Art	• Renaissance: sculptural balance (L1) • Using different values of complementary hues (L1) • Using line and texture in drawing (L2) • Using linear perspective (L1) • Da Vinci: using value (L1) • Michelangelo: using proportion (L1) • Using shape in a visual symbol (L4)	• Using color, form and texture in drawing (L3) • Using color, shape and texture in design (L4) • Using principles and elements in church design (L1) • Rubens: creating movement (L1) • Creating mood with line (L1) • Baroque: flowing movement (L1) • Caravaggio: use of light (L1)
Aesthetics/ Art Criticism	• Examining Your Work (L2, L4) • Developing realistic painting (L1) • Describing the **Mona Lisa** (L1) • Defining **Madonna** (L1) • Describing **Michelangelo's Pietà** (L1) • Understanding symbolism (L3)	• Examining Your Work (L2, L4) • Caravaggio: shocking realism (L1) • Watteau: imaginary sound (L3) • Chardin: painting with affection (L3) • Goya: shocking war scenes (L3) • Expressing mood in drawing (L3) • Rococo: make-believe world (L3)
Art History	• Introduction of **Renaissance** (L1) • Map of Renaissance Italy (L1) • Understanding the importance of **Florence** during the Renaissance (L1) • The reality of **Masaccio's** work (L1) • Introducing **da Vinci** (L1) • Introducing **Raphael** (L1) • Introducing **sculpture** (L1) • Describing the **Northern Renaissance** (L3) • Locating **Flanders** (L3) • Defining **symbolism** (L3) • Defining oil paint (L3) • Describing **van Eyck's** precision (L3) • **Van der Weyden:** emotional scenes (L3)	• Introducing the **Counter-Reformation** (L1) • Defining **Baroque** (L1) • **Caravaggio's** use of light (L1) • Baroque influence spreads to **Spain, northern Europe** (L1) • **Velázquez** uses blurring (L1) • **Rubens** leads trend for action and feeling (L1) • Dutch prefer **genre painting** (L1) • **Portrait** defined (L1) • **Leyster's** portraits (L1) • **Rembrandt's** portraits (L1) • **Paris** becomes center of art (L3) • Locating Paris (L3) • **Louis XIV** affects art (L3) • Building **Versailles** (L3) • **Watteau** starts **Rococo** art (L3) • **Vigée-Lebrun:** flattering portraits (L3) • **Chardin:** domestic scenes (L3) • Etching defined (L3) • **Goya** (L3)
Media and Techniques	• Pencil, paper, ruler, paint (L1) • Pencil, paper, and drawing (L2) • Pencil, paper, and drawing (L3) • Pencil, paper, paint, and designing (L4)	• Pencil, paper, construction paper, white crayon (L2) • Found object, pencil, paper, tempera (L3) • Pencil, paper, cardboard, scissors, glue, stapler, scraps (L4)
Studio Production	• Making a triangular design (L1) • Making a pencil drawing (L2) • Making a precise drawing (L3) • Designing a visual symbol (L4)	• Drawing expressive hands (L2) • Painting a common object (L3) • Constructing a Rococo shoe (L4)
Safety		
Artists	• Castagno, Masaccio, da Vinci, Raphael, Michelangelo (L1) • da Vinci (L2) • Van Eyck, Van der Weyden (L3) • Van Eyck (L4)	• Gentileschi, Borromini, Caravaggio, Velázquez, Rubens, Leyster (L1) • Rembrandt (L2) • Le Vau, Hardouin-Mansart, Watteau, Vigée-Lebrun, Chardin, Goya (L3) • Watteau (L4)

Scope and Sequence Chart

	Chapter 13 *Native American Art*	Chapter 14 *European Art of the Early 1800s*
Elements and Principles of Art	• Using shape in design (L1) • Weaving: changing color and pattern (L2) • Houser: changing color and pattern (L2) • Kenojuak: use of balance (L4) • Howe: using line, shape and color (L3) • Using line and shape (L4)	• Delacroix: use of line (L1) • Using elements of art in stage set (L2) • Monet: use of color (L5) • Rodin: using texture (L3) • Using color for emphasis (L3) • Using color, value, intensity (L4) • Warm vs. cool colors (L4)
Aesthetics/ Art Criticism	• Describing **Petroglyphs** (L1) • Examining Your Work (L2, L4) • Describing the **Pueblo Kachinas** (L3) • Pottery: abstract decoration (L3) • Namingha: aesthetic view (L3) • Sand painting: abstract drawing (L3) • Designing an abstract print (L4)	• Examining Your Work (L2, L4) • Romanticism: exotic subjects (L1) • Impressionism: a new view (L3)
Art History	• **Native American Groups** (L1) • Locating the **Pueblo** culture (L1) • Examining the **pueblos** (L1) • **Northwest Coast** culture (L1) • **Totem pole** defined (L1) • **Plains** Indian culture (L1) • **Woodlands** culture (L1) • Carving **false face masks** (L1) • Introducing current **Native American** art (L3) • Making **polychrome pots** (L3) • Explaining **sand painting** (L3) • Studying **Houser's sculpture** (L3) • **Cannon's** paintings (L3) • Painting of **Howe, Namingha** (L3)	• Explaining the **French Revolution** (L1) • Defining **Neoclassic art** (L1) • Introducing **Romantic art** (L1) • England: **Turner** landscapes (L1) • Explaining the **Salon** (L3) • Defining **art movement** (L3) • Introducing **Impressionist painting** (L3) • Defining Impressionism (L3) • Describing **Monet's** use of light (L3) • Describing **Renoir's** portraits (L3) • **Morisot:** capturing mood (L3) • Introducing **Impressionist sculpture** (L3) • **Rodin:** using uneven surfaces (L3)
Media and Techniques	• Paper, pencil, watercolor markers (L1) • Describing the loom (L2) • Coat hangers, masking tape, fibers, tapestry needles (L2) • Making a jar using molding and carving (L3) • Pencil, eraser, cardboard, knife, glue, brayer, tablespoon (L4)	• Paint, paper, watercolors and drawing (L1) • Pencil, paper, tempera, shoe box, mat board, scissors, glue (L2) • Found object, paper, pencil, crayon (L3) • Paper, pencil, white paper, tempera (L4)
Studio Production	• Painting a story (L1) • Making a round weaving (L2) • Making an Inuit-style print (L4)	• Sketching a mood (L1) • Designing a stage set (L2) • Drawing a point of interest (L3) • Painting a landscape (L4)
Safety		
Artists	• Houser (L1) • Lewis, Tafoya, Cannon, Howe, Namingha, Dallas (L3) • Kenojuak (L4)	• Renoir, David, Delacroix, Turner (L1) • David (L2) • Monet, Renoir, Morisot, Rodin (L3) • Monet (L4)

Scope and Sequence Chart

	Chapter 15 *Art of the Late Nineteenth Century*	Chapter 16 *Art of the Early Twentieth Century*
Elements and Principles of Art	• Using brush strokes to show form (L1) • **Arbitrary** vs. **optical** color use (L1) • Using elements and principles in painting (L2) • Using texture in drawing (L3) • Using elements and principles in expressive painting (L4) • Cézanne: using colors for harmony (L1) • Van Gogh: use of color and texture (L1) • Gauguin: using line and color (L1) • Ryder: the source of light (L2) • Cassatt: using light for mood (L3) • Tanner: using hue, value, shape (L4)	• Using elements of art in non-objective art (L1) • Using elements of art to create unity (L1) • Light and dark values (L1) • Braque: using texture and unity (L2) • Sloan: using emphasis (L3) • Bellows: creating movement (L3) • Curry: using emphasis (L3) • Fauvism: using bold color (L1) • Cézanne: seeing form in nature (L1) • Lipchitz: using texture and harmony (L1) • Kandinsky: using only color, shape, line (L1)
Aesthetics/ Art Criticism	• Examining Your Work (L2, L4) • Degas: creating mood (L1) • Describing style of Seurat (L2) • Eakins: using reality (L3) • Post-Impressionism: aesthetic view (L1) • Homer: the story teller (L3) • Ryder: dreamlike images (L3) • Cassatt: Impressionist (L3)	• Examining Your Work (L2, L4) • Expressing mood in a collage (L1) • Expressionism: innermost feelings (L1) • Describing and interpreting **Kirchner's** work (L1) • Describing **Kollwitz** prints (L1) • Kandinsky: non-objective art (L1) • The Eight: realistic painting (L3)
Art History	• Defining **Post-Impressionism** (L1) • **Cézanne:** working with color patches (L1) • **Van Gogh:** capturing feeling (L1) • **Gauguin:** using unusual color (L1) • **Seurat:** using **Pointillism** (L1) • Introducing **American art** (L3) • Defining **realism** (L3)	• **Fauvism** (L1) • **Matisse:** use of color (L1) • Introducing **Expressionism** (L1) • Introducing **Cubism** (L1) • **Picasso:** founder of Cubism (L1) • **Braque** (L1) • **Lipchitz:** Cubist sculpture (L1) • Defining **The Eight** (L3) • Defining **The Ashcan school** (L3) • **Sloan** (L3) • **Bellows** (L3) • **Stieglitz:** photography as a new art form (L3) • Introducing **Regionalism** (L3) • **Curry** (L3) • Introducing art in Mexico (L3) • Defining **muralist** (L3) • **Rivera** (L3)
Media and Techniques	• Bottle, paper, pencil, tempera (L1) • Paper, pencil, tempera (L2) • Paper, pencil, watercolor paint, brushes, tempera, pen, India ink (L4)	• Collage (L1) • Chalk and drawing (L2) • Magazines, tracing paper, pencil, paper, India ink (L3) • Paper, pencil, foam tray, brayer, water-based printing ink (L4)
Studio Production	• Drawing with color patches (L1) • Making a Post-Impressionist painting (L2) • Using texture in drawing (L3) • Making an expressive watercolor (L4)	• Creating a photo collage (L1) • Making a Cubist chalk drawing (L2) • Making an expressive abstract design (L3) • Making an action print (L4)
Safety	• Using safe paints (L2)	• Using chalk safely (L2) • Using fixative safely (L2)
Artists	• Degas, Cézanne, van Gogh, Gauguin (L1) • Seurat (L2) • Eakins, Homer, Ryder, Cassatt (L3) • Tanner (L4)	• Kandinsky, Matisse, Kirchner, Kollwitz, Lipchitz (L1) • Braque (L2) • Sloan, Bellows, Stieglitz, Curry, Rivera (L3) • Bellows (L4)

Scope and Sequence Chart

Chapter 17
Art of Today

Elements and Principles of Art	• Creating optical illusion with line and shapes (L4) • Creating harmony (L1) • Using line to create tension (L1) • Using texture in sculpture (L1) • Creating unity and variety in sculpture (L1) • Using positive and negative shape (L3)
Aesthetics/ Art Criticism	• Examining Your Work (L2, L4) • Chirico: dreamlike picture (L1) • Magritte: realistic dream style (L2) • Gorky: abstract view (L3) • Lawrence: social protest (L3) • Interpreting Hanson (L3)
Art History	• Introducing **Duchamp** and **Dada** (L1) • Defining **Surrealism** (L1) • Defining **Abstract Expressionism** (L3) • Defining **Hard-Edge painting** (L3) • Defining **social protest painting** (L3) • Defining **New Realism** (L3) • Defining **Op Art** (L4) • Defining **technology** (L5) • Defining **multi-media art** (L5) • Kinetic art (L5)
Media and Techniques	• Paper, pencil, crayons or chalk and drawing (L1) • Pencil, sketching paper, tempera (L3) • Bleach, dark construction paper, cotton swab (L3) • Pencil, sketching paper, illustration board, India ink, pen, nibs (L4)
Studio Production	• Drawing a Surrealist Scene (L1) • Painting a Surrealist Style (L2) • Experimenting with action painting (L3) • Blending Hard-Edge and Op Art (L4)
Safety	
Artists	• Stella, De Chirico, Miró, Klee, Marini, Hepworth, Moore (L1) • Magritte (L2) • Gorky, Kelly, Lawrence, Wyeth, Calder, Nevelson, Hanson, Frankenthaler (L3) • Davis (L4) • Pfaff, Paik, Skoglund (L5)

Handbook

Aesthetics/ Art Criticism	• Examining Your Work (L1, L2, L3, L4, L5)

Technique Tips

Drawing Tips
- Making gesture drawings
- Making contour drawings
- Drawing with oil pastels
- Drawing thin brush lines
- Making an enlarging grid
- Using shading techniques
- Using sighting techniques
- Using a viewing frame
- Using a ruler

Painting Tips
- Cleaning a paint brush
- Making natural earth pigments
- Mixing paint: value and color
- Working with poster paints
- Working with watercolors

Printmaking Tip
- Making a stamp printing

Sculpting Tips
- Working with clay
- Joining clay
- Making a clay mold
- Mixing plaster
- Working with papier-mâché
- Making a paper sculpture

Other Tips
- Measuring rectangles
- Making a mat
- Mounting a two-dimensional work
- Making rubbings
- Scoring paper
- Making a tissue paper collage
- Working with glue

Studio Production
- Creating a computer-type drawing (L1)
- Making a coil pot (L2)
- Making a photo essay (L3)
- Designing a false face mask (L4)
- Designing a space colony (L5)

Safety

Career Exploration
- Art director, art teacher, computer graphics specialist, editorial cartoonist, exhibit and display designer, graphic designer, industrial designer, interior designer, magazine designer, medical illustrator, museum curator, photojournalist, special effects designer, urban planner

Artists
- Cézanne, Giotto, Goya, Lewis, Leyster, Michelangelo, Miró, Monet, Morisot, Nevelson, Ryder, Rivera, Stieglitz, Tanner

Designing a Quality Art Program

Teachers need to be keenly aware and responsive to the physical, intellectual, and social-emotional development of the middle school student in order to appropriately plan for instruction. The following strategies are suggested to help the teacher organize the chapters and lessons in the order that best meets the needs of their students.

- **Set goals.** The key to a quality art program is knowing your students and then deciding what you want them to learn. The Pacing Chart and the Scope and Sequence Chart in *Understanding Art* highlight topical emphases and suggest sequential development of material. In addition *Understanding Art* outlines specific objectives at the beginning of each chapter, which tells students what they will be learning. Teachers need to plan specific objectives to meet the general goals of a quality art education program. It is best if the objectives are behaviorally written. Use the curriculum guides developed by your school, school district, and/or state to create your own specific program.

- **Create lessons that divide the entire period.** Subdivide the time available for classroom instruction into a number of modules. These modules can vary in length and will, of course, depend on the activity to be completed. For example, introduce a new concept through slides or give a short demonstration, give an assignment, have students participate in a summary of the lesson, and assign a homework assignment before dismissing the class.

- **Offer a concise and clearly formulated structure for all activities.** Students must know exactly what is required of them for each specific activity. Give them as many "clues" as possible; for example, write instructions on the board, have them repeat your directions, give a handout, show a completed example, and so on. Do not assume that students can see the interrelationships between steps. Give students detailed step-by-step instructions and then show them how the steps are connected.

- **Provide variety within the class time.** Variety is achieved by having the various phases of the art program accomplished within the given period. For instance, the lesson can include slides or a portion of a video combined with a studio production activity and concluding with class discussion. You must recognize that providing variety maintains student enthusiasm and interest.

- **Give explanations for each activity.** Students must know what they can expect to learn from a certain activity.

- **Provide motivation and readiness techniques.** Once students know what is expected of them, you must make an extra effort to provide motivational techniques to get students involved in the lesson focus. In his book *Emphasis Art* (1985), Wachowiak suggests the following motivational resources:

  — Reproductions of paintings, sculpture, prints, and crafts that can supplement, illuminate, and intensify the objectives of the lesson.

  — Photographs, in color or black and white, that can extend the students' visual repertoire of experiences.

  — Color slides of paintings, drawings, sculpture, prints, architecture, and crafts; of design elements in nature and constructed objects; of creative work by children worldwide; of examples illustrating technical stages in a project; of people in active work, in sports, and in costume; and of animals, birds, fish, insects, and flowers.

  — Filmstrips and video tapes on artists, art history, and art techniques.

  — Films, TV films, and tapes that relate to the art project undertaken.

  — Books (stories, plays, poems, and biographies) and periodicals that can help both teachers and students toward a richer interpretation of the art project undertaken.

  — Recordings (disk or tape) of music, dramatizations, poetry, sounds of geographic regions—city and country, nature's forces, forest and jungle—and sounds of machines, planes, ships, trains, rockets, circuses, and amusement centers.

  — Guests invited to art class as inspiration, such as police officers, fire fighters, and nurses; performers such as clowns, dancers, pantomimists, and musicians with their instruments; and scuba divers, pilots, athletes in uniform, and, if possible, an astronaut outfit.

— Resource and sketching trips to science, natural, and historical museums; art museums; university and college art studios; farms; factories; wharves; airports; observatories; bus and train stations; bridge and dam sites; national parks; zoos; shopping malls; boat marinas; air shows; amusement parks; and historical monuments. Be sure field trips are planned in advance. Visit the sketching site beforehand, if possible, to check on hazards and permits. Clear permission with the school principal so that parental approval can be obtained and travel arrangements can be expedited. If necessary, arrange for parent chaperones.

— Models for art-class drawing projects may include animals, birds and fish, flowers and plant life, dried fall weeds, beehives, bird's nests, insect and butterfly collections, terrariums, pets, rocks and pebbles, fossils, coral, seaweed and seashells, skeletons of animals, and assorted still-life material: fruits and vegetables, including gourds; lanterns; kettles; teapots; vases; old clocks; bottles; fish net; old lamps; assorted fabrics for drapery; musical instruments; bicycles and motorcycles; and old hats, shoes, and gloves. Vintage automobiles can be sketched in school parking lots.

— Artifacts from other cultures and countries: masks, wood carvings, costumes, textiles, ceramics, toys, dolls, puppets, kites, armor, fans, and paper umbrellas.

— Examples of children's art in varied media from worldwide sources.

— Demonstrations of art techniques by teacher and students.

— Introduction of a new art material or tool or a new use for commonly employed art materials.

— Planned exhibits and bulletin board displays that relate to the art project in process.

— Assorted devices and equipment to help expand the students' awareness and visual horizons: microscopes, prisms, kaleidoscopes, touch-me kinetics, magnifiers, color machines, liquid light lamps, telescopes, microscopic projectors, computers, mirrors, and black light.

- **Use recall and transition strategies.** Help students connect material they have already learned with new material. Open-ended questions are a particularly effective technique. An effective lesson for pupils is to provide several activities designed to accomplish an objective. For example, if students were to learn about van Gogh, show a video about his art; have them study about the time period and cultural context of his life; have them learn about color, color mixing, and painting techniques by viewing his art; and then maybe have them create a painting in his style or of a similar subject matter.

- **Within the class structure, be flexible.** Middle school/junior high art teachers are most often structured and organized. They spend a great deal of time preparing challenging art lessons, but they need to be flexible. Sometimes it may be necessary to reteach a concept, or a conflict may arise, or some interesting question is asked that needs further exploration. Be flexible within the prescribed time limits.

- **In the concept development process, move from concrete to abstract.** Always begin with the specific or concrete examples, and then move to the more abstract, general, or theoretical. Concrete examples are exact and can often be something students can touch—a reproduction of an art work, a model, an advertisement, various media, or objects.

- **Ask effective questions to reach the objectives of each lesson.** Teachers should refine their questioning techniques. In preparation for teaching, plan several key stimulating questions that serve to promote students' critical thinking skills and to maintain student interest. You may want to evaluate your questions by asking:
  — Do the questions I ask elicit concepts?
  — Are the questions focused on the lesson objectives?

— Are they clear?
— Do I ask questions only one time?
— Do the questions promote critical thinking skills?
— Do I wait enough time after asking each question?

- **Provide an evaluation or summary.** There should be a summary at the end of each activity and also at the end of the class. You should help students see what they learned during the lesson and prepare them for the next step. This also provides an opportunity for students to ask questions.

Creating a Positive Learning Environment

Understanding Art provides a variety of activities to help the teacher create a positive learning environment and to support the concepts presented in the text. You will need to select those activities that best suit your teaching methods and the needs, and interests, maturity level, and artistic abilities of your students.

The following suggestions can help art teachers structure the classroom to create a positive learning environment for all students.

- Accept students as they are and encourage students to reach their maximum level of potential.
- Become familiar in detail with the specific learning styles of your students and employ media that will help them achieve success.
- Find out about the students' previous art education programs.
- If possible, obtain assistance from a teacher's aide to help with individual or organizational problems that may occur in the art classroom.
- Art teachers are often required to write and implement an individualized educational plan for students with special needs. Find out if this is the case in your school.

Teaching Students with Varying Ability Levels and Learning Styles

In most art classrooms there is a wide range of ability levels and learning styles. It becomes critical that teachers identify the various abilities within the classroom and adapt instructional materials to meet the needs. Below are additional suggestions for teaching students with varying ability levels and learning styles.

The Hearing Impaired
- Learn sign language—at least a few basic words.
- Use the chalkboard or other visuals to highlight key art concepts, vocabulary words, or terms.
- Give the students your lecture notes or ask a good student to make copies of his or her notes.
- Speak normally and look directly at a hearing-impaired student when you are speaking.
- Write instructions for activities on the chalkboard, or hand out written instructions.
- Encourage as much verbal interaction as possible.

The Visually Impaired
- Emphasize art experiences that promote kinesthetic manipulation and multisensory stimulation.
- Assign student helpers.
- Provide opportunities for students to tape-record assignments or to complete them orally.
- Tape-record each chapter of the textbook for the students' use.
- Administer tests orally.
- Let students move around the art classroom freely so that they can get close to displays or three-dimensional visuals located in the room.

The Learning Disabled
- Provide an organized environment.
- Make expectations and directions clear and realistic.
- Give large amounts of positive reinforcement that indicate the students' strengths.
- Encourage small-group participation.
- Encourage students to participate in discussions.
- Avoid assigning these students to seats around distracting students.
- Provide positive feedback whenever possible.

The Physically Challenged
- If necessary, rearrange the classroom to accommodate the students' needs.
- Encourage these students to participate in physical activities whenever possible.
- Allow sufficient time for completion of a task.
- Plan studio projects that can be broken down into sequential and manageable tasks.

The Gifted and Talented

- Be patient and nurture these youths' playfulness because this contributes to their cognitive development.
- Avoid overstructuring tasks and time for gifted students; they need the freedom to come up with solutions.
- Demand and challenge these students. It is always good to give verbal positive reinforcement, but they should work for it.
- Encourage students to think about and use metaphors in their art work.
- Establish an art honorary society as an effective way for gifted students to receive special recognition.
- Expose these students to quality art work created by others. Do not let these students be content to compare their work with that of peers.
- The general consensus regarding teaching the gifted is to let them work independently. So-called gifted students should be given the same assignments the other students are given, but they should be challenged to stretch the possibilities of the assigned project or theme to the fullest.

The Limited-English Proficiency Student

Students with limited English proficiency may not have problems with mastering art content. Their difficulty may be only with the English language. The following teaching strategies will help you provide a welcoming positive learning environment:

- Allow students to become familiar with the structure of English. Even if students make grammatical mistakes, praise their efforts. Provide a classroom environment in which students can experiment with English.
- Students can often understand more than they can say. Students may be able to construct simple sentences but have difficulty with idioms, figures of speech, and words with multiple meanings. Take time to explain yourself, or involve the other students in the explanation.

- If you assign art reports or other writing assignments, expect to see a mixture of English with their native language. Bear in mind that at this stage, helping an adolescent gain confidence and building self-esteem are valuable educational goals.
- Provide peer learning by grouping English-proficient students with students who have a limited proficiency. Encourage students to work in small groups or in pairs to teach one another various art skills.

Teaching Art to Students From All Cultural Backgrounds

Art teachers are faced with the challenge of teaching art and all its cultural contexts to a changing wide range of ethnic groups. Art teachers respect and appreciate ethnic diversity and whenever possible should adapt teaching strategies, curriculum content, and the classroom environment to best meet individual student's needs. The teacher should be committed to multicultural education and to a culturally pluralistic view. In cultural pluralism people with different ethnic backgrounds retain many of their cultural traditions but also adapt to predominant North American social values, the English language, and many other aspects of life. Within this view people can possess their particular ethnic perspective and still identify with the general policies of this society.

A quality multicultural-sensitive art program should begin to help students do the following:

- Celebrate the diversity of individuals and cultures as seen through their art.
- Understand different world views and concepts expressed through art in various cultures.
- Understand how the cultural mores affect art.
- Understand the different subcultures within a core culture and explore the differences in the ways those subcultures express themselves through art.
- Understand the roles of artists in different cultures.
- Understand how art affects changes within a culture and also how it sometimes maintains the status quo.

- Understand how the physical environment has affected the visual arts.
- Understand the support (for example, financial, educational, and so on) given for the visual arts and the impact made within a culture.
- Help students make connections with other subjects (such as social studies, religion, history, or economics).
- Understand both *what* art is and *why* it was made.

The following are some sample activities that could be used in getting students to explore cultural contexts:

- Visit an art museum and have students pretend they are cultural anthropologists. They could work individually or in a group. Have them pick three or four art works and compare them and the cultures they represent.
- Have students pick a theme such as nature, color, religion, wooden objects, life/death, utility and find related works of art through library research or by visiting a museum. Ask students to compare and contrast the expressions of the theme in the various works.
- Have students pick a particular aspect of one culture and compare it with the same aspect of another culture. For example, students could compare the fiber arts of two cultures.

Below is a series of specific questions that can be helpful in exploring the cultural contexts of art works.

- What are the ideas, emotions, values, and/or qualities being transmitted through the art work?
- What does the work tell the viewer about the person who created it (that is, rank, status or role in his or her culture)?
- What does this piece tell the viewer about the culture it was created in?
- Does the art work tell the viewer anything about the style of the culture?
- Is the art form now extinct?
- Is the art considered popular, traditional, or avant-garde?
- Was this art produced because of ethnic revitalization or simply as an economic response to the perceived desires of the consumer?

- Was this work an innovation? If so, why did it come about?
- Why would one culture put more emphasis on the shape of a bowl, another on the pictorial decoration, another on size, another on texture, and so on?
  1. Does this difference indicate specific availability of materials, knowledge of tools, or specific needs of their personal, social, or religious life?
  2. Are these differences related to date, climate, or trade patterns?
  3. To what degree do differences depend on the skills and dedication of the individual artist?
- What evidence can be found that one culture has learned from (been acculturated with) another culture?
  1. Is there a similarity in utilitarian objects or pictorial subject matter?
  2. Is there a similarity in the treatment of materials?
  3. Is there a similarity in emphasis on the depiction of the human figure or of other subject matter?

Teaching Critical Thinking in the Art Classroom

Helping students to think critically is one of the major goals of education. Critical thinking can be defined generally as the process of logically deciding what to do, create, or believe.

Creative thinking requires the ability to identify and formulate problems, as well as the ability to generate alternative solutions. Fluency (quality of ideas), flexibility (variety of ideas), originality (unusual or unique ideas), and elaboration (details for the implementation of ideas) are necessary components of creative thinking.

The following assumptions underlie the teaching of thinking:

- All students are capable of higher-level thinking.
- Thinking skills can be taught and learned in the art classroom.
- Appropriate expectations for logical thinking are based on physiological maturation, social experiences, and the knowledge level of the students.

- Students can be taught to transfer thinking skills from the art content area to an internalized process applicable to a variety of new learning.

How do you teach thinking skills in the art classroom? Teachers need to reflect on their instructional strategies used in daily art lessons and include opportunities for students to reason and think about what is being learned.

Bloom's taxonomy is generally the most widely recognized scheme for levels of thinking. Each of Bloom's categories includes a list of various thinking skills. Here are some examples:

- **Knowledge:** define, recognize, recall, identify, label, understand, examine, show, collect.
- **Comprehension:** translate, interpret, explain, describe, summarize.
- **Application:** apply, solve, experiment, show, predict.
- **Analysis:** connect, relate, differentiate, classify, arrange, check, group, distinguish, organize, categorize, detect, compare, infer.
- **Synthesis:** produce, propose, design, plan, combine, formulate, compose, hypothesize, construct.
- **Evaluation:** appraise, judge, criticize, decide.

The art class is a fertile content area to help students develop critical and creative thinking skills. Begin by knowing the cognitive level of the students in your classroom and realize that not all questions or interactions need to be initiated by the teacher. Dialogue among peers is a way to promote critical thinking. Having students discuss, debate, explain, decide, or creatively solve problems increases critical thinking skills. Encourage students to generate answers to solve their own problems, create their own art projects, and be responsible for their own learning.

The following are some examples of critical thinking questions:

- **Knowledge**—the identification and recall of information:
  — Who, what, when, where, how . . . ?
  — Describe an art work.
- **Comprehension**—the organization and selection of facts and ideas:
  — Retell in your own words . . .

  — What is the main idea of . . . ?
  — Create an art work that demonstrates . . .
- **Application**—the use of facts, rules, principles:
  — How is . . . an example of . . . ?
  — How is . . . related to . . . ?
  — Demonstrate through . . . art activity . . .
- **Analysis**—the separation of a whole into component parts:
  — What are the parts or features of . . . ?
  — Classify . . . according to . . .
  — How does . . . compare/contrast with . . . ?
- **Synthesis**—the combination of ideas to form a new whole:
  — Construct a . . .
  — What would you predict/infer from . . . ?
  — What might happen if you combined . . . with . . . ?
  — Design a . . .
- **Evaluation**—the development of opinions, judgments, or decisions:
  — What do you think about . . . ?
  — Prioritize . . .
  — Criticize this art work.

Implementing Cooperative Learning

In the same way that society is made up of groups such as sports teams, families, and political parties, learning in the classroom is most effective when students cooperate to achieve a common goal within an art lesson.

Cooperative learning is when students are assigned to work in small heterogeneous groups of four or five. Student groups are chosen by the teacher. The major difference between cooperative learning and traditional group projects is that the completion of a project and mastery of a lesson are dependent upon each student's contributions to the team effort. When graded, each group is given a team score based on an average of each individual's grade.

The recognition of teams that clearly meet the goals and criteria set by the teacher is an important aspect of cooperative learning. Students that are lazy cannot easily get by with utilization of this teaching strategy. The situation is designed so that the *group* may achieve recognition and success as a team—individual members encourage each other to complete the specific tasks at hand.

Cooperative learning is an ideal strategy to employ in the art classroom. Not only are the learning experiences effective with studio activities but they can also be used to teach art history, art criticism, and aesthetic concepts.

Relating Art to Other Content Areas

Interdisciplinary teaching is central to the middle school/junior high concept. Efforts to integrate and interrelate the many areas of the school curriculum have a long history and are supported by a large amount of research. Interdisciplinary programs are organized in many different ways and involve various degrees of curriculum integration. Below is a listing of a few ways that art teachers can encourage and participate in such approaches.

- **Total staff approach.** This involves a school-wide theme approach to interdisciplinary learning. In this format art teachers must seek ways to relate both instruction and curriculum to the chosen theme.
- **Interdisciplinary teams.** Having an interdisciplinary event or course of study undertaken by a team of three to five teachers is the approach used most often. Because few teachers have been prepared for this type of planning and teaching, the following list of steps outlined in *Interdisciplinary Teaching in the Middle Grades*, (1990) by Gordon F. Vars, may be helpful.
  1. Review goals and objectives for that grade level and/or subjects.
  2. Review curriculum scope and sequence. Determine degree of flexibility.
  3. Determine the type of interdisciplinary unit that will be attempted: correlated, fused, or purely problem-centered without restriction as to subjects covered.
  4. Brainstorm themes, topics, or problem areas that: (a) fit the given curriculum, (b) are interdisciplinary, and (c) appear to be relevant to students.
  5. Seek student reactions and input.
  6. Select one or two themes, topics, or problem areas for further development.
  7. Explore the contributions of each subject area to the unit, including pertinent content, skills, and learning activities.
  8. Develop an overall framework or outline for the unit.
  9. Locate learning materials and other sources. Invite students to help.
  10. Plan procedures for evaluating student learnings.
  11. Determine logistics:
      a. Time frame; full-time or part-time each day?
      b. Student groupings.
      c. Rooms and other facilities needed.
      d. Equipment needed.
  12. Carry out the unit, seeking student involvement along the way and at its conclusion.
  13. Evaluate the unit.
- **Self-contained and block-time classes.** This approach gives one teacher responsibility for the so-called academic subjects, with students traveling to art and other similar classes. Whenever possible, art teachers should work with self-contained classroom teachers to interrelate appropriate content. Block-time teachers should also work closely with art teachers to make connections whenever possible.

There are basically three ways to interrelate different subject areas.

- **Correlation.** Correlation arises out of cooperative planning among teachers even if they are not officially members of a team. Correlation only requires that teachers try to present related material at the same time. Through merely a change in the sequence of their materials, students can benefit from reinforcement of learning. This approach shows students how various subjects are related.
- **Fusion.** Fusion, or unified studies, as it is sometimes referred to, is often organized around a theme. For example, a class called "World History" may be offered, which would include art, music, literature, and dance.
- **Core.** Core is a type of curriculum that focuses on helping students deal with their immediate problems or issues of significance to them.

Both students and their teachers vary in their needs and characteristics, so schools should use a variety of approaches. Art teachers need to be aware of the various approaches and actively participate in the interdisciplinary process.

Teachers or teams inevitably develop interdisciplinary units in their own unique ways, but they can benefit from examining units developed by others. Teachers are urged to keep informed of new developments through reading professional journals and attending workshops and conferences.

A few sources especially appropriate for middle school teachers are described below:

1. National Resource Center for Middle Grades Education, University of South Florida, EDU 115, Tampa, FL 33620. Reproducible interdisciplinary units available for purchase. Write for current list. As new units become available, they are announced in the Resource Center's newsletter, *Middle Grades Network*.

2. National Association for Core Curriculum, Inc. 404 White Hall, Kent State University, Kent, OH 44242. Units of various lengths are sold at cost.

3. ERIC Document Reproduction Service, Computer Microfilm Corporation, 3900 Wheeler Avenue, Alexandria, VA 22304. Units occasionally appear in this source and are available in either microfiche or photocopy form. Titles are listed in *Resources in Education*, under the descriptor "Teaching Guides (for Teachers)" (052).

4. Association for Supervision and Curriculum Development, 125 North West Street, Alexandria, VA 22314. Resource units and interdisciplinary units occasionally appear among the curriculum materials displayed at the annual ASCD convention.

5. National Middle School Association, 4807 Evanswood Drive, Columbus, Ohio 43229-6292. How to design quality units may be found in their publication.

Providing Sources of Inspiration

Art teachers are generally receptive to a variety of resources that are available to them to help in the development of new units or lesson plans or to augment existing lessons. The following is a list of ideas that may serve as sources of inspiration:

- **Artist-in-residence programs.** These programs provide students with the rare opportunity to witness an artist at work.
- **Arts councils.** Art councils provide many educational programs that may offer unique possibilities.
- **Art teacher associations.** By becoming a member of your state association or the National Art Education Association you will have the opportunity to make interesting contacts. These associations sponsor conferences and seminars that offer a mixture of workshops, visits to schools, lectures, exhibitions, and social events.
- **Museums and galleries.** Both offer the opportunity to view various exhibitions. Museums also often offer educational services, slide presentations, and special docent tours. You can even find interesting inspirational materials in their gift shops.
- **Inservice training.** Many school districts offer special workshops on art education. Organize these yourself; have an idea-sharing session with teachers in your area.
- **Multicultural or cross-cultural experiences.** Learn about or visit an area in North America you are not familiar with, or travel to another country and visit art education programs, museums, and the like there.
- **Environment.** From the natural and human-made environment you can get many ideas.
- **Other.** Book stores, antique shops, junk stores, shopping malls, parks, historic homes, industries (especially those related to the art field), interesting speakers, poetry, music, dance, theatre, and so on.

Evaluating Performance

Many schools require written tests as well as performance grades. Although written tests should be only one part of the total evaluation of the art student's performance, the art teacher should approach testing as creatively as possible. Below are some guidelines to follow if you want to use test items other than those included in this program.

- Always build some success into each test. Place a few simple items that everyone will be able to answer at the beginning of the test. The positive reinforcement received from answering the first questions correctly may overcome students' fear of tests.

- The test items should span a range of cognitive levels instead of being limited to the recall of facts. The following list gives examples related to visual art for each level.
  - **Knowledge:** This level requires the recall of facts, terminology, dates, events, or titles of art works. It also involves the recall of simple processes such as cleaning a brush, mixing colors, and/or classifying works according to style. The highest level of knowledge required is knowledge of universals and abstractions.
  - **Comprehension:** In visual art this level may include diagramming, explaining, summarizing, and/or predicting outcomes.
  - **Application:** This level relates to the proper use of materials. It can be tested, for example, by asking students to describe how to make a glue print or what steps must be followed to join clay.
  - **Analysis:** An example of this level of cognitive learning is the analysis step in art criticism. Analysis can deal with the students' work as well as with reproductions of works by master artists.
  - **Synthesis:** At this level students display their ability to use a combination of concepts or elements to solve a visual problem. This creative level can be tested by asking students to produce designs expressing a particular emotion. Synthesis is much more open-ended than the previous levels. In art, it is usually tested in an art production activity rather than by a verbal problem.
  - **Evaluation:** Critically examining an art work requires judging and giving reasons for the judgment.

  By using various cognitive levels in designing tests, you will be able to distinguish the achievement levels of students.
- Keep the reading level of tests low so that you are testing art knowledge and not reading ability. Make your tests as visual as possible, using drawings and reproductions. For example, you can test knowledge of color theory in several ways that do not require reading. You may put three reproductions on a bulletin board, number each work, and ask the students which one contains cool colors. This question is a better test of the student's understanding of cool colors than asking them to name these colors. Ask the students to describe how to change the value of a hue, to use paint to mix a light value of a hue, or to find a magazine picture showing a light value of a specific hue.
- You could also display several reproductions identified with numbers and ask the students to recognize different color concepts by listing which reproduction uses high-intensity colors, which shows a large area with a light value of red, or which uses a complementary color scheme.
- Essay tests require high-level thinking in which students must reorganize knowledge. Be sure to make expectations for the answers clear for these tests. For example, ask for at least four works of art using a technique, or similarities and differences between two artists' works. Ask essay questions about the students' work as well as works of the masters.

Other Evaluation Methods

The following suggestions are based on classroom practices of experienced teachers. Not all of them are appropriate for every situation. Try the ones you think will work for you.

1. Daily participation grades: As the class works, quickly give each student a check in your roll book for satisfactory participation, a check-plus for exceptional work, a check-minus for below average participation, and a minus or zero for inadequate work.
2. Anecdotal records: At the end of the day, take a few minutes to record any outstanding student behavior, either positive or negative.
3. Daily journals: Have students record what they have done in class each day. These journals may be part of the students' notebooks. At the end of the grading period, they will help you remember what students have accomplished. The entries in the journals do not have to be elaborate. For example, they might be as simple

as "I helped Joe mix colors to make a color wheel," or "Continued working on my expressive painting."

4. Performance criteria for creative work: Grading criteria should be planned and explained to students before they start an activity. One way to grade an art work is to assign percentages out of a total of 100 to each item in the "Examining Your Work" feature in the text (plus others you want to add). Although the subjective aspect of grading art cannot be eliminated, it can be reduced by using performance criteria. You might decide to give A's for exceeding objectives, B's for meeting all of them, C's for completing a certain number, and so on.

5. Written evaluations: When you grade major works, whether they are verbal or visual, take the time to write evaluations of strengths and weaknesses.

Finally, remember that students' talent should not influence evaluation. Each student should be graded on his or her specific achievements. A student with little natural ability who struggles to draw a still life should be recognized for his or her effort. However, a talented student who does not finish the assignment or turns in careless work should not be given a high grade. (At the same time, don't penalize the gifted student for being able to produce work in little time.) Since most art classes are a good place to practice mainstreaming, they will often contain students with a wide range of abilities. Tailor your expectations to fit the different levels of your students' capabilities.

Classroom Environment and Management

Although they tend to be taken for granted, a classroom's environment and organization are a part of the instruction process for the art teacher. Teachers working with junior high students are confronted daily with problems of discipline. By providing an effectively designed physical environment, many problems can be prevented and students will have the opportunity to learn responsible behavior. Researchers in the areas of environmental psychology, architecture, interior space design, communications theory, and sociology have developed a large body of information that can assist the art teacher in guiding environmental decisions. Art teachers need to understand that the spatial arrangement of the art classroom has a major impact, not only on discipline, but also on the effectiveness of teaching in general.

Classroom Organization

Quality art programs continue the traditional studio experiences, which include diverse laboratory activities. Pupils learning about art production need to be provided a safe, comfortable, and organized area in which to work in these various media.

In addition, the classroom needs to be designed so that quality learning outcomes may be achieved in the study of art history, art criticism, and aesthetics. Every art teacher develops her or his own style for organizing, arranging, and effectively using classroom space. The following points are suggested in order to have a quality art education program:

- Organize the room so that there are distinct areas where certain activities always take place.
- Pay attention to the amount of space needed by pupils so that they may work effectively.
- When students are required to clean up by using the sink, the proximity of student work areas should be considered.
- Map out specific procedures to expedite cleanup.
- Cluster storage and work areas so that travel around the room by students is limited.

- Arrange your supplies, and label shelves where materials are to be stored.
- Provide the least restrictive setting for the activities you plan.
- Pay attention to your floor plan—where storage is located and general traffic flows.
- Tell students your classroom rules, such as where supplies are stored, to put away things where they found them, and so on.
- Make sure the desks or tables are arranged so that the teacher can easily view each student.
- Arrange the room so that there is easy movement around the room. Try to prevent congestion around sinks, door, or other areas.
- Emphasize order and respect for equipment and materials; have students apply the "golden rule."
- Have students avoid unnecessary trips around the room. Be clear as to where you want them to be in the room.
- Make sure you can have eye contact with everyone in the class.
- Set up a "home base" location for student tables or desks. If student desks or tables are moved around for a particular activity mark the original location in some way, such as with tape or paint on the floor, so that they can be easily returned.
- Make your room interesting and aesthetically pleasing! A carefully designed room sends a message to students that you care about art and about their learning experiences.
- Have a wide variety of items around your room to make it interesting (for example, plants; shells; fossils; artifacts from other cultures; lots of visuals; still-life materials; interesting garage sale, junk store, or junk yard finds, and so on).

On the following pages are suggested floor plans for a classroom, a darkroom, and storage/kiln room.

Safety in the Classroom

Because there are many potential health hazards in the art classroom, the art teacher must be particularly careful. It is *very important* that

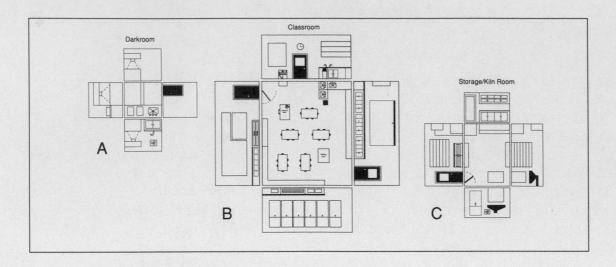

Darkroom

Classroom

Storage/Kiln Room

A

B

C

Darkroom

Door to Classroom

A

Storage/Kiln Room

Fireproof
Locker

Cabinets

Kiln

Kiln

Door to Classroom

Kiln

C

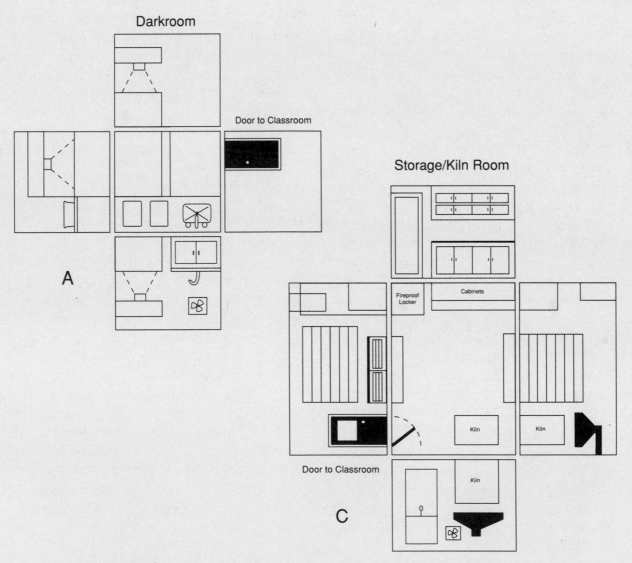

Classroom

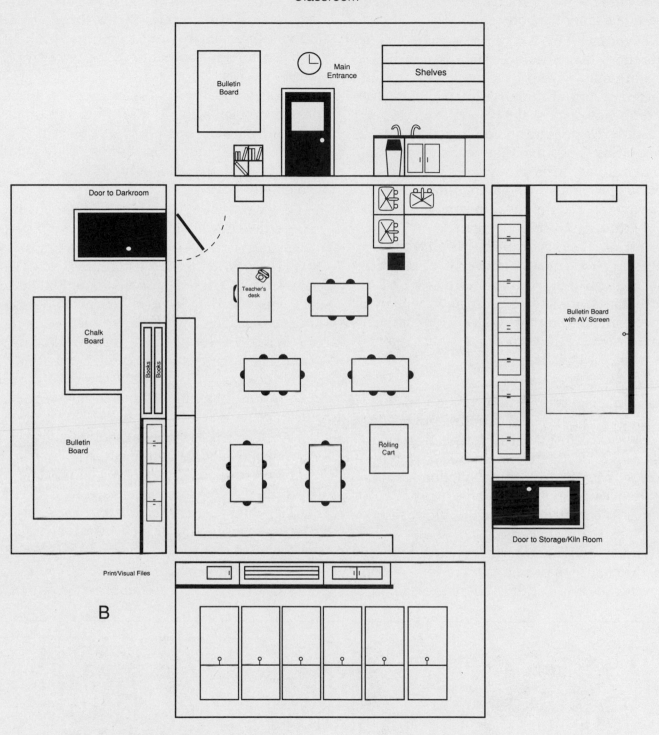

Bulletin Board

Main Entrance

Shelves

Door to Darkroom

Chalk Board

Books

Books

Bulletin Board

Teacher's desk

Rolling Cart

Bulletin Board with AV Screen

Door to Storage/Kiln Room

Print/Visual Files

B

every teacher become aware of how to minimize health risks in the art classroom. Listed below are the major routes by which hazardous materials enter the body.

- **Skin contact.** This is a common route of entry into the body. Substances such as acid, bleach, and organic solvents destroy skin upon contact. There are certain chemicals that go even deeper and may even enter the bloodstream (for example, turpentine and methyl alcohol).
- **Inhalation.** The inhalation of toxic fumes, dust, smoke, spray mists, and vapors may cause serious problems—damaging lungs and airways, and sometimes affecting the whole body through the blood stream.
- **Ingestion.** Serious problems result from ingesting toxic materials directly or indirectly (such as through mouth contact with hands, drawings, implements, food, and the like that have come into contact with such materials). Do not let young adults chew on pencils, paintbrushes, and the like.

Labeling

Labeling can provide information on any potentially dangerous art supplies, but teachers need to be aware of what various labels mean. The label "non-toxic," for example, does not guarantee a product's safety. According to federal regulations, toxicity means that a single exposure can be fatal to adults. The effect on children, who are more likely to be harmed by dangerous substances, is not considered in this definition. Also, the chance of developing chronic or long-term illnesses is not addressed by the legal definition of toxicity. Repeated exposure to non-toxic materials is not always safe. Many dangerous substances, such as asbestos, can legally be defined as non-toxic. Also, some art supplies, particularly those manufactured by small or foreign companies, may be improperly labeled as non-toxic.

Not all products whose labels provide chemical components but have no warnings or list no information at all are safe to use. Since manufacturers are not required to disclose ingredients, products without this information or warnings are potentially hazardous.

For more complete information on the presence of hazardous substances in art supplies, teachers may request a Material Safety Data Sheet (OSHA Form 20) from the manufacturer. This sheet provides information on potential health and fire hazards, a list of chemicals that might react dangerously with the product, and a list of all ingredients for which industrial standards exist. The manufacturer should supply this sheet on request, and a local public health official or poison control center technician can help interpret the information.

Art teachers can also take advantage of voluntary labeling standards developed by the art materials industry. The Art and Craft Materials Institute (ACMI) administers a voluntary testing and labeling program that helps to ensure the safety of those who work with art materials. This system uses the labels CP, AP, and HL.

CP (Certified Product) and AP (Approved Product) labels are used mainly on products

MEETS PERFORMANCE STANDARDS

Saftey labels approved by the Art and Craft Materials Institute (ACMI).

designed for younger children, while HL (Health Label) is used on products intended for older children and adults. Products labeled CP, AP, or HL are certified in a program of toxicological evaluation by a medical expert to contain no materials in sufficient quantities to be toxic or injurious to humans or to cause acute or chronic health problems. Products labeled CP, in addition, meet specific requirements of material, workmanship, working qualities, and color. HL means that the product is certified to be properly labeled in a program of toxicological evaluation by a medical expert. The Art and Craft Materials Institute makes available a list of institute-certified products. For a copy, or for more information on the Institute's certification program, write to:

> The Art and Craft Materials Institute
> 715 Boylston Street
> Boston, MA 02116

Common Toxic Processes and Materials

As shown above, many techniques and materials art teachers use are *very* dangerous. For the elementary level a restriction to AP- or CP-approved products is fine, but middle school/junior high art teachers will want to provide their students with more challenging techniques and media. Be aware of the potential risks in such offerings and take heed of the following:

- **Paint.** Some paints that are commonly used may be carcinogenic (for example, chromate and cadmium). The dangers of using lead pigments are well known and documented. If possible, do not use these inorganic pigments.

  Turpentine and other solvents, especially the ones used for varnishes and lacquers are *very* toxic. These should only be used with extreme caution and proper ventilation. Acrylic emulsions contain small amounts of formaldehyde and ammonia. Without proper ventilation, they may cause throat and lung irritations.

- **Ceramics.** Clay itself may be toxic. If people inhale silica dust or Kaolin dust over a prolonged period of time, it may cause silicosis. Whenever possible, use talc-free clay and asbestos-free talcs.

When mixing clay from powder, make sure to use an exhaust system and/or a toxic dust respirator. If clay dust is covering the studio, *never* try to sweep up the clay. Use a wet mop or HEPA-type vacuum cleaner.

When mixing glazes, wear a toxic dust respirator. Spraying glazes should be done only with a spray booth exhausted to the outside. It is important to stress to students to keep glazes off their skin.

- **Jewelry.** Local ventilation is a must. Teachers should purchase only lead-free enamels. Heated enamels give off infrared radiation, so teachers should require students to use infrared goggles to protect their eyes from injury.

- **Printmaking.** Local exhaust is required to prevent the accumulation of dangerous toxic vapors. Whenever possible, use water-based inks for all silk screening.

  With intaglio and lithography, the major danger is contact with the acids and the toxic gases given off when etching copper or zinc. Students should *never* mix acid baths. Rubber gloves, aprons, and face protectors should be worn when working with acids. Acid baths should have proper ventilation hoods over them.

- **Photography.** It requires proper ventilation. Hands should never be put into developer, stop-baths, or fixers. Use tongs. Kodak recommends at least ten changes of room air per hour for black-and-white processing.

- **Art materials in general.** Rubber cement contains large amounts of toxic hexane, which causes many serious health problems. Substitute other adhesives whenever possible. If students use a spray fixative, they should use it outside or in a spray booth.

  Over-heated wax for batik or encaustic may release dangerous fumes and formaldehyde. Watch for explosions or fires when using a hot plate, open flame, or iron.

- **Equipment.** Students should be carefully instructed in the proper use of drills, potters' wheels, paper cutters, printing presses, grinders, air brushes, knives, etc. Items should be labeled as dangerous. Require students to learn the proper procedures of equipment use, and make them take a test before using the equipment.

General Safety

There are certain guidelines to be followed in selecting art supplies to be used in the classroom. Perhaps the most important is to know what the materials are made of and what potential hazards exist. If a material is improperly labeled, or if adequate information cannot be obtained about it, don't use it. The following rules are also helpful:

- Be sure that all materials used by younger students (age 12 and under) have the CP or AP label and that materials used by older children and adults are marked HL.
- Don't use acids, alkalies, bleaches, or any product that will stain skin or clothing.
- Don't use aerosol cans because the spray can injure lungs.
- Use dust-producing materials (such as pastels, clays, plasters, chalks, powdered tempera, pigments, dyes, and instant papier-mâché, except the premixed cellulose type) with care in a well-ventilated area. Better yet, avoid using them at all.
- Avoid using solvents (including lacquers, paint thinners, turpentines, shellacs, solvent-based inks, rubber cement, and permanent markers) in the art room.
- Avoid using found or donated materials unless the ingredients are known.
- Avoid using old materials. Many art supplies formerly contained highly dangerous substances, such as arsenic, or raw lead compounds, or high levels of asbestos. Older solvents may contain chloroform or carbon tetrachloride.

Working conditions in the art room also affect safety. A disorderly, confused art room leads to unsafe conditions, particularly when there are many people working close to each other. Controlling the buildup of litter and dust, ensuring that tools are in good condition, and keeping the work space reasonably organized not only help prevent common accidents but also make it easier to recognize and eliminate other hazards. An orderly art room is absolutely essential to the students' and teacher's safety.

Following the above measures will provide a safe and healthy art environment. However, some students who, for one reason or another, run a higher risk of injury will need special precautions. It's a good idea to identify high-risk students at the beginning of each school term by sending questionnaires to parents and checking school records. Teachers are urged to plan programs with these students' limitations in mind.

The safety of students with some physical impairments must also be considered. Visually impaired students, for example, tend to get closer (sometimes within one or two inches) to the work in order to see it and are more likely to inhale fumes or dust. Also, they are less likely to notice spills. Some activities that create noise, such as hammering or using machinery, may be unsuitable for the hearing impaired. Asthmatics already have difficulties in breathing and should not be exposed to dust or fumes. Students with motor impairments may manipulate materials with their feet or mouths, making accidental ingestion or absorption more likely and cleanup more difficult.

Students who are mentally impaired may have trouble understanding rules for art room safety and may require extra supervision. Some students with emotional disturbances might deliberately abuse art supplies. Students who are taking medication or undergoing chemotherapy should be medically evaluated for possible interactions between their medications and art materials.

More information on safety in the art environment is available from The Center for Occupational Hazards, a national nonprofit clearinghouse for research and information on health hazards in art. For more information, or to subscribe to their newsletter, which covers a variety of topics on art safety, write to:

The Center for Occupational Safety
5 Beekman Street
New York, NY 10038

Resources in the Community

The community is an excellent resource for the art teacher. There are a wealth of opportunities available for enriching art instruction through the use of community resources. Every art teacher should create a notebook of resources.

The following are suggested contents for a resource notebook. Under each topic list the place, address, telephone number, contact person, hours, cost, topics covered, recommended group size, and grade-level suitability.

- **Museums/Galleries.** An obvious resource would be art museums and galleries. They often offer many educational programs. Larger museums often have an educational staff that will perform a variety of services for you.
- **Historical Sites.** Historic homes or buildings are particularly useful in teaching architectural concepts.
- **State and National Parks and Monuments.** State and national parks provide wonderful educational services.
- **Public and Social Services.** Public recreation areas may be used in a variety of ways. Various parks, lakes, and riverfront areas may be used also for picnic lunches while on a field trip.
- **Institutional Services.** College and university art departments will be an invaluable resource.
- **Industry and Business.** Think of each one in your community, and see how each could be useful to you. Your local newspaper and Chamber of Commerce are good resources.
- **Government Resources.** City or state art councils are an excellent resource for you. Check to see whether your city has an Office of Cultural Affairs. Many cities put out a cultural events list.
- **People.** There are many people in your local area who would be happy to come to your class or let you visit their studio. Include, of course, artists of every kind. Think about craftspeople, for example, quiltmakers, basketmakers, potters, or furniture makers.

Public Relations

It is important that a quality art program is visible to those in the school, school district, and community. If you desire strong support for your program, consider the following:

- Are you committed to the idea of public relations and convinced of its importance?
- Have you recruited the proper people (for example, parents, school board members, key community figures, etc.) for support?
- Have you planned a public relations program for the school year (for example, exhibitions, Youth Art Month activities, etc.)?
- Have you prepared hand-out materials to tell about your art program accomplishments, goals, how your program contributes to the community, etc?
- Have you committed at least a small portion of your art budget to "selling" your program so that you can eventually get more financial and other types of support?
- Does your art program have an image problem? Have you outlined steps that could be taken to improve this image?
- Do your principal, board members, media, and community leaders know about your quality art program? Have you personally contacted these individuals?
- Are other media contacts, local art museum or art councils familiar with the exciting things happening in your program?
- Do you work with other teachers in your school, county, or district to promote art education?
- When you hold special events (such as exhibitions, special field trips, etc.) do you contact the radio, newspaper, or television to offer suggestions for stories or photos?
- Have you contacted local community businesses or community organizations for support for your program? Many companies and organizations will give you free materials or money—they sometimes like taking on a special project (for example, helping send children to a special art exhibit).

Public Relations Strategies

One of the most effective public relations strategy is to display your students' art works. The following are teacher-tested ideas for displaying art work both within the school and throughout the community and creating support for the program.

- Use bulletin boards and display cases in halls at school as concept teaching boards. You could display projects from a "Studio Experience" activity with the title "Art Concepts." Type a brief explanation of the activity and mount it to accompany the display. You will be surprised at how many people will take the time to read the explanation of the concept that is illustrated.
- Have a "teacher's choice" work selected each year by a panel of judges, frame it, and place it on permanent display in the office. In a few years you will have an interesting collection.
- Get permission to hang framed students' work in high-traffic areas around the school building, such as offices, the lunchroom, the teachers' lounge, the library, and entrance halls. These pieces could be products of the Studio Lessons that students have had time to carefully plan and finish. These art works can be changed several times throughout the school year.
- Hold an exhibit at the end of each semester or at the end of the year. Send out invitations, have a guest book, and invite honored guests. Take photos and send them to the local newspaper.
- Contact local banks, other businesses, and government offices to display framed pieces. Volunteer to have your students paint store windows for special occasions.
- Hold an exhibit at the local mall.
- Encourage your students to participate in community art festivals and exhibits.
- Create public art to make community members notice your program. Paint a mural on the walls around a construction site, make relief tiles and mount them on a wall, stitch some banners, or weave wall hangings.

- Join and actively participate in the local art association. It can be a valuable source of contacts, information, and possible funding for special programs.
- Get a local art association or art-related business to sponsor your class. Its members or employees could not only donate money but also help you collect found items such as magazine pictures and fabric scraps for projects, hang art works for shows, or go with your class on a weekend trip to a museum.
- Organize a parents' support group. Even if you don't hold meetings, send out newsletters. Although everyone is busy, some parents will be interested enough in art education to volunteer help with your class.
- Speak to community groups in order to develop an interest in your art program; for example, the PTA, garden clubs, civic groups. Show slides of students' works, have students tape a narrative to accompany the slides explaining how and why they created their art works, or make a videotape of yourself teaching the class.
- Be involved with Youth Art Month activities. Contact the National Art Education Association, 1916 Association Drive, Reston, VA 22091-1590, for further information.

Notes

Understanding Art

A Sunday Afternoon on the Island of La Grande Jatte, 1884-85, by Georges Seurat was chosen for the cover design because of the luminous beauty of the work. Seurat began the work at the age of 25 and spent two years executing the final painting, which stands at six-and-a-half feet tall and ten feet long and includes 40 human figures. Before he finally completed the large canvas, he had done twenty drawings at the site or from models in his studio and thirty small paintings that were rapidly executed with broad brushstrokes.

An enterprise of this scope was unique among the painters dominated by the Impressionist vision. Most of them chose to work rapidly in order to capture fleeting effects in a short time. Apparently, under the dots, there is a layer of pigment that has been applied broadly, showing much the same technique as in his painting sketches. That is why white from the canvas does not show through.

The luminosity in Seurat's work comes about because of the technique he developed, which uses pointillist brushstrokes of pure pigment mixed in complementary and contrasting patterns to create optical color mixture in the eyes of the viewer.

Understanding Art

Gene Mittler, Ph.D.
Professor of Art
Texas Tech University

Rosalind Ragans, Ph.D.
Associate Professor Emerita
Georgia Southern University

GLENCOE

Macmillan/McGraw-Hill

Lake Forest, Illinois   Columbus, Ohio   Mission Hills, California   Peoria, Illinois

Send all inquiries to:
Glencoe Division, Macmillan/McGraw-Hill
15319 Chatsworth Street
P.O.Box 9609
Mission Hills, CA 91346-9609

ISBN 0-02-662286-6 (Student Text)
ISBN 0-02-662287-4 (Teacher's Wraparound Edition)

2   3   4   5   6   7   8   9   95   94   93   92

Editorial Consultants

Nancy C. Miller
Booker T. Washington High School
for the Performing and Visual Arts
Dallas, Texas

Jean Morman Unsworth
Art Consultant to Chicago
Archdiocese Schools
Chicago, Illinois

Contributors/Reviewers

Josephine Julianna Jones
Booker T. Washington High School
for the Performing and Visual Arts
Dallas, Texas

Johanna Stout
Art Teacher
New Caney High School
New Caney, Texas

Studio Lesson Consultants

Acknowledgments: The authors wish to express their gratitude to the following art coordinators and specialists who participated in the field test of the studio lessons.

Thomas Beacham, Telfair County High School, McRae, GA; Kellene Champlain, Fulton County Schools, Fulton, GA; Jane Dixon, Highlands Junior High School, Jacksonville, FL; Karen Roach Ford, Tecumseh Middle School, Lafayette, IN; Nadine Gordon, Scarsdale High School, Scarsdale, NY; Margie Ellen Greer, Ridgeway Junior/Senior High School, Memphis, TN; Barbara Grimm, Taylor Road Middle School, Alpharetta, GA; Ken Hatcher, Douglas Anderson School of the Arts, Jacksonville, FL; Annette Jones, Fletcher Junior High School, Jacksonville Beach, FL; Frances Kovacheff, Charles N. Scott Middle School, Hammond, IN; Geri Leigh, Stanton College Preparatory School, Jacksonville, FL; Nellie Lynch, Duval County Schools, Jacksonville, FL; Sandra Moore, John Sevier Middle School, Kingsport, TN; Bunyon Morris, Marvin Pittman Laboratory School, Statesboro, GA; Virginia Marshall Ramsey, Mabry Middle School, Marietta, GA; Joanne Rempell, Bradwell Institute High School, Hinesville, GA; Lahwana Reynolds, Glen Hills High School, Augusta, GA; Jane Rhoades, Georgia Southern College, Statesboro, GA; Julia Russell, Memphis City Schools, Memphis, TN; Barbara Shaw, Cobb County Schools, Cobb County, GA; Linda Smith, Millen Middle School, Millen, GA; Carolyn Sollman, Eminence School, Eminence, IN; Catherine Stalk, North Augusta High School, North Augusta, SC; Nancy Walker, Colonial Junior High, Creative & Performing Arts School, Memphis, TN; Betty Womack, William James Middle School, Statesboro, GA; Shirley Yokley, Tennessee Department of Education, Nashville, TN.

Photography Credits

Contents

viiT, Richard Lindner. *Rock-Rock*. Dallas Museum of Art, Dallas, Texas.
   Gift of Mr. & Mrs. James H. Clark.
viiB, André Derain. *The River Seine at Carrieres-sur-Seine*. Kimbell Art Museum.
viiiT, Milton Resnick. *Genie*. Whitney Museum of American Art,
   New York, New York.
ixT, Katsushika Hokusai. *View of Mt. Fuji from Seven-Ri Beach*. Metropolitan
   Museum of Art, New York, New York. Rogers Fund.
ixB, Earring. National Geographic Society, Washington, D.C.
xT, Myron. *The Discus Thrower*. Museo Nazionale Romano, Rome, Italy.
xB, Tamil Nadu. *Shiva, King of the Dancers* (Nataraja). Los Angeles County
   Museum of Art, Los Angeles, California. Given anonymously.
xiT, Africa, Nigeria. Court of Benin, Bini Tribe. *Mounted King and Attendants*.
   The Metropolitan Museum of Art, New York, New York.
   The Michael C. Rockefeller Memorial Collection. Gift of Nelson A. Rockefeller.
xiiT, Raphael. *The Small Cowper Madonna*. National Gallery of Art,
   Washington, D.C. Widener Collection.
xiiB, Judith Leyster. *Self-Portrait*. National Gallery of Art, Washington, D.C.
   Gift of Mr. & Mrs. Robert Woods Bliss.
xiiiT, Tony Dallas. *Koshare Clown*. Kachina Doll. Joan Cawley Gallery, Santa Fe,
   New Mexico.
xiiiB, Berthe Morisot. *In the Dining Room*. National Gallery of Art,
   Washington, D.C. Widener Collection.
xivT, Rosa Bonheur. *Plowing in the Niverne*. Fontainebleau, Chateau.
xivB, William Glackens. *Family Group*. National Gallery of Art,
   Washington, D.C. Gift of Mr. & Mrs. Ira Glackens.
xvT, Jacob Lawrence. *Tousaint L'Overture Series*. Fisk University.
xvB, Jan Steen. *The Drawing Lesson*. The J. Paul Getty Museum.

Text

R.A. Acharya/Dinodia, 114; Art Resource, New York, 25T, 85B, 178; Bill
Ballenberg, ixB, 89L; Gary Braash, 73TL, 73BL, 73R; Jack Breed, 201R; Digital
Art/Westlight, 304; Laima Druskis, 299L; Rick Fowler, selected student works;
Robert Frerck/Odyssey/Chicago, 55B, 83T, 84T, 84B, 90L, 105T, 105B, 115B, 122B,
122TL, 122TR, 146, 147T, 148, 150R; Ann Garvin, 297L, 297R, 298L, 298R, 299L,
299R, 301L, 301R, 302L, 302R, 303L; Giraudon/Art Resource, New York, xivT, 46,
49T, 65, 149, 187; Jack Stein Grove/PhotoEdit, 91T; Paul Hartman, 28; Erich
Lessing/PhotoEdit, 96, 111, 106L; Herbert Lotz, xiiiT, 200; Ray Lutz, 196L; Bruno
Maso/Bill Roberts/PhotoEdit, 185T; Douglas Mazonowica, 52; Stephen
McBrady/PhotoEdit, 300R; Henry Nelson, 20T; John Neubauer/PhotoEdit, 152;
Nimatallah/Art Resource, 100R; Odyssey, 115B; M. Richards, 303R; Bill
Roberts/PhotoEdit, 150L, 153B; Scala/Art Resource, New York, xT, 61, 85T, 100L,
101T, 107T, 154B, 163T, 165T, 169, 172, 179L, 188; Tektronix, 300L; Susan Van
Etten/PhotoEdit, 73R; Westlight/Comnet, 50B; Nick Wheeler/Black Star, 60; R.
White, 49B.

Illustrations

Michael Rowley

Maps

The Mazer Corporation

CONTENTS

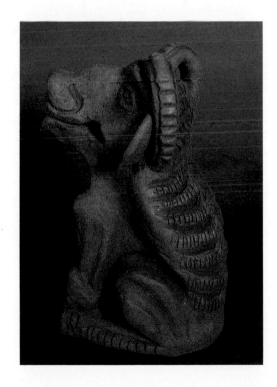

LISTING OF STUDIO LESSONS BY MEDIA

Understanding Art

The Language of Art

Chapter Scan

TRB Resources

- 1-1 *Gabriele Münter,* (artist profile)
- 1-10 Chapter Test
- Color Transparency 1
- Color Transparency 2

TEACHING THE CHAPTER

Introducing the Art Work

Direct the students' attention to Gabriele Münter's *Staffelsee In Autumn.* Inform them that Gabriele Münter was one of the founders of the German Expressionism movement, and she painted in the late nineteenth and early twentieth centuries. Because the official art academies were closed to women, Münter attended Wassily Kandinsky's Phalanx school in Munich where she was introduced to Post-Impressionism. Kandinsky became her companion and the two settled in the village of Murnau in the Bavarian Alps, where she was influenced by the local folk arts and crafts, and the Alpine landscape. Münter felt that while in Murnau she moved beyond merely painting nature—to painting the essence of nature.

Gabriele Münter began working in the Impressionist style, then began to assimilate the principles of Post-Impressionism and Fauvism to create her own personal style which became part of the German Expressionist movement. Her style is characterized by broad, flat areas of color, intense color contrast, and bold and simple compositional designs. Münter, along with Kandinsky, Von Werefkin, Klee, Marc, and Jawlensky became known as the Blau Reiter group.

▲ Gabriele Münter has made use of the elements of art to create a dramatic picture. Notice how she leads your eye from the foreground to the hills in the distance. How does her use of color make you feel?

Gabriele Münter. *Staffelsee in Autumn.* 1923. Oil on board. 34.9 x 48.9 cm (13¾ x 19¼"). National Museum of Women in the Arts, Washington D.C. Gift of Wallace and Wilhelmina Holladay.

The Language of Art

To learn how a watch works, you might take it apart and study the pieces. While the parts are spread out before you, however, the watch cannot run. Only when the parts are in place will the familiar ticking tell you the watch is working.

Like watches, works of art are made up of parts. When an artist skillfully puts the pieces of an art work together, it succeeds as art. That means that the parts work together to make a unified and visually pleasing whole. In this chapter you will learn about these parts and how they can be organized, as in the painting at the left, to make a pleasing whole.

OBJECTIVES

After completing this chapter, you will be able to:
- Define and recognize the elements of art.
- Make an abstract design, experimenting with the elements of art.
- Identify the principles of art.
- Use the elements of art and principles of art in a studio experience.

WORDS YOU WILL LEARN

balance	proportion
color	rhythm
emphasis	shape
form	space
harmony	texture
line	unity
movement	variety
non-objective art	

ARTISTS YOU WILL MEET

Marc Chagall	Richard Lindner
Charles Demuth	Gabriele Münter
William Harnett	Auguste Renoir
Grace Hartigan	Vincent van Gogh

Examining the Art Work

Explain to students that this painting is organized in blocks of color which accentuate the cutout effect of the landscape. The regular flat brush strokes and the unifying use of color create intense colors and sharp contrast.

Point out the way the color is used to create unity. For example, the blue hue of the houses in the foreground is repeated in the color of the lake, and then again in the mountains and sky which appear in the background. Explain that Münter used intense and expressive color contrasts to create an expressive mood in her work. Suggest that the bold, vibrant colors infused with low- and high-intensity yellow tones create a cheerful, appealing, and serene mood. Suggest that her choice of color communicates many things to the viewer, such as the Staffelsee is a quiet, clean and picturesque setting.

Discussing the Art Work

Ask students to explain how Münter's flat brush strokes and blocks of color influence the texture of the work. Point out how the painting has a smooth, soft visual texture, which is consistent with the mood that is suggested through the choice of colors.

Ask students to think about what influences of Impressionism and Post-Impressionism they might be able to identify in this work. Point out the way the background mountains contain patches of color, creating the impression of foliage rather than the detailed realism of foliage. Ask: What time of the year do you think it is? Besides the title of the painting, what other clues in the painting suggest what time of year it is? Point out the importance placed on light in this work, as it plays off of the trees and grass. Also mention the emphasis on color to create mood, rather than merely to portray objects as they appear to the eye.

Tell students that in this chapter they will learn to define and recognize the elements and principles of art. They will also create an abstract design and use the elements and principles of art in creating their own works of art.

1

Building Self-Esteem

Tell students that in this chapter they will be learning the language of art. Ask whether any in the class have traveled to a country where the language was different from their own. Ask: What did it feel like to be asked a question and not know what was asked or how to answer? Art has a language of its own, words that refer to the visual elements (or basic parts) and to the principles (the guidelines for putting the parts together.) You can learn the individual words of a language, but unless you know how to put the words together to make sentences, you cannot communicate very well. Learning the language is a necessary and interesting part of mastering any new skill. Tell students that knowing how to use the language of art will help them to appreciate the work of others. Learning how to use the visual language will help them communicate their own creative ideas in a new and powerful way.

The Elements of Art

LESSON PLAN
(pages 2–5)

Objectives
After completing this lesson, students will be able to:
• Recognize and define the elements of art.
• Work with the art elements using various methods and materials.
• Make abstract designs by experimenting with the art elements.

Supplies
• Patches of colored paper.
• Straight pins
• Reproductions of art work of various types and periods.
• White glue.
• Sketch paper.
• Watercolors.
• A variety of brushes.

TRB Resources
• 1-2 *The Elements of Art*, (reproducible master)
• 1-3 *Space in Painting*, (reproducible master)
• 1-4 *A Dozen Right Answers*, (art history)
• 1-5 *Feel the Space of a Japanese Home*, (appreciating cultural diversity)

TEACHING THE LESSON

Getting Started
Motivator. Give students different color patches of primary, secondary, or intermediate colors in various values and intensities, making sure that each student has a different color of patch. Have students pin the patches to their clothing and arrange themselves in a color circle. Explain the relationships of the colors in monochromatic, analogous, warm, and cool color schemes. Ask the students to group themselves in these relationships and identify the groups representing the various schemes.

Art is a powerful language. Through it, artists communicate thoughts, ideas, and feelings. Like most languages, the language of art has its own special vocabulary. Unlike other vocabularies, however, the vocabulary of art is not made up of words. Rather, it is made up of visual elements. The visual elements include color, line, shape, form, space, and texture.

COLOR

Have you ever noticed it is harder to see colors when the light is dim? Color relies on light. In fact, **color** is *what the eyes see when light is reflected off an object*.

Color has three properties, or traits. These are:

• **Hue**. Hue is the name of a color, such as red, blue, or yellow. Hues are arranged in a circular format on a color wheel. Red, yellow, and blue are the primary hues. They are equally spaced on the color wheel. (See Figure 1–1.) Look at the picture in Figure 1–2. How many different hues, or colors, can you find in this work? Which ones can you name?
• **Value**. Value is the lightness or darkness of a hue. The value of a hue can be changed by adding white or black. Can you point out different values of any one color in the picture in Figure 1–2?

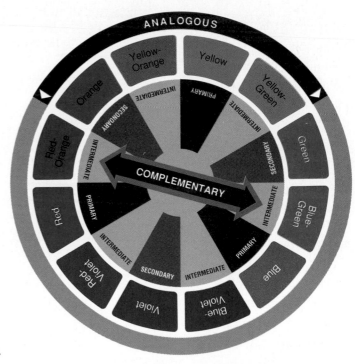

▶ **Figure 1–1   Color Wheel.**

Classroom Management Tip
An overhead projector is a valuable teaching aid. The overhead enlarges images to make materials easily visible to a large group while leaving the teacher free to observe and interact with the class. Information can be presented on transparencies and kept on file for future review. Printed illustrations can be lifted from clay-coated magazine pages by adhering the printed side to a sheet of clear, adhesive-backed acetate and soaking off the paper from the back. In addition to projecting all kinds of prepared materials, the overhead provides a good way to illustrate the visual elements and to experiment with composition. Cut shapes and found objects can be projected onto a screen and moved around to create various types of balance. Yarn, string, and rods become lines, and color experiments can be added by the use of gels and colored acetate. Line and texture drawing may be demonstrated with markers on a sheet of plexiglass or acetate placed on the projector.

- **Intensity**. Intensity is the brightness or dullness of a hue. Pure hues are high-intensity colors. Dull hues are low-intensity colors. Which objects in Figure 1–2 would you describe as high in intensity? Which would you describe as low in intensity?

Colors can be combined to produce many interesting and striking results. Artists make use of different types of color schemes to create different effects. Following are some of the color schemes that trained artists use:

- **Monochromatic** (mahn-uh-kroh-**mat**-ik) **color scheme**. This scheme uses different values of a single hue. For example, dark

green, medium green, and light green make a monochromatic scheme.

- **Analogous** (uh-**nal**-uh-gus) **color scheme**. This scheme uses colors that are side by side on the color wheel and share a hue. Look at the color wheel in Figure 1–1. What colors share the hue red?

- **Warm or cool color scheme**. Warm color schemes — with red, yellow, and orange colors — remind us of the sun and warmth. Artists use blue, green, and violet — cool color schemes — to make us think of cool items such as ice or grass.

▲ **Figure 1–2** Notice how Harnett has captured a realistic scene using the elements of space, form, and texture. Would he have been as successful in showing depth if he had painted a lighter background?

William Michael Harnett. *Munich Still Life*. 1882. Oil on canvas. 62.5 x 76.8 cm (24⅝ x 30¼"). Dallas Museum of Art, Dallas, Texas.

Vocabulary. Help the students to develop definitions for the vocabulary terms listed on page **1**. Have them make a vocabulary chart that includes all of the terms and definitions. Keep the chart on permanent display and add new terms and definitions as they are learned. Have the students keep a copy of the chart in their sketchbooks for reference and review.

Developing Concepts

Exploring Aesthetics. Explain to the students that artists selectively use the art elements to achieve the effect that they want. Show students a variety of art reproductions including drawings, prints, graphic designs, paintings, sculptures, and crafts. Ask them to list the elements they find in each of the examples. Discuss the reasons why artists might choose the elements that they do. Ask students to imagine the effect of removing, changing, or adding an element in one of the examples.

Using Art Criticism. Have students choose an illustration from the text and write a short description of the work, the elements that it uses, and the effect that those elements create. Have them decide the artist's purpose in making the work and the point of view that it takes. Discuss the variety of works that artists create and the many different purposes behind those art works.

Understanding Art History. Explain to students that visual elements have been used by artists ever since the first primitive drawings were made. Have students find examples of cave art and report on the elements that they find. Show examples of art work from various periods and discuss artists' use of the elements.

Background Information
There are several ways to work with color in addition to the familiar pigment mixing. For example, theaters use sets of transparent gels to filter stage lighting and create various color effects. The color separation process, used in the printing industry, depends on a different set of primaries to mix printing ink. Scientists separate the colors of light by bending the light through a prism. Have students explore some of the applications of color.

Note
Explain to students that the elements have been analyzed, organized, and used in many ways, but they are not inventions of the artist. They are natural elements that artists have learned to use as an alternative language. Emphasize that the use of visual elements as an art language is common to all cultures and is a normal part of every child's development. Helping students to understand the elements will give them new methods of applying them.

LINE

An element of art that can be used to send different messages to viewers is a line. **Line** is defined as *the path of a moving point through space*. You can draw lines on paper or scratch a line in wet clay with a tool. Lines can be seen in your environment, such as the web of a spider or the railing on a stair.

There are five main kinds of lines:

- Horizontal lines, which run parallel to the ground, appear to be at rest.

- Vertical lines—lines that run up and down—seem to show dignity, formality, and strength.
- Diagonal, or slanting, lines signal action and excitement.
- Zigzag lines, which are made from combined diagonal lines, can create a feeling of confusion or suggest action.
- Curved lines express movement in a graceful, flowing way.

▶ **Figure 1–3** Color, line and shape are successfully combined to create the appearance of a three-dimensional form. Why do you think Chagall has shown the violinist floating?

Marc Chagall. *Green Violinist.* 1923–1924. Oil on canvas. 198 x 108.6 cm (78 x 42¾"). Solomon R. Guggenheim Museum, New York, New York. Gift of Solomon R. Guggenheim.

4 📖 Lesson 1 *The Elements of Art*

4

Look again at Figure 1–2 on page **3**. How many different lines can you find? In what directions do these lines go?

In art, line quality and line variation influence the viewer's reaction to a work of art. Line quality is the unique character of the line. It can be affected by the tool or medium used to produce the mark or by the particular motion of the artist's hand. Line variation describes the thickness or thinness, lightness or darkness of a line.

SHAPE AND FORM

Every object—a cloud, a house, a pebble—has a shape. **Shape** is *an element of art that refers to an area clearly set off by one or more of the other elements of art*. Shapes are limited to two dimensions—length and width.

All shapes belong to one of two classes:

- **Geometric** (jee-uh-**meh**-trik). Geometric shapes look as though they were made with a ruler or drawing tool. The square, the circle, the triangle, the rectangle, and the oval are the five basic geometric shapes. Look at the painting in Figure 1–3. Can you find any geometric shapes?
- **Organic**. Also called free-form, organic shapes are not regular or even. Their outlines may be curved or angular, or they may be a combination of both, to make free-form shapes. Organic shapes, such as clouds and pebbles, are usually found in nature. Can you find any organic shapes in Figure 1–3?

Like shapes, forms have length and width. Forms also have a third dimension, depth. **Form** is *an element of art that refers to an object with three dimensions*. With the forms found in works of art, such as sculpture and architecture, you can actually experience the three dimensions by walking around or into the works.

SPACE

All objects take up space. **Space** is *an element of art that refers to the distance between, around, above, below, and within things*. Which objects in Figure 1–3 appear closest to you? Which seem to be farther back in space?

In both two- and three-dimensional works of art, the shapes or forms are called the positive area. The empty spaces between the shapes are called negative spaces. The relationship between the positive and negative space will affect how the art work is interpreted.

TEXTURE

Run your fingers over the top of your desk or work table. You are feeling the surface's texture. **Texture** is *an element of art that refers to the way things feel, or look as though they might feel, if touched*.

Imagine you could touch the objects in the picture in Figure 1–2 on page **3**. Which of them do you think would feel smooth? Do any look rough or uneven?

✔ CHECK YOUR UNDERSTANDING

1. What are the three properties of color?
2. What message do vertical lines send to a viewer? What message do diagonal lines send?
3. What is the difference between shape and form?
4. What is the difference between the positive area and the negative area in a work of art?
5. Define *texture*.

Following Up

Closure. Collect and display "Studio Experience" exercises. Discuss with students the variety of effects in the collection. Review vocabulary terms and definitions.

Evaluation. 1. Review students' written responses to the "Check Your Understanding" questions. 2. Quiz students on terms and definitions. 3. Evaluate student descriptions of elements in an art work.

Reteaching. Have students study a variety of natural objects to find examples of the elements. Have them record the shapes, colors, lines, and textures in sketchbooks.

Enrichment. Have students find the mathematical definitions of various geometric shapes and the formulas for drawing them. Have them try some of the formulas to make designs.

Answers to "Check Your Understanding"
1. Three properties of color are hue, the name of the color; value, the lightness or darkness of the hue; and intensity, the brightness or dullness of the hue.
2. Vertical lines convey dignity, formality and strength to the viewer. Diagonal lines signal action or excitement.
3. The difference between the elements of shape and form is that shapes are limited to two dimensions; length and width. Form refers to an object with three dimensions: length, width, and depth.
4. Positive areas are occupied by objects in a work of art; negative areas are the empty spaces between the objects.
5. Texture is the element of art that shows how the surface of an object might feel if it were touched.

Using the Elements of Art

Using the Elements of Art

LESSON PLAN
(pages 6–7)

Objectives

After completing this lesson, students will be able to:
• Create a non-objective design that uses all of the elements of art.
• Analyze a non-objective design and discern the various elements of art.

Supplies

• Pencils.
• Rulers.
• Sheets of white drawing paper, 18 x 24 inches (45 x 60 cm).
• Colored markers.
• Colored pencils.
• Crayons.
• Yarn.
• Strips of construction paper.
• Black and white photos.

> **TRB Resource**
> • 1-6 *The Elements in Your Life,* (studio)

TEACHING THE LESSON

Getting Started

Motivator. Show students a large sheet of white paper and explain that it represents a space to be used in organizing a picture or design. Ask them to write short descriptions of pictures they might make on the paper. Discuss the descriptions and add as many details as possible. List on the blackboard all examples of visual elements that are mentioned in the descriptions.

Building Vocabulary. Discuss the term *non-objective art.* Display examples of art works that have clearly identifiable subjects and examples of abstract art, and make sure that students can categorize each example properly. If you wish, include some examples of art works that may initially appear to be non-objective but do have a subject upon closer inspection or to viewers who understand that style of art. Examples include paintings that Kandinsky made shortly before World War I and the fertility motifs on Neolithic pottery.

Sometimes artists create **non-objective art**. These are *works in which no objects or subjects can be readily identified*. Figure 1–4 is such a work. This one is by Grace Hartigan. She has combined several elements of art in this work to create unusual effects.

WHAT YOU WILL LEARN

This is the first of many studio lessons. In these lessons you will use your creative skills and experiment with different media. You will create many works of art that may be displayed.

For this first studio experiment, you will create a non-objective design using all the elements of art. You will use pencil, felt-tip markers, colored pencils, and crayons. (See Figure 1–5.)

WHAT YOU WILL NEED

• Pencil and ruler
• Sheet of white drawing paper, 18 x 24 inches (46 x 61 cm)
• Colored markers, colored pencils, and crayons

WHAT YOU WILL DO

1. Using one continuous pencil line, make a design that fills the sheet of drawing paper. Allow your pencil to drift off the edge of the paper and return. Try to create a design that has both large and small shapes.
2. Using the ruler, divide your paper into eight equal rectangles. Each should measure 6 x 9 inches (15 x 23 cm). Number the eight boxed areas lightly in pencil. You may order the numbers any way you like (Figure 1–6).

▲ **Figure 1–4   Hartigan has painted a non-objective work that shows several elements of art combined to make a pleasing whole. What elements can you identify in this painting?**

Grace Hartigan. *The Faraway Places.* 1974. Oil on canvas. 228.6 x 166.4 cm (90 x 65½″). McNay Art Museum, San Antonio, Texas. Purchase made possible by a grant from the National Endowment for the Arts with matching funds, Marion Koogler.

3. Using primary *hues* of crayons, color the shapes in Area 1. (See the color wheel on page **2**.)
4. Using light and dark *values* of colored pencils, color in the shapes in Area 2. Using bright and dull *intensities* of colored pencils, color in the shapes in Area 3.
5. Using the pencil, go over the *lines* in Area 4. Make some of the lines straight and others curved. Try pressing down on the pencil for some of the lines. This will give a thicker, darker result.

Background Information

The history of Grace Hartigan's bold, gestural, and colorful paintings reflects the tension between her natural artistic impulses and the prevailing aesthetic fashions during the 1950s and later. During her childhood, Hartigan spent long hours observing the itinerant gypsies who camped near her house. After arriving in New York City in 1946, she saw a strong similarity between the caravans, bonfires, and flashy clothing of the gypsies and the colorful world of pushcart peddlers and pickle barrels on the city's Lower East Side. She took New York street life as her subject, but in the 1950s she allowed herself to be persuaded by successful abstract artist colleagues who told her that she wasn't selecting sufficiently serious subject matter. Hartigan did not return to the realist material for which she had such an affinity until the late 1960s.

6. Using pencil, crayons, colored pencils, or markers, create three different *textures* in Area 5.

7. Using the markers, draw outlines around *shapes* in Area 6. Fill in some of the shapes with the markers. Leave the others white.

8. Use pencil to add a new shape that overlaps the existing shapes in Area 7 to show *space*. Add to this feeling of space by using colored pencil to color this shape in a bright hue. Color the other shapes in dull hues.

9. Using the pencil, shade the shapes in Area 8 little by little. Try to make these shapes look like rounded, three-dimensional *forms*. (For information on shading, see Technique Tip **6**, *Handbook* page **278**.)

10. Display your design. See if other members of your class can identify the different art elements found in each area.

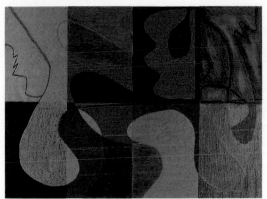

▲ Figure 1–5 Student work. Non-objective design.

OTHER STUDIO IDEAS

- On a sheet of white paper, create a second design using geometric shapes. Complete your design as before using only tempera paint as your medium.
- ●● Draw a simple still life using *lines* to create each of the *shapes*. Overlap some shapes to add a feeling of *space*. Choose three hues to add *color* to your picture.

EXAMINING YOUR WORK

- **Describe** Tell which element each area of your design highlights. Identify the media you used to create the different areas.

- **Judge** State whether your design clearly highlights each element of art. Tell which section of your design you think is the most successful. Explain your answer.

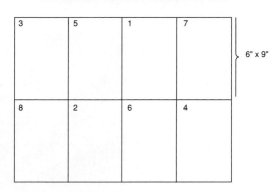

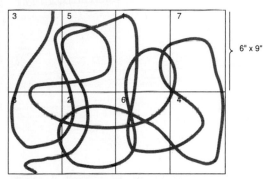

▲ Figure 1–6 Drawing the elements of art.

Gradual and sudden changes in value should be used to make some shapes look like three-dimensional *forms*. Create different rough and smooth *textures*. Exhibit your finished work in class. Identify and discuss each of the art elements used.

Lesson 2 *Using the Elements of Art* 7

Developing Concepts

Exploring Aesthetics. Have students explore the effects of horizontal, diagonal, and curved lines by using yarn and thin strips of construction paper to make various arrangements on a sheet of white paper. Ask students to describe what feelings the different arrangements represent. You can also ask the students to illustrate words such as placid, excitement, explosion, stately, and bold.

Developing Studio Skills. Have students continue their collection of examples of visual elements. Ask them to look for black and white photos so that they can start a collection of patches showing different values. They can match these values by using drawing pencils and black watercolor paint. Have students make a third collection of texture samples (some of which may be rubbings of textures), which they can reproduce by using drawing pencils and markers.

Following Up

Closure. Discuss the variety of effects that students achieved in their "Studio Lesson" exercise.

Evaluation. 1. Review students' responses to "Examining Your Work." 2. Assess the students' collections of examples of visual elements.

Reteaching. Help students to discover the visual elements in Figure 1-4, and ask them to describe the feeling of the work.

Enrichment. Have groups of students research the work of various artists who created non-objective works. Ask them to report back to the class why their artist chose to work non-objectively and which visual elements where most important to that artist.

Classroom Management Tip
Art teachers sometimes need to be scavengers. Design problems are often worked out more easily by using a number of identical parts that can be moved around to try different compositional arrangements and various applications of art principles. Sometimes such materials are available as scrap from manufacturers. Check the factories and shops in your community for usable goods including cardboard, wood, fabrics, and packing materials. Consult students for leads on locating other scrap items.

LESSON PLAN

Objectives

After completing this lesson, students will be able to:

• Recognize and define the principles of art.
• Use the principles of art to organize the elements of art.
• Apply principles of art to the creation of works of art.

Supplies

• Black squares of paper for an overhead projector layout; or black squares of felt and a white feltboard.
• Round objects such as buttons and washers.
• Cut paper shapes.
• Magazines and newspapers.
• White glue.
• Construction paper.
• White drawing paper, 18 x 24 inches (45 x 60 cm).
• Large sheet of white paper, or a white cloth sheet.
• Scissors.
• Thin sticks.
• Yarn.

> **TRB Resources**
> • 1-7 *How a Work of Art "Works,"* (reproducible master)
> • 1-8 *The Language of Art in Your Home,* (aesthetics/ art criticism)

TEACHING THE LESSON

Getting Started

Motivator. Show students an evenly spaced arrangement of black squares on either the overhead projector or on a feltboard. Ask students to suggest changes that they feel would make the composition more interesting. Ask them to move, change, or add shapes and lines and to try to arrange the elements so as to develop the various kinds of aesthetic balance. Ask students to describe the effects of each alteration and to discuss the principles involved. Ask them to identify the center of interest created by each change.

The Principles of Art

If you want to use a language, knowing the vocabulary is not enough. You must also know how the words go together. You must know the rules of grammar for that language.

The same is true of art. Instead of rules of grammar, the language of art has art principles. These principles, or guidelines, govern how artists organize the visual elements to create a work of art.

The principles of art include balance, variety, harmony, emphasis, proportion, movement, and rhythm.

▶ **Figure 1–7   This picture combines familiar images from our modern rock culture. What are some of the images? What do you think the artist is trying to say about this culture?**

Richard Lindner. *Rock-Rock.* 1966. Oil on canvas. 177.8 x 152.4 cm (70 x 60"). Dallas Museum of Art, Dallas, Texas. Gift of Mr. & Mrs. James H. Clark.

8   📖   Lesson 3   *The Principles of Art*

Background Information

The way we understand and use the elements and principles of art today comes largely from the ideas and systems developed in a German school of design known as the Bauhaus. Established by Walter Gropius in 1919, the Bauhaus emphasized basic elements, materials, and structures. By 1926, when the school moved to a new glass and steel building in Dessau, the Bauhaus had secured a worldwide reputation for design research and education. Master craftspeople in many fields of art were hired to teach there. All students participated in an introductory program of creative experiments that stressed free manipulation, originality, and sensitivity to the individual qualities of different materials. The Bauhaus also tried to revive the old craft guild concept of the designer-producer and to form a partnership between designers and machine age manufacturers. Although the Bauhaus failed to achieve this goal, the school changed the way artists and architects thought about design.

BALANCE

If you have ever carried a stack of dishes or books, you know the importance of balance. In art, balance is also important. **Balance** is *a principle of art concerned with arranging elements so no one part of a work overpowers, or seems heavier than, any other part.* In art, balance is seen or felt by the viewer.

In works of art, three kinds of balance are possible. They are formal balance, informal balance, and radial balance. In works of art with formal, or symmetrical (suh-**meh**-trih-kuhl), balance the two halves are mirror im-ages. In works with informal, or asymmetrical (ay-suh-**meh**-trih-kuhl), balance two unlike elements seem to carry equal weight. For example, a small shape painted bright red will balance several larger items painted in duller reds.

Radial balance occurs when elements or objects in an art work are positioned around a central point. Study the art works in Figures 1–7, 1–8, and 1–9. Which uses formal balance? Which uses informal balance? Which uses radial balance?

▲ **Figure 1–8** This painting creates a certain mood or feeling about the girl playing the guitar. How has Renoir combined the element of color and the principle of balance to create a pleasing portrait?

Auguste Renoir. *Young Spanish Woman with a Guitar.* 1898. Canvas. 55.6 x 65.2 cm (21⅞ x 25⅝"). National Gallery of Art, Washington, D.C. Ailsa Mellon Bruce Collection.

Vocabulary. Guide the students in developing working definitions of the words balance, variety, harmony, emphasis, proportion, movement, rhythm, and unity. Have them add the terms to the vocabulary chart and to their sketchbook lists.

Developing Concepts

Exploring Aesthetics. Scatter cut shapes and round objects at random on a white cloth sheet or large piece of white paper on the floor or on a table. Ask students to describe the effect, identify the type of balance illustrated, and try to pick out a center of interest. If they find one, ask them to explain why it attracts their attention. Select a student to move the pieces around to develop a formal balance. Ask another student to change the arrangement to develop a feeling of rhythm in the composition. Have various students work with the materials to create a visual sense of movement and of the other principles. Discuss with the students the changes that take place in the developing composition.

Using Art Criticism. Have students choose an illustration from the text and write a brief description of the elements they find in the composition and the principles that are used. Ask them to decide which of the elements is most important in developing the work's composition and mood. Have them identify the focus of the composition and explain how the artist makes it important and leads the viewer's eye to it. Ask them to decide whether the artist was successful in establishing and supporting the center of interest.

Classroom Management Tip

A collection of simple cameras can be very useful in the classroom. With a little instruction, students can use them to explore subject matter, record images, and illustrate their reports. Students who are studying the use of art principles in their school and community can find and record examples more easily with a camera. Some students who are hesitant about their artistic talents in other media find the medium of photography considerably less intimidating. Cameras are also ex-cellent aids to observation. By framing a subject, the viewfinder allows the photographer to focus on important parts of a composition and eliminate unwanted background elements. Students who carry a camera are more aware of the visual details of their environment and more apt to record them. Furthermore, students can use cameras to record images that will be used later in a studio project.

▲ Figure 1–9   Van Gogh has blended many elements and principles of art in this work. Notice how he has used the elements of color and line to create a feeling of movement. How has he created balance?

Vincent van Gogh. *The Starry Night*. 1889. Oil on canvas. 73.7 x 92.1 cm (29 x 36¼"). Collection, The Museum of Modern Art, New York, New York. Acquired through the Lillie P. Bliss bequest.

VARIETY

The same routine day after day can become dull. The same color or shape repeated over and over in an art work can become equally dull. To avoid dullness, artists use the principle of variety in their works. **Variety** is *a principle of art concerned with combining one or more elements to create interest by adding slight changes*. By giving a work variety, the artist heightens the visual appeal of the work.

Look again at the picture in Figure 1–7. How does the artist's use of color add variety to the work? Which other elements are used to add variety?

HARMONY

If too little variety can become boring, too much variety can create chaos. Artists avoid chaos in their works by using the principle of harmony. **Harmony** is *a principle of art concerned with blending elements to create a more calm, restful appearance*.

Of the two paintings in Figures 1–7 and 1–8, which has greater harmony? Which elements does the artist use to introduce harmony to the work?

10   📖   Lesson 3   *The Principles of Art*

EMPHASIS

To attract a viewer's attention to important parts of a work, artists use the principle of emphasis. **Emphasis** is *making an element in a work stand out*. Emphasis can be created by contrast or by extreme changes in an element.

Look once more at Figure 1–8. What has been done to emphasize the face of the young woman?

PROPORTION

Have you ever tasted a food that was so salty you couldn't eat it? The problem was one of proportion. **Proportion** is *the principle of art concerned with the relationship of one part to another and to the whole*.

The principle of proportion is not limited to size. Elements such as color can be used in differing proportions to create emphasis. It is used this way in Figure 1–7. Which color is used in greatest proportion?

MOVEMENT

You may not have realized it, but when you look at a work of art your eye moves from part to part. Artists use the principle of movement to lead the viewer's eyes throughout the work. **Movement** is *the principle of art used to create the look and feeling of action and to guide a viewer's eye throughout the work of art*.

Study yet again the paintings in Figures 1–7, 1–8, and 1–9. How have the artists used line and shape to move your eyes throughout the works?

RHYTHM

Often artists seek to make their works seem active. When they do, they call upon the principle of rhythm. **Rhythm** is *the principle of art concerned with repeating an element to make a work seem active or to suggest vibration*. Sometimes to create rhythm, an artist will repeat not just elements but also the same exact objects over and over. When this is done, a pattern is formed.

Compare the works in Figures 1–7, 1–8, and 1–9. Which uses the principle of rhythm? What element is repeated?

UNITY IN ART

When you look at works of art, it may be difficult to determine where one part ends and the other begins. Instead, the piece of art works together as a whole. It has unity. **Unity** is *the arrangement of elements and principles with media to create a feeling of completeness or wholeness*. You will sense this unity as you look at works of art in which artists use the elements and principles with skill, imagination, and sensitivity.

✔ CHECK YOUR UNDERSTANDING

1. What are principles of art?
2. Name three kinds of balance. Describe each kind.
3. What principles do artists use to prevent works from being static?
4. How can emphasis be created in a work of art?
5. Define *movement*.

Lesson 3   *The Principles of Art*   **11**

Following Up

Closure. Review with students art principle terms and definitions. Have the groups present their designs from the problem in "Developing Studio Skills," explain what their problem was, and show how they solved it. Collect and display the designs.

Evaluation. 1. Review students' written responses to the "Check Your Understanding" questions. 2. Have the students critique the designs produced in the "Studio Experience." 3. Quiz students on terms and their definitions, and have them identify the design that illustrates each principle.

Reteaching. Review with students the various steps they made in the classroom composition "Motivator" exercise that illustrated the different design principles. Guide a discussion based on the following questions: Where did the creative process begin? What were the steps in that process? Which of the arrangements would you call art? Must art necessarily be done on purpose to qualify as art? Can something be aesthetically stimulating and yet not be art?

Enrichment. Explain to students that formal balance is based on mathematics and that the field of geometry includes methods for developing a great variety of designs. Have the students consult the school's math department to locate the formulas and tools necessary for making radial and other formal balance arrangements. After they have tried these techniques, have them analyze examples of radial design and try to determine which formulas were used to make them.

Answers to "Check Your Understanding"

1. The seven principles artists use to organize the visual elements of a work of art are balance, variety, harmony, emphasis, proportion, movement, and rhythm.
2. The three kinds of balance are formal or mirror-image; informal or asymmetrical, where two unlike elements seem to carry equal weight; and radial, where objects are arranged around a central point.
3. Artists can use movement and rhythm to prevent an art work from looking static.
4. Emphasis can be created by using contrast or extreme change in an element.
5. Movement is the principle used to create a feeling of action and to lead the viewer's eye throughout the art work.

Using the Principles of Art

LESSON PLAN
(pages 12–13)

Objectives
After completing this lesson, students will be able to:
• Create a design that imaginatively illustrates their name and embodies all the principles of art.

Supplies
• Sheets of scrap paper.
• Pencils.
• Rulers.
• Erasers.
• White drawing paper, 18 x 24 inches (45 x 60 cm).
• Watercolor paints.
• A variety of brushes.
• Tempera paints.
• Paint mixing trays.
• Construction paper.
• Scissors.

TRB Resource
• 1-9 *Be an Interior Designer*, (cooperative learning)

TEACHING THE LESSON

Getting Started
Motivator. Have students brainstorm all the associations that come to mind when they think about their name or nickname. Have them list the different ideas for reference during the Studio Lesson.

Building Vocabulary. Have students study Figure 1-10. List the principles of art on the board, and ask students to identify where each one can be found in Demuth's painting.

Developing Concepts
Exploring Aesthetics. Discuss with students how much of our environment consists of products that have been designed according to the principles of art. Among the examples that you can discuss are buildings, furniture, automobiles, and household appliances. Have students find good examples of the use of art principles in manufactured goods. Ask them to bring in pictures or items and report to the class how these goods illustrate art principles.

12

Using the Principles of Art

Artists use the language of art in different and often highly imaginative ways. Figure 1–10 gives us painter Charles Demuth's (duh-**mooth**) view of a fire engine racing through a rain-swept city at night.

Notice that the artist has not attempted to create a true-to-life picture. There are no clear images of trucks, wet streets, or darkened buildings. Rather, Demuth has captured the *idea* of those images. Look closely and you can almost hear the screaming of Engine Company 5's siren. You can almost see the red truck's lights flashing.

▲ **Figure 1–10   Charles Demuth creates amazing impact by using simple images. What do you notice first when you look at this picture?**

Charles Henry Demuth. *I Saw the Figure 5 in Gold*. 1928. Oil on composition board. 91.4 x 75.6 cm (36 x 29¾"). The Metropolitan Museum of Art, New York, New York. The Alfred Stieglitz Collection.

WHAT YOU WILL LEARN
You will create the "idea of your name." You will do this through a design made up of the letters of your name or nickname. All the principles of art will be used in your design. You will use watercolor paint and tempera paint in your work. (See Figure 1–11.)

WHAT YOU WILL NEED
• Sheets of scrap paper
• Pencil, ruler, and eraser
• Sheet of white drawing paper, 18 x 24 inches (46 x 61 cm)
• Watercolor paint and several brushes
• Tempera paint and mixing tray

WHAT YOU WILL DO
1. On scrap paper, practice making block letters of different sizes and shapes. Focus only on the letters in your name or nickname. Working lightly in pencil, create a design with the letters on the sheet of drawing paper. Arrange for some of the letters to overlap and some to go off the page. Fill the entire sheet of paper. (See Figure 1–12.)
2. Using the ruler, divide your paper into eight equal rectangles. Each should measure 6 x 9 inches (15 x 23 cm). Number the eight boxed areas lightly in pencil in any order you like.
3. Using the pencil and eraser, draw in or erase lines to rearrange the shapes in Area 1 so they have formal *balance*. Fill in some of the shapes with pencil.
4. Using a *variety* of hues of tempera, paint the shapes in Area 2.
5. Using no more than three hues, paint the shapes in Area 3. Repeat one of these colors over and over to add *harmony*.

Background Information
Charles Demuth's painting *I Saw the Figure Five in Gold* demonstrates the influence of several twentieth-century art movements and was itself the ancestor of yet another movement. Demuth (United States, 1883–1935) was friendly with Marcel Duchamp and other Cubists who lived in New York during World War I, and his relationship with them is reflected in the faceted and geometric forms. Demuth's later development of a style known as Precisionism, strongly influenced by the clean lines and architectural emphasis of Futurism, can also be seen in Figure 1-10. The most direct precedent to this work, however, is found in the luminescent cables, energetic diagonals, and crystalline spaces of Joseph Stella's painting *Brooklyn Bridge*. Demuth's canvas ultimately formed part of the heritage of Pop artists. Pop artist Robert Indiana even honored Demuth with a variation entitled *The Demuth Five*.

6. Identify the most interesting shape in Area 4. Using the brightest hue, paint this area to give *emphasis* to this shape. Paint other shapes with dull hues.

7. Using the pencil and eraser, rearrange the shapes in Area 5 to create *rhythm*. Use watercolors to paint the shapes.

8. Using watercolors, paint the shapes in Area 6. Increase the *proportion* of one of the colors you use. Notice how doing this *emphasizes* that color.

9. Using the pencil and eraser, rearrange the shapes in Area 7 to create a sense of *movement* in any direction. Use watercolors to paint the shapes. Pick colors that will add to the feeling of movement.

10. Rearrange similar shapes in Area 8 to create a pattern. Pick one color of tempera to paint the shapes in Area 8. Paint the nearest shapes. Paint the other shapes, adding white to lighten the value of the hue. (For information on mixing paint to change value, see Technique Tip **12**, *Handbook* page **280**.) In this way the shapes will appear to create rhythm.

11. Display your design and identify the different principles of art found in each area.

▲ Figure 1–11 Student work. Design using your name.

OTHER STUDIO IDEAS

- On a sheet of white paper, create a second design. This work should be based on your initials. Focus on the part of your first design that you found most interesting.

- **Describe** Tell where the different letters of your name or nickname are found in your design. Identify the art media you used to create the different areas.
- **Analyze** Name the principle of art highlighted in each area of your design.
- **Judge** Tell whether your design clearly highlights each principle of art. Tell which section of your design you think is the most successful. Explain your answer.

SAFETY TIP
Remember to check paints for safety labels. The labels *AP* (for Approved Product) and *CP* (for Certified Product) mean the paint does not contain harmful amounts of poisonous substances. An *HL* label (for Health Label), on the other hand, warns that the paint contains poisonous ingredients and is dangerous to use.

▲ Figure 1–12 Design using the principles of art.

Lesson 4 *Using the Principles of Art* **13**

Developing Studio Skills. An exercise in dividing and reconstructing a shape can help students develop new shapes and find new ways to work with composition. Ask students to select a geometric shape and cut it out of construction paper. Have them divide their shape into seven segments by drawing straight lines and cutting the segments apart. Have them reassemble the parts to form a new arrangement that exemplifies unity and harmony. The segments may be spread out in a manner that suggests movement, and one or more parts may be colored or textured to provide contrast. Ask students to explain the principles that they used in reconstructing their original shapes.

Following Up

Closure. Have the students discuss whether they find conceptual art works such as Figure 1-10 as satisfying as more straightforward illustrations of a subject.

Evaluation. Assess how well each student illustrated the art principles in his or her Studio Lesson. 2. Evaluate each student's ability to relate the art principles to the manufactured object that he or she presented to the class. 3. Review students' responses to "Examining Your Work."

Reteaching. Have students examine Figure 1-10 in terms of the art principles. Ask them to identify which principles make this a successful painting.

Enrichment. Point out to the students the red "Bill," the "Carlo" in gold lights, and the "W. C. W." that appear in Figure 1-10. Explain that the poet William Carlos Williams was an old friend of Demuth. Have students look up the Williams poem that inspired Demuth's painting of a fire truck. Ask them if they find Demuth's picture as pleasing as Williams did.

Note
Help the students understand the importance of organization in art. Emphasize the concept that art making is not accidental. It is a purposeful synthesis of the art elements and principles. Reiterate to students that the principles are the basis of composition and that they are the means by which an artist can develop a composition's center of interest and create a sense of space and distance.

Classroom Management Tip
Although Figure 1-12 does not show the grid lines, students will be dividing the page into eight rectangles as they did for the Studio Lesson on pages **6-7**. Remind students that they have already learned to divide their 18 x 24 inch (46 x 61 cm) paper into eight equal rectangles. Figure 1-6 shows how to divide the long sides into four six-inch segments and the short sides into two. These will give them eight 6 x 9 inch (15 x 23 cm) rectangles which they can number in any order they desire.

ANSWERS TO "CHAPTER 1 REVIEW"

Building Vocabulary

1. color
2. line
3. texture
4. shape
5. form
6. balance
7. variety
8. harmony
9. emphasis
10. rhythm
11. proportion
12. unity
13. movement
14. non-objective art
15. space

Reviewing Art Facts

16. The elements of art are color, line, shape, form, space, and texture.
17. Hue indicates a color's name and place on the color wheel.
18. The two different kinds of shapes are geometric and organic, or free-form.
19. Non-objective art is art without an identifiable subject.
20. Symmetrical balance is formal balance. It occurs when the two halves are mirror images. Asymmetrical balance, or informal balance, occurs when two unlike objects seem to carry equal weight.

Thinking About Art

1. Diagonal lines would be used because they suggest action. Curved lines could be used to create a calm, peaceful scene.
2. Organic shapes are more likely to be found in nature.
3. Shape and form both have dimensions of length and width. Form has the additional dimension of depth.

CHAPTER 1 REVIEW

BUILDING VOCABULARY

Number a sheet of paper from 1 to 15. After each number, write the term from the box that best matches each description below.

balance	proportion
color	rhythm
emphasis	shape
form	space
harmony	texture
line	unity
movement	variety
non-objective art	

1. What the eyes see when light is reflected off an object.
2. Path of a moving point through space.
3. The way things feel, or look as though they might feel, if touched.
4. An area clearly set off by one or more of the other elements of art.
5. An object with three dimensions.
6. Arranging elements so no one part of a work overpowers, or seems heavier than, any other part.
7. Combining one or more elements to create interest by adding slight changes.
8. Blending elements to create a more calm, restful appearance.
9. Making an element in a work stand out.
10. The repeating of an element to make a work seem active or to suggest vibration.
11. The relationship of one part to another and to the whole.
12. The arrangement of elements and principles with media to create a feeling of completeness or wholeness.
13. The principle of art used to create the look and feeling of action and to guide a viewer's eye throughout the work.
14. Art works in which no objects or subjects can be readily identified.
15. The distance between, around, above, below, and within things.

REVIEWING ART FACTS

Number a sheet of paper from 16 to 20. Answer each question in a complete sentence.

16. What are the elements of art?
17. Which of the three properties of color refers to a color's name and place on a color wheel?
18. What are the two different kinds of shapes?
19. What is non-objective art?
20. What is symmetrical balance? What is asymmetrical balance?

THINKING ABOUT ART

On a sheet of paper, answer each question in a sentence or two.

1. **Extend.** What kind of lines would you use in creating a picture of an action-packed horse race? What kind of lines would you use in creating a calm, peaceful picture of a lake and trees? Explain your answers.
2. **Analyze.** Which type of shapes, geometric or organic, are you more likely to find in nature? Why do you suppose this to be the case?
3. **Compare and contrast.** What do the elements of shape and form have in common? In what ways are the two different?

MAKING ART CONNECTIONS

1. **Science.** Make a list of the elements of art you have learned about in this chapter. Choose an object from nature that shows examples of these elements. Beside each art element listed, write a one- or two-word description of the natural object you chose.
2. **Language Arts.** Writers use words to express ideas. Choose three words from the elements and principles of art and write a paragraph expressing these ideas.

CHAPTER 1 REVIEW

LOOKING AT THE DETAILS

The detail shown below is from Gabrielle Münter's *Staffelsee in Autumn*. Study the detail and answer the questions below.

1. Give examples of types of shapes that you see in this work. Are they free-form or geometric shapes?
2. How is color used to create unity?

3. Where is the emphasis in this detail? Look at the entire work on page **xviii**. Has the emphasis changed? Explain your answer.
4. What does the artist's choice of color communicate about this scene?

Gabriele Münter. *Staffelsee in Autumn*. 1923. Oil on board. (Detail.) 34.9 x 48.9 cm (13¾ x 19¼"). National Museum of Women in the Arts, Washington, D.C. Gift of Wallace and Wilhelmina Holladay.

The Media of Art

Chapter Scan

TRB Resources

- 2-8 Chapter Test
- Color Transparency 3
- Color Transparency 4

TEACHING THE CHAPTER

Introducing the Art Work

Direct students' attention to M.C. Escher's *Drawing Hands*. Inform the students that Maurits Cornelius Escher was a Dutch graphic artist of the twentieth century. He studied printmaking at the School for Architecture and Decorative Arts in Haarlem, Holland and worked with lithographs and wood engravings. Escher considered the universe to have a definite structure within the mathematical laws of nature, and in turn, had a deep aversion to disorder and unfinished representation. He balanced perfect forms and definite structure with the idea of illusion. Normal expectations of perspective are violated by the illogical structures of his works. Escher not only mastered his craft, but had a thorough understanding of the properties of the media and the materials he used. He frequently created many preliminary drawings before creating a final print.

Examining the Art Work

Explain to students that Escher created a three-dimensional image which seems to rise out of a two-dimensional drawing. Point out how the artist created the illusion of three dimensional form. This is contrasted with the shapes of the cuffs and paper, which appear to be flat and sketched due to their lack of dimension. Point out how Escher emphasized the element of line by having the tip of the pencil appear to be drawing the outline of the cuff. This line leads the viewer's eye to the other hand and the tip of the pencil which emphasizes the drawing of the other cuff outline. Explain how these lines also create a circular movement in the work.

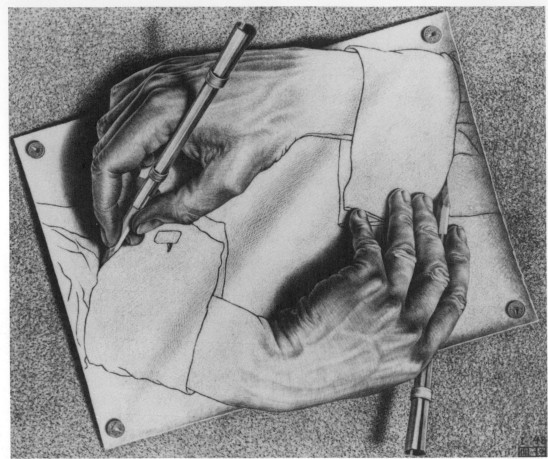

▲ The artist was famous for creating "impossible" buildings and landscapes. In what way is this work impossible?

M. C. Escher. *Drawing Hands*. Lithograph. M. C. Escher Heirs/Cordon Art. Baarn, Holland.

The Media of Art

You may think of an artist as someone who paints. While it is true that many artists are painters, paint is just one material artists use. Some artists prefer to work with the tools and materials of sculpting. Others prefer to work with the tools and materials of architecture. Still others would rather work with the tools used to create the picture at the left.

In this chapter you will learn about the many different materials of the artist's profession.

OBJECTIVES

After completing this chapter, you will be able to:
- Name the ways in which drawing, painting, and printmaking media are used in art.
- Explain the basic methods of printmaking and sculpting.
- Explain the basic uses of architecture.
- Name and describe some important crafts.
- Create art work using different art media.

WORDS YOU WILL LEARN

architecture	medium of art
binder	mixed media
crafts	pigment
edition	printmaking
freestanding sculpture	relief sculpture
	solvent

ARTISTS YOU WILL MEET

Barbara Aubin	Helen Frankenthaler
Isabel Bishop	Antonio Gaudi
Mary Cassatt	Vinnie Ream Hoxie
Paul Cézanne	John Marin
Abastenia St. Leger Eberle	Joan Miró
M. C. Escher	Gertrud and Otto Natzler

Stress that a three-dimensional object coming from a two-dimensional drawing is only an illusion, since the viewer understands that it is impossible for this to take place.

Discussing the Art Work
Ask students to think about why Escher chose the media of the lithograph and why he omitted the element of color. Suggest that if Escher used painting he would not have been able to create the sharp fine lines he used in the hands. These lines give the appearance of realism. If Escher used the medium of sculpture the illusion would completely loose its' meaning. Remind students that the lack of color heightens the contrast in the work and stresses the illusion of drawing by making the cuffs appear as if they were an unfinished sketch. If color had been added to the hands and not the cuffs, the illusion would have been lost.

Tell students that in this chapter they will learn about the various media of drawing, painting, printmaking, sculpting, architecture, and crafts. They will create their own art works using different art media.

17

Building Self-Esteem
Tell students that in this chapter they will be making a mixed-media project. During the planning stage, they will be asked to select some lines from a favorite poem, song, or saying. Ask them to focus on some area in which they have a special skill or interest. Urge them to brainstorm and write down as many words, ideas, and visual images as they can. Help them realize that creating a work of art is always more fascinating and absorbing when they select a subject they love. Tell them to let their imaginations take them wherever they will. Remind the class that artists who have felt strongly about a subject have used color and visual symbols to convey the message and mood. In this project, they will have the opportunity to experiment with and use many media in imaginative ways.

Objectives

After completing this lesson, students will be able to:
- Define the term *medium of art.*
- Name four different kinds of painting media.
- Name four methods of making prints.

Supplies

- Variety of drawing and painting media.
- Sketch paper.
- Index cards.
- Painting tools such as brushes, palette knives, sponges, drawing paper.

> **TRB Resource**
> - 2-1 *The Medium is the Message,* (aesthetics/art criticism)

TEACHING THE LESSON

Getting Started

Motivator. Distribute different kinds of drawing media to the students. Have them experiment with the media. Ask: How are the media different from each other? What kinds of lines do they make? Have the students work with partners, discussing what they have discovered about the different media. Ask students which media they prefer and why.

Vocabulary. Have students make notecards with the names of different painting media—oil paint, tempera, watercolor, and acrylic—on one side and the definition on the reverse side of the card. Divide students into groups and have them quiz each other. Then have them take a brief vocabulary test.

Drawing, Painting, and Printmaking

As you have read, when artists set out to create, they are faced with many choices. One of the most important is the decision of which medium to use. A **medium of art** is *a material used to create a work of art*. Paint, which you used in the studio lessons in Chapter 1, is one medium. Pencil and crayon, which you also used, are two others. When we speak of more than one medium at a time, we use the plural *media*.

▲ **Figure 2–1 Works created with pastels sometimes seem like paintings. What does this work have in common with a painting? How is it different?**

Mary Cassatt. *Sleepy Baby.* c. 1910. Pastel on paper. 64.7 x 52.0 cm (25½ x 20½″). Dallas Museum of Art, Dallas, Texas. Munger Fund.

When artists use several different media, such as pen and ink and watercolor, they create a mixed media work of art. **Mixed media** means *the use of more than one medium in a work of art.*

In this lesson you will learn about the media used in drawing, painting, and printmaking.

DRAWING

If you have ever scribbled with a pen or pencil, you have used drawing media. Pen, pencil, charcoal, and chalk are some of the media used to draw. The picture in Figure 2–1 was made using another medium, pastels. This is a soft, chalky medium. Notice how delicately the artist has used this medium to capture her subject.

The Purpose of Drawing

Artists use drawing for different purposes. One is to create finished works of art, such as the one you have just seen. Another use is to help plan projects. Artists often make studies, or sketches, for their works. Look at the drawing in Figure 2–2. This was done by French artist Paul Cézanne (say-**zahn**) as a study for the painting in Figure 2–3. Can you match up the figure in the drawing with one in the painting?

PAINTING

Like other artists, painters use a wide variety of media. Before a painter begins a work, he or she chooses a type of paint and an appropriate surface on which to work. Canvas, paper, or fabric are three surface materials that painters use.

Background Information

During the Renaissance artists planned and executed drawings before producing large art works. It was during this period that the widespread use of drawing media began. The media most often used were silverpoint, pen, charcoal, and chalk. During the sixteenth century, wash drawings were most popular. This method actually used a painting medium to produce drawings. Also popular was the reed pen. In the following centuries, the pencil achieved great popularity, and it was used almost exclusively by the nineteenth century. The Romantic artists, however, preferred pen and ink or brush and ink to render their drawings. In modern times the common pencil is most widely used by Western artists.

▲ Figure 2–2 Cézanne used pencil and watercolors for his study of a card player. Did he use all the detail captured in this sketch for his painted version?

Paul Cézanne. *The Card Player.* 1892. Pencil and watercolor. 53.4 x 36.4 cm (20¼ x 14⁹⁄₁₆"). Museum of Art, Rhode Island School of Design, Providence, Rhode Island. Gift of Mrs. Murray S. Danforth.

Regardless of the type of paint, all paint has three basic parts:

- **Pigment** (pig-muhnt) is *a finely ground, colored powder that gives every paint its color.*
- **Binder** is *a liquid that holds together the grains of pigment.* The binder is what makes the pigment stick to a surface.
- **Solvent** is *a material used to thin a paint's binder.* The thickness or thinness of a paint depends on the amount of solvent used. Turpentine is the solvent in oil paints. Water is the solvent in watercolors. Solvents are also used to clean brushes.

Painting Media

Every medium of painting has its own unmistakable look. Some of the most commonly used media are the following:

- **Oil paint.** Oil paint takes its name from its binder, linseed oil. Turpentine is its solvent. Because oil paint dries slowly, the artist is able to blend colors right on the canvas. The painting in Figure 2–3, which you have already examined, was painted with oils.

◀ Figure 2–3 Did the medium make a difference in how Cézanne painted the figures in his oil painting? Compare the man in the sketch with the one in the final version.

Paul Cézanne. *The Card Players.* Oil on canvas. 65.4 x 81.9 cm (25¾ x 32¼"). The Metropolitan Museum of Art, New York, New York. Bequest of Stephen C. Clark.

Developing Concepts

Exploring Aesthetics. Ask the students to look at Figures 2-2, 2-4, and 2-6. Ask them how each work of art is different. Is printmaking an art form that is equivalent to painting? Is drawing as much an art form as painting? How might each art work change if it were executed in a different medium? Encourage students to express their opinions and to explain their responses.

Understanding Art History. Discuss the printmaking techniques of the ancient world. Explain to the students that the prehistoric cave art of 25,000 years ago incorporates printmaking. The artist smeared a hand with paint and pressed it against the wall. Negative prints were also made by dotting paint around the hand. The meaning of these handprints is controversial. Nevertheless, they are the only images that we have of the prehistoric cave artists.

Understanding Art History. Have students research how new techniques and inventions allow artists to make new kinds of art. For example, a process for making multicolored prints was developed in the eighteenth century, which allowed inexpensive color prints to be made for the first time. Another possible topic of investigation is the nineteenth century invention of the tin paint tube, which permitted artists to work outdoors for long periods of time and encouraged a whole new generation of landscape artists to paint directly from their subjects instead of only working from sketches and memory.

Lesson 1 *Drawing, Painting, and Printmaking* **19**

Background Information

Like many of America's finest eighteenth- and nineteenth-century artists, Mary Cassatt (United States, 1845–1926) spent the majority of her life in Europe. There she was associated with the Impressionist group. The lightness of her palette, her free brush strokes, and the intimate, contemporary nature of her subject matter all constitute Cassatt's exploration of the Impressionist style. During the period from 1879 to 1886, when she exhibited four times with the Impressionists, Cassatt took many of her models from her family, several members of whom came to live with her in Paris in 1877. As the Impressionists suffered criticism in 1886 at the hands of a new and more radical generation of artists, Cassatt began to develop a more monumental style by relying less on the Impressionist perception of spontaneity and more on elegant drawing and stable picture arrangements. In her search for a more timeless subject, Cassatt increasingly came to paint the traditional mother and child theme, albeit with a modern sensibility.

▶ Figure 2–4   Study the painting on the right. Can you find spots in the picture where the artist seems to have used a lot of solvent? Do you remember what the solvent for watercolor is?

John Marin. *Sunset, Casco Bay.* 1936. Watercolor on paper. Wichita Art Museum, Wichita, Kansas. Ronald P. Murdock Collection.

- **Tempera** (**tem**-puh-ruh). Some of the earliest paintings on record were made with tempera. A mixture of pigment, egg yolk, and water, tempera is very hard to use. The school tempera you used in the studio lesson in Chapter 1 is a different type. It is also called poster paint.
- **Watercolor.** Watercolor is named for its solvent. Its binder, gum arabic, is a gummy plant matter. Watercolor gives paintings a light, misty quality. Look at the painting in Figure 2–4. Notice how the sun rays seem to "melt" into the sky and water.
- **Acrylic** (uh-**kril**-ik). A quick-drying water-based paint, acrylic is a very popular medium among painters today. Acrylics are synthetic, or manufactured, paints that were introduced in the 1950s. Because its solvent is water, acrylic is easy to use. More important, it offers the artist a wide range of pure, bold colors. Notice the lively splashes of color in the work in Figure 2–5.

▲ Figure 2–5   Do you think this artist was interested in painting a clear and real-looking subject? If not, what do you think she was interested in?

Helen Frankenthaler. *Interior Landscape.* 1964. Acrylic on canvas. 266.4 x 235.3 cm (104⅞ x 92⅝"). San Francisco Museum of Modern Art, San Francisco, California. Gift of The Women's Board.

20   📖   Lesson 1   *Drawing, Painting, and Printmaking*

Background Information
Color Field painter Helen Frankenthaler inherited the large scale and abstract, gestural strokes of the Abstract Expressionists, but none of their sense of psychic chaos, imminent doom, and infernal gyrating energy. Her work explores more tranquil waters and is composed of floating fields of color, scattered fountains of color on bare canvas, and sometimes areas of pulsating, warm earth tones. Her compositions of light and color seem to express a desire for a spiritual transcendence that does not necessarily deny the pleasures of the visual and sensual world. Frankenthaler pours her paint directly onto a canvas laid out on the floor. The pools of paint flow outward, but she channels the paint with sponges, wipers, and other tools. Although she is guided in part by the serendipitous intersections that occur between edges of paint pools, Frankenthaler insists that the artist should know how to work with the accidental and not rely on an accident to create the art by itself.

PRINTMAKING BASICS

Over the centuries artists have searched for new ways to create art. Around 2,000 years ago the Chinese developed a form of art called **printmaking**. This is *a technique in which an inked image from a prepared surface is transferred onto another surface*, such as paper or fabric.

There are three basic steps in printmaking. First, the printmaker creates a printing plate by altering a surface to create an image. Next, ink is applied to the plate. Finally, the printmaker transfers the ink to the paper or cloth by pressing the plate against the surface to be printed and then pulling the paper or cloth off the plate.

These steps may be repeated many times for a given plate. *A series of identical prints made from a single plate* is called an **edition**.

Printmaking Methods

There are four main methods of making prints. These are:

- **Relief printing**. In relief printing, the image to be printed is raised from a background. A medium used often in relief printing is wood.
- **Intaglio** (in-**tal**-yoh). Intaglio may be thought of as the reverse of relief printing. In this method, the image to be printed is scratched or etched into a surface. (See Figure 2–6.) The plates for intaglio prints are often made of metal.
- **Lithography** (lith-**ahg**-ruh-fee). To make a lithograph, the artist draws the image to be printed on a limestone, zinc, or aluminum slab with a special greasy crayon. Lithography lets the artist blend, little by little, light and dark values of a hue. The art on page **16** is a lithograph.
- **Screen printing**. To make a screen print, the artist transfers the design through various processes on a silk screen. The areas not to be printed are blocked off so that a kind of stencil remains. Screen prints that are handmade by an artist are also known as serigraphs (**ser**-uh-grafs).

✔CHECK YOUR UNDERSTANDING

1. Define *medium of art*.
2. Name three media used in drawing.
3. What are the three basic parts, or ingredients, of paint?
4. Name three media used in painting.
5. Name and describe two printmaking methods.

◄ **Figure 2–6** Notice how the use of line and shapes can be effective in different media, as in this intaglio print.

Isabel Bishop. *Men and Girls Walking*. 1969. Aquatint on paper. 21.3 x 29.2 cm (8⅜ x 11½"). National Museum of Women in the Arts, Washington, D.C. Gift of Mr. and Mrs. Edward P. Levy.

Lesson 1   *Drawing, Painting, and Printmaking*   📖   **21**

LESSON PLAN
(pages 22–23)

Objectives
After completing this lesson, students will be able to:
• Define the term mixed media.
• Explain harmony and rhythm.
• Plan and create a mixed media design.

Supplies
• Examples of mixed-media designs.
• Pencils and sketch paper.
• Found materials.
• Magazines; envelopes; and scissors.
• White glue.
• Construction paper or lightweight posterboard of various colors, cut into sheets of 12 x 18 inches (30 x 45 cm).
• Watercolor markers, thick- and thin-tipped.
• Crayons, colored pencils, and watercolor paints.
• Examples of graphic art.

> **TRB Resource**
> • 2-2 *Mixed-Media Studio,*
>   (studio)

TEACHING THE LESSON

Getting Started
Motivator. Begin by showing the students examples of various mixed-media designs. Ask them to identify the different media used in each design. Have them discuss the elements involved in unity, including harmony, balance, and rhythm. Ask: How do the artists use the different media? What effects are created? How does a mixed media work differ from one made with just one medium?

Vocabulary. Have the students look up the words *rhythm* and *harmony* in the dictionary. Ask them how these definitions apply to the art they have seen. Have them discuss the concepts of rhythm and harmony in the music world, and ask if they can apply the same ideas to art. Point out the visual and verbal elements in Aubin's work. Ask how the relationship of the words and pictures create harmony and rhythm.

22

Creating Mixed-Media Art

Study the mixed-media work of art in Figure 2–7. Notice how the artist has united visual and verbal symbols. The letters are woven into the design so that their shapes are as important as their meanings. They are not written in neat rows that are easy to read, but are integrated into the surface of the work.

Some of the visual symbols are directly related to the words, while other symbols just fit the design. Some visual symbols have been drawn and painted by the artist, or have been printed with rubber stamps. Others are made with decals, lace, and stamps. Notice that some of the letters are written and printed by the artist. Stick-on letters or those cut from magazines and glued on are also used.

WHAT YOU WILL LEARN
You will create a mixed-media design uniting visual and verbal symbols in the manner of Aubin. Weave the letters into the design so that their shapes are as important as their meanings. Use the principle of rhythm to create a sense of visual movement in the work. Use harmony of shape, color, and texture to unify your work.

▲ **Figure 2–7   The artist, Barbara Aubin, created a dream-like mood in this work. What other sources of inspiration do artists use in getting ideas for their art?**

Barbara Aubin. *I Dreamed I Saw a Pink Flamingo in the Salle de Bain*. 1981. Mixed media on paper. (Detail.) 45.7 x 61 cm (18 x 24").

Background Information
Collage was first used by early Cubists and Dadaists. The Cubists were concerned with the essence of an object and painted a subject from various perspectives to express the idea of that object. In later phases of Cubism, decorative, or rococo, elements are evident. During this phase Picasso first introduced elements other than paint onto the canvas. The Dada movement saw this use of collage as an expression of their theories of art. They intended to outrage and shock the art world, and one way to do this was to introduce non-paint media into a painting. Marcel Duchamp (French-born, 1887–1968) was the most famous of the Dadaists. He eventually abandoned oil painting to make art out of objects that he had found. He felt his role as an artist was to bring these elements together and arrange them at random.

WHAT YOU WILL NEED

- Pencil and sketch paper
- Found materials
- Magazines, scissors, and white glue
- Envelope
- Construction paper or lightweight poster board, 12 x 18 inches (30 x 46 cm), in a color of your choice
- Watercolor markers, thick and thin-tipped
- Crayons, colored pencils, and watercolor paints

WHAT YOU WILL DO

1. Select some lines from a favorite poem, song, story, or saying. The words may be your own or something you have read. Write the words on your sketch paper.
2. Make sketches of objects and scenes to go with your words.
3. Look through magazines and cut out interesting shapes, letters, or printed words for your work. Collect found materials that fit your ideas. Keep all the small cutouts in an envelope. Select a color for your background.
4. Notice how Aubin has used the letters as design elements. They are not written in neat rows that are easy to read, but are woven into the composition as shapes. Make some rough sketches to plan your design on your sketch paper. Repeat shapes to create movement that makes the viewer's eyes move through the work. Plan for harmony by using monochromatic or analogous colors as well as related shapes and textures. Select your best idea, and sketch it lightly on your construction paper or poster board.

EXAMINING YOUR WORK

- **Describe**   Identify the media you used. Read the phrase you chose, and explain why you chose it. Describe the visual images you chose to go with the words.
- **Analyze**   What shapes did you repeat to create rhythmic movement? How did you use color, shape, and texture to create harmony?
- **Judge**   Did you create a unified design? Are the verbal symbols and visual images equally important? If not, how could the unity of the work be improved?

---

5. Place the found objects and cutouts on your design. Do not glue them down. Take time to arrange and rearrange your words and images until you are satisfied. Then glue them down.
6. Use a variety of media to draw and paint the remaining images and words. For example, use paints to fill large spaces, and use fine-line markers to draw thin lines.
7. Place your work on display with that of your classmates. Look for works in which the words and pictures are unified.

OTHER STUDIO IDEAS

- Select one key word from current events. Cut out the word itself and photographs illustrating that word from newspapers and magazines. Create a mixed-media work in the same manner as described in this lesson.

- ●● Make another mixed-media work combining art media with recyclable found materials. You may integrate words cut from recyclable newspaper, but do not let the words dominate your work.

Lesson 2   *Creating Mixed-Media Art*   **23**

Classroom Management Tip
Colored pencil markings are often difficult to erase with an ordinary rubber or plastic eraser. Try to purchase erasable colored pencils for art projects. A particularly erasable brand, which is available in a wide range of colors, is the Col-Erase series manufactured by FaberCastell.

Sculpture, Architecture, and Crafts Media

Drawings, paintings, and prints created as two-dimensional works often appear to have roundness and depth. Some works of art have *real* roundness and depth. These works, which have height, width, and depth, are known as three-dimensional works.

In this lesson you will learn about three areas of art—sculpture, architecture, and crafts—in which three-dimensional works are created. You will learn about the media used in making such works.

SCULPTURE

Sculpture is art that is made to stand out in space. All sculpture is of one of two types, freestanding or relief. Also called sculpture "in the round," **freestanding sculpture** is *sculpture surrounded on all sides by space*. It is meant to be seen from all sides. The work in Figure 2–8 is an example of freestanding sculpture.

Relief sculpture, on the other hand, is *sculpture only partly enclosed by space*. It is flat along the back and is meant to be viewed only from the front. The work in Figure 2–9 is an example of relief sculpture.

Sculpting Methods

Sculptors use four basic methods or techniques in their work. These are:

* **Carving**. Carving is cutting or chipping a shape from a mass. Often stone and other hard materials are used in carving. The sculpture in Figure 2–8 was carved from a block of marble.

▲ Figure 2–8 Hoxie used a very hard medium and was still able to portray fabric falling in soft folds. How does the light help?

Vinnie Ream Hoxie. *Abraham Lincoln*. 1870. Marble. 210.8 cm (6′11″) high. United States Capitol Art Collection.

Background Information
Architects create, among other things, structures for religious uses. The creation of churches, temples, and other houses of prayer is always an expression of religious belief. The different architectural styles in which churches and temples have been built illustrates this idea. The Romanesque churches of Europe are massive structures that to the medieval person suggested the strength and power of the Church. Gothic architecture is lighter and more flexible than Romanesque buildings. Gothic churches soar into the air; some are as tall as skyscrapers. This draws the eye heavenward. Renaissance church architecture is characterized by concern with correctness of proportion and reflects the idea of humanity's nobility.

▲ Figure 2–9   Notice how the horses seem to be galloping in this relief sculpture. This frieze circles the top of a famous Greek temple known as the Parthenon.

Horsemen Riding at a Gallop. Parthenon. British Museum.

- **Casting**. In casting, a melted-down metal or other liquid substance is poured into a mold to harden. Bronze is a material often used in casting. (See Figure 2–10.)
- **Modeling**. In modeling, a soft or workable material is built up and shaped. Clay is the material used most often in this sculpting method.
- **Assembling**. Assembling is gathering and joining different kinds of materials. Wood, wire, glue, and nails are a few of the materials used in assembling. The figure on page 28 is an example of assembling.

▶ Figure 2–10   How did the sculptor show movement in this figure? Would you have needed the title to tell you the wind was blowing?

Abastenia St. Leger Eberle. *The Windy Doorstep.* 1910. Bronze. 34.5 x 24.4 x 16 cm (13⅝ x 9⅝ x 6⅜"). Worcester Art Museum, Worcester, Massachusetts.

Lesson 3   *Sculpture, Architecture, and Crafts Media*   📖   **25**

▶ **Figure 2–11** This is a
unique example of architecture.
Notice how the architect
repeated the pointed arch shape
in the towers, emphasizing the
height of the structure.

Antonio Gaudi. *Church of the
Sacred Family.* Barcelona, Spain.

ARCHITECTURE

All art is made to be seen. Some art is
made to be used as well as seen. Works of art
known as architecture fit into this second category. **Architecture** is *the planning and creating of buildings.* The success of a work of
architecture is measured partly by how well
it does the job it was meant to do and partly
by its appearance.

The Uses of Architecture

Since earliest times, a chief form of architecture has been the creation of dwelling
places. This has by no means been the only
type, however. Two other examples have
been the artistic creation of the following
kinds of buildings:

• **Structures for prayer.** The building of
temples, churches, and other houses of
worship dates to the dawn of history. The
unusual house of prayer shown in Figure

2–11 was begun in the late 1800s. It is still
under construction. Notice how this
unique building seems almost to be
reaching toward the sky.
• **Structures for business.** With the spread
of civilization in ancient times came the
need for places to carry on business. In
our own time that need is often met by
vertical creations such as skyscrapers.

CRAFTS

In ages past, artists worked not only out of
a desire to create but also out of a need to
provide items required for everyday use.
Clothing, cooking pots, and whatever other
goods people needed were handmade.

Artistic craftspeople still make functional
items that are often considered aesthetically
pleasing works of art. The useful and decorative goods these artists make, and *the different areas of applied art in which craftspeople work*
are called **crafts**.

26   Lesson 3   *Sculpture, Architecture, and Crafts Media*

Craft Areas

Craftspeople today, like those long ago, work in a number of special areas. Some of these are:

- **Pottery**. This is the making of objects from clay. Before objects of pottery can be used, they must be hardened by heat, or fired. This takes place in a special oven called a kiln. Ceramics is the name of objects made in this fashion. The vase shown in Figure 2–12 is an example of modern American ceramics.
- **Weaving**. This is the interlocking of fiber strands to create objects. Fibers such as wool, cotton, plant materials, and synthetic materials are used in weaving. Weaving is done on a special machine called a loom, which holds the threads in place as they are woven together. The weaving in Figure 2–13 was done by twentieth-century Spanish artist Joan Miró (zhoh-**ahn** mee-**roh**).
- **Glassblowing**. This is the shaping of melted glass into objects. Glassblowers work by forcing air through a tube into globs of melted glass.

▲ **Figure 2–12** The Natzlers are famous for their glazes. They called this a crater glaze.

Gertrud Natzler/Otto Natzler. *Pilgrim Bottle*. c. 1956. Earthenware. 33 x 43 cm (17 x 13"). Los Angeles County Museum of Art, Los Angeles, California. Gift of Howard and Gwen Laurie Smits.

▲ **Figure 2–13** This weaving shows large areas of color against a textured background. Can you see a woman in the tapestry?

Joan Miró, Josep Royo. *Woman*. 1977. Dyed New Zealand Wool. 105.3 x 604.3 cm (415 x 238"). National Gallery of Art, Washington, D.C. Gift of the Collectors Committee and George L. Erion.

✔ CHECK YOUR UNDERSTANDING

1. What are the two main types of sculpture?
2. What are the four basic sculpting methods?
3. Define *architecture*. How is the success of a work of architecture measured?
4. Define *crafts*. Name three areas in which craftspeople work.

Following Up

Closure. Ask students to write short paragraphs about their "Studio Experience" work. Their paragraphs should include responses to the following questions: Which was easier to make—the two-dimensional art, or the three-dimensional art? What are the benefits of each kind of art? Which do you prefer? What would you choose to be if you could be anything—a painter, an architect, a sculptor, or a craftsperson? Why?

Evaluation. 1. Review the students' written responses to the "Check Your Understanding" questions. 2. Read the students' paragraphs about the "Studio Experience" work.

Reteaching. Have each student choose a category—architecture, sculpture, or crafts—and research a contemporary artist who works in that area. Ask the students to find out what the artist has to say about his or her work, and why he or she does it. Have the students share their results with the class. Guide a class discussion about the different points of view.

Enrichment. Have students bring in an example of one of their hobbies. Ask: Are any of these hobbies fine art? Are any applied art? Ask the students to describe why they enjoy the hobbies they do. Or, ask a local crafts club to demonstrate a simple craft for the students.

Answers to "Check Your Understanding"

1. The two main types of sculpture are freestanding and relief.
2. The four methods used by sculptors are carving, casting, modeling, and assembling.
3. Architecture is the planning and creating of buildings. The success of a work of architecture is measured partly by how well it does the job it was meant to do and partly by its appearance.
4. The term crafts refers to the different kinds of applied arts techniques used by artisans and the functional and decorative products they make. Three areas craftspeople work in are pottery, weaving, and glassblowing.

LESSON PLAN
(pages 28–29)

Objectives
After completing this lesson, students will be able to:
• Plan and create an environmental design.
• Define the terms *environment* and *recycle*.

Supplies
• Index cards.
• Found materials.
• Pins.
• White glue; transparent tape; and scissors.
• Markers.
• School acrylics and paint brushes.
• Heavy cardboard, cut into 18 x 18 inch (45 x 45 cm) squares.

> **TRB Resources**
> • 2-5 *Japanese Sculptors Today,* (appreciating cultural diversity)
> • 2-6 *Evolution of Assembly Architecture,* (art history)
> • 2-7 *Designs for Assembly,* (reproducible master)

TEACHING THE LESSON

Getting Started
Motivator. Organize a trip to the school grounds, and have students collect objects to use in their environmental designs while they clean up the area. Discuss the principle of decomposition and ask which objects will eventually decompose. Describe how paper and similar products are less harmful to the environment than plastic. Discuss ways in which students could help clean up the environment—keeping school grounds clean, recycling in their homes, or simply cutting down on the amount of garbage that they create. Ask students if they know about any local recycling efforts and how they could be helped.

Creating an Environmental Design

Today we are all concerned about our environment. Some people have invented a way to recycle used tires by building playgrounds with them. (See Figure 2–14.) These areas are fun, and they are also visually pleasing. They have visual unity.

WHAT YOU WILL DO
Working in teams of three to five, you will design and construct models of playground equipment using found materials. You will organize this equipment on a heavy cardboard base that represents the ground. The forms you create must invite children to crawl through, jump over, climb up, and balance upon. You must also consider space in this plan. Consider how children will move around the area. Place equipment pieces with space for the children to move around the area.

▶ **Figure 2–14   Recycled tires provide safe and inviting playground equipment. What other products might be given a second life in parks and playgrounds?**

Background Information
Louis Kahn (United States, 1901–1974) summed up how planning is important to architecture. "If I were to define architecture in a word," he said, "I would say that architecture is a thoughtful making of spaces." It is important for the architect to keep in mind the nature of people's activities. Kahn's two largest commissions demonstrate both his success and failure with his own ideas. The Richards Building, constructed for scientists doing experiments, suffers because the rooms are of uniform size. Experiments that require more space, therefore, sometimes spill over into the halls. In addition, there is too much light for experiments that must be conducted in darkness. Kahn's Salk Building, however, suits its purposes well. It is criticized because, however, it is too beautiful for a medical clinic!

WHAT YOU WILL NEED

- Found materials
- White glue, transparent tape, pins, and scissors
- Markers, school acrylics, paint brushes, and construction paper
- Piece of heavy cardboard, 18 x 18 inches (46 x 46 cm) or larger

WHAT YOU WILL DO

1. Collect a large assortment of found materials such as corks, wood scraps, and plastic containers.
2. Brainstorm with your class for ideas about things young children would like to play on in a playground.
3. Divide into small groups of three to five students. Work together as a team to solve problems. Look over the found materials you have collected. Experiment with the forms. Try different ways to combine objects until they look like something to climb up, crawl through, swing on, balance upon, or jump over. When you are satisfied with the forms, glue them together. Since white glue takes time to dry, you might want to secure some pieces with pins or tape until the glue dries.
4. You may decorate some pieces with markers, paint, or construction paper.
5. Get out the cardboard base, and arrange your model equipment on the base. Remember to consider the necessary space between different pieces of equipment. When you are satisfied with the arrangement, glue the equipment to the base.
6. Decorate the base by painting it or gluing sand to it to make it look like earth. You might turn twigs into trees by adding

EXAMINING YOUR WORK

- **Describe** Identify the found materials you collected, and point to the ones you used. Explain how the brainstorming session helped in the planning stages. Tell how your group worked together. Describe the equipment you constructed. What can a child do on each piece?
- **Analyze** Explain how you decided to arrange the space for each piece.
- **Interpret** What did you name your playground? Why?
- **Judge** Tell whether your design was successful.

green paper leaves. You may even make some cutouts of people to play on the playground. (See Figure 2–15.)

7. Give your playground a name, and put it on a sign. Place your work on display with the other model playgrounds. Which ones invite you to play?

▲ Figure 2–15   Student work. Environmental design.

OTHER STUDIO IDEAS

- Create a playground using paper sculpture techniques to create the forms. (See Technique Tip **21**, *Handbook* page **284**.)

- ●● Use found materials to create a model of a shelter for travelers who have been stranded on a desert island.

Lesson 4   *Creating an Environmental Design*   **29**

ANSWERS TO "CHAPTER 2 REVIEW"

Building Vocabulary

1. medium of art
2. pigment
3. binder
4. solvent
5. printmaking
6. edition
7. freestanding sculpture
8. relief sculpture
9. architecture
10. crafts
11. mixed media

Reviewing Art Facts

12. Artists use drawing for sketches during the planning stage and for finished works of art.
13. The three steps in printmaking are making the plate by altering the surface to create an image; applying ink to the plate's surface; transferring ink to the paper or cloth.
14. A lithograph is a print made from a metal or stone plate that has been drawn on with a greasy crayon. A serigraph is a print made by forcing ink through unmasked areas of a silk screen. A woodcut is a relief print made from the raised surfaces of a wood block.
15. Freestanding sculpture is a substitute term for "in the round."
16. In the casting method of sculpture, melted-down metal is poured into a mold.
17. Three types of architecture are dwellings, churches, and business structures.

Thinking About Art

1. Responses will vary. Advantages and disadvantages listed should take into consideration the time element and how the artist wants to blend the paints.
2. No. The original work of art, whether it is a plate for a print or a mold for sculpture, is one of a kind. Duplicates of the original have the same attributes and will be judged by the same criteria.
3. Modeling and carving could be used at different stages; modeling to build the basic shape, carving for details.
4. Responses will vary. Students might mention any two of the following: Theaters, libraries, museums, sports facilities, airports, train stations, factories, and so forth.

BUILDING VOCABULARY

Number a sheet of paper from 1 to 11. After each number, write the term from the box that best matches each description below.

architecture	medium of art
binder	mixed media
crafts	pigment
edition	printmaking
freestanding sculpture	relief sculpture
	solvent

1. A material used to create a work of art.
2. A finely ground powder that gives every paint its color.
3. A liquid that holds together the grains of pigment in paint.
4. A material used to thin a paint's binder.
5. A technique in which an inked image from a prepared surface is transferred onto another surface.
6. A series of identical prints made from a single plate.
7. Sculpture surrounded on all sides by space.
8. Sculpture partly enclosed by space.
9. The planning and creating of buildings.
10. The different areas of applied art in which craftspeople work.
11. The use of more than one medium in a work of art.

REVIEWING ART FACTS

Number a sheet of paper from 12 to 17. Answer each question in a complete sentence.

12. What are the two main ways in which artists use drawing?
13. Describe the steps in printmaking.
14. What is a lithograph? What is a serigraph? What is a woodcut?
15. What is "in the round" a substitute term for?
16. In what method of sculpting is a melted-down metal poured into a mold?
17. What are three types of architecture?

THINKING ABOUT ART

On a sheet of paper, answer each question in a sentence or two.

1. **Compare and contrast**. Some paints, as you learned, dry slowly and others dry quickly. What would be some of the advantages and disadvantages of each type?
2. **Extend**. In attempting to define *art* over the centuries, scholars have often noted that an art work is a one-of-a-kind creation. Does accepting this view rule out prints as a form of art? Explain your answer.
3. **Analyze**. Which of the methods of sculpting you learned about would be best for making a sand castle? Explain your choice.
4. **Extend**. Name two kinds of structures not mentioned in this chapter that architects create. Look through books and magazines and bring examples to class.

MAKING ART CONNECTIONS

1. **Social Studies.** Many people today create crafts as a leisure activity. Try to find an individual you know who is interested in a craft. Interview him or her and make a report for your class. Tell how the craft affects the life of the person.
2. **Science.** Find out how the study of anatomy contributes to the work of a sculptor. Compare an anatomical drawing from a science book to a freestanding sculpture of the same subject. What similarities and differences do you see?

CHAPTER 2 REVIEW

LOOKING AT THE DETAILS

The detail shown below is from M. C. Escher's *Drawing Hands*. Study the detail and answer the following questions.

1. What did the artist accomplish by combining a highly detailed hand with the unfinished sketch of a cuff?
2. Would it have been possible for Escher to show as much realistic detail if he had used oil paints?
3. Which parts of the drawing depict three-dimensional form and which show only shape? Why?
4. Look at the entire work on page **16**. What is lost by looking at only the detail?
5. Looking at the entire work, which element of art does the artist emphasize and how?
6. What is it about this work that appears to be "impossible"?

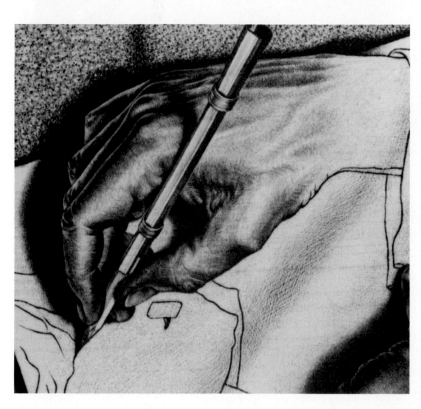

M. C. Escher. *Drawing Hands.*
Lithograph. (Detail.) M. C.
Escher Heirs/Cordon Art. Baarn,
Holland.

CHAPTER 3

Art Criticism, Aesthetics, and Art History

Chapter Scan

TRB Resources

- 3-9 Chapter Test
- Color Transparency 5
- Color Transparency 6

TEACHING THE CHAPTER

Introducing the Art Work

Direct students' attention to Georges Rouault's *Christ Mocked by Soldiers*. Inform them that Georges Rouault was a French painter and engraver in the late nineteenth and early twentieth centuries. Rouault aligned himself with the Fauves for a short period of time. However, he never felt that their ideas were compatible with his own and he set out to discover his own creativity. Rouault was concerned for the corrupt state of the world and he hoped for spiritual renewal through a revitalized religious faith. His paintings, regardless of their subject, represented that hope. The bulk of his work, particularly after 1913, contained religious subjects and was painted with great determination. Rouault never tried to create a handsomely finished work. Instead, he sought to express his innermost feelings through his painting. Rouault was so preoccupied with his spiritual intentions that he felt no need to innovate in form or color, therefore he had little influence over the younger painters of his time, who were more concerned with technique than moral attitudes. Rouault is considered to be the greatest religious painter since Rembrandt.

▲ Early in his career Georges Rouault worked for a maker of stained glass. What makes this painting look like a stained-glass window?

Georges Rouault. *Christ Mocked by Soldiers*. 1932. Oil on canvas. 92.1 x 72.4 cm (36¼ x 28½"). Museum of Modern Art, New York, New York. Given anonymously.

Tell students that as a young man Rouault had been trained as a stained glass worker, and evidence of that training can be seen in his paintings. Point out the thick black outlines and how they resemble the lead in stained glass. Explain to students how the hard, opaque brush strokes and slashes of color add texture to the painting as well as contribute to its mood. Explain that the artist used dark colors, thick, heavy lines and unusual, exaggerated shapes to create a painful, cruel, somber, even savage mood.

CHAPTER 3

Art Criticism, Aesthetics, and Art History

Imagine you were visiting the museum where the painting on the left is hung. What questions might you ask as you look at the painting? You might ask:

- With what media and how was the painting made?
- What elements and principles of art are used?
- How does the painting make me feel?
- Who is the artist, and when and where was the art work made?

What other questions might you ask? In this chapter you will learn how to find your own answers to the questions about works of art.

OBJECTIVES

After completing this chapter, you will be able to:

- Describe the four steps used in art criticism.
- Identify three aesthetic views.
- Explain the four steps used by art historians.
- Create paintings based on art criticism and art history.

WORDS YOU WILL LEARN

aesthetic view
art criticism
art history
composition
content
style
subject

ARTISTS YOU WILL MEET

James Brooks
Edward Hopper
Pablo Picasso
Georges Rouault
Jan Steen
Beatrice Whitney van Ness

Discussing the Art Work

Ask students how they think Rouault viewed the soldiers. Point out how the soldiers caricatural forms set against ominous shadows and the shape of the Christ figure contains most of the light in the work. Suggest that by painting the figures of the soldiers in this way Rouault revealed their inner ugliness or cruelty.

Ask students to study Rouault's use of space. Point out the soldier in the upper right hand corner. Tell students that rather than appearing to be behind the Christ figure, the soldier seems to be practically on top of his shoulder. The soldiers seem to be looming over and encroaching on the Christ figure. Explain that Rouault's work lacks spatial depth. Suggest that since his work is more abstract, the lack of depth adds to the intensity of the mood.

Tell students that in this chapter they will learn the steps used by art critics and art historians. Explain that they will learn how to judge a work of art based on aesthetic views. Using the theories of art criticism and art history, students will create their own works of art.

33

Art Criticism and Aesthetics

LESSON PLAN
(pages 34–37)

Objectives
After completing this lesson, students will be able to:
• Define art criticism.
• Describe three aesthetic views.
• Identify the four steps of art criticism.

Supplies
• Sketch paper; pencils.
• White drawing paper.
• Watercolor markers.
• Erasable colored pencils.
• Charcoal pencils.
• Kneaded rubber erasers.
• White glue.
• Assortment of magazines.

> **TRB Resources**
> • 3-1 *Art and Plenty of It,* (reproducible master)
> • 3-2 *Aesthetics: Another Side,* (appreciating cultural diversity)
> • 3-3 *Invent Your Own Chair,* (studio)

TEACHING THE LESSON

Getting Started

Motivator. Have students select a large, clear reproduction of a painting in a book or at a local museum. Have them first write down what they notice in their choices. Then have them sketch their painting on plain paper. Ask them to list at the bottom of their sketches things that they noticed only after sketching the work. Ask: Did you see details that you initially overlooked? Discuss the importance of careful observance of art criticism.

Vocabulary. Discuss what the word *criticism* means in everyday usage. How is the meaning of *art criticism* different? Point out that although artists may sometimes be offended by what an art critic says about their art, art criticism does not necessarily entail a negative evaluation.

34

Art Criticism and Aesthetics

You have heard the saying "Don't judge a book by its cover." What this saying means is that to judge something fairly, you need to have all the facts. It is not enough to look at the surface of the object. You need to dig beneath the surface — to understand as much as you can about the object.

In this lesson you will learn ways of looking at art that will help increase your understanding and appreciation of it.

ART CRITICISM

Have you ever looked at a work of art and wondered if there was more to the painting than you understood? You may have asked yourself this question when you looked at Figure 3–1. Works of art are sometimes like mysteries. Solving art mysteries is one of the jobs of people in the field called art criticism. **Art criticism** is *studying, understanding, and judging works of art*.

In carrying out their work, art critics often use a four-step system. The four steps are describing, analyzing, interpreting, and judging.

► **Figure 3–1   In describing this art work, what element would you choose to discuss first? What do you think the artist was most interested in as he created this oil painting?**

James Brooks. *Rasalus.* 1959. Oil on canvas. 167.6 x 202.6 cm (66 x 79¾"). Whitney Museum of American Art, New York, New York.

Background Information
James Brooks was one of a group of painters known as Abstract Expressionists. A movement that sprang up in the United States shortly after World War II, Abstract Expressionism simultaneously gained instant recognition and caused confusion and anger. The roots of this new movement can be traced back to the works of Kandinsky, Picasso, and especially the Surrealists. Abstract Expressionists rejected the idea of realistic subject matter. They thought of the picture sur-face as a flat wall and emphasized the physical action it took to paint it. Painting was compared to life itself—an ongoing endeavor in which one undergoes ordeals and faces challenges that require a series of decisions. Instead of carefully planned brush strokes, Abstract Expressionists dribbled, spilled, spattered, and splashed paints onto their canvases. As they applied colors in this way, they looked for and emphasized emerging areas of interest that added structure to their work.

Describing an Art Work

In describing an art work, the critic notes certain key facts. These include the following:

- **The size of the work, the medium, and the process used.** The credit line gives the viewer information about the size of the work and the medium used. It also lists the process, such as serigraph or woodcut.
- **The subject, object, and details.** The **subject** is *the image viewers can easily identify in an art work.* The subject answers the question "What do I see when I look at this work?" The subject in Figure 3–2 is a group of people, probably a family, at a holiday gathering. What other objects and details might the art critic mention? What subject, object, and details would be described in Figure 3–3 on page **36**?

- **The elements used in the work.** Look again at Figure 3–2. Line and color are two of the elements of art that play an important part in this work. Can you identify the other art elements? What elements can you point out in Figure 3–3?

Notice that while every work of art uses elements, not all have subjects. Figure 3–1 is a painting without a recognized subject. Because such works are not "about" something, some viewers are uncertain how to describe them. These viewers should learn to focus attention on the elements of art. This is what the critic—or anyone else—will see in this work. This is called describing the formal aspects of the work.

◄ **Figure 3–2** Notice the title of the work. What American holiday is similar to the one being celebrated in this picture? What do you think the man at the right is pointing to?

Jan Steen. *Eve of St. Nicholas.* c. 1667. Canvas. 81.9 x 70.5 cm (32¼ x 27¾"). Rijksmuseum, Amsterdam.

Developing Concepts

Exploring Aesthetics. Have the students study the Rouault painting pictured on page **32**. Ask the students whether Rouault's use of the art elements recalls any other medium. Explain that Rouault spent part of his youth apprenticed to a stained glass artisan. Have the students describe how Rouault took the art elements that he learned in the medium of stained glass and used them later in oil painting.

Using Art Criticism. Have students choose a picture from this lesson and imagine that they are professional art critics. Direct them to use four steps of art criticism to write short reviews of their chosen art works. Read aloud the different critical evaluations of each picture. Discuss how critics may legitimately arrive at different opinions of a given art work.

Understanding Art History. Discuss the hidden moral message in Figure 3-2. Point out to students that many of Jan Steen's artistic peers also sought to include a moralizing precept in their pictures. Have small groups of students research other seventeenth-century Dutch paintings, such as those created by Gerard Ter Borch, Pieter de Hooch, and Jan Vermeer to find out what moral rules they contain.

Background Information

The seventeenth-century Dutch painter, inn keeper, and amateur actor Jan Steen was a master of genre scenes or pictures of daily life, of which hundreds have been attributed to him. Good-humored and sharply observant, Steen consistently created paintings that carried an obvious moral message, one that was often repeated in the form of an inscription tacked to the wall in the painting. At least half of Steen's works lament the folly to which children are prey when their parents and other adults don't raise them properly. Other typical Steen themes include lovesick maidens who use illness as an excuse to visit with their doctor-beau and groups of merry people who have forgotten that they will someday die. Despite the somber nature of Steen's messages, he was sympathetic rather than cruel to those who erred, and many of his paintings are quite humorous. Furthermore, Steen did not hesitate to include himself in his paintings, where he frequently appears as a lighthearted carouser.

▲ **Figure 3–3   Is this work successful because it looks lifelike or because it expresses an idea or mood? Why is it necessary to use more than one aesthetic view when judging works of art?**

Beatrice Whitney van Ness. *Summer Sunlight*. c. 1936. Oil on canvas. 99.1 x 124.5 cm (39 x 49"). National Museum of Women in the Arts, Washington, D.C. Gift of Wallace and Wilhelmina Holladay.

Analyzing an Art Work

In analyzing an art work, the critic focuses on the work's composition. **Composition** is *the way the art principles are used to organize the art elements of color, line, shape, form, space, and texture.* Look once again at the painting in Figure 3–2 on page **35**. Find the long loaf of bread in the lower left and the chair in the lower right. Notice how the diagonal lines of these and other objects lead your eye to the center of the picture. There you find a small child grinning and looking out at you. The child is one of the most important figures in the work. How are the elements organized in the painting in Figure 3–3?

Interpreting an Art Work

In interpreting an art work, the critic focuses on the work's **content**. This is *the message, idea, or feeling expressed by an art work.* Each art critic may interpret an art work differently, according to individual feelings. Your interpretation of an art work will be based on your personal opinions and experiences.

Look once more at Figure 3–2. Notice that the grinning child is pointing at another child, who is crying. It appears that this second boy has received no presents. His smiling sister holds his wooden shoe in which his gifts were to be placed. But the shoe holds only a hickory stick instead of presents. Maybe the artist's message to children of all ages is that gifts come only to those who behave. What mood or feeling does the painting in Figure 3–3 communicate to you?

Judging an Art Work

In judging an art work, the critic tells whether the work succeeds. He or she answers the question "Is this a successful work of art?"

How, exactly, the critic answers this question depends on his or her particular aesthetic (ess-**thet**-ik) view. An **aesthetic view** is *an idea, or school of thought, on what is important in a work of art.* Such views help critics better understand and explain the meaning of art to others.

AESTHETICS AND ART

Through the ages, scholars have put forth many different aesthetic views. The following are three common ones:

- **The subject view.** In this aesthetic view, a successful work of art is one with a lifelike subject. Look yet again at the picture in Figure 3–2. The members of the family are painted to look like real people. Critics holding this aesthetic view would praise this work for being true to life. How do you think these same critics would react to the painting in Figure 3–3? How would they judge the painting in Figure 3–1?
- **The composition view.** In this view, what is most important in an art work is its composition. Notice how light and dark

values of hue in Figure 3–2 create a feeling of depth. Critics taking this view would praise the artist's use of the elements and principles of art to create a visually pleasing design. How do you suppose these same critics would respond to the work in Figure 3–3? How might they react to the picture in Figure 3–1?

- **The content view.** In this view, what counts most is the content, or the mood or feeling, an art work communicates. Critics supporting this view would praise the work in Figure 3–2 for the joyous holiday mood it captures. What do you imagine these critics would have to say about the painting in Figure 3–3? What might their response be to the painting in Figure 3–1?

Keep in mind that few critics limit themselves to a single aesthetic view. Most feel that learning as much as possible from an art work requires keeping an open mind. How might a critic accepting all three views above react to the painting that opened this chapter on page **32**?

✓ CHECK YOUR UNDERSTANDING

1. What is art criticism? Name the four steps used by art critics.
2. What are subject, composition, and content?
3. What is an aesthetic view?
4. Describe the three commonly held aesthetic views detailed in this lesson.

Closure. Have each student briefly state to the class what he or she thinks is most important in a work of art. Ask: Is there one aesthetic view that best expresses your outlook on art?

Evaluation. 1. Review students' written responses to the "Check Your Understanding" questions. 2. Evaluate students' critical reviews of an art work. 3. Assess the group reports on moral messages in Dutch paintings.

Reteaching. Have students select a studio project that they completed in this class and write a short art critical review of it. Have them clearly label the four steps of art criticism in their review.

Enrichment. Have students read short art reviews that you have gathered from local newspapers or national magazines such as *Art in America, ArtNews, New Art Examiner, Arts,* and *Artforum.* Select the simplest and most clearly written examples and, if possible, choose reviews that are accomplished by an illustration of the art under discussion. Have the students try to identify the four steps of art criticism in each review.

Answers to "Check Your Understanding"
1. Art criticism is studying, understanding, and judging art works. The four steps art critics use are describing, analyzing, interpreting, and judging.
2. The *subject* of an art work is the image viewers can easily identify. *Composition* is the way the art principles are used to organize the art elements of color, line, shape, form, space, and texture. *Content* is the message, idea, or feeling express.
3. An aesthetic view is an idea or school of thought on what is important in a work of art.
4. The three most commonly held aesthetic views are subject, composition, and content. In the *subject* view, a successful work of art is one with a realistic or lifelike subject. The *composition* view values most the artist's use of composition to create a harmonious art work. In the *content* view, what counts most is the content, or the mood conveyed to the viewer.

Painting an Expressive Scene

LESSON PLAN
(pages 38–39)

Objectives
After completing this lesson, students will be able to:
- Describe how the formal elements of an art work contribute to its expressive qualities.
- Appreciate and imitate stylistic features of Edward Hopper's art.

Supplies
- Pencils and erasers.
- White drawing paper, 8 x 13 inches (20 x 33 cm).
- Tempera paints.
- Variety of brushes.
- Mixing trays.
- Still life or simple diorama.
- Several hand-held light sources, such as a flashlight.

> **TRB Resource**
> - 3-4 *Edward Hopper*, (artist profile)

TEACHING THE LESSON

Getting Started
Motivator. Have students describe their neighborhood on an early Sunday morning. Encourage them to identify every possible detail of the scene. Discuss which details would best convey the atmosphere of this scene if it were painted.

Developing Concepts
Exploring Aesthetics. Ask students to identify the source of lighting in Figure 3-4. Explain that Hopper often took advantage of striking or unusual lighting effects in his art. Discuss the expressive quality of Hopper's lighting. Set up a still life or simple diorama. Darken the room and use a flashlight to demonstrate how different degrees and angles of illumination can dramatically change the mood of the subject.

38

STUDIO **LESSON 2** STUDIO

Painting an Expressive Scene

Study the painting in Figure 3–4. The work is by American painter Edward Hopper. How do you think an art critic would react to this painting? What is the work's subject? What elements are emphasized? What principles are used to organize the elements? What mood or feeling does the work express? Does the work succeed? Why, or why not? One last question: How do you think the painting would look if the artist had extended its left boundary?

WHAT YOU WILL LEARN

You will create a painting that continues the row of empty shops in Figure 3–4. You will use the same hues, values, and intensities in your work. You will create harmony by repeating the same vertical and horizontal lines. You will add variety by placing a circular shape somewhere in your work. Finally, you will try to capture the same feeling of loneliness. (See Figure 3–5.)

WHAT YOU WILL NEED

- Pencil, sketch paper, and eraser
- Sheet of white drawing paper, 8 x 13 inches (20 x 33 cm)
- Tempera paint and several brushes
- Mixing tray

WHAT YOU WILL DO

1. Imagine the scene in Figure 3–4 as it might appear if the artist had continued it on the left side. Make several pencil sketches of possibilities you imagine. Use horizontal and vertical lines like the ones in the painting to outline shapes. For variety, include somewhere in each sketch an object with a circular shape. (Did you discover the circular shape in Hopper's painting when you examined its elements?) Let your imagination guide you.

▶ **Figure 3–4** Can you find the circular shape in this painting? How does this shape add variety to the work? What has the artist done to give the work harmony?

Edward Hopper. *Early Sunday Morning.* 1930. Oil on canvas. 88.9 x 152.4 cm (35 x 60"). Whitney Museum of American Art, New York, New York. Gertrude Vanderbilt Whitney Funds.

38 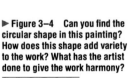 Lesson 2 *Painting an Expressive Scene*

Background Information
On several occasions, Edward Hopper (United States, 1882–1967) stated his belief that art is an expression of the artist's emotional life and subconscious. He once wrote, "I believe that the great painters, with their intellect as master, have attempted to force this unwilling medium of paint and canvas into a record of their emotions. I find any digression from this large aim leads me to boredom." Because he stressed the importance of the artist's personality, art historians have taken great pains to gain information about Hopper's personal life as a key to interpreting his art. Although camouflaged by a strong sense of privacy, Hopper emerges from his letters, interviews, and casual comments as a romantic man. Several of his paintings provide direct evidence of his nostalgic attitude toward couples courting. The great majority of critics, however, have seen only loneliness in his paintings, an emphasis that Hopper lamented. As he once said in response to critical writings on his art, "The loneliness thing is overdone."

2. Place the sheet of drawing paper along-side the photograph of Figure 3–4. Line up the paper so that it touches the left edge of the photograph. Starting at the edge of the paper, carefully continue the horizontal lines of the buildings and side-walk. Working lightly in pencil, draw details from the best of your sketches.

3. Mix tempera colors to match the hues, values, and intensities of Figure 3–4. Use a brush to fill in the shapes of your drawing with color. (For information on using a brush see Technique Tip **4**, *Handbook* page **277**.)

4. Allow time for your painting to dry. Display the finished work alongside those created by other members of your class. Discuss your works using the steps in art criticism.

▲ Figure 3–5 Student work. Expressive scene.

OTHER STUDIO IDEAS

- Imagine you live in the apartment above the barbershop in the work in Figure 3–4. Complete a perspective drawing of things you might see looking out the window of your apartment. Before you begin your drawing, think about the feeling your work will express.

EXAMINING YOUR WORK

- **Describe**   Point out the row of buildings and empty streets in your picture. Explain how they resemble the buildings and streets in Figure 3–4. Identify the hues, values, and intensities in your work. Show where these same elements are found in Figure 3–4.
- **Analyze**   Explain how you used the principles of harmony and variety. Point to places in Figure 3–4 where these same principles have been used.
- **Interpret**   Ask other students to describe the mood expressed by your picture. See if they are able to identify a mood of loneliness.
- **Judge**   Tell whether your picture looks like the one in Figure 3–4. State whether it uses many of the same elements and principles. Tell whether your work is successful in expressing the same mood of loneliness.

●● Complete another painting of the same street scene, this one titled *Late Saturday Night*. Show how the scene might come alive on a Saturday night. Include people, cars, and other objects. Change the hues, values, and intensities of color to create a mood of excitement.

Lesson 2   *Painting an Expressive Scene* **39**

Using Art Criticism. Explain that art critics do not always agree on the message or feeling embodied in a particular art work. For example, many critics characterize Hopper's view of an urban street in Figure 3-4 as lonely and even anxious. Others have called it peaceful, a quiet beginning to a calm Sunday. Have students write a short paragraph in which they give their interpretation of this painting. Invite them to share their opinions with the class.

Following Up

Closure. Ask students how they liked imitating the style of another artist. Did Hopper's way of rendering a street scene come naturally? Were they tempted to paint it differently than Hopper might have? Have students explain their responses.

Evaluation. 1. Review students' responses to "Examining Your Work." 2. Review the students' written interpretations of Figure 3-4.

Reteaching. Have students bring in magazine and newspaper pictures that convey the feeling of loneliness. Have the students share their findings. Discuss the many different ways in which an artist might express a single mood.

Enrichment. Explain to students that Hopper was one of a number of early twentieth-century artists who painted distinctively American subjects. Have groups of students investigate other members of this group, such as Georgia O'Keeffe, Thomas Hart Benton, Charles Burchfield, Grant Wood, and Marsden Hartley. Ask the groups to determine what mood the artist that they researched was most interested in expressing. Have students share and compare their results.

LESSON 3

Art History

Look briefly again at the painting in Figure 3–4 on page **38**. Having created an "extension" to the work, you now have a better understanding of its composition and content. What do you know about its artist, Edward Hopper? When and where did he live? Did his other paintings look like the one in Figure 3–6? Is he thought to be an important artist?

Answering these and similar questions is the goal of art history. In this lesson you will learn ways of answering these questions.

▲ **Figure 3–6   What makes this work more than just a realistic picture of two people in a room? How do these people behave toward each other? How do their actions make you feel?**

Edward Hopper. *Room in New York*. 1932. Oil on canvas. 71.1 x 91.4 cm (28 x 36"). Sheldon Memorial Art Gallery, University of Nebraska, Lincoln, Nebraska. F. M. Hall Collection.

LESSON PLAN
(pages 40–41)

Objectives
After completing this lesson, students will be able to:
• Understand the difference between art criticism and art history.
• Define *style*.
• Describe the kinds of information that an art historian discovers.

Supplies
• Several prints of paintings from a variety of art historical periods, including works by twentieth-century realists.

> **TRB Resources**
> • 3-5 *Rhythms of the Ages,* (reproducible master)
> • 3-6 *Art Through the Ages,* (art history)

TEACHING THE LESSON

Getting Started

Motivator. Have students bring in a photo of themselves. Discuss what someone might think about a person in a photo if that were all the information available about the subject. Ask: What if there were a series of photos that ranged from infancy through old age? Point out to students that they would know a lot more, but many questions would be left unanswered. Ask students how someone would go about collecting more information about the subject of a photo. Draw a parallel between their responses and an art historian's use of interviews, letters, diaries, comparisons with similar images or ones made during the same period, and knowledge of the culture in which an art work was produced.

Vocabulary. Guide the students to a working definition of *style*. Relate the everyday association of style and fashion with the text definition of style as a personal approach to expression, the art elements, and the art principles. Ask students whether an art work can ever be said to lack a style. Have them explain their responses.

40

Note

Explain to students that art historians sometimes disagree with each other about the interpretation or importance of particular art works and movements. Art historians may even change their own minds during the course of their careers in art history. For example, it wasn't until a decade or two ago that works by female artists were given the same kind of scholarly attention that was accorded art made by their male peers. Major textbooks on the history of Western art were published without a single mention of female artists, despite the fact that over half of art school graduates since World War II have been female. Other art that has received increased respect from art historians includes medieval art, which was once thought to be childish and unsophisticated, and Third World art, which used to be relegated to museums of natural history instead of art museums.

ART HISTORY AND YOU

To understand an art work completely, you need to do more than just look at it. You need to look beyond it. You need to know when and where the work was done. You need to know something about the artist who created it. Searching of this sort is the job of people in the field of art history. **Art history** is *the study of art from past to present*.

When they study art, art historians often use the same four steps art critics use: they describe, analyze, interpret, and judge. Unlike art critics, however, art historians do not use these steps to learn *from* art. They use them to learn *about* art.

Describing an Art Work

In describing an art work, art historians answer the questions "Who?" "Where?" and "When?" In other words, "Who painted the work, and when and where was it painted?" Look at the painting in Figure 3–6. Acting as an art historian, you can answer the first two of these questions by reading the credit line. The "who" is, again, Edward Hopper. The "when" is 1932. A visit to your school or local library will give you more information about the artist. There you will find that Hopper was an American painter who lived from 1882 to 1967.

Analyzing an Art Work

In analyzing an art work, the historian focuses on questions of style. **Style** is *an artist's personal way of using the elements and principles of art and expressing feelings and ideas in art*. Two typical questions the historian asks when analyzing a work are the following:

- What style did the artist use?
- Did the artist use the same style in other works?

Look again at the painting in Figure 3–6. An art historian would describe the style of this work as realistic. Compare this work with Figure 3–4 on page **38**. Would you say that both are done in a realistic style? Do you sense the same feeling of quiet loneliness in each?

Interpreting an Art Work

In interpreting an art work, the historian tries to determine how time and place may have affected the artist's style. Usually, this requires some research on the art historian's part. A trip to the library would reveal that:

- The painting in Figure 3–6 was completed during a period called the Great Depression.
- The Depression was a time during the 1930s when many people were out of work and money was scarce.
- To many people living through the Depression, the future looked hopeless.

In this work, Hopper captures the loneliness many people felt during that bleak time. The painting shows two people in a room. Notice that they do not face one another. Each, in fact, seems to be ignoring the other. A large door seems further to separate them. The people share the room but little else. Each is neglected and alone.

Judging an Art Work

In judging an art work, the historian notes its place in all art history. The historian decides whether the work and its artist make an important contribution to art. One way in which an artist can make a contribution is by introducing new materials or perfecting a style. Hopper is noted for developing a style that captured the mood of the times more effectively than most artists of that period.

✔CHECK YOUR UNDERSTANDING

1. What is art history?
2. Explain *describing, analyzing, interpreting,* and *judging* as the terms are used by art historians.
3. Define *style*.

Developing Concepts

Exploring Aesthetics. Have the students write a short paragraph that compares Hopper's use of the elements and principles of art in Figures 3-4 and 3-6.

Understanding Art History. Explain to students that art historians are sometimes called upon to decide whether a certain art work is a forgery or has been incorrectly attributed in the past. Display a variety of reproductions of paintings, being careful to cover any visible credit lines. Ask the students to pick out which, if any, of the prints are by Hopper. Have them explain how they judged whether the style and other features of each print were or were not similar to the works by Hopper that are reproduced in their text.

Following Up

Closure. Review with students the differences between art criticism and art history.

Evaluation. 1. Review students' written responses to the "Check Your Understanding" questions. 2. Review students' paragraphs comparing the two Hopper reproductions.

Reteaching. Have students pretend that their research into Hopper revealed that he had spent a portion of his life hiding out from the police because of a crime that he had committed. Ask: How might such information change an art historian's interpretation of Figure 3-6?

Enrichment. Have students visit a library and meet with a librarian who can show examples of the various materials that art historians consult while researching an art work. The materials might include primary sources such as letters, diaries, and old sketchbooks, and secondary sources such as a dictionary of symbols, a variety of art magazines and journals, and an index of articles published on a given artist.

Answers to "Check Your Understanding"
1. Art history is the recorded study of art from past to present.
2. When art historians *describe* an art work, they answer the questions, "who," "where," and "when." In *analyzing* a work, they focus on style, the artist's way of presenting the elements and ideas. *Interpreting* consists of determining how time and place may have affected the artist's subject and style. In *judging* a work, the art historian notes its place in all art history and tries to determine whether the work and the artist have made an important contribution.
3. Style is an artist's personal way of using the elements and principles of art and expressing feelings and ideas.

Painting in the Cubist Style

Painting in the Cubist Style

LESSON PLAN
(pages 42–43)

Objectives

After completing this lesson, students will be able to:

• Evaluate the art principles and elements in a Picasso work.

• Produce a composition based on the Cubist stylist principles.

Supplies

• Tracing paper, pencils, and rulers.

• White drawing paper, 8 x 24 inches (20 x 60 cm).

• Tempera paints and a variety of brushes.

• Mixing trays.

TRB Resources

• 3-7 *Where Do Ideas Come From?,* (aesthetics/art criticism)

• 3-8 *A Survey on Creative Thinking,* (cooperative learning)

TEACHING THE LESSON

Getting Started

Motivator. Referring to Figure 3-7, discuss with students the following quote by Picasso: "From the point of view of art there are no concrete or abstract forms, but only forms which are more or less convincing lies. . . . Cubism is no different from any other school of painting. The same principles and the same elements are common to all. The fact that for a long time Cubism has not been understood and that even today there are people who cannot see anything in it, means nothing. I do not read English, an English book is a blank book to me. This does not mean that the English language does not exist . . ." (1923)

Vocabulary. Have students look up the definition of *Cubism* in a dictionary. Discuss why Figure 3-7 is called *cubist.* Ask students whether they would have named this movement differently.

Study the painting in Figure 3–7. Think about how an art historian would react to this work. Begin by describing the work. Who is the artist? When was the painting done? The style, Cubism (**kyoob**-izm), grew out of a wish to show objects from many different angles at once. Would you guess that Cubist works like this changed the course of art history? Why, or why not?

WHAT YOU WILL LEARN

Using tempera, you will enlarge and re-create a section of the painting in Figure 3–7 or of another Cubist painting. You will use the same colors, lines, shapes, and textures in your work that were used in the original. You will use the principles of variety, harmony, and rhythm to organize these elements. Your section will be added to those completed by your classmates to form a large version of Figure 3–7. (See Figure 3–8.)

WHAT YOU WILL NEED

• Tracing paper, pencil, and ruler
• Sheet of white drawing paper, 8 x 24 inches (20 x 61 cm)
• Tempera paint and several brushes
• Mixing tray

▶ **Figure 3–7 Why do you think this artist is among the best known in the history of art? Which aesthetic view would you use when judging this work of art?**

Pablo Picasso. *First Steps.* 1943. Oil on canvas. 130.2 x 97.1 cm (51¼ x 38¼"). Yale University, New Haven, Connecticut. Gift of Stephen C. Clark.

Background Information

Cubism is the first truly twentieth-century artistic style. Heralded by Picasso's 1907 work *Demoiselles d'Avignon,* Cubism involved entirely new approaches to the treatment of pictorial space and to the representation of emotions and states of mind. Picasso (Spanish-born, 1881–1973) and fellow Cubists broke away from two major features of Western art ever since the Renaissance: the classical model of rendering the human figure, and the spatial illusionism of one-point perspective.

Undoubtedly, Picasso's familiarity with sculpture from the Ivory Coast and other French colonies helped him treat the human form in a more radically conceptual fashion than was possible within the confines of the Renaissance paradigm. The result was not only the reduction of body parts to geometrical forms and the loss of a normal scale of human proportion, but also a means of suggesting three-dimensional relationships that would not hinge on the convention of illusionistic, one-point perspective.

WHAT YOU WILL DO

1. Lay a sheet of tracing paper over the painting in Figure 3–7. Using pencil, lightly and carefully trace the lines and shapes of the picture.
2. Using a ruler, divide your drawing into sections measuring 3 x 1 inches (8 x 3 cm). Your teacher will assign you one of the sections. Enlarge and draw freehand the lines and shapes of your section onto the sheet of drawing paper. Stay as close as you can to the original work.
3. Mix tempera colors to match the hues used in Figure 3–7. (For information on mixing paints, see Technique Tip **12**, *Handbook* page **280**). As you work, try also to use the same lines, textures, and shapes found in the original painting.
4. When your section is dry, add it to those completed by other members of your class. Compare your class effort with the original work. Decide whether it is made up of the same features as the original.

► **Figure 3–8** Student work. Cubist style painting using another Cubist work.

OTHER STUDIO IDEAS

- Make another painting of your section of Figure 3–7. This time limit yourself to different values of a single hue. Be prepared to discuss in what ways this new version is different from the original.
- ●● Pick another painting from this chapter. Using tracing paper, copy a section of the work measuring 2 x 2 inches (5 x 5 cm). Enlarge the drawing to fit a larger square sheet of drawing paper. Paint the section using tempera. See if classmates can identify the original work of art and the section of the work you used.

EXAMINING YOUR WORK

- **Describe** Identify the objects in your section of the class painting. Show where these same objects are found in the matching section of the original art. Point out the colors, lines, textures, and shapes in your section. Show where these same elements are found in the matching section of the original.
- **Analyze** Explain how you used the principles of harmony, variety, and rhythm. Point out places in the matching section of the original where these same principles have been used.
- **Judge** Tell whether your section of the painting blends in with those completed by classmates. If it does not, explain why. Tell whether the class effort as a whole succeeds. Explain your answer.

Developing Concepts

Understanding Art History. Have students research the period of time during which Picasso painted and identify other painters who worked in a similar style. Have them select one of these artists and write a short paragraph that explains why their choice is considered a Cubist artist.

Appreciating Cultural Diversity. Point out to students that Picasso's experiments with new ways of representing three-dimensional forms were inspired by contact with non-Western art. Have students investigate African sculpture and report back to the class any similarities that they see between Picasso's art and African tribal art.

Following Up

Closure. Ask students to describe how an art historian would go about researching Figure 3-7. Would an art historian be thrown off the track if he or she were researching the composite "Picasso" made by the class? 2. Using "Examining Your Work," have students evaluate their work.

Evaluation. 1. Review students' paragraphs on Cubist artists. 2. Review student reports on Picasso and African art. 3. Review students' responses to "Examining Your Work."

Reteaching. Have students briefly characterize the artistic styles of Hopper and Picasso and state which one they prefer or if they like them equally well.

Enrichment. Explain to students that Picasso's contribution to twentieth-century art went far beyond experimenting with non-illusionistic representation. Have students investigate Picasso's *Bull* sculpture, which highlighted the aesthetic properties of ordinary handlebars, and his metal guitar sculpture, which inaugurated a tradition of sculpture that took on a banal subject and was composed of cheap materials.

Note
Students may find the numerous steps involved in art historical analysis to be overwhelming and laborious. Encourage them through the first few attempts at art historical investigation, and point out how much more is known about a painting by the addition of even a single fact or insight. Have them break down their research into the four steps to make the process manageable. Students may inadvertently leap to the last two steps, but will be pleasantly surprised how much easier their conclusions arrive after they have patiently undertaken the first two steps.

BUILDING VOCABULARY

Number a sheet of paper from 1 to 7. After each number, write the term from the box that best matches each description below.

aesthetic view	content
art criticism	style
art history	subject
composition	

1. Studying, understanding, and judging works of art.
2. The image viewers can easily identify in an art work.
3. The way the art principles are used to organize the elements of art in an art work.
4. The idea, feeling, mood, or message expressed by an art work.
5. An idea, or school of thought, on what is important in a work of art.
6. The study of art from past to present.
7. An artist's personal way of using the elements and principles of art and expressing feelings and ideas in art.

REVIEWING ART FACTS

Number a sheet of paper from 8 to 17. Answer each question in a complete sentence.

8. What is *describing*, as the term is defined by art critics? What are two key facts a critic would note when describing a work?
9. What is *analyzing*, as the term is defined by art critics?
10. What is *interpreting*, as the term is defined by art critics?
11. What question is asked by art critics when judging a work?
12. Summarize the three aesthetic views discussed in the chapter.
13. What are three questions an art historian would answer when describing a work?

14. What are two typical questions an art historian would ask when analyzing a work?
15. What is *interpreting*, as the term is defined by art historians?
16. What questions do art historians ask when interpreting an art work?
17. What do art historians decide during the judging stage?

THINKING ABOUT ART

On a sheet of paper, answer each question in a sentence or two.

1. **Interpret.** Could two art critics using the four-step system of art criticism come up with different judgments of a work? Explain your answer.
2. **Interpret.** Is any one step in art criticism more or less important than any other step? Which step? Explain your answer.
3. **Extend.** Art, it is often said, is not created in a vacuum. To which lesson in this chapter does this statement apply? Explain your answer.
4. **Analyze.** Give an example of events taking place in the world right now that could affect an artist's style.
5. **Compare and contrast.** In what ways is the judging of art similar for art critics and art historians? In what ways is the task different?

MAKING ART CONNECTIONS

1. **Social Studies.** Visit the library and learn what you can about the artist of the sculpture in Figure 2–8 on page **24**. How would an art historian say that time and place affected the artist's work?
2. **Language Arts.** Pretend you are an art critic. Write an article you could submit to a magazine judging the work in Figure 3–4 by Edward Hopper.

CHAPTER 3 REVIEW

LOOKING AT THE DETAILS

The detail shown below is from Georges Rouault's *Christ Mocked by Soldiers*. Study the detail and answer the following questions.

1. What mood do you sense in this work? What elements of art are used to convey this mood?
2. Which aesthetic view would you use in judging this work? Give reasons to support your answer.

3. What would an art historian discuss when analyzing this painting?
4. Compare Rouault's style in this painting with Jan Steen's style in Figure 3–2 on page 35. What differences do you see?

Georges Rouault. *Christ Mocked by Soldiers*. 1932. Oil on canvas. (Detail.) 92.1 x 72.4 cm (36¼ x 28½"). Museum of Modern Art, New York, New York. Given anonymously.

3. Answers may vary. They should show students understand that Lesson 3 on art history focuses attention on how time and place affect subject matter in art.
4. Responses will vary. They can include observations about war versus peace or other art forms, including music, dance, theater and television.
5. Responses will vary. They should show students understand critics will judge works subjectively based on aesthetic views held and that historians focus on more objective criteria.

ANSWERS TO "LOOKING AT THE DETAILS"

1. Student answers may vary. The mood is somber, painful, and cruel. The artist uses color, line and shape to convey the mood.
2. Either the composition or content view. Student explanations may vary. Some possibilities include: For the composition view, one could look at the way the Christ figure is centered in the foreground of the work and painted in the lighter colors to emphasize him and to give the darker figures, positioned on either side and looking at him, a feeling of hardness. For the content view, one could look at the downcast eyes of the Christ figure and the grotesque features of the soldiers which create the painful mood of mocking.
3. The art historian would discuss the style the artist used in this work and look at the artist's other works to see if the same style was used.
4. Student answers may vary. Steen's work portrays realism both in its detail and in use of color. It also shows depth. Rouault's work is more abstract, using color in subtle and rough ways to create a mood. Rouault's work appears textured and lacks depth. He also uses thick black outlines to define his figures, while Steen uses fine lines.

Chapter Evaluation

The goal of this chapter is to develop students' understanding of the steps that an art critic and an art historian use in evaluating works of art. Students are then able to use the steps of art criticism when evaluating their works of art. Possible methods of evaluation include:

1. Divide the class into groups of four, assigning two of the students in each group to act as art critics and the other two to act as art historians. Have each group evaluate their work of art based on art criticism or art history and report to the class.
2. Have students use the steps of art criticism and evaluate a work of art that they have created.
3. Have students complete Chapter 3 Test (TRB, Resource 3-9).

Art of Earliest Times

Chapter Scan

TRB Resources

- 4-10 Chapter Test
- Color Transparency 7
- Color Transparency 8

TEACHING THE CHAPTER

Introducing the Art Work

Direct students' attention to the *Funerary Feast*, Stele of Nefertia-bet. Inform them that this work was taken from the tomb of Princess Nefertiabet in Giza, Egypt. Princess Nefertiabet lived during the fourth dynasty in Egypt. One of the great achievements of this dynasty was the idea of building a royal tomb. Since the pharaoh was seen as a link to the gods, he was privileged to grant offerings for funerary rites. It was customary that above the door lintel to the tomb there was a representation of the deceased at the dining table. The Egyptians be-lieved that the dead would step out through this door to receive the fu-nerary offerings. The most impor-tant desire of mortal men was for life after death, which was guaran-teed to those who were granted a tomb by the king. At the end of the fourth dynasty, the dining table scene was transferred to the inte-rior of the tombs.

Examining the Art Work

Have students identify the seated figure and point out how not all of the body parts are shown from the same angle. Tell students that they will learn why the artist portrayed the figure in this way. Also explain that if the ancient Egyptian artist was free to choose which way his figures would face, he painted the subjects facing in the right direction, as opposed to the left. Suggest that this may be related to the fact that Egyptian script starts from the right.

▲ Ancient Egyptians portrayed figures' faces in profile, following strict artistic rules.

Funerary Feast, Stele of Nefertiabet. Old Kingdom, 4th Dynasty. Painted limestone. The Louvre, Paris, France.

Art of Earliest Times

You have heard the saying "a picture is worth a thousand words." This saying holds true especially for pictures like the one at the left. This is a photograph of an art object from the ancient world. Such pictures, and the objects themselves, are like windows on life at the dawn of civilization. Ancient art tells us, often in ways that words cannot, about how people lived and what they believed.

In this chapter you will study and learn about art from the distant past.

OBJECTIVES

After completing this chapter, you will be able to:

● Define the term *culture*.
● Describe life during ancient times.
● Tell what kinds of art were created during ancient times.
● Create art works with media in the art styles of early civilizations.

WORDS YOU WILL LEARN

culture
hieroglyphic
megaliths
post and lintel system

stele
urban planning
ziggurat

Point out how the rows of images and repeated patterns in the right half of the work create rhythm. Have students note the open hands of the figure. Explain that ancient Egyptians represented hands as open and closed doors. They also often portrayed clenched fists to indicate a male figure, representative of strength.

Discussing the Art Work
Ask students to think about what some of the individual images in the work might mean such as the birds and the falcons on the hunting tree in the upper right. Explain that often images of birds, desert animals, hunting and husbandry were included in an attempt to keep the memory of earthly existence alive for the deceased.

Ask students to identify some of the other objects in the art work. Explain that an art historian looking at this work would gain insight into the types of objects this culture valued and the symbolism they used. Ask students to identify other objects that are clues into how the Egyptians reasoned.

Tell students that in this chapter they will learn about life and art during ancient times in Egypt, China, India, and Mesopotamia. They will also create art works in the art styles of early civilizations.

Building Self-Esteem
Tell students that in this chapter they will be learning about the development of art from about 30,000 B.C. until about 2500 B.C. During that time-span, men and women evolved into groups who had language, clothing, and formal shelters. In addition, they developed art forms to decorate their utensils, homes, and public places. One of the oldest Indian art forms is shown on page **59**. These small tiles, or seals, measured only about 1.5 inches on all sides (3.8 cm), but they showed many varieties of intricately carved animals as well as what appeared to be early letter forms. There was often a pierced "boss" at the back to accommodate a cord. Ask: Could these have been an early form of belt or neck adornment? Let students reflect upon the fact that human beings have created art from earliest times. Even prehistoric men and women found time to celebrate their lives. Ask the students to develop a list of reasons they have to celebrate their lives.

LESSON PLAN
(pages 48–51)

Objectives
After completing this lesson, students will be able to:
- Define *culture*.
- Describe life in ancient times.
- Tell what kinds of art were created in early times.
- Describe the difference between Paleolithic and Neolithic societies.

Supplies
- Found natural objects (such as stones, shells, pieces of wood, chunks of clay).
- Sharp tools.
- Crayons.
- Markers.
- Chalk.

TEACHING THE LESSON

Getting Started
Motivator. Ask the students to describe their image of ancient life. Explain that ancient people had the same feelings that people experience today, such as love, fear, and hunger. Ask the students how they can learn more about prehistoric culture. Write the word *artifact* on the board. Tell the students that archaeologists use artifacts to gain information about early civilizations, which made no written records. Point out that the first three letters of artifact are ART. The art of prehistoric people is an important source of information about their daily life. Talk about the differences between the Old Stone Age and the New Stone Age. Ask: Do you think there may have been a Wooden Age? Why would we lack evidence of this?

Vocabulary. Write the words *Paleolithic*, *Neolithic*, and *Monolith* on the board. Explain that "lith" means stone. Ask whether any students have heard of lithography, a printing technique in which prints are made from inked stones.

LESSON 1

Prehistoric Art

As long as there have been people, there has been art. The need to create has always been a driving force among people. In this lesson you will look at prehistoric art. This is art dating back to the time before people kept written records. By studying this art, you will find out about the civilizations of early times. You will learn about their **culture**, or *ideas, beliefs, and living customs*.

ART OF THE OLD STONE AGE

The earliest art works modern experts have uncovered date back to the Old Stone Age. Also known as the Paleolithic (pay-lee-uh-**lith**-ik) period, the Old Stone Age lasted from around 30,000 until about 10,000 B.C.

The lives of people during the Old Stone Age were filled with danger, hunger, and fear. Each day meant a new struggle just to survive. In the winter they searched for shelter against the snow and cold. In the summer they battled the heat and the sudden rains that flooded their caves. Those lucky enough to survive were old by age 40. Few lived past their fiftieth year.

Painting

Many of the Old Stone age art works that have lasted into recent times are paintings. The animal painting in Figure 4–1 is one such work. It was discovered on the wall of a cave in France. Others like it have been found in Spain and elsewhere in western Europe. Examples of cave art have been found on every continent, from the Sahara desert to the Arctic. Notice also how lifelike the animals look.

No one knows the real reason behind the creation of paintings like this one. Such works have always been found deep within caves, far from entrances and daylight. Their

▲ Figure 4–1 The cave which houses this painting was discovered by two boys playing ball. What do you suppose was their first reaction to this painting?

Cave painting. c. 15,000–10,000 B.C. Lascaux, Dordogne, France.

location has led experts to think they were not created merely as decoration. Some think the paintings played a part in hunting rituals. Many have imagined scenes like the following . . .

The evening meal over, the men of the tribe stood. The boy—now a man—stood with them. One by one, they moved away from the warm cooking fires and into the cool, shadowy depths of the cave. Suddenly the boy felt himself being shoved to his knees. As he groped forward, he found himself crawling through a narrow passageway.

By and by, the path widened again. In the distance ahead, the boy could see the glow of a fire. Soon he found himself in a great hall lighted by torches. On one wall was a huge bison. In the flickering light, the beast seemed to be charging toward him. The boy's heart raced.

As the boy watched with wide eyes, an artist began creating a second bison. With a sharp-ended stick, the artist scratched the outlines of the animal into the wall. Using clumps of fur and moss, he filled in the body with a variety of reds and browns. Using a bit of coal, he added a single fierce eye.

Background Information
The cave paintings found in France are remarkably similar to prehistoric paintings from many other parts of the world, including Spain and North America. For example, the stenciled hand is one of the most common prehistoric images, and it appears worldwide. Some symbols found in the French caves, such as the symbol of bear paw marks, have remained unintelligible until a very similar mark elsewhere has provided a clue. In every region where prehistoric art is found, the manner of representing a man is the same virtual stick figure. Bulls and other commonly painted animals also bear a strikingly universal resemblance. Careful attention is invariably given to depicting the horns, antlers, and feet.

▲ Figure 4–2   These figures were found in a chamber one mile underground. In what ways did their location help preserve them?

Clay Bison from Le Tuc d'Audoubert Cave, France. c. 17,000 B.C. Archeological Museum, Madrid, Spain.

At last the second beast was finished. The men, now excited about the promise of tomorrow's hunt, began to chant. The boy chanted with them. He picked up the spear his father had carved for him. With his fellow hunters, he attacked the "spirit" of the bison up on the wall, just as he would attack the real bison during the hunt.

Sculpture and Crafts

Old Stone Age artists were skilled not only at painting, but equally talented at sculpture and crafts. Notice the attention to detail in the bison shown in Figure 4–2. These remarkable sculptures, which are thought to date to around 15,000 B.C., were modeled out of clay.

The necklace in Figure 4–3 was found in an ancient grave. It is made of animal teeth and shells. Stone, ivory, and bone were some other media used by early sculptors and craftspeople.

▲ Figure 4–3   During prehistoric times, there were many animals to hunt. Bear and lion teeth such as those in this necklace were easy to find.

Bear-tooth necklace. c. 13,000 B.C. Private collection.

Developing Concepts

Exploring Aesthetics. Art of the Paleolithic age was quite realistic. By carefully painting animal pictures, Paleolithic people hoped to receive power from those animals and perhaps become better hunters. Sometimes animals were seen as protectors, and their particular attributes were adopted by different tribes or clans. Ask your students which animal characteristics might have been especially prized by prehistoric people. Explain that during the Neolithic period, artists used symbolic, geometric forms and began to represent their beliefs about the spiritual forces behind events. These geometric forms can be seen in Neolithic pottery.

Understanding Art History. Ask your students whether they have ever lain back and looked at passing clouds. Did they see shapes in those clouds? Just as they saw shapes, so did early people see shapes in the rocks of their cave homes. The firelight may have enhanced those images and inspired some prehistoric artists.

Understanding Art History. Show your students photos of Stonehenge, one of many stone circles found in northern Europe. Explain to your students that the sun rises between the two upright lintels on the summer solstice. This is the longest day of the year, usually occurring on June 21 or 22. Discuss the reasons why the longest day of the year might be important to a Neolithic or agricultural society.

Background Information

Today no scholar doubts the existence of hundreds of cave paintings. A century ago, however, authorities scorned the claims made by Spanish archaeologist Don Marcelino Sautuola, whose 12-year-old daughter accidentally discovered the first known cave paintings. They even accused Sautuola of forgery. Three main arguments were leveled against Sautuola's claim. It was thought impossible that prehistoric people were capable of painting so well, given the crude implements that cave people were thought to have used. Authorities also doubted that any pigments could have lasted over 15,000 years. Finally, experts could think of no reason why Paleolithic people, who lived only near the entrances of their caves, would devote so much effort to decorating the ceilings and walls of places that they didn't live in or visit. The battle continued for 15 years, until excavations at French sites yielded fine prehistoric wall engravings that could be dated to everyone's satisfaction.

ART OF THE NEW STONE AGE

People gradually began to change as civilizations moved into the New Stone Age. Prehistoric peoples stopped wandering and formed villages. They learned to raise livestock and started growing their own food. Ways of making art changed, too.

Crafts

In the area of crafts, people learned to spin fibers, weave, and make pottery. Figure 4–4 shows a vase made about 6000 B.C. Note the potter's use of formal balance in this piece. Notice how the geometric design and balance combine to give the work a sense of unity.

▲ **Figure 4–4** What steps did the maker of this work take to obtain harmony? How was variety achieved?

Neolithic pottery. Vase with flat base. Ceramique armoricaine. St. Germainen Lays.

▲ **Figure 4–5** Some scholars believe this circle of stone was built as an accurate calendar. What other purpose might it have served?

Stonehenge. Salisbury Plain, Wiltshire, England.

Architecture

The New Stone Age, or Neolithic (nee-uh-lith-ik) period, also saw the first attempts at architecture. One kind of early building took the form of *large stone monuments* called **megaliths** (**meg**-uh-liths). The most famous of these is Stonehenge in England (Figure 4–5). This style of construction demonstrated the **post and lintel system**. This is *an approach to building in which a crossbeam is placed above two uprights*. As with the early cave paintings, the reason behind the creation of Stonehenge is unknown. As much a mystery is how the stones, many of which weigh 50 tons, were set in place. To this day, we can only guess and wonder.

▲ Figure 4–6   Student work. Image on natural object.

✔CHECK YOUR UNDERSTANDING

1. Define the term *culture*?
2. Describe life during the Old Stone Age.
3. What is a possible explanation for the creation of the cave paintings?
4. What changes in the way people lived took place in the New Stone Age?
5. What is a megalith? What is the name of the most famous megalith? Where is it found?

Painting Using Earth Pigments

Painting Using Earth Pigments

LESSON PLAN
(pages 52–53)

Objectives
After completing this lesson, students will be able to:
• Name earth pigments and the color each one represents.
• Create unusual effects with different tools.
• Design and complete a scene representing their daily life.

Supplies
• Pencils and sketch paper.
• Yellow chalk.
• White paper, 12 x 18 inches (30 x 46 cm).
• Mortar and pestle.
• Natural pigments.
• School acrylic paint.
• A variety of brushes and palettes.
• Diluted white glue.
• Several small jars, palette knives.
• Water and paper towels.
• Bark, twigs, cloth, and the like for applying paint.

TEACHING THE LESSON

Getting Started

Motivator. Explain to students that artists of prehistoric times used natural pigments such as ground rocks and minerals. Have students gather around you as you demonstrate grinding the pigments. Ask them to speculate about the resulting colors. Explain the purpose of the glue and what a binder does. Ancient artists used animal fat and blood for binders. Demonstrate how to add the binder.

Vocabulary. Show students tubes of yellow ochre or burnt umber oil or watercolor paints. Explain that earth pigments are still used by artists today. Many potters use pigments called oxides to glaze their bowls and pots.

When prehistoric artists created their cave paintings, they weren't able simply to open paint jars. They made use of natural sources of pigment around them. For reds, browns, and golds, they mixed ground-up earth minerals in animal fat, vegetable juices, and egg whites. For black they used charcoal from burned firewood. Minerals like these do not fade over time as other materials do. Notice how the painting in Figure 4–7 has kept its brilliant color for 15,000 years.

WHAT YOU WILL LEARN
You will create a painting about your environment using earth pigment paints that you have made from local earth minerals. At least half the paint you use in your work will be made from natural earth pigments. Use thin and built-up layers of this paint to obtain different textures that will add variety to your painting. For the remaining paint, you will use two hues of school acrylics plus black and white. (See Figure 4–8.)

WHAT YOU WILL NEED
• Pencil and sheets of sketch paper
• Yellow chalk
• Sheet of white paper, 12 x 18 inches (30 x 46 cm)
• Natural pigments
• School acrylic paint, several brushes, and palette
• Diluted white glue and a small jar
• Painting knife
• Water and paper towels

▶ Figure 4–7 This horse is often called the Chinese horse. It resembles work done a few centuries ago.

Horse from Cave Painting. Lascaux, Dordogne, France.

Background Information
The purpose of the Lascaux animal paintings still puzzles scholars. It is possible that they were created, not to foster a killing hunt, but as part of a fertility ritual that would increase the number of animals. One theory is that the paintings were executed deep inside caves because such deep, dark places could best represent the womb of the earth from which all living things sprang.

Note
If students visit Lascaux, France, they can go inside an exact replica of the cave. The original cave used to be open to the public. It had to be closed, however, because the humidity caused by the breathing of so many visitors caused fungi and mold to grow inside the cave. Nevertheless, many of the other sites of prehistoric cave painting in Europe are still open to the general public or to those who have written for permission in advance.

WHAT YOU WILL DO

1. Collect and grind your own earth pigment. (See Technique Tip **11**, *Handbook* page **280**.)
2. Make several sketches of scenes from your environment that would make good use of these colors. White sand would be good for a beach scene. Gray dirt could be used to show city sidewalks. Reddish-brown colors would work well for brick walls. Look at the colors you have, and let the colors give you ideas.
3. Select your best sketch. Using yellow chalk, draw the outline shapes of your sketch on the sheet of white paper.
4. Choose the colors of paint you will use. Remember to limit yourself to two hues of school acrylic, plus black and white. Prepare the earth pigment paints. Take care to mix no more than what you will use in a single day.
5. Paint your scene. Experiment with different ways of using the earth pigments. For a thin smooth area, use only the liquid part of the paint. For a built-up, textured area, make a thick binder using extra glue and add plenty of powder. Apply the thick paint with the painting knife.
6. Display your work when it is dry. Look for ways in which your work is similar to and different from those of your classmates. Take note of any unusual effects created using the earth pigments.

EXAMINING YOUR WORK

- **Describe** Tell what scene from your environment you chose to make. Identify the different earth colors you used. Name the hues of school acrylic paint you used.
- **Analyze** Point out areas in which you used thick and thin layers of paint to create different textures. Explain how these different textures add variety to your picture.
- **Interpret** Explain why this scene represents your environment.
- **Judge** Tell whether you feel your work succeeds. Explain your answer.

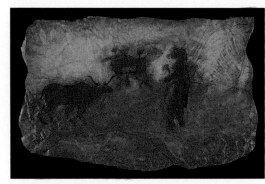

▲ Figure 4–8 Student work. Earth pigments.

OTHER STUDIO IDEAS

- Create a small non-objective design using earth pigment and white school acrylic.

- •• Using white glue from the bottle, squeeze out a design on a sheet of paper. Sprinkle powdered pigment onto the lines to create a form of sand painting. Shake off excess powder.

Art of Ancient Egypt

Art of Ancient Egypt

During prehistoric times the chief enemy of the human race was nature. Unfriendly weather and fierce beasts of prey kept early humans always on their guard. By the time people began keeping written records, they had a new enemy. That enemy was other people.

As tribes learned to herd animals and grow crops, they also learned to live in harmony with their surroundings. This peaceful balance was upset by population growth. Small tribes began to fight over grazing land and soil suitable for growing crops. They were forced to band together into more organized groups for protection and also to be able to produce more food. By around 3000 B.C. four major civilizations had developed at different points on the globe. The ancient civilizations of Egypt, China, India, and Mesopotamia (mes-uh-puh-**tay**-mee-uh) emerged at this time.

In this lesson you will learn about the culture and art of ancient Egypt.

ANCIENT EGYPTIAN CULTURE

Ancient Egypt developed along the banks of the Nile before 3000 B.C. Find this area on the map in Figure 4–9. This civilization lasted for almost 3000 years. The arts of ancient Egypt reflect the endurance and solid foundation of that culture.

Egypt was ruled by a leader called a pharaoh (**fehr**-oh). The pharaoh was not merely a king in the eyes of the Egyptian people, he was also a god. After death he was believed to join other gods, whom the Egyptians identified with forces of nature. The afterlife of the pharaoh and other important people is a theme running through much of ancient Egyptian art.

Architecture

There can be little doubt that ancient Egypt's greatest achievement in art was in architecture. Figure 4–10 shows the civilization's most remarkable achievement of all, the great pyramids. These magnificent structures were built as tombs for the pharaohs. Thousands upon thousands of workers toiled for decades to build a single pyramid. Today the pyramids remain among the true wonders of the world.

Proof of the genius of later Egyptian architects is found in temples like the one in Figure 4–11. This temple is named in honor of the Egyptian sun god, Re (**Ray**). Apart from their beauty, temples like this were among the first buildings ever to use the post and lintel system. What structure of the New Stone Age that you studied also used posts and lintels?

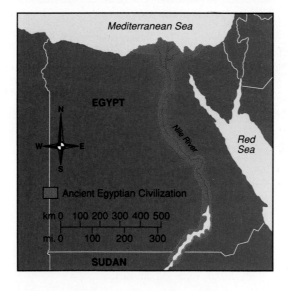

◄ Figure 4–9   Ancient Egypt.

LESSON PLAN
(pages 54–57)

Objectives
After completing this lesson, students will be able to:
• Discuss the importance of religion and the afterlife to ancient Egyptians.
• Discuss the purpose of a pyramid.
• Describe the difference between a relief sculpture and a tomb painting.

Supplies
• Recordings of popular songs describing Egyptian life.
• Clay and rolling pins.
• Tools for modeling clay.
• Pencils.
• Strips of white paper, 12 x 8 inch (30 x 20 cm).

TRB Resources
• 4-1 *Ceramic Brick Relief,* (cooperative learning)
• 4-2 *Artist of Ancient Times,* (artist profile)

TEACHING THE LESSON

Getting Started

Motivator. Play recordings of two popular songs that describe Egyptian life: "Walk Like an Egyptian," by the Bangles, and "King Tut," by Steven Martin.

Vocabulary. Have the students consult a large dictionary to look up the root words of *hieroglyphics.* Discuss why Egyptian writing was called "sacred" by the Greeks. Note that hieroglyphics were used only on monuments, tomb and temple walls, statues, and funerary stelae. A cursive script known as hieratic writing was used for everyday purposes.

Background Information
The pyramids and other funerary structures reflect the beliefs of the aristocratic group associated with the immortal pharaohs. Little is known about the afterlife beliefs of other Egyptians. Royal Egyptians, however, believed that their own lives would continue in another world. The lavish tombs and temples attest to their hope of eternal life, which was thought to parallel a deceased person's earthly life. Because the dead were considered to be still carrying out their daily tasks, food, weapons, and servant figurines were placed in royal tombs.

◄ Figure 4–10   In ancient times, these pyramids were each covered with a layer of polished white limestone. What do you suppose happened to this outer layer?

Sphinx and Pyramid of Khafre. c. 2600 B.C. Giza.

▲ Figure 4–11   It is thought that the post and lintel system dates back to prehistoric times. Trees and bundles of stalks may have served as the first posts and lintels.

Built by Amenophis III. *Temple of Luxor.* Pylon and Hypostyle Hall. Egypt.

Developing Concepts

Understanding Art History. Lead a discussion on the pyramids of Giza, possibly the most familiar architectural forms in the world. Tell students that the Great Pyramid of Cheops (*key*-ops) is almost 500 feet high and is a maze of tiny passageways and a few small rooms. This maze was intended to confuse and trap looters who wanted the jewels and precious art objects that were buried with the king. Nevertheless, the tombs at Giza were plundered. Ask students whether they can figure out a better way to safeguard the pyramids. Explain that later tombs were carved into the sides of hills. After the death of a pharaoh, the door was sealed and disguised with rubble.

Appreciating Cultural Diversity. Discuss with students the team nature of Egyptian artistic production. Point out that Egyptian artists worked as members of a team of professional craftspeople that usually included an "outline scribe" who marked out the preliminary drawing, a person who chiseled the relief, and a third artist who added the paint. Artists in many other cultures have also worked as a team. In some societies, however, artists work by themselves. Discuss the advantages and drawbacks of each way of creating art. Have students investigate whether the following artists worked alone or as part of a team:

- The Irish monks who created the *Book of Kells* in the ninth century.
- Peter Paul Rubens, a seventeenth-century Netherlandish painter.
- Georgia O'Keeffe, a twentieth-century North American painter.

Background Information

Much Egyptian art was destined to be buried in a tomb, but this does not mean that it was not intended to be seen and appreciated. Only a few portions of a tomb, such as the burial chamber, were made inaccessible. Visitors to the remaining parts were encouraged to offer prayers and present offerings in the tomb. Therefore, at least a few of the tomb reliefs were on view, and some of the sculptures were visible. Egyptians also created beautiful jewelry, minor art objects, and wall paintings for their homes.

▲ **Figure 4–12   Much of the information we have about daily life in Egypt comes from paintings on walls and coffins found in tombs.**

Egyptian. *Fishing Scene: Attendants with harpoons and string of fish.* 1436–1411 B.C. Wall painting from the Tomb of Kenamun. 43.5 x 53 cm (17 x 21"). Egyptian Expedition of The Metropolitan Museum of Art, New York, New York. Rogers Fund.

Background Information
Egyptian hieroglyphics, some of which derive from representations of objects, are an art form in themselves. Whether they were elaborately painted and carved or not, the hieroglyphics were generally spaced so as to form attractive patterns, frequently in square or rectangular clusters. Egyptians even permitted the order in which the signs appeared in a word to be altered if that improved the word's appearance in the painting or relief. The Egyptian system of writing was also flexible in other ways. Ideograms were generally placed at the ends of words composed of several phonetic symbols. In art, however, large scale figures might themselves stand in for the final ideogram. For example, the written names of men and women were terminated by a male or female figure. In a funerary relief where the deceased is depicted, the final ideogram of the deceased's name would be omitted because the picture was considered to have completed the name.

Sculpture

In Egypt it became customary to decorate the tombs of rich or important people. Often this was done with painted relief sculptures. An example of this type of art appears in the relief that opened this chapter (page 46). This is a **stele** (**stee**-lee), a *carved upright stone slab used as a monument*. Each frame shows a different part of a person's life or preoccupation for the afterlife. The frame closest to the top shows the subject seated at his own funeral banquet.

Painting

The wall paintings found in the tombs of royalty and the wealthy tell us about the daily life of the Egyptians. Figure 4–12 shows a typical Egyptian painting. Scenes from the buried person's life were painted on the walls. Notice that some body parts are painted as they would appear from the side. The head, arms, and legs are three such parts. Other parts appear as they would if we were seeing the people head-on. The single eye and shoulders demonstrate this. These views show the strict rules that artists of ancient Egypt followed. One of these was to show every body part from its most visible angle.

STUDIO EXPERIENCE

Look once again at the stele on page 46. Notice the rows and columns of small birds and other shapes. Experts today know these to be examples of **hieroglyphic** (hy-ruh-**glif**-ik), *an early form of picture writing*. In this writing system, shapes stand not for sounds, as in our modern alphabet, but for ideas. (A heart shape, for instance, might be used to mean "love.") Here the symbols provide a written record of the achievements of the stele's subject.

Imagine that you are a citizen of a future civilization who has been called upon to create a new writing system. As you begin to work on this task, remember that you know nothing of modern alphabets. Think about what ideas you will need to express in your culture. Create a shape for each idea. When your system is complete, write a sentence in it. See if anyone in your class can read the message.

✔ CHECK YOUR UNDERSTANDING

1. When did ancient Egypt come into being? How long did the civilization survive?
2. Who were the pharaohs? What part did they play in the art of ancient Egypt?
3. Name two achievements in ancient Egyptian architecture.
4. What is a stele?
5. How did Egyptian artists show the human figure in their work? What was their reason for doing this?

Following Up

Closure. Have students view Figure 4-12 and make up a story that describes what the panel figures might be saying or thinking. Ask: What other attendants might have been pictured on the wall of the tomb?

Evaluation. 1. Review the students' written responses to the "Check Your Understanding" questions. 2. Review students' stories, and share several with the class.

Reteaching. Ask your students to think of a popular saying, perhaps from a television show or commercial. Have them draw a bumper sticker that communicates the saying in hieroglyphics.

Enrichment. Have students find out what artifacts were discovered in the tomb of King Tutankhamun. The enormous quantity of treasures found include belongings that he might be expected to enjoy in the afterlife, amulets to protect him during his journey in the underworld, and tools to perform any labors that the gods might request.

Answers to "Check Your Understanding"
1. Ancient Egypt came into being before 3000 B.C. It lasted for almost 3000 years.
2. A pharaoh was a leader who ruled with absolute power. The afterlife of the pharaohs and other important people is a theme running through much of ancient Egyptian art.
3. Two achievements of ancient Egyptian architecture were the creation of the great pyramids and the development of the post and lintel system for use in temples.
4. A *stele* is a carved upright stone slab used as a monument.
5. The human figure was depicted with some body parts shown head on and some viewed from the side. The reason for this was that artists were bound by strict rules, one of which was to show every body part from the most familiar angle.

Ancient China, India, and Mesopotamia

LESSON PLAN
(pages 58–61)

Objectives
After completing this lesson, students will be able to:
- Name the four ancient civilizations that developed simultaneously.
- Discuss the artistic achievements of early Chinese civilization.
- Describe a ziggurat.

Supplies
- Erasers and utility knives.
- Stamp pads.
- Poster paint and brushes.
- White paper.
- Milk carton.

TRB Resources
- 4-3 *The King Tut Discovery*, (appreciating cultural diversity)
- 4-4 *The Silk Road*, (art history)
- 4-5 *China Today*, (appreciating cultural diversity)
- 4-6 *Uncovering Ancient Life*, (aesthetics/art criticism)
- 4-7 *Time Line*, (reproducible master)

TEACHING THE LESSON

Getting Started
Motivator. Talk to your students about Indiana Jones and the popular action movies. Explain that these films give a fictionalized account of the field of archaeology, which nonetheless could be an exciting career. Brainstorm the difficulties and rewards of an archaeologist's life.

Vocabulary. Look up the definition of the word "civilization." Discuss why the ancient Egyptians, Chinese, Indians, and Sumerians are said to have developed civilizations. Have your students write a short paragraph that gives their understanding of the word civilization and explains whether Neolithic and Paleolithic cultures should be called civilized.

Ancient China, India, and Mesopotamia

Like Egypt, the ancient civilizations of China, India, and Mesopotamia each developed in a river valley. Like Egypt, each had a king and a religion that was based on nature.

Yet, despite some similarities, each civilization had its own separate culture and ways of making art. In this lesson you will learn about the culture and art of these civilizations.

ANCIENT CHINESE CULTURE

The first Egyptian pyramids were built around 2600 B.C. Around that time another new civilization was emerging a continent away, in the Yellow River valley. Can you find the Yellow River on the map in Figure 4–13? This civilization, China, is still alive today. It boasts the oldest continuous culture in the history of the world.

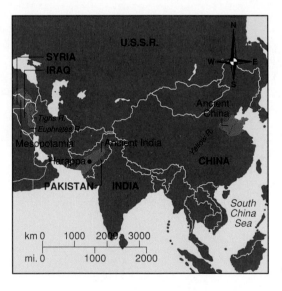

◀ Figure 4–13   Ancient China, India, and Mesopotamia.

The history of China, until modern times, is divided into periods known as dynasties. Dynasties are named for ruling families of emperors. The first of these, the Shang dynasty, began around 1766 B.C. The last of them, the Ch'ing, ended in fairly recent times. Like the history of China itself, the art of China is grouped by dynasties.

ANCIENT CHINESE ART

The ancient Chinese were skilled in all areas of art. Legends show that Chinese artists were creating pictures as early as 2200 B.C. The works we have today were made in bronze and on stone and pottery instead of silk or paper, which has not survived. The architecture of this early period has also vanished, though large building foundations have been unearthed.

Sculpture and Crafts

The single greatest achievement of early Chinese artists was their work in bronze. A bronze pitcher dating from the Shang Dynasty is shown in Figure 4–14. Like most art of the time, the work is covered with motifs and squared spirals. Experts today believe the spirals to stand for clouds, rain, or water. What do these images seem to say about the ancient Chinese view of nature?

Background Information
Ancient bronze vessels are never unearthed in perfect, polished condition. They are covered by a surface film called the patina, which forms on copper and bronze that has been exposed to earth or a damp atmosphere for an extended period of time. Depending on the composition of the soil in which they were buried, Shang dynasty Chinese bronzes may have a glossy black or smooth green patina and be encrusted with red (cuprite), deep blue (azurite), or green (malachite) deposits.

Background Information
Shang dynasty bronzes were embellished with a number of characteristic motifs, some of which were placed in a horizontal band and some of which covered the entire surface. Among the most common decorative features were dragons, birds, the thunder scroll, the cloud scroll, a bowstring ornament, small circles, vertical ridges, and a variety of animals including the ox, the sheep, the goat, and the cock.

ANCIENT INDIAN CULTURE

Like that of the Shang dynasty, the culture of ancient India remained a legend until modern times. In 1856 railroad workers laying track in the Indus River valley made a discovery. Near the city of Harappa (huh-**rap**-uh), they found a hill of crumbling fired clay bricks. These bricks date to between 2500 and 1500 B.C. Can you find the city of Harappa on the map in Figure 4–13? In what modern country is it located?

In addition to bricks, the railroad workers found a number of small relief carvings in soapstone. One of these is shown in Figure 4–15. These carvings are the oldest examples of Indian art.

Did you notice the odd lines and shapes above the animal form? These are known to be letters from an ancient system of writing. Scholars have yet to decipher the Harappan language.

◀ **Figure 4–14** Would you describe the images shown on this pitcher as realistic? If not, how would you describe them?

Chinese. Ritual Wine Vessel, with Spout. Shang Dynasty, 14th Century B.C. Bronze. 21.6 cm (8½"). The Metropolitan Museum of Art, New York, New York. Gift of Ernest Erickson Foundation, Inc.

◀ **Figure 4–15** Soapstone seals may have been used as personal adornment. Could the symbols have identified the owner?

Soapstone seal from Mohenjo-daro showing a Brahmani bull. Harappan culture. c. 2300–1750 B.C. 3.5 cm (18½"). British Museum, London, England.

Developing Concepts

Exploring Aesthetics. Have students look at Figure 4-17. Ask students why the artist made the eyes of this statue so large. Point out how the clasped hands draw attention to the face. Discuss the other ways in which the artist has focused the viewer's attention on the face.

Using Art Criticism. Have students look at Figure 4-15 and identify the animal that is pictured. Ask students to compare it with those in Figure 4-1: Which animals are more realistically rendered? What feeling is conveyed by each style? Which elements of an animal's body are emphasized and which parts are omitted on the Chinese vessel?

Understanding Art History. Explain to students that the Shang dynasty was quite rich in material culture. It possessed a well-developed form of writing, technically accomplished wheel-made pottery, developed bronze casting, fine jade carving, and stone sculpture executed in the round. Have groups of students research Shang dynasty sculpture. Ask them to find out what kinds of bronze pieces are especially plentiful and whether the decorations are mere designs or are meaningful symbols.

Developing Studio Skills. Have students examine Figure 4-15. Ancient Indians used chiseled and drilled seals as amulets to stamp their agreements. Have students use utility knives to carve personal seals out of rubber erasers. Then have them print the seals with ink or paint on plain paper to make "official" stationery.

Background Information

The Sumerians constructed ziggurats in the belief that mountaintops were the dwelling places of their gods. Lacking real mountains on the Mesopotamian plain, the Sumerians had to create their own artificial ones to provide a suitable home for their gods. The cult statues placed inside the ziggurat temple were believed to embody the deities that they depicted. Sumerians also made statues of worshippers to send prayers and messages to the gods in their place.

▲ **Figure 4–16** Perhaps the most famous ziggurat of all is the one recorded in the Bible. It is the tower of Babylon.

Ziggurat at Ur, Iraq.

Architecture

In 1922 a second ancient city was found in the area of Harappa. Its name is Mohenjo-Daro (moh-hen-joh-**dahr**-oh), which means "Hill of the Dead." The city is believed to have had a population of 35,000.

Mohenjo-Daro is an early example of the art of **urban planning**. This is *arranging the construction and services of a city to best meet its people's needs*. The ancient city had wide, open streets dividing it into large blocks about the size of four football fields. There were homes, shops, and large buildings thought to be houses of worship.

MESOPOTAMIAN CULTURE

The culture of Mesopotamia was more the culture of a region than of a people. The region was the fertile crescent of land between the Tigris (**ty**-gruhs) and Euphrates (yoo-**frayt**-eez) Rivers. This land is shared today by Syria and Iraq. (See Figure 4–13.) The people of Mesopotamia lived in city states that each had their own king. Sometimes these city states fought with each other and one would become more powerful.

60   Lesson 4   *Ancient China, India and Mesopotamia*

The first important group to live in Mesopotamia was the Sumerians (soo-**mehr**-ee-uhns). Where the Sumerians came from is unclear. There is evidence that they learned to control the floods that were common in the fertile crescent. They also built strong walled cities, each with its own king.

The Sumerians were the first people to have a system of writing. Called cuneiform (kyoo-**nee**-uh-form), the system was made up of wedge-shaped characters. The Sumerians did not have paper so they wrote the cuneiform upon clay tablets.

Other city states that later became important were Babylon and Assyria.

Architecture

At the center of the Sumerian city, and of their form of art, was the **ziggurat** (**zig**-uh-rat). This was *a stepped mountain made of brick-covered earth*. A temple honoring the god of the city was placed at the top of the ziggurat. Figure 4–16 shows a ziggurat dating from 2100 B.C. What other ancient building does the ziggurat resemble?

Sculpture

As with other ancient cultures, the tribes of Mesopotamia often expressed their religious beliefs in their art. Study the sculpture in Figure 4–17. This marble figure stands for a Sumerian goddess or worshipper. This work has been dated from between 2700 and 2600 B.C. What other art that you studied in this chapter was completed around the same time? How does the style of that work compare with this?

▲ Figure 4–17 This figure is typical of Sumerian sculpture. Notice the large eyes and the hands clasped in prayer.

Statua di Donna. The Iraq Museum, Baghdad, Iraq.

CHECK YOUR UNDERSTANDING

1. What are dynasties? How do they relate to the art of China?
2. How was the Harappan culture of ancient India discovered?
3. Why is the ancient city of Mohenjo-Daro important?
4. What is a ziggurat? In what culture were ziggurats built?

Following Up

Closure. Have students select their favorite art work pictured in this lesson and write a short paragraph explaining their choice. Invite them to share their paragraphs with the class.

Evaluation. 1. Review students' written responses to the "Check Your Understanding" questions. 2. Review student paragraphs.

Reteaching. Mohenjo-Daro was carefully planned to meet the needs of those who dwelled there. Have the students draw a map of their neighborhood on the board. Ask whether the layout reflects any principles of urban planning and whether the ideas of Mohenjo-Daro still seem relevant today.

Enrichment. Invite an urban planner, an archaeologist, or an art historian who specializes in ancient art to explain his or her work. If such professionals are not available, have students investigate the phenomenon of desertification. Ask them to find areas of the world today that, like the Indus Valley, are being lost to the encroaching desert.

Answers to "Check Your Understanding"
1. Dynasties are periods of history in China. The art of China is grouped by dynasty.
2. The Harappan culture of ancient India was discovered by railroad workers who uncovered a hill of crumbling clay bricks.
3. The ancient city of Mohenjo-Daro is important because it was one of the first examples of urban planning.
4. A *ziggurat* was a stepped mountain made of brick-covered earth. Ziggurats were built by the Sumerians, the first group to live in Mesopotamia.

Creating a Picture Story

LESSON PLAN
(pages 62–63)

Objectives
After completing this lesson, students will be able to:
- Draw and paint in the style of the ancient Egyptians.
- Explain characteristics of Egyptian tomb art.

Supplies
- Comic strips from a Sunday newspaper.
- Pencils, erasers, and sketch paper.
- Watercolor paints and watercolor brushes (suggested sizes are #2, #3, and #8).
- Sheets of white paper, 18 x 24 inches (45 x 60 cm).
- Containers for water.
- Paper towels.
- Candle (optional).
- Prints of images from all cultures studied so far.

> #### TRB Resources
> - 4-8 *Making Papyrus,* (reproducible master)
> - 4-9 *Media of Earliest Times,* (studio)

TEACHING THE LESSON

Getting Started

Motivator. Display comic strips from a Sunday newspaper. Have students discuss the ways in which Figure 4-18 is like the comics and how the two are different.

Developing Concepts

Exploring Aesthetics. Artistic balance and a sense of realism were not prized by Egyptian artists who painted tomb walls. The goal was to render the most complete possible cycle of events so that the spirit of the deceased person could watch them. In most cases, people are not shown at a particular moment of action, but in a posture that typifies that task. Have students

---

Creating a Picture Story

Egyptian artists, as you have read, followed strict rules when they worked. One rule required that they show human body parts from their most familiar angle. Another required artists to make the most important people in a work the largest. Both these rules are followed in the wall painting in Figure 4–18. The important man and woman at the left are observing a hunting and fishing scene. The smaller figures are the servants. The painting tells a story.

WHAT YOU WILL LEARN

You will paint a picture story about the important events in your life. You will use the rules of Egyptian art shown in Figure 4–18. (For example, make your proportions larger to emphasize your importance.) Select lines and shapes to look stiff and dignified. Use contrasting colors to draw attention to the center of interest. Do *not* show depth of space in your painting. Instead, give it the same flat look as an Egyptian work. (See Figure 4–19.)

▲ **Figure 4–18** Notice that little shading was used. The pictures look flat, as though they are cut from paper.

Wall painting from the Tomb of Nakht. *Nakht and his Wife.* Egypt. c. 1425 B.C. The Metropolitan Museum of Art, New York, New York.

Background Information
Egyptian tomb artists worked under less than ideal conditions. It is a mystery how they managed to paint so precisely in the innermost chambers of tombs, which are either very dim or entirely devoid of light. Experts suggest that they held special tapers impregnated with oil or fat to light the walls while they worked. Egyptian artists also used surprisingly crude brushes.

Some were fashioned out of lengths of palm ribs beaten to produce very stiff bristles. Examples that have been found, still clogged with old paint, do not look at all suitable for elaborate work.

WHAT YOU WILL NEED

- Pencil, sheets of sketch paper, and an eraser
- Watercolor paints and several watercolor brushes, some thick and some thin
- Sheet of white paper, 18 x 24 inches (46 x 61 cm)
- Paper towels

WHAT YOU WILL DO

1. Brainstorm with your class about ideas for your story painting. Some possibilities might be a birthday party, a school dance, a ride on your bike, a family get-together, passing an important test, and taking part in a class play or athletic event. You may want to pick more than one event for your work.

2. Study the figures in Figure 4–18. Make some rough pencil sketches that show figures in the same way. These should help you plan not only the story but also the size, location, and proportion of figures. The pictures do not have to read across the paper like the lines in a story. Rather, you may, if you like, place the most important scene in the center. Let your imagination guide you.

3. Choose your best plan. Working lightly in pencil, sketch it on the sheet of white paper.

4. Use your watercolors to paint the scene. Using your brushes, paint the areas. Take care not to smear any areas of paint. (For information on using watercolors, see Technique Tip **14**, *Handbook* page **281**.)

5. When your work has dried, display it. See if any of your classmates can "read" your picture story.

OTHER STUDIO IDEAS

- Create a second story painting. This time, tell your story in a straight line using a rectangular strip of paper.

●● Work in small groups to create a story painting mural. Choose events that relate to a famous leader. Use school acrylic paint to color your mural.

EXAMINING YOUR WORK

- **Describe** Describe the events in your painting. Tell how you used size to emphasize the most important person — you.
- **Analyze** Tell whether your lines and shapes give a feeling of stiffness. Explain how you used contrasting color to create a center of interest. Tell how you used proportion to emphasize yourself.
- **Interpret** State whether a viewer will be able to "read" your picture story and identify the important events in your life. Give your work a title.
- **Judge** Tell whether you feel your work succeeds. Explain your answer.

▲ Figure 4–19   Student work. Picture story.

 Lesson 5   *Creating a Picture Story*   **63**

compare the drawings of Nahkt and his wife with the other people in Figure 4-18. Why is the couple shown larger? Are all of the figures equally stiff and formal? Why might underlings be drawn with less dignity than royal persons? Also point out how all the space is used. Discuss the advantages of filling all the space in a painting.

Understanding Art History. Explain to the students that Egyptian artists followed strictly established rules that had religious significance. For example, because the sculptures, paintings, and relief sculptures of the dead were intended to act as substitutes for the body in the afterlife, the artist was careful to render all parts of the body. Have students research the other rules that guided Egyptian artists and report their findings to the class. Discuss whether socially and religiously imposed rules helped the Egyptians to create more powerful art or whether the rules inhibited creative expression.

Following Up

Closure. Have the students write a short paragraph about their story and critique their work. Ask them to consider whether their work looks Egyptian? Why, or why not? You may want to crumple the work and carefully burn the edges with a candle to make it resemble ancient papyrus.

Evaluation. 1. Review the students' paragraphs. 2. Review the students' studio projects taking into account the following: Do they use hieratic proportion? Are the figures presented according to Egyptian postural conventions? Is all the negative space filled in?

Reteaching. Present prints of images from all of the cultures studied so far. Have the students identify where each work was produced and explain their reasons.

Enrichment. Have students find several good color photographs of Egyptian painting. Discuss the pigments that produced the brilliant colors that have survived in much ancient Egyptian painting. Almost all of the pigments were made from natural mineral substances. The white came from chalk, the black was soot that was scraped from the bottom of cooking pots, the red is from iron oxides, the green is from copper, and the blue is a compound of silica, copper, and calcium.

Classroom Management Tip
Be careful when using a candle to burn the edges of art work. Hot wax can spill out of a tipped candle and cause a burn. Do not let students "age" their own art work.

ANSWERS TO "CHAPTER 4 REVIEW"

Building Vocabulary

1. culture
2. megaliths
3. post and lintel system
4. stele
5. hieroglyphic
6. urban planning
7. ziggurat

Reviewing Art Facts

8. Another name for the Paleolithic period is the Old Stone Age; it began about 30,000 B.C.
9. The cave painting's location deep within caves led experts to think they were not created for decoration alone.
10. Old Stone Age artists used clay, teeth, bone, shells, stone, and ivory. (Students may name any three items.)
11. People began to spin, weave, and make pottery. They also began to build monuments.
12. The mysteries are why Stonehenge was built and how the huge stones were set in place.
13. Egyptian artists showed every body part from its most familiar angle. Artists were bound by strict rules.
14. China, India, and Mesopotamia each developed in a river valley and each had a king and a religion based on nature.
15. The greatest achievement of early Chinese artists was their bronze pieces.

Thinking About Art

1. The soapstone carvings are the oldest examples of Indian art, and they contain letters from an ancient system of writing.
2. Art themes from around 3000 B.C. might include activities from daily life, ceremonies, and the beginnings of written language and storytelling.
3. Answers will vary, but students should show they understand the difference between realistic drawings, such as those shown in the cave paintings and Harappan seals, and symbolic art such as the Egyptian paintings and Chinese crafts.

BUILDING VOCABULARY

Number a sheet of paper from 1 to 7. After each number, write the term from the box that best matches each description below.

culture	stele
hieroglyphic	urban planning
megaliths	ziggurat
post and lintel system	

1. The ideas, beliefs, and living customs of a people.
2. Large stone monuments, such as Stonehenge in England.
3. Approach to building in which a crossbeam is placed above two uprights.
4. Carved upright stone slab used as a monument.
5. An early form of picture writing
6. Arranging the construction and services of a city to best meet its people's needs.
7. Stepped mountain made of brick-covered earth.

REVIEWING ART FACTS

Number a sheet of paper from 8 to 15. Answer each question in a complete sentence.

8. What is another term for the Paleolithic period and when did it begin?
9. What fact about the cave paintings has led experts to suspect they were not created for decoration alone?
10. Name three media used by sculptors and craftspeople during the Old Stone Age.
11. How did the style of art change by the time of the Neolithic period?
12. What are two mysteries surrounding Stonehenge?

13. How did ancient Egyptian artists show the human body in their works? Why?
14. Name two ways in which ancient China, India, and Mesopotamia were like ancient Egypt.
15. What was the greatest achievement of early China?

THINKING ABOUT ART

On a sheet of paper, answer each question in a sentence or two.

1. **Summarize.** From a historical standpoint, why are the soapstone carvings of the Harappan culture important?
2. **Extend.** Suppose you learned of the discovery of a new civilization dating to 3000 B.C. Based on your reading of this chapter, what themes might you expect to find running through its art?
3. **Compare and contrast.** Some art scholars, you will recall, believe a successful art work is one with a realistic subject. Which of the ancient periods and civilizations you studied would appeal most to such a person? Which would appeal least? Explain your answers.

MAKING ART CONNECTIONS

1. **Mathematics.** Construction of the ancient pyramids was based on specific mathematical formulas. This is one reason why they have existed so long. Look up *pyramid* in an encyclopedia. Explain how math was involved in designing these architectural structures.
2. **Social Studies.** Choose a personality from current events. Imagine this person living in an ancient culture. Plan an appropriate monument to honor this figure.

LOOKING AT THE DETAILS

The detail shown below is from the Stele of Nefertiabet, *Funerary Feast*. Study the detail and answer the following questions using complete sentences.

1. What are some universally recognizable images in this work?
2. This painting is from an ancient culture. Can you guess what is being shown here?
3. How does art history help you to understand this work?
4. How might this work of art help you understand ancient Egyptian figure drawing styles?

Funerary Feast, Stele of Nefertiabet. Old Kingdom, 4th Dynasty. Painted limestone. (Detail.) The Louvre, Paris, France.

ANSWERS TO "LOOKING AT THE DETAILS"

1. Student answers may vary. Some possible items include the table, chair, human figure, bird, and pitcher.
2. Student answers may vary. The viewer might guess correctly that it is a type of meal or ritual, or the viewer could also guess that it is a game or test of some sort.
3. Art history helps in understanding this work by providing information about the culture who created it. Their strong belief in the afterlife and the fact that this is a painting in a tomb helps us define this image as a funeral banquet as opposed to another kind of meal.
4. Students answers may vary. This work of art would give us more detailed knowledge of the objects they valued, of how they prepared for the afterlife, what symbols they used to communicate, their creative interpretation of the human form and perhaps a clue into how they reasoned, among other things.

Chapter Evaluation

The goal of this chapter is to develop students' understanding and appreciation of early civilizations and the artistic achievements of these groups. Methods of evaluation include:

1. Display slides or photographs of the following objects: Egyptian pyramids, ziggurats, bronze vessels, and so forth. Have students identify the civilization that is associated with each artistic achievement.
2. Set up a class debate in which students compare and contrast the life of early civilizations to life today.
3. Have students complete the Chapter 4 Test (TRB, Resource 4-10).

The Art of the Far East

Chapter Scan

TRB Resources

- 5-10 Chapter Test
- Color Transparency 9
- Color Transparency 10

TEACHING THE CHAPTER

Introducing the Art Work

Direct students' attention to the Chinese painting *Evening In Spring Hills*. Inform them that this landscape painting was created in China in the 1100s. Explain that in China, after the tenth century, an increasing interest in landscape painting led to a decline in the use of strong colors. Artists felt that the strong colors were not suited to nature's real hues and that bright colors obscured fine brush work. These artists placed greater importance on the skilled manipulation of the brush. This mastery of brush work was considered necessary in order to give vitality to the painting. Chinese painters practiced for years to develop the necessary control of executing delicate, swift strokes. Every artist worked to perfect his brush work until it bore an imprint as personal as his handwriting.

The goal of Chinese painters was to capture the spirit, as well as the form, of their subject. In the Buddhist faith, the Chinese visualized the physical universe—earth and sky—as a unit. They believed that the earth was surmounted by the canopy of heaven, studded with the fiery stars that control human destiny.

▲ Why do you think the artist chose to show so much sky in the painting? Describe everything you see in this work. Does the picture show only natural objects?

Unknown. Fan Mounted as an Album Leaf. *Evening in Spring Hills*. Southern Sung Dynasty. 1127–1278. Ink and color on silk. 24.8 x 26.1 cm (9¾ x 10¼"). The Metropolitan Museum of Art, New York, New York. Gift of John M. Crawford, Jr., in honor of Alfreda Murck.

Art of the Far East

"East is East and West is West, and never the twain shall meet." These words, penned a century ago by a well-known British poet, express a view still sometimes heard. In truth, the twain — or two — opposite sides of our planet — hold much in common. They both express their feelings about their culture in paintings and through art.

Can you read the message in the Chinese silk painting at the left? In the pages ahead you will learn about the art of China and Japan.

OBJECTIVES

After completing this chapter, you will be able to:
- Describe the role of religion in the art of China and Japan.
- Identify key developments in Chinese painting, sculpture, and crafts.
- Identify key developments in Japanese architecture, sculpture, painting, and printmaking.
- Create art objects that record experiences or events in your world.

WORDS YOU WILL LEARN

glaze   scroll
pagoda   Ukiyo-e
perceive   woodblock printing
porcelain   Yamato-e
screen

ARTISTS YOU WILL MEET

Chao Meng-fu   Kiyotada

Examining the Art Work

Tell students that this Chinese landscape painting was created by brushing ink and watercolors on silk. Point out the fine lines used to create the human figures, the canopy, and the surrounding foliage. Explain to them that line is the basic structural element of all Chinese painting, as opposed to light and shadow which is used more in Western art. Emphasize the subtle blending of colors in the work and the way the human figures blend into the surroundings rather than stand apart from them. Suggest that this could illustrate the Buddhist belief that humans are one with nature. Point out the use of space in this work and explain that the Chinese paid special attention to achieving a sense of three-dimensional space.

Discussing the Art Work

Ask students whether they think the vast amount of negative space is important to this painting. Point out how the large block of negative space pushes the land and people to the bottom of the work. Suggest that the negative space is not that at all, but instead a real and important force or universe greater than earthly life. Explain how this conforms to the Buddhist belief system and to the artist's goal of capturing the spirit of his beliefs in his work.

Ask students to think about the placement of the human figures in this work. Have students identify how the figures are placed in the center of the work, suggesting that they are part of nature. Since their faces and forms are undefined, they could represent every man.

Tell students that in this chapter they will learn about the role of religion in Chinese painting and they will be able to identify key developments in Chinese and Japanese art. They will also create art objects reflecting their own world and experiences.

Building Self-Esteem

Tell students that in this chapter they will be learning about the art of China and Japan by seeing art objects from ancient times. They will also have the opportunity to create some art projects that record experiences or events in their own world. Ask whether the class knows what a time capsule is and what kinds of objects are placed in time capsules today. Ask what they might include in selecting objects most commonly associated with teen interests of today. What do the choices we make in the areas of music, art, and extra-curricular activities say about us? If a time capsule were opened in the year 2100, what conclusions might be drawn about teen lifestyles of the late 1900s? The student work shown on page **77** might have shown the artist's actual room or dream room. Ask students to imagine the life of their dreams; life as it *might* be. Let them reflect on what actions they can take to reach their goals. Ask what items they would include in their time capsule if they were to reach the goals in their "life as it might be."

LESSON 1

The Art of China

LESSON PLAN
(pages 68–69)

Objectives

After completing this lesson, students will be able to:

- Describe the role of religion in the art of China.
- Identify key developments in Chinese painting, sculpture, and crafts.
- Take time to perceive natural objects and then make pen-and-ink drawings of them.

Supplies

- Slide or display-size photograph of a Chinese sculpture of Buddha (if available).
- Two pieces of pottery: one either earthenware or stoneware, the other porcelain.
- Natural objects, such as leaves, rocks and pine cones (brought in by students, if possible); sheets of white drawing paper; brushes; ink.
- Objects of various shapes and sizes, such as mugs, apples, rulers, vases, and so on.

TRB Resources
- 5-1 *Chinese Dynasties and Art Forms,* (art history)
- 5-2 *Oriental Views in Design,* (reproducible master)

TEACHING THE LESSON

Getting Started

Motivator. Introduce the lesson by displaying a slide or photograph of a Chinese sculpture of Buddha. Let students describe the work and, if they can, identify the subject. Encourage students to share what they know about Buddhism and meditation; you may want to explain that Buddhism is a religion that emphasizes the oneness of humans with nature and that meditation is a practice of focusing thoughts on a single idea. Tell students that in this lesson they will learn about Chinese art and how it has been influenced by Buddhism and meditation.

Vocabulary. Display an object of simple pottery (either earthenware or stoneware) and one of porcelain. Help students discuss the differences, and introduce the term *porcelain.*

68

The Art of China

The Chinese have a long history of being highly creative. Two thousand years before the invention of the seismograph, they were recording earthquakes. Long before the first Texas oil wells were drilled, they were drilling holes 2000 feet deep. The compass and kite are two other early Chinese inventions.

Added proof of the Chinese gift for creating can be found in their art. In this lesson you will learn about the important contributions they have made.

MODERN CHINESE CULTURE

The "modern" period of Chinese civilization is thought to have begun with the Han dynasty. This dynasty lasted from 206 B.C. to A.D. 220. To this day, the Chinese still refer to themselves as the "Han people."

During this period a new religion came to China, called Buddhism (**boo**-diz-uhm), which stressed the oneness of humans with nature. An important part of Buddhism is meditation, focusing one's thoughts on a single object or idea. This experience allows the person to know the inner beauty of the object or idea. Chinese art of the last 2000 years has been greatly influenced by Buddhism and meditation.

Scroll Painting

The Chinese were the first people to think of "picture painting" as honorable work. This was because many artists were also scholars. They wrote with brushes that could make thick and thin lines. They used the same brush and line technique to paint pictures. They painted fans, pages of books, and scrolls. A **scroll** is *a long roll of illustrated parchment or silk.* Some scrolls were meant to hang on walls. Other scrolls were made of long rolls of silk or paper. They were meant to be unrolled a little at a time and read like a book.

Like other Chinese artists, scroll painters began a work only after a long period of meditation. The work itself was an attempt to capture a feeling, not an image. Shapes and figures were limited to the barest essentials. The artist included only those lines and shapes needed to capture the mood of the scene. (See Figure 5–3 on page **70**.)

Landscape Painting

The earliest Chinese paintings were filled with images of people illustrating the beliefs that people should live together peacefully and be respectful of their elders. With the influence of a new religion, the focus of painting began shifting away from humans and toward nature. By around A.D. 1100, the landscape was the main theme of Chinese painting.

The work that opened this chapter on page **66** is a landscape painting. Look closely at the work. Can you find a covered deck, or pavilion (puh-**vil**-yuhn), nestled within the hills? Studying the painting more closely still, do you see two small shapes inside the pavilion? These are meant to be seen as the heads of people. What statement is the artist making about the place of humans in nature?

Sculpture

For many centuries important people in China were buried in tombs with objects they could use in the afterworld. These figures were made from clay. Many, like the horses in Figure 5–1 were of animals. Notice how the artist uses line and movement to create the feeling of action.

After the collapse of the Han dynasty, China fell into chaos. It remained this way until the mighty T'ang (**tahng**) dynasty rose to power some 400 years later. It was during this new dynasty that Chinese sculpture flourished.

Background Information

Like the architects, playwrights, astronomers, writers, and gardeners, the artists of China strove to reflect nothing less than a universal model in their works. Chinese philosophy involved a flat world sandwiched by an underground network of vital fluids and heavenly stars that governed destiny. The Chinese organized and balanced these features in their philosophies, actions, and arts. With skilled brush strokes, Chinese painters delineated landscapes, portraits, and narratives in their attempt to capture the spirit and logic of the world.

In their pursuit of expressing the spiritual tensions as well as the physical forms of their subjects, Chinese painters focused their abilities on brush-work. Finding that simple lines could convey movement, vigor, and emotion, the artists practiced their brushing until they achieved personal and powerful techniques. As a result, both Chinese painting and calligraphy share a precise but fluid quality that suggests both refinement and spontaneity, instilling a static art form with spirit and energy.

▲ Figure 5–1 Both the ladies and horses are shown in action in this work. Centuries ago they played similar games to what we do today.

Four Ladies of the Court Playing Polo. Tang Dynasty. A.D. 618–906. Painted terra cotta. Nelson-Atkins Museum of Art, Kansas City, Missouri.

Crafts

The T'ang dynasty was followed in A.D. 960 by another powerful dynasty, the Sung (**soong**). Landscape painting soared to new heights during the Sung dynasty. So did the making of **porcelain** (**pore**-suh-luhn), *a fine-grained, high-quality form of pottery.* Porcelain is made from a fine and fairly hard-to-find white clay called kaolin (**kay**-uh-luhn).

Work in porcelain reached its highest point ever during the Ming dynasty (1368–1644).

▲ Figure 5–2 The blue pigment came from Persia. Unless the timing was precise, the blue could turn black or brown during the firing.

Pair of Vases, Meiping. Reign of Xuande. Ming Dynasty. 1426–1435. Porcelain with underglaze blue decoration. Nelson-Atkins Museum of Art, Kansas City, Missouri.

STUDIO EXPERIENCE

Chinese artists, you have learned, began a work only after long meditation on an object. This helped the artist capture the mood he wanted to show. In other cultures artists approach subjects of works in a similar way. They train themselves to **perceive**, or *look deeply at the subject.* This allows them to think about and study the properties of the subject that might otherwise go unnoticed.

Bring a natural object, such as a leaf, rock, or pine cone, to class. Sit silently for five minutes and study the object from every angle. Notice the object's lines, form, and textures. Do the lines curve around the form? Is the object rough or smooth? Are there shiny highlights? Now place the object out of sight. Using brush and ink, draw what you perceived on a sheet of paper.

The remarkable matched vases shown in Figure 5–2 date from this period. The painted dragon designs are protected by a *glass-like finish,* or **glaze**, on these Ming porcelains. What kind of balance does each of the vases have? What kind of balance do they have as a matched set?

✔ CHECK YOUR UNDERSTANDING

1. Name two inventions credited to the early Chinese.
2. What religion was introduced to China during the Han dynasty?
3. What is meditation? What has been its role in Chinese art of the last 2000 years?
4. What are scrolls?
5. What art form flourished during the T'ang dynasty and during the Sung dynasty?
6. What art form reached its highest point during the Ming dynasty?

Lesson 1   *The Art of China*   📖   **69**

Developing Concepts

Exploring Aesthetics. Help students discuss their ideas about appropriate subjects for paintings: Are landscapes as interesting—or important—as portraits? Which painting subjects do you like best? Why? Do you see beliefs reflected in all paintings—or only in paintings of certain subjects? Must a painting have a religious subject in order to be a religious painting? Encourage students to share and support various points of view.

Understanding Art History. Have students form three groups, and ask each group to research pottery created in China during one of these dynasties: T'ang, Sung, Ming. Let each group share and discuss its findings with the class.

Following Up

Closure. Have students write paragraphs about their "Studio Experience" work. Ask them to respond to these questions: How did you feel as you studied the object? What did you learn about the object during that time? How clearly did you remember the object as you were drawing it? How would your drawing have been different if you had not spent time studying the object?

Evaluation. 1. Review students' written responses to the "Check Your Understanding" questions. 2. Read students' paragraphs about their "Studio Experience" work.

Reteaching. Work with small groups of students to discuss tomb objects. Begin by having group members describe what they see in Figure 5-1. Then ask: Why do you think these clay horses were buried in a tomb? What other objects would you expect to find in a tomb? How do you think the use of tomb objects affected the work of all artists in a culture?

Enrichment. Display various manufactured and natural objects—a vase, a ruler, an apple, a pencil, a leaf, and so on. Let students study one object and write a complete description of it—without naming the object. Can other students identify the object from the description?

Answers to "Check Your Understanding"

1. Three inventions credited to the early Chinese are the compass, kite, and hot air balloon.
2. During the Han dynasty, the religion of Buddhism was introduced to China.
3. Meditation is focusing one's thoughts on a single object or idea. This experience helps a person to perceive the inner beauty of the object or idea.
4. A scroll is a long roll of illustrated parchment or silk.
5. During the T'ang dynasty, sculpture began to flourish. The Sung dynasty featured landscape painting and the making of porcelain objects.
6. Work in porcelain reached its peak during the Ming dynasty.

Making a Scroll

Objectives

After completing this lesson, students will be able to:

- Plan and create original scroll paintings in the style of Chinese painters.
- Describe, analyze, interpret, and judge their own scrolls.

Supplies

- Sheets of drawing paper, colored pencils.
- Small pieces of drawing paper, markers, pieces of string.
- Sheets of white paper, 1 x 6 feet (30 cm x 2 m); pencils; watercolor markers; transparent tape; dowels, 14 inches (36 cm); pieces of ribbon, 24 inches (61 cm).
- Reproductions of several Chinese paintings (if available).
- Sheets of drawing paper, brushes, ink.
- Several similar natural objects, such as small branches.

TRB Resource

- 5-3 *Hokusai Sketch,* (reproducible master)

TEACHING THE LESSON

Getting Started

Motivator. Begin by having students work in small groups. Ask the members of each group to select a specific location they are all familiar with, such as the school grounds or a field in a local park. What mood or feeling do they have when recalling that location? Have group members work together to draw a picture of the scene, emphasizing the feeling or mood it creates for them. Then have each group share its work with the rest of the class.

Vocabulary. Ask students to recall the definition of *scroll.* (Refer them to page **68** if necessary.) Then have them write the definition on small pieces of drawing paper, roll the paper to form scroll shapes, and tie their scrolls with string.

Look at the Chinese scroll painting in Figure 5–3. The work is by Chao Meng-fu (chow meng-foo), a leading scroll painter of the Yuan dynasty. Though the artist trained himself to paint quickly, his work was meant to be viewed slowly. The viewer was meant to meditate on each scene as the artist did before creating it.

WHAT YOU WILL LEARN

You will create a scroll recording the events of a nature walk in the manner of the Chinese painter. Record scenes of your walk on a long strip of paper, using pencils and markers. Leave large areas of negative space around the shapes. Shapes to be emphasized will be filled with color. (See Figure 5–4.)

WHAT YOU WILL NEED

- Sheet of white paper, 1 x 6 feet (30 cm x 2 m)
- Pencil, watercolor markers, and transparent tape
- 2 dowels, 14 inches (36 cm)
- Piece of ribbon, 24 inches (61 cm)

WHAT YOU WILL DO

1. Set aside time to walk slowly through your school and around the school grounds. Gaze at objects and scenes as though you are seeing them for the first time. Stop as necessary to perceive the visual impression of the texture of a bush or the color of a flower. Try to focus on the feeling or mood each scene communicates. This feeling may come to you in a small detail, such as the texture of a wall or the line of the path you walk.

▲ **Figure 5–3**   **How is space treated differently here than in Western paintings?**

Chao Meng-fu. Handscroll: *Twin Pines, Level Distance.* Yuan Dynasty. Early 1300s. Ink on paper. (Detail.) 25.4 x 127.3 cm (10 x 42½″). The Metropolitan Museum of Art, New York, New York. Gift of the Dillon Fund.

Background Information

Chinese artists intended scrolls to be viewed in portions. Unlike Western painters, who rely primarily on composition and subject matter to affect audiences, the Chinese scroll artists force viewers to study their works actively. As the scroll is slowly revealed to the viewer, the relationships of height, depth, and direction draw the audience's interaction. By involving the viewer in this way, the Chinese scroll painter recreates his or her own visionary process in the audience's mind.

The dominating subject matter for Chinese scroll art is the landscape. The scroll provides the artist with an excellent medium for presenting a panoramic view of nature. If any human ingredients are included, they are overwhelmed by the natural elements. Villages and boats are portrayed in a miniature scale to emphasize their insignificance in comparison to the huge landscapes. The treatment of civilization in scroll art reminds the viewer that while he or she perceives the scaled-down world in the art work, nature exists on an even larger scale.

2. Roll the large sheet of paper into a scroll. Close your eyes and try to picture one of the scenes and the mood attached to it. Keep the lines, shapes, colors, and textures uppermost in your mind. Unroll 10 inches (25 cm) of your scroll and, using pencil, very lightly draw the scene. The scene should not fill the section of paper. You should, in other words, have plenty of negative space around shapes and objects.

3. Using markers, trace over the pencil lines. Make sure no pencil marks are left showing. Fill in the shapes you want to emphasize with color. Do not color everything in the scene.

4. When you are satisfied with your work, unroll another 10 inches (25 cm) of scroll. Close your eyes again and try to picture another scene. Again record the scene in pencil and trace over the lines with markers. Continue to work in this fashion until you have used up all your paper.

5. Using tape, fasten each end of your scroll to a dowel. Roll up the scroll and tie it with the ribbon.

6. Exchange scrolls with a friend. Study the works slowly and silently. See if you can identify the scenes in the other person's work.

OTHER STUDIO IDEAS

- Using a brush and one hue of watercolor, paint the scenes in your scroll.
- ●● Create a vertical scroll. Start with the scene at ground level in front of your feet. Shift your eyes upward little by

EXAMINING YOUR WORK

- **Describe**   Tell what scenes you chose to show. State whether your work has any pencil lines showing.
- **Analyze**   Point to the places where you used negative space in your scroll. Point to places where you used color for emphasis. Identify other elements you used.
- **Interpret**   Show features in your work that would help a viewer understand how it captures a mood. Identify the different moods of the scenes.
- **Judge**   Tell whether you feel your work succeeds. Explain your answer.

▲ Figure 5—4   Student work. Scroll painting.

little. The last scene in your scroll should be the sky. At each level, search for and include details that capture the mood of the scene.

Lesson 2   *Making a Scroll*   🎨   **71**

Background Information
While painters recreated the natural world in their silken and paper scrolls, gardeners were also shaping their plots to reflect the greater cosmos. By using stones and water as symbols, and assembling trees, shrubs, and flowers, the skilled gardener could reproduce the variety of relationships that characterized the body and universe according to the Chinese tradition. During the early Chou dynasty, kings and lords even stocked their huge gardens with animals as a symbol of status.

By 300 B.C., however, the well-tended garden came to represent spiritual peace rather than economic or social power. Chinese intellectuals adopted Taoist and Buddhist ideals, revering gardens as places to worship. While the vegetation and landscaping still mirrored the universe, they served as reminders of the simplicity and balance of nature. The natural elements that once represented division and struggle now symbolized unity and harmony. Even today, China's gardens still convey wholeness and peacefulness.

Developing Concepts

Exploring Aesthetics. Guide students in discussing the scroll painting in Figure 5-3: What mood or feeling does this work communicate to you? How do you feel the work communicates that feeling?

Using Art Criticism. Have students examine the scroll painting in Figure 5-3 and, if possible, reproductions of several other Chinese paintings. Point out the use of negative space in these works. Ask: What purpose do you think this negative space serves? How is color used in these paintings? What effect does this use of color have?

Developing Studio Skills. Remind students that many Chinese artists were also scholars; they used the same brushes to write and to draw pictures. Let students experiment with this technique. Have each student choose a favorite quotation and use a brush and ink to write that quotation on a sheet of drawing paper. Then have each student use the same brush to make a pen-and-ink drawing to illustrate the quotation.

Following Up

Closure. Let students work with partners to discuss their scrolls, following the steps in "Examining Your Work." Then have each student write a short paragraph judging his or her own scroll.

Evaluation. Review students' scrolls and read their paragraphs about their own work.

Reteaching. Have students form groups, and give each group a natural object, such as small branch or a small houseplant. Ask the members of each group to sit silently and study their natural object for several minutes. Then have them discuss the object as they perceive it, and work together to write a brief description of it. Let each group present its description to the rest of the class. Then lead students in comparing their descriptions and in discussing how working as a group influenced their perception.

Enrichment. Ask volunteers to find and share reproductions of Chinese calligraphy. Help students discuss this form of writing and compare it to drawing or painting. Are some examples of calligraphy works of art? Is all calligraphy art? Why, or why not? Encourage students to express and support various points of view.

71

LESSON 3

The Art of Japan

LESSON PLAN
(pages 72–75)

Objectives

After completing this lesson, students will be able to:

• Describe the role of religion in the art of Japan.
• Identify key developments in Japanese architecture, sculpture, painting, and printmaking.
• Make a headband with a painted decorative design.

Supplies

• Slides or photographs of examples of Japanese architecture, including interiors and gardens.
• Long pieces of white paper or cloth (to use as headbands), pencils, school acrylic paints, and brushes.
• Sheets of drawing paper, colored pencils.

TRB Resources

• 5-4 *Aesthetics and Japanese Art,* (aesthetics)
• 5-5 *Opening Japan to the World,* (art criticism)
• 5-6 *Plan a Nō Performance,* (cooperative learning)
• 5-7 *Oriental Customs,* (appreciating cultural diversity)
• 5-8 *Hokusai,* (artist profile)

TEACHING THE LESSON

Getting Started

Motivator. To help students begin thinking about Japanese culture and art, display slides or photographs of Japanese architecture; include photographs of the interiors of traditional Japanese homes and gardens. Encourage students to describe what they see, to compare these settings with modern American buildings, homes, and gardens, and to discuss their reactions to the Japanese settings. Then ask: What mood or feeling do you think these buildings, rooms, and gardens create? What do they tell you about the interests of the Japanese people? What do they suggest to you about the art works created in the Japanese culture?

The Art of Japan

The history of Japanese art began around 5000 B.C. In the years that followed, art influenced every aspect of Japanese life. In this lesson you will learn about the one-of-a-kind culture and art of the "floating world" called Japan.

JAPANESE CULTURE

Japan makes its home on an island group in the South Pacific. Find Japan on the map in Figure 5–5.

In most civilizations, art follows culture. In a sense, the reverse is true of Japan. In A.D. 552 the ruler of a kingdom in nearby Korea sent the Emperor of Japan a gift. The gift was a piece of art. More specifically, it was a bronze figure of the Buddha (**bood**-uh), the founder of Buddhism. Along with the sculpture came priests to spread Buddhist teachings. Eventually the people of Japan came to accept this new religion. They also learned about different ways of making art. For the next 250 years Japanese art would show strong traces of Korean, Chinese, and other Asian styles.

Architecture

Before the arrival of the bronze Buddha, the only Japanese art worth noting was prehistoric. Clay objects created by artists of the ancient Jomon (**joh**-muhn) culture are thought to date as early as 3000 B.C.

The first important Japanese art of "modern" times began being created in A.D. 594. These were magnificent Buddhist temples like the one shown in Figure 5–6. These temples were designed by Chinese or Chinese-trained architects and show a strong Chinese influence. Since the islands have little usable rock, wood was the main building material, except for the roofs which were made from tile. One of the most interesting features of early Japanese temples was the **pagoda** (puh-**gohd**-uh). This is *a tower several stories high with roofs curving slightly upward at the edges.* Figure 5–7 shows a pagoda from one of the greatest temples of the day. It is exactly like the first pagoda built at this temple. What does this fact reveal about the design of the building and how the Japanese feel about the past?

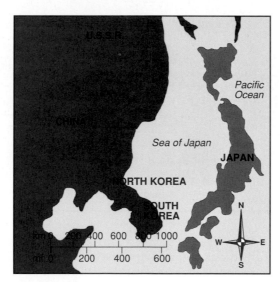

◀ Figure 5–5   Japan.

Background Information

Considered by its believers to be "the way of the gods," Shinto is the oldest practiced religion in Japan. Ancestors and Kami, gods found in all forms of nature, are honored with prayers and gifts. Shinto ceremonies stress the importance of the simple aspects of life such as peace, health, and harvests. Because the religion values only basic human necessities—it does not emphasize an afterlife, for example—it has remained pertinent in Japan for the last two thousand years.

The impact of the Shinto religion reflects noticeably in Japanese art. The *torii,* a wooden gateway used as an entrance to a Shinto shrine, blends Japanese artistic and religious convictions. The gate itself consists of two pillars under an inverted arch that resembles the roof of a pagoda. This frame symbolizes the sky and its supporting posts. Within the structure is a secondary horizontal bar, representing the earth. This simple gate functions as an entrance to the shrine, but symbolizes physical and spiritual relationships to its guests.

▲ **Figure 5–6** At least 10,000 pieces of the art of the period have been stored at this temple for over a thousand years.

Nara Todai-Ji Temple. c. A.D. 600. Japan.

▲ **Figure 5–7** Structures like these were used to store religious items.

Nara Horyu-Ji Temple Pagoda. A.D. 700. Japan.

Sculpture

The Japanese of this early period modeled small sculptures out of clay. They also carved images of wood and cast them in bronze. Most, like the one in Figure 5–8, featured the figure of the Buddha. As a new emperor came into power he would order a new Buddha to be cast. Each emperor would order his Buddha to be made larger than before to emphasize the emperor's own importance.

▲ **Figure 5–8** Why do you think sculptures like this are found outdoors?

Bronze Buddha of Todai-Ji. Japan.

Vocabulary. Help students discuss the two Japanese terms introduced in this lesson: *Yamato-e* and *Ukiyo-e*. Let students find the definitions in the Glossary or in the text. To help students understand *Yamato-e*, point out that it contrasts with *Kara-e*, which means "pictures of Chinese themes." Ask: Why do you think this new painting style was important in the Japanese culture? What changes did it mark? Then ask about the style called Ukiyo-e: What do you think the "floating world" of this style might be? In what ways could it be related to Japanese geography? In what ways could it be related to the subjects of the art works?

Developing Concepts

Exploring Aesthetics. Guide students in examining and discussing the woodcut shown in Figure 5-10: What is the subject of the work? How are the elements of line and color used? What other visual elements can you identify in this woodcut? Which principles of art are used to organize the elements? What idea or feeling does the work communicate to you?

Then raise the more general subject of woodblock printing: Are all the prints made from a woodblock works of art? Why, or why not? Is the woodblock itself a work of art? Why, or why not? Point out that Japanese woodblock printing developed in response to the popularity of the Ukiyo-e style of art; they made more works available for more people. Ask: Is popularity an important aspect of art? Should art be popular? Why, or why not?

Using Art Criticism. Let students work in groups to discuss the Yamato-e painting shown in Figure 5-9. Have group members describe the work: How big is it? In what medium was it created? What people and objects do you see? What is happening? What art elements are used in the work? Then have the group members analyze the work: How have the principles of art been used to organize the elements in the work? Finally, have each student write a short interpretation of the work, answering this question: What is the meaning, mood, or feeling of this painting?

Lesson 3   *The Art of Japan*   📖   **73**

Background Information

Like other Japanese art forms, the Japanese tattoo has an established and symbolic tradition. Tattooing was a rite of passage for children and newlyweds among the Ainu, early inhabitants of Japan. Samurai warriors were tattooed to receive good fortune and protection from evil spirits. As in Japanese prints, the tattooed images of tigers, flowers, and gods relied on elemental themes to provide balance and meaning. Flames could have symbolized a mood, an energy, or a god in a particular tattoo.

Balance, style, and scale—images often covered an entire back or limb—have profoundly affected modern tattooing. In Japan, where tattoo art is now a mostly underground practice, a dragon or samurai image on one's back is as traditional as the anchor or "mom" tattooed on an American's forearm. The disreputable but fascinating tattoo art of Japan would eventually inspire western tattoo artists with its subject matter and scope in the 1970s.

Painting

In 784 Japan entered its golden age of art. During this period, which lasted some 400 years, countless new temples were built. The period also witnessed, around 898, the birth of a new painting style. Its name, **Yamato-e** (yah-**mah**-toh-ay), means *pictures in the Japanese manner*. Paintings done in this style were the first true examples of pure Japanese art.

Figure 5–9 shows a Yamato-e painting. The work is a scroll. What scene is shown in this painting? In what ways is the work different from a Chinese scroll painting? In what ways is it similar?

Another important form of painting was the decoration of screens. A **screen** is *a partition used as a wall to divide a room*. The use of screens made it easy to rearrange a house and use space efficiently. Most screens were painted with Chinese subjects.

Printmaking

The outbreak of civil war brought the golden age to an end in 1185. Japan remained in a state of political unrest for the next 430 years. The art of these stormy times focused both on the harsh realities of war and on escaping those realities. When peace came at last, another new style of art came with it. This style was called **Ukiyo-e** (oo-**kee**-yoh-ay), meaning *pictures of the floating world*. These pictures show different ways the Japanese enjoyed life.

The demand for art works in the new style was great. To meet this demand, artists turned to a new technique, **woodblock printing**. This is *making prints by carving images in blocks of wood*. The prints, or woodcuts, were made by a team of artists and craftspeople. Figure 5–10 shows a woodcut in the Ukiyo-e style. Notice the artist's use of strong lines and flat areas of color. Both were typical of such works. Equally typical was the balance shown here. What kind of balance has the artist of this print used?

▲ Figure 5–9   This scroll shows an important person of the day, an ambassador, on a journey. Which figure do you think is the ambassador? Explain your answer.

Unknown. Illustrated Handscroll of *Minister Kibi's Trip to China* (Kibi diajin nitto emaki). 12th Century. Ink and color on paper. 32.2 x 244.2 cm (12⅞ x 96⅛"). Museum of Fine Arts, Boston, Massachusetts. William Sturgis Bigelow Collection.

▲ **Figure 5–10** Can you find the figure's feet? Can you find the artist's signature?

Torii Kiyotada. *An Actor of the Ichikawa Clan.* Woodcut, hand colored. 28.6 x 15.2 cm (11¼ x 6"). The Metropolitan Museum of Art, New York, New York. Harris Brisbane Dick Fund.

◀ **Figure 5–11** What do you think the purpose of these headbands might have been? What is the purpose of headbands today?

Headbands for Nō costumes. Japanese. Edo Period. 1615–1867. Embroidered in silk on satin., 40 x 3.2 cm (15¾ x 1¾"). The Metropolitan Museum of Art, New York, New York. Gift of Mr. and Mrs. Teigi Ito.

STUDIO EXPERIENCE

The print in Figure 5–10 is of a Kabuki (kuh-**boo**-kee) actor. Kabuki is a form of popular Japanese theater. Notice the richly decorated costume. Another Japanese stage tradition with even more spectular costumes is the Nō (**noh**) drama. Figure 5–11 shows the type of headbands worn by a Nō actor. Notice the highly decorative pattern in the headband. Design a decorative pattern related to an important activity in your life. If, for example, you are in the school band, the pattern might be made up of musical notes. If you are in the math club, the pattern could be made up of mathematical symbols. Using school acrylic paint, transfer the pattern to a headband made of paper or cloth.

✔ CHECK YOUR UNDERSTANDING

1. What important event in the history of Japanese art happened in A.D. 552?
2. What is a pagoda?
3. When did the golden age of Japanese art begin? What painting style came into being during that period?
4. What is Ukiyo-e? What technique was most commonly used for Ukiyo-e art works?

Creating a Time Capsule

Objectives

After completing this lesson, students will be able to:
- Make clay models of a teen's room, including furniture and other details.
- Describe, analyze, interpret, and judge their own clay models.

Supplies

- Sheets of sketch paper, pencils.
- Pencils; notepads; sheets of sketch paper; guide sticks, each about 1/2 inch (13 mm) thick; newspaper; clay; rolling pins, needle tools; modeling tools; rulers; sheets of plastic; slip; scissors; scraps of fabric.

> **TRB Resource**
> - 5-9 *Woodblock Print,* (studio)

TEACHING THE LESSON

Getting Started

Motivator. Begin by posing these questions: What message does your room at home communicate to others? What does it say about you? What do you think the average American teenager's room says about American teenagers? Encourage students to share and discuss their ideas. Then have each student sketch a room that communicates who American teens are and what they are interested in. Let students work in small groups to compare and discuss their sketches.

Vocabulary. Review with students the definitions of *proportion* and *variety* as principles of art. Ask: How are proportion and variety used in works of art to help express moods or feelings? Why do artists use proportion and variety to organize visual elements? What kinds of messages can artists communicate by consciously not using one of these principles in a work of art?

Creating a Time Capsule

Look at the object in Figure 5–12. This clay sculpture of a horse is from the ancient culture of Japan. Studying objects like these, you have learned, teaches us about past civilizations.

Imagine that students of your school have been asked by community leaders to create clay objects. These are to be buried in a time capsule to tell future cultures about our own. Working in small groups, you will create a clay model of a teenager's room. You may use your own room at home or you may invent the room of your dreams. In the room you will include objects that represent the lifestyle of your group.

▲ **Figure 5–12** Would you describe this horse as realistic? Do you think the surface would feel rough or smooth to the touch? Does the work communicate any particular feeling?

Horse sculpture. Japanese. A.D. 200–500. Terra cotta. 59.7 x 66 cm (23½ x 26"). The Cleveland Museum of Art, Cleveland, Ohio. Gift of Mrs. Henry Norweb.

WHAT YOU WILL LEARN

You will make and join together clay slabs to create a teen's room. Your model will have a floor and three walls. Furniture and other details will be modeled from clay. In designing your room you must consider the elements of space, shape, form, and texture. Use the principles of proportion and variety to organize the elements. (See Figure 5–13.)

WHAT YOU WILL NEED

- Pencil, notepad, and sheets of sketch paper
- 2 guide sticks, each about 1/2 inch (13 mm) thick
- Newspaper
- Clay
- Rolling pin, needle tool, modeling tools, and ruler
- Sheet of plastic
- Slip (a mixture of water and clay used for joining clay pieces) and container of water
- Scissors and scrap of fabric

WHAT YOU WILL DO

1. On the notepad, list the furniture, objects, and details your room will have. Note also the different shapes, forms, and textures you will use. Make pencil sketches of the room and its contents.

Classroom Management Tip

You may wish to review with students the different forms of clay—plastic clay, slip, leather hard, and bisqueware. Explain that plastic clay is clay that is wet enough to be worked but dry enough to hold its shape. Slip is clay with enough water added to make it runny. Slip is used to glue together shaped pieces of damp clay. Leather hard clay is clay which is still damp but too hard to model. Pieces of leather hard clay can be joined with slip. Greenware is very dry clay that will break easily. Bisqueware is fired pottery that is hard but still not ready to use.

2. Set up the guide sticks 10 inches (25 cm) apart on the sheet of newspaper. Using the slab method, place the clay between these two guide sticks. Flatten the lump with the heel of your hand. Resting a rolling pin on the guide sticks, roll out the clay. This will help keep the thickness of the slab even. Using a ruler and knife or other sharp object, make four rectangles, each measuring 10 x 10 inches (25 x 25 cm). Cover the slabs loosely with the sheet of plastic. Leave them out overnight to firm up to the leather hard stage. This is the stage where clay is still damp but too hard to model.

3. The next day, score one of the slabs along three of its edges. This slab is to be the floor. Working a slab at a time, score each of the other slabs along its bottom. Use slip to join the walls to the floor. (For information on joining clay slabs and pieces, see Technique Tip **17**, *Handbook* page **281**.)

4. Model the furniture and other objects and details. Use proper joining methods for such tasks as adding legs to chairs. Using slip, attach the furniture and other objects to the floor.

5. When the clay is totally dry, fire the work. Complete your room by adding details — window coverings and a bedspread, for example — cut from the fabric.

6. Display your finished work. Look for similarities and differences between your work and that of other students.

EXAMINING YOUR WORK

- **Describe** Point to the floor and walls of your room. Describe the furniture and details you chose to include. Tell whether you followed the rules for making clay slabs and joining pieces.
- **Analyze** Show where you used the elements of space, shape, form, and texture. Explain how you used the principles of proportion and variety. Point out examples of each.
- **Interpret** Show what features in your work would help a viewer of the future understand this to be a teenager's room.
- **Judge** Tell whether you feel your work succeeds. Explain your answer.

▲ Figure 5–13 Student work. Model of teen's room.

OTHER STUDIO IDEAS

- Choose a room in your school. Some possibilities are the gym, the cafeteria, or the art room. Think about what furniture and other objects you find in that room. Make a clay model of the room.

- ● Make a clay model of a whole single-story building. You might base your work on an actual building in your town or city, or you might invent your own. Think about what furniture and other objects you would find in each of the rooms. Add these details to your work.

Lesson 4 *Creating a Time Capsule* **77**

BUILDING VOCABULARY

Number a sheet of paper from 1 to 9. After each number, write the term from the box that best matches each description below.

glaze	scroll
pagoda	Ukiyo-e
perceive	woodblock
porcelain	printing
screen	Yamato-e

1. A long roll of illustrated parchment or silk.
2. A fine-grained, high-quality form of pottery.
3. A glass-like finish on pottery.
4. Look deeply at a subject.
5. A tower several stories high with roofs curving slightly upward at the edges.
6. An art style which means "pictures in the Japanese manner."
7. An art style which means "pictures of the floating world."
8. Making prints by carving images in blocks of wood.
9. A partition used as a wall to divide a room.

REVIEWING ART FACTS

Number a sheet of paper from 10 to 15. Answer each question in a complete sentence.

10. With what dynasty is the "modern" period of Chinese civilization sometimes connected?
11. What was the goal of Chinese scroll painting?
12. During which dynasty did work in porcelain reach its highest point?
13. Who sent the Emperor of Japan a gift in 552? What was the gift?
14. What date is associated with the earliest Jomon examples of Japanese art?
15. What culture strongly influenced the design of the first Buddhist temples in Japan? Where did the architects who designed these temples come from?

THINKING ABOUT ART

On a sheet of paper, answer each question in a sentence or two.

1. **Interpret.** Review the three aesthetic views that you studied in Chapter 3 (see page **37**). Tell how art critics of the three different views would each react to the painting that opened the chapter (see page **66**).
2. **Analyze.** It has been said that no artist works in a vacuum. Name three events or happenings you read about in this chapter that support this statement. Explain your choices.
3. **Analyze.** Look at the scroll painting in Figure 5–3. Review the four stages of work in the art historian's job (see page **41**). Then describe the scroll painting.

MAKING ART CONNECTIONS

1. **Language Arts.** A type of Japanese poetry called haiku is influenced by meditation on subjects in nature. Look in the library for some examples of haiku. Find out the style and form of a haiku poem. Try to create some haiku of your own.
2. **Social Studies.** Look in the encyclopedia or history books to learn about the Great Wall of China. Find out when it was constructed and why. Prepare a short oral report for your class. Explain some of the features of the Great Wall, such as how and where it was constructed.

CHAPTER 5 REVIEW

LOOKING AT THE DETAILS

The detail shown below is from the Chinese painting *Evening In Spring Hills.* Study the detail and answer the following questions using complete sentences.

1. Do you think that the time period in which the artist lived influenced the subject matter of this work? Explain your answer.
2. How do you think Buddhism influenced this artist's choice of color?
3. In what way does negative space reveal something about the beliefs of this artist and his/her culture?
4. Look at the entire work on page 66. Notice how the proportion of the negative space compared to the objects in the painting provides balance. What type of balance is this called?

Unknown. Fan Mounted as an Album Leaf. *Evening in Spring Hills.* Southern Sung Dynasty. 1127–1278. Ink and color on silk. (Detail.) 24.8 x 26.1 cm (9¾ x 10¼"). The Metropolitan Museum of Art, New York, New York. Gift of John M. Crawford, Jr., in honor of Alfreda Murck.

Chapter 5 Review **79**

Art of Pre-Columbian America

Chapter Scan

TRB Resources

- 6-10 Chapter Test
- Color Transparency 11
- Color Transparency 12

TEACHING THE CHAPTER

Introducing the Art Work

Direct students' attention to the Zapotec funerary urn dating back to A.D. 500–700. Inform them that the Zapotecs were one of the oldest civilized peoples of Mexico whose culture sprang up in Monte Alban, Oaxaca. This culture assimilated cultural elements from the Olmecs. Monte Alban was the central place of worship consisting of temples, courts and pyramidal clusters which made up a great architectural complex built upon the flat top of a mountain, overlooking the valley of Oaxaca. Zapotec artists specialized entirely in funerary urns. The urns acted as guardians in front of the entrances to graves and stone sepulchral chambers, but they have also been found in temples without any association to burials. Still today, little is known about their social function and no recorded instance of anything has been found inside these urns. Since the ancient artists were the servants of religion, these urns probably represented some deity. They were sculpted human forms adorned with some form of headdress. In many cases the most important component was a variety of feathers in the headdress.

▲ The headdress on this figure stands for an ancient goddess. What kind of balance was used in creating this work?

Mexican (Zapotec) from Monte Alban. Funerary Urn. A.D. 500–700. Terra cotta with traces of polychrome. Nelson-Atkins Museum of Art, Kansas City, Missouri.

Art of Pre-Columbian America

Can you name an important event that took place in the year 1492? If you said this was the year Columbus discovered the New World, you were *almost* right. In 1492 Christopher Columbus did explore the lands in the western hemisphere. Long before Columbus's arrival, however, civilizations were developing in this part of the globe. Many tribes and peoples were already living there. All were part of a rich heritage or culture, and all created art, such as the work shown at the left. In this chapter you will learn about these peoples and their art.

OBJECTIVES

After completing this chapter, you will be able to:

- Name and describe four major Pre-Columbian cultures.
- Identify the contributions the various Pre-Columbian cultures made to the art world.
- Work in the art styles of early Mesoamerican peoples.

WORDS YOU WILL LEARN

adobe	genre pieces
artifacts	monolith
effigy	motif
funerary urn	stylized

Examining the Art Work

Explain to students that this urn is representative of other Zapotec urns—the male human figures wearing an elaborate headdress. Point out the faces within the headdress and explain that the feminine features of the faces suggest that this headdress represents the worship of a goddess.

Explain to students that the artist created rhythm in this work through the use of repeated patterns of feathers and other unusual shapes on the headdress.

Ask students to point out the symmetrical balance of the headdress combined with the asymmetrical balance of the figure.

Explain that the round, thick features of the figure's face are characteristic of the culture.

Discussing the Art Work

Ask students to identify the method of sculpting they think the artist used to create this figure. Point out how many of the shapes on the headdress, with the exception of the faces, have dimension but a flat surface. Explain that the Zapotecs used the assembling method. Zapotec potters controlled the water content of their clay with great precision to prevent warping during firing. Few other early American potters were as skilled in this area.

Ask students to describe the mood the work displays. Point out the strength of the main figure that is necessary in order to support a headdress of that size. Point out the serious facial features of the main figure, and the serene features of the faces in the headdress.

Tell students that in this chapter they will learn about four major Pre-Columbian cultures and their contributions to the art world. Students will also create works in the art styles of early Mesoamerica.

81

Building Self-Esteem

The studio lesson found on page **86** in this chapter teaches students to make a cylinder-shaped container. The decoration consists of a figure wearing symbols representing some special interest in the student's life. A repeated pattern is to be applied in the style an ancient Mexican culture used to decorate its artifacts. Help students focus on the meaning of the word *symbol*: an object used to represent something. Choosing a *personal* symbol means first identifying some special interest or skill. Ask students to think about one or two things they do well or would *like* to do well. Give them the option of choosing a personal goal and selecting a set of symbols representing that goal if they do not have a special area of interest at the present time. This container could then represent a goal and could serve as a personal inspiration to work toward that goal.

Art of Mesoamerica

LESSON 1

LESSON PLAN
(pages 82–85)

Objectives
After completing this lesson, students will be able to:
- Name and describe four Pre-Columbian cultures of Mesoamerica.
- Identify the contributions made by those four Pre-Columbian cultures to the art world.

Supplies
- Reproductions of various American art works; include two- and three-dimensional works from North, Central, and South America.
- Wall map of the Americas (if available).
- Pencils, sheets of drawing paper, colored markers, scissors.

TRB Resources
- 6-1 *Aztec School Calendar,* (cooperative learning)
- 6-2 *Aztec Calendar Details,* (reproducible master)
- 6-3 *The Aztec Gold Culture and Cortes* (art history)

TEACHING THE LESSON

Getting Started
Motivator. Introduce this lesson by displaying reproductions of art works from various parts of America, produced during various periods. Begin with a relatively familiar work by a painter from the United States (Winslow Homer, for example). Let students discuss what they see in the work and then ask: Is this an American work of art? Why, or why not? Use the same process to introduce works created in Central and/or South America within the past 150 years and then to introduce older works created by native peoples in North, Central, and/or South America. (It is not necessary to represent every area or all periods or styles; five or six different works of art should be sufficient.) Then help students generalize about what they have experienced: Where is America? What is an American work of art? When have American works of art been created?

Art of Mesoamerica

You can probably guess the meaning of the word *Pre-Columbian*. This term means "before Columbus." However, art historians use the term in a special way. They use it to refer to the art of early Mexico, Central America, and South America. Less is known about the cultures of these regions than about most others you have studied so far. This is because scientists have only recently begun to find and examine evidence of them.

In this lesson you will read about four major cultures of ancient Mexico and Central America. These are the Olmec, West Mexican, Mayan, and Aztec cultures.

OLMEC CULTURE

The Olmec (**ol**-mek) people lived on the Gulf of Mexico nearly 3000 years ago. Find the center of their civilization on the map in Figure 6–1. Olmec culture is often called the

▲ Figure 6–1 Mesoamerica.

"mother culture" of Mexico. This is because the **artifacts**, or *simple handmade tools or objects,* found in the region where the Olmecs lived are the most ancient. The artifacts left by the Olmecs had an influence on all the civilizations that were to follow.

Like other Pre-Columbian civilizations, the Olmecs were not a prehistoric race. They had a very important culture and a very accurate calendar. They also left behind a number of interesting works of art.

Sculpture

Among the most interesting of the Olmec creations are four huge human heads carved from rock. These were discovered at La Venta, a center for religious ceremonies. One of these sculptures is shown in Figure 6–2. Notice the childlike features on this giant face. The full lips, which seem almost to be pouting, are typical of the Olmec style.

WEST MEXICAN CULTURE

After the Olmecs, the next oldest civilization seems to have been that of West Mexico. The center of West Mexican culture was the city of Colima (koh-**leem**-uh). Find Colima on the map in Figure 6–1. For many years scientists ignored this region. Much of what we know of West Mexican culture was discovered when scientists studied the artifacts accidentally turned up by grave diggers.

Sculpture

Among the West Mexican art that has surfaced are many small clay sculptures of dogs. One of these is shown in Figure 6–3. Study the figure. Would you describe the work as realistic?

Background Information
Little is known about the Olmec culture that carved the series of gigantic heads resting in La Venta, Mexico. Standing taller than their sculptors, the heads possess surprisingly fleshy features. The soft contours of the huge eyes, noses, and mouths create an organic effect that is framed by the parallel lines of tight-fitting helmets on each sculpture. These framed organic shapes would characterize art of later cultures in the southern half of Mexico and northern Central America.

Ensuing Mesoamerican cultures would also share the religion-inspired treatment of humans and animals of the Olmecs. The Olmec pantheon included gods with human and animal elements. The widespread appearances of half-human, half-jaguar figures indicates that religion played a big role in the arts as well as other aspects of Olmec life. Because they flourished early, from about 800 B.C. to A.D. 600, and shared many practices with future cultures, the Olmecs are considered to be a "mother culture" to the area.

◀ Figure 6–2 Records show that this 40-ton (40,000-kg) stone head was moved 60 miles (96 km), through swampland. What does this tell you about the Olmecs?

Olmec Head. 1500–800 B.C. Basalt. La Venta Archeology Museum, Mexico.

At one time these sculptures were thought to be **genre** (**zhahn**-ruh) **pieces**. These are *art works that focus on a subject or scene from everyday life*. It is now known that ancient Mexicans viewed dogs as having special powers. Specifically, the animals were believed to serve the dead. A sculpture of this type is called an **effigy** (**eff**-uh-jee), *an image that stands for ideas or beliefs*.

MAYAN CULTURE

The first great Pre-Columbian civilization was that of the Mayas (**my**-uhs). By around A.D. 800 their empire covered the Yucatán (yoo-kuh-**tahn**) peninsula, modern Belize (buh-**leez**), Guatemala, and Honduras. Find these places on the map in Figure 6–1. The Mayas were gifted mathematicians. They had the most accurate calendar of any people in history. They were also great builders. The Mayas erected huge temples and cities with tools of wood, stone, and bone.

▲ Figure 6–3 This is a hollow clay form. The swollen lower body is typical of Colima figures.

Effigy Vessel. c. A.D. 250. Ceramic. Fowler Museum of Cultural History, UCLA, Los Angeles, California.

Understanding Art History.
Have students form six groups, and ask each group to learn more about one of these topics: the Mayan writing system, the Mayan calendar, the Mayan religion, the Aztec writing system, the Aztec calendar, the Aztec religion. Have the members of each group research their assigned topic; then have them discuss the effect that aspect of culture had on the culture's works of art. Ask each group to prepare and present a visual display summarizing what they have learned.

Developing Studio Skills.
Guide students in discussing the variety of gods and goddesses that were central to the religions of Pre-Columbian Mesoamericans. Then ask students to imagine the kinds of gods and goddesses people of a Pre-Columbian culture might create to deal with modern life in the United States. What aspects of life would each god or goddess be concerned with? How would each god or goddess look? What kinds of headress, jewelry, and animals would adorn each god or goddess?

Follow this class discussion by having each student draw an original god or goddess in the style of Pre-Columbian cultures. Have them draw the head and decorations in pencil; then have them outline the drawing with a black marker and use bright markers to color in the drawing. Ask students to write the name of the god or goddess beneath the drawing. Then have them cut out their drawings, including the names. Display all the images in a row on the walls of the classroom— just as the Pre-Columbian Mesoamericans used the images of their gods and goddesses to decorate their architecture.

▶ Figure 6–4 The project to dig up this ancient city is one of the biggest in history. Why do you think scientists spend so much time and effort digging up lost civilizations?

Mayan-Tikal Site. Jaguar Temple. c. A.D. 800. Peten, Guatemala.

Architecture

In the late 1800s scientists digging in northern Guatemala made an important discovery. They found traces of an ancient city. Today this Mayan city, Tikal (tih-**kahl**), is known to have covered an area of 50 square miles (130 sq km). That is roughly the size of Boston. The city is thought to have been home to some 55,000 people. Figure 6–4 shows a view of the site.

Mayan architects not only built outward but they also built upward. Look again at Figure 6–4. The pyramid in the foreground has a temple on top of it. It is typical of many temples built throughout the Mayan civilization. Two others have been discovered at Tikal alone. How many tops of them can you find above the trees in this picture? Amazing structures like these rose at times to heights of 175 feet (53 m). What kind of balance did Mayan architects use in designing these impressive temples?

Sculpture

Most of the Mayan sculpture that has lasted is relief carvings on buildings and monuments. In the early stages of the Mayan civilization, these carvings were mostly simple and realistic. In some later temples a more complex, geometric style came to be the rule. Study the relief sculpture in Figure 6–5. This is a staircase dating to around A.D. 755. Notice the symbols and writings that fill the background. These artists have not left any negative space.

▲ Figure 6–5 This relief carving is from a stairway that was 50 feet (15 m) wide and had 72 steps. Each step was 18 inches (45 cm) high. Since a collapse in 1800, only 32 of the stairs remain.

Mexico Chiapas. Mayan Palenque Glyphs. A.D. 600–900.

Background Information
Like modern Americans, the Mayas were very concerned about appearance. With the dual purposes of social status and spiritual discipline, they regularly practiced body modification. Children's heads were shaped by wooden molds in an attempt to nurture an ideal profile. Tattoos were popular for both men and women, and body paint was used to show status, reflect fashion, or repel insects. Ears, noses, and lips were pierced and ornamented, and ears were often stretched.

While the Mayan ideals of beauty may seem bizarre, it is important not to be condescending or judgmental. Modern liposuction, plastic surgery, hair transplants and figure enhancements are all comparable to Mayan practices. Modern men and women endure dangerous diets and strenuous exercises to become attractive. When considering that the Mayan practices had spiritual goals, the modern American notion of beauty might actually seem less sophisticated.

▲ **Figure 6–6** This sculpture and its base are decorated with a number of designs. Can you see any that look like flowers?

Xochipilli, Lord of the Flowers. Aztec. National Museum of Anthropology, Mexico City, Mexico.

▲ **Figure 6–7** The stone was more than a calendar. It told the story of the universe. It stated when the Aztec world began and predicted when it would end.

The Aztec Calendar Stone. c. 1500. Tenochtitlán National Museum of Anthropology, Mexico City, Mexico.

AZTEC CULTURE

The largest of the cultures of ancient Mexico and Central America was the Aztec. This civilization emerged sometime between A.D. 1200 and 1325. The Aztecs were a small, warlike tribe. Like other Pre-Columbian peoples, they were very religious. When their god told them to leave their comfortable homeland and settle where they saw an eagle perched on a cactus, they did. A swampy island, which they called Tenochtitlán (tay-noch-tee-**tlahn**), became the center of their great empire. By the time Spanish conquerors arrived in 1519, their island city covered over 25 square miles (66 sq km). Today we know the city, which is no longer on an island, as Mexico City. Find Mexico City on the map in Figure 6–1.

Sculpture

The Aztecs adopted many of the ways of making art used by the people they conquered. They carved huge ceremonial sculptures like the one shown in Figure 6–6. This sculpture is one of 1600 gods and goddesses in the Aztec religion.

One unusual piece of Aztec art is the calendar stone, shown in Figure 6–7. The work is so called because its rim is decorated with signs for the 20 days of the Aztec month. The stone measures 12 feet (3.6 m) in diameter and weighs over 24 tons (22,000 kg).

✔ CHECK YOUR UNDERSTANDING

1. Which culture is the mother culture of Mexico?
2. What is a genre piece? What is an effigy?
3. What was the first great Pre-Columbian civilization? What huge structures did the people of this civilization build?
4. What is the calendar stone? What Pre-Columbian civilization created the calendar stone?

Lesson 1 *Art of Mesoamerica* 📖 **85**

Making A Clay Urn

Objectives

After completing this lesson, students will be able to:

- Make cylinder-shaped clay containers that exhibit formal balance and repeating patterns.
- Describe, analyze, interpret, and judge their own clay containers.

Supplies

- Pencils; sheets of sketch paper; guide sticks, each about 1/2 inch (13 mm) thick.
- Newspaper; clay; rolling pins; rulers; needle tools.
- Paper towels; modeling tools; slip; containers of water; plastic bags; glaze or school acrylics (optional).

TRB Resource

- 6-4 *Mexican Primitive Sculptors,* (appreciating cultural diversity)

TEACHING THE LESSON

Getting Started

Motivator. Begin by letting students share and discuss their responses to these questions: Which of your interests and activities are most important to you? What shapes and objects symbolize your interests and activities? Encourage all students to participate. Then explain that students will use these ideas in creating their own art works.

Vocabulary. Have students use dictionaries or the Glossary at the back of the text to find the meaning of *motif.* Then help students discuss how the word is used in reference to musical and literary—as well as visual—works of art.

Developing Concepts

Exploring Aesthetics. Guide students in discussing the funerary urn shown on page **80**: What motif covers the urn? What visual elements can you identify in that motif? Which principles of art have been used to organize those elements? What feeling or idea does the work communicate to you?

Look again at the work that opened this chapter on page **80**. It is a **funerary (fyoo-nuh-rehr-ee) urn,** *a decorative vase or vessel found at burial sites.* Compare it with the clay vessel in Figure 6–8. The works were created by different Pre-Columbian cultures, but they have much in common. Both use formal balance and are covered with a repeated motif (moh-**teef**). A **motif** is *part of a design that is repeated over and over in a pattern or visual rhythm.* Finally, both works are rich with symbols that had special meaning for members of their cultures.

WHAT YOU WILL LEARN

You will make a cylinder-shaped container at least 6 inches (15 cm) high using the clay slab method. You will decorate your container with a figure wearing symbols that represent your life. You will use formal balance and repeating patterns in your work. The pattern will be in the style of an ancient Mexican culture. You may paint your figure using school acrylics, or you may glaze it. (See Figure 6–9.)

WHAT YOU WILL NEED

- Pencil and sheets of sketch paper
- 2 guide sticks, each about 1/2 inch (13 mm) thick
- Newspaper
- Clay
- Rolling pin, ruler, needle tool, paper towel, and modeling tools
- Slip (a mixture of water and clay used for joining clay pieces), and container of water
- Plastic bag
- *Optional:* Glaze or school acrylics

WHAT YOU WILL DO

1. Brainstorm with your classmates for ideas for personal symbols to be used to decorate your figure. For example, if you play football, the figure could be wearing a helmet. You could decorate the helmet with a pattern of footballs for a headdress. If your major interest is math, the headdress might be covered with numbers. The hands might hold pencils and a notebook to symbolize the student. Make pencil sketches of the figure and the different decorations you will use.

▲ **Figure 6–8 What relationship do you suppose existed between the figure of the clay vessel and what it was used for?**

Pottery jar with removable head. Teotihuacan, Mexico. American Museum of Natural History, New York, New York.

Background Information

Located on what is now the northwest coast of Italy, the Etruscans reigned from about 800 B.C. to about 400 B.C. Today, most of the knowledge about Etruria has been gathered from tombs. Buried beneath mounds of dirt or masonry, vaults held wall paintings and reliefs of scenes from Etruscan life. Paintings have included joyful occasions such as hunting, fishing, and comforting images, including pet dogs. In contrast to the formal Egyptian form or classic Greek technique, the Etruscan depictions are vigorous and lifelike.

The sculpture and pottery in Etruscan tombs are found in the forms of urns and sarcophagi. Etruscan artists characterize the deceased in sculpted limestone, bronze, or *terra cotta.* Whether the Etruscans' buried art was designed to comfort the dead or furnish them in the afterlife, it succeeds in capturing their life's essence.

2. Set up the guide sticks 6 inches (15 cm) apart on the sheet of newspaper. Using the slab method, make a rectangle, 6 x 12 inches (15 x 30 cm). Keep the unused clay damp by covering it with a lightly moistened towel. Score the short edges of your rectangle. Carefully bend your slab into a cylinder. Apply slip to the scored surfaces and press them together. Smooth both the inside and outside surfaces of the cylinder along the seams.

3. Using a portion of the remaining clay, roll out a slab measuring 10 inches square (65 sq cm). Stand the cylinder on top of the square. Using the needle tool, lightly trace around the cylinder. Score the surface of the circle you have created and the edges of the cylinder. Apply slip, and press the two surfaces together. Add a thin coil of clay inside your cylinder along the bottom. Press it gently into the seam to make the cylinder stronger. Cut off the excess clay from around the base of the cylinder.

4. Model the head, arms, legs, and headdress for your figure. Attach them using scoring and slip. With modeling tools add patterned markings to create rhythm to your work. Note that you may need to support the head and headdress as the work dries. Prop these in place using an object of the right height.

5. When your clay container is bone dry, fire it in a kiln.

6. *Optional*: Glaze or paint the fired container using acrylics.

7. Place the finished work on display. See if your friends can guess what the decorations on your work stand for.

EXAMINING YOUR WORK

- **Describe**   Show that your container is at least 6 inches (15 cm) high. Show that the parts are properly joined. Describe the figure and symbols you used to decorate your container. Identify the hues used to color your figure.
- **Analyze**   Describe the kind of balance you used. Identify the repeating rhythmic pattern in your work.
- **Interpret**   Identify the features of your work that are similar to those of the ancient Mexican culture you used as a model. Explain how the symbols represent your life.
- **Judge**   Tell whether you feel your work succeeds. Explain your answer.

▲ Figure 6–9   Student work. Clay urn.

OTHER STUDIO IDEAS

- Make a second container, this time using the medium of paper. (For information on making paper sculptures, see Technique Tip **21**, *Handbook* page **284**.)

●● Using construction paper or poster board, design and make a piece of jewelry in the style of the Mesoamerican cultures.

Lesson 2   *Making a Clay Urn*   **87**

Developing Studio Skills.
Let students explore a different method of working with clay to create small animal figures. Begin by helping them review the dog sculpture shown in Figure 6-3 (page **83**). Ask students to select other animals of which they might create sculptures in a similar style. Encourage students to discuss and sketch their ideas. Then demonstrate the pinch method of modeling clay: Roll clay into a ball, and use a thumb to start digging into the ball. Gradually pinch the clay to a thickness of about 1/4 inch (6.5 mm) in all sides. Then turn and shape the clay to create the head and body of an animal. After the demonstration, let students work on their own sculptures, discussing their responses and technical problems with one another.

Appreciating Cultural Diversity.
Ask volunteers to research and then share responses to the following questions: Which other cultures have used funerary urns? How did artists in those cultures create the urns? How did they decorate the urns?

Following Up

Closure. Let students work with partners to discuss their own clay containers, following the steps in "Examining Your Work." Then have students write short analyses of their partners' containers.

Evaluation. Review students' clay containers and read their analyses of their partners' containers.

Reteaching. Work with small groups of students to review the meaning of the term *motif*. Then help group members identify and discuss other examples of motifs. Encourage them to look around the classroom and at other art works reproduced in the text: What motifs do you see? How can you recognize them as motifs? How are they used?

Enrichment. Have each student write a story about explorers in the future who unearth the clay container he or she created.

Background Information
The Aztecs founded Tenochtitlan, which is now Mexico City, in about 1325 and established an empire spreading over central and southern Mexico. Inspired by a sacrificial religion, the Aztecs pursued an aggressive way of life, reflected in their art. Paintings and sculptures depict the Aztec gods and their sacrifices, showing hands, hearts, souls, snakes, and eagles. Unfortunately, most Aztec art was destroyed by the Spaniards who had conquered the empire by 1521.

One sculpture that remains is the Aztec Calendar Stone. Arranged around *Tonatiuh*, the sun god, the twelve foot diameter stone lists the days and months and indicates occasions for sacrifice or celebration. Because their religion states that the sun god had died to create man, the Aztecs believed that they had to repay the god in human blood. While the circular calendar stone was possibly used as a receptacle for human hearts sacrificed to Tonatiuh, the Aztecs never used the circle shape in wheel form as a tool or method of transportation.

Art of the Andes

LESSON PLAN
(pages 88–91)

Objectives
After completing this lesson, students will be able to:
• Name and describe four Pre-Columbian cultures of the Andes.
• Identify the contributions made by those four Pre-Columbian cultures to the art world.

Supplies
• Slides or display-sized photographs of Machu Picchu (if available); wall map of South America or of Peru (if available).
• Sheets of white drawing paper, colored pencils, pieces of sturdy cardboard (such as corrugated cardboard), tape, scissors, yarn in various colors.

> #### TRB Resources
> • 6-5 *Peruvian Cloth Factory*, (reproducible master)
> • 6-6 *The Inca Gold Culture*, (aesthetics/art criticism)
> • 6-7 *Latin American Artists*, (appreciating cultural diversity)

TEACHING THE LESSON

Getting Started

Motivator. Begin by displaying slides or photographs of Machu Picchu (if available) or by having students look at the photograph in the text, Figure 6-16. Let students share and discuss their ideas about these fascinating ruins. Then explain that Machu Picchu was built by members of another Pre-Columbian culture, farther south than the Mesoamericans. These were the Incas, who lived in and around the area that is now Peru. If a wall map is available, have volunteers point out Peru and the city Cuzco; Machu Picchu is about 50 miles (80 km) northwest of Cuzco. Tell students that, when the Spanish invaders conquered this area in the sixteenth century, they built over most Incan cities; however, Machu Picchu was not discovered by the Spaniards. In fact, the city remained hidden until 1911.

88

Art of the Andes

Taken together, the four major cultures of Mesoamerica spanned a period of several thousand years. While these civilizations were developing, parallel developments were taking place in the Andes (**an**-deez) Mountains of South America.

In this lesson you will read about the culture and art of the Chavín, Moche, Tiahuanaco, and Inca Tribes.

CHAVÍN CULTURE

The earliest of the Andes civilizations, the Chavín (chuh-**veen**), made their home in the highlands of present-day Peru. The discovery of artifacts places the beginning of Chavín civilization at around 1000 B.C. Their name is taken from their ceremonial center, Chavín de Huántar (**hwahn**-tahr). Today stone pyramids and stone sculpture can still be found at that site. Find this place on the map in Figure 6–10.

Crafts

Like other Andean cultures, the Chavín held the jaguar to be sacred. Images of the cat turn up in much of their art.

One area of art in which the Chavín were especially skilled was crafts. The clay jaguar pitcher in Figure 6–11 is an example of one of their works. Notice the unusual stirrup-shaped spout. This design feature, used by later Andean cultures, was typical of Chavín pottery.

▲ **Figure 6–11** This hollow vase is decorated with relief designs. Why do you think the Chavín developed the stirrup spout?

Peru. Stirrup-Spout Vessel, Feline. 700–500 B.C. Ceramic. 23.5 x 14.1 x 20.9 cm (9⅛ x 5⅝ x 8⅛"). The Metropolitan Museum of Art, New York, New York. Michael C. Rockefeller Memorial Collection.

▲ **Figure 6–10** Andean Cultures.

Moche People
Inca People
Tiahuanaco People

km 0 100 300 500 700
mi. 0 100 300 500

Background Information
Originally used as a ceiling decoration, the Raimondi Stone is now one of the best known art works of Chavín de Huántar, Peru, and portrays a stocky figure wearing a towering headdress and holding two staffs. This god displays typical Chavín conventions, integrating many animal aspects in his appearance. His feet are eagle talons and his hands have feline claws. Snakes emanate from his staff, headdress, and waist. The Chavín artists demonstrate an impressive level of detail and great imagination with this intricate stone monolith. When the stone is seen upside-down, the headdress is revealed to be a series of serpents, while the once scowling countenance grins as if the viewer has been let in on a secret. The snake heads emerge from one another's jaws, and additional serpents loom from within the staffs. The dual nature of the Raimondi Stone indicates not only the cleverness of Chavín artists, but the complexity of their religion as well.

▲ Figure 6–12   The figure is the size of a thumb. It wears a movable nosepiece and carries a movable war club.

Earring. National Geographic Society, Washington, D.C.

Another way in which this object is typical is in the stylized look of its subject. **Stylized** means *simplified or exaggerated to fit a specific set of rules of design*. Did you notice the circles on the head and body? These were meant to stand for the jaguar's spots.

MOCHE CULTURE

West Mexican culture developed roughly between A.D. 100 and 700. Approximately these same years, interestingly, mark the rise and fall of Moche (**moh**-chay) culture. The Mochica (moh-**cheek**-uh), as these people were called, lived on the northern coast of what is now Peru. Find this area on the map in Figure 6–10.

The Mochica were farmers who irrigated the strips of desert between the Andes and the Pacific Coast. They grew corn, beans, squash, and peanuts. They built great pyramids and platforms with **adobe** (uh-**doh**-bee), or *sun-dried clay*. Here they buried their nobles.

▲ Figure 6–13   This stirrup-spout vessel represents a deer. It shows two figures having a conversation. One has the head of a frog.

Peru, Moche. Stirrup-Spout Vessel in the Form of a Seated Deer. A.D. 200–500. Ceramic. 27.9 cm (11″). The Metropolitan Museum of Art, New York, New York. Gift of Nathan Cummings.

Crafts

The Mochica buried fine works of gold and pottery with their dead. One of these, a gold and turquoise earring, is shown in Figure 6–12. The object was found in 1987 in a tomb near Sipan (see-**pahn**), Peru. The tomb is one of few untouched by thieves that scientists have located. In it, they discovered the remains of a warrior-priest, several servants, and a dog. Did you notice the headdress and necklace worn by the human figure on the earring? One of the skeletons in the tomb was dressed in much the same way.

In the design of their pottery, the Mochica borrowed from the Chavín. A Mochica stirrup-spout pitcher is shown in Figure 6–13. Compare this object with the jaguar pitcher in Figure 6–11. Which spout do you find more graceful? Which of the two ways of showing figures do you find the more stylized?

Vocabulary. Help students consider the vocabulary words presented in this lesson. Begin by asking about the word *stylized*: From what shorter English word is *stylized* formed? How does the word *style* help you understand the word *stylized*? Then ask volunteers to look up *adobe* in a dictionary. Ask: From what language does the word *adobe* come? Why do you think we use a Spanish word for this kind of building material? Finally, ask students about *monolith*: What prefix do you recognize at the beginning of this word? In what other words is the same prefix used? What does the prefix mean? How can understanding this prefix help you understand the word *monolith*?

Developing Concepts

Exploring Aesthetics. Have students compare the Chavín stirrup-spout pitcher shown in Figure 6-11 and the Moche stirrup-spout pitcher shown in Figure 6-13. How are the two works similar—and different—in subject? How is the use of visual elements similar in the two works? How is it different? Which principles of art are used to organize the elements in each work? Do the two works communicate the same idea or feeling to you? If so, what is that idea or feeling? If not, how are the messages of the two works different?

Using Art Criticism. Guide students in discussing the two examples of weaving: Figure 6-15 from the Tiahuanaco culture and Figure 6-17 from the Incan culture. Ask: What do you see in each work? How are the principles of art used to organize the elements in each weaving? What mood, idea, or feeling does each suggest to you? What function is each work intended to serve? How successfully do you believe each work serves that function? Then ask students to compare these two Andean vessels with the Mesoamerican vessel in Figure 6-3: How are the works alike? What are the most important differences?

Background Information

While funerary urns were often created for the dead in Pre-Columbian Mexico, vessels were also made for everyday use. Between 200 B.C. and 600 A.D., the Moche culture developed in northern Peru where they fashioned their famous portrait jars. The *Mochica* potters created a staggering amount of vessels without the use of the potter's wheel and molded heads with a variety of expressions. Slender stirrup-shaped spouts allowed them to transport the often multi-chambered pots easily.

The heads themselves were sculpted quite remarkably. Possessing natural contours and expressions that range from intense, military gazes to spirited, laughing grins, the vessels were lavishly decorated with paints. Some of the most interesting caricatures display exaggerated features creating a comical effect. The spouts rose from military helmets, religious ornament, or other headgear. Later heads were adorned with designs on the ceramic surfaces.

TIAHUANACO CULTURE

The Tiahuanaco (tee-uh-wahn-**ahk**-oh) civilization developed around the time the Mayas were coming to power. The Tiahuanaco made their home in the Andes highlands of modern Bolivia, just below Lake Titicaca (tee-tee-**kahk**-uh). Find Lake Titicaca on the map in Figure 6–10.

Architecture

Like the Mayas, the Tiahuanaco were master builders. They built a great ceremonial center using stones of the region. The crowning jewel of this center was a stone gateway rich with relief carvings. The impressive work was a **monolith**, *a structure created from a single stone slab.* A detail of the gateway is shown in Figure 6–14. The large figure at the upper right is a winged god. Who do you imagine the smaller figures in the left half of the work are? What do you think they are doing?

Crafts

The unusually dry climate of the Andes highlands has helped preserve another side of Tiahuanaco art. That is the civilization's work in weaving. Figure 6–15 shows a detail from a shirt of the culture. Notice how many colors the weaver used. Would you describe the shapes in this design as organic or geometric?

▲ Figure 6–14   What kind of design has the artist used in this pattern — geometric or organic?

Tiahuanaco. Gate of Sun Creator-God Virachocha. (Detail.) Pre-Colombian. A.D. 600. Aymara Culture. Bolivia.

INCAN CULTURE

About 1450 the Incas conquered the other Andean tribes. The Incan empire stretched more than 2500 miles (4023 km) from north to south. It included present-day Peru plus parts of Ecuador, Chile, Argentina, and Bolivia. Find these countries on the map in Figure 6–10. Each tribe the Incas conquered was forced to learn their language, Quechuan (**kech**-wahn). Today 6 million people speak this language.

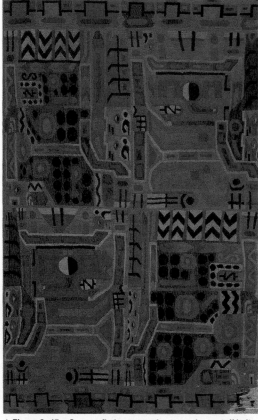

▲ Figure 6–15   Can you find a crowned cat carrying a staff in its paw? Notice how the details change slightly in each creature.

Peru, Coastal Huari-Tiahuanaco. Shirt Section. A.D. 600–1000. Wool, cotton. 53.5 cm (21"). The Metropolitan Museum of Art, New York, New York. Michael C. Rockefeller Memorial Collection.

Background Information
Welcoming people to commercial or religious centers, portrayals of gods were often carved above Tiahuanaco gateways in a combination of art and architecture. Artists could convey the relative importance of the depicted gods by scaling them appropriately, making the lesser deities shallower, centering or raising the placement of the important figures, or assigning numbers of attending characters. The Tiahuanaco sculptors prevent potentially cluttered scenes by composing the figures geometrically or arranging them around a greater god. The successful blending of aesthetics and religion is noteworthy.

Tiahuanaco tapestries also deserve recognition for their colorful appearance and delicate style. The Tiahuanaco artists used motifs on their monolith gateways and other carved art. Like the engravings, the textiles first seem complex and disjointed, but closer inspection reveals a focus on one central figure. It is simply repeated. These tapestries show that Pre-Columbian artists created art in every media.

▲ Figure 6–16   This town was built quickly. Yet it stood up to all invaders. What does this reveal about the skill of its builders?

Machu-Picchu, Peru.

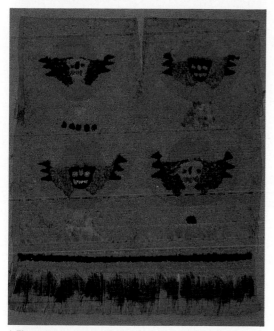

▲ Figure 6–17   Some of the feathers in this work are from tropical birds that lived far from the Incan capital of Cuzco. Some experts believe that this demonstrates that the Inca may have carried on trade with other civilizations.

Peru, South Coast. Pre-Inca period. A.D. 800–1300. Tunic. Feathers on canvas. 75.9 x 59.1 cm (29⅞ x 23¼"). The Metropolitan Museum of Art, New York, New York. Fletcher Fund.

The Incas never developed a true writing system. They did, however, develop a method for counting called quipu (**kee**-poo). In quipu, knotted strings were used to stand for numbers. These knots were also used as memory aids in reciting Incan history. The Incas' abilities with numbers is reflected in their art. Incan artifacts were made with great mathematical precision.

Architecture

The Incas were masters of shaping and fitting stone. They were also highly skilled urban planners. Proof of both talents can be found in the walled city of Machu Picchu (**mahch**-oo **peek**-choo). Figure 6–16 provides a view of this ancient city. Built on a mountainside to discourage would-be attackers, the city has withstood five centuries of earthquakes. The stones of its buildings were so carefully matched a knife blade cannot be slipped between any two.

Crafts

Like the Tiahuanaco, the Incas were also gifted weavers. Figure 6–17 shows a woven panel covered with feathers. The colors in the work are the natural ones found in the feathers. Why do you think the Incas chose feathers to decorate their works?

✔CHECK YOUR UNDERSTANDING

1. Which Andean tribe was the earliest? When did it come into being?
2. What is the meaning of *stylized*? What art works did you study in this lesson that were stylized?
3. For what types of art work are the Tiahuanaco best known?
4. The Incas were masters of what type of skills?

Appreciating Cultural Diversity.   Many different cultural groups are known for their skillful weaving. Among these groups are ancient Egyptians, Persians, and Native Americans. Have volunteers work in pairs or small groups to read about and, if possible, find photographs of the works created by the weavers of each culture. Then ask the volunteers to discuss their research with the rest of the class.

Following Up

Closure.   Guide the class in discussing the four Pre-Columbian cultures of the Andes and the art works they created. How are the art works of these cultures alike? What is unique about the art created by each culture? How are the art works of the Andean cultures similar to—and different from—those created by the Mesoamerican cultures? Encourage all students to contribute to this discussion; help students use specific examples to support the ideas they express.

Evaluation.   1. Review students' written responses to the "Check Your Understanding" questions. 2. Consider their contributions to the "Closure" discussion.

Reteaching.   Work with small groups of students to review the four Pre-Columbian cultures of the Andes. Ask each group member to imagine herself or himself as a member of one of these groups and to describe what life would be like. Remind students to refer to the text and the reproductions of art works to develop and add detail to their descriptions.

Enrichment.   Ask students to imagine themselves as the archaeologists who first found and explored the hidden city of Machu Picchu. To stimulate their thinking, ask questions such as these: Why were you exploring that area? What had you expected to find? How did you feel when you first saw the ruins of Machu Picchu? What did you imagine about the lives of the people who had built and lived in the city? Then ask students to write journal entries recording the events and their reactions on the day of the discovery.

Answers to "Check Your Understanding"

1. The Chavín was the earliest Andean civilization. It came into being about 1000 B.C.
2. Stylized means simplified or exaggerated to fit a specific set of rules of design. The Chavín clay jaguar pitcher and the Mochica stirrup-spout pitcher were decorated with stylized art.
3. The Tiahuanaco were master builders and constructed a great ceremonial center featuring a monolith stone gateway. They were also weavers.
4. The Incas were masters of shaping and fitting stone. The stones of buildings in the walled city of Machu Picchu were so carefully matched that a knife blade could not be slipped between any two. The Incas also developed a method for counting, called *quipu*.

Making a Stylized Motif

Making a Stylized Motif

LESSON PLAN
(pages 92–93)

Objectives
After completing this lesson, students will be able to:
- Create stylized motifs that could be used in designs for fabric or wallpaper.
- Describe, analyze, interpret, and judge their own motif designs.

Supplies
- Pencils; sheets of sketch paper; sheets of white paper, 6 x 9 inches (15 x 23 cm); sheets of construction paper in assorted colors, 12 x 18 inches (30 x 46 cm); rulers; scissors; white glue.
- Long sheets of butcher paper, pencils, tempera paints, brushes.

> ### TRB Resources
> - 6-8 *Figure Wall Hanging,* (studio)
> - 6-9 *Frida Kahlo,* (artist profile)

TEACHING THE LESSON

Getting Started
Motivator. Refer students to the student art works in Figure 6-19 and 6-20. Ask them to identify the motifs that are used in the works and discuss how the art works were created.

Vocabulary. Review with students the meanings of the terms *motif* and *stylize.* Then help them discuss the process of stylizing a figure: Do you make the figure look as much like nature as possible, or do you change it to look less natural? What kinds of line changes can be used to help stylize a figure?

Developing Concepts
Exploring Aesthetics. Have students discuss and compare the Incan stylized motif in Figure 6-18 and the student's stylized motif in Figure 6-19: How are they similar? What are the most important differences? What feeling or idea does each communicate to you?

Animals, as you have seen, play an important role in Pre-Columbian art. Look at Figure 6–18. The artist has used a stylized pairing of a man and animal as a motif. Notice how the man in the motif is holding a torch. Notice also how the motif is repeated through the use of shapes and colors.

WHAT YOU WILL LEARN
You will pick two related objects that are important in modern life. You will stylize and combine these into a motif that could be used in a design for fabric or wallpaper. Pick colors that add harmony to your design and carry over shapes from one object to the other to create a feeling of unity in your design. (See Figure 6–19.)

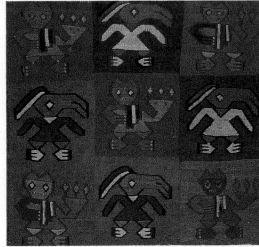

 Figure 6–18 Motifs may be simple or complex. Which word would you use to describe the motif in this shirt? Can you find motifs in any of the items of clothing you are wearing right now?

Peru. Textile fragments. Late Chimu. c. A.D. 1000. Cotton, wool. The Metropolitan Museum of Art, New York, New York. Gift of Henry G. Marquand.

WHAT YOU WILL NEED
- Pencil and sketch paper
- Sheet of white paper, 6 x 9 inches (15 x 23 cm)
- Sheets of construction paper in assorted colors, 12 x 18 inches (30 x 46 cm)
- Ruler, scissors, and white glue

WHAT YOU WILL DO
1. Brainstorm with members of your class to identify objects associated with late twentieth-century living. Some possibilities are cars, telephones, computers, and radios. Pick one object that holds particular importance for you. Then think of a second object that in some way is related to it. A car, for example, might be paired with a gasoline pump; a telephone might be paired with a teenager.
2. Make rough pencil sketches for a motif that combines the objects you picked. Connect the two in some manner. The curly wire of a telephone, for instance, could become the hair of a teenager. Draw one of the objects larger than the other. If possible, simplify some of the larger shapes or forms to geometric ones. Carry one or more shapes from one object over to the other. (Notice how the diamond shapes appearing as eyes on the animal in Figure 6–18 also appear on the man.) This will help lend a feeling of unity to your design.
3. Pick your best motif. Transfer it to the sheet of white paper. Draw the design large enough to fill most of the paper. Cut it out. This is your motif pattern.
4. Pick hues of construction paper that suit the mood of your design. Use one of these colors to serve as a background for

---

Background Information
While animals are attractive artistic subjects, the Mayas primarily treated animals as equals and not just as patterns. Mayas avoided offending or mistreating other creatures because, like humans, animals maintained varying relationships with magic. Any specific animal could be a disguised sorcerer or a powerful deity. Mayans gave extra respect to dogs, which they kept as pets.

The serpent was especially significant according to Mayan beliefs. As a magical creature, the dragon provided shamans with the ability to perceive and interpret revelations during religious ceremonies. Snakes were common in the depictions of a ruler, where they symbolized a governor's rightfulness, and a feathered and bearded serpent represented the Mayan god *Kikulcan* (*Quetzalcoatl* to other Pre-Columbian cultures).

your work. Using the ruler and working lightly in pencil, divide a sheet in this color into four equal boxes.

5. Trace your motif pattern onto your remaining sheets of construction paper. You will need four copies in all. You may use the same color for each motif or use a different color for each. (See Figure 6–20.) Using scissors, carefully cut out the motifs you have drawn.

6. Experiment with arranging your motifs in the four boxes on your background sheet. Try turning two of the motifs upside down. When you have found an arrangement that satisfies you, glue the motifs in place.

7. Use leftover scraps of construction paper to make designs for your motif. Whatever designs you add to one must appear on all others.

8. Place your work on display. Can you identify the stylized objects in your classmates' works?

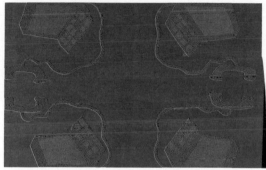

▲ Figure 6–19   Student work. Stylized motif.

EXAMINING YOUR WORK

- **Describe**   Tell what objects you chose for your motif. Tell how you connected them. State whether you stylized your objects. Identify the hues you selected.
- **Analyze**   Tell how the colors you picked add harmony to your design. Point out the shape or shapes you carried from one object to the other to create unity.
- **Interpret**   Name one or more ways in which your design might be used. Tell whether your design is similar in style to the one in Figure 6–18.
- **Judge**   Tell whether you feel your motif succeeds. Explain why you feel it does or does not.

▲ Figure 6–20   Student work. Stylized motif.

OTHER STUDIO IDEAS

- Create another motif that might be used as your personal letterhead. The motif should sum up who you are. Avoid using initials or other letters.

- ●● Use the same motif and use tempera to paint it.

Lesson 4   *Making a Stylized Motif*   **93**

Developing Studio Skills. Let students work in groups to plan and paint murals with stylized motifs that make statements or suggestions about the school. Have group members begin by selecting two related objects that are important to the school and its students. Then have them draw and make a pattern for a stylized motif based on their objects. Using their pattern, have group members draw and then paint the motif on their sheet of butcher paper. Display these murals in the school halls or other open areas.

Appreciating Cultural Diversity. Stylized motifs were important in the art works of the Pre-Columbian cultures. Ask students to consider how similar motifs are used in our modern culture. Have each student bring in at least one example of the uses of stylized motifs; suggest that advertising, packaging, and fabrics might be good sources.

Following Up

Closure. Let students work in groups to compare and discuss their stylized motifs. What similarities can they identify? What makes each design unique? Then let students post their designs on classroom bulletin boards, explaining as they do so what they like best about their own work.

Evaluation. Review students' motif designs. Also consider their contributions to the group discussions and their evaluations of their own work.

Reteaching. Work with small groups of students. Guide group members in experimenting with different motif possibilities using geometric shapes cut from construction paper. How does using different shapes affect the mood of the design? How can you change the mood by changing the color of some—or all—of the motifs?

Enrichment. Have students research a facet of the Pre-Columbian culture and present their findings to the class.

Background Information

While the ancient cultures in West Mexico did not demonstrate the trademark architectural achievements or stone sculpting skills of the Aztecs, Mayas, or Incas, they still established a unique and noteworthy artistic culture. Unscavenged Nayarit, Jalisco, and Colima tombs yield tools, clothes, weapons, mirrors, and, most importantly, ceramics. The buried pottery of West Mexico affords a glimpse at the area's past and provides examples of excellent ancient artistry.

In contrast to the Mesoamerican tradition of sculpting gods and other polymorphic beings, the artists of West Mexico present humans and animals in typical circumstances. The stylized plump figures hug, sing, and play instruments. Animals are not combined with humans to create deities, but are shown in their natural but pudgy states. Similarly, the sculptors cleverly utilize human and animal anatomy to create artistic and functional containers.

BUILDING VOCABULARY

Number a sheet of paper from 1 to 8. After each number, write the term from the box that best matches each description below.

adobe	genre pieces
artifacts	monolith
effigy	motif
funerary urn	stylized

1. Simple handmade tools or objects.
2. Art works that focus on a subject or scene from everyday life.
3. An image that stands for ideas or beliefs.
4. A decorative vase or vessel found at burial sites.
5. Simplified or exaggerated to fit a specific set of rules of design.
6. Sun-dried clay.
7. A structure created from a single stone slab.
8. Part of a design that is repeated over and over in a pattern or visual rhythm.

REVIEWING ART FACTS

Number a sheet of paper from 9 to 17. Answer each question in a complete sentence.

9. What does the term *Pre-Columbian* mean? How do art historians use the term?
10. What is an artifact?
11. Why is the Olmec culture often called the "mother culture" of Mexico?
12. What city was the center of West Mexican culture?
13. What ancient city did scientists discover in northern Guatemala in the late 1800s? To what culture did this city belong?
14. What was the largest civilization of ancient Mexico and Central America?
15. What animal did the Chavín hold to be sacred?
16. What design feature did the Chavín create in their works that was later used by other cultures?
17. Why was Machu Picchu built on a mountainside? What evidence can be used to support the claim that the builders were talented architects?

THINKING ABOUT ART

On a sheet of paper, answer each question in a sentence or two.

1. **Summarize.** Tell how developments taking place throughout Pre-Columbian America were expressed through the art of the following time periods: 1000 B.C. to A.D. 100; A.D. 300 to 1000; A.D. 1000 to 1500.
2. **Compare and contrast.** Which of the two cultures of Mesoamerica that you read about were most alike? Which were the least alike? Support your answers with information from the chapter.
3. **Compare and contrast.** Review what you learned about the great Egyptian pyramids in Chapter 4. Which of the Pre-Columbian cultures built pyramids for the same reason? Which built pyramids for other reasons?

MAKING ART CONNECTIONS

1. **Language Arts.** Imagine you are touring the parts of present-day South America you studied in this chapter. Write a letter to a friend back home expressing your reactions to the art of ancient peoples of the region. Use the descriptions and pictures from this chapter as a starting point.
2. **Social Studies.** Research interesting facts and traditions of the Incan or Aztec cultures. Report your findings to the class.

LOOKING AT THE DETAILS

The detail below is of a Mexican funerary urn. Study the detail and answer the following questions using complete sentences.

1. Describe how the elements of line and texture are used in this sculptural piece.
2. What type of balance occurs in this detail? Compare the detail to the chapter opening on page 80. What type of balance would you use to describe the entire sculptural piece?
3. Identify a pattern that is repeated in the headdress.
4. What sculpting methods do you think were used in creating this work?

Mexican (Zapotec) from Monte Alban. Funerary Urn. A.D. 500–700. Terra cotta with traces of polychrome. (Detail.) Nelson-Atkins Museum of Art, Kansas City, Missouri.

ANSWERS TO "LOOKING AT THE DETAILS"

1. The sculptural piece is made up of mostly curved flowing lines. Texture is created by the use of the hard rough surface of the medium and the relief of the shapes.
2. Symmetrical balance occurs in this detail. When students describe the balance of the entire sculptural piece, they will identify it as symmetrical balance. (You may wish to explain that it is approximate symmetry.)
3. Students may identify the figure's heads in the headdress that are repeated or the repetition of lines and shapes.
4. A subtractive method of sculpting was used in this work.

Chapter Evaluation

The purpose of this chapter is to introduce students to four major Pre-Columbian cultures and to identify the artistic contributions of the various cultures. Some possible evaluation techniques include:

1. Ask students to compare and contrast the culture and art of Pre-Columbian civilization to Egyptian civilization.

2. Divide the students in groups of three or four. Have each group identify as many motifs as they can find in the classroom. Give a prize to the group who identifies the most.
3. Have students complete Chapter 6 Test (TRB, Resource 6-10).

95

Art of Greece and Rome

Chapter Scan

TRB Resources
- 7-11 Chapter Test
- Color Transparency 13
- Color Transparency 14

TEACHING THE CHAPTER

Introducing the Art Work

Direct students' attention to the photograph of the Parthenon, Temple of Athena. Inform them that the Parthenon is a temple built on the Acropolis in Athens, Greece. The Acropolis, which means "high city" in Greek, consists of seven buildings overlooking the city of Athens. The Parthenon is the largest structure built in 447 B.C. on the highest point of the Acropolis. The principal architect was Iktinos who supervised the nine-year construction process. The entire structure was built of Pentelic marble, and in its time the Parthenon contained many magnificent statues, friezes, and ornamentation. The building shone with color. Over the centuries, the interior of the Parthenon had been repeatedly remodeled, but the exterior remained intact with all its sculptures in place until 1687. At that time, the Turks used it as a powder magazine and during their war with the Venetians, a mortar shell struck the building, blowing out its center. The Parthenon is considered the supreme monument of Greek architecture.

▲ This temple was once used as a Christian church and then as a mosque. Later it was used to store ammunition. It was partly destroyed when an artillery shell exploded in its center.

The Parthenon. Temple of Athena. 5th Century B.C. Acropolis, Athens, Greece.

Art of Greece and Rome

Look up Greece in an almanac, and you will learn it has a population of about 10 million. Look up Rome, and the information will be similar.

Facts like these, while useful, do not begin to tell the story. They tell nothing of the mighty powers that Greece and Rome once were. They tell nothing of their contributions to art. One of these contributions is shown at the left. Do you know its name?

In this chapter you will learn about Greece and Rome and study some of the art works created by ancient artists.

OBJECTIVES

After completing this chapter, you will be able to:
* Identify the contributions of the ancient Greeks and Romans to the history of art.
* Name some important works by ancient Greek and Roman artists.
* Paint in the style of Greek and Roman artists.
* Model in the architectural style of ancient Greece and Rome.

WORDS YOU WILL LEARN

amphora	frieze
aqueduct	round arch
concrete	triumphal arch

ARTISTS YOU WILL MEET

Myron	Phidias

Examining the Art Work

Tell students that the Parthenon is perfectly proportioned. Explain that it displays symmetrical balance by equidistant spacing of the same number of columns on each of the opposing sides of the building.

Explain to students how the vertical columns and the negative space between the columns create rhythm. Point out how the vertical lines in the columns and the vertical line patterns contribute to a sense of rhythm.

Point out the Doric structure of the building and explain how the architect used the columns for structural as well as artistic purposes.

Discussing the Art Work

Ask students what kind of mood they sense in this structure. Point out the sense of unity and harmony which gives a graceful appearance. Suggest that the placement of the building on the highest point on the Acropolis along with its tall, imposing vertical columns gives the viewer the impression of strength and grandeur. Ask students to think about what the solid marble structure might feel like. Suggest that the weight and coolness of the solid marble gives the viewer a sense of the monumental.

Explain that the columns and other reliefs were all hand carved with extreme precision. Ask the students to think about the strength of the commitment these people had to their city and its goddess Athena.

Tell students that in this chapter they will learn about important art works and contributions of the ancient Greeks and Romans to the history of art. They will also create their own paintings and architectural models in the style of ancient Greece and Rome.

Building Self-Esteem

The first Olympic Games were held in Greece on the Olympia plain around 776 B.C. They lasted five days and were held every four years. The prize given to winners was a garland of wild olives, but as in today's Olympic games, victorious athletes earned great honor and esteem. The games deteriorated when Rome succeeded Greece as a military power and were finally banned by decree of Roman Emperor Theodosius in A.D. 394, after having been celebrated for over one thousand years.

Mention that many Greek sculptors depicted athletes and athletic events. In *The Discus Thrower,* shown on page **100,** the sculptor Myron suggests motion by showing the instant of pause between two actions. The figures shown in Greek sculpture of this kind captured the ideal human figure and the intense concentration it takes to excel. It wasn't until 1896 that the Olympic games were revived, once again giving athletes a chance to compete. As in ancient Greece, one of the awards earned for giving their personal best is great honor and esteem.

LESSON 1

Art of Ancient Greece

LESSON PLAN
(pages 98–101)

Objectives
After completing this lesson, students will be able to:
- Identify the contributions of the ancient Greeks to the history of art.
- Name some important works by ancient Greek artists.
- Make symmetrical cutouts of the shapes of Greek vases.

Supplies
- Pencils, colored pencils, sheets of drawing paper.
- Large sheets of white paper, pencils, scissors.
- Square sheets of construction paper, pencils, rulers, colored markers.

TRB Resources
- 7-1 *Time Line,* (reproducible master)
- 7-2 *Capital Cartoon,* (reproducible master)
- 7-3 *Greek Capitals,* (art history)
- 7-4 *The Three Periods of Greek Art,* (art history)
- 7-5 *The Elgin Marbles,* (art criticism)
- 7-6 *Phidias,* (artist profile)

TEACHING THE LESSON

Getting Started

Motivator. Explain to students that they will be studying the art work of the ancient Greeks and that one of the most familiar forms of ancient Greek art is sculpture. Ask students to think about these questions: What do you already know about Greek sculpture? What subjects do many Greek sculptures show? How are those subjects depicted? How do you think the art elements of color, line, form, shape, space, and texture were used in ancient Greek sculpture? Let students discuss their ideas with partners; then have the partners work together (using pencils and/or colored pencils) to draw their ideas about ancient Greek sculpture. Finally, have all the students share and compare their drawings.

Why study events that happened over 3000 years ago in a country the size of Arizona? Why bother learning the names of artists whose works no longer exist? The reason in both cases is that the country — Greece — was the birthplace of Western civilization. The influences of ancient Greek culture and art can still be felt and seen today.

In this lesson you will learn about that culture and art.

THE BEGINNING OF GREEK CULTURE

The story of ancient Greece begins around 1500 B.C. It was around this time that different groups from the north settled in the region bordering the Aegean (ih-**jee**-uhn) Sea. Find the Aegean on the map in Figure 7–1.

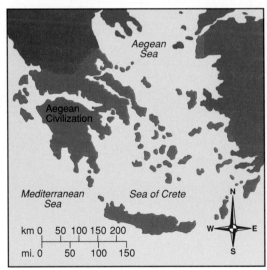

▲ **Figure 7–1   Aegean Civilization.**

Greece never became a nation. Instead, the tribes that formed it remained small, separately ruled powers called city-states.

Part of the reason for this was geography. High, rocky mountains and miles of sea divided the different city-states. Two other, and more important, factors were self-pride and jealousy. It was loyalty to their own and distrust of others that prevented the city-states from banding together to form a nation.

One of the largest and most powerful of the city-states was Athens. Athens was also the most important in the history of art.

Architecture

The artists of Greece valued above all else grace, harmony, and precision. These qualities are present in the work that opened this chapter on page **96**. This famous building is the Parthenon. The Parthenon was a temple built in honor of the Greek goddess Athena (uh-**thee**-nuh). It stood along with other temples on a sacred hill known as the Acropolis (uh-**krop**-uh-luhs). (See Figure 7–2.) The word *acropolis* means "high city."

The Parthenon is thought to be the most perfect building ever created. Take a moment to study this art treasure. Like other works of Greek architecture, it uses the post and lintel system. Do you remember learning about this system of building in Chapter 4? Can you find the posts in the Parthenon? Can you find the lintels?

Background Information
Acropolis is a term used to name the highest and most easily defended part of any ancient Greek city. The most famous acropolis, of course, is the Athenian Acropolis (shown in Figure 7-2). The four major monuments still to be seen on the Athenian Acropolis were erected during a major building project initiated by Pericles during the fifth century B.C.

The largest and best-known monument on the Athenian Acropolis is the temple of Athena Parthenos, usually called the Parthenon. The temple was designed by two architects, Iktinos and Callicrates, and constructed between 447 and 432 B.C.

The other three remaining monuments on the Athenian Acropolis are the Propylaea, the temple of Athena Nike, and the Erechtheum. The Propylaea is a monumental gateway to the Acropolis; it was designed by Mnesicles and built between 437 and 432 B.C. The Temple of Athena Nike, only 18.5 x 27 feet (5.64 x 8.34 m), is considered an outstanding example of the Ionic order.

▲ Figure 7–2   The Acropolis rises 500 feet (150 m) above Athens. It was once filled with magnificent buildings.

Acropolis, Athens, Greece.

Sculpture

Sculpture was another of the outstanding achievements of ancient Greek art. At first sculptures were stiff and awkward. In time, however, as Greek sculptors gained skill and confidence, they began creating works that were remarkably lifelike and natural. Figure 7–3 shows one such work. Notice the attention to detail. Even the veins in the arm have been made to stand out in sharp relief. Carved in marble, sculptures like this looked even more realistic because sometimes their surfaces were painted.

Another example of Greek sculpture can be found in Figure 2–9 on page **25**. This long horizontal relief carving is a frieze (**freez**) from the Parthenon. A **frieze** is *a decorative band running across the upper part of a wall.* See how the horses almost seem to gallop across the work. The carving of this frieze was over-

seen by a sculptor named Phidias (**fid-ee-uhs**). Art historians agree that Phidias was among the greatest of all Greek sculptors. One of his most famous works was a magnificent statue of the goddess Athena created for the Parthenon. Made of gold and ivory, the statue rose 40 feet (12 m) to the ceiling. Sadly, this statue and almost all of Phidias's other individual works have been lost. The only knowledge we have of them comes through ancient written descriptions.

Painting and Crafts

Even more famous than the sculptors of ancient Greece were its painters. Like the sculptors, the painters sought to make their pictures as realistic as possible. None of the works of the great Greek painters have survived, however. As with the sculpture of Phidias, these works exist for us only in the words of ancient writers.

Lesson 1   *Art of Ancient Greece*   📖   **99**

Understanding Art History.
Remind students that artists do not work in isolation; they always build on—or react to—the works of artists before them. What were the works of art from which the ancient Greeks learned and developed? Have groups of volunteers research Minoan and Mycenaean art. Ask them to find answers to these questions: When and where did the Minoan and Mycenaean artists work? What art forms did they work in? What subjects did the works portray? Then have the groups present their findings to the rest of the class, sharing photographs of Minoan and Mycenaean art works if possible.

Developing Studio Skills.
Ask one or two volunteers to read and then tell the rest of the class about the ancient Cretan labyrinth. Explain that labyrinth (or maze) designs have been found on ancient Greek pottery and in mosaics made to decorate Greek pavements and homes. Have students use square sheets of paper to draw their own labyrinth designs. They should begin by folding their papers in half. If students want to create circular maze designs, they should cut their folded papers into half circles and then unfold the papers to make full circles. Ask students to use the folds in their papers as guidelines to plan and draw symmetrical maze designs. Suggest that students use dark blue or black markers to draw the lines that form their mazes and that they use brighter shades to decorate the labyrinth pathways. This use of color will make their completed designs resemble the mosaic work used by the ancient Greeks.

Appreciating Cultural Diversity. Ask students to compare the Parthenon pictured on page **96** (and again on the Acropolis in Figure 7-2) with the Buddhist temple pictured in Figure 5-6 (page **73**). How are these two temples alike? What are the most important differences between them? What do those differences imply about the differences between the cultures of Japan and ancient Greece?

Some examples of ancient Greek painting do exist, however, in the pictures found on surviving pottery. The earliest Greek vases were decorated with bands of geometric patterns. One of these objects is shown in Figure 7–4. Found in a cemetery in Athens, this **amphora** (**am**-fuh-ruh), or *twin-handled vase*, was used as a grave marker. The small scene toward the center shows a burial ceremony.

Human figures were later added to the decorations on vases. At first these were little more than stick figures. Later they became more realistic and lively. Often the subjects were gods and goddesses or popular heroes. Scenes from sports and battles were also popular. The amphora in Figure 7–5 shows runners in a race. Notice how the repeated pattern of running figures adds a sense of movement. The curved surface of the vase adds to this feeling. Vases like this were sometimes used as prizes at the games held each summer in Athens. They were filled with olive oil from sacred groves and presented to victorious athletes.

▲ Figure 7–3 **The original statue by Myron is known only through descriptions and reconstructed copies. Notice how the sculptor used balance and rhythm to show harmonious form.**

Myron. *The Discus Thrower.* Roman copy of a bronze original of c. 450 B.C. Life-size. Museo Nazionale Romano, Rome, Italy.

▲ Figure 7–4 **Notice the geometric patterning. Does this design remind you of those created by any cultures you have read about? If so, which ones? This vase was used as a grave marker in much the same way tombstones are used today.**

Amphora. Geometric Style. Athens National Museum, Athens, Greece.

Developing Perceptual Skills
Make a photocopy of several Greek vases which depict various scenes. Glue each copy on a separate color of construction paper and then cut the copy into sixteen shapes to create a puzzle. Give each student one or more of the puzzle pieces. Ask students to write down or sketch how they think the remainder of the picture might look. After they have completed their description or sketch, have them get together with their classmates to put the puzzles together. Did any of the students' descriptions or sketches closely resemble the actual piece? Compare this to the tasks that archaeologists encounter when they attempt to visualize their discoveries of broken pieces.

▲ **Figure 7–5** The surface of the vase is curved. In what way does this add to the lively scene in the painting?

Amphora. Runners in a Race. Etruscan. Vatican Museum.

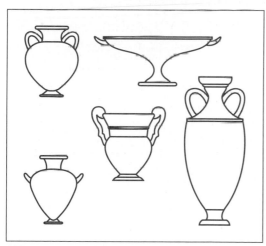

▲ **Figure 7–6** Examples of Greek vase shapes.

STUDIO EXPERIENCE

Greek craftspeople designed their pottery for many different purposes. They created large jars for storage and delicate cups for drinking. Examples of these and other vase shapes are shown in Figure 7–6.

Fold a large rectangular sheet of white paper in half. Pick one of the vase shapes in Figure 7–6. Place the point of your pencil at the folded edge of the paper. Draw *one half* of the vase as accurately as you can. Make sure your drawing ends at the crease. Leaving the paper folded, cut your vase shape out along the line you have drawn. When the paper is unfolded, you will have a symmetrical cutout of the vase.

✔ CHECK YOUR UNDERSTANDING

1. Why did the city-states of ancient Greece never join together to form a nation?
2. What three qualities did the artists of Greece value most?
3. What was the Parthenon? On what sacred hill is it found?
4. What is a frieze? What famous artist oversaw the work on the Parthenon's frieze? What other contribution to the Parthenon did he make?
5. What sorts of designs were painted on early Greek vases? What was painted on later Greek vases?

Following Up

Closure. Have students form small groups. Ask the members of each group to compare and discuss the shapes they cut in the "Studio Experience" activity. Then have them consider how their ideas about ancient Greek art works have changed: How accurate were the pictures you drew at the beginning of this lesson? (See "Motivator" activity.) If you were to draw those pictures again, what would you change?

Evaluation. 1. Review students' written responses to the "Check Your Understanding" questions. 2. Consider their contributions to their "Closure" group discussions.

Reteaching. Work with small groups of students to review and discuss what they have learned about the art of ancient Greece. Then ask: How do you think our modern way of life is influenced by the culture of ancient Greece? What ancient Greek influences can you see in the art and architecture of our times? Encourage all group members to contribute to this discussion.

Enrichment. Have students work in small groups to research some of the gods and goddesses of Greek mythology. Who were the most important deities? How were they depicted in the art of ancient Greece? Then have each group select a story from Greek mythology to share with the rest of the class. Let group members choose a method of presentation; they might consider writing and illustrating the story, giving an oral report, painting a mural, or performing a skit. Encourage group members to include their own sketches of Greek art works or photographs of Greek art works in the presentations. Then have each group share its presentation of a story from Greek mythology.

Answers to "Check Your Understanding"
1. Two reasons why the city-states of ancient Greece never formed a nation were: rugged geography separated areas; loyalty to their own and jealousy of others prevented the tribes from banding together.
2. The artists of Greece valued grace, harmony, and precision.
3. The Parthenon was a temple built to honor the Greek goddess Athena. It is found on the Acropolis.
4. A frieze is a decorative band running across the upper part of a wall. Phidias oversaw the work on the Parthenon frieze. His other major contribution was a 40 foot gold and ivory statue of the goddess Athena.
5. Geometric designs were painted on early Greek vases. Later, human figures were added.

Making a Painting for a Greek Vase

LESSON PLAN
(pages 102–103)

Objectives
After completing this lesson, students will be able to:
• Plan and paint scenes that might appear on amphoras.
• Describe, analyze, interpret, and judge their own paintings.

Supplies
• Cutouts of vase shapes (made by students for "Studio Experience" in previous lesson).
• Pencils; sheets of sketch paper; scissors; sheets of white paper, 18 x 24 inches (45 x 61 cm); black tempera paint; brushes in several sizes; mixing trays.
• Clay, slip.

> **TRB Resource**
> • 7-7 *The Golden Rectangle*, (cooperative learning)

TEACHING THE LESSON

Getting Started

Motivator. Display the cutouts of vase shapes created by students during the previous lesson. (See "Studio Experience," page **101**.) Let students identify the shapes and then discuss and compare them. How are the shapes alike? What distinguishes some of the shapes? What moods or feelings do different shapes suggest? What subjects might seem most appropriate on each of the different shapes?

Vocabulary. Help students review the terms *aesthetics* and *aesthetic views:* What does the study of aesthetics involve? What three different aesthetic views do aestheticians adopt? Why do many students of aesthetics consider all three aesthetic views?

Making a Painting for a Greek Vase

Art critics, you will recall, judge works in terms of different aesthetic views. Look carefully at the Greek amphora pictured in Figure 7–7. How might a critic stressing the importance of the subject of a work react to this vase? Do the figures on the vase look real? Are their actions lifelike?

Think next about how a critic emphasizing composition might respond to the work. Can you find the *X* made of real and imaginary lines? Do you notice how these lines link the warriors to each other and to the amphora's handles? Note, finally, how a critic stressing content might react to this vase. Did you notice the two women at either side of the work? Could these be the mothers of the two warriors? Could it be they are weeping and pleading for their sons to stop fighting?

A measure of this amphora's greatness is that it succeeds in terms of all three aesthetic views.

WHAT YOU WILL LEARN

You will use tempera to paint one of the following: a scene of warriors in battle, a wedding, an athletic event. Your picture will have at least two figures. Make these figures as realistic as you can. Use the principle of movement to organize the lines and shapes. Finally, your scene will communicate a meaning, mood, or feeling. Paint your scene on a vase cutout like the one you made for the Studio Experience in Lesson 1. (See Figure 7–8.)

WHAT YOU WILL NEED

• Pencil and sheets of sketch paper
• Scissors
• Sheet of white paper, 18 x 24 inches (45 x 61 cm)
• Black tempera paint, several brushes, and mixing tray

▲ **Figure 7–7** **This is one of two scenes of combat painted on this vase. Both show warriors of the Trojan war. Have you ever heard of that war? Do you know which sides fought in it?**

Black Figured Panel Amphora. Painter of the Medea Group, Greek. 520–510 B.C. Terra cotta, glazed. Lip 19.7 x Base 16.4 x Height 46.4 x Diameter 27.9 cm (Lip 7¾ x Base 6⁷⁄₁₆ x Height 18¼ x Diameter 11"). Dallas Art Museum, Dallas, Texas. Munger Fund.

SAFETY TIP

When a project calls for paints, use watercolors, liquid tempera, or school acrylics. If you must use powdered tempera, wear a dust mask. Try also to work away from other class members.

Background Information
Greek vases in various shapes were designed for storing water, oil, or wine and as funerary vases. The funerary works, usually quite large, served as grave markers and as vessels through which offerings could be poured onto the graves; these vases had no bottom.

The earliest vases date from the Geometric Period of Greek art (about tenth to eighth century B.C.). The paintings on these vases are abstract, geometric designs created in black on the light-colored clay; toward the end of this period, figures of animals and humans were included within the design.

During the Archaic Period (seventh to sixth century B.C.), human figures were central to most vase paintings, which often depict scenes from Greek legends. The figures were painted as silhouettes in black (or red) and then a sharp instrument was used to incise details.

Vase painters of the Classical Period (about fifth to fourth century B.C.) began to use perspective and shading.

WHAT YOU WILL DO

1. Pick one of the three themes for your painting. Make several pencil sketches of scenes that have this theme. Use the vase painting in Figure 7–7 as a model. In your design, create real and imaginary lines that add a sense of movement to it. Keep your design simple. Make sure to emphasize the figures in it. Choose your best sketch.

2. Review the vase shapes in Figure 7–6 on page **101**. Decide which of the shapes would be best suited to your sketch. Using scissors, create this shape out of the large sheet of white paper. Follow the instructions given in the Studio Experience on page **101**.

3. Transfer your sketch to the cutout. Using a fine-pointed brush and black tempera, trace over the outlines of your figures. Carefully paint around lines that are to appear within figures. These lines will appear white in the finished painting.

4. Decorate and paint the rest of your vase using black only. (*Hint*: The neck, handles, and foot of the vase are well suited to decorations.)

5. When your vase painting is dry, display it. Note ways in which it is similar to and different from those created by your classmates.

EXAMINING YOUR WORK

- **Describe**   Tell which of the three scenes you picked for your work. Describe the shape of amphora you chose. Tell whether the figures in your work look lifelike.
- **Analyze**   Tell whether you used the principle of movement to organize the lines and shapes in your picture. Tell whether the shape of the vase is well suited to the picture you created.
- **Interpret**   State whether your picture communicates a meaning, mood, or feeling. Note whether your classmates are able to identify this mood or feeling.
- **Judge**   Tell whether you feel your work succeeds. Explain your answer.

▶ **Figure 7–8   Student work. Greek vase painting.**

OTHER STUDIO IDEAS

- Create a myth or legend about the event shown in your painting. Write it on an index card to be placed alongside your vase.

- ●● Create a second vase painting using two hues of tempera. Use one hue for the figures and a contrasting earth-toned hue, such as burnt orange, for the background.

Lesson 2   *Making a Painting for a Greek Vase*   **103**

Developing Concepts

Exploring Aesthetics. Let students work in groups to discuss the content of the amphora shown in Figure 7-7: What message or feeling do you think the painting on this vase is intended to communicate?

Developing Studio Skills. Let students work with partners or in small groups to discuss how they might make their own amphoras out of clay. Then let them work with clay and slip to try the technique they have chosen. When the amphoras are fully shaped, have students allow them to sit until they are bone dry; then fire students' works in a kiln. Encourage students from different groups to compare and discuss their works and the techniques they used.

Appreciating Cultural Diversity. Let students examine the amphora shown in Figure 7-7 and the funerary urns shown on page **80** and in Figure 6-8 on page **86**. How are the vessels from ancient Greece and from Pre-Columbian American alike? What are the most important differences? What do these works tell about the two different cultures? What influences on our own culture and art can you identify?

Following Up

Closure. Have students work in small groups to discuss their paintings. Let each member present his or her painting to the rest of the group, following the steps in "Examining Your Work."

Evaluation. Review students' paintings and consider their contributions to the "Closure" group discussions.

Reteaching. Ask students to write paragraphs explaining what they like best about Greek art or culture. Then have students work in groups to compare and discuss their responses.

Enrichment. Ask groups of students to research ancient Greek plays. Where were the plays performed? What kinds of masks did the actors wear? What was the purpose of these masks? What subjects and themes did the plays present? Ask each group to select an interesting method of presentation (such as a short play or a mural) and use that presentation to share its information with the rest of the class.

LESSON PLAN
(pages 104–107)

Objectives
After completing this lesson, students will be able to:
• Identify the contributions of the ancient Romans to the history of art.
• Name some important works by ancient Roman artists.
• Draw triumphal arches that include freestanding sculpture and relief carvings.

Supplies
• Slides or large photographs of the city of Rome.
• Sheets of drawing paper, pencils.
• Sheets of white paper, 6 x 6 inches (15 x 15 cm); pencils; scraps or pieces of construction paper in various colors; scissors; glue.

TRB Resources
• 7-8 *Roman vs. Greek Aesthetics,* (aesthetics)
• 7-9 *Pompeii—A Buried City,* (appreciating cultural diversity)
• 7-10 *Draw in Perspective,* (studio)

TEACHING THE LESSON

Getting Started
Motivator. Introduce this lesson by showing students slides or photographs of Rome as it can be seen today. Try to include scenes that show ancient structures beside modern buildings, traffic, and the business of modern daily life. Let students discuss what they see in the photographs. Ask them to describe how this looks like any large modern city and to explain what sets it apart. Then ask: What do we mean when we talk about Rome? Guide students in discussing Rome as a city in Italy, Rome as an ancient culture and civilization, and Rome as the center of the Roman Empire.

Ask students to study the map of ancient Rome in Figure 7-9. Which Rome does this map show? How does it help explain the fact that Roman structures and works of art can be seen in modern Spain, France, Egypt, and other countries outside Italy?

104

Art of Ancient Rome

The Greek city-states were not only unable to band together to form a nation, they were also unable to keep the peace among themselves for long. Frequent outbreaks of fighting over a 1300–year period weakened the country. It made Greece helpless against attack from outside forces. Finally in 197 B.C., Greece fell to the Romans.

Although the Greek empire was defeated, Greek influence continued. The Romans were influenced by Greek ideas about art and used them in their own works.

In this lesson you will learn about some of those works.

ANCIENT ROMAN CULTURE

By the time of its takeover of Greece, Rome was the greatest power in the civilized world. At its peak, the city had a population of over one million people. Find this city on the map in Figure 7–9.

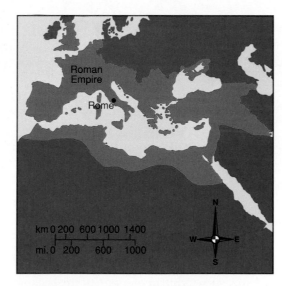

◀ **Figure 7–9   Ancient Rome.**

Rome was a city of contrasts. There were magnificent public buildings, baths, and parks, but there were also narrow streets crammed with shabby dwellings.

The Romans were a practical-minded people. They were more interested in such things as engineering, law, and government than in art. Romans did, however, make some very important contributions to the world of art.

Architecture

Rome's greatest contributions were in the field of architecture. Among its accomplishments were:

• **Concrete.** This *mixture of powdered minerals and small stones* was used to create buildings with great domes and ceilings. One such building is shown in Figures 7–10 and 7–11. This is the Pantheon. It was a temple built to honor all the Roman gods. Concrete made it possible for Roman architects to build a huge dome over this temple. The Pantheon is the largest domed building from ancient times still standing.

• **The round arch.** This *curved arrangement of stones over an open space* opened up new building possibilities. A series of round arches could be used to build bridges and other structures.

104   Lesson 3   *Art of Ancient Rome*

Note
The Roman arch improved upon the post-and-lintel system favored by the Greeks. The post and lintel limited builders in terms of the space it could bridge. A stone lintel could not be used to span a wide space because it would break. Unlike a lintel, an arch is made of a number of bricks or cut stones. These are held in place by a wooden form until the top stone, called a *keystone,* is fit into place. The space that can be spanned in this manner is much greater than the space bridged by a lintel. However, an arch needs the support of another arch or wall. For this reason, the Romans created a series of smaller arches to replace the single large arch.

◄Figure 7–10   Greek temples were built to be "used" only by their gods. Roman temples like this one were built to be used by the people for prayer. The building is large enough to hold 3000 people.

Restored by Hadrian. Pantheon Facade and Piazza della Rotunda. A.D. 118–125. Rome, Italy.

◄Figure 7–11   The dome of the Pantheon soars to a height of 144 feet (44 m). The hole at its center is the building's only source of light. Though the hole looks small, it is actually 30 feet (9 m) across.

Restored by Hadrian. Pantheon Interior. A.D. 118–125. Rome, Italy.

Vocabulary. Have students use dictionaries to find the derivations of these words: *arch, aqueduct, concrete.* From what ancient language are all these English words derived? What language was spoken by the people who first built rounded arches, constructed aqueducts, and made concrete? What is the meaning of the Latin words from which these English words come?

Developing Concepts

Exploring Aesthetics. Guide students in examining and discussing the Pantheon, shown in Figures 7-10 and 7-11: How do you imagine you would feel toward this building? What kind of space can you see inside the Pantheon? How do you think that space would make you feel once you were in the building? What message or feeling does this work of art communicate to you?

Then read aloud the following quotation; it has been attributed to the emperor Hadrian, at whose direction the Pantheon was constructed: "My intention had been that this sanctuary of All Gods should produce the likeness of the terrestrial globe and of the stellar spheres." Ask students to restate Hadrian's intentions in their own words and to discuss whether they feel the Pantheon succeeded in fulfilling those intentions.

Using Art Criticism. Help students discuss the portrait sculpture shown in Figure 7-14 and compare it to the Greek sculpture shown in Figure 7-3 on page **100**. Ask: What do you see when you look at this Roman sculpture? Who is the subject of the work? How does this subject compare to the athlete shown in the Greek sculpture? What mood or message does the Roman portrait sculpture communicate to you? How is that mood or message different from the one communicated by the Greek sculpture? Is the Roman sculpture a successful work of art? Why, or why not? Is it any more—or less—successful than the Greek sculpture? Why?

Background Information

The Pantheon, constructed under the rule of Hadrian and completed around A.D. 125, was built to honor all the Roman gods. It is considered one of the first buildings intended to emphasize the space of the interior rather than the form of the exterior. The spacious rotunda rises to a graceful dome that suggests the sky itself. The building has no windows; the only source of light is a large oculus (or "eye") at the top of the dome.

The proportions of the Pantheon's space have been widely praised for their harmony. The diameter of the rotunda is equal to the height of the building, measured from the floor to the top of the dome. The height of the walls is equal to the height of the dome above them.

The Pantheon was constructed primarily from concrete and bricks. The walls of the rotunda are 20 feet (6.1 m) thick, and the dome was formed by rotating a series of rounded arches above the circular walls. The oculus helped reduce the weight of the dome to decrease pressure on the Pantheon's walls.

▲ Figure 7–12   Aqueducts like this one sloped ever so slightly. This allowed gravity to carry the water on its way.

Pont du Gard. 20–16 B.C. Near Nimes, France.

▲ Figure 7–13   Would you describe the design of this work as simple or complicated? What elements of art were used in the work? What principles were used?

Arch of Constantine. A.D. 312–15. Rome, Italy.

- **The aqueduct** (ak-wuh-duhkt). This *network of channels, meant to carry water to a city*, was another type of structure that used round arches. The aqueduct in Figure 7–12 was built to carry water over a valley 600 yards (548 m) wide. This impressive structure is 160 feet (48 m) high. Note how the arches are placed side by side. This allowed them to support each other and carry the weight to the ground.
- **The triumphal** (try-**uhm**-fuhl) **arch**. This was *a monument built to celebrate great army victories*. The largest ever built was the Arch of Constantine, shown in Figure 7–13. The round arch was used here by the ancient Romans for purely decorative reasons. Notice how the structure uses three round arches. The emperor and his officers would ride chariots or horses through the large center one. Foot soldiers would march through the smaller side arches as the people of Rome cheered.

Sculpture

Like the Greeks before them, the Romans aimed for realism in their sculpture. A number of the works that remain are portrait sculptures. One of these is pictured in Figure 7–14. Study this work. Notice the care the sculptor has taken to capture not just lifelike detail but also the features of a specific individual. The eyes look as though they might blink at any moment. What mood or feeling does this sculpture communicate?

The Romans also excelled at relief sculpture. The ones shown in Figure 7–15 are from the Arch of Constantine. These reliefs tell of the deeds of the emperor in battle. What events seem to be taking place in the section of the story shown?

106   📖   Lesson 3   *Art of Ancient Rome*

Note
Roman baths were more than public swimming pools. They were huge buildings containing libraries, shops, gymnasiums, restaurants, and walkways. In many ways they were like the shopping malls of today.

Note
Eleven aqueducts from 10 to 60 miles long carried about 270 million gallons of water to Rome daily. The one in Figure 7-12 was also used as a bridge. It is still in use today.

▲ **Figure 7–14** What is there about this face that makes it look like someone you might see on the street?

Bust of Philip the Arab dressed in a toga. A.D. 244–249. Marble. Vatican Museum, Rome, Italy.

◄ **Figure 7–15** Many of the relief carvings on this arch were taken from earlier monuments. Some of the figures on them were changed so they would look more like the emperor Constantine.

Arch of Constantine. A.D. 312–15. (Detail.) Rome, Italy.

✔CHECK YOUR UNDERSTANDING

1. What led to the downfall of Greece? When was Greece finally conquered?
2. What were Rome's three main contributions to the history of architecture?
3. What was the Pantheon?
4. What is an aqueduct? What is a triumphal arch? What was the triumphal arch used for?
5. What was a key aim of Roman sculpture?

Making a Model of a Roman Triumphal Arch

LESSON PLAN
(pages 108–109)

Objectives
After completing this lesson, students will be able to:
- Build models of triumphal arches.
- Describe, analyze, interpret, and judge their own models.

Supplies
- Drawings of triumphal arches (made by students for "Studio Experience" in previous lesson.)
- Empty cardboard boxes, as for soap or cereal; tape; large sheets of construction paper in various colors, including gray and black; pencils; scissors; white glue; old magazines featuring sports illustrations; scraps of heavy cardboard.
- Clay, modeling tools.

TEACHING THE LESSON

Getting Started
Motivator. Let each student present, either to the whole class or to a small group, the triumphal arch he or she drew for the "Studio Experience" in the previous lesson. Encourage students to discuss and compare their designs, noting the subjects depicted, the lines and shapes shown, the kinds of balance used, and the moods or messages communicated.

Vocabulary. Help students review the term *triumphal arch* (introduced in the previous lesson). What were triumphal arches built to celebrate? How many arches did they include? How were those arches used?

Making a Model of a Roman Triumphal Arch

Art critics often approach their study of architecture just as they do the study of paintings or sculptures. They begin by describing what they see, and then they analyze the ways the principles have been used to organize the elements. After that they interpret the meanings, moods, and feelings the work communicates. Finally, they judge whether the work succeeds and explain why. Doing this helps the critic understand and appreciate a work of architecture.

Look at the triumphal arch pictured in Figure 7–16. What do you think an art critic would say about this arch during each of the four steps of art criticism? How would you, as an art critic, describe, analyze, interpret, and judge it?

▲ Figure 7–16 What type of balance do you see in this triumphal arch? How is proportion used?

Arch of Septimus, Roman Forum.

WHAT YOU WILL LEARN

You will build a model of a triumphal arch out of cardboard and construction paper. Your arch will have all the features outlined in the Studio Experience in Lesson 3. You will use a variety of different shapes and forms. Some of these will be repeated to add harmony. Your work will have formal balance. (See Figure 7–17.)

WHAT YOU WILL NEED

- Empty cardboard soap or cereal box, taped shut
- Large sheets of colored construction paper, including gray and black
- Pencil, scissors, and white glue
- Assortment of magazines featuring sports illustrations
- Scraps of heavy cardboard

WHAT YOU WILL DO

1. Place the cardboard box down flat on a sheet of gray construction paper. With the pencil, trace around the box. Hold a second sheet of gray construction paper firmly against the first. Using scissors, carefully cut through both sheets along the line you drew. Glue the sheets to the front and back of the box. Cover the top and side panels of the box with gray construction paper.
2. Look back at the drawing you made for the Studio Experience in Lesson 3. Doubling two sheets of black construction paper, cut out two large rounded arches and four smaller ones. Glue these arches in place on the front and back of the box. Use your drawing as a guide.

Background Information
The people of ancient Rome did not barter; they purchased goods and services and paid their taxes with coins. Many of these Roman coins were intricate works of art created in gold, in silver, or even in copper covered with silver. To make the coins official, highly trained artisans imprinted them with images of Roman emperors, temples and other buildings, altars, gates, aqueducts, tombs, fountains, harbors, and lighthouses.

The Roman coins provide one source of information about the appearance of ancient buildings that have been altered or lost completely. The public currency of ancient Rome includes images of more than 200 buildings; the coins of provincial cities records 800 more structures.

One particularly interesting Roman coin, minted in A.D. 81, shows the Roman Colosseum, which was completed during Titus's reign. The relief work on the coin shows a bird's-eye view of the famous amphitheater, including the arched opening to the emperor's box and a fountain beside the building.

3. Use construction paper to create columns and other decorations. Glue these in place.
4. Look through the sports magazines. Locate black-and-white photographs showing scenes of the sport you chose for your design drawing. Look for action shots that focus on athletes. Cut these out and trim them to fit on your arch. Glue those that are to work as reliefs directly to the arch. Glue those that are to work as free-standing sculpture to small scraps of heavy cardboard before gluing them in place on the arch. This will make them seem to project outward in space.
5. When the glue has dried, display your arch. Compare your work with that of your classmates.

SAFETY TIP

Be very careful when using cutting tools such as scissors and knives. Pick these up only by the handle, never by the blade. Make sure also to offer the handle when you are handing the tool to another person.

OTHER STUDIO IDEAS

- On a large sheet of poster board, draw the outline of a triumphal arch using a black felt-tipped marker. Decorate the arch with magazine cutouts standing for a personal victory. Possibilities include learning to play a musical instrument, making one of the school's athletic teams, or being accepted to a school club.

EXAMINING YOUR WORK

- **Describe**   Point out the round arches on the front and back of your arch. Point out the columns. Point out the two different types of sculpture.
- **Analyze**   Tell whether your arch has formal balance. Identify the variety of shapes and forms you used. Tell whether these add harmony to the work.
- **Interpret**   State whether your arch tells the story of an important team win. Tell whether it communicates pride in this victory.
- **Judge**   Tell whether you feel your work succeeds. Explain your answer.

▲ Figure 7–17   Student work. Triumphal arch.

- Create another triumphal arch, this time out of clay. Use the clay slab method. Be sure to use proper joining techniques. Use a clay tool to carve decorations and relief sculptures on your arch.

Lesson 4   *Making a Model of a Roman Triumphal Arch*   **109**

Note
For students creating a triumphal arch using the clay slab method, review the following stages of clay: Plastic clay—clay wet enough to hold its shape. Slip—clay with water added to make it runny. Slip is used to glue together shaped pieces of damp clay. Leather hard clay—clay which is still damp but too hard to model. Pieces of leather hard clay can be joined with slip. Greenware—very dry clay that will break easily. An object at the greenware stage is ready to be fired. Bisqueware is fired pottery that is hard but still not ready to use. Glazeware is pottery coated with powdered chemicals that melt during firing into a hard, glass-like finish.

Developing Concepts

Using Art Criticism. Have students work with partners to answer the question posed in the text about the triumphal arch shown in Figure 7-16: How would you, as an art critic, describe, analyze, interpret, and judge it? Let the partners write brief responses.

Understanding Art History. Ask the class: Were the Romans the only people who built triumphal arches? Have you seen photographs of more recent triumphal arches? Encourage students' responses; then have them find photographs and read about the world's largest triumphal arch, the Arc de Triomphe de l'Etoile in Paris. How is it similar to the Roman triumphal arches shown in Figures 7-13 and 7-16? How is it different?

Developing Studio Skills. Let students experiment with modeling clay to create relief sculpture that might be used to decorate their triumphal arches.

Following Up

Closure. Have students write short responses to the four sets of instructions in "Examining Your Work." Then let each student present his or her arch to the rest of the class, explaining the work as directed in the "Analyze" section.

Evaluation. Review students' models of triumphal arches, read their responses to the "Examining Your Work" instructions, and listen to their presentations and analyses of their work.

Reteaching. Work with small groups of students to review the structure and purpose of Roman triumphal arches: What new development in Roman architecture made the construction of these arches possible? For whom were triumphal arches built? What do the triumphal arches tell us about the art and culture of ancient Rome?

Enrichment. Let students work in small groups to discuss their responses to this question: What creations in our culture serve purposes similar to those served by the triumphal arches of ancient Rome? Then ask the members of each group to select one modern work they consider comparable to Rome's triumphal arches. Have group members plan and make a presentation that shows the similarities.

Building Vocabulary

1. frieze
2. amphora
3. concrete
4. rounded arch
5. aqueduct
6. triumphal arch

Reviewing Art Facts

7. Loyalty to their own and jealousy of others as well as rugged geography were two reasons why the Greek city-states never banded together.
8. Athens was the largest and most powerful city-state.
9. The Acropolis was a sacred hill. The word *acropolis* means "high city."
10. The Parthenon was built to honor the goddess Athena.
11. Sometimes the Greeks painted the surfaces of their sculptures.
12. Phidias was one of the greatest Greek sculptors.
13. Romans made their greatest art contributions in the area of architecture.
14. Concrete made it possible to build the dome of the Pantheon.
15. The round arch appeared in aqueducts, bridges, and triumphal arches.

Thinking About Art

1. The figure is preparing to throw the discus. His state is one of intense concentration.
2. Similarities can include such items as: both were built as temples and were considered outstanding examples of architecture. Differences include post and lintel system vs. dome, being built to honor one Greek goddess vs. to honor all Roman gods, and only one still stands in its entirety.
3. Elements include line, form space, and texture. Principles include balance, proportion, and harmony.
4. Answers will vary. Students can mention architecture; Greeks and Romans both valued grace, harmony and precision as shown in the Parthenon and the Pantheon. They can also mention sculpture, with both cultures valuing realism as shown in the Discus Thrower and the bust of the Arab.

BUILDING VOCABULARY

Number a sheet of paper from 1 to 6. After each number, write the term from the box that best matches each description below.

amphora	frieze
aqueduct	round arch
concrete	triumphal arch

1. A decorative band running across the upper part of a wall.
2. A twin-handled vase.
3. A mixture of powdered minerals and small stones used in building.
4. A curved arrangement of stones over an open space.
5. A network of channels meant to carry water to a city.
6. A monument built to celebrate great army victories.

REVIEWING ART FACTS

Number a sheet of paper from 7 to 15. Answer each question in a complete sentence.

7. What are two reasons why the Greek city-states never banded together?
8. Which was the largest and most powerful of the Greek city-states?
9. What is the Acropolis? What does the word *acropolis* mean?
10. What goddess was the Parthenon built to honor?
11. To make their sculptures appear even more realistic, what did the Greeks do?
12. Who was Phidias? Name two contributions he made to the Parthenon.
13. In what area of art did the Romans make their greatest contribution?
14. What made possible the building of the dome on the Pantheon?
15. Name two structures in which the Romans used the round arch.

THINKING ABOUT ART

On a sheet of paper, answer each question in a sentence or two.

1. **Interpret.** Look again at the sculpture in Figure 7–3 on page **100**. Tell what you think this figure is doing. Decide what word you would use to describe his feelings at this moment. Explain your answer.
2. **Compare and contrast.** Using the Parthenon and Pantheon as models, list the similarities and differences between Greek and Roman temples.
3. **Analyze.** Examine the aqueduct shown in Figure 7–12 on page **106**. What art elements can you identify in this structure? What principles of art have been used to organize the elements?
4. **Extend.** The Romans, you read, were influenced by Greek ideas about art and used them in their own works. In which area of art do you find this influence to be most evident? Support your answer with facts and examples of specific works from the chapter.

MAKING ART CONNECTIONS

1. **Social Studies.** In this chapter you learned that the Romans were very interested in law and government. In an encyclopedia or other library resource, read about these areas. Search for ties between Rome's system of government and its architecture. Write a short report on your findings.
2. **Language Arts.** Ancient Greece and Rome had rich traditions in mythology. Often, myths were formed to explain events like the origin of man or the change of seasons. Create a myth expressing your own ideas about a natural event.

LOOKING AT THE DETAILS

The detail shown below is of the Parthenon, Temple of Athena. Study the detail and answer the following questions using complete sentences.

1. Which elements of art are used to create harmony in this structure?
2. Compare this detail with Figure 7–12 on page **106**. What similarities as well as differences do you see in the architect's use of the elements and principles of art?
3. What architectural form is used to provide rhythm in this structure?
4. What two purposes did the architect have in mind in his use of the columns?

The Parthenon. Temple of Athena. 5th Century B.C. (Detail.) Acropolis, Athens, Greece.

Art of India and Islam

Chapter Scan

TRB Resources

- 8-10 Chapter Test
- Color Transparency 15
- Color Transparency 16

TEACHING THE CHAPTER

Introducing the Art Work

Direct students' attention to *The Feast of Sadeh.* Explain that in Islam the art of calligraphy ranks foremost among the arts even above painting. Tell students that in their religion painting was considered a "lazy art," and therefore was a private art. During the fourteenth century in Islam, painting and calligraphy merged in the form of illustrated storytelling. It wasn't until the second half of the fifteenth century that some painters finally began to sign their works.

Often, more than one artist worked on a single picture, but the work was always known by the master artist's name.

Characterized by a love of detail, Islamic art has a uniform style and a certain degree of sameness to the Western viewer's eye.

Rocks, trees, flowers and wispy clouds are seen throughout Islamic painting, and gardens are the Persian artist's passion.

Examining the Art Work

Point out the definite border drawn by the artist and the deliberate way the artist extends the subject beyond that border. Explain to the students that in early Islamic painting the artist confined himself to the area within the border, but as painting progressed it became a common practice to extend beyond the border.

▲ This miniature painting celebrates the discovery of fire by an early king. Only the skin coats give a clue that this is a scene from the Stone Age. Notice how every space in this miniature is filled with objects and patterns.

Sultan Muhammad. *The Feast of Sadeh.* c. 1520–1522. Colors, ink, silver and gold on paper. 27.4 x 23 cm (9½ x 9¹⁄₁₆″). The Metropolitan Museum of Art, New York, New York. Gift of Arthur A. Houghton, Jr.

Art of India and Islam

In a way, the frame around a work of art is like a window. The miniature painting on the left does not always stay within the limits of its frame. Notice which parts break free, and which parts stay inside the frame.

This is from a book that illustrates the legends of Iran and its leaders. The artist used intricate details and rich colors to enhance this story. What do you think the curved lines at the bottom of the painting represent?

You will learn to interpret images like this one in the pages to come.

OBJECTIVES

After completing this chapter, you will be able to:

- Identify the major Indian contributions to architecture and sculpture.
- Explain how Islamic culture began.
- Identify the major Islamic contributions to painting, architecture, and crafts.
- Create a design in the Hindu style.
- Make an art work in the Islamic style.

WORDS YOU WILL LEARN

arabesques
batik
calligraphy
collage

mihrab
minaret
mosque
stupas

ARTISTS YOU WILL MEET

'Abd Allah Musawwir
Sultan Muhammad

Tamil Nadu

Point out the Persian rugs, the calligraphy, the elaborate composition and the highly decorative and stylized landscapes. Explain that these are characteristic of the Islamic art style. Point out the flat style of the work and explain that this is also characteristic of Islamic art. Have students note the tiny pattern used to fill in the background space which contributes to a lack of depth in the work, but it also creates a sense of unity. Emphasize the unique composition of the art work and the vivid color of the work.

Discussing the Art Work
Refer students to the individual scenes within the work. Ask them to think about how the scenes are interrelated. Explain that each scene is self-contained and each expresses a part of the story, creating its own mood. Combined scenes interrelate to tell a story.

Ask students to think about how they would read this story through the pictures. Point out the circular pattern of the work, with the exception of the figures in the upper left. Ask students to identify the man and the animals at the bottom of the work, and how they appear to be moving toward the left. Suggest that most of the figures lead the viewer's eye in a clockwise direction.

Tell students that in this chapter they will learn about the major Indian and Islamic contributions to art. They will also create their own works of art in the Hindu and Islamic art style.

113

Building Self-Esteem
Tell students that in this chapter they will be learning about some of the art forms created in India. One of these is an open cast-metal sculpture called the *Tree of Life and Knowledge* which shows a number of animal and bird forms sacred to the Hindus. On page **117** is a Studio Experience in which students can create their own personal tree of life. Have the class think about what they value in their lives. Ask: What processes do you use to make life choices? Is there a connection between these choices and how you feel about yourself? Help students focus on choosing areas of interest: sports, hobbies, nature, special friends or family members. Then remind students about choosing symbols to represent these choices. After students have made their selections and completed their personal tree of life, they will have a memento showing symbols of their values.

Art of India

LESSON PLAN
(pages 114–117)

Objectives
After completing this lesson, students will be able to:
• Identify the major Indian contributions to architecture and sculpture.
• Explain how the religions of Hinduism and Buddhism have influenced the art of India.
• Identify and describe stupas.
• Draw personal designs inspired by the *Tree of Life and Knowledge.*

Supplies
• Wall map of the world (if available).
• Sheets of drawing paper, pencils, fine-tipped markers.
• Pieces of Indian embroidered fabric (if available), small pieces of plain dark fabric, yellow chalk, needles, embroidery thread in bright colors.

TRB Resource
• 8-1 *Religion and Aesthetics,* (aesthetics/art criticism)

TEACHING THE LESSON

Getting Started

Motivator. Begin by displaying a world map and asking volunteers to point out India on the map. Ask: Of what continent is it a part? What other countries are India's neighbors? Then have students form groups in which to share their ideas about India. Ask the members of each group to brainstorm facts and feelings about India: What comes to mind when you think of this country? Let one of the group members record all responses; encourage everyone to participate. After several minutes of brainstorming, give students in each group time to discuss and evaluate their ideas: How does their knowledge of India compare to their knowledge of other countries? What do they already know about the art of India? What do they hope to learn?

India is a land of opposites. It is a country of snow-capped peaks and tropical lowlands, of parched deserts and rain-soaked valleys.

Yet, for all its differences, India is a land joined by the strong religious beliefs of its people. These beliefs have in large measure shaped Indian art since the dawn of civilization. In this lesson you will learn about the religion and art of India.

THE RELIGIONS OF INDIA

Indian culture has long been guided by two religions. One of these, Buddhism, you read about in Chapter 5. The other, and older, of India's religions, Hinduism (**hin**-doo-iz-uhm), has its roots in prehistoric times. It was as an outgrowth of Hinduism that Buddhism emerged around 500 B.C.

Unlike Buddhism, Hinduism is not based on the teachings of a single leader. Rather, it is the collected ideas and beliefs of many peoples and cultures over thousands of years. A key belief of Hinduism is that the individual can come to know the powers of the universe through worship. Another is that the soul never dies. Instead, it is reincarnated (ree-uhn-**kahr**-nayt-uhd), or reborn, into a lower or higher life form depending on a person's behavior during his or her previous life.

Hinduism and Buddhism—sometimes together, sometimes separately—have influenced Indian art over the last 2500 years.

Architecture

Among the earliest, and most important, examples of modern Indian architecture are **stupas** (**stoop**-uhs), which are *beehive-shaped domed places of worship.* These were built by Buddhist architects to honor their religion's founder and other important leaders. Each stupa was reached through four gates covered with relief sculptures. Figure 8–1 shows the Great Stupa at Sanchi (san-**chee**). Find Sanchi on the map in Figure 8–2. Completed before A.D. 1, this impressive structure rises to 50 feet (15 m) at its highest point. Notice the contrast between the dome's smooth surface and the detailed carvings of the gate.

▶ Figure 8–1   Believers would pass through one of the gates, then slowly walk around the dome. All the while they would meditate. Do you recall what meditation is?

The Great Stupa. c. A.D. 1. Sanchi, India.

Note
Although the relief carvings on the stupa's gates tell of the life of Buddha, the figure of Buddha never appears. His presence is hinted at, rather, through "reminders," such as his footprints and empty throne.

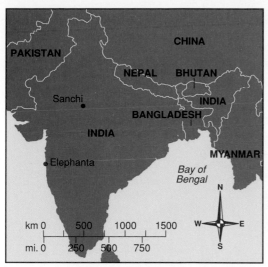

▲ Figure 8–2   India.

No less impressive were the great temples Hindu architects created some 600 years later. One of the most striking facts about these temples is how some of them were built. They were cut directly into solid natural rock formations.

Figure 8–3 shows an important achievement of Hindu temple building. This amazing structure was cut from a hilltop by many craftspeople. Its hall, almost 100 feet (30 m) square, is decorated with deeply carved religious panels. Yet, like other early Hindu temples, it was made to be viewed mainly from the outside. To the Hindus, a temple was as much sculpture as it was architecture.

▲ Figure 8–3   On entering the hall, visitors would come upon three gigantic heads. Standing for important Hindu religious figures, these heads were each nearly 14 feet (4 m) high.

Rock Cut Temple, India.

Lesson 1   *Art of India*   115

▲ **Figure 8—4   Some of the Buddhas created during this period had an unmistakably Greek look. This was the result of a conquest of parts of India in 327 B.C. by Alexander the Great, a powerful general who admired Greek art.**

Gautama Buddha in Contemplation. India, Gandharan. 1st-3rd Century A.D. Black schist. 73 cm (28¾"). Yale University Art Gallery, New Haven, Connecticut. Anonymous gift through Alfred R. Bellinger.

116   📖   Lesson 1   *Art of India*

Sculpture

Many sculptures, such as the work in Figure 8–4, show the Buddha seated in meditation. Look closely at this sculpture. Notice the dot on the forehead, the seated pose, and the unusually long earlobes of the figure. All are standard features of the Buddha image, each having its own special meaning. The earlobes, for instance, are a reminder of the heavy earrings the Buddha, who was born an Indian prince, wore before he gave up worldly possessions.

In sharp contrast to the weighty stone Buddha figures are the light, open sculptures of cast metal created later by Hindu sculptors. One of these works, the *Tree of Life and Knowledge*, is pictured in Figure 8–5. This sculpture expresses the Hindu belief in the creative force of the universe. Many animals were sacred to the Hindus, especially the cow. Can you find the cows in this work? What other creatures and birds do you notice? What kind of balance has the sculptor used?

◀ **Figure 8–5** The "tree of life" ties in with the Hindu belief in reincarnation. Since Hinduism teaches that animals have souls, they too can be reborn into higher or lower forms.

Tree of Life and Knowledge. Southern India, Late 1500–1600 A.D. Bronze. Nelson-Atkins Museum of Art, Kansas City, Missouri. Given anonymously.

STUDIO EXPERIENCE

Look once again at Figure 8–5. Each animal in the work plays a special part in the Hindu view of life. The goose at the end of each branch, for example, stands for the soul's ability to "take flight." The five-headed serpent at the center is a sign of evil and danger.

With a pencil and fine-tipped markers, create your own tree of life. Use the same kind of balance noted in the *Tree of Life and Knowledge*. Fill the branches of your tree with objects that play a part in your personal happiness. Some possibilities are pets, signs of favorite pastimes (a tennis racquet, for example), or good-luck charms. Create decorative patterns of repeated objects similar to the patterns in Figure 8–5. See whether classmates can guess the importance of objects based upon where they appear on your tree.

✔CHECK YOUR UNDERSTANDING

1. What are two key beliefs of Hinduism?
2. What is a stupa?
3. How was the temple shown in Figure 8–3 created?
4. Name three standard features of early Indian Buddhist sculptures.

Following Up

Closure. Have students work in small groups to share their ideas about Indian art. How is it similar to traditional Western art forms with which you may be more familiar? What distinguishes Indian art from European art? Which aspects of Indian art do you find most interesting? How can understanding Indian art help you understand and appreciate art of Europe, the Americas, and other cultures? How can understanding Indian art help you when you plan and create your own works?

Evaluation. 1. Review students' written responses to the "Check Your Understanding" questions. 2. Consider their contributions to the "Closure" group discussions.

Reteaching. Let students work with partners or in small groups to discuss their own "Studio Experience" drawings and compare them to the *Tree of Life and Knowledge* shown in Figure 8-5. What does your own drawing reflect about your interests and your life? How does it reflect the style of the *Tree of Life and Knowledge?* What are the most important differences between your drawing and the drawings made by other students? What are the most important differences between the *Tree of Life and Knowledge* in Figure 8-5 and the drawings made by all the students?

Enrichment. Ask volunteers to learn more about the gods of Hinduism and their representation in sculpture and other art forms. Let the volunteers work together to present their findings to the rest of the class; encourage them to include slides or photographs in their presentation if possible.

Answers to "Check Your Understanding"

1. Two key beliefs of Hinduism are reincarnation and that an individual can come to know the powers of the universe through worship.
2. A stupa is a beehive-shaped, domed temple.
3. The temple was cut from a hilltop by many craftspeople.
4. Three standard features of early Indian Buddhist sculpture included a dot on the forehead, a seated pose, and unusually long earlobes.

LESSON PLAN
(pages 118–119)

Objectives
After completing this lesson, students will be able to:
- Paint dancing figures in the style of Hindu sculpture.
- Describe, analyze, interpret, and judge their own work.

Supplies
- Pieces of batik fabric or clothing made from batik (or photographs of batik).
- Pencils; sketchbooks; yellow chalk; facial tissue; sheets of heavy white paper, 12 x 18 inches (30 x 45 cm); thick, creamy tempera paint in a variety of bright hues; thick and thin watercolor brushes; waterproof black ink; trays or pans measuring at least 12 x 18 inches (30 x 45 cm); thick pads of newspaper; polymer gloss medium.
- Art books that include reproductions of Indian art.

TRB Resource
- 8-2 *Batik Print,* (reproducible master)

TEACHING THE LESSON

Getting Started

Motivator. Display samples of batik (or photographs of batik). Let students describe the fabric and discuss other examples of batik they may have seen. Ask: How do you think batik is created? Let students discuss their ideas. Then, unless some of the students are familiar with batik and can explain it to the class, give a simplified explanation of the process: A design is painted onto washed cotton fabric with melted wax; then the fabric is dyed; when the fabric is dry, the wax is scraped or boiled away.

Vocabulary. Ask volunteers to look up the noun *batik* in a dictionary: From what language does the word come? What two meanings does the noun have?

Making a Tempera Batik

Hindu art is full of contrasts. Study the sculpture in Figure 8–6. This is Shiva (**shee-vuh**), one of three main gods of the Hindu religion. Notice the contrast between the vertical calm of Shiva's head and the diagonal movement of his arms, legs, and body. His pose captures the feeling of Hindu dance.

WHAT YOU WILL LEARN

You will create a painting of a dancing figure based on the style of the Hindu sculpture. You will use the contrast of vertical calm and diagonal movement. You will use the principle of rhythmic repetition to make your work decorative. You will add contrast and unusual effects to your work using a tempera batik (buh-**teek**) method. **Batik** is *a method of designing on fabric using wax and dyes.* (See Figure 8–7.) Your finished batik will express a mood of excitement.

WHAT YOU WILL NEED
- Pencil and sketchbook
- Yellow chalk and facial tissue
- Sheet of heavy white paper, 12 x 18 inches (30 x 45 cm)
- Thick, creamy liquid tempera paint in a variety of bright hues
- Thick and thin watercolor brushes
- Waterproof black ink
- Tray or pan measuring at least 12 x 18 inches (30 x 45 cm)
- Thick pads of newspaper
- Polymer gloss medium

WHAT YOU WILL DO

1. Study the sculpture of Shiva. Notice the placement of the arms and legs. Make rough sketches creating your own design for a dancer moving in the Hindu style.
2. Using yellow chalk, lightly draw your best dancing figure to fill your paper. Use rhythmic repetition to decorate the figure.
3. Go over your lines to make them wider. Trace over all your lines heavily with a layer of chalk.

◀ **Figure 8–6** Every part of this sculpture has a meaning. The arch and its three-tongued flames stand for the universe and its destruction by fire. The drum in the figure's "upper right" hand stands for the sound of the bang beginning the universe.

Tamil Nadu. *Shiva, King of the Dancers* (Nataraja). Chole Dynasty, 10th Century. Bronze. 76.2 x 57.1 x 17.8 cm (30 x 22½ x 7"). Los Angeles County Museum of Art, Los Angeles, California. Given anonymously.

Classroom Management Tip

Tempera Batik is a resist method. The tempera paint coats the paper to resist the ink. When it is washed off, unusual crackle effects occur. It is important that the paint be thick, or it will not resist the ink. Do *not* use anything but creamy liquid tempera for this process.

The paint must be thick to resist the ink. The paint MUST dry 24 hours or more. If you ink too soon the bottom layer of paint may not be dry.

The dust may smear over the paint in rubbing. That's okay. The heavy layer of chalk must be removed because it might resist the ink.

If the ink is stuck in places that need to be uncovered, it can be removed by rubbing very gently with a soft brush, or a very gentle touch of the fingers.

The paper is very fragile when wet. If a wrinkle occurs do not try to remove it. Wait until the painting is dry, and then press it with a cool iron.

4. Paint all the shapes, both positive and negative, with bright hues and light values. Do not paint over the chalk lines. Instead carefully paint up to them, but do not cover them. Put down a thick layer of paint. If necessary go over all the colors a second time. Set your work aside to dry at least 24 hours.

5. Gently rub off the thick layer of chalk with the facial tissue. Using a thick, soft brush cover the whole painting with one layer of black waterproof ink. Move the brush across the surface in one direction only. Rubbing it back and forth may dissolve the paint. When you have finished, dab any spots you missed with a brush loaded with ink. Allow the work to dry again 24 hours or longer if possible.

6. When the paper is dry, place it, ink side up, in the tray. Gently pour water over your work to cover it. After several minutes, pour off the water by tilting the tray. Add more water. Repeat this process until the ink has worn off in spots, leaving a crackling effect like you see in batik fabric.

7. Pick up your paper very carefully by two corners. Set it down flat on a thick pad of newspaper to dry.

8. *Optional:* Coat your work with a layer of clear, glossy polymer medium. This will make the colors look richer and it will protect the ink from flaking off.

OTHER STUDIO IDEAS

- Do a second version of your Hindu pattern, this time using a monochromatic color scheme with tempera paint. Describe in what ways this design differs from your original.

EXAMINING YOUR WORK

- **Describe** Identify the figure in your design. Did you follow all the technique directions?
- **Analyze** Explain how your figure shows movement. Explain how you used contrast of line and value. Tell whether you have created a decorative quality by using rhythmic repetition.
- **Interpret** Describe the mood of this work. Explain how this mood is shown. Give your work a title.
- **Judge** Tell whether you feel your work succeeds. Explain your answer.

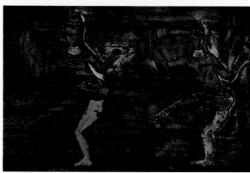

▲ Figure 8–7   Student work. Tempera batik.

- ● Draw the figure and cover it with a chalk line pattern. Paint between the lines and paint the negative space.

Lesson 2   *Making a Tempera Batik*   🎨   **119**

Developing Concepts
Exploring Aesthetics. Guide students in discussing the sculpture of Shiva in Figure 8-6: What principles have been used to organize the visual elements in this work? What message or mood do you think this sculpture was intended to communicate? What idea or feeling does it communicate to you now? Is this sculpture a work of art? Why, or why not?

Developing Studio Skills. Ask a group of volunteers to read about safe techniques for making batik cloth at home. Have these volunteers experiment with creating batiks. Let them share the results with the rest of the class.

Appreciating Cultural Diversity. Let groups of students read about the special fabrics created in other cultures, such as the cotton fabrics of various African groups and the silks of China and Japan. Let these groups share their findings—including photographs, if possible—with the rest of the class.

Following Up
Closure. Let students work with partners to discuss their designs, following the steps in "Examining Your Work." Then have students write short paragraphs interpreting their own designs, responding to the "Interpret" instructions.

Evaluation. Review students' designs and read their interpretations of their own work.

Reteaching. Ask small groups of students to share and discuss what they like most about the art of India. Then have group members browse through art books, identifying and showing examples of Indian art: Which visual elements can they identify in each art work? What principles have been used to organize those elements?

Enrichment. Remind students that their batiks were intended to express a mood of excitement. Then ask each student to write a short story or poem inspired by his or her batik.

Background Information
Followers of the Hindu religion usually accept a multitude of gods; the most important deities, however, are Shiva, Vishnu, and Brahma.

The god Shiva has many aspects and many forms. He is at once terrible and graceful; he is the destroyer of the world in the endless cycle of destruction and re-creation. Shiva is the god of death; he is also the god of dance and love.

The dancing Shiva shown here expresses the rhythmic cycle of destruction and renewal. Every portion of the sculpture is rich with symbolism. One left hand holds the flame of spiritual light that burns away the veils of illusion. The other left hand points with the "teaching" gesture to the raised left foot, which represents release. One right hand shows the fear-dissolving pose, while the other holds the drum that beats eternity's rhythms. Under Shiva's right foot lies forgetfulness, which takes away the memory of past lives.

LESSON PLAN
(pages 120–123)

Objectives
After completing this lesson, students will be able to:
- Explain how Islamic culture began.
- Identify the major Islamic contributions to painting, architecture, and crafts.
- Define the terms *calligraphy, arabesque, mosque, mihrab,* and *minaret.*
- Create their own small samples of knotted-pile rugs.

Supplies
- A small Persian rug (if available) or photographs of Persian rugs.
- Strips of lightweight cardboard, scissors, glue, tapestry needles, yarn.
- Sheets of drawing paper, pencils, black ink, small brushes.

TRB Resources
- 8-3 *Adapting Styles,* (appreciating cultural diversity)
- 8-4 *The Prayer Rug,* (appreciating cultural diversity)
- 8-5 *Persian Miniatures,* (art history)
- 8-6 *Bringing the East to the West,* (cooperative learning)
- 8-7 *Make Your Own Miniature,* (studio)

TEACHING THE LESSON

Getting Started
Motivator. If you have a small Persian rug available for display, put it out where students can examine it closely. If a real rug is not available, show slides or photographs of several rugs. Let students identify and describe what they observe: What kinds of patterns are woven into the rug? What colors are used? How would you describe the texture of the rug? If some students are familiar with Persian rugs, let them describe other rugs and share what they know about where and how the rugs are made. Explain to the class that Persian rugs are one of the outstanding contributions of Islamic art; students will learn about other contributions as they study this lesson.

Art of Islam

Around A.D. 600 Hinduism, which had lost favor in India with the rise of Buddhism, began making a comeback. During this same period another religion was taking shape 2000 miles (3220 km) to the east. This new religion would grow into one of the world's largest, with some half billion followers. Its name is Islam (**iz**-lahm).

THE GROWTH OF ISLAM

The birthplace of Islam is the city of Mecca (**mek**-uh), located on the Arabian peninsula. Can you find Mecca on the map in Figure 8–8? There in A.D. 613 a merchant named Muhammad (moh-**ham**-uhd) began preaching a faith centering on one god. This god, called Allah, had revealed himself to Muhammad during meditation. People who came to share Muhammad's beliefs recognized him as Allah's holy messenger. They, themselves, were called Muslims (**muhz**-luhms).

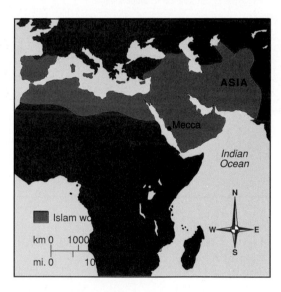

ASIA

Mecca

Indian
Ocean

Islam wo

km 0   1000
mi. 0   10

◄ **Figure 8–8   The lands of Islam.**

Muhammad's lifelong dream was a world united under Islam. By the early 700s, his followers had spread his message to the Middle East, North Africa, Europe, and Asia.

Painting
The Koran (kuh-**ran**) is the bible of Islam, recording the beliefs of Muhammad. A page from the Koran is shown in Figure 8–9. Some of the finest examples of early calligraphy (kuh-**ligg**-ruh-fee) are found in this book. **Calligraphy** is *a method of beautiful handwriting sometimes using a brush.* Notice the circular gold decorations among the flowing letters. **Arabesques** (ar-uh-**besks**) are the *swirling geometric patterns of plant life used as decorations.* These became a popular decoration because the early Muslim teachings forbade picturing humans or animals.

Architecture
Muhammad taught that dying in battle for the faith guaranteed Muslims entrance into Paradise. As a result, Islam was often spread through force rather than preaching. Each new conquest was celebrated by the building of a **mosque,** *a Muslim house of worship.* By the 800s the Muslim capital of Córdoba (**kord**-uh-vuh), Spain, alone was reported to have 300 mosques.

120   Lesson 3   *Art of Islam*

Note
Islam is the Arabic word for "surrender." Muhammad was disturbed by his fellow Arabs' practice of worshiping many different idols. His goal was to have them "surrender to the will of one God."

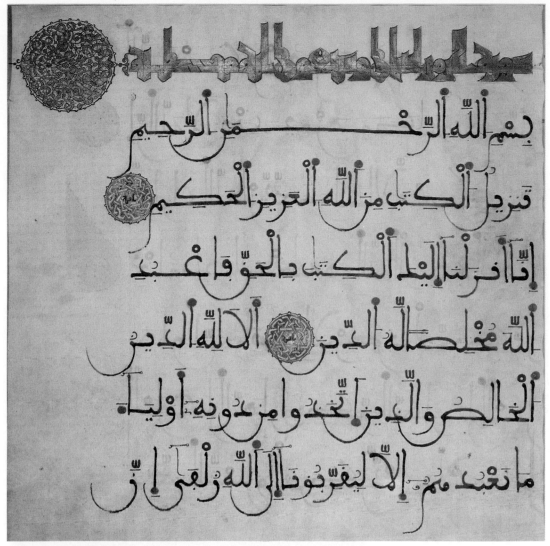

▲ **Figure 8–9** Calligraphy means "beautiful writing." The work that opened this chapter on page 112 also makes use of calligraphy. Can you find it in among the figures?

Leaf from Qur'an (Koran), in Maghribi Script. Islamic, North African. c. 1300. Ink, colors and gold on parchment. 53.3 x 55.8 cm (21 x 22"). The Metropolitan Museum of Art, New York, New York. Rogers Fund.

Figures 8–10 and 8–11 show two views of a Spanish mosque begun in the 700s. In Figure 8–10 you can see a **mihrab** (**mee**-ruhb), which is *a highly decorated nook found in a mosque*. Covered with calligraphic inscriptions from the Koran, the mihrab is found on the wall closest to the holy city of Mecca. The origin and purpose of the mihrab is still a mystery. Some scholars feel it may honor the place where Muhammad stood in his own house when he led his followers in prayer. It became a standard feature of all mosques. Rising above the outside of such mosques are found one or more minarets (min-uh-**rets**). A **minaret** is a *slender tower from which Muslims are called to prayer* five times a day. Can you

Vocabulary. Have volunteers use dictionaries to look up the words *calligraphy* and *arabesque*. From what two ancient Greek words does our word *calligraphy* come? What is the meaning of those two Greek words? How can they help you understand what calligraphy is? What is the meaning of the word from which *arabesque* is derived? Which definition of *arabesque* relates to visual arts and which relates to the art of ballet? What connection can you see between those two meanings of the word?

Developing Concepts

Exploring Aesthetics. Have students work in groups to examine and discuss the page from the Koran shown in Figure 8-9: What do you see in this work? How does it make you feel? What purpose was this page intended to serve when it was created? What feeling or message does it communicate to you now? What distinguishes this page as a work of art?

Using Art Criticism. Guide students in discussing the Spanish mosque shown in Figures 8-10 and 8-11. Remind students that works of architecture are usually considered examples both of fine art and of applied art. Let students describe, analyze, and interpret the mosque as shown in these two photographs. Then ask students to judge the work both as fine art and as applied art.

Understanding Art History. Ask students to research the Taj Mahal, shown in Figure 8-12: When and where was it built? Who had it built, and for what reason? What does the location of the Taj Mahal indicate about the spread of Islam? Then let students compare and discuss what they have learned.

Background Information

The main religious building of Islam is the mosque. Our word *mosque* comes from the Arabic word *masjid,* which means "a place to kneel down or to prostrate one's self." Every mosque must be oriented toward Mecca, the birthplace of Muhammad. In addition, a mosque must have a courtyard, a mihrab, a gate, and at least one minaret.

Statues or other visual depictions of human and animal forms are not found within mosques; most decoration takes the form of geometric and floral motifs on the walls of the mosque. The floor is usually covered with carpets or reed matting on which worshipers kneel and touch their foreheads to the ground.

As Islam spread to various countries, the styles in which mosques were constructed grew more varied. Worshipers built their mosques to reflect their local culture and style as well as their religious beliefs. Among the most famous mosques are the Suleymaniye Mosque in Istanbul, Turkey and the Imam Mosque in Isfahan, Iran.

▲ Figure 8–11   What feeling does this seemingly endless row of columns and arches communicate?

The Great Mosque and Roman Bridge. Cordoba, Spain.

▲ Figure 8–10   Muslims always turn toward Mecca while praying. The mihrab, placed inside a mosque, is a pointer to this holy city.

The Great Mosque of Abd ar-Rahman. 8-12th Century. Moorish. Mihrab with arched dome. Cordoba, Spain.

► Figure 8–12   This work was built by a Muslim leader as a memorial to his wife. Notice the perfect symmetry of the building and all that surrounds it.

Taj Mahal, garden and pools. c. 1650. Agra, India.

122   Lesson 3   *Art of Islam*

find the minarets in the famous structure in Figure 8–12? Do you know the name and location of this famous building?

Crafts

One of the most outstanding contributions of Islamic art is the knotted-pile, or Persian, rug. Persian knots in this type of rug are so close together that when the pile (raised loops of yarn) is all worn away the colors of the design are still visible. Figure 8–13 shows a Persian rug dating from 1550. This object uses 18 different shades of wool. Notice the care the weaver has used in balancing the complex design. Can you name the type of pattern running through this carpet?

▲ **Figure 8–13   A single rug would take one craftsperson many years to complete.**

Iranian. Prayer rug. 16th Century. Wool, cotton, silk. 161.3 x 108 cm (63½ x 42½"). The Metropolitan Museum of Art, New York, New York. Mr. and Mrs. Isaac D. Fletcher Collection. Bequest of Isaac D. Fletcher.

STUDIO EXPERIENCE

Look again at Figure 8–13. A feature common to rugs like this is the Persian knot, illustrated in Figure 8–14. Using knots like these, the weaver was able to create an unusually tight weave.

Make a very small cardboard loom and make a warp. (See Chapter 13, Lesson 2, for a description of how to make a warp.) Using a tapestry needle and yarn, alternate rows of Persian knots with rows of tabby (simple over, under, over, under) weave.

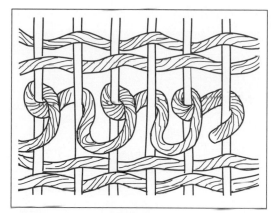

▲ **Figure 8–14   Persian knot diagram.**

✔CHECK YOUR UNDERSTANDING

1. Who was Muhammad? When and where did he begin preaching his new faith?
2. What are followers of Muhammad called?
3. What is the Koran? What is calligraphy?
4. What is an arabesque? Why did arabesques become popular?
5. What is a mosque? What are two standard features of mosques?
6. What kind of rugs are Islamic artists famous for?

Following Up

Closure. Have students write a paragraph in response to this question: Which form of Islamic art do you find most interesting? Be sure students include explanations of their ideas in these paragraphs. Then have students meet in small groups to read and discuss their paragraphs. Group members should also share the small samples of Persian carpets they made in the "Studio Experience" activity. How has each student used the combination of Persian knots and tabby weave?

Evaluation. 1. Review students' written responses to the "Check Your Understanding" questions. 2. Read their paragraphs about Islamic art and listen to their "Closure" group discussions.

Reteaching. Let groups of students work together to review the most important features of Islamic architecture. Then have group members browse through books that include photographs of Islamic structures; ask them to identify photographs of mosques, minarets, and mihrabs. Then have them compare different mosques: How are the buildings alike? What makes each unique?

Enrichment. Have students form research teams in which to learn about the Islamic religion and culture. Let the students in each team choose four or five questions that interest them and then organize themselves to find answers to those questions. Ask the members of each research team to summarize what they have learned in written or oral reports.

Answers to "Check Your Understanding"

1. Muhammad was a merchant. He began preaching his faith about A.D. 613 in Mecca.
2. Followers of Muhammad are called Muslims.
3. The Koran is the bible of Islam. Calligraphy is a method of decorative handwriting using a brush.
4. Arabesques are swirling geometric patterns of plant life used as decoration. These became popular because Muslim teachings forbad picturing animals or humans.
5. A Mosque is a Muslim house of worship. Two standard features of mosques are mihrabs and minarets.
6. Islamic artists are famous for knotted-pile, or Persian, rugs.

Making a Collage in the Islamic Style

Objectives

After completing this lesson, students will be able to:
- Create collages with several scenes organized in the manner of Islamic miniature paintings.
- Describe, analyze, interpret, and judge their own collages.

Supplies

- Several collages (including student works if possible) and/or reproductions of collages.
- Pencils; sheets of sketch paper; rulers; scissors; sheets of white paper or poster board, 22 x 28 inches (56 x 71 cm); variety of patterned fabrics and papers; white glue; colored pencils; small pieces of white drawing paper.
- Magazines (provided by students if possible), tracing paper, pencils.

> **TRB Resources**
> - 8-8 *Islamic Geometric Designs*, (reproducible master)
> - 8-9 *Creating an Islamic Design*, (studio)

TEACHING THE LESSON

Getting Started

Motivator. Show the class several collages, and encourage students to discuss their own experiences in making and viewing collages. What makes collages different from other kinds of art works? How can collages be similar to paintings? Explain to students that, though collage is a modern art form, they will be making collages in the style of ancient Islamic paintings.

Vocabulary. Ask students to use dictionaries to find the derivations of the words *miniature* and *collage:* What is the meaning of the Latin word from which our English word *miniature* comes? Are the origins of this word related to size or to the use of color? What is the meaning of the French word from which we get *collage?* How does that meaning help explain the technique of making a collage?

Making a Collage in the Islamic Style

Look at the Islamic miniature painting in Figure 8–15. Everything seems to be flat on the picture plane. The colors are intensely bright. How many different scenes or images do you see? Notice how the artist presents many points of view in the same work of art. A variety of patterns are used to fill the background spaces. Shapes, colors, and patterns are emphasized. By doing so, the illusion of depth is not felt.

◄ Figure 8–15 This is a page of a book meant to be held in the hand and studied closely. Notice the patterns, rhythmic designs, and bright colors. Some of the pigments for the work were made by grinding precious metals such as gold and silver.

'Abd Allah Musawwir. *The Meeting of the Theologians.* c. 1540–1549. Colors on paper. Bokhara. Nelson-Atkins Museum of Fine Arts, Kansas City, Missouri.

WHAT YOU WILL LEARN

In this lesson you will create a **collage**, *an art work made up of bits and pieces of two-dimensional materials pasted to a surface.* Your collage will focus on several scenes related to a current event or activity. The work will be organized, however, in the manner of a flat, patterned Islamic miniature painting. You will use bright colors, decorative patterns, and flat shapes as in Figure 8–15. You will create the background shapes using patterned fabrics and papers. People and other objects can be made by drawing and painting them on white paper. See Figure 8–16.

WHAT YOU WILL NEED

- Pencil, sketch paper, ruler, scissors
- Sheet of white paper or poster board, 22 x 28 inches (56 x 71 cm)
- A variety of patterned fabrics and papers
- White glue, colored pencils
- Small pieces of white drawing paper

Background Information

Because early Islamic artists could not depict the figures of humans or animals, they developed a style of flat, abstract designs to be used in a variety of works. Best known is the arabesque, which comes from the Italian word meaning "Arab-like." These swirling, interlaced designs are apparently based on plant shapes, but the forms of leaves, branches, and vines have been transformed into scrolls, spirals, and curves. Such arabesque designs were first used during the 900s in all Muslim countries. Arabesques and other geometric designs have been used to decorate the walls of buildings, tiles, miniature paintings, rugs, metalware, and other craft objects.

Less stylized arabesques have also been used in European art. Arabesques were used in ancient Greek art works. They also became important forms of ornamentation during the Renaissance, when humans and figures were often portrayed interwoven with the swirling plant forms.

WHAT YOU WILL DO

1. Brainstorm with classmates for ideas that could best be explained by showing several different scenes. For example, to show a football game you might have one scene of a huddle, one of a tackle, and one of the ball being kicked. Pick an event, such as a school dance, a parade, or a wedding. Make pencil sketches of different objects and scenes from the event you picked.

2. Make a plan to arrange your best ideas within rectangles of different sizes. Using the ruler and pencil, lightly draw these rectangles on the poster board.

3. Measure each shape and cut out patterned fabric or paper to fit each shape. As you select each pattern for the background, consider how one will look next to another. Look for contrast in the fabric so that you can see the distinction between each shape. If you wish, you may draw and color patterns in some of the spaces. Glue the pieces of fabric and paper to the poster board.

4. Draw and color figures and objects to place in each scene. Measure first to be sure that the figure will fit inside its area. Cut out the drawn objects and glue them onto the design.

5. When the glue is dry display your work. See whether classmates can guess what event your collage celebrates.

▶ Figure 8–16   Student work. Collage in the Islamic style.

EXAMINING YOUR WORK

- **Describe**   Identify the different scenes and objects related to your events. Explain why you placed each scene or object where you did.
- **Analyze**   Show where you used contrast in your design. Identify how you used the element of space. Explain how the many different patterned areas made your work look different from other art works you have created.
- **Interpret**   State what feeling or mood your work communicates to viewers.
- **Judge**   Tell whether you feel your work succeeds. Explain your answer.

OTHER STUDIO IDEAS

- Working as part of a group of four students, make another collage. This time use a larger sheet of poster board.

- ●● Pick an American legend or hero, such as Paul Bunyan, Daniel Boone, or Betsy Ross. Organize the events of the person's life in a second collage.

Lesson 4   *Making a Collage in the Islamic Style*   **125**

Developing Concepts

Using Art Criticism. Guide students in examining and discussing the Islamic miniature painting shown in Figure 8-15: What do you see when you look at this work? How is it similar to other paintings you have studied? What makes it different? What message or mood do you think this painting is intended to communicate? Do you think this painting is a successful work of art? Why, or why not?

Developing Studio Skills. To prepare for drawing small figures to use in their collages, let students trace small photographs or drawings from magazines.

Appreciating Cultural Diversity. Ask a group of volunteers to read about the illuminated manuscripts of medieval Europe. Let these volunteers discuss their findings with the class, showing reproductions if possible. Then help the class consider how these European works are similar to—and different from—the Islamic miniature paintings.

Following Up

Closure. Give each student an opportunity to present his or her collage to the rest of the class. During these presentations, ask students to analyze their own collages, responding to the instructions in "Examining Your Work." Encourage students to ask questions and make positive comments about one another's collages.

Evaluation. Review students' collages in the Islamic style and listen to their presentations of their own work.

Reteaching. Work with groups of students as they compare their collages with the Islamic miniature painting shown in Figure 8-15. Why is collage a good art form for creating works that echo the style of this kind of miniature painting? Which collages best capture the feeling of Islamic miniature paintings? Would you have found it harder—or easier—to imitate this style in a painting? Why?

Enrichment. Let students try creating original drawings or paintings in the style of Islamic miniature paintings.

Building Vocabulary

1. stupas
2. batik
3. calligraphy
4. arabesques
5. mosque
6. mihrab
7. minaret
8. collage

Reviewing Art Facts

9. Buddhism and Hinduism have played a major role in the art of India.
10. Hindu temples like the one in Figure 8-3 were sometimes cut from a hilltop.
11. The long earlobes on the Buddha sculptures were a reminder of the heavy earrings he wore before giving up worldly possessions.
12. The *Tree of Life and Knowledge* expresses the Hindu belief that many animals are sacred, especially the cow.
13. The god of Islam is called Allah. He revealed himself to Muhammad during meditation.
14. Calligraphy was used in the Koran.
15. Muslims built a mosque to celebrate each new conquest.
16. Persian knots are so close together that when the pile has worn away the colors of the design remain visible.

Thinking About Art

1. Students may disagree with the statement. They should cite the steps an art critic and an art historian would use to judge a work of art in order to understand it.
2. Buddhist stupas were domed and beehive-shaped; Hindu temples were cut from solid rock formations. Both could contain relief sculpture.
3. Answers will vary. Students should show they know the elements and the principles and can accurately identify them in a work of art.
4. The answer should address the amount of detail and the huge size of the interior, neither of which are apparent from the photographs. Seeing a work of art first hand intensifies its impact.

CHAPTER 8 REVIEW

BUILDING VOCABULARY

Number a sheet of paper from 1 to 8. After each number, write the term from the box that best matches each description below.

arabesques	mihrab
batik	minaret
calligraphy	mosque
collage	stupas

1. Beehive-shaped domed places of worship.
2. A method of designing on fabric using wax and dyes.
3. A method of beautiful handwriting sometimes using a brush.
4. Swirling geometric patterns of plant life used as decorations.
5. A Muslim house of worship.
6. A highly decorated nook found in a mosque.
7. A slender tower from which Muslims are called to prayer.
8. An art work made up of bits and pieces of two-dimensional materials pasted to a surface.

REVIEWING ART FACTS

Number a sheet of paper from 9 to 16. Answer each question in a complete sentence.

9. What two religions have played a major role in the art of India over the last 2500 years?
10. How were Hindu temples like the one shown in Figure 8–3 created?
11. What is the explanation for the unusually long earlobes found on Buddha sculptures?
12. What Hindu belief is revealed in the *Tree of Life and Knowledge* sculpture?
13. What is the name of the god of Islam? How did Muhammad come to know this god?
14. In what book central to the Islam faith was calligraphy used?
15. What buildings did Muslim conquerors raise after each new conquest?
16. What can you see in Persian rugs that reveals the special weaving method with which they were made?

THINKING ABOUT ART

On a sheet of paper, answer each question in a sentence or two.

1. **Interpret.** Read the following statement: "To appreciate fully a work of religious art you must be a member of the religion." Tell whether you agree or disagree. Defend your position with information and examples from this and other chapters.
2. **Compare and contrast.** What common features can you find between Buddhist and Hindu temples? What differences between the two can you note?
3. **Analyze.** Pick one art work from the chapter. Note how the elements of art and principles of art were used in the work. Identify the way they were used.
4. **Extend.** Look once more at the inside view of the mosque in Figure 8–10. How would the experience of walking through this building differ from the experience of seeing it in a photograph? What does this difference reveal to you about ways of looking at art?

MAKING ART CONNECTIONS

1. **Social Studies.** Like Islam, Buddhism spread far from its birthplace. Compare the Japanese sculpture of Buddha you studied in Chapter 5 on page **73** with Figure 8–4. List the ways the two works are alike and different. Note standard style features of each. Identify the influences of culture that led to these similarities and differences.
2. **Language Arts.** Create a verse for a greeting card. Write your poem using a calligraphy style.

LOOKING AT THE DETAILS

The detail shown below is from Sultan Muhammad's *The Feast of Sadeh*. Study the detail and answer the following questions using complete sentences.

1. Can you see evidence of a renowned Islamic craft in this painting?
2. If you were not aware of the origin of this painting and a credit line was not available, what clues do you see that might tell you that it is an Islamic work of art?

3. How would you describe the mood of the top figure? Is the same mood expressed by the lower figure? Explain your answer.
4. Look at the entire work on page **112**. Do you think this painting is meant to be "read" in a clockwise or counter clockwise direction? Explain your answer.

Sultan Muhammed. *The Feast of Sadeh*. c. 1520–1522. Colors, ink, silver and gold on paper. 27.4 x 23 cm (9½ x 9¹⁄₁₆"). The Metropolitan Museum of Art, New York, New York. Gift of Arthur A. Houghton, Jr.

ANSWERS TO "LOOKING AT THE DETAILS"

1. The Persian rug, upon which the top figure is seated, is evidence of the Islamic craft of carpet weaving.
2. The calligraphy, the lack of depth, the portrayal of more than one scene, and the patterns used to fill the background spaces, are all clues which might suggest that this is an Islamic art work.
3. Student answers may vary. Some considerations might include: The mood of the top figure is demanding, authoritative, strong, important, and wealthy. The mood of the lower figure differs from the mood of the top figure in that it expresses a mood of hard work, weariness, subservience, and a laboring lifestyle.
4. This painting is meant to be read in a clockwise direction because most of the figures' faces and body positions lead the viewer's eye in that direction. Also the animals at the bottom center of the work appear to be moving to the left, along with the man, which then lead the viewer to the two figures at the left which direct the eye to the central figure, then down to the right figures, etc.

Chapter Evaluation

The goal of this chapter is to develop students' understanding of the Indian contributions in architecture and sculpture, and to identify major Islamic contributions to art. Some possible evaluation techniques include:

1. The illusion of depth is not felt in Islamic miniature painting. Have students analyze a miniature painting and explain how the artist has not created a sense of depth.

2. Write the chapter vocabulary words and their definitions on a sheet of paper. Cut the terms and definitions apart and place them in an envelope. Prepare one envelope for each student. Have the students open the envelope and match the term with the definition.

3. Have students complete Chapter 8 Test (TRB, Resource 8-10).

Art of Africa

Chapter Scan

TRB Resources
- 9-10 Chapter Test
- Color Transparency 17
- Color Transparency 18

TEACHING THE CHAPTER

Introducing the Art Work

Have students refer to the *Dance Headdress*. Inform them that this sculpture comes from the Ibo tribe of West Africa. Explain that most African art works were created for use in various ceremonies, which incorporated physical art pieces with music, dancing, and poetry. For the artists, the meaning in their works lay in the part they played in these ceremonies. This art work was kept in shrines and only seen by the people during these special rituals. The African sculptor spent years in strenuous apprenticeship learning how to use the tools and materials of his art. The sculptor was supposed to use symbolism which was understood by everyone in his village. Masks and headdresses were created to establish the presence of specific spirits for particular ceremonies. It was believed that because of the headdress, the dancer became possessed by the spirit. Explain that with the introduction of trading, Christianity, Western education and urbanization into Africa, the Ibo people no longer adhere to their traditional views.

▲ This headdress was to be worn as a sign of magical power. The section over the cap stands for a tribal altar. The birds signal the presence of ghosts.

Africa, Nigeria, Ibo Tribe. Dance Headdress. Wood, paint, metal, fiber. 47 x 32.7 x 27.7 cm (18½ x 12⅞ x 10⅞"). Dallas Museum of Art, Dallas, Texas. The Eugene & Margaret McDermott Fund.

Art of Africa

Africa's past is shrouded in mystery. Until recent times there were no written documents and contacts with peoples from other lands were limited. Even the wood figures and masks of the past no longer exist. They were destroyed by the damp climate and wood-eating insects.

Most of the African art you see in museums today was made within the past 100 years. Works like the one pictured at the left are more than a tribute to the imagination and skill of recent African artists. They are our only clues to the works of generations of artists who came before.

OBJECTIVES

After completing this chapter, you will be able to:
- Describe the figures in wood and bronze made by African tribal sculptors.
- Name the three kinds of masks made by African tribal sculptors.
- Work with different media to create abstract and imaginative art objects.

WORDS YOU WILL LEARN

abstract work papier-mâché
face mask shoulder masks
headpieces

Examining the Art Work
Tell students that this sculpture is considered tribal art—traditional art produced by Africans for Africans within the framework of the tribal system of values. Point out the sharp visual texture of the work. Explain that the long vertical points represent ram horns, symbolizing strength and aggression, and the circular layers of small triangles symbolize the idea of rank and prestige. The birds symbolize natural power. Tell students that if the sculpture is viewed from the front, it exhibits symmetrical balance. There are equal numbers of horns, triangles and birds on either side of the head.

Discussing the Art Work
Ask students to identify how rhythm is achieved in this work. Point out how the triangles, birds, and horns form an even, circular pattern. Explain how this creates an even rhythm representational of the drum, which was the key instrument of the dance. Explain how the lower row of triangles, which point down and away from the bell shape, along with the bird heads facing down, create a sense of movement.

Ask students to think about how this sculpture makes them feel. Remind the students that the African culture believed that the spirit was in the headdress and suggest that the sculptor succeeded in creating the illusion that this piece is restraining an intense force within itself—a power trying to burst out. Also point out how the dark color emphasizes the mood of strength, power, seriousness and force.

Tell students that in this chapter they will learn about wood and bronze figures and different kinds of masks made by African tribal sculptors. They will also work with different media to create their own art objects.

129

Building Self-Esteem
Tell students that in this chapter they will see masks and headpieces created by African artists. In many cases, tribe members attached great magical importance to these masks and used them to try to influence the spirit world. Some of the masks were crafted for use in ceremonies to ensure a good harvest; others were made to help protect the tribe from the baffling forces of nature. Although many of these masks and carvings were made in the nineteenth and twentieth centuries, the tribes creating them were relying on ceremonies and superstitions to help them cope with a reality they did not understand. Help students discuss the reasons for ceremonies of a kind that might be considered futile by other cultures. Make the point that, although the masks and ceremonies didn't affect the outcome of the harvests, the artifacts and the stories behind them are a valuable contribution to our understanding of cultural diversity.

Objectives

After completing this lesson, students will be able to:
- Describe the wood and bronze figures made by African tribal sculptors.
- Define the term *abstract work*.
- Draw themselves, creating figures that reveal their personalities rather than their appearances.

Supplies

- Wall map of Africa (if available).
- Pencils, sheets of drawing paper.
- Photographs of animals, sheets of drawing paper, sheets of tracing paper, markers.
- An adz, or photograph of an adz.

> **TRB Resources**
> - 9-1 *Beauty in Pattern*, (aesthetics/art criticism)
> - 9-2 *Yoruba Twin Sculptures*, (aesthetics/art criticism)

TEACHING THE LESSON

Getting Started

Motivator. Have students work in groups to begin sharing and discussing their ideas about Africa and African art. First, have members of each group brainstorm a list of words that come to mind when they think of Africa. Encourage all group members to contribute, and have one member record all the ideas. Then have all students compare the ideas listed by their groups. Display a map of Africa (if available) and ask: How many different countries can you identify in Africa? Which groups included names of African countries on your lists? Do any of your lists include names of African tribal groups? Do any include works of art created by African artists? What else did you include in your lists? As students respond, emphasize that Africa is a large continent with a diverse population and a rich history of art; explain that students will learn more about Africa and African art as they study this lesson.

130

The Figure Sculptures of Africa

Africa is the second largest continent in the world. It is more than three times the size of the United States. Yet, until Portuguese explorers came in the late 1400s, little about Africa was known. To this day the continent's distant past remains cloaked in mystery.

THE CULTURES OF AFRICA

The peoples of Africa below the Sahara live in many different tribes and kingdoms. The location of the larger of these tribes is shown on the map in Figure 9–1. Each tribe has its own language, customs, and religion.

Each tribe has also made its own unique contribution to the world of art. Many of these contributions have taken the form of sculpted human figures and masks. In this lesson you will read about the human figure sculptures created by African artists.

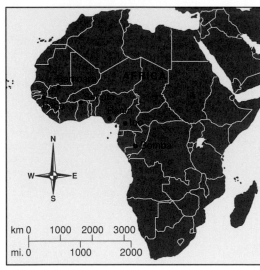

▲ Figure 9–1 Africa.

Carved Wood Figures

A favored medium of the African tribal sculptor was wood. Most carvings were made from a single log. The original shape of the log was often suggested in the finished work. Many were rubbed with natural oils to heighten the beauty of the work. This was also thought to add to the carving's magical powers.

Figure 9–2 shows a carving by an artist of a west African tribe. Like all African wood figures, the work is boldly carved. It is also typically abstract. An **abstract work** is *a work in which the artist uses a recognizable subject but portrays it in an unrealistic manner*.

▲ Figure 9–2   Carvings like this were not done to please their owners. They were done for the sake of the spirit who lived inside the carving.

Africa, Ivory Coast, Senufo Tribe. Bird. 19th-20th Century. Wood. 121.2 cm (47½"). The Metropolitan Museum of Art, New York, New York. The Michael C. Rockefeller Memorial Collection. Gift of Nelson A. Rockefeller.

Background Information

The art of Africa cannot be simply defined by a set of rules, but it can be contrasted with the European version of the arts. While European art is generally meant to be a lasting expression of an individual's perspective, African art work is meant to be used for specific occasions or purposes and doesn't reflect the creator as much as it fulfills a certain need. The differing attitudes towards the arts delineate a cultural and fundamental difference between the egocentric Europeans and the tribal Africans. While the European arts represent an artist's view of society, African arts are meant to function in society.

The figurine is a typical form of African art. When asked to carve figures to bring luck, prosperity, or divining powers, an artist would be inspired more by appropriateness than personal vision. Unfortunately, the utilitarian aspects of African art that make it unique from the European perspective have also made it hard to come by. After they have served their purposes, works are usually discarded or allowed to deteriorate.

Figure 9–3 shows a Senufo carving. This one appears to be a man on a horse. Actually, it is much more than that. Legend has it that the rider is a magician. His powers allow him to travel between the spirit world and the real world. Notice how this carving seems almost to reveal the artist at work. You can almost picture the artist's knife slashing the forms of horse and rider from the log. The finished work captures the dignity and pride of the rider with his shoulders back and his chest and chin thrust forward.

◄ Figure 9–3 In creating figures like this, the artist would perform certain rituals. One was making an offering to the tree the wood was taken from.

Africa, Ivory Coast, Senufo Tribe. Equestrian Figure. 19-20th Century. Wood, patination. 32.5 x 7.3 x 22.3 cm (12¾ x 3 x 8¾"). Dallas Museum of Art, Dallas, Texas. Gustave and Franyo Schindler Collection. Gift of the McDermott Foundation.

Lesson 1 *The Figure Sculptures of Africa* 📖 **131**

Vocabulary. Have volunteers look up the word *abstract* in dictionaries and read the various definitions. Ask: How are these different definitions related to each other? Which definition of *abstract* is used to tell about works of art? Where and when have you seen abstract works of art? How are they different from realistic or naturalistic works? How are they different from non-objective works?

Developing Concepts

Exploring Aesthetics. Guide students in examining and discussing the two carved wood figures shown in Figures 9-2 and 9-3. Ask: What are the most important similarities between the two works? What are the most important differences? Then let students describe the subject of each work, identify and describe visual elements, and name the principles used to organize those elements. Then ask about each sculpture: What message or mood does this work communicate to you? Is it a work of art? Why, or why not? Is the tribal sculptor who created it an artist? Why, or why not?

Using Art Criticism. Have students work in small groups to discuss the bronze sculpture shown in Figure 9-4. Members of each group should discuss and try to agree on responses to these questions: What is the subject of this work? What visual elements have been used in this sculpture? What principles of art organize those elements? What is the effect of those principles? What meaning or message is the work intended to communicate? Is this a good or successful work? Why, or why not? Have one member of each group take notes; then let that student summarize the group's responses for the rest of the class.

Note
Point out to students that the continent of Africa is very large—three times the size of the United States. Refer them to the world map on pages **314-315**. Ask them to compare the size of the African continent with North and South America. Ask if any students have traveled across the United States by plane or car. Let them share their experience of how great the distance seems when driving. Then remind them that most African tribes traveled by foot from one location to another, therefore they were not apt to go very far from their tribal location. This contributed to the isolation of tribes and the fact that they each maintained their own language, religious beliefs, and customs.

Understanding Art History.

Explain to students that the sculptures of the Benin Empire (such as the one shown in Figure 9-4) are among the most famous examples of African art. The sculptors of Benin, most of whose work was created between the sixteenth century and the nineteenth century, probably learned the techniques of casting from the sculptors of Ife. Ife is in southwestern Nigeria; from about the eleventh century until the seventeenth century, Ife was the seat of the Yoruba kingdom. Many art historians think that the sculptures of both Benin and Ife can be traced back to the Nok culture, centered in what is now northern Nigeria; examples of Nok sculpture have been dated between the fifth century B.C. and the second century A.D. Ask groups of volunteers to research the cultures and the sculpture of Benin, Ife, and Nok. Then let the volunteers share their findings with the rest of the class, and encourage all students to discuss the relationships between these cultures.

Developing Studio Skills.

Let students experiment with drawing abstract figures. First display photographs of various animals. Have each student choose a specific animal and make a clear contour drawing of it. Be sure students recognize that these drawings are realistic. When students are satisfied with their initial work, have them place sheets of tracing paper over the realistic drawings. Then, using the realistic drawing underneath as a guide, have students make abstract drawings of their chosen animals. Encourage students to simplify lines and forms and to use straight lines and angles in place of curves whenever possible. Finally, have students work in small groups to compare and discuss their realistic and abstract drawings of animals.

▲ Figure 9–4 The sculptor effectively shows mood through the use of texture and composition in this work.

Africa, Nigeria. Court of Benin, Bini Tribe. *Mounted King and Attendants*. c. 1550–1680. Bronze. 49.5 x 41.9 x 11.3 cm (19½ x 16½ x 4½"). The Metropolitan Museum of Art, New York, New York. The Michael C. Rockefeller Memorial Collection. Gift of Nelson A. Rockefeller.

132   📖   Lesson 1   *The Figure Sculptures of Africa*

Cooperative Learning

Along with the research asked for in the section on "Understanding Art History," ask for volunteers to find information on bronze casting. Urge this group to focus on what materials and techniques are used to make the mold for a casting as well as the ingredients and equipment necessary to make and melt the components of bronze. Let this group of students present their information to help the class appreciate the complexity of the casting shown in Figure 9-4.

Cast Bronze Figures

In the spring of 1897 a shipload of bronze sculptures arrived in England. The works showed a skill at casting equal to that of any sculptor of the day. Imagine the excitement of the art community upon discovering these marvelous bronzes.

These sculptures were made by artists of the Benin (buh-**neen**) Empire. Among the most remarkable of the works were reliefs used to decorate the wooden pillars of the palace. One of these appears in Figure 9–4. It shows the powerful king of the tribe on horseback. Two servants protect him from the sun with their shields. Two others support him with their hands, while still another supports the king's feet with his head. Notice the sculptor has made the figure of the king larger than those of the servants. This was done to emphasize the king's importance. What ancient culture that you read about had a similar practice?

Not all bronze castings by African artists are reliefs. Some, like the sculpture in Figure 9–5, are freestanding. Bronze heads like this one were placed on an altar as memorials to the king's ancestors. Notice the lifelike quality of this sculpture. What kind of balance has the artist used?

◀ **Figure 9–5   Bronze sculptures like this show the skill of the tribal artist. Notice the varied patterns on this sculpture.**

Africa, Nigeria. Court of Benin, Bini Tribe. Head. c. 1550. Bronze. 23.5 x 22 x 22.9 cm (9¼ x 8⅝ x 9"). The Metropolitan Museum of Art, New York, New York. Bequest of Nelson A. Rockefeller.

Lesson 1   *The Figure Sculptures of Africa*   📖   **133**

STUDIO EXPERIENCE

Study Figures 9–2 and 9–3 again. Works like these were created to honor family ancestors. The artist always focused on giving a strong sense of who the person was.

Suppose you lived in a place where images of past relatives were kept in every home. Think of how you would like future generations of your family to remember you. Then complete a pencil drawing of yourself as seen from the front. Show yourself in an activity that reveals your personality. The figure does not need to be a perfect likeness. It must, however, tell viewers about the kind of person you were. Try to use facial expression and stance as the artists in Figures 9–2 and 9–3 have done. Your personality, not your appearance, should be shown.

✔CHECK YOUR UNDERSTANDING

1. Explain why the art of each African tribe has been a unique contribution to the art world.
2. What is the meaning of abstract work?
3. In what year did the bronze sculptures from Africa reach Europe? How did the Europeans react upon seeing these works?

Appreciating Cultural Diversity. African sculpture had an important impact on the works of Western European artists, particularly during the early years of the twentieth century. Have volunteers read about the works of Amedeo Modigiani, Henri Matisse, Georges Braque, and Pablo Picasso: What and how did each artist learn about African sculpture? How can the influence of African sculpture be seen in the artists' works? Ask the volunteers to make short presentations to the rest of the class, displaying reproductions of African and European art works if possible.

Following Up

Closure. Let students browse through the text and identify examples of sculpture from other cultures. Then ask: How is African sculpture similar to the sculpture created by artists in other cultures? What are the most important differences?

Evaluation. 1. Review students' written responses to the "Check Your Understanding" questions. 2. Evaluate their contributions to the "Closure" discussion.

Reteaching. Help students learn about and discuss the tools and techniques used by African sculptors. Show students an adz (or a photograph of an adz), the tool most commonly used by African carvers. Let students imagine how it might feel to carve figures from wood with this tool: What might the advantages—and disadvantages—be? Then ask one or two volunteers to read about and report on the lost wax technique of casting bronze.

Enrichment. Explain to the class that, when the bronze sculptures from Benin were first shown in Europe in 1897, many people assumed that the works had been influenced—or even created—by Portuguese artists. This theory was widely accepted for more than thirty years. Help students discuss the impact of this idea: Why do you think this theory was accepted? What does it show about European attitudes? Can you as a student of art today learn anything from this theory? If so, what can you learn?

Answers to "Check Your Understanding"

1. The art of each African tribe has been a unique contribution to the art world, because each tribe has its own language, customs, and religion.
2. An abstract work is art with a recognizable subject portrayed in an unrealistic manner.
3. African bronze sculptures reached Europe in 1897. The Europeans reacted with excitement upon seeing these marvelous bronzes.

Abstract Self-portrait Cutout

LESSON PLAN
(pages 134–135)

Objectives
After completing this lesson, students will be able to:
• Create abstract cardboard cutout self-portraits.
• Describe, analyze, interpret, and judge their own self-portraits.

Supplies
• Sheets of drawing paper, pencils.
• Pencils; sheets of sketch paper; pieces of cardboard, 6 x 12 inches (15 x 30 cm); rulers; scissors; tempera paints in black and white; brushes; white shellac; scraps of heavy cardboard; transparent tape.
• Sheets of drawing paper, watercolors, brushes.

TRB Resource
• 9-4 *Contemporary Totems,* (studio)

TEACHING THE LESSON

Getting Started
Motivator. To prepare for making their abstract cutouts, have students draw several views of a human face, practicing ways of dividing it into geometrical planes. Suggest that they begin by sketching an oval and then use corners and angles to replace the oval's curves. Help students discuss different geometric shapes—rectangles, triangles, squares, diamonds, octagons—that might be drawn to represent different parts of a face. Then have students experiment with several drawings of a face on a single sheet of drawing paper. Let them select the work they like best and add shading to the planes in that face. Finally, ask groups of students to compare and discuss their drawings: Which techniques do they consider most effective?

Vocabulary. Help students review the definition of *harmony* as a principle of art. Then ask: What can harmony help add to a work of art? What possible disadvantages can be associated with harmony? What techniques can artists use to achieve harmony?

Abstract Self-Portrait Cutout

The African figure sculptures you studied in Lesson 1 were made to honor past tribe members. They were also made to hold the spirits of past tribe members. Figure 9–6 shows another of these figure sculptures. Notice that, like other African standing figures, it is highly abstract. This work goes a step further, however. The artist here has simplified the human figure into a series of flat shapes and simple forms. You may be able to see how this abstract style had an effect on the later development of cubism in European art.

▲ **Figure 9–6   Did you notice how the features have been stylized? What has been done to simplify the figure?**

Africa, Zaire. Buye style. 19th-20th Century. Wood, kaolin. (Detail.) 77.5 x 28.9 x 21.6 (30½ x 11⅜ x 8½"). The Metropolitan Museum of Art, New York, New York. The Michael C. Rockefeller Memorial Collection. Gift of Nelson A. Rockefeller.

WHAT YOU WILL LEARN
You will create an abstract cardboard cutout self-portrait as seen from the front. Show yourself in a posture or activity that tells something about your personality. You will use flat shapes and simple forms for body parts and features. You will give the work a three-dimensional look by painting certain parts of the figure in black and white. You will add harmony by using only sharp-angled shapes and forms. (See Figure 9–7.)

WHAT YOU WILL NEED
• Pencil and sheets of sketch paper
• Piece of cardboard, 6 x 12 inches (15 x 30 cm)
• Ruler and scissors
• Black and white tempera paint
• Brushes and polymer gloss medium
• Scrap of heavy cardboard and transparent tape

WHAT YOU WILL DO
1. Look back at the drawing you made for the Studio Experience in Lesson 1. Do another drawing, this time replacing all curved lines with straight ones. Simplify the facial expression, but make sure your new version still shows a pose or expression that tells viewers about the kind of person you are. Make several sketches.
2. Draw the best of your sketches on the piece of cardboard. Use the ruler to make sure all the lines in your drawing are straight. Take care also to create shapes that are flat and angled.

Background Information
While the abstract portraiture of African art may not exactly be indicative of how Africans have actually looked throughout history, it does reveal a lot about African society and spirituality. The imagination and creativity demonstrated by African artists in their depictions of the human form suggest that their world view included aspects that go beyond the visual senses.

Unrestricted by the formal conventions held by European artists, the Africans were free to convey the natural energies that they believed to animate all people, and not just the individual physical characteristics of a subject.

3. Using the scissors, cut out your shape. Add more straight lines *within* the shapes on your cutout. These should suggest flat surfaces at different angles to each other. This will make the shapes seem more like three-dimensional forms.

4. Study the carving in Figure 9–6. Decide which shapes in your work could be painted either black or white to give it a sense of depth. Paint the cutout with black and white tempera.

5. When the paint has dried, apply a coat of polymer gloss to your cutout. Cut a wedge shape from the scrap of heavy cardboard. Using tape, attach the wedge to the back of your cutout. This will allow you to stand the cutout for display.

▲ Figure 9–7   Student work. Abstract self-portrait.

EXAMINING YOUR WORK

- **Describe**   Tell how you created your cutout to be a standing figure as seen from the front. Tell whether your work is abstract. Explain why your work is considered an abstract piece.
- **Analyze**   Point out the flat shapes and simple forms in your work. Identify the places where you used black or white paint to add a three-dimensional look to the work. Explain why the use of angled shapes and forms throughout adds harmony to the work.
- **Interpret**   Show what features in your work would help a viewer understand what kind of person you are.
- **Judge**   Identify what is most successful about your cutout. Explain whether the work succeeds because of its abstract look. Tell whether its success arises out of your use of art elements and principles. State, finally, whether its most successful feature is the message it communicates about you as a person.

OTHER STUDIO IDEAS

- On a sheet of white paper, make a pencil drawing of another standing figure. The subject this time should be a friend or relative you admire. Decide what qualities you admire most in the person. Decide how best to show these qualities in your work.

- ● Make another cardboard cutout, this time of a figure on horseback. Your figure should exhibit an emotion or feeling, such as pride, humility, or anger. Use the sculpture in Figure 9–3 on page **131** as your model. Again, simplify each of the figures into a series of flat shapes and forms. Paint your cutout with two complementary colors.

Lesson 2   *Abstract Self-Portrait Cutout*   **135**

Using Art Criticism. Guide students in briefly describing, analyzing, and interpreting the sculpture shown in Figure 9-6. Then let students discuss and support their responses to these questions: Is the sculpture successful in depicting its subject? Is it successful in using the principles of art to combine the visual elements into an interesting whole? Is it successful in communicating a feeling or idea to the viewer?

Developing Studio Skills. Have students plan and paint realistic portraits of themselves. These portraits should show the same posture or activity portrayed in their abstract cutouts. These works, however, should show their appearance as clearly as possible; students should strive to use natural shapes and colors. Display these watercolor portraits beside the students' abstract cutouts, and encourage students to discuss the differences between the two kinds of self-portraits.

Following Up

Closure. Let students work with partners to discuss their self-portrait cutouts, following the steps in "Examining Your Work." Then have students write paragraphs about their own cutouts, responding to the instructions in the "Judge" section of "Examining Your Work."

Evaluation. Review students' abstract self-portrait cutouts and read their paragraphs judging their own work.

Reteaching. Work with small groups of students to discuss their abstract cutouts: How is the principle of harmony evidenced in each work? Then have group members review the African sculptures shown in Figures 9-2 on page **130**, 9-3 on page **131**, 9-4 on page **132**, 9-5 on page **133**, and 9-6 on page **134**: Has harmony been used to organize the visual elements in each work? How is it evidenced? What message does it help to communicate?

Enrichment. Have students write stories or essays to go with their cutouts, explaining how they would like future generations of their families to remember them.

Background Information
By utilizing simple shapes and forms to enhance physical appearances, African sculptors captured the moods and feelings of their subjects, giving viewers an emotional experience instead of a mere visual one. Often carved to commemorate the dead, the abstract sculptures stirred feelings, reminding the mourner of the life energies that had once invigorated the deceased and still arouse the living. Although it would be undermined by European colonialism, the dynamic and expressive style of African art would eventually be explored and emulated by such notable European artists as Braque and Picasso.

135

The Masks of Africa

LESSON PLAN
(pages 136–139)

Objectives
After completing this lesson, students will be able to:
• Name the three kinds of masks made by African tribal sculptors.
• Make simple masks and describe the experience of wearing them.

Supplies
• African masks or photographs of African masks, recording of traditional African music (if available).
• Pieces of thin cardboard, scissors, staplers, construction paper, tempera paints, brushes, found objects, glue.
• Large brown paper bags, cardboard boxes, scissors, tempera paints, brushes, scraps of fabric and/or construction paper, found objects, glue.

TRB Resources
• 9-5 *Geometry of African Masks,* (reproducible master)
• 9-6 *Picasso and the African Mask,* (art history)
• 9-7 *African-American Artists,* (appreciating cultural diversity)
• 9-8 *Contemporary African Art,* (appreciating cultural diversity)

TEACHING THE LESSON

Getting Started
Motivator. Introduce the lesson by displaying African masks (or reproductions or photographs of African masks). Explain that masks were used as part of various tribal ceremonies; often these ceremonies included music, dancing, and chanting or singing. As students examine the masks, play recordings of traditional African music and/or read the following "Drum Call" from Zaire:

The Masks of Africa

African tribespeople had several ways of relating to the spirit world through art. One, which you read about in Lesson 1, was through figure sculptures. Another was through masks. Like the figure sculptures, the masks made by African tribal artists were richly carved. They are among the finest and most remarkable art forms of Africa. The masks also had great magical importance attached to them.

The artists of Africa created three different types of masks. These were the face mask; the headpiece, or headdress; and the shoulder mask.

▲ Figure 9–8 How do you think a dancer wearing this mask would appear to onlooking tribespeople?
_____
Africa, Chumbanndu, Buluba. Face Mask. American Museum of Natural History, New York, New York.

THE FACE MASK

The **face mask** was *a mask worn to hide the identity of the wearer*. The wearer even changed his or her voice so as not to be recognized. An example of a face mask is shown in Figure 9–8. Animal furs, feathers, and shells are included in its decoration.

The face mask was used in a number of different tribal ceremonies. Sometimes these ceremonies were held to protect the tribe from the unknown forces of nature. Others were intended to ensure a good harvest. Once the ceremony began, the tribespeople wearing masks would dance to rhythmic music. Seen by flickering firelight, these masked dancers were sometimes frightening and sometimes amusing. Always they were exciting.

THE HEADPIECE

Not all African masks were made to hide the wearer's identity. The headpieces created by artists of the Bambara tribe of west Africa were made with an abstract animal design. **Headpieces** were *masks carved of wood and worn on the head like a cap*. In Bambara culture the antelope is a symbol for a rich harvest and appeared as the model for their headpieces. Figure 9–9 shows examples of these headpieces.

Bambara headpieces were used in a ritual performed when a new field was readied for planting. This ritual honored Tyi Wara, a mysterious being who was credited with having taught the Bambara how to plant and grow crops. The design of the headpiece was meant to blend the speed and grace of the antelope with the powerful spirit of Tyi Wara. Study the headpiece in Figure 9–9. What element in the work is used to capture a feeling of grace? What art element is used to capture a feeling of power?

Background Information
When admiring the artistry and craftsmanship of an African mask, it is easy to regard it as simply a sculpture and forget that it is only one element of an entire ceremony. Most often worn with a full costume and accessories, the African mask is usually donned for social or religious purposes. Amongst the Dan tribe in West Africa, the wearer of a policeman mask, for example, would serve as a policeman. The Dan also used masks in religious activities to represent spirits and gods.

Because they are worn by performers, African masks require extra care in their construction. Mask makers have to observe functional needs as well as aesthetic customs. The wearers must be able to stand, dance, and perform acrobatics while wearing the traditional garb. Even the most graceful, athletic performers require masks that provide adequate ventilation, allow freedom of motion, and preserve stability. When considering the many demands on the mask maker, artistic notions such as atmosphere, movement, and balance acquire additional meaning.

▲ **Figure 9–9** The antelope on the right is male. Notice its beautiful, flowing mane. The female carries a baby on her back.

Africa, Mali, Bamana Tribe. Two Antelope Headpieces. 19th-20th Century. Wood, metal bands. Left: 71.2 x 30.9 x 5.4 cm (28 x 12⅛ x 2⅛"). Right: 90.7 x 40 x 8.5 cm (35¾ x 15¾ x 3⅜"). The Metropolitan Museum of Art, New York, New York. The Michael C. Rockefeller Memorial Collection. Gift of Nelson A. Rockefeller.

All of you, all of you
come, come, come, come,
let us dance
in the evening
when the sky has gone down river
down to the ground.
Ask students to imagine the feelings these ceremonies might evoke in participants and observers: How would the masks affect the people who wore them? How would they affect the people who were watching? Encourage students to share and discuss their responses. Explain that students will learn more about different kinds of African masks as they study this lesson.

Vocabulary. Introduce the names of the three different kinds of masks presented in this lesson: *face masks, headpieces, shoulder masks*. Let students suggest the likely meaning of each term. Then have them check the definitions and look at the photographs in the text.

Developing Concepts

Exploring Aesthetics. Have students work with partners to select and discuss one of the African masks shown in Figures 9-8, 9-9, and 9-10. Ask partners to discuss their responses to these questions about their chosen mask: What is the subject of this work? Which elements of art can you identify and describe? Which principles of art have been used to organize those visual elements? What message or mood do you think this mask is intended to communicate?

After the partners' discussions, help the entire class consider each mask. Ask: What distinguishes this mask as a work of art? Encourage students to share and support various points of view.

Using Art Criticism. Have students select photographs of several face masks (perhaps from the display used in the "Motivator" activity or perhaps from books featuring photographs of African art). Let students work in groups to compare the different face masks they have found and the face mask shown in Figure 9-8: What purpose do you think each mask was created to serve? How successfully does each mask serve that purpose? What message or mood does each mask communicate to you now? What elements and principles of art contribute to the communication of that message or mood?

Note
Each face mask worn in a tribal ritual stood for a different spirit. The Africans believed that the dancer actually *changed into* that spirit during the ritual.

Note
Africans thought the magic to "live on" in a mask. For this reason masks continued to be used even when they were old and crumbling.

Understanding Art History.
Ask students to read about the arts and crafts being created in Africa now. Volunteers may want to explore these and other topics: stone sculpture, wood carving, pottery, handwoven textiles, painted murals, mosaics, beadwork, basketry, jewelry. Ask volunteers to share their findings with the rest of the class. Then encourage students to discuss the influence of traditional figure sculptures and masks on the works being created by African artists today.

Developing Studio Skills.
Have students work in small groups to discuss their ideas for making headpieces and shoulder masks. Make available materials such as large paper bags, cardboard boxes in various sizes, paints, and found objects such as buttons, beads, feathers, and so on. Ask group members to work together in planning what kind of mask to make, what construction techniques to use, and what decorations to include. Then have them carry out their plans together. Let the members of each group share their headpiece or shoulder mask with the rest of the class.

Appreciating Cultural Diversity. Point out to students that masks are used by people in many different ethnic groups. Have pairs or small groups of volunteers research the masks made by various Native American groups and by Polynesian, Micronesian, and Australian peoples. Ask all the volunteers to share their findings with the rest of the class, explaining how masks are made and used, and displaying photographs or drawings if possible. Then guide the class in discussing the most important similarities and differences among the kinds of masks.

THE SHOULDER MASK

Face masks were meant to cover the face of the wearer. Headpieces were meant to cover the wearer's head. The third kind of African mask, shoulder masks, were meant to do both. **Shoulder masks** were *large, carved masks made to rest on the shoulders of the wearer.*

They are sometimes called helmet masks. A shoulder mask of the Baga tribe is shown in Figure 9–10. It was used during a dance performed as part of a ceremony to guarantee a successful harvest. Notice how the face in this work is highly stylized.

▲ **Figure 9–10   Masks are meant to be seen in motion. They were thought to have great magical powers.**

Africa, Guinea, Baga Tribe. Headdress. 19th-20th Century. Wood. 122.6 x 40.9 x 70.3 cm (48¼ x 16⅛ x 27⅝"). Dallas Museum of Art, Dallas, Texas. The Gustave and Franyo Schindler Collection. Gift of the McDermott Foundation in honor of Eugene McDermott.

Background Information
Like the mask makers, African textile weavers demonstrate great care and craftsmanship in their art. While European methods have been introduced to Africa, pre-colonial techniques still flourish, as evidenced by modern spinners, weavers, and dyers. Spinners use wool, silk, cotton, and raphia (a palm fiber) to make yarn, fiber, and thread. Then, weavers utilize horizontal or vertical looms to create fabrics. Finally, dyers add color with indigo, cola nuts, and other natural pigments.

Using styles, colors, and patterns, African textile artists can convey rank, occasions, and purposes in the clothes they fashion. For example, red can be associated with blood and war—or success and achievement—in some cultures. More specifically, weavers of the *Berber* region often embroider figures that defend against the evil eye. Patterns representing mirrors, hands, and sharp objects all negate the effects of any malevolent glares that may fall upon the wearer.

The wearer of a shoulder mask peered out through holes cut in the chest. Like face masks and headpieces, shoulder masks were part of a complete costume. Long strips of fiber were used to cover the body of the wearer. Unlike the other masks, shoulder masks were quite heavy, often weighing 75 pounds (34 kg) or more. When the mask was in place, the wearer stood over 8 feet (243 cm) tall. Wearing such a mask called for very strong performers. Even so, they could perform in rituals for only a short time.

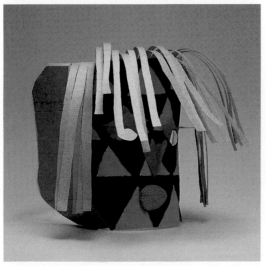

▲ Figure 9–11   Student work. Cardboard mask.

STUDIO EXPERIENCE

What happens when you cover your face with a mask? Do you feel and act differently? Can you hide your identity from others when the mask is in place?

Design a mask using thin cardboard. Cut strips of the material and staple them into cones and cylinders large enough to fit over your head. (See Figure 9–11.) Cut holes or slits to see through. Use construction paper, tempera paint, and found objects to create face features and decorations. Compare your mask with those created by classmates.

✔ CHECK YOUR UNDERSTANDING

1. What are face masks? What were face masks used for?
2. What role did the antelope play in Bambara culture? Who or what was Tyi Wara?
3. In what way were shoulder masks different from face masks and headpieces?

Following Up

Closure. Have students wear their "Studio Experience" masks as they present their work to the rest of the class. Let each student explain the techniques used and describe the finished mask he or she is wearing. Then have students write paragraphs in response to this question: How did wearing your mask change the way you felt about yourself, your work, and your audience?

Evaluation. 1. Review students' written responses to the "Check Your Understanding" questions. 2. Listen to students' mask presentations and read their paragraphs in response to the "Closure" question.

Reteaching. Work with small groups of students to review the images and uses of African masks. Then have group members work together to create a story to go with one of the masks they have studied. Once they have planned their story, let them decide on a method for presenting it to the rest of the class. Possible methods include putting on a skit, acting out a pantomime, drawing a mural, writing the story. Can group members think of other methods? Let them choose one method and then plan and make their presentation.

Enrichment. Some of the richest gold mines in the world are located in the African continent. Have students select and research a topic related to gold in Africa. Possible topics: history of gold mining techniques; specific tribes that have mined and used gold; African gold figures; African gold jewelry. Ask students to summarize their findings in written or oral reports.

Answers to "Check Your Understanding"
1. The face mask was worn to hide the identity of the wearer. The masks were used during various tribal ceremonies.
2. In Bambara culture, the antelope is a symbol for a rich harvest. Tyi Wara was a mysterious being credited with having taught the Bambara how to grow crops.
3. Shoulder masks covered the head and face, could weigh up to 75 pounds, and made the wearer appear to be 8 feet tall.

Making a Mood Mask Relief

The goal of African artists was to make expressive art. Masks were meant to communicate a mood or feeling to the viewer. Study the helmet mask shown in Figure 9–12. It is known as the "Firespitter." What mood does this half-animal, half-human mask communicate?

WHAT YOU WILL LEARN

You will create a mask relief that communicates a particular feeling or mood. You will model your mask out of papier-mâché (pap-yay-muh-**shay**). **Papier-mâché** is *a sculpting technique using newspaper and liquid paste*. You will use a variety of different shapes, forms, and textures. You will exaggerate the proportions of the shapes and forms used for the face features. Your shapes and forms will be organized into patterns to decorate the whole mask. (See Figure 9–13.)

Africa, Ivory Coast, Senufo Tribe. Helmet Mask. 19th-20th Century. Wood. 94 cm (35⅝"). The Metropolitan Museum of Art, New York, New York. The Michael C. Rockefeller Memorial Collection. Gift of Nelson A. Rockefeller.

◄ **Figure 9–12** Notice the care with which this work was designed. Real and imaginary lines of the horns, tusks, and mouth are used to unify the work.

WHAT YOU WILL NEED

- Pencil and sheets of sketch paper
- Heavy-duty aluminum foil and newspaper
- Masking tape and a large sheet of cardboard
- Non-toxic commercially prepared papier-mâché paste or white glue
- Plastic mixing bowl and water
- Newspaper torn into strips about 1/2 inch x 1 1/2 inches (13 x 39 mm)
- Fine-grain sandpaper
- Scissors or other sharp cutting tool
- Tempera paint and brushes
- Yarn, cloth, and cotton for decoration
- Polymer gloss medium

WHAT YOU WILL DO

1. Pretend that you belong to a tribe that has been having a series of misfortunes. The crops are dying and the water supply is low. Create a mask to be used in a ceremony your tribe might perform to restore your tribe's good fortune.
2. Do sketches for a mood mask expressing joy and happiness to attract the spirit of good fortune. Exaggerate the proportions of the features of the face. Use lines and shapes to create decorative patterns.

LESSON PLAN
(pages 140–141)

Objectives
After completing this lesson, students will be able to:
- Use papier-mâché to create mask reliefs that communicate particular feelings or moods.
- Describe, analyze, interpret, and judge their own mask reliefs.

Supplies
- Sheets of drawing paper, colored pencils.
- Pencils; sheets of sketch paper; heavy-duty aluminum foil; newspaper; masking tape; large sheets of cardboard; non-toxic commercially prepared papier-mâché paste or white glue; plastic mixing bowls; water; torn strips of newspaper, about 1/2 inch x 1 1/2 inches (13 x 39 cm); fine-grain sandpaper; scissors or other sharp cutting tools; tempera paints; brushes; yarn, cloth, and cotton for decoration; polymer gloss medium.

> **TRB Resource**
> - 9-9 *Appliqué Class Quilt*, (studio)

TEACHING THE LESSON

Getting Started

Motivator. Begin by explaining that, in this lesson, students will create masks that express specific moods. Have each student use colored pencils to sketch at least three different masks expressing three different moods. Then let groups of students compare and discuss their sketches. Encourage students in each group to continue working together, sharing and discussing ideas, as they create their own mood mask reliefs.

Vocabulary. Let students discuss their own experiences in working with papier-mâché. Based on their experiences, what definition of the term can they develop? Let them check their definition against that given in the text. Also have volunteers look up *papier-mâché* in dictionaries: From what language does the word come? What does it mean in that language?

140

Background Information
Although it combines animal and human features, the Firespitter looks neither animal nor human. When it was worn, a burning coal was placed in its open jaws. The wearer blew on this to produce smoke and sparks that came out through the mouth and nose. This, along with its half-animal, half-human appearance, made the Firespitter a frightening sight.

The Firespitter's awesome appearance should not keep the students from noticing how well it is designed. Have them notice how effectively the elements and principles have been used to create a visually appealing work of art.

3. Cut a sheet of heavy-duty aluminum foil large enough to cover your face. Using your fingers, gently press the foil around your eyes, nose, and mouth.

4. Place the foil mask on the cardboard and stuff wads of newspaper under it. This will help it keep its shape when the papier-mâché is applied. Using masking tape, fasten the stuffed foil to the cardboard.

5. Follow the instructions for applying papier mâché in Technique Tip 20, *Handbook* page 283. As you work, take care not to press too hard on the foil. If you do, the raised areas may collapse. Set the mask aside overnight to dry.

6. The next day sand your mask lightly with the fine-grain sandpaper. Trim the edges with scissors and carefully cut holes or slits for eyes. If you do not wish to wear your mask you might want to paint the eyes on your mask instead.

7. Look back at your sketches. Working in pencil, transfer the other face features and decorative patterns from your best sketch.

8. Pick colors of tempera paint for your mask. Your color choices should emphasize the joyous mood of the work. Paint your mask and add yarn, cloth, or cotton to create texture. Apply a coat of polymer gloss to add sheen to the mask.

SAFETY TIP

Avoid using wallpaper paste and similar glues for your work in papier-mâché. These glues have poisons in them that can enter the body through the skin.

OTHER STUDIO IDEAS

• Create a ritual to go with your mask. Invent a tribe name and an aspect of nature or of an animal that the mask honors. Share this information with your class in an oral demonstration.

EXAMINING YOUR WORK

• **Describe**   Point to the different face features of your mask.
• **Analyze**   Identify where your mask has a variety of different shapes, forms, and textures. Explain how shapes and forms are organized into decorative patterns. Point out the exaggerated proportions of shapes and forms in the face features of your mask.
• **Interpret**   Point to the features in your work that would help a viewer understand its joyous mood. Explain how exaggeration helped communicate this mood.
• **Judge**   Tell whether you feel your work succeeds. Identify the best features of your mask.

▲ Figure 9–13   Student work. Mood mask.

•• Design another mask for another tribal ceremony. Perhaps the ceremony is intended to ensure a successful hunt or to frighten away evil spirits. Exhibit your mask in class. Ask if anyone can name the kind of ceremony in which it would be used.

Lesson 4   *Making a Mood Mask Relief*   **141**

ANSWERS TO
"CHAPTER 9 REVIEW"

Building Vocabulary

1. abstract work
2. face mask
3. headpieces
4. shoulder masks
5. papier-mâché

Reviewing Art Facts

6. Portuguese explorers came to Africa in the late 1400s.
7. Wood was the favorite medium of African tribal sculptors.
8. Two reasons for rubbing wood carvings with oil was to heighten the beauty and to add to the carving's magical powers.
9. The Benin tribe created the bronze sculptures.
10. African artists created face masks, headpieces, and shoulder masks.
11. Face masks were used to ensure a good harvest and to protect the tribe from the unknown forces of nature. Bambara headpieces were used in a ritual when a new field was prepared for planting.
12. The Bambara credited a mysterious being Tyi Wara with having taught them about planting.
13. Shoulder masks weighed up to 75 pounds.

Thinking About Art

1. Answers can include the cultures in India, Egypt, Mesoamerica, Andes, and the prehistoric cave dwellers.
2. Answers will vary, but students can include chapter opening (Nigerian Headdress) and Figure 9-4 (Benin bronze) as least stylized, and Figure 9-9 (Mali wood headpieces) and Figure 9-10 (Baga headdress) among the most stylized. Their answers should indicate they know what stylized and realistic mean.
3. Similarities among the two works are: stylized figures, made of wood, and defined features. Difference among the two works is: Figure 9-3 is a statue and Figure 9-12 is a helmet mask.
4. Students can include such words as abstract, stylized, decorative, fierce, frightening, magical, majestic.

BUILDING VOCABULARY

Number a sheet of paper from 1 to 5. After each number, write the term from the box that best matches each description below.

abstract work	papier-mâché
face mask	shoulder masks
headpieces	

1. A work in which the artist uses a recognizable subject but portrays it in an unrealistic manner.
2. A mask worn to hide the identity of the wearer.
3. Masks carved of wood and worn on the head like a cap.
4. Large, carved masks made to rest on the shoulders of the wearer.
5. A sculpting technique using newspaper and liquid paste.

REVIEWING ART FACTS

Number a sheet of paper from 6 to 13. Answer each question in a complete sentence.

6. When did Portuguese explorers first come to Africa?
7. What is the favored medium among African tribal sculptors?
8. What two reasons did African sculptors have for rubbing their wood carvings with oil?
9. Which African tribe created the remarkable bronze sculptures that arrived in Europe in 1897?
10. What three kinds of masks were created by African artists?
11. Name two ceremonies in which face masks were used. In what ceremonies were Bambara headpieces used?
12. What mysterious being did the Bambara credit with having taught them about planting?
13. Why did rituals calling for shoulder masks require strong tribe members?

THINKING ABOUT ART

On a sheet of paper, answer each question in a sentence or two.

1. **Extend.** You read in this chapter that the antelope has a special meaning among the Bambara of Africa. In what other cultures that you read about were animals important?
2. **Analyze.** Which of the works in this chapter do you find the most stylized? The least stylized? Explain your answer.
3. **Compare and contrast.** Look back at the works in Figures 9–3 and 9–12. Both were created by artists of the Senufo tribe. Make a list of the similarities and differences between the two objects.
4. **Interpret.** Select three words that you think best describe African art. Write these on a sheet of paper. Compare your choices with those made by other members of the class. Which words were used most often?

MAKING ART CONNECTIONS

1. **Social Studies.** You read in this chapter that the different African tribes each have their own religion. Look up Africa in an encyclopedia in the school library. Learn what you can about African tribal religions and about the role of religion in art. Share your findings with the class in the form of a brief oral report.
2. **Science.** Artists all over Africa were able to choose from a large variety of wildlife for inspiration. List some animal forms unique to the continent of Africa. Choose an animal that interests you and research its habitat and lifestyle. Write a one-page report on your animal.

CHAPTER 9 REVIEW

LOOKING AT THE DETAILS

The detail shown below is from the sculpture *Dance Headdress*. Study the detail and answer the following questions using complete sentences.

1. What is the visual texture of this work?
2. What mood is the artist communicating in this sculpture? What elements and principles of art help to create this mood?
3. Note the expression on the figure's face, and the title of the work. What does this sculpture tell you about how this culture feels about dance?
4. What elements of art are combined to create harmony?

Africa, Nigeria, Ibo Tribe. Dance Headdress. Wood, paint, metal, fiber. (Detail.) 47 x 32.7 x 27.7 cm (18½ x 12⅞ x 10⅞"). Dallas Museum of Art, Dallas, Texas. The Eugene & Margaret McDermott Fund.

Chapter 9 Review **143**

ANSWERS TO "LOOKING AT THE DETAILS"

1. The visual texture is sharp and smooth.
2. Student answers may vary. Some possible answers include: The mood is one of strength, seriousness, and movement. The bold dark color of the work, the sharp thick shapes, harmony and symmetrical balance all indicate a strong, serious mood. The repeating patterns of the spikes, "birds," and negative space create rhythm and movement.
3. This culture treats dance as a ritual. They take dance seriously and perhaps even feel a sense of power from it.
4. The artist created harmony by using repeating patterns of form. The large spikes create harmony around the sculpture and the small spikes create it around and vertically. The face of the figure and the face on the headdress are on the same line to create harmony. And the birds symmetrically repeat.

Chapter Evaluation

The goal of this chapter is to develop students' understanding of the type of art created by African artists. Some possible evaluation techniques include:

1. Have students discuss the various uses and types of African masks. Ask them to create an imaginative story that describes the legends associated with one of the masks.

2. Ask students to review the art work within the chapter. Have them make pencil sketches of a sculptural piece or headdress that is reflective of the culture.

3. Have students complete Chapter 9 Test (TRB, Resource 9-10).

Art of the Middle Ages

Chapter Scan

TRB Resources

- 10-10 Chapter Test
- Color Transparency 19
- Color Transparency 20

TEACHING THE CHAPTER

Introducing the Art Work

Direct students' attention to the photograph of the Cathedral of Leon, Spain. Inform them that the word *cathedral* refers to a church of any size that contains a bishop's chair. The architectural features associated with cathedrals were developed during the Gothic period. Pointed arches and vaults, large amounts of glass in the walls, and an overall feeling of great height are the most common features of Gothic architecture. Cathedrals were the largest structures in the cities of their time. The Gothic architect, although relying on the compass and square in drafting and on geometric formulas, worked in an essentially intuitive manner. Gothic engineering was not a science but an art and the gifts required for it were more similar to those of the visual artist than the architect. Today, the roles of architect, engineer, builder, and contractor often do not coincide, but Gothic architects performed all of these roles, which is one reason why their buildings embody such grandness and intensity.

▲ Notice how the vertical lines of this church act as arrows pointing upward toward heaven.

Cathedral of Leon. Leon, Spain.

Art of the Middle Ages

The period of history beginning about A.D. 500 is known by several names. One is the Middle Ages. Another is Medieval (mid-**ee**-vuhl) times. A third name sometimes given to these years is the Dark Ages. In the world of art, however, the times were anything but dark. Sculpture and painting were used to express ideas of the times. Architecture found expression in magnificent churches. Sculpture and stained glass were used to add splendor to these buildings. Do you know what structures like the one at the left are called?

OBJECTIVES

After completing this chapter, you will be able to:
- Tell how life in Romanesque times affected the art of the period.
- Identify the role of Romanesque sculpture and illuminations.
- Describe the contributions of Gothic artists to architecture and painting.
- Work with Romanesque and Gothic styles of architecture and sculpture.

WORDS YOU WILL LEARN

buttress	gargoyle
castles	illuminations
cathedral	pointed arch
fresco	stained glass

ARTIST YOU WILL MEET

Giotto di Bondone

Examining the Art Work

Explain to students that the lines of the cathedral take the viewer's eye up toward the sky—the heavens. Explain that the cathedral was constructed as an image of the Heavenly Jerusalem. The architectural innovations of the Gothic period were brought about in an attempt to create a more grand place to worship. The goal of the architect was to create a house of the Lord on earth. The structure of the cathedral used strong upward lines, prominent statuary, and vivid stained glass to create a feeling of sheer scale and magnificence. Point out the relief sculpture. Explain that it provides texture as well as ornamentation to the outside of the building.

Discussing the Art Work

Tell students that great care and many decades went into the construction of a single cathedral. Ask them to think about the teamwork, commitment, and craftsmanship necessary to successfully complete such a building. Ask students if they can name some of the types of craftspeople involved in the construction of a cathedral. Explain that apart from the architect, some of the other craftspeople were quarryworkers, stone cutters, sculptors, mortar makers, masons, carpenters, blacksmiths, roofers, and glass makers.

Explain that space, light, line, and geometry create the transcendent atmosphere of the building and the structural features—rib vaulting, pointed arches, and flying buttresses—make possible the visual factors.

Tell students that in this chapter they will learn how life in the Romanesque and Gothic times affected art styles.

145

Building Self-Esteem

In this chapter students will have the opportunity to design and model a gargoyle. This sculpture will combine the characteristics of several animals. In addition, students will incorporate some grotesque features. Help them understand the concept behind the grotesque features on Gothic gargoyles. During the 1300s, when it became possible to put windows in cathedrals, the church became a place where architectural decoration became popular. Stained glass windows told Bible stories, and statuary depicted Bible characters. Because many parts of the roof were sharply sloped, it was necessary to develop a method of carrying away from the building great amounts of rain water. What better way than to combine a spout with sculpture telling yet another story? Let the spouts look like evil spirits fleeing from under the eaves of the church, driven out by the ceremonies within. Point out the similarities between this design concept and that of the primitive African masks they just studied. Urge students to let their imaginations fly.

Art of the Romanesque Period

History teaches many meaningful lessons. One is that even the most powerful empires, in time, weaken and crumble. Rome was no exception. The Roman Empire fell to invading armies around A.D. 400. Both the style of life as well as the art of this period were affected by these historical changes. Temples and palaces were torn down and the stone was used to build fortresses to keep out the invaders.

Shortly before Rome fell, the practice of Christianity became widely accepted. The Catholic Church stood as the single most important influence in western Europe. Its influence on people and events was widespread throughout the span of history now called the Middle Ages. The art and architecture at the end of the Middle Ages is divided into two periods: the Romanesque (roh-muh-**nesk**), from around 1050 to around 1150, and the Gothic from around 1150 to about 1500. In this lesson you will learn about the art of the Romanesque period.

LIFE IN ROMANESQUE TIMES

Warfare was common during the Romanesque period. Since land was the main source of power and wealth, kings and rich landowners were forever fighting among themselves to protect or add to their holdings.

Architecture

To protect themselves, the rich lived in **castles,** or *fortlike dwellings with high walls and towers*. These castles were often protected further by a moat and drawbridge. One of these structures is pictured in Figure 10–1. Notice how sturdy the castle looks even now, some 600 to 700 years after it was built. The structure has few windows. Why do you suppose this is so? Do you think the builder was more interested in constructing a structure that was comfortable or well fortified?

▶ **Figure 10–1   Early castles like this were massive and strong. They were also dark and drafty. Instead of windows, narrow slits were cut into the walls. These helped those inside detect, and attack, intruders.**

La Calahorra Castle. Andalucia, Spain. 16th Century.

Sidebar (left column)

LESSON 1

Art of the Romanesque Period

LESSON PLAN
(pages 146–149)

Objectives
After completing this lesson, students will be able to:
• Tell how life in Romanesque times affected the art.
• Identify the role of Romanesque architecture, sculpture, and illuminations.
• Draw illustrations in the style of illuminations.

Supplies
• Sheets of sketch paper, colored pencils.
• Sheets of drawing paper, pencils, oil pastels.
• Reproductions of illuminated manuscripts featuring decorated capital letters, sheets of white paper, pencils, tempera paint, brushes.

TRB Resources
• 10-1 *Charlemagne and the Manuscript,* (aesthetics)
• 10-2 *Tapestry Details,* (reproducible master)
• 10-3 *Chart of Lettering,* (reproducible master)
• 10-4 *Learn Calligraphy,* (studio)

TEACHING THE LESSON

Getting Started
Motivator. Introduce this lesson by asking students to imagine what life in a castle might have been like: What would your castle have looked like from the outside? How would the inside of your castle have looked? What kinds of activities would have kept you busy if you had lived in a castle? Let students think about these questions and then make sketches to show their ideas about castles and the lives of the people who lived in them. Encourage students to share and discuss their sketches. Then have them look at the castle shown in Figure 10-1: How do their sketches compare to the massive, dark castle shown in the photograph?

146

Background Information
The post and lintel structure of windows and doors has been used since the earliest buildings were erected. The Egyptians used post and lintel structures in tombs; the ancient Greeks and Romans used them in temples; Europeans used them in churches. Today the post and lintel structure is still the most common way of building an opening without losing structural strength or stability.

There is, however, a problem with post and lintel structures: the stress on the lintel can cause it to crack. This problem was solved by Roman and European architects, as well as Eastern architects, through the use of arches. The arch allows the weight of a building to be distributed differently, and so is inherently stronger. Arches have often survived in buildings after the walls have fallen down.

▲ **Figure 10–2** High, thick walls and towers protected those living in this city. Only a few well-protected gates allowed people to enter or leave the city.

Walled City of Carcassone. c. 1100. Southern France.

The leaders and rulers lived in the castles during the Middle Ages. Communities of people living outside the castles were left open to attack. For this reason, whole towns and cities were surrounded by walls for protection. At first these walls were made of wood. In the 1100s and 1200s stone began to be used. One of the most impressive of these walled cities is shown in Figure 10–2. Today this city looks much as it did during the Middle Ages.

During this time the Catholic Church also had a great influence on the architecture. As early as A.D. 400 churches were springing up in towns and villages across Europe. All, like the one shown in Figures 10–3 and 10–4, were low and thick-walled. Windows, which might weaken the walls and bring the heavy stone roof crashing down, were avoided. As a result, these churches were dark and somber inside.

▲ **Figure 10–3 (Left)** and **Figure 10–4 (Right)** Thick walls and lack of windows made these churches look like forts, or fortresses. This may be the origin of the phrase "fortresses of God," used to describe these churches.

Anersall-Romanesque Church.

Vocabulary. Have students use dictionaries to learn about the derivation of the word *castle:* What is the meaning of the Latin word from which our English word *castle* comes? How does that meaning relate to the castle shown in Figure 10-1?

Developing Concepts

Exploring Aesthetics. Have students examine and discuss the illumination shown in Figure 10-6 on page 149: What idea or feeling does this work communicate to you? How do you respond to this painting? How do you think the people for whom it was painted responded to it? Was this a work of art when it was first painted? Why, or why not? Is it a work of art now? Why, or why not?

Using Art Criticism. Guide students in discussing the sculptures on the Santa Maria la Real Church, Figure 10-5 on page **148**: What makes these sculptures part of the church building? What makes these sculptures stand out as individual works? How would you judge these works in terms of subject, in terms of composition, and in terms of content?

Understanding Art History. Help students consider the importance of illumination: How are illuminations different from the illustrations you find in modern books? How were the books of the Middle Ages different from modern books? Why do you think artists stopped creating illuminations?

Following this discussion, let groups of volunteers research these topics: production of books during the Middle Ages, styles of illumination, ancient illuminations, development of movable type. Then have the volunteers share their findings with the rest of the class.

Cooperative Learning
Combat during the Middle Ages took great strength and endurance. Knights on horseback wore over 50 pounds of armor. Their helmets alone weighed up to 11 pounds. They wore all this while charging each other at full gallop holding a horizontal lance measuring half the length of a telephone pole! Have students work in small groups and research the different types of armor and present their findings to the class.

Note
The rounded arches common to the Romanesque style of architecture presented another problem: Rounded arches of different widths must start their curve at different points in order to support the weight of a building, so arches of different widths could not all be of the same height. This construction difficulty was overcome during the Gothic period by the use of the pointed arch.

Sculpture

The Church was also responsible for the development of sculpture during this period. Since most people were unable to read, sculpture was used to teach religion. The exteriors of churches were covered with reliefs and statues like the ones in Figure 10–5. These sculptures portrayed the same Bible teachings that were taught verbally. Look closely at Figure 10–5. Notice the detailed figures shown in the half-round space above the doorway.

▶ **Figure 10–5 Sculptures on the outside of churches were meant to remind people to lead good lives.**

Santa Maria la Real Church. 13th Century. Sanguesa, near Pamplona, Spain.

Background Information
During the Romanesque period, most illuminations were created by monks for use in monastic settings. Manuscripts were copied onto vellum; typically the first letter of each page or the first page of each section was illuminated. The monks used bright colors in combination with silver or gold leaf.

The most commonly decorated works were the Bible and psalm books. Liturgical books were also illuminated, and during the latter part of the Romanesque period, some works describing the lives of saints and certain scientific works were decorated with illuminations. Another change took place in the late Romanesque period: a few trained lay people worked with monks in creating illuminated manuscripts.

Painting

In addition to being portrayed in sculpture, the teachings of the Church were spread through hand-lettered books, which contained illuminations. **Illuminations** are *hand-painted book illustrations*. For nearly a thousand years, these illustrations were the most important paintings created in Europe. Figure 10–6 shows an illumination from a prayer book. The work shows a scene from the life of Moses. In the illustration, Moses is looking up to receive the word of the Lord. His upturned face and outstretched arms suggest his willingness to accept the teachings for his people. Would you describe the work as realistic? What do you suppose was the artist's main goal in creating this illumination? Which aesthetic view would you use if someone asked you to judge this work?

▲ Figure 10–6   The story in this work was told simply so it could be understood by anyone who knew the Bible. The picture does not look real because the story was more important to the artist than was a lifelike subject.

Illuminated Page of the Bible. *The Tablets of the Law.* 13th Century. Psalter of Ingeburg of Denmark. France.

STUDIO EXPERIENCE

The story illustrated in Figure 10–6 is from the Old Testament. Notice how the artist in portraying this story includes only those details needed in its telling.

Working in pencil, draw an illustration of a scene from a favorite story from literature or a movie. As in the illumination, leave out all unnecessary details. Keep your figures flat, and outline them with a variety of thick and thin black lines. Add bright colors to your picture with oil pastels. Share your finished work with classmates. See if anyone can identify the scene or story you have illustrated.

✔ CHECK YOUR UNDERSTANDING

1. In what century did Rome fall? What became the single most important influence in western Europe after its collapse?
2. When did the Romanesque period begin? When did it end?
3. What fact of life in the Middle Ages led to the building of castles?
4. Why were Romanesque churches thick-walled and without windows?
5. What was the purpose of sculpture during the Romanesque period? What other art form had the same purpose?

Following Up

Closure. Let each student share his or her "Studio Experience" illustration with the rest of the class. Encourage students to discuss each illustration as it is presented: What do you see in this drawing? What scene or story do you think it illustrates? What is the most successful aspect of this work? Then let students review the castle sketches they made at the beginning of this lesson (see "Motivator"). Ask students to write short paragraphs in response to these questions: How have your ideas about castles changed? What is the most important thing you have learned about life in Romanesque times?

Evaluation. 1. Review students' written responses to the "Check Your Understanding" questions. 2. Evaluate students' participation in the "Closure" class discussion, and read their paragraphs about castles and life in Romanesque times.

Reteaching. Work with small groups of students to review the most important features of Romanesque architecture, sculpture, and painting. Then point out that the word *Romanesque* originally meant "in the Roman manner." Help group members discuss this meaning: Why might the word have been used? To what extent is it descriptive of Romanesque art and architecture?

Enrichment. Remind students that, in many parts of Europe, buildings from the Middle Ages are still standing—and still in use. Ask students to work with partners or in small groups to explore European cities where Romanesque castles, churches, and walls can be seen. Suggest that they use travel books as well as art books and history books in their research. Then have each pair or group describe a short tour through Romanesque Europe.

Answers to "Check Your Understanding"

1. Rome fell around the fifth century. The church then became the governing force in Western Europe.
2. The Romanesque period began in 1050 and ended about 1150.
3. Warfare to gain land led kings and rich landowners to protect themselves by building fort-like dwellings with high walls and towers.
4. Roman churches were thick-walled and windowless because windows would have weakened the walls.
5. Since most people were unable to read, sculpture was used to teach religion. Hand-lettered books containing many illustrations served the same purpose.

Objectives

After completing this lesson, students will be able to:
• Design their own Romanesque castles and create reliefs of them.
• Describe, analyze, interpret, and judge their own castle reliefs.

Supplies

• Pencils; notepads; sheets of sketch paper; sheets of cardboard, 12 x 18 inches (30 x 45 cm); scissors; tape; heavy wrapping cord; white glue; sheets of aluminum foil, 16 x 20 inches (41 x 50 cm).
• Cardboard tubes (such as those inside rolls of wrapping paper), self-hardening clay (no firing needed), white glue, scissors, sheets of aluminum foil.

> **TRB Resource**
> • 10-5 *Sculpture — From Romanesque to Gothic,* (art history)

TEACHING THE LESSON

Getting Started

Motivator. Let students begin by discussing what they know about Romanesque castles. Ask groups of students to discuss their ideas; together, group members should list at least eight adjectives that describe Romanesque castles. Also have them list at least eight specific features of castles.

Vocabulary. Write the word *battlement* on the chalkboard. Ask students to think about the word and guess its meaning. Let a volunteer check the definition in a dictionary. Then have students look at the castles shown in Figures 10-7 and 10-8. Let them identify the battlements and discuss how they were used.

Developing Concepts

Using Art Criticism. Guide students in discussing the two castles shown in Figures 10-7 and 10-8. Remind students that works of architecture are considered both fine art and applied (functional) art. Ask: Are these castles successful works of fine art? Why, or why not? Are they successful works of applied art? Why, or why not?

Romanesque Castle Relief

Castles, as you have read, were common in Europe during the Romanesque period. Two more of these structures are shown in Figures 10–7 and 10–8. The ridged geometric pattern along the top of each is called a battlement. Can you guess what battlements were used for? Can you identify any other features in these castles?

WHAT YOU WILL LEARN

You will design a castle of your own. You will create a relief of your castle using heavy cord and aluminum foil. Focus on the use of line to highlight the different features of your castle. Use the element of line to add harmony to your design. (See Figure 10–9.) Your castle should look strong and safe.

WHAT YOU WILL NEED

• Pencil and notepad
• Sheets of sketch paper
• Sheet of cardboard, 12 x 18 inches (30 x 45 cm)
• Scissors, tape, and heavy wrapping cord
• White glue
• Sheet of aluminum foil, 16 x 20 inches (41 x 50 cm)

WHAT YOU WILL DO

1. Begin by studying the castles in Figures 10–1 (on page **146**), 10–7, and 10–8. On your notepad, list the features common to these buildings. One common feature

▲ **Figure 10–7 How many features can you find that helped make these castles safe?**

Castle at Penafiel, Spain. c. 14th Century.

▲ **Figure 10–8 See caption for Figure 10–7.**

Gothic Castle on Rio Esla, south of Leon, Spain. 15th Century.

 150 Lesson 2   *Romanesque Castle Relief*

Background Information

The first European castles were probably erected during the ninth century; the first stone castles were built during the eleventh century. The thick, sturdy walls served to keep the people within the castle safe—and to notify outsiders that here was the home of a wealthy, powerful noble.

A castle was usually built on a hillside or an artificial mound and surrounded by high, turreted walls. These walls had to be thick enough to withstand attack and, at the top, wide enough

to provide space for those defending the castle. Within the walls were residence and support buildings, providing housing for the noble family and all their retainers.

After the introduction of gunpowder in Europe, the castle ceased to serve its defensive purpose. Gradually, manor houses replaced castles as the residences of the wealthy landowners.

in the castles shown here, for example, is the battlement. On a sheet of sketch paper, make several drawings of an original castle. Show the building as it appears from the front. Draw all the features included on your list.

2. Choose your best design. Make a line drawing of this sketch on the sheet of cardboard. Fill the surface of the cardboard with your drawing.
3. Glue cord along the lines in your drawing. To do this, squeeze a thin band of glue along the line. Press the piece of cord into place. Repeat this process until all lines are covered.
4. Small pieces of cardboard can be glued to your castle design to give it more detail.
5. Cover your design with the sheet of aluminum foil. Wrap the foil around the ends and sides of the cardboard. Using tape, fasten the foil to the cardboard along the back.
6. Using the end of your pencil, carefully but firmly press down on the foil along the cord lines and around the cardboard shapes. Display your finished work to your class. Note ways in which your castle relief is similar to and different from those of other class artists.

EXAMINING YOUR WORK

- **Describe**   Point out the features of your castle listed on your notepad.
- **Analyze**   Tell whether the use of line adds harmony to your design.
- **Interpret**   State whether your castle communicates the ideas of strength and safety. Tell whether the castle shown would succeed in protecting those inside from attackers.
- **Judge**   Tell whether you feel your work succeeds. Explain your answer.

▲ Figure 10–9   Student work in progress. Castle relief.

OTHER STUDIO IDEAS

- Spray your castle with black paint. When the paint is dry, lightly rub the relief with steel wool. This will remove the paint from the raised surfaces, creating an interesting effect.

- Create another castle relief, this time out of a continuous piece of 14-gauge steel wire. Show each feature in your castle by bending and twisting the wire until it has the right shape.

Lesson 2   *Romanesque Castle Relief*   **151**

Developing Studio Skills. Let students study the statues on the Santa Maria la Real Church, Figure 10-5 on page **148**, and then make their own statues in a similar style. Have them use cardboard tubes for the statue bodies, and form heads, necks, shoulders, arms, and hands from self-hardening clay. Once the clay additions have hardened, have students glue them to their tubes. Then have students add long, draped robes of aluminum foil to their statues. Display all the students' statues in a group, and encourage them to examine and discuss one another's work.

Appreciating Cultural Diversity. In what other parts of the world did people build castles? Why did those people build castles? What did their castles look like? Ask volunteers to read about castles of other cultures, such as those built in Japan (during the Momoyama period) and those built in ancient Egypt. Let these volunteers give a brief presentation to the rest of the class.

Following Up

Closure. Let students present their castle reliefs to the rest of the class, describing, analyzing, interpreting, and judging as instructed in "Examining Your Work."

Evaluation. Review students' castle reliefs and listen to their presentations of their own work.

Reteaching. Work with groups of students to examine and discuss their castle reliefs: Which aspect of each work is most important in suggesting a Romanesque structure? Next, guide group members in discussing other media they might use in creating castle reliefs of models of castles. Encourage a variety of ideas. Then ask: Which media would be best adapted to creating a Romanesque work? Why?

Enrichment. Let students work in groups to make up stories set in castles. Then have group members choose a means of communicating their story—a series of paintings, a short play, or an illustrated booklet, for example. Have the groups prepare their stories and share them with the rest of the class.

Classroom Management Tip

Before students begin to form a wire relief, they should cover both ends of the wire with masking tape or electrician's tape. While working, they should wear protective goggles. Both of these tips will help prevent them from scratching or poking their eyes and skin while they work.

LESSON 3
Art of the Gothic Period

LESSON PLAN
(pages 152–155)

Objectives
After completing this lesson, students will be able to:
- Describe the contributions of Gothic artists to architecture and painting.
- Identify and explain the importance of the pointed arch and the flying buttress.
- Make paper models of rose windows.

Supplies
- Slides or display-size photographs of a Romanesque church (or other structure) and a Gothic church (or other structure).
- Sheets of sketch paper, pencils, sheets of black construction paper, white chalk, scissors, sheets of construction paper in various colors, white glue.
- Small cardboard boxes, scissors, tempera paints, brushes.

TRB Resources
- 10-6 *Imagine the Life of an Artist in the Middle Ages,* (appreciating cultural diversity)
- 10-7 *Architectural Styles,* (reproducible master)
- 10-8 *Giotto,* (artist profile)
- 10-9 *Playing Card Designs,* (cooperative learning)

TEACHING THE LESSON

Getting Started
Motivator. Begin by showing students a slide or large photograph of a Romanesque church. Ask students to brainstorm a list of words that describe the structure and the feelings it evokes. Record all their ideas on the chalkboard. Then show a slide or photograph of a Gothic church. Again, let students brainstorm a list of descriptive words, and record all their suggestions. After both lists are complete, let students identify the first church as an example of Romanesque architecture; identify the second as an

152

Art of the Gothic Period

Throughout history an important part of creating art has been solving problems. A key problem facing artists of the Romanesque period was mentioned in Lesson 1. This was figuring out how to build walls that could both contain windows and support a heavy roof.

Romanesque builders never solved this problem. Architects of the Gothic period did, however. In this lesson you will learn about this and other contributions of artists of the Gothic period.

▲ **Figure 10–10** The hundreds of sculptures lining this huge cathedral were meant to be seen up close. To this day, visitors can climb up to the roof and walk among the many carvings.

Milan Cathedral. Begun 1386. Milan, Italy.

LIFE IN GOTHIC TIMES

Toward the end of the Romanesque period, Europe began to change. With the growth of trade, money replaced land as the measure of wealth. Castles became unpopular as cities grew and thrived. Many of these cities developed into large population centers by the year 1200.

The Church continued to have a great effect on the people as well as on the art of these new European cities.

Architecture

One structure that exists as a great contribution of Gothic artists is the cathedral. A **cathedral** is *a large, complex church created as a seat of office for a bishop.* The bishop would have several parishes, or congregations, under his leadership. An example of one of these huge structures opened this chapter (page **144**). Another is shown in Figure 10–10. Notice the openness of both these buildings. Notice how both seem to soar upward. Magnificent works of architecture like these were possible thanks to two improvements made by Gothic French architects. These were:

- **The pointed arch.** The **pointed arch** is *a curved arrangement of stones reaching up to a central point.* Gothic architects found that the vertical shape of this design feature allowed it to carry weight downward. Examine the inside view of a cathedral in Figure 10–11 and find the pointed arches.
- **The flying buttress.** A **buttress** (buh-truhs) is *a brace or support placed on the outside of a building.* Such supports are said to "fly" when they arch out over other parts of a building. In Gothic cathedrals, flying buttresses took on some of the load of the heavy roof. Which structures in Figure 10–12 are flying buttresses?

Note
The term "Gothic" was coined by later critics looking back on the art of the period. The word traces to the name of a tribe of savages—the Goths—that helped bring about Rome's downfall. The critics meant the term as an insult.

◀ **Figure 10–11** The weight of the roof is carried by the pointed arches and transferred to columns inside the building. Can you find the pointed arches in this church?

Avila Cathedral. Avila, Spain.

▶ **Figure 10–12** Flying buttresses like these helped make thick solid walls unnecessary in Gothic cathedrals. What replaced these walls?

Notre Dame Cathedral. Paris, France.

Lesson 3　*Art of the Gothic Period*　📖　**153**

Vocabulary. To help students understand the noun *buttress*, ask them about the verb: Suppose someone says, "You need facts to buttress your argument"; what is another word for *buttress* in that sentence? Then help students work from their understanding of the verb to suggest their own definition of the noun: A buttress is an architectural structure. What do you think the function of that structure is? Finally, have students check their definition with the definition given in the Glossary at the back of the text.

You may also want to ask several volunteers to select and bring to class photographs of buildings with buttresses. Let the volunteers show the photographs, and have the class identify which are plain and which are flying buttresses.

Developing Concepts

Exploring Aesthetics. Have students examine and discuss Giotto's fresco shown in Figure 10-14: What is the subject of this painting? What do you think Giotto intended to communicate with this art work? What message or mood does the work communicate to you? How do you think the subject, composition, and content of this work might have been different if Giotto had used a different medium, such as stained glass or oil paints?

Then ask students to compare this fresco with the illumination shown in Figure 10-6 (page **149**): What similarities do you see? What are the most important differences? How did each artist use shape, texture, and color? How would you compare the moods of the two works?

Using Art Criticism. Guide students in discussing the stained glass window shown in Figure 10-13: How do you imagine the colors in this work change with changes in sunlight? What do the colors of the glass contribute to the message of the work? What do you think the artist's purpose was in creating this work? When the stained glass window was designed and created, was it an object of fine art or applied art? Why? Which do you think it is now? Why?

Background Information

The making of stained glass was one of the greatest of Medieval art forms. For color, artisans added minerals to the glass while it was still in the molten state. In this way, the glass was stained rather than painted and it was very bright. Small pieces of this stained glass were then joined together with lead strips and reinforced with iron bars. Often, the lead strips and iron bars were made as part of the design.

These stained glass windows were an ideal way of instructing the congregation. With stories about the lives of Christ, the Virgin Mary, and the saints, the stained glass brings to mind the beautifully colored illuminations found in Medieval manuscripts. In cathedrals such as those at Chartres and Reims in France and Leon in Spain, huge areas are devoted to stained glass.

Crafts

The pointed arch and flying buttress did away with the need for solid walls. They also opened up the possibility of having many windows in churches and cathedrals. This created yet another outlet for expression by artists and craftspeople of the day. Brilliantly colored stained glass windows like those in Figure 10–13 began gracing the walls of cathedrals. **Stained glass** is made of *colored glass pieces held in place with lead strips.* These windows filled the cathedrals with softly tinted light. The pictures in these windows, focusing on religious figures and events, also helped teach the Bible. Do you recall which art forms of the Romanesque period showed Bible stories?

▲ **Figure 10–13** The lead strips appear as dark lines in the finished design. Do you feel these lines add to or take away from the beauty of the work? Explain your answer.

Stained Glass from Cathedral of Leon — *Head of a Prophet*. Leon, Spain.

► **Figure 10–14** What has the artist done to make the people in this work look lifelike? What has he done to emphasize the woman, child, and donkey?

Giotto. *The Flight Into Egypt.* c. 1305–06. Fresco. Arena Chapel, Padua, Italy.

Background Information
Giotto di Bondone (Italy, *c.* 1267–1337) is often credited with breaking from the flat, Byzantine style and establishing a concern with pictorial space. Giotto's work was highly acclaimed even in his lifetime. Contemporaries and near-contemporaries, such as Dante and Boccaccio, praised Giotto highly, and the Florentine painter Cennino Cennini (Italy, *c.* 1370–*c.* 1440) wrote that "Giotto translated the art of painting from Greek to Latin."

Tradition claims that Giotto studied with Cimabue (Italy, 1240–1302), though many art historians now consider it more likely that he was a student of Pietro Cavallini (Italy, *c.* 1250–*c.* 1330). Giotto surely surpassed his teacher—whatever the teacher's identity—in his modeling of convincing human figures and in his depiction of human behavior.

In Giotto's lifetime, his most famous work was the mosaic of *Christ Rescuing the Apostles in a Storm* in St. Peter's in Rome. Unfortunately, only fragments of that original work now remain.

Painting

The Gothic style of building cathedrals never fully caught on in Italy. There churches continued to be built in the Romanesque manner with large, unbroken walls. Instead of stained glass, religious decoration was added with a form of painting known as fresco. **Fresco** (fres-koh) is *a painting created when pigment is applied to a section of wall spread with fresh plaster. Fresco* is the Italian word for "fresh." This technique required the artist to work quickly before the plaster dried. The pigment was absorbed and the painting was permanently preserved.

The work in Figure 10–14 is a fresco. It is one of a series found on the walls of a chapel in Padua, Italy. All were done by a gifted artist named Giotto (**jah**-toh). Take a moment to study this work. In creating this and other frescoes, Giotto wished to do more than tell Bible stories. His goal was to make the people in his pictures come alive. His genius was such that a century would pass before an artist of equal skill would appear.

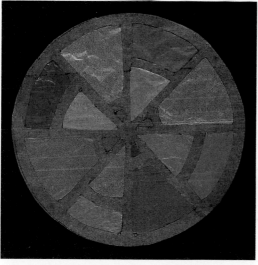

▲ Figure 10–15   Student work. Rose window design.

STUDIO EXPERIENCE

Make a pencil sketch based on a rose window design. Rose windows sometimes appear on the front of a church or cathedral. They are round, so your design should have either symmetrical or radial balance. Leave out all unnecessary details in your work. Transfer your sketch to a sheet of black construction paper. Go over all the lines with white chalk. Make some of the lines thicker than others.

Using scissors, cut out all the spaces between the chalk lines. Cut out patches of tissue paper in the shape of the spaces, only slightly larger. Pick different colors of paper for different spaces. Using white glue, attach these patches to the construction paper along their edges. *Optional:* You may want to use two thicknesses of black construction paper and sandwich pieces of tissue paper between the outlined areas. Turn your work over to reveal your own stained glass window. (See Figure 10–15.)

✔CHECK YOUR UNDERSTANDING

1. What problem faced architects of the Romanesque period? What two improvements allowed Gothic architects to solve this problem?
2. What is a cathedral?
3. What is stained glass? For what purpose did Gothic artists use stained glass?
4. What is a fresco? How was it done?
5. Who was Giotto? What was his goal?

Lesson 3   *Art of the Gothic Period*   155

Answers to "Check Your Understanding"

1. The problem facing Romanesque architects was how to build walls that could both contain windows and support a heavy roof. Gothic French architects began to use the pointed arch and the flying buttress.
2. A cathedral is a large, complex church created as a seat of office for a bishop.
3. Stained glass art is colored pieces of glass held in place with lead strips. Stained glass windows illustrated with religious figures and events helped teach the Bible.
4. A fresco is a painting created when pigment is applied to a section of wall spread with fresh plaster.
5. Giotto was a gifted fresco artist. His goal was to create paintings that made the people look lifelike.

Making a Gothic Gargoyle

LESSON PLAN
(pages 156–157)

Objectives
After completing this lesson, students will be able to:
- Use clay to model and carve gargoyles that have imaginary proportions.
- Describe, analyze, interpret, and judge their own gargoyles.

Supplies
- Sheets of sketch paper, pencils.
- Pencils; sketchbooks; slips of paper; small boxes; clay; clay modeling tools; burlap or other cloth cut into squares, 14 x 14 inches (36 x 36 cm); glaze in several colors (optional).

TEACHING THE LESSON

Getting Started

Motivator. Before students turn to the lesson, ask them to imagine and then sketch pictures of fantastic creatures. Their works may be related in some ways to real animals, but encourage students to be as imaginative as possible. When they have finished their sketches, let students share and discuss their work: Which creatures are most fantastic? What mood does each sketch create? Which creatures seem friendly and inviting? Which are frightening? Then have students look at the gargoyles in Figure 10-16: What distinguishes these gargoyles as fantastic creatures? What mood do they create? How are the creatures in their sketches similar to these gargoyles?

Vocabulary. Have a volunteer look up *gargoyle* in a dictionary and read the complete entry to the rest of the class. The derivation shows that *gargoyle* is related to the word *gargle:* What is the link between these two words? (Remind students, if necessary, of the practical purpose that gargoyles served.)

Making a Gothic Gargoyle

If you look up to the highest point of a Gothic cathedral, you will see creatures known as gargoyles. Look at Figure 10–16. A **gargoyle** is *a projecting ornament on a building carved in the shape of a fantastic animal or grotesque creature.* Gargoyles were made of carved stone and metal. They were meant to look like spirits fleeing, or being driven, from the holy building. However, these strange creations actually served a very practical purpose. They are really rain spouts that carried rainwater from the roof of the cathedral.

Creating these fascinating, sometimes frightening creatures required a great deal of imagination. In this lesson you will have an opportunity to design a gargoyle like the ones that appeared on Gothic cathedrals. (See Figure 10–17.)

WHAT YOU WILL LEARN

You will use clay to model and carve a gargoyle that will have imaginary rather than realistic proportions. Surface patterns will be created with a variety of textures to suggest fur, hair, scales, or feathers. Your model will be a freestanding sculpture.

WHAT YOU WILL NEED

- Pencil and sketchbook
- Slips of paper and small box
- Clay and clay modeling tools
- Burlap or cloth cut into sections, 14 x 14 inches, (36 x 36 cm)

▶ **Figure 10–16** How do you suppose someone of Gothic times would have felt to look up and find these odd-looking figures overhead?

Gargoyles at Narbonne, France.

Background Information
Originally, a gargoyle was a plain drain pipe; the pipe was important in protecting the walls of a building from rainwater that might accumulate on the roof. During the Middle Ages, stonemasons began creating grotesque figures—usually part human and part animal—around these pipes.

Grotesque gargoyles probably have their roots in the architecture of ancient Greece. Marble or terra cotta lion's heads were often placed along the edges of the roofs. These lions had open mouths through which water could drain.

Gargoyles are commonly found along the roof or eaves of Gothic buildings. They served an important purpose, because the cathedrals, palaces, and other structures of the time had no gutters. They were also a popular form of decoration. Some gargoyles projected as much as 3 feet (91 cm) from the side of the building.

Grotesque figures used simply as building decorations—not as drain pipes—are not gargoyles but chimera.

WHAT YOU WILL DO

1. Find examples of gargoyles in books from the library. Make a list of the animals or parts of animals used in these gargoyles.
2. On three separate slips of paper, write the name of a different animal. Place these slips of paper, along with those completed by other students, in a box.
3. Pass the box around the room. Without looking, pick out two slips.
4. Complete several pencil sketches in which you combine the animals named on your slips of paper to create a gargoyle design. Use your imagination to draw a creature unlike anything seen in real life. Add details such as hair, fur, scales, and feathers.
5. Complete a three-dimensional version of your gargoyle in clay. Begin by modeling the basic form of the gargoyle. Add details using both modeling and carving techniques.
6. Add interesting textures and surface patterns with modeling tools. These can be made to look like hair, fur, scales, feathers, or a combination of these.
7. Hollow out your model so it will dry more quickly and thoroughly. Work from the back to create a channel through the sculpture that exits through the open mouth. This channel can represent the passage through which rainwater would flow in a real gargoyle.
8. Fire your sculpture.
9. *Optional:* You may wish to add color by glazing in one or several colors. After glazing, fire the gargoyle again.

OTHER STUDIO IDEAS

- If you choose not to glaze your gargoyle, shoe polish may be applied to the fired piece and rubbed to a shine with a soft cloth.

•• Make another gargoyle, this time as a relief sculpture. Use the slab method. Trace your design onto the soft clay with a pencil. Use modeling tools to carve your picture out of the clay. Add textures to the surface of your relief.

EXAMINING YOUR WORK

- **Describe**   Show how your gargoyle combines more than one animal. Does it have fantastic proportions?
- **Analyze**   Did you use a variety of actual textures to create an interesting surface pattern?
- **Interpret**   Does your gargoyle resemble any animal seen in real life? How does it make you feel?
- **Judge**   Does your sculpture look as though it belongs as a decoration of a Gothic cathedral?

▲ Figure 10–17   Student work. Gargoyle.

Lesson 4   *Making a Gothic Gargoyle*   **157**

Developing Concepts

Using Art Criticism. Guide students in discussing the gargoyles shown in Figure 10-16: What purpose do you think the creator of these gargoyles intended them to serve? How do you think people of the Middle Ages felt when they looked at these gargoyles? How do you feel when you look at them? Do you think the gargoyles were created as works of fine art or works of applied art? Which do you consider them now? Why?

Understanding Art History. Ask a group of students to read and think about the development of gargoyles. Remind students that at first the term *gargoyle* referred simply to an unadorned spout. When were gargoyles first used? How did the gargoyle figures develop? How did gargoyles change after the introduction of the lead drain pipe in the sixteenth century? Have the students present an illustrated history of gargoyles to the rest of the class.

Appreciating Cultural Diversity. In what other parts of the world have sculptors created figures of fantastic creatures? Ask each student to find and share with the class at least one photograph of the figure of a fantastic creature from another culture.

Following Up

Closure. Let students work in small groups to compare and discuss their gargoyles. Then have students write interpretations of their own gargoyles, responding to the questions in the "interpret" section of "Examining Your Work."

Evaluation. Review students' gargoyles, consider their participation in the "Closure" group discussions, and read their interpretations of their own work.

Reteaching. Let students work in small groups to review the most important features of Gothic art and architecture: How are they similar to the art and architecture of the Romanesque period? What are the most important differences?

Enrichment. Ask students to find out more about the term *Middle Ages:* What are the middle ages "in the middle of"? Who first used the name for this period? What other terms have been used to name this period?

Handbook Cross-Reference

Remind students of the different forms of clay. Plastic clay is clay that is wet enough to be worked but dry enough to hold its shape. Slip is clay with enough water added to make it runny. Slip is used to glue together shaped pieces of damp clay. Leather hard clay is clay which is still damp but too hard to model. Pieces of leather hard clay can be joined with slip. Greenware is very dry clay that will break easily. Bisqueware is fired pottery that is hard but still not ready to use.

Refer students to Technique Tips 16 and 17, *Handbook* pages **281** and **282** for additional information about working with clay.

BUILDING VOCABULARY

Number a sheet of paper from 1 to 8. After each number, write the term from the box that best matches each description below.

buttress	gargoyle
castles	illuminations
cathedral	pointed arch
fresco	stained glass

1. Fortlike dwellings with high walls and towers.
2. Hand-painted book illustrations.
3. A large, complex church created as a seat of office for a bishop.
4. A curved arrangement of stones reaching up to a central point.
5. A brace or support placed on the outside of a building.
6. Colored glass pieces held in place with lead strips.
7. A painting created when pigment is applied to a section of wall spread with fresh plaster.
8. A projecting ornament on a building carved in the shape of a fantastic animal or grotesque creature.

REVIEWING ART FACTS

Number a sheet of paper from 9 to 13. Answer each question in a complete sentence.

9. Name three common features of a Romanesque castle.
10. What was the purpose of the sculptures found on the outside of Romanesque churches?
11. Where were illuminations found? What were they used for?
12. Under what circumstances can a buttress be said to "fly"?
13. What subjects appeared in the stained glass windows of Gothic cathedrals?

THINKING ABOUT ART

On a sheet of paper, answer each question in a sentence or two.

1. **Analyze.** Look back at the picture of a castle in Figure 10–1. What changes in society would have had to take place in order for this building's architects to add more windows?
2. **Compare and contrast.** What are the most important differences between Romanesque churches and Gothic cathedrals?
3. **Extend.** Imagine yourself walking through one of the Gothic cathedrals pictured in this chapter. What feature do you think would impress you most?

MAKING ART CONNECTIONS

1. **Language Arts.** Acting as an art critic, describe, analyze, interpret, and judge the illumination in Figure 10–6 on page **149**. Use these questions to guide you: Do the people in the picture look lifelike? Why, or why not? Which elements of art are important in this picture? What clues tell you this is a religious work? In judging the work, tell whether your reaction is based on subject, composition, or content.
2. **History.** Find the term *fresco* in an encyclopedia or art history book in your library. Learn as much as you can about how frescoes are made and what difficulties fresco painters experienced. If you can, make photocopies of several different frescoes showing the range of possibilities within the medium. Share your findings with your class in an audiovisual presentation.

CHAPTER 10 REVIEW

LOOKING AT THE DETAILS

The detail shown below is from the Cathedral of Leon, Spain. Study the detail and answer the following questions using complete sentences.

1. What direction do the lines of the cathedral take the viewer's eye? Do you think this is effective for a cathedral? Explain your answer.
2. Compare the visual texture of this structure with the one in Figure 10–1 on page **146**. How do they differ?
3. Is there another art form besides architecture used in this structure?
4. If you were not aware of the period in which this cathedral was built, what clues would you use to estimate when it was built?

Cathedral of Leon. (Detail.) Leon, Spain.

ANSWERS TO "LOOKING AT THE DETAILS"

1. The lines lead the viewer's eye dramatically up toward the sky. This is appropriate for a cathedral, since it is a place of worship and gives the interpretation of reaching toward the heavens.
2. The visual texture of the cathedral is sharp and textured with relief sculpture and carvings. The visual texture of the castle is smooth and flat.
3. Relief sculpture is another art form used in this structure.
4. Romanesque builders never solved the problem of how to build walls that could contain windows and support a heavy roof simultaneously. Cathedrals didn't exist as such before the Gothic period. The cathedral was an architectural contribution of the Gothic artists who came up with the pointed arch, shown in this structure.

Chapter Evaluation

The purpose of this chapter is to develop students' understanding of Romanesque and Gothic styles of art and to create works of art depicting these styles. Some possible evaluation techniques include:

1. Have students pretend that they are artists producing works of art during the Romanesque times. Ask them to write a short paper describing how this time in history influences their work.
2. Refer students to the vocabulary terms listed on page **145**. Have students divide a sheet of paper into 8 equal squares. In each square have them draw a sketch showing that they understand the meaning of the vocabulary term.
3. Have students complete Chapter 10 Test (TRB, Resource 10-10).

Art of the Renaissance

Chapter Scan

TRB Resources

- 11-10 Chapter Test
- Color Transparency 21
- Color Transparency 22

TEACHING THE CHAPTER

Introducing the Art Work

Direct the students' attention to Andrea del Castagno's *Portrait of a Man*. Inform them that Andrea del Castagno was an Italian painter in the fifteenth century. As a youth, Castagno left his home near Tuscany and went to Florence to be trained as an artist, where he was inspired by the works of Masaccio. Before he reached the age of twenty-five, he was among the most celebrated painters of his time. Castagno was commissioned to paint frescoes for various churches, stained glass windows for a cathedral, numerous portraits, and was also known to have been painting in the Vatican Library in Rome. Castagno is part of a group of painters who established numerous innovations that are associated with all Renaissance painting. Castagno's deepest interest was man. The figures Castagno painted in his frescoes are strong types, solidly constructed with powerful hands, yet with faces full of spiritual expression.

Examining the Art Work

Tell students that this portrait is remarkable not only for its striking portrayal of a strong personality, but also from a historical point of view. Explain that Florentine artists were accustomed to painting their portraits in profile. This portrait appears to be the earliest example of a portrait in which the subject is painted from a nearly frontal view.

▲ Notice how the change little by little from light to dark values makes this face seem three-dimensional. By using a three-quarter view the artist makes the face seem to project out toward the viewer.

Andrea del Castagno. *Portrait of a Man*. c. 1450. Oil on wood. 54 x 40.5 cm (21¼ x 15⅞"). National Gallery of Art, Washington, D.C. Andrew W. Mellon Collection.

Art of the Renaissance

The years following the Middle Ages in Europe were a time of great growth and discovery. Trade spread, and so did knowledge. New discoveries were made in every field, including science and geography. One of the most startling was the discovery of the New World by Christopher Columbus.

The period also saw great discoveries in art. Among the most important were exciting new ways of adding realism to works. The painting at the left makes use of one of these techniques. In the pages to come, you will learn about others.

OBJECTIVES

After completing this chapter, you will be able to:
- Identify artists of the Italian Renaissance and describe their contributions.
- Identify the contributions of artists working in northern Europe during the Renaissance.
- Use details and symbolism in studio experiences.

WORDS YOU WILL LEARN

linear perspective	Pietà
Madonna	Renaissance
oil paint	symbolism

ARTISTS YOU WILL MEET

Andrea del Castagno	Raphael
Jan van Eyck	Leonardo da Vinci
Masaccio	Rogier van der
Michelangelo	Weyden
Buonarroti	

Point out the brilliant colors in the work and sweeping curved lines. Ask students to notice the ring on the subject's little finger, the authoritative position of the hand and the facial expression which shows a man of great willpower and determination. Explain how these details, along with the deep red color, create an intense and powerful mood filled with a sense of drama. Explain that the details Castagno chose to portray give the viewer the impression that this individual is a powerful figure in society. Point out the numerous folds of flowing cloth suggesting the status and wealth of the individual.

Discussing the Art Work

Ask students how the eyes of the man in the painting affect them. Point out how the subject appears to be looking at the viewer and suggest that this creates an involvement between the viewer and the subject. Point out the way the eyes appear to be looking down at the viewer, rather than straight at him or her. Suggest that this is consistent with the mood and personality of the subject. He is looking out from an elevated perspective, one of self-importance, thus presenting himself as an authority over the viewer, one who commands respect.

Ask students to think about how Castagno saw this man. Explain that during the Renaissance, portraiture was characterized by an intense, even pitiless, insight into the model.

Tell students that in this chapter they will learn about the artists of the Renaissance and their contributions. They will also incorporate details and symbolism into their own works of art.

161

Building Self-Esteem

Tell students that in this chapter they will learn about a period called the Renaissance. It was during this period that a Flemish painter named Jan van Eyck developed oil paints. This discovery made it possible to work on a painting over a long period of time, because oil dries very slowly. Painters began to include very realistic detail, which hadn't been possible with water-based paints. Artists also started to use perspective to give their works a three-dimensional quality and began to draw their subjects showing deep emotion. These challenges required more mental effort than ever before. Artists had to concentrate very deeply on what they saw in order to paint convincingly. During the lesson on still life, help students to understand the techniques of shading and overlapping. Encourage them to set up as simple an arrangement as they feel they can handle, given the time. Let them know that depicting an object in a very realistic way will require intense concentration and attention to detail.

LESSON PLAN
(pages 162–165)

Objectives
After completing this lesson, students will be able to:
- Describe the style of Italian Renaissance art.
- Name several Italian Renaissance artists.
- Explain the terms *Madonna*, *Pietà*, and *linear perspective*.

Supplies
- Pencils, rulers, and sheets of white paper.
- School acrylic paints or tempera; paint brushes.
- Paper for making simple scrapbooks.
- Magazines and markers.

> ### TRB Resources
> - 11-1 *Renaissance Costumes*, (reproducible master)
> - 11-2 *Leonardo da Vinci*, (artist profile)
> - 11-3 *Drawing the Figure*, (reproducible master)
> - 11-4 *The Renaissance Artist and Anatomy*, (studio)

TEACHING THE LESSON

Getting Started

Motivator. Have students examine Figure 11-2. Tell them how this painting of the Trinity was so lifelike to fifteenth-century people that when they saw it for the first time they became frightened and ran from the church. Discuss how photography has accustomed people to highly realistic representations. Then ask students if they have seen a hologram. Discuss what kinds of holographic images could frighten them if unexpectedly encountered. If possible, go to an art or science museum that displays a hologram.

Art of the Italian Renaissance

During the Middle Ages the teachings of the Catholic Church were the focus of much of the art work. By the beginning of the 1400s, however, artists gradually began to change their style. After centuries of creating religious works, artists began to paint pictures to look as realistic as possible. The emphasis was not always on religious subjects. This time is known as the **Renaissance** (ren-uh-sahns), *a period of great awakening*. The word renaissance means "rebirth."

THE RENAISSANCE IN ITALY

The shift in interests that took place during the Renaissance was especially noticeable in Italy. There, a number of cities grew into trading and business centers. One of these, Florence, became the capital of Europe's cloth trade and home to its richest bank. Find Florence on the map in Figure 11–1.

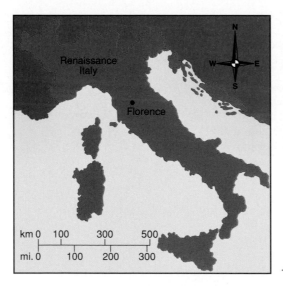

◄ Figure 11–1   Renaissance Italy.

Florence also became a center for art during the Renaissance. In this lesson you will read about the contributions of its artists.

Painting

Among the people living in Florence during the early 1400s was a young artist named Masaccio (muh-**zahch**-ee-oh). Masaccio continued where Giotto had left off a century earlier. He made the figures in his works seem solid and real. (See Figure 11–2.)

Masaccio also sought to add a true-to-life, three-dimensional quality using a technique called linear perspective (puhr-**spek**-tiv). **Linear perspective** is *the use of slanted lines to make objects appear to extend back into space*. (See Figure 11–3.) The technique was discovered by an architect and friend of Masaccio named Filippo Brunelleschi (fi-**leep**-oh broon-uhl-**ess**-kee).

The artist adds to this realistic appearance by giving the subject an expression of genuine grief. This combination of three-dimensional form and emotion became a trademark of Renaissance art.

Masaccio died suddenly at the age of 27. Some believe he may have been poisoned by a jealous rival. Luckily, there were other artists with the talent to build upon Masaccio's discoveries. One of these was a man whose talents were not limited to art. He was also skilled in science, literature, and music. The name of this gifted man was Leonardo da Vinci (lee-uh-**nard**-oh duh **vin**-chee).

Background Information
Renaissance painters were usually employed by an individual or a small group who exercised a great degree of control over the artist's work. Occasionally a painter was employed by a prince and paid a regular salary to execute whatever works the prince desired. Contracts between clients and artists in the fifteenth century show that artists were often required to base their work on a preliminary drawing that had been discussed in advance. A donor might specify the subject of a work, and then the artist would produce a preliminary drawing modified according to the client's wishes. In the late fifteenth century, many Italian Renaissance patrons wished to dissociate themselves from the nouveau riche and so they preferred art works that emphasized pictorial skill over the use of flashy and expensive pigments such as gold and ultramarine.

◄ Figure 11–2 Look at this painting and identify where Masaccio has used slanted lines to produce a three-dimensional quality.

Masaccio. *The Holy Trinity.* c. 1428. Fresco. Church of Santa Maria Novella, Florence, Italy.

▼ Figure 11–3 Diagram showing linear perspective. Linear perspective is based on a trick the eyes play on us. This trick causes the sides of a highway, for example, to seem to come together in the distance. The point at which such lines appear to meet at the horizon is called the vanishing point.

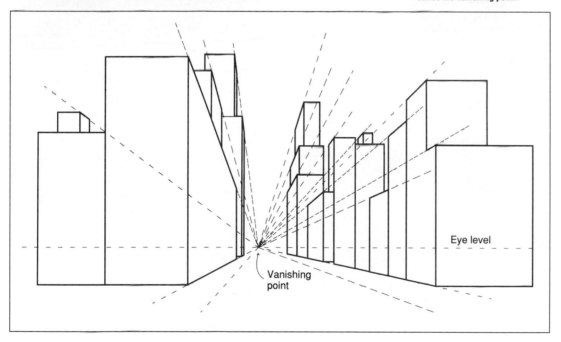

Eye level

Vanishing point

Vocabulary. Divide the class into groups that will research the Renaissance. Each group should assemble a scrapbook of information about the Renaissance, including a list of famous people and artists, sketches of clothing worn by Renaissance people, notes on how people lived, forms of entertainment, sketches of buildings erected, and other findings. Have students present their scrapbooks to the class. If you wish, play Renaissance-period music in the background during their presentations.

Developing Concepts

Exploring Aesthetics. Have students look through magazines and select pictures that are based on linear perspective. Suggest that they tear the pictures out and use markers to draw slanted lines indicating where the space recedes to a vanishing point.

Using Art Criticism. Refer students to Figure 11-4 and have them write down possible thoughts that may be going through the mind of the sitter. Then have students read aloud their interpretations as expressively as possible. Discuss how Renaissance aristocrats valued the appearance of serenity. Then have them compare Figures 11-2 and 11-4 and ask students how the Renaissance admiration for stoicism, dignity, and nobility is reflected in the figure of Christ.

Understanding Art History. Appoint three students to act as curators at a museum that is considering the acquisition of one of the art works illustrated in this lesson. Each curator should defend why one of the works is an excellent example of Renaissance art and would be a valuable addition to the museum's collection. The rest of the students should act as the board of trustees. The trustees should closely question the curators' statements and then take a vote on which piece the museum will purchase.

Background Information
Masaccio is regarded as the first important artist of the Italian Renaissance. Masaccio took the innovations of Giotto and developed them further to produce a style that became the trademark of the Italian Renaissance. It was a style that owed a great deal to the fresco painting technique that continued to be popular throughout Italy. The Gothic architectural style, with its walls of glass, did not appeal to Italians. They preferred the solid walls and cool, dark interiors of the Romanesque style. The walls of their churches were covered with bright mosaics and large frescoes. While painters in northern Europe were making intricate stained glass windows and manuscript illuminations, Italian artists such as Masaccio were doing huge wall paintings on the interiors of their churches.

Leonardo's most famous work is a portrait, the *Mona Lisa*. Figure 11–4 shows another of his haunting portraits. In this painting Leonardo uses light and dark values in the manner developed by Giotto and Masaccio. The blending is so precise, however, that it is impossible to tell where one value ends and the next begins. Notice how these gently changing values help make the sad face seem three-dimensional. Notice how the figure of the woman stands out dramatically against the dark background.

Leonardo was recognized as a great artist even in his own day. Artists from all over flocked to Florence in the hopes of learning from him. One of these was a young painter named Raphael (**raf**-ee-el). Figure 11–5 is one of over 300 Madonnas that Raphael painted. A **Madonna** is *a work showing the Virgin Mary with the Christ Child*. In this one, Leonardo's influence can be seen in the soft change from light to dark values. Notice the expressions of the faces of the different people. How would you describe each one?

Sculpture

Like Leonardo, Michelangelo Buonarroti (my-kuh-**lan**-juh-loh bwon-nar-**roe**-tee) excelled in many fields, including poetry, painting, and architecture. As an artist, however, he thought of himself as a sculptor first. One of Michelangelo's greatest and best-known works is his *Pietà* (pee-ay-**tah**), pictured in Figure 11–6. A **Pietà** is *a work showing Mary mourning over the body of Christ*. Michelangelo carved his *Pietà* when he was 24 years old.

Study this work. Can you find anything unusual about the proportion of the two figures? Did you notice that Mary is much larger than her son, a full-grown man? In fact, if the figure were to stand, she would be nearly 9 feet (3 m) tall! Michelangelo purposely planned the sculpture this way. He wanted the viewer to focus on the work's mood—not on Mary's struggle to support the weight of Jesus' body. How would you describe the mood of Michelangelo's *Pietà*?

▲ **Figure 11–4**   Who is this woman, and why is she so sad? Some historians claim she was the daughter of a rich banker abandoned by the man she loved.

Leonardo da Vinci. *Ginevra de 'Benci*. c. 1474. Wood. 38.8 x 36.7 cm (15¼ x 14½"). National Gallery of Art, Washington, D.C. Ailsa Mellon Bruce Fund.

▲ **Figure 11–5**   Where has the artist used linear perspective? How has the use of linear perspective added to this painting?

Raphael. *Madonna and Child Enthroned with Saints*. Tempera on wood. 169.2 x 169.5 cm (66⅝ x 66¾"). The Metropolitan Museum of Art, New York, New York. Gift of J. Pierpont Morgan.

Background Information
Italian Renaissance frescoes were created by the rapid application of a water-based paint to wet patches of wall plaster. The artist could only work on the amount of wall that would remain wet for that work day. (Because of this time restriction, viewers today can see ridges that define each day's worth of painting.) A fresco painter began by making a drawing on the wall. These preliminary drawings were first discovered when conservators removed frescoes that were damaged in World War II. The drawings were of limited usefulness because they were obscured after a thin coat of plaster was applied. Once paper was invented in the mid-fifteenth century, artists could make life-size cartoons that helped artists efficiently plan frescoes. The cartoons were applied to the wall and pricked with colored dust to provide guide lines.

▲ **Figure 11–6** Notice that the two figures—one horizontal, the other vertical—seem almost to form a pyramid. Can you trace the lines of that pyramid with your finger?

Michelangelo. *Pietà.* c. 1501. Marble. St. Peter's Basilica, Rome, Italy.

▲ **Figure 11–7** Triangles and pyramids used for balance.

STUDIO EXPERIENCE

Many Renaissance artists followed a triangular or pyramid plan to balance their work. This was used to organize the main figures in their works. This triangle plan can be found in the *Pietà*. (See Figure 11–7.) Can you find a similar plan in any other works seen in this lesson?

Using pencil and ruler, draw a large triangle on a sheet of white paper. Within this shape, fit one or more of the letters that make up your initials. Fill as much of the space inside the triangle as you can. Use only straight, ruled lines for your letters.

Now continue some of the lines beyond the triangle to the edge of the paper. This will divide the rest of your composition into various shapes. Paint the shapes within the triangle with different values of a single hue. Paint the outside shapes with different values of the complementary hue.

✔CHECK YOUR UNDERSTANDING

1. How did the art in Europe at the beginning of the 1400s differ from that of the Middle Ages?
2. What was the Renaissance? What city was its center in Italy?
3. What is linear perspective? Who discovered it? Who was one of the first artists to use it in a painting?
4. What is remarkable about the portraits painted by Leonardo da Vinci?
5. What is a Madonna? What Renaissance artist was influenced by Leonardo in his painting of Madonnas?
6. What is a Pietà? What is unusual about the use of proportion in Michelangelo's *Pietà*?

Lesson 1   *Art of the Italian Renaissance*   📖   **165**

LESSON 2

Drawing a Still Life

LESSON PLAN
(pages 166–167)

Objectives

After completing this lesson, students will be able to:

• Describe some of Leonardo da Vinci's many interests.
• Create a highly detailed drawing of a found object.
• Use overlapping objects and other means of creating the illusion of space in a drawing.

Supplies

• Pencils and sketch paper.
• Sheets of white drawing paper, 12 x 18 inches (30 x 46 cm).
• Examples of da Vinci's sketches.
• Objects that possess a variety of textures, such as scraps of velvet or silk, ridged seashells, pieces of wood, and various plants.
• Wide variety of drawing materials suitable for rendering different textures.

TEACHING THE LESSON

Getting Started

Motivator. Show students examples of pages from Leonardo da Vinci's notebooks. List on the board all the different subjects that interested him, including architecture, mathematics, botany, sculpture, painting, anatomy, poetry, literature, music, geology, and hydraulics. Have students look around the classroom and create a page of notes and sketches such as Leonardo might have made if he were sitting there.

Developing Concepts

Exploring Aesthetics. Have students imagine that Leonardo was once friends with someone who had been blind since birth. In order to share his visual world with the friend, Leonardo needed to talk about how things looked and felt. Have students describe five things that Leonardo would have wanted to share with his blind friend.

Drawing a Still Life

Many artists use sketch pads to record sights and ideas that interest them. In his lifetime Leonardo da Vinci filled some 100 sketchbooks with drawings on many subjects. Some of these were of storm clouds. Some were of rock formations and the action of waves. Some — like the one in Figure 11–8 — were of the human body. What sets Leonardo's drawings apart was how precisely he captured every detail of an object. Clearly, this Renaissance master had remarkable powers of concentration.

WHAT YOU WILL LEARN

You will make a pencil drawing of a still life, using your powers of concentration to make the drawing as accurate as possible. Gradual and sudden changes of value will be used to suggest rounded and angular forms. Space will be shown by overlapping these forms. Differences in texture will be emphasized. (See Figure 11–9.)

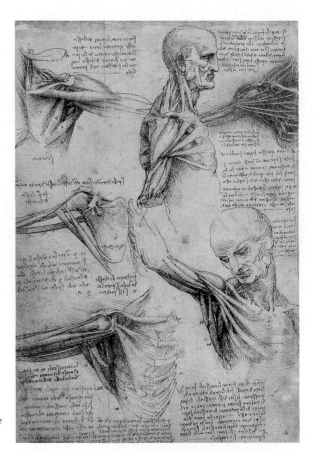

▶ **Figure 11–8 Leonardo was left handed. He wrote the notes you see backward to keep his ideas private. A mirror was needed to read them.**

Leonardo da Vinci. *Studies of Male Shoulder.* Royal Library, Windsor Castle, England.

Background Information

Leonardo da Vinci was the first artist to systematically study the structure of the human body. One of his means of investigation was dissection, a practice that he developed to an unprecedented degree. He is said to have dissected bodies during a time when the practice was outlawed and subject to severe punishment. Dissection helped Leonardo to learn how arms and legs bend and how muscles shift as the body moves. He was especially interested in the head, particularly how the eye sees and the mind reasons. He searched for the part of the brain where the senses meet, believing that this was where the soul would be found. Despite his fascination with the human form, Leonardo did not approve of artists who exaggerated musculature in their works—he accused such artists of making bodies look like "sacks of nuts."

WHAT YOU WILL NEED

- Pencil and sheets of sketch paper
- Sheet of white drawing paper, 12 x 18 inches (30 x 46 cm)

WHAT YOU WILL DO

1. Bring an unusual found object to class, something that is broken or in some other way altered. Possibilities are a crushed can, a broken toy, or an old hand tool.

2. Set your object on a table in front of you. Place the point of your pencil on a sheet of sketch paper. Without taking your eyes off the object, begin to draw it. Attempt to feel the lines of the object with your pencil as you draw. Concentrate on and draw each object in accurate detail. Make several more drawings on the same sheet until your work looks like your object.

3. Working with four other students, arrange your five objects in an interesting way. Some of the objects should overlap others. Make a drawing of the arrangement. Concentrate on overlapping objects to create an illusion of space. (See Technique Tip **2**, *Handbook* page **277**.)

4. Carefully draw the key lines of your sketch onto the large sheet of drawing paper. Include in this finished version as many details as you can, including differences in texture. Use your pencil to add gradual and sudden changes of value to show rounded and angular forms.

5. Display your work along with those of your classmates. Discuss how this drawing has helped you to better see details.

OTHER STUDIO IDEAS

- Do a still life drawing of a familiar object, such as your shoe, to fill an entire sheet of paper. Select a single color of tempera and add white and black to create gradual changes of value to show rounded forms. Use abrupt changes of value to show angular forms.

•• Color in another still life with pastels. Vary the pressure with which you apply the pastel to your paper. This will create differences in value and add to the three-dimensional look of the forms. Use color also to further emphasize the textures of forms.

EXAMINING YOUR WORK

- **Describe** Tell what objects you sketched. Point to the features of your drawing that would help others identify the objects.
- **Analyze** Point to the objects in your still life that overlap others. Explain whether this overlapping adds a feeling of space to the work. Tell how gradual and sudden changes of value suggest rounded and angular forms. Show the different textures you have emphasized.
- **Interpret** Give a name to your work that reflects the feelings you experienced while doing it.
- **Judge** Tell whether you feel your work as a whole succeeds as an accurate still life. Point to the most successful parts of your drawing. Explain why you think these parts are successful.

▲ Figure 11–9   Student work. Still life.

Note

You may wish to discuss the many factors that made it difficult for a fifteenth-century Italian woman to obtain the proper training to work as an artist. During the Renaissance, artists were expected to have more than the usual seven-year apprenticeship. They needed a liberal arts education which included travelling to major art centers, studying mathematics and the laws of perspective, and understanding ancient art and literature. It was also expected that artists would study the male nude model, which no proper lady could ever admit to having seen. This level of education and ability to travel for adequate training was extremely difficult for women to obtain. Among the very few women artists to have succeeded in developing professional careers as artists are the provincial nobleman's daughter Sofonisba Anguissola, Sofonisba's sister Lucia, and the artist's daughter Lavinia Fontana.

Art of the Northern Renaissance

LESSON PLAN
(pages 168–171)

Objectives
After completing this lesson, students will be able to:
• Describe the preparation and advantages of oil paint.
• Define symbolism.
• Characterize the style of Northern Renaissance art.
• Name two Northern Renaissance painters.

Supplies
• Drawing pencils and sheets of white drawing paper.
• Pigments, linseed oil, and turpentine; jar and stick for mixing.
• Tempera and watercolor paints; paint brushes, markers.
• Magazines.
• Several garments in different styles.
• Magnifying glasses.

TRB Resources
• 11-5 *Dürer's Perspective Technique,* (reproducible master)
• 11-6 *Invention of the Modern Mind,* (aesthetics)
• 11-7 *Renaissance and Exploration,* (appreciating cultural diversity)
• 11-8 *A Classical Rebirth,* (art history)

TEACHING THE LESSON

Getting Started

Motivator. Have students discuss or present objects that symbolize something important to them. They should explain what the item symbolizes and how it came to have that meaning for them. Present a symbolic object of your own.

Art of the Northern Renaissance

The shift from a Gothic to a Renaissance art style happened in northern Europe later than in Italy. The changes were also slower to develop and found different forms of expression.

In this lesson you will read about the contributions of Renaissance artists of northern Europe.

THE RENAISSANCE IN THE NORTH

The Northern Renaissance was concentrated in the area of Europe known as Flanders. It had as its center the modern Belgian capital of Brussels. Find Flanders and the city of Brussels on the map in Figure 11–10.

▲ Figure 11–10 Renaissance Europe.

The art of the Northern Renaissance continued to make use of several Gothic techniques and features. One of these was symbolism. **Symbolism** is *the use of an image to stand for a quality or an idea.* A dog, for example, was a symbol of loyalty; a lily could mean purity.

In other ways Northern Renaissance artists experimented with new ideas. This was especially true in the area of painting.

Painting

The most important contribution of the Northern Renaissance was a new painting technique. Artists discovered that **oil paint**, *a mixture of pigment, linseed oil, and turpentine*, gave them a slow-drying paint. This oil-based paint was far easier to use than tempera. It allowed the artist to work more slowly and add more details. Colors, moreover, could be mixed right on the canvas.

Jan van Eyck

The person often credited with discovering the oil painting technique was a Flemish artist named Jan van Eyck (**yahn** van **ike**). Like painters working in Italy, those in the North were fascinated with precision. Van Eyck was no exception. He would spend hours using the smallest brushes he could find to paint patterns of bark on a tree or the blades of grass in a meadow. Notice the attention to detail in the brilliantly colored work in Figure 11–11. Look especially at the textures of the robe and jeweled crown on the figure at the left. The paint is applied so skillfully that not a single brush stroke can be seen. Do you know what Bible story this work illustrates? Do you recall where you saw this event before?

Background Information
Art conservators are sometimes forced to transfer a painting from its original surface to a better one. This is necessary in cases where a poor quality canvas or wood panel has begun to deteriorate and where environmental factors such as excessive dryness, humidity, or cold have caused the paint to crack and fail to adhere to the original support. Wood panels, such as the one that was originally part of Figure 11-11, are particularly vulnerable to changes in the climate. The transfer of a painting is a major operation that is only resorted to after preventive measures, such as thinning a panel to reduce the strength of a warp, have proved useless. Unfortunately, some attempts at transferring paintings have caused the ruin of the works in question. For example, paintings have been transferred from wood to plastic surfaces that reacted poorly with the paint composition. It is sometimes preferable to simply accept the fact that an old painting is warped or cracked.

◄ **Figure 11–11** **The work is rich with symbolism. The tiles on the floor show scenes from the Old Testament telling of the coming of the Messiah. A dove, symbol of the Holy Spirit, follows a path of light streaming through an open window. The light stands for Christ.**

Jan van Eyck. *The Annunciation.* 1434–1436. Oil on wood transferred to canvas. 90.2 x 34.1 cm (35⅜ x 13⅞"). National Gallery of Art, Washington, D.C. Andrew W. Mellon Collection.

Vocabulary. Demonstrate how to mix a pigment, linseed oil, and turpentine to create *oil paint.* Point out that the pigment does not actually dissolve—it remains suspended in the vehicle, and when it is applied to a canvas or panel it stays on the surface instead of soaking in like a dye. Have students create small demonstration panels of oil paint, tempera, and watercolor swatches. Compare the different effects of each medium after the panels dry.

Developing Concepts

Exploring Aesthetics. Have students compare van Eyck's and van der Weyden's representations of the human figure with magazine photographs of people. Discuss the differences between the realism of highly detailed Northern Renaissance paintings and the realism of photographs.

Using Art Criticism. Have students describe the use of art elements and art principles in Figure 11-12, paying particular attention to the postures of the people in the work. Ask: Which figures are upright and which are placed on a diagonal? Why are the outermost figures on each side positioned along a curve? Why did van der Weyden place Mary's left hand so close to Christ's right hand? Discuss the different emotional reactions of the people. Do any of them feel the same way?

Using Art Criticism. Discuss the design principles of Mary's robe in Figure 11-11. Ask students how the robe's line, texture, and ornament combine to present Mary in a particular way. Compare the effect of Mary's robe to that of other dress styles, such as a ruffled pink gown, jeans and a tee shirt, and a black leather motorcycle outfit. How does the design of each garment influence the way its wearer is perceived? If possible, bring in examples of each of the garments that are discussed.

Note

Students who are familiar with the New Testament may enjoy trying to identify each of the figures in Rogier van der Weyden's painting in Figure 11-12. Christ's body is supported by Joseph of Arimathea, who wears a red tunic and hose. St. John is dressed in red and is reaching to help the Virgin Mary, who wears a blue gown. Nicodemus faces the viewer and wears a gold brocade robe. The woman at the far right side of the painting is Mary Magdalene. The woman covering her eyes at the left side of the work is Mary, the mother of James and Joseph. The young assistant on the ladder and the man holding a container of ointment are unidentified. The woman in green could be Mary, the wife of Clopas, who is mentioned in the gospel of John.

▲ **Figure 11–12** How is the artist's treatment of the Crucifixion different from how an artist of the Romanesque period would have treated it?

Rogier van der Weyden. *Descent from the Cross.* c. 1435. Museo del Prado, Madrid, Spain.

Rogier van der Weyden

Another important Northern Renaissance painter is Rogier van der Weyden (roh-**jehr** van duhr **vyd**-uhn). Van der Weyden was greatly influenced by van Eyck. Like van Eyck, he was able to reproduce each hair, each stitch in his paintings. Unlike van Eyck, whose pictures are calm and quiet, van der Weyden painted powerful, emotional scenes.

One of these is shown in Figure 11–12. In this picture, 10 life-size figures are placed in a shallow nook. The nook is just wide enough to hold them. The wall behind pushes the figures forward, bringing them closer to the viewer. In this way the artist forces the viewer to look at and experience this emotional scene from the Bible. Notice how the different people are reacting to the death of Christ. What has just happened to the woman in the blue dress in the foreground?

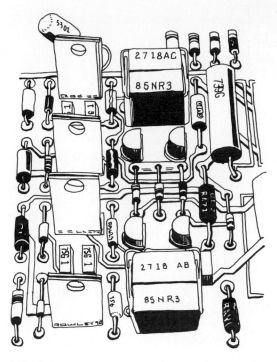

▲ Figure 11–13   Student work.   Detail drawing.

STUDIO EXPERIENCE

Look again at the paintings by van Eyck and van der Weyden in Figures 11–11 and 11–12. Notice how every last detail is captured in sharp focus.

Using your imagination, do a detailed drawing of a new, complicated electronic gadget. The item might be a new type of hand-held computer, a compact disc player, or other device. In your drawing include all the features and parts, such as dials and speakers. These should be drawn in sharp focus. Fill a whole sheet of paper with your drawing. (See Figure 11–13.)

✔CHECK YOUR UNDERSTANDING

1. What area became the center of the Northern Renaissance?
2. What Gothic feature continued to be used by Northern Renaissance artists?
3. What was a major contribution of artists of the Northern Renaissance? Who is credited with having discovered it?
4. In what ways were the religious paintings of Jan van Eyck and Rogier van der Weyden similar? In what ways were they different?

Following Up

Closure. Review the characteristics of Northern Renaissance painting and ask students to express their personal reactions. Do they feel moved by the pictures? Are the stories interesting or boring? How much do they feel they have in common with the people of van Eyck's and van der Weyden's time?

Evaluation. 1. Review the students' written responses to the "Check Your Understanding" questions. 2. Evaluate presentations on religious figures in non-Western art. 3. Review students' "Studio Experience" work.

Reteaching. Have students compare Figure 11-11 with a medieval and an Italian Renaissance painting of the same theme. List on the board the differences and similarities in the settings, gestures, garments, moods, and use of symbols. Ask: Do annunciation paintings from various times seem to express different ideas and feelings about Mary and her life?

Enrichment. Invite a professional art conservator from a local art museum or art restoration business to speak to the students. Have him or her discuss the profession, the experience of transferring paintings to new surfaces (as was done to Figure 11-11), and filling in decomposed or otherwise missing parts of an art work. If possible, the speaker should show slides or examples of his or her work.

Answers to "Check Your Understanding"
1. Brussels, in Flanders, became the center of the Northern Renaissance.
2. Northern Renaissance artists continued to use the Gothic feature of symbolism.
3. A major contribution was the use of oil paint. Flemish painter Jan van Eyck was credited with discovering the medium.
4. Jan van Eyck and Rogier van der Weyden's realistic styles were similar. Their choices of subject matter were different. Jan van Eyck's pictures are calm and quiet; van der Weyden painted powerful, emotional scenes.

LESSON PLAN
(pages 172–173)

Objectives
After completing this lesson, students will be able to:
- Explain the meaning of symbols used by Jan van Eyck.
- Identify symbols found in modern life.
- Create a visual symbol for a shoe company.

Supplies
- Pencils and sheets of sketch paper.
- Rulers; scissors; and shoe box lids.
- Sheets of white paper, 12 x 18 inches (30 x 46 cm).
- Tempera paints and brushes; white glue.
- Variety of shoes to augment those supplied by students.
- Photos of couples at their wedding ceremonies, culled from bridal magazines.

> **TRB Resource**
> - 11-9 *Create Your Own Renaissance Society,* (cooperative learning)

TEACHING THE LESSON

Getting Started

Motivator. Have students examine their belongings and clothing for evidence of a company's symbol or logo. Sketch the different symbols on the board. Discuss how the design of each symbol expresses the spirit or other quality of the item on which it is found. Ask: Does it hint that the product is sexy, healthy, prestigious, or environmentally sound?

Understanding Art History. Ask students how an art historian who had never heard of Jan van Eyck would go about placing Figure 11-14 in its historical context. List all of the clues on the board. Have students consult a history of fashion to confirm that this is a mid-fifteenth-century work.

172

Designing a Visual Symbol

Symbolism, as you have read, was an important feature of Northern Renaissance art. Its importance can be seen in the picture by Jan van Eyck in Figure 11–14. The painting, which shows a wedding ceremony, is heavy with symbols. The dog stands for the loyalty the marriage partners have promised each other. The single burning candle in the chandelier symbolizes the presence of God at the event. Even the shoes on the floor have meaning. They have been removed to show that the couple is standing on ground made holy by the exchange of vows.

Symbolism is as popular today as it was over 500 years ago. Think of all the symbols you see every day for cars, fast-food chains, and brands of clothing. Can you think of other products in our culture that use symbols? What symbols do these products use?

Imagine you have been asked to design a symbol for a shoe company. The design is to be colorful, detailed, and easy to recognize. It is also to be strictly visual—without any lettering.

WHAT YOU WILL LEARN

You will create a visual symbol for a shoe company. You will use repeated flat shapes to give harmony to your design. Variety will be obtained by making the shapes in different sizes. Use color to emphasize the most important shoe in your design. (See Figure 11–15.)

WHAT YOU WILL NEED

- Pencil and sheets of sketch paper
- Ruler and scissors
- Shoe box lid
- Sheet of white paper, 12 x 18 inches (30 x 46 cm)
- Tempera paint and several brushes
- White glue

WHAT YOU WILL DO

1. Look at the table of shoes that your teacher has arranged.
2. Make several pencil sketches of the shoe pile. Use only lines in your sketches. Do not fill in any of the shapes with shading.

▲ **Figure 11–14** The translation of the words above the mirror is: "Jan van Eyck was here." Experts have put forth the idea that this painting might have been an official wedding document. If it was, what importance would these words have?

Jan van Eyck. *Giovanni Arnolfini and His Bride.* 1434. National Gallery, London, England.

Background Information
Giovanni Arnolfini was a rich Italian merchant who lived in Flanders. Since he was from the city of Lucca, it is probable that he became wealthy by selling the beautiful silk brocade for which that town was famous. But, like many other Italians in Flanders, he no doubt sold other luxury goods as well and may have worked as a banker. When Giovanni Arnolfini decided to marry Jeanne de Chenay in 1434, he looked for the best artist available to paint a picture of their wedding. That artist, Jan van Eyck, made the couple and their wedding immortal. The bride and groom solemnly face the witnesses to the ceremony. Giovanni raises his right hand as if he is saying an oath, while his bride places her right hand in his left. Her frail body seems lost in the full, fur-lined dress. Her curving posture may look odd, but at the time it was considered quite fashionable to stand that way. Of the two figures, Giovanni is painted in a much more natural fashion. Given the opportunity to examine the actual painting, viewers could see the stubble on his chin.

3. Choose the best of your sketches and study it. Using the ruler, draw a rectangle around the part of your sketch that seems most interesting. This is to be your design.

4. Using the ruler, measure the length and width of the shoe box lid. Rule off a rectangle with the same measurements on the sheet of white paper. With scissors, cut out the rectangle.

5. Draw your design sketch on the rectangle, filling the space. Keep the shapes flat to give your design harmony. Make some of the shapes larger than others to add variety. Pick out one shoe that you would like to emphasize. Add details to this shoe.

6. Paint your design using tempera. Paint the different shoes so they look flat. Use a contrasting hue for the shoe you want to emphasize.

7. When the paint is dry, glue your painting to the shoe box lid. Display your finished work along with those of your classmates. Include some professionally designed shoe box lids in the display. Discuss which of the designs works best as a symbol for a shoe company. Try to identify the reasons for your opinions.

EXAMINING YOUR WORK

- **Describe** Tell whether you can instantly identify your design as a symbol for shoes. Are the shoes in your design easily recognized?
- **Analyze** Tell whether you used only flat shapes in your design. State whether the repeated use of these flat shapes adds to the harmony of the design. Point out the different-sized shapes in your work. Explain how these add variety to the design. Point out the one shoe you emphasized. Tell what you did to emphasize this shoe.
- **Interpret** Tell whether your design is unique enough to be identified with a particular shoe company.
- **Judge** Tell whether you feel your work succeeds. Explain your answer. Tell what changes you would make if you had a chance to do the design over.

▲ Figure 11–15 Student work. Design of a visual symbol.

OTHER STUDIO IDEAS

- Think of a brand name for the shoes your design symbolizes. From a contrasting color of construction paper, cut letters that spell out this name. Glue the letters to the shoe box lid so that they fit the overall design.

- ● With pencil, transfer your shoe design to a sheet of white paper. Go over all the pencil lines with India ink. Fill in the shapes of your design with as many textures as possible using only closely spaced ink lines.

Lesson 4 *Designing a Visual Symbol* **173**

Classroom Management Tip
Linseed oil and the usual additives to oil paints have no significant hazards. The pure driers that are sometimes used, however, can be dangerous. Lead and manganese driers are poisonous if inhaled, ingested, or absorbed into the bloodstream through the skin. Cobalt driers are slightly toxic through skin contact and somewhat more so when inhaled. The least toxic driers are cobalt linoleate and oleate.

Using Art Criticism. Compare Figure 11-14 with contemporary photos of couples at their wedding ceremonies. Have students discuss the ideas, values, and emotions expressed in van Eyck's work. Ask: Are they different than those emphasized in modern wedding portraits?

Appreciating Cultural Diversity. Have students research wedding ceremonies in various cultures and write a paragraph on the different kinds of visual symbols that are part of these ceremonies.

Following Up

Closure. Ask students to briefly state whether they prefer paintings that have symbols to be decoded. Ask: Do symbols make an art work more interesting or fun to look at? Do symbols make it harder to understand art from a different time and place? Point out that van Eyck's contemporaries did not have to research to understand the meaning of his symbols, which were as much a part of their culture as the language they spoke.

Evaluation. 1. Have students review their shoe company symbols using "Examining Your Work" as a guide. 2. Assess the paragraphs on wedding symbols in other cultures.

Reteaching. Discuss the visual symbols that are a part of modern weddings. List them on the board. If necessary, refer again to the bridal magazine photos to remind students of the importance of rings, flowers, a white dress, and other accessories of a traditional American wedding.

Enrichment. Invite a graphic designer who has worked on corporate logos to speak to the class. Have him or her discuss the various stages a symbol goes through before it reaches its final form. Ask whether the public always responds to a company symbol in the way that the designer anticipated.

ANSWERS TO "CHAPTER 11 REVIEW"

Building Vocabulary

1. Renaissance
2. linear perspective
3. Madonna
4. Pietà
5. symbolism
6. oil paint

Reviewing Art Facts

7. Florence in the 1400s was the capital of Europe's cloth trade, the home of its richest bank, and a center for art.
8. Masaccio was a painter. He was remembered for being the first painter to use linear perspective to give his paintings a three-dimensional quality.
9. Leonardo da Vinci was skilled in science, literature, and music as well as art. (Students may choose two.)
10. Leonardo influenced Raphael to use subtle blending of light and dark values.
11. Michelangelo made Mary much larger than Jesus in his Pietà to intensify the mood of mourning.
12. Many Renaissance artists used a triangle or pyramid plan to balance their work.
13. Northern Renaissance artists continued to use the Gothic feature of symbolism.
14. Jan van Eyck is credited with discovering oil paint.

Thinking About Art

1. Answers will vary but should include the shift to realism, introduction of three-dimensional form and emotion into painting (Masaccio), discovery of oil paint (van Eyck), and continued use of symbolism.
2. Answers will vary. Both paintings have many realistic details as well as many symbols. The Annunciation has more details. Students will list different items.
3. Similarities include the use of symbolism, love of accurate details, three-dimensionality, and emotion. Differences include media: fresco painting in Italy and oils in northern Europe.

BUILDING VOCABULARY

Number a sheet of paper from 1 to 6. After each number, write the term from the box that best matches each description below.

linear perspective	Pietà
Madonna	Renaissance
oil paint	symbolism

1. A period of great awakening.
2. The use of slanted lines to make objects appear to extend back into space.
3. A work showing the Virgin Mary with the Christ Child.
4. A work showing Mary mourning over the body of Christ.
5. The use of an image to stand for a quality or an idea.
6. A mixture of pigment, linseed oil, and turpentine.

REVIEWING ART FACTS

Number a sheet of paper from 7 to 14. Answer each question in a complete sentence.

7. Name three things the city of Florence was noted for in the 1400s.
8. Who was Masaccio? What is he remembered for?
9. Name two areas besides art in which Leonardo da Vinci was skilled.
10. In what way can Leonardo's influence be seen in the works of Raphael?
11. What is unusual about the proportions of the two figures in Michelangelo's *Pietà*?
12. What geometric shape did Renaissance artists use as a way of planning their works?
13. What feature of Gothic art did Northern Renaissance artists continue to use in their works?
14. What Northern Renaissance painter is credited for discovering oil paint?

THINKING ABOUT ART

On a sheet of paper, answer each question in a sentence or two.

1. **Interpret.** Read the following statement: "Art of the present would not be possible without art of the past." Describe three facts about artists or events of the Renaissance that you would use to support this statement.
2. **Analyze.** Look once again at the two paintings by Jan van Eyck (Figures 11–11 and 11–14). Which has the most lifelike details? Which particular details struck you as looking most like a photograph?
3. **Compare and contrast.** In what ways were the art styles of the Renaissance in Italy and in the North similar? In what ways were they different?

MAKING ART CONNECTIONS

1. **Language Arts.** Artists of the Renaissance were greatly influenced by the art of ancient Greece and Rome. Pick a painting or sculpture that you studied in Chapter 7. Choose another from the present chapter. Write a short report noting where Greek or Roman influences were strongest in Renaissance art. Discuss how breakthroughs during the Renaissance allowed artists to expand their horizons still further.
2. **Social Studies.** Michelangelo, as you read in this chapter, was gifted in many fields. Two of these were painting and architecture. In an art history book or encyclopedia, read about his contributions in these two areas. Note names of specific projects and, if possible, make photocopies of pictures of the works. In addition, gather details of Michelangelo's life. Combine your findings with information on his sculpture into a book.

LOOKING AT THE DETAILS

The detail shown below is from Andrea del Castagno's *Portrait of a Man*. Study the detail and answering the following questions using complete sentences.

1. How does color affect the mood in this painting?
2. What details has the artist used to contribute to a mood of wealth and authority?
3. How do you, as a viewer, feel in the presence of this work?
4. Do you think Castagno involves the viewer in this work of art? Explain your answer.

Andrea del Castagno. *Portrait of a Man*. c. 1450. Oil on wood. (Detail.) 54 x 40.5 cm (21¼ x 15⅞"). National Gallery of Art, Washington, D.C. Andrew W. Mellon Collection.

1. The deep colors create a bold mood. The dominant red color creates a sense of drama, power, and intensity.
2. Other details the artist has used include the ring and the position of the hand (a symbol of wealth and authority), the facial expression, and the numerous folds of flowing cloth.
3. Students' responses may vary. Possible answers include: In the presence of this work the viewer may feel fearful, shy, reserved, respectful, in awe or uncomfortable.
4. Castagno involves the viewer in this work because the subject's eyes look out toward the viewer and engage the viewer's eyes.

Chapter Evaluation

The goal of this chapter is to develop students' understanding of the artists and art styles created during the Renaissance. Some possible evaluation techniques include:

1. Distribute reproductions of works of art that depict linear perspective. Ask students to analyze and explain how linear perspective is used in the art work.
2. Working in small groups, have students compare and contrast the art produced by Italian Renaissance artists with the art produced by the artists in northern Europe.
3. Ask students to write a paragraph describing symbolism and giving two examples.
4. Have students complete Chapter 11 Test (TRB, Resource 11-10).

European Art of the 1600s and 1700s

Chapter Scan

TRB Resources

- 12-10 Chapter Test
- Color Transparency 23
- Color Transparency 24

TEACHING THE CHAPTER

Introducing the Art Work

Direct students' attention to Artemisia Gentileschi's *Judith and the Maidservant with the Head of Holofernes*. Inform them that Artemisia Gentileschi was an Italian painter during the early 1600s. The social conventions of her day restricted education for women and tended to exclude them from training and practicing in the arts. Gentileschi was instructed by her artist father, who was strongly influenced by the works of Caravaggio and passed that influence on to Artemisia. Artemisia Gentileschi had a successful career and helped to propagate Caravaggio's style through the Italian peninsula. The Caraveggesque style was characterized by theatrical depictions of the human form illuminated by a strong or single light source against dark backgrounds, and also showed a fascination for the horrific and gruesome. Gentileschi was known as a portrait artist in her day, but today, her reputation rests on an impressive group of religious paintings.

▲ Notice the striking use of light in this work. Notice also the work's size: it is over 6 feet (2 m) high. That the figures are larger than life adds to the impression the painting makes on its viewer.

Artemisia Gentileschi. *Judith and Maidservant with the Head of Holofernes*. c. 1625. Oil on canvas. Detroit Institute of Art, Detroit, Michigan.

European Art of the 1600s and 1700s

"What goes around comes around." Have you ever heard this saying? The truth behind it is clear from events in Europe following the Renaissance. There, in the 1500s, a religious revolution took place — only to be followed a century later by another.

This second revolution resulted in a new peaceful atmosphere. It also resulted in a new wave of artists and new ways of making art. The picture at the left was done in a style of the age. Can you identify any of its features? You will soon be able to recognize them.

OBJECTIVES

After completing this chapter, you will be able to:

- Explain what new ways of creating art were brought about by the Counter-Reformation.
- Identify features of the Baroque style and name important artists who practiced it.
- Describe features of the Rococo style and identify important artists of the period.
- Create art works in the expressive style of Rembrandt.
- Experiment with art in the Rococo style.

WORDS YOU WILL LEARN

Baroque
etching
facade

portrait
Rococo

ARTISTS YOU WILL MEET

Francesco Borromini
Michelangelo Merisi
    da Caravaggio
Jean-Baptiste Siméon
    Chardin
Artemisia Gentileschi
Francisco Goya
Judith Leyster

Rembrandt van Rijn
Peter Paul Rubens
Louis Le Vau and Jules
    Hardouin-Mansart
Diego Velázquez
Élisabeth Vigée-
    Lebrun
Antoine Watteau

177

Art of the 1600s

When Rome collapsed, you will recall, the Catholic Church became more influential. It remained this way until the early 1500s, when the Church's power began to slip. A group of Christians led by a man named Martin Luther splintered off from the Church in revolt to form their own religion.

Objectives

After completing this lesson, students will be able to:
• Describe the Protestant Reformation and Counter-Reformation movements.
• Characterize Baroque art and architecture.
• Name Baroque artists from northern and southern Europe.

Supplies

• Popular magazines.
• Objects for a candlelit scene.
• Paints and brushes.
• Sheets of white paper, 18 x 24 inches (30 x 46 cm).

TRB Resources

• 12-1 *Out of the Picture*, (reproducible master)
• 12-2 *The Art of Light*, (reproducible master)
• 12-3 *Study Dutch Genre Paintings*, (cooperative learning)
• 12-4 *Baroque Sculpture*, (aesthetics/art criticism)

TEACHING THE LESSON

Getting Started

Motivator. Ask students to give examples from their own experience of telling a passionate, dramatic story in order to persuade someone. Perhaps a student has regaled his or her parents with a description of the dire consequences of not being permitted to attend a particular social event. Discuss when a cool and logical approach is most persuasive and when a dramatic story works best. Draw a parallel between their responses and the Counter-Reformation church's belief that emotionally charged accounts of Biblical tales were necessary to persuade people to remain within the Catholic Church.

▲ **Figure 12–1** Study the changing light and dark values on the surface of this church. What principles are used to organize these different values?

Francesco Borromini. San Carlo alle Quattro Fontane. c. 1665–1676. Rome, Italy.

The Protestant Reformation, as this movement was called, drew many people away from the Catholic Church. In an effort to win them back, the Church started its own reform movement in the 1600s. This movement, which began in Italy, is known as the Counter-Reformation.

Art was an important part of the Counter-Reformation. Artists were called upon to create works that would renew religious spirit. A sense of flowing movement is one feature of a new art style of the day, **Baroque** (buh-**rohk**), or *an art style emphasizing movement, contrast, and variety*.

ARCHITECTURE AND PAINTING

In architecture the call to renew religious spirit was answered by, among others, an artist named Francesco Borromini (fran-**ches**-koh bor-uh-**meen**-ee). The church pictured in Figure 12–1 won Borromini great fame. He created the **facade** (fuh-**sahd**), *the outside front of a building*, to express his art. Do you notice how the surface seems to flow — first in, then out, then in again? Notice how the structure looks almost as though it were modeled from soft clay. This helps create a pattern of light and dark values across the whole facade. The Baroque emphasis on movement is also seen in painting of the period. Although the style originated in Italy, it spread to Spain and northern Europe.

Italy

The leader of the Baroque style in Italy was a young painter named Michelangelo Merisi da Caravaggio (kar-uh-**vahj**-yo). One of his key contributions was the use of light in a daring new way. This ability is combined with the artist's skill as a storyteller in the picture in Figure 12–2. Take a moment to study the work, which pictures the burial of

---

Background Information

The Counter-Reformation is generally said to have begun with the Council of Trent in 1545. At this time the Catholic Church realized that it was having problems and initiated eighteen years of council sessions. Several of those gatherings dealt specifically with the relationship between art and religion. The bishops decided that images should remain in churches as a "Bible of the illiterate," however, nudity in religious pictures was no longer acceptable. Since the Pope himself owned a large collection of paintings of mythological stories that necessitated nude figures, the Council made an exception for him. The Council also decreed that images of Mary and Christ should be placed in churches and venerated, and that paintings should not have a seductive character. Finally, scenes of the passion of Christ and his crucifixion were to be rendered as realistically as possible so that the viewer could empathize more easily.

Christ. It is as if a spotlight has been shone on real actors on a stage. Find the man holding Christ's legs. This man, whose eyes meet yours, draws you into the painting. Notice the puzzled expression on his face. He seems about to ask you to identify yourself. Perhaps he will also ask if you intend to merely watch or to help in laying Christ in his tomb. In this way, Caravaggio makes you feel that you are a part of the drama.

Caravaggio's style influenced the work of many other Italian painters of the day. Among them was a woman named Artemisia Gentileschi (ahr-tuh-**meez**-ee-uh jent-uhl-**ess**-kee). Like Caravaggio, Gentileschi used light and shadow to add excitement to her paintings. One of these opens this chapter (page **176**). The work shows the Bible hero

Judith in the tension-filled moments after she has slain an enemy of her people. A servant is seen placing the victim's severed head in a sack. Suddenly Judith, still clutching her sword, raises a hand in warning. Have the two been discovered? They wait silently, afraid to move. The light from a single flickering candle creates the only movement in the hushed tent. It reveals the anxious faces of the two women staring into the darkness.

Spain

Not all Baroque paintings showed such tense, dramatic movement. Movement of another sort is found in the works of Spanish painter Diego Velázquez (dee-**ay**-goh vuh-**las**-kuhs). One of these, a simple painting of a woman sewing, is pictured in Figure 12–3. Examine this painting. Note how the fingers of both hands are blurred. This helps show that her fingers are moving rapidly as she sews.

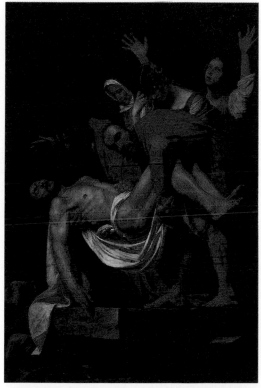

▲ Figure 12–2 **Light is used to emphasize the most important details of this picture. These details are shown in shocking realism. Notice that even the soles of Christ's feet are painted to look dirty.**

Caravaggio. *The Deposition*. 1604. Vatican Museum, Pinacoteca, Rome, Italy.

▲ Figure 12–3 **The young woman in this picture may be the artist's daughter. She is known to have married one of his pupils.**

Diego Velázquez. *The Needlewoman*. c. 1640–1650. Oil on canvas. 74 x 60 cm (29⅛ x 23⅝"). National Gallery of Art, Washington, D.C. Andrew W. Mellon Collection.

Lesson 1 *Art of the 1600s* 📖 **179**

Understanding Art History.
Have students study Figure 12-4. Point out the Virgin Mary's hefty proportions. Ask students to hypothesize why Rubens painted her so large. Explain that large-bodied women were considered highly attractive in this era, and show other paintings by Rubens to illustrate this fact. Have students page through magazines and pull out examples of what are considered ideal female bodies today. Emphasize how standards of attractiveness vary according to time and place.

Developing Studio Skills.
Set up a scene that is lit by a single candle. Have the light fall diagonally from outside of the picture frame. If at all possible, include a person in the scene who is engaged in a tense or exciting action. Have students paint the scene and attempt to render the shadows and dramatic lighting in the manner of Gentileschi's painting at the chapter opening on page **176**.

Appreciating Cultural Diversity.
Discuss the sculptural qualities of Borromini's facade in Figure 12-1. Then have students research Hindu temples in northern India, such as the Lingaraja temple in Bhubaneshwar and the Lakshmana temple in Khajuraho, and religious architecture in Cambodia, such as the temple of Angkor Wat. These buildings also have highly sculptural exteriors. Help students characterize the ways in which the facades of these buildings embody some of the same elastic, rhythmic, and three-dimensional qualities as San Carlo alle Quattro Fontane in Rome.

▲ **Figure 12–4   Nothing seems to stand still in this painting. You are made to feel as though you are witnessing a moment in time.**

Sir Peter Paul Rubens. *The Assumption of the Virgin*. c. 1626. Wood. 125.4 x 94.2 cm (49⅜ x 37⅛"). National Gallery of Art, Washington, D.C. Samuel H. Kress Collection.

Background Information
Of all the European artists of the seventeenth century, Peter Paul Rubens most completely captured the exciting spirit and rich effects of the Baroque style. While still a young man, he spent eight years in Italy. There he came to know sixteenth-century Italian painting and the works of Caravaggio. When he returned to his native Antwerp he set up a studio that soon became the busiest in Europe. Assisted by many helpers, Rubens turned out portraits, religious pictures, and mythical scenes. He also gained fame as a diplomat and as a man of learning.

Northern Europe

The major talents in Northern Europe, you will remember, developed during the Renaissance. This trend continued into the 1600s, led by a Flemish painter named Peter Paul Rubens. No other Baroque artist came close to Rubens in capturing the action and feeling of the new style. Notice his use of line in the work in Figure 12–4. The picture shows the Virgin Mary rising toward heaven. Can you find the line—partly real, partly imaginary—beginning in the raised arm of the figure at the left? Where does this line lead? What kind of line is it? Notice how the line pulls the viewer into the work, making him or her feel present.

In neighboring Holland, which remained a Protestant stronghold, a new subject matter for paintings was busily being explored. Genre pictures showing simple scenes from daily life were preferred over religious paintings. Another type of painting being introduced was the **portrait**, *a painting of a person.* A gifted young painter named Judith Leyster (**lye**-stuhr) specialized in portraits, using quick, dazzling brush strokes. This allowed her to catch the fleeting expressions on the faces of her subjects. Figure 12–5 shows a portrait she did of herself. Note how she seems to smile out of the picture at the viewer. Could she be eager for the viewer's reaction to the painting she is working on?

▲ **Figure 12–5** By the time she was 17, the artist was already gaining fame as a painter. Later in life, as a married woman with three children, she painted less. She died when she was only 50.

Judith Leyster. *Self Portrait*. c. 1635. Canvas. 72.3 x 65.3 cm (29⅜ x 25⅝"). National Gallery of Art, Washington, D.C. Gift of Mr. & Mrs. Robert Woods Bliss.

✔CHECK YOUR UNDERSTANDING

1. What was the Protestant Reformation? Who was its leader?
2. What was the Counter-Reformation?
3. What new art style arose during the period of the Counter-Reformation? What are the main features of this style?
4. What was a main contribution of Caravaggio?
5. Name a major Baroque painter of northern Europe.
6. What is a portrait? What artist that you read about specialized in painting portraits?

Following Up

Closure. Ask students to briefly state whether they prefer Renaissance or Baroque art. Have them explain their responses.

Evaluation. 1. Review students' written responses to the "Check Your Understanding" questions. 2. Assess students' paragraphs on van Eyck as a Baroque artist. 3. Evaluate the fabricated Leyster documents.

Reteaching. Review the style of Borromini's facade in Figure 12-1. Then have students select a local building and redraw its facade in the manner of Borromini. Make sure that they bring their textbook so that they can refer to the specific features that they will incorporate.

Enrichment. Have students research how Rubens ran his studio, including his use of assistants to complete commissions for very large works. Discuss which parts of Figure 12-4 Rubens probably worked on personally and which parts he may have given his approval on after they were completed by others.

Answers to "Check Your Understanding"

1. The Protestant Reformation was a movement away from the Catholic Church by a group of Christians who wanted to form a new religion. Martin Luther was the leader of this movement.
2. The Counter-Reformation, led by the Catholic Church, was a movement launched to win back people who had left the Church.
3. The new art style that arose during the Counter-Reformation was called the *Baroque Style.* It was characterized by movement, contrast, and variety.
4. Caravaggio's main contribution to the art of the period was the use of light in a new and daring way.
5. Flemish painter Peter Paul Rubens was a major Baroque painter from Northern Europe.
6. A portrait is a painting of a person.

Objectives

After completing this lesson, students will be able to:
- Describe the expressive qualities of various hand positions.
- Create an expressive drawing of hands.
- Use three-dimensional shading techniques.

Supplies

- Pencils and sketch paper.
- Sheets of black construction paper, 9 x 12 inches (23 x 30 cm).
- White crayons.

> **TRB Resources**
> - 12-5 *Rembrandt and The Night Watch,* (art historian)
> - 12-6 *Chiaroscuro Ink Drawing,* (studio)

TEACHING THE LESSON

Getting Started

Motivator. Ask students to think of a body posture that reflects a particular feeling. Have each student assume their posture in turn and see if the rest of the class can guess what emotion is being expressed. Discuss the phenomenon of body language and its importance to artists. Ask: Do the students notice in their daily life how people position their bodies? Is body language something that they respond to on an unconscious level?

Developing Concepts

Using Art Criticism. Explain to students that Figure 12-6 was painted as one of a pair of portraits. The companion portrait is Rembrandt's *Man with Gloves.* Have students find a reproduction of this work. Discuss how the portraits work as a pair. Ask: Are the sitters' characters more apparent when the portraits are viewed in tandem? How has Rembrandt used the art elements and principles to enhance the psychological dimension of these pictures?

182

Drawing Expressive Hands

The leading Dutch painter of the 1600s is a man named Rembrandt van Rijn (**ryn**). Figure 12–6 shows a portrait by this master. The artist uses a soft light to highlight the main parts of the picture. The subject, you will notice, is not beautiful. She seems, however, not to care about this. She is not bothered by the fact that others may be more attractive. If anything, she appears to be at peace with the world and her place in it. Notice how even her hands mirror this gentle calm. The artist has managed to make them look totally relaxed and at rest.

WHAT YOU WILL LEARN

You will make a drawing of your hand on black construction paper. Draw the hand to express a particular feeling. White crayon will be used to emphasize the three-dimensional form of the hand. (See Figure 12–7.)

WHAT YOU WILL NEED

- Pencil and sheets of sketch paper
- Sheet of black construction paper, 9 x 12 inches (23 x 30 cm)
- White crayon

► **Figure 12–6** The artist uses a straight horizontal line in the center of this picture. He separates the linen scarf from the lady's clothing. Do you remember what kind of mood a straight line like this calls to mind?

Rembrandt van Rijn. *Portrait of a Lady with an Ostrich-Feather Fan.* c. 1660. Canvas. 99.5 x 83 cm (39¼ x 32⅝"). National Gallery of Art, Washington, D.C. Widener Collection.

182 Lesson 2 *Drawing Expressive Hands*

Background Information

In 1648, a treaty with Spain divided the Netherlands into two parts. Flanders in the South remained Catholic and a territory of Spain. But Holland in the north, which was largely Protestant, finally gained its independence from Spain. In Holland, the Baroque style had little impact. Although some features appear in Dutch art (notably the Caravaggesque lighting in works by Gerrit van Honthorst and Hendrick Terbruggen), the Baroque was limited mainly to Catholic countries, where it was the style of the Counter-Reformation. Dutch Protestants did not want religious sculptures or paintings in their churches, and this presented a problem for artists. They had to find new subject matter for their art. The average Dutch citizen enjoyed a comfortable home and profitable business. It became clear that there was a good market for paintings that spoke of these Dutch successes as well as for works that would remind Dutch businessmen of their loyal, hardworking wives, their polite, obedient children, and their good-natured friends.

WHAT YOU WILL DO

1. Brainstorm with your classmates on ways hands can show different moods and feelings. Some possibilities for discussion are surprise, anger, sadness, joy, and nervousness. Choose one of these moods or feelings. Do not tell anyone in your class which one you have picked.

2. Pose the hand you do not use to draw with in a way that shows the mood you have selected. It might be relaxed, clenched, or distorted in some way. With your drawing hand, make pencil sketches of the posed hand. Make your drawings as accurate as you can.

3. Still using pencil, draw the best of your sketches on the sheet of black paper. Make the drawing large enough to fill the sheet.

4. Switching to white crayon, add highlights to your drawing. Begin by coloring lightly. Gently blend the crayon around the fingers and other hand parts to make them look three-dimensional and lifelike. (For information on shading techniques, see Technique Tip 6, *Handbook* page 278.) Press lightly when coloring shadowed areas. Press harder on the crayon when coloring the most highly lighted areas.

5. Place your finished drawing on display with those of other students. Decide which of the drawings are most lifelike. Are your classmates able to guess the feeling or mood your hand drawing expresses?

EXAMINING YOUR WORK

- **Describe**   Tell whether your drawing looks like your hand. Identify its most realistic features.
- **Analyze**   Show where you used white crayon to highlight your drawing. State whether the light and dark values emphasize the three-dimensional form of the hand.
- **Interpret**   Tell whether your drawing expresses a particular mood or feeling. Tell whether viewers were able to identify this feeling.
- **Judge**   Identify the best feature of your drawing. Tell whether it is the realistic appearance of your work, the use of light and dark to give a sense of roundness, or the expressive content of your drawing.

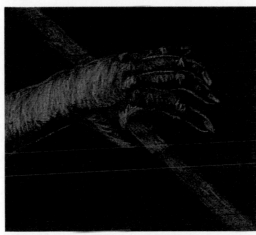

▲ Figure 12–7   Student work. Expressive hands.

OTHER STUDIO IDEAS

- Make another drawing of an expressive hand, this time using charcoal on white paper. Use the charcoal as you did the chalk, both for drawing and shading.

- ●● Blending values of a single hue of tempera, paint a large picture of your hand. Create a range of values from very dark (for shading) to very light (for the most lighted areas).

Lesson 2   *Drawing Expressive Hands*   **183**

Art of the 1700s

LESSON PLAN
(pages 184–187)

Objectives
After completing this lesson, students will be able to:
• Describe the reign of Louis XIV.
• Characterize the Rococo style.
• Name several Rococo artists.
• Explain how Goya's art changed after 1808.

Supplies
• Pencils.
• Tempera paint and brushes.
• Sheets of white paper, 12 x 18 inches (30 x 46 cm).
• Popular women's magazines.
• Colored drawing pencils.
• Recording of music from the Rococo period.

TRB Resources
• 12-7 *Vigée-Lebrun,* (artist profile)
• 12-8 *Bag Wigs,* (reproducible master)
• 12-9 *Bag Wigs Three Feet High,* (appreciating cultural diversity)

TEACHING THE LESSON

Getting Started
Motivator. Have students imagine that they are very wealthy, unemployed, and required to attend numerous entertainments run by the head of state. Ask them whether they would eventually become bored. If so, what might remove some of the tedium? Draw a parallel between students' responses and the eighteenth-century court's fascination with romance, elaborate ornament, and extravagant expenditures.

Vocabulary. Invite a printmaker to speak to the class about various forms of printmaking, including *etching.* The speaker should present examples of prints executed in each printmaking technique so that students can appreciate their different qualities. The speaker should also demonstrate the method of etching.

Just as events of the 1500s brought in the Baroque style, so events of the 1600s brought about its end. The most important of these was the crowning of one of history's most colorful, pleasure-loving rulers. Because this king chose the sun as his emblem, he became known as the Sun King.

In this lesson you will learn about this king, the period in which he lived, and the new art style that he helped inspire.

EUROPE IN THE LATE 1600s
During the 1600s France emerged as Europe's strongest and wealthiest nation. Its capital, Paris, became the center of art. Find this city on the map shown in Figure 12–8.

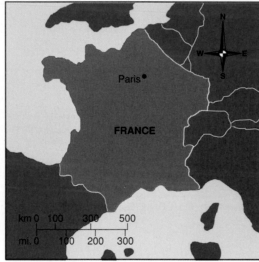

▲ **Figure 12–8** France.

The force behind these changes was a powerful king with very rich tastes. He was Louis XIV, who ruled France for over 70 years. Louis' tastes were to help chart the course Western art would follow over the next 100 years.

Architecture
The beginnings of the new art style were put into motion in 1661. That year Louis ordered architects to build him the biggest, most elaborate palace in the world. It was built at Versailles (vuhr-**sye**), a short distance from Paris (Figure 12–9).

No photograph can begin to do the Palace of Versailles justice. The building covers 15 acres and contains enough rooms to house 10,000 people. The landscaped gardens around the palace cover another 250 acres. In Louis' time, 4 million flower bulbs were brought in each year from Holland to fill these gardens with the flowers the king loved.

Painting
Life for the king and his friends at Versailles was happy and carefree. This mood gave rise to a new style of art in the early 1700s. This style, which has come to be called **Rococo** (ruh-**koh**-koh), is *an art style stressing free, graceful movement; a playful use of line; and bright colors.*

The first artist to create works in the Rococo style was a painter named Antoine Watteau (an-**twahn** wah-**toh**). Watteau's pictures show a make-believe world peopled by untroubled members of France's ruling class. The painting in Figure 12–10 is one such picture. Like the figures in Watteau's other works, the people in this one appear to have not a care in the world. They are shown in a parklike garden listening to music. Notice

---

Background Information
The establishment of concord and prosperity in Europe made it unnecessary for Louis XIV to continue patronizing the heavily propagandistic Baroque style. Lightness and ease became attractive in both art and social relations in the court world. Louis, however, still kept the aristocracy close at hand in Versailles and required their participation at innumerable receptions, dances, and informal daytime gatherings. The aristocracy's power was effectively dampened by this method, but Louis still faced the problem of keeping them entertained. According to historian Stephen Jones, "It was necessary to create a world in which the occupations of the idle appeared important." Romance and political intrigue proved to be potent remedies against boredom among the courtiers. Painters such as Watteau succeeded in part because they were able to portray the lighthearted ideals and preoccupations of court life in an appealing fashion.

▲ Figure 12–9   The gardens at Versailles also included a small zoo with unusual animals and birds. Louis XIV spent nearly three-fourths of all taxes collected to pay for this and other luxuries of his palace.

Louis Le Vau and Jules Hardouin-Mansart. Palace at Versailles, France.

◀ Figure 12–10   Watteau's paintings are meant not only to be seen but also to be heard. With a little imagination you can hear the soft strumming of a guitar and the breezes rustling the leaves on trees.

Antoine Watteau. *The Vista*. 1716. Oil on canvas. 47 x 56 cm (18½ x 22"). Museum of Fine Arts, Boston, Massachusetts. Maria Antoinette Evans Fund.

Developing Concepts

Exploring Aesthetics. Tell students that the great majority of eighteenth-century intellectuals strongly objected to Rococo art on the grounds that it was frivolous and lacking in serious moral purpose. Divide students into debating teams. One side should defend paintings such as those by Watteau and the other side should say why they are worthless, if not morally harmful. If possible, display reproductions of works by Rococo artists Francois Boucher and Jean-Honore Fragonard as reference points during the debate.

Using Art Criticism. Have students examine Figure 12-11. Explain that commissioned portraits often represent the sitter as he or she would ideally want to be perceived. Ask students how Vigée-Lebrun presented the lady in a flattering manner. Then have students find and study images of women in magazine ads, such as those that promote cosmetics. Help students see how the ads reflect modern notions of beauty and glamour, just as Vigée-Lebrun's society portraits show how women were supposed to look in the late eighteenth century.

Understanding Art History. Have students investigate other paintings by Watteau, especially ones that are set in a garden or park. Ask students to write a paragraph that characterizes the mood of these works and explains why such scenes were so popular with Rococo period dealers and collectors.

Background Information

Watteau's *The Vista* is an example of a so-called fête galante painting. Fêtes galantes represent a gathering of people, usually in a park. The people are having a good time conversing, listening to music, and flirting with one another. The people in these pictures are not aristocrats, who would never dress so flimsily or sit on the grass, at least not until the late eighteenth century. Often the scene includes a statue that represents the thoughts of those who are standing near it. For example,

Watteau frequently painted fêtes galantes that contained a statue of a woman with a long lock of hair. This statue symbolizes opportunity, according to a contemporary saying that one should "seize opportunity by her locks."

▲ Figure 12–11   The artist lived to be 87. When she died, her will called for a relief carving of a painter's palette and brush on her tombstone.

Élisabeth Vigée-Lebrun. *Portrait of a Lady.* 1789. Wood. 107 x 83 cm (42⅛ x 32¾"). National Gallery of Art, Washington, D.C. Samuel H. Kress Collection.

▲ Figure 12–12   Chardin painted many scenes like the one in this work. Each treats familiar scenes and ordinary objects with respect and affection.

Jean-Baptiste-Siméon Chardin. *The Kitchen Maid.* 1738. Canvas. 46.2 x 37.5 cm (18⅛ x 14¾"). National Gallery of Art, Washington, D.C. Samuel H. Kress Collection.

that the viewer seems to be looking at this scene from far off. What reason might the artist have had for removing us — and himself — from the events in the painting?

The members of the French ruling class enjoyed having their portraits painted. An artist who met this demand was Élisabeth Vigée-Lebrun (ay-**lee**-zah-bet vee-**zhay**-luh-**bruhn**). Before she was 20, Vigée-Lebrun had painted many important nobles. By the time she was 25, she was named the queen's personal portrait painter. Vigée-Lebrun's portraits often put the subject in a very favorable light. She also reveals, in works like the one in Figure 12–11, how successful a simple pose can be. Notice how the young woman appears to be watching and listening *to you*. How flattering this is. No doubt this attention adds to a warm feeling about her.

Another side of French life was shown in the Rococo paintings done by Jean-Baptiste Siméon Chardin (**zhahn**-bah-**teest** see-may-**ohnh** shahr-**danh**). His genre pictures take the viewer into the simple homes of everyday people. One of these works, Figure 12–12, shows a woman preparing a meal. She seems to be lost in dreamy thought as she works. Everyone has had similar experiences when a sound or image sets the mind wandering for a few moments. Notice how the artist blends mellow colors and carefully painted still-life objects to communicate a quiet mood. The world of Chardin's art is one where time stands still and nothing disturbs the peacefulness. The viewer is able to observe simple domestic scenes treated with respect and affection.

Background Information
Marie Louise Élisabeth Vigée-Lebrun is one of history's most celebrated women artists. Before she was twenty, she had studied in a convent and had received private art lessons from colleagues of her artist father. She had also painted portraits of important members of the French aristocracy. By the age of twenty-five, she was employed by Queen Marie-Antoinette, whose portrait she painted often. On the night the queen and king were arrested, Vigée-Lebrun escaped from Paris. The French Revolution did not stop her career, however. She continued to work in other European capitals and was flooded with commissions. She earned a huge sum of money, a great portion of which was devoted to paying off her husband's gambling debts. Vigée-Lebrun's easy, charming portraits present sitters to their best advantage. They also preserve for posterity a picture of the aristocratic way of life as it faded from history.

ROCOCO ART IN SPAIN

The Rococo style in painting was not limited to France. In Spain the style was picked up by a free-thinking artist named Francisco Goya (fran-**sis**-koh **goy**-uh). Through his early forties, Goya painted softly lighted portraits of people from Spanish high society. A glimpse of the horrors and suffering of war, however, changed all that.

In 1808 French troops attacked Spain. The bloody scenes Goya witnessed prompted a series of etchings. An **etching** is *an intaglio print made by scratching an image onto a specially treated copper plate*. The etching in Figure 12–13 shows a French firing squad taking aim at a captured war prisoner. The figures and weapons stand out against a darkened sky. Goya's view of war is stripped of brave warriors and glorious victories. It is a shocking vision of death and destruction.

▲ Figure 12–13 How do you suppose viewers in the 1800s reacted to the manner in which Goya chose to express scenes like this in his work?

Francisco de Goya. *Cornered (From the Disasters of War)*. Barbares, Paris, France. Bibliotheque Nationale.

STUDIO EXPERIENCE

Look once again at the painting in Figure 12–12 by Jean-Baptiste Siméon Chardin. The artist, it might be said, changes the ordinary into the extraordinary. With a little imagination, you can do the same.

Find a small ordinary object. Focus your search on something you would not usually think of in connection with a painting. Some examples are a clothespin, a nail, or a safety pin. Study the object carefully, and then draw it on a sheet of white paper. The drawing should totally fill the page. It should also be as accurate as you can make it. Use tempera to add color. Work at capturing the color, form, and texture of the object. Paint the background a dark color so the object will stand out boldly.

✔CHECK YOUR UNDERSTANDING

1. What country became the center of art in the late 1600s? What king helped bring about the change?
2. What new art style grew out of the carefree life of the ruling class at Versailles? What are the main features of works done in this style?
3. What kinds of paintings were created by Antoine Watteau? What kind of paintings were done by Élisabeth Vigée-Lebrun and by Jean-Baptiste Siméon Chardin?
4. What are etchings? What events prompted Goya's etchings of war-related scenes? What do these etchings tell about Goya's view of war?

Following Up

Closure. Play a recording of music from the Rococo period such as Mozart's fourth and fifth violin concertos. Ask students if they discern any parallels between the music and the art of the 1700s.

Evaluation. 1. Review students' written responses to the "Check Your Understanding" questions. 2. Assess paragraphs on Watteau paintings. 3. Evaluate drawings of a Versailles-style garden. 4. Review reports on a lavish non-European building. 5. Review students' "Studio Experience" assignments.

Reteaching. Tell students that some art historians have found the roots of Rococo style in Rubens's paintings. Have students re-examine Figure 12-4 on page **180** and discuss the features that resemble elements of the Rococo art illustrated in this lesson.

Enrichment. Show students reproductions of the high society portraits that Goya created early in his career as an artist. Compare them with Figure 12-13 and characterize the mood of each. Then have students write a short story in which a dramatic event leads to a completely new outlook on life.

Answers to "Check Your Understanding"
1. France became the center of art in the late 1600s. Louis XIV helped bring about the change.
2. The new art style of the ruling class at Versailles was called the *Rococo* style. It was characterized by free, graceful movement, playful use of line, and bright colors.
3. Antoine Watteau painted pictures showing a make-believe world peopled by untroubled members of France's ruling class. Élisabeth Vigée-Lebrun painted portraits of the ruling class and was named the queen's personal portrait painter. Jean-Baptiste Siméon Chardin focused on life in the simple homes of everyday people.
4. An etching is an intaglio print made by scratching an image onto a specially treated copper plate. Goya communicated his view of war by emphasizing death and destruction.

Constructing a Rococo Shoe

The 1700s were, above all else, a period of high fashion. It was said that if a woman left Paris on a short vacation, she would return to find all her clothes outdated. Hairdos grew taller and taller, and so did the heels on shoes—men's as well as women's. Architects began raising doors higher so people could pass through. Paintings by Antoine Watteau, like the one in Figure 12–14, mirror this concern for fashion. The figures in this painting look almost like fashion dolls.

Imagine that the president of a modern-day shoe company has decided to stage a contest. Designers are to come up with ideas for a shoe. It is to be of a type that might be found on the foot of a figure in a Watteau painting.

WHAT YOU WILL LEARN

You will design and create a Rococo shoe using cardboard and scrap materials. Use a variety of colors, shapes, and textures to create a highly decorative pattern. Your finished shoe will be a three-dimensional form. (See Figure 12–15.)

WHAT YOU WILL NEED

- Pencil and sheets of sketch paper
- Sheets of lightweight cardboard
- Scissors, heavy cardboard scraps, white glue, and stapler
- Pieces of brightly colored, richly patterned cloth
- Scrap materials, such as buckles, laces, bows, and sequins

► Figure 12–14 This painting shows a group of aristocrats about to leave the legendary island of romance. Notice the delicate figures, rich costumes, and dreamlike setting. These, along with the soft colors, are typical of Watteau's Rococo style.

Antoine Watteau. *Embarkation from Cythera.* 1717–1719. Charlottemburg Museo, The Louvre, Paris, France.

LESSON PLAN
(pages 188–189)

Objectives
After completing this lesson, students will be able to:
- Describe clothing and hairstyles of the 1700s.
- Design a shoe that incorporates Rococo features.

Supplies
- Pencils and sketch paper; scissors.
- Heavy cardboard scraps; white glue, and staplers.
- Pieces of brightly colored, richly patterned cloth.
- Scrap materials, such as buckles, laces, bows, and sequins.
- Video of the film *Amadeus.*

TEACHING THE LESSON

Getting Started
Motivator. Have the students watch a scene from the film *Amadeus* that includes clear views of Rococo clothing and hairstyles. The ballroom scene near the beginning of the film is a good choice, and even includes a look at Mozart's shoes. Discuss the most prominent features of fashions from that era. Ask: In what ways do the costumes in *Amadeus* resemble the outfits shown in Watteau's painting?

Developing Concepts
Understanding Art History. Have students research the significance of the Venus statue located at the right-hand side of Figure 12-14. Tell them that in Rococo art, as in Baroque art, a statue represents the thoughts of the people standing near it. Have students write a short paragraph that discusses the role played by the goddess of love in this scene.

Background Information
Watteau's fête galante painting *Embarkation from Cythera* was the work that he presented to obtain membership in the Academy. It represents an island dedicated to love and the worship of Venus. The goddess of love was said to have first stepped on firm ground at Cythera, which is a real island in the Mediterranean. All the protagonists in this painting are couples, and the work should be read as the same couple rendered three times, thereby introducing a passage of time. The staff and little capes worn by the people show they have gone on a pilgrimage to Cythera to seek a land where romance lives forever. According to historian Stephen Jones, "The thrill for the aristocrats who saw such a picture may have lain in the implication that some high romantic aspiration inspired their own elegant but pointless existence."

WHAT YOU WILL DO

1. Make several pencil sketches of a shoe as seen from the side. Make your design as elaborate and unusual as you can. Use exaggerated heels, soles, laces, and decorative features. Let your imagination guide you.
2. Choose your best sketch. Draw the outline of the shoe on a sheet of cardboard. Make the shoe lifesize. Carefully cut out the shoe.
3. Place your cutout on a second piece of cardboard. Holding it firmly in place, carefully cut around it, creating a second identical shoe.
4. Glue strips of heavy cardboard between the two shoe cutouts. These will be hidden inside, and will give you the basic form of a shoe.
5. Using pieces of cloth in different colors and patterns, cover the shoe form. Curve the cloth pieces around the heel of the shoe and across the top and the toe. Staple the cloth in place. (*Hint:* Cutting the cloth scraps small will help add to the decorative look of the shoe.) Glue buckles, bows, laces, and other scrap items in place as added decoration.
6. When the glue is dry, place your shoe on display. Compare your finished shoe with those of your classmates.

EXAMINING YOUR WORK

- **Describe** Tell whether your finished object can be recognized as a shoe. State whether it has a heel, sole, and other shoe parts. Explain how your shoe is a three-dimensional form.
- **Analyze** Point out the variety of colors, shapes, and textures in your work.
- **Interpret** Identify the kind of person who would wear the shoe you designed. State whether you could imagine the shoe on the foot of a subject in Figure 12–14.
- **Judge** Tell whether you feel you have succeeded in creating a Rococo shoe. State whether you feel it would win the shoe company contest. Explain why.

▲ Figure 12–15   Student work. Rococo shoe.

OTHER STUDIO IDEAS

- Create a shoe box with a design in the same Rococo style as your shoe. Follow the instructions given in Lesson 4 of Chapter 11.
- How would an ancient Egyptian, Greek, or Roman shoe differ from your Rococo shoe? Select a period you have read about, and design a shoe that reflects that period in a humorous way. Do this as a painting using tempera colors. Display your work, and ask if anyone can identify the period you selected.

Lesson 4   *Constructing a Rococo Shoe*   **189**

Appreciating Cultural Diversity. Have students investigate and write a paragraph on a non-European style of clothing that possesses a highly decorative or ornamental aesthetic. Some possibilities are the clothing of the Sioux, Latin American festival garments, Indian saris, and imperial Chinese fashions.

Following Up

Closure. 1. Remind students that Rococo fashions were made entirely by hand. One clothing historian stated that fashion design and the craftsmanship that goes into clothing has declined ever since the Rococo period when clothes and accessories began to be mass-produced by machine. Ask students if they agree with this statement. 2. Have students use "Examining Your Work" to critique their student art work.

Evaluation. 1. Review students' Rococo-style shoes. 2. Assess paragraphs on the Venus statue in Figure 12-14. 3. Evaluate paragraphs on non-European clothing.

Reteaching. Have students examine reproductions of Francois Boucher's paintings of Madame de Pompadour, the mistress of Louis XV and a fashion trendsetter for Europe. List on the board all of the elements of her dress and shoes and discuss how they are characteristic of the Rococo period.

Enrichment. Have students consider the question of whether people today are as concerned with fashion styles as they were in the 1700s. Students should take into account factors such as the amount of money spent on clothing, how much people notice what others wear, how important it is to wear fashionable styles, and how often people discuss fashion. Have students write a page that states their conclusions and the reasons for them.

Background Information

In the eighteenth century, the French court at Versailles dictated the fashions of European footwear. Women were taught to lift their skirts to show off their dainty shoes and ankles. Such shoes had a curved heel and were frequently embellished with jewelry and embroidery. Buckles and ties over the instep were also typical. One of the most characteristic Rococo shoes, however, was the backless silk and lace mule, which exemplified the softness and sexual charm of women's dress during the Rococo period. Naturally, women also needed sturdier shoes for walking outdoors and clogs for traveling in bad weather. During the peak of the Rococo era, from 1740 to 1770, fashionable men wore heeled shoes with large silver or diamond buckles that complemented their colorful garments. By the 1780s, footwear became more informal and facilitated a greater freedom of movement. Extremely high heels and the odd walk that went with them were no longer seen except at court.

ANSWERS TO "CHAPTER 12 REVIEW"

Building Vocabulary
1. facade
2. Baroque
3. portrait
4. Rococo
5. etching

Reviewing Art Facts
6. The Baroque style of architectural art was practiced by Borromini.
7. Caravaggio's key contribution was the use of strong light and shadow.
8. Caravaggio's style most influenced Gentileschi.
9. Genre paintings were in demand in Holland during the 1600s.
10. Judith Leyster specialized in portrait painting.
11. Antoine Watteau was the first artist to create Rococo paintings.
12. Élisabeth Vigée-Lebrun was named the queen's personal portrait painter.
13. Chardin painted scenes of the simple homes of everyday people.
14. Goya painted portraits of people from Spanish high society through his forties.

Thinking About Art
1. Students should notice texture in the fabrics, flesh, hair, stone, plants.
2. Similarity exists in the artists' choice of women as portrait subjects, capturing the mood of the moment, showing detail. Differences lie in the areas of how detail is shown, brush stroke technique, and how subject is presented. Answers will vary on which is preferred. Students should show they understand the aesthetic view they have chosen.

CHAPTER 12 REVIEW

BUILDING VOCABULARY

Number a sheet of paper from 1 to 5. After each number, write the term from the box that best matches each description below.

Baroque	portrait
etching	Rococo
facade	

1. The outside front of a building.
2. An art style emphasizing movement, contrast, and variety.
3. A painting of a person.
4. An art style stressing free, graceful movement; a playful use of line; and bright colors.
5. An intaglio print made by scratching an image onto a specially treated copper plate.

REVIEWING ART FACTS

Number a sheet of paper from 6 to 14. Answer each question in a complete sentence.

6. What architectural art style was practiced by Francesco Borromini?
7. What was a key contribution of Caravaggio to the art of the 1600s?
8. What artist's style most influenced the work of Artemisia Gentileschi?
9. What kinds of paintings were in demand in Holland during the 1600s?
10. What kinds of paintings were the specialty of Judith Leyster?
11. Who was the first artist to create Rococo paintings?
12. To what post was Élisabeth Vigée-Lebrun named as a young woman?
13. What side of French life of the 1700s is revealed in the paintings of Jean-Baptiste Siméon Chardin?
14. What sorts of paintings did Francisco Goya create through his early forties?

THINKING ABOUT ART

On a sheet of paper, answer each question in a sentence or two.

1. **Analyze.** Turn again to Caravaggio's painting of Christ's burial (Figure 12–2). Notice the artist's use of texture to add variety to the work. How many different textures can you find? On what objects in the work are these textures found?
2. **Compare and contrast.** Look once again at the portraits by Judith Leyster (Figure 12–5) and Élisabeth Vigée-Lebrun (Figure 12–11). Tell in what ways the two works are alike. Explain how they are different. Which of these two artists' works do you find most successful? Explain your decision by referring to one or more aesthetic views.

MAKING ART CONNECTIONS

1. **Music.** The Baroque style was not limited to art. It is also found in music of the period. Working as part of a team of students, (1) find and tape-record a musical composition by the famous Baroque composer Johann Sebastian Bach (**yo**-hahn suh-**bast**-ee-uhn **bahk**), and (2) find and photocopy other works by several Baroque artists you learned about in this chapter. Stage a sound-and-sight presentation before your class.
2. **Social Studies.** Several of the painters you read about in this chapter created genre, rather than religious, works. Rembrandt, during the 1600s, was one. Chardin, during the 1700s, was another. Find a third genre artist from either of the two periods. Imagine that this person were living today. Based on what you know of the artist, describe what a twentieth-century work by him or her might look like. Give details about both the subject and style of the work.

LOOKING AT THE DETAILS

The detail shown below is from Artemisia Gentileschi's *Judith and the Maid Servant with the Head of Holofernes*. Study the detail and answer the following questions using complete sentences.

1. How does the artist pull the viewer into the drama of the scene?
2. How is light used to affect the mood of this work of art?
3. Compare this detail with Figure 12–2 on page **179**. How is the use of light similar? How is it different?

4. Compare this work with Figure 12–14 on page **188**. What differences do you see in the use of the elements of space and texture?
5. Look at the entire work on page **176**. If the artist had shown more of the room and placed the women farther into the scene, how do you think this would have changed the mood of the work? Explain your answer.

Artemisia Gentileschi. *Judith and Maidservant with the Head of Holofernes*. c. 1625. Oil on canvas. (Detail.) Detroit Institute of Art, Detroit, Michigan.

ANSWERS TO "LOOKING AT THE DETAILS"

1. The use of light and dark shadows pulls the viewer into the drama of the scene.
2. Light is used to create a mysterious feeling or mood in the work of art.
3. Light is used in a similar way in both the detail and in Figure 12-2 by creating a strong feeling of drama. In Figure 12-2 light is used to emphasize the most important details. In the detail on this page light is used to draw attention to the subjects.
4. Comparing this work with Figure 12-14, students will note numerous differences in the use of space and texture. Students' responses will vary, but may include: Figure 12-14 has shown a larger part of a scene and portrayed rich textured costumes. In contrast, the detail on this page has isolated one part of the scene and has ommitted fine detail.
5. Students' responses will vary.

Chapter Evaluation

The goal of this chapter is for students to identify the contributions of artists working during the 1600s and 1700s in Europe. Methods of evaluating results include:

1. Ask students to divide a sheet of paper into five sections. Using the medium of their choice, have them demonstrate their understanding of each of the following terms: Baroque, etching, facade, portrait, Rococo.

2. Have students write a short paper describing the contributions of one of the artists presented in the chapter.
3. Have students complete Chapter 12 Test (TRB, Resource 12-10).

Native American Art

TRB Resources

- 13-10 Chapter Test
- Color Transparency 25
- Color Transparency 26

TEACHING THE CHAPTER

Introducing the Art Work

Direct students' attention to Allan Houser's *Sacred Rain Arrow.* Inform them that Allan Houser is a contemporary Apache Indian sculptor. Houser studied at the Indian School at Santa Fe, New Mexico and then remained in Santa Fe and worked as a free-lance artist. His first job of notoriety was to paint a mural of the life of his people for the Department of the Interior in Washington, D.C. During World War II, Houser traveled to California, where he became interested in the media of sculpture. He has worked successfully in a variety of styles and has mastered the media of bronze, metal, and stone in his sculptural designs.

Houser's designs are contemporary yet firmly rooted in the special tradition of his Native American forefathers. Houser draws inspiration from both past and present, but like all successful artists, his sculpture transcends race and language.

▲ The artist is a teacher of sculpture. His advice to students is to go out and find their own styles.

Allan Houser. *Sacred Rain Arrow.* 1988. Bronze. 249 x 99 x 78.7 cm (98 x 39 x 31"). Glenn Green Galleries, Phoenix, Arizona.

Native American Art

In history books the part of the globe we live in is called the New World. To the people who have dwelled in this region since earliest times, there is nothing new about it. Some of these groups — from Central and South America — you learned about in Chapter 6.

In this chapter you will read about the first people of North America. You will learn about their culture. You will learn, finally, about the proud traditions that have led to the making of art works like the one shown on the left.

OBJECTIVES

After completing this chapter, you will be able to:

● Name and describe five major groups of Native Americans.
● Identify the contributions to art the different Native American cultures have made.
● Identify Native American artists working today.
● Create art in the style developed by the Native Americans.

WORDS YOU WILL LEARN

coiled pot	pueblos
cradle board	sand painting
Kachina doll	tepee
loom	totem pole
petroglyphs	warp
polychrome	weft

ARTISTS YOU WILL MEET

T. C. Cannon	Kenojuak
Tony Dallas	Lucy Lewis
Allan Houser	Dan Namingha
Oscar Howe	Margaret Tafoya

193

Examining the Art Work

Tell students that the Native American is Houser's favorite subject. As a boy, Houser listened to his father tell stories of his adventures with Chief Geronimo, which caused a deep attachment to his ancestral background. Explain that Allan Houser values his heritage and cultural background. Point out the strength and conviction depicted in the work. Explain that Houser has created anticipated movement through the position and action of the figure. This movement is further accentuated by the bent arm and the visible tension in the muscles. Point out the way the artist contrasts the element of line, for example, the curved line of the bow contrasts with the straight line of the arrow. He also contrasts form—the straight arm with the bent arm and the long flowing hair with the square jaw. Explain that these contrasts add to the anticipated movement and sense of strength in the work.

Discussing the Art Work

Ask students to think about the mood of this work and how it depicts some of Houser's values as well as those of his people. Point out the precision of the lines and how the forms powerfully create a sense of physical strength, athletic ability and dexterity. Ask students to look closely at the facial expression of the figure and the way it is balanced gracefully and steadily on one knee. Suggest that this communicates a sense of vast concentration, determination, agility and accuracy. Suggest that these may be qualities that Houser seems to value by depicting this figure with such intensity and grace. Also suggest that the Native American shooting toward the stars may express the human desire to reach the peak of endeavor. Explain that these human qualities transcend time.

Tell students that in this chapter they will learn about the different Native American cultures, their artists and their contributions to art. They will also create their own art work in the Native American style.

Building Self-Esteem

In this chapter students will be learning about the first people who inhabited North America and some of the art forms they developed. The totem pole is described on page **196**. Tell students that the word *totem* was applied originally to an animal or other object held sacred by a tribe or individual. The animal or object was then adopted as their own symbol. This custom has its counterpart in the symbols that nations chose. The American eagle, the thistle of Scotland, and the lion of Great Britain are examples. Let each student choose a personal symbol or totem. Maybe they can run very fast, are good at math, or have a musical talent. The object or animal should be selected for its symbolic link to the skill. Discuss what might have influenced the Native Americans to select the specific totems they chose. Have students draw their totem in the same stylized way the totem pole figures were designed. This symbol can be planned as a personal logo. Let the class share their totems and what they symbolize.

LESSON PLAN
(pages 194–197)

Objectives
After completing this lesson, students will be able to:
- Name and describe four major groups of Native Americans.
- Identify the contributions to art made by the different Native American cultures.
- Draw narrative pictures in the style used by the Plains Indians.

Supplies
- Wall map of the world.
- Newspapers and news magazines, sheets of drawing paper, pencils, watercolor markers.
- Clay, sheets of newspaper, clay tools (optional), glaze (optional).
- Sheets of drawing paper or outline maps of the United States, pencils, fine-line markers.

> ### TRB Resources
> - 13-1 *History of the Mimbres Society,* (art history)
> - 13-2 *Mimbres Designs,* (reproducible master)
> - 13-3 *The Richness of Tribal Variety,* (cooperative learning)

TEACHING THE LESSON

Getting Started

Motivator. Display a map of the world, and ask volunteers to point out the approximate route sailed by Christopher Columbus: Where did he intend to sail? Was he headed in the correct direction? What was in his way?

Then ask: Who was living in North America when Columbus arrived? What did he call these people? Why? What do you think they called themselves? What collective name do you think these people prefer now? Why? (If necessary, help students mention specific tribal names as well as the terms Native Americans, Tribal People, and Original People.) How do you think these different collective names affect people's perceptions of the Native Americans?

194

LESSON 1

Native American Art of the Past

When Christopher Columbus reached North America in 1492, he thought his ships had landed on the east coast of India. He referred to the natives he found living there as Indians. Today these first settlers of the United States and Canada are called Native Americans.

In this lesson you will study four of the major Native American groups: the Pueblo, Northwest Coast Indians, Plains Indians, and Woodlands Indians. You will look at the art they produced hundreds of years ago and see how their contributions influence Native American art today.

PUEBLO CULTURE

In prehistoric times the Pueblo (poo-**eb**-loh) people settled in what is now known as the Four Corners region of the United States. Find this region on the map in Figure 13–1. Like other Native American groups, the Pueblo are believed to have come from Asia.

Scientific records show they probably came by way of the Bering Sea some 20,000 to 30,000 years ago.

"The People," as the early Pueblo called themselves, were farmers. They wore clothes woven from cotton, had a democratic form of government, and traded with other cultures.

Crafts

It was through trade with Mexico around A.D. 400 that the Pueblo learned to make pottery. The earliest kind of pot, called a **coiled pot**, was *a pot formed by coiling long ropes of clay in a spiral*. An example of such a pot is shown in Figure 13–2. The careful pinching together of the coils was meant to be both decorative and useful. In what ways is this type of pot similar to the ones made by the Chavín of South America? (See Figure 6–11 on page **88**). In what ways is it different?

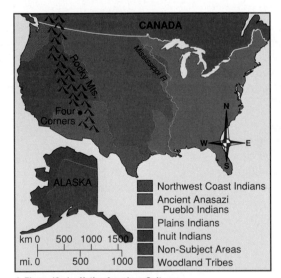

▲ Figure 13–1   Native American Cultures.

Map legend:
- Northwest Coast Indians
- Ancient Anasazi Pueblo Indians
- Plains Indians
- Inuit Indians
- Non-Subject Areas
- Woodland Tribes

▲ Figure 13–2   Pots like this had to be able to hold water, which was precious in the dry hot southwestern desert. The pots were also used to store food and were buried with the dead to help them in the afterlife.

Coil pot. Pueblo. A.D. 1050–1200. Exterior: coiled neck; pinched coil underbody and base; lug handles on each side of neck; smoothed interior. 27.9 x 26.7 cm (11 x 10½"). Courtesy of the School of American Research, Indian Arts Research Center, Santa Fe, New Mexico. Gift of Maria Chabot, Albuquerque, New Mexico.

194   Lesson 1   *Native American Art of the Past*

Note

The Four Corners region of the United States is located where the boundaries of Utah, Colorado, New Mexico, and Arizona come together. The Native Americans who settled in this region are thought to be Asians who traveled across the Asian continents to the Bering Sea. They crossed into what is now Alaska and made their way south along the West Coast and then inland. Have students look at the map of the world on pages **314** and **315** and estimate the number of miles these people traveled before settling in the Southwest United States. Ask students if any have participated in a walk-a-thon and how far they walked. Let them reflect on the fortitude these early settlers must have had in order to travel thousands of miles on foot, carrying their belongings with them.

Petroglyphs

Although they were farmers, the early Pueblo also hunted for food. To ensure a good hunt, they made **petroglyphs** (peh-truh-glifs), or *rock carvings and paintings*, of their prey. This, they believed, would allow them to capture the animal's spirit. Can you think of another culture you learned about that shared this belief?

Examine the petroglyph of a bighorn sheep in Figure 13–3. Would you describe the work as realistic? Would you say it is stylized?

Architecture

The early inhabitants of the southwestern United States lived in round pit houses dug into the earth and covered with branches. Over the years the Indians learned to build with adobe, mud, and straw. When the Spanish arrived in the Southwest in 1540, they found *stacked, many-family dwellings made of adobe*. The Spaniards called these **pueblos**, after the Spanish word for "village." The same word was also used to refer to the Native American builders of these dwellings. Study the pueblo in Figure 13–4 on page **196**. Notice how the structure seems to grow out of the earth. What modern form of dwelling in our own culture has a purpose similar to the pueblo?

◄ Figure 13–3 Petroglyphs like these have survived for many centuries.

Petroglyph: Bighorn Sheep. A.D. 900–1100. Three Rivers Site, New Mexico.

NORTHWEST COAST INDIAN CULTURE

The coastal sections of British Columbia and the states of Washington, Oregon, and northern California are rich with plant and animal life. Rain for growing crops is plentiful, and cooling sea breezes keep temperatures mild. It is no doubt these features appealed to several groups of people heading south before 7000 B.C.

Today the collected groups of the region are known by the name of Northwest Coast Indians. Find the area settled by these early cultures on the map in Figure 13–1.

Like the Pueblos, the Northwest Coast Indians made use of the resources around them. They used the tall trees of the area to make boats and logs for houses. They also used the trees to make art.

Sculpture

No art form is more unmistakably Native American than the totem pole. A **totem pole** is *an upright log carving picturing stories of different families or clans*. The word *totem* means "spirit or guardian." Figure 13–5 on page **196** shows a totem pole carved by an artist of a Northwest Coast tribe. Typically, this pole is meant to be read from top to bottom. The top figure identifies the clan to which the pole belongs. Notice how the facial features have been stylized to fit the available space.

PLAINS INDIAN CULTURE

Not all peoples who arrived here in Pre-Columbian times set up permanent villages. Some were wanderers who moved from place to place as the food supply dwindled. One such group was the people known as the Plains Indians.

Vocabulary. Have students use dictionaries to explore the meanings and derivations of the vocabulary words introduced in this lesson: From what two ancient Greek words does our word *petroglyph* come? What is the meaning of those two words? How can they help you understand the definition of *petroglyph*?

From what language does the word *pueblo* come? What is the meaning of the word?

From what language is our word *totem* derived? What is a totem? What is a totem pole?

From what language does the word *tepee* come? What is the relationship between the derivation and the meaning of the word?

Developing Concepts

Exploring Aesthetics. Help students examine and discuss the Northwest Coast totem pole shown in Figure 13-5: What do you see in this work? What visual elements can you identify? Which principles of art have been used to organize those elements? What message do you think the totem pole is intended to communicate? Are you able to fully understand that message? Why, or why not? What mood or feeling does the work convey to you? Do you think the person who created this totem pole considered the work an example of fine art or an example of applied art? Why? Which do you consider it? Why?

Using Art Criticism. Have students discuss and compare two works by the Plains people: the cradle board shown in Figure 13-6 and the hide painting shown in Figure 13-7. What function was each work created to serve? How successfully does it serve that function? Is each a successful work of art? In terms of which aesthetic view do you consider the works successful? Why?

Background Information

Sometimes pots made by the coil method are smoothed so it is not possible to tell that they were constructed with coils. Other times the ropes of clay are only partially flattened so they show on the outside. Whatever form of final decoration, the coils themselves must contain just the right balance of clay and water. If they are too dry, they will crack when they are bent. If there is too much water in the clay, the ropes will not be firm enough to stand the weight of those above, and the pot will not hold its shape. Point out to students how the pot shown in Figure 13-2 has relatively vertical sides. Let them compare this example with those by Lucy Lewis in Figure 13-12 on page **201**. Ask if they think the Lewis pots were made by the coil method or, perhaps, made on a potter's wheel. Let them discover, as they read the text, that Lewis also made her pots by hand. Their curved sides show she is a master of her craft.

Understanding Art History.
Have students form four groups, and ask each group to research one of these topics about the Pueblo people: their farming methods, including irrigation techniques; the development and construction of their multistory pueblos; the cycle of ceremonies throughout a year; the use and designs of their petroglyphs. Then have the groups present their information to the rest of the class, and encourage discussion among all groups.

Developing Studio Skills.
Ask volunteers to find and share photographs of other clay coiled pots from the Pueblo culture. Then let students make their own clay coiled pots. Have them begin by rolling coils of clay, about 1/2 to 3/4 inch (1.3–2 cm) thick. Then have them place their coils on newspaper and begin winding them to form first the base and then the sides of their coiled pots. Suggest that students press their coils down as they work to make firm pots. Once they have shaped the pots, have students carefully smooth their pots, holding one hand inside the pot and the other on the outside. After pots have dried to the leather hard stage, students may want to use clay tools to incise designs in their work. After the pots have been fired, students may want to glaze them.

Appreciating Cultural Diversity. Help students compare the cultures of the Pueblo people and the Plains Indians: What were the most important differences between the lives of people in these two groups? How was the architecture of the two groups different? What differences in their crafts can you identify? What do you think accounts for these differences? Encourage all students to participate in this discussion; ask interested students to do further research and to share their findings with the class.

▲ Figure 13–4   Most Pueblo people live in ordinary houses today. Some still return to a family pueblo, however, for holidays.

Pueblo Dwellings. c. 1100. Taos, New Mexico.

The Plains Indians made their home in the large area bounded by the Mississippi River and the Rocky Mountains. Find these boundaries on the map in Figure 13–1. The Plains Indians hunted the bison. As the herds moved, so did the Plains people, dragging their possessions behind them on their custom-made sleds.

Architecture

Among the belongings the Plains people carried with them was the tepee. A **tepee** (**tee**-pee) was *a portable house*. As a rule, the tepee was cone-shaped and made of rawhide patches stretched over poles. The hides were covered with designs symbolizing the forces of nature.

At its base a tepee could range anywhere from 12 to 30 feet (4 to 9 m) in diameter. A large tepee contained about as much space as a standard living room of today. How many people do you think could live comfortably in such a space?

Crafts

Like the tepee, the crafts created by the Plains people were made to be easily carried. An example is the object pictured in Figure 13–6. This is a **cradle board**, *a harness worn on the shoulders and used to carry a small child.*

▲ Figure 13–5   Totem poles like this can symbolize a marriage, a birth, or a death. Sometimes a great chief was buried inside a totem pole.

Northwest Coast Totem Pole. Kwakiutl. c. 1900. Channing, Dale, Throckmorton Gallery, Santa Fe, New Mexico.

Notice the care that went into the woven design. What kinds of shapes—organic or geometric—has the artist used in this design? What natural materials are used to decorate the cradle board?

WOODLANDS CULTURE

The Woodlands made up the largest cultural group of Native Americans. They settled in North America east of the Mississippi River. The Woodlands people combined hunting and gathering with primitive farming. The Iroquois, made up of six different Woodlands groups, combined to form the

Background Information
Most of the Plains people lived in tepees, houses that provided several important advantages. Tepees were easy to erect—at least for experts. Even large tepees could be assembled or disassembled within minutes. Tepees were also easily portable; a dog or horse could pull the tepee poles attached to a drag frame, and the hides could be loaded onto the poles. The top of a tepee could be left open, providing a smokehole above the central fire; the top could also be tightly shut to keep out wind and rain. During cold weather the tepee could be lined with additional hides to keep the residents warm; during hot weather the bottom portion of the tepee could be partly rolled up to admit breezes. In addition, the buffalo hides of the tepee could be readily decorated; even beads and quills could be worked into the tepee decorations.

Plains people were not the only Native Americans to build tepees. Natives in Canada and along the Northeast coast built tepees covered with birch bark.

highly organized Iroquois nation. Their most spectacular art works were wooden False Face masks, carved from living trees, and believed to hold live spirits. (See Studio Lesson 4, *Handbook* pages **310–311**.)

▲ **Figure 13–6** Even though their life was hard, the Plains Indians took great pride in their art. What features of this work reveal this pride?

Ute Cradle Board. c. 1870. Buffalo hide, trade beads. Channing, Dale, Throckmorton Gallery, Santa Fe, New Mexico.

◄ **Figure 13–7** This hide tells stories from the artist's own life. Can you tell what is taking place in this scene?

Exploits of a Sioux Leader. c. 1870–1875. Hide Painting. Phillbrook Museum of Art, Tulsa, Oklahoma. Gift of Kills Eagle.

STUDIO EXPERIENCE

Plains Indians painted tales of their battles on skins. An example of one such work is shown in Figure 13–7. Notice that the artist has used a bird's-eye view in telling this tale.

Look through a newspaper or magazine for coverage of an important event in your city or in the world. On a sheet of paper, sketch the story behind this event. Use the Plains style illustrated in Figure 13–7. Carefully outline each object in your design. Color the work using watercolor markers. Compare your finished work with those of classmates. Which picture tells its story most clearly? Which is closest in style to the work in Figure 13–7?

✔ CHECK YOUR UNDERSTANDING

1. In what region did the Pueblo settle? Where are they and other Native American groups believed to have come from?
2. What are coiled pots? What are petroglyphs?
3. What form of architecture gave one Native American group its name? Why was this word chosen?
4. For what unmistakably Native American form of art are the Northwest Coast Indians known?
5. What are tepees? Why did the Plains Indians have a need for tepees?

Lesson 1   *Native American Art of the Past*   📖   **197**

Following Up

Closure. Ask each student to write a short response to this question: What are the most interesting or important new facts you have learned about Native Americans and their cultures? Then lead a class discussion in which students share their responses and react to one another's ideas.

Evaluation. 1. Review students' written responses to the "Check Your Understanding" questions. 2. Read students' responses to the "Closure" question and consider their contributions to the class discussion.

Reteaching. Work with groups of students to review the major contributions of the four Native American cultures presented in the lesson. Then have students sketch simple outline maps of the United States, or provide them with outline maps. Ask them to draw four symbols on their maps—each an appropriate symbol of the Pueblo culture, the Northwest Coast Indian culture, the Plains Indian culture, or the Woodlands culture—each on the part of the map where Native Americans of that culture lived.

Enrichment. Ask students to imagine that they are Native Americans witnessing the first arrival of European explorers: How do these newcomers look to you? What are the strangest aspects of their appearance and behavior? What—if anything—makes them seem familiar or friendly? What do they ride? How are they dressed? What kinds of weapons do they carry? What unusual foods do they eat? How do you and the other members of your tribe react? Let students work in small groups to write or draw their responses to these and/or similar questions.

Answers to "Check Your Understanding"

1. The Pueblo settled in what is now known as the Four Corners section of the United States. They and other Native American groups are believed to have come from Asia.
2. Coiled pots were formed by coiling long ropes of clay in a spiral until a pot or vase had been made. *Petroglyphs* are rock carvings of prey made by the Pueblo to ensure a good hunt.
3. Pueblo was the form of architecture that shared its name with one group of Native Americans. The stacked, many-family dwelling took its name from the Spanish word *pueblo*, which meant "village."
4. The Northwest Coast Indians are known for their totem poles.
5. A tepee was a cone-shaped portable house. The Plains Indians were nomadic and needed to carry their shelters with them.

LESSON PLAN
(pages 198–199)

Objectives
After completing this lesson, students will be able to:
• Plan and make round weavings on looms made from coat hangers.
• Describe, analyze, interpret, and judge their weavings.

Supplies
• Slides or large photographs of Native American blankets and rugs (including, if available, slides or photographs of looms).
• Small loom already warped (if available) or a simple loom made from cardboard.
• Wire coat hangers, masking tape, assorted fibers, blunt tapestry needles.
• Sheets of drawing paper, pencils, colored pencils or markers.

TEACHING THE LESSON

Getting Started
Motivator. Let students begin by sharing their ideas about Native American weavings. Then show slides or large photographs of several blankets and rugs woven by Native Americans; if possible, also show slides or photos of Native American weavers working at their looms. Let students describe and discuss what they see in each work. Then explain to students that they will be making their own weavings.

Vocabulary. Show students a small warped loom. (If you don't have a loom, you can make a simple notched cardboard frame and wrap the warp around it.) Let volunteers identify the loom and the warp (or introduce these names to students). Then demonstrate the tabby weave, going over and under the warp with the weft. Again, let volunteers name the weft, or introduce this name yourself.

198

Making a Round Weaving

Some Native American craft styles and techniques are borrowed from other cultures. One you have learned about is Pueblo pottery, which came from artists in Mexico. Another craft, which also became an important art medium to many Native American cultures, is weaving. Woven materials were used for clothing and blankets. They were often highly decorated and expressed the artists' beliefs, customs, and traditions. Study the decorative weaving shown in Figure 13–8. It was created on a **loom**, or *frame holding a set of crisscrossing threads*. The loom holds two sets of threads. The **warp** threads are *threads running vertically and attached to the loom's frame*. The **weft** threads are those *threads passed horizontally over and under the warp*. The weaver of the object in Figure 13–8 was able to change colors and patterns by using different weaving techniques. This weaving was created on a circular loom.

▲ Figure 13–8   Student work. Round weaving.

WHAT YOU WILL LEARN

You will make a round weaving on a loom made from wire coat hangers. Plan a color scheme for your weaving, and use weaving techniques to change colors in your design. Use a complementary, monochromatic, or analogous color scheme.

WHAT YOU WILL NEED

• 2 wire coat hangers
• Masking tape
• Assorted fibers
• 2 or more blunt tapestry needles

WHAT YOU WILL DO

1. Make a frame for your loom by putting two wire coat hangers together and bending them to form a flat circle. Connect the hangers in two places around the circle with masking tape. Bend the hook on one of the hangers into a loop. This will be used to hang your completed work.
2. Pick the colors of fiber you will use in your weaving. Choose a complementary, monochromatic, or analogous color scheme. Set the fibers aside.
3. Tie a long strand of fiber to your frame using an overhand knot. Wrap the fiber strand completely around the frame using half-hitch knots. (See Figure 13–9.) Thread the end of your fiber strand through a needle. Pull it through several of the knot loops to keep the fiber from coming undone. Cut off any extra fiber.

Background Information
The basic techniques of weaving were probably first used in basketry, one of the world's oldest crafts. Evidence shows that the native peoples who lived in what we now know as Utah were creating twined baskets by 7500 B.C. and had begun making coiled baskets by 7000 B.C.

Nearly all Native American groups made baskets; they used their baskets for storing and transporting food and even for cooking. Some of the baskets were so tightly woven that they could be used for carrying seeds or water.

Most Native Americans wove designs into baskets, of natural or geometric forms or human figures.

In the Northeast, baskets were made from sweet grass, hardwood, and cedar. In the Plains they were made from hazel and buffalo grass. Basket makers in the Southwest used yucca leaves, rushes, cattails, willow, and sumac; and in California and the Northwest they used squaw grass, cedar, and spruce.

4. Create a warp by attaching a single long strand of fiber to the frame. Pass this across the circle at different points. Make sure each pass of the warp fiber crosses the center of the loom. (See Figure 13–10.) After six passes, begin a seventh. This time, take the warp strand only as far as the center. Tie all passes at this point.

5. Working from the center out, begin the weft using a tabby (over and under) weave. After several circuits, switch to one of the other techniques detailed in Figure 13–10. Experiment to create different color shapes or designs. You may leave some open spaces where the warp is not covered.

6. Display your weaving along with those done by classmates. See if you can identify the weaving techniques used in different works.

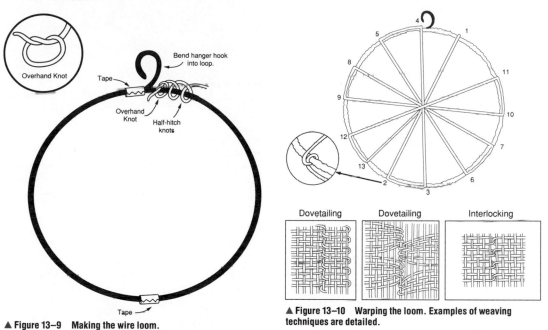

▲ Figure 13–9   Making the wire loom.

OTHER STUDIO IDEAS

- Make a second weaving, this time picking a different type of color scheme. Emphasize texture by using different fibers.

- ●● Use a heavy-duty paper plate as a loom. Make an uneven number of notches around the edge. Warp it following the instructions in the lesson. Create a second weaving.

EXAMINING YOUR WORK

- **Describe**   Explain how you created a loom using two wire coat hangers. Identify the different color shapes you created by switching weaves.
- **Analyze**   Describe the shape of your loom. Tell what kind of color scheme you picked. Name the colors you used. Tell how you used weaving techniques to change the colors in your design.
- **Interpret**   Explain how the colors you chose help communicate a certain mood to viewers. Give your work a title.
- **Judge**   Tell whether your work succeeds. State what you might do differently in a second attempt at the assignment.

Dovetailing   Dovetailing   Interlocking

▲ Figure 13–10   Warping the loom. Examples of weaving techniques are detailed.

Lesson 2   *Making a Round Weaving*   **199**

Developing Concepts

Exploring Aesthetics. Show students a photograph of a Navajo rug (or, if possible, display the rug itself). Ask them to compare the Navajo rug with a manufactured rug: What are the most important differences between the two rugs? Do you consider one a work of art? Why? Are all handmade rugs works of art? Are all rugs woven by Native Americans works of art? If rugs were manufactured in a traditional Navajo design, would they be works of art? Encourage students to express various points of view, and remind them to present examples and facts to support their ideas.

Understanding Art History. Ask a group of volunteers to research the history and development of looms among Native Americans of the Southwest. Then have the volunteers present their findings, using photographs or drawings if possible, to the rest of the class.

Developing Studio Skills. Ask students to study the designs used in woven blankets or rugs of a particular cultural group. Then have students sketch their own designs in the style of that group, and use colored pencils or markers to complete their designs.

Following Up

Closure. Let students work in small groups to compare and discuss their weavings. Then have students write their responses to the "Interpret" section of "Examining Your Work."

Evaluation. Review students' weavings, consider their participation in "Closure" group discussions, and read their interpretations of their own work.

Reteaching. Work with groups of students to review Native American weavings: How do they differ from other woven works with which students are familiar?

Enrichment. Ask students to work in small groups to learn about the uses of natural dyes. What colors did Native American weavers use? Which plants provided those colors? How was the dying accomplished? Encourage interested groups to experiment with natural dyes.

Native American Art Today

LESSON PLAN
(pages 200–203)

Objectives
After completing this lesson, students will be able to:
- Identify Native American artists working today.
- Discuss works of both traditional and modern Native American art.

Supplies
- Photographs of pottery created by modern American artists, only some of whom are Native Americans; reproductions of paintings created by modern American artists, including some Native Americans.
- Sand, tempera paint, sheets of newspaper, pieces of cardboard, white glue, small brushes.
- Reproductions of paintings by Georgia O'Keeffe and of photographs by Alfred Stieglitz.

TRB Resources
- 13-4 *From Chief Seattle,* (reproducible master)
- 13-5 *Naming a Native American,* (appreciating cultural diversity)
- 13-6 *Ritual—A Life of Aesthetics,* (aesthetics)
- 13-7 *Coil Pot,* (studio)

TEACHING THE LESSON

Getting Started
Motivator. Show students photographs of pottery created by living American artists; some of the works should be by Native American artists, and others should be by Americans of other origins. Present each work, and let students describe and discuss it, but do not identify the artist. After students have viewed all the works, ask: Were any of these pieces of pottery created by Native American artists? If so, which pieces? What makes you think so? Encourage students to share and discuss various points of view; then identify the works by Native American artists.

LESSON 3

Native American Art Today

During the 1700s and 1800s America was explored and settled by newcomers from Europe. Native Americans fought to keep the lands they had lived on for generations. Their efforts were unsuccessful. As the land was developed by Europeans, the Native American population dwindled. Those who remained were eventually forced to live in limited areas called reservations.

Although the original Native American way of life has been lost, their art lives on. Many Native American artists working today continue the traditions of earlier artists.

TRADITIONAL NATIVE AMERICAN ART

Traditional art is art based on past forms and ideas. Some designs and techniques used by traditional artists today date from over a thousand years ago.

Crafts

Pueblo legend tells of supernatural spirits called Kachina (kuh-**chee**-nuh) who once lived among the people. The Kachina taught the Pueblo how to live in harmony with nature. This legend gave rise long ago to the making of Kachina dolls. A **Kachina doll** was *a hand-carved statuette used to teach children about Pueblo rituals.* Figure 13–11 shows a Kachina doll created in this century. Like the dolls of old, this object uses formal balance. What toys of our own culture does this remind you of? What idea or mood does it communicate to the viewer?

Another tradition carried forward by craftspeople today is pottery. The **polychrome**, or *many-colored*, pots in Figure 13–12 are by Lucy Lewis, a leading twentieth-century Native American potter. Lewis cre-

ated these pots using the same skills she learned as a child watching her elders. Each step was carefully done by hand, from digging the clay to grinding the minerals for the paints she used. She worked without the aid of a potter's wheel. Look closely at these works. The patterns on the surface are adaptations of prehistoric designs. What images do you see in these abstract decorations?

▲ Figure 13–11   The Pueblo believe there are between 300 and 400 Kachinas. Can you think of another culture you learned about that believed in a great many spirits?

Tony Dallas. *Koshare Clown*. Kachina Doll. Joan Cawley Gallery, Santa Fe, New Mexico.

Note
Let students compare the decorative methods used on the Lewis pots in Figure 13-12 with the Tafoya jug shown in Figure 13-13. Lewis applied painted designs to the outside of her pieces. Before applying the paint, she carefully smoothed the outside surface, using a wooden or bone paddle to rub the clay while it was at the leather hard stage. Margaret Tafoya drew her water serpent design on the pot and then used carving tools to cut and remove parts of the clay. In order to do this, she had to know exactly how thick the walls of her pot were so she wouldn't cut all the way through. Both design techniques take a very steady hand. The examples show the superb skill of these Native American artists.

▲ Figure 13–12   The artist learned to make pots from an aunt. What other skills besides art are learned through tradition?

Lucy Lewis. Polychrome Pots. Lewis Family. c. 1989/90. Acoma, New Mexico.

▲ Figure 13–13   In what ways is this water jar similar to the ones by Lucy Lewis? How are they different?

Margaret Tafoya. Jar. 1965. Blackware. 43 x 33 cm (17 x 13"). National Museum of Women in the Arts. Gift of Wallace & Wilhelmina Holladay.

Margaret Tafoya is another Native American artist who has also preserved the traditional methods with modern experimental techniques. She has created the pottery water jar shown in Figure 13–13 using a method of intaglio molding and carving. Her jar is decorated with an ancient water-serpent design.

Painting

Some ancient art techniques still practiced today are associated with health and well-being. One of these, sand painting, is part of a healing ritual. **Sand painting** is *the pouring of different colors of powdered rock on a flat section of earth to create an image or design*. Examine the sand painting pictured in Figure 13–14. As with all creations of this type, this one is abstract in design.

▲ Figure 13–14   Works like this are temporary; a new one is made from scratch for each ritual.

Sand Painting. Medicine men placing feathers. American Museum of Natural History, New York, New York.

Lesson 3   *Native American Art Today*   📖   **201**

202

MODERN NATIVE AMERICAN ART

Not all Native American artists of the twentieth century have been content to follow tradition. Some have struck out in new directions, using new media and techniques.

Sculpture

One of the most influential Native American artists at work today is Allan Houser (**ha**-oo-zohr). A Chiricahua Apache (chir-uh-**kah**-wuh uh-**pach**-ee), Houser was born in Oklahoma in 1914. As a child, he listened intently to stories about his people. After studying art, he went on to retell—usually in stone or bronze—the stories he had heard. Study the sculpture by Houser that opened this chapter, on page **192**. Can you imagine a story about this young warrior? How has Houser used line to move your eyes around the statue?

Painting

Portrait and landscape paintings are not parts of Native American art tradition. However, both played major roles in the brief life and career of twentieth-century painter T. C. Cannon. Cannon, a member of the Kiowa (**ky**-uh-waw) tribe, was born in 1946. A student of Allan Houser, he painted traditional subjects in brightly colored modern-day settings. Typical of his work is the portrait in Figure 13–15. Note the strong sense of design. What kind of detail has the artist shown in the man's clothing?

▶ **Figure 13–15 The subject of this painting seems to exist in two worlds. How does the artist show this?**

T. C. Cannon. *Turn of the Century Dandy.* 1976. Acrylic on canvas. 152.4 x 132.1 cm (60 x 52"). Aberbach Fine Arts, New York, New York. Private Collection.

202 Lesson 3 *Native American Art Today*

In the painting shown in Figure 13–16, another artist, Oscar Howe, breaks with painting traditions imposed upon Native Americans by European teachers. Traditionally, Indians did not use a realistic style. They believed that they could not depict nature as well as the Creator had made it. They depicted the spirit of animals and plants in symbolic, stylized designs. Howe uses line, shape, and color to show excitement. He expresses the powerful energy of the spirit of victory.

The painting by Dan Naminga, Figure 13–17, is yet another example of the blending of contemporary subject and traditional styles. This time the artist paints modern dwellings in a rich, colorful landscape.

▲ Figure 13–17 The work is an interpretation of modern times, yet it reveals strong feelings on the artist's part for the land and nature. What aesthetic view would you take in judging this work? Why?

Dan Namingha. *Hopi Dwelling*. Acrylic on canvas. 102 x 102 cm (40 x 40″).

▲ Figure 13–16 What story do you imagine this dancer is telling?

Oscar Howe. *Victory Dance*. Philbrook Museum of Art, Tulsa, Oklahoma.

✔CHECK YOUR UNDERSTANDING

1. What is traditional art?
2. What is a Kachina doll?
3. What is sand painting? For what is sand painting used?
4. In what area of art does Allan Houser specialize?
5. What was the art specialty of T. C. Cannon?

Appreciating Cultural Diversity. Ask volunteers to find and bring to class reproductions of paintings by Georgia O'Keeffe and photographs by Alfred Stieglitz. Display these works, and ask students to compare them with the works of Native American artists studied in this lesson: What similarities in subject can you identify? How are the uses of visual elements and principles of art similar? What are the most important differences between the works by O'Keeffe and Stieglitz and those by the Native American artists? Are O'Keeffe's paintings more similar to the works of the Native American artists or to Stieglitz's photographs? Encourage students to make specific comparisons between individual works of art and to express and support various opinions.

Following Up

Closure. Have students meet in small groups to compare and discuss their responses to these questions: If you were a Native American artist working today, which style would you choose to work in? What would be your most important reasons for making that choice?

Evaluation. 1. Review students' written responses to the "Check Your Understanding" questions. 2. Consider their contributions to the "Closure" group discussions.

Reteaching. Work with groups of students, helping them review what they have learned about modern Native American artists. Then have group members discuss T.C. Cannon's painting, *Turn of the Century Dandy*, shown in Figure 13-15: What message does this painting communicate? In what ways is this painting representative of the works created by today's Native American artists?

Enrichment. Have students work in small groups to research the jewelry created by different groups of Native Americans: What kind of jewelry is being created today? How is it made? How is it related to the culture's traditions? Let each group share its findings with the rest of the class.

Answers to "Check Your Understanding"
1. Traditional art is art based on past forms and ideas.
2. A Kachina doll is a hand-carved statuette used to teach children about Pueblo rituals.
3. Sand painting is the pouring of different colors of powdered rock on a flat section of earth to create a design. Sand paintings were used as part of a healing ritual.
4. Allan Houser, a Chiricahua Apache, specialized in using stone or bronze to retell stories about his people.
5. T.C. Cannon specialized in portrait and landscape painting, two areas not part of the Native American art tradition.

Inuit-Style Print

Another Native American group that has been around since earliest times is the Inuit (**in**-yuh-wuht). You probably know these people of Canada and Alaska better as Eskimos. The name "Eskimo" was used by explorers from other lands. The people from this group call themselves the Inuit. The Inuit have a tradition of carving bone, ivory, or stone to create abstract views of images from nature. This tradition is being upheld by artists working today. The print in Figure 13–18 is by a leading Inuit artist named Kenojuak (kuh-**noh**-joo-ak). Like all Native American artists, she combines nature, religion, and her own imagination.

WHAT YOU WILL LEARN

You will design a print based on your school mascot or some other school symbol. Your print will be abstract in design and should use line and shape to express your feelings about the animal. You will make an edition of three prints. (See Figure 13–19.)

WHAT YOU WILL NEED

- Pencil, eraser, and sheets of sketch paper
- 2 pieces of corrugated cardboard, 8 x 10 inches (20 x 25 cm)
- Paper-cutting knife and white glue
- Water-based printing ink
- Shallow pan and soft brayer
- Paper for printing
- Tablespoon

▶ **Figure 13–18   What kind of balance has the artist used? Is the subject in the work readily identifiable?**

Kenojuak. *Owls, Ravens and Dogs.* Courtesy of Dorset Fine Arts, Toronto, Ontario, Canada.

LESSON PLAN
(pages 204–205)

Objectives
After completing this lesson, students will be able to:
- Design and make printing plates for Inuit-style prints and make editions of three prints.
- Describe, analyze, interpret, and judge their own prints.

Supplies
- Photographs of several different examples of Inuit art, including if possible carved soapstone figures, carved ivory figures, masks, ivory record sticks, wood carvings, prints.
- Pencils; erasers; sheets of sketch paper; pieces of corrugated cardboard, 8 x 10 inches (20 x 25 cm); utility knives; white glue; water-based printing ink; shallow pans; soft brayers; sheets of paper for printing; tablespoons.

TRB Resources
- 13-8 *Kenojuak,* (artist profile)
- 13-9 *Inuit Sculpture,* (art criticism)

TEACHING THE LESSON

Getting Started

Motivator. Display photographs of Inuit art works. Try to include works in several different media, such as soapstone, ivory, wood, bone; try to include carved figures, record rods, masks, and prints. Display the art works, and let the students describe them and their reactions to them. Then ask: What group of people do you guess might have created these works? What are your reasons for guessing that cultural group? Guide students in identifying the Inuit people and in using the term *Inuit* rather than *Eskimo.*

Vocabulary. Review with students the definition of a *print:* What steps are involved in making a print? What tools and equipment are needed? What is an edition? How are the prints in an edition numbered?

Background Information
The traditional Inuit home is the igloo, a dome-shaped structure built from blocks of snow. The first step in constructing an igloo is selecting an area of hard, deep snow. The next step is digging a round pit in this area, cutting out blocks of the hard snow, and setting the blocks around the edges of the pit. These snow blocks are usually about 3 feet (90 cm) long, 2 feet (60 cm) high, and 1 foot (30 cm) thick. The home builder forms a spiraling wall, which rises and narrows to form a dome. Loose snow is used to fill in any cracks between the blocks. The builder cuts a doorway into the dome, digs a trench leading to the doorway, and covers the trench with a tunnel of snow blocks to keep the wind from blowing directly into the igloo. Inside, platforms of packed snow are covered with hides and used as areas for sitting and sleeping. A fire provides enough warmth for the residents without melting the igloo walls.

Though the igloo is an important part of Inuit tradition, nearly all Inuit people now live in wooden homes.

WHAT YOU WILL DO

1. On sketch paper, do a drawing of the animal you chose. On a second sheet of sketch paper, create an abstract design based on your first sketch. Leave out all unneeded details. Use line and shape to express feelings. Round shapes can express gentleness, diagonal lines can show danger or quick movement.
2. Transfer your design to a piece of corrugated cardboard. Using the paper-cutting knife, carefully cut out the design. Glue it to the second piece of cardboard to form a printing plate.
3. Squeeze out a small amount of ink into the pan. Roll the brayer back and forth in the ink to coat it evenly. Roll the brayer lightly over your printing plate. If you press down too hard, you might collapse the relief.
4. Place a clean sheet of paper on your plate. Gently rub the paper with the back of the spoon or your fingertips. Work quickly. Carefully remove the print. Set it aside to dry. Repeat the process twice more to make an edition of three prints. When all the prints are dry, sign and number them.
5. Display your finished prints alongside those of classmates. Decide which design you feel best captures the appearance and the spirit of your school mascot.

EXAMINING YOUR WORK

- **Describe** Identify the sources of your ideas for abstraction. Identify the unnecessary details you eliminated to create an abstract design.
- **Analyze** Tell which elements stand out most in your design.
- **Interpret** State what feelings toward your mascot your print expresses. Identify the features that help communicate those feelings.
- **Judge** Tell whether you feel your work succeeds. If you could redo your work, tell what changes, if any, you would make.

▲ Figure 13–19   Student work. Inuit-style print.

OTHER STUDIO IDEAS

- Make another print, this time using a darker-colored ink. Explain how this changes the mood of the work.

●● Work with three or four classmates. On a large sheet of paper, create a repeated pattern incorporating all your plates.

Lesson 4   *Inuit-Style Print*   **205**

Developing Concepts

Understanding Art History. Have students research the traditional Inuit lifestyle: Where and how do Inuit people live? What kinds of living conditions do they face? What special adaptations have they made to those conditions? What kinds of work do men and women do? How many people still maintain traditional lifestyles? How many have adopted the European-American ways of life? How do some Inuit try to live in both cultures? Let students compare their findings and then discuss their responses to this question: How is the traditional Inuit way of life reflected in Inuit art?

Appreciating Cultural Diversity. Ask a group of volunteers to find out more about Inuit masks and to compare them to tribal masks of Africa: How are they alike in appearance and in function? What are the most important differences?

Following Up

Closure. Let each student present his or her Inuit-style prints to a group of classmates, describing, analyzing, interpreting, and judging the work as instructed in "Examining Your Work." Encourage group members to make positive comments about one another's prints.

Evaluation. Review students' Inuit-style prints and consider their contributions to the "Closure" group discussions.

Reteaching. Help groups of students discuss their own prints and compare them to Kenojuak's print, *Owl, Ravens, and Dogs,* Figure 13-18: How does her print reflect the Inuit traditions? In what ways are your prints similar to hers?

Enrichment. Explain that Kenojuak, like many other Inuit artists, is a member of an artists' cooperative; hers is the West Baffin Eskimo Cooperative Limited, formed more than 30 years ago. Ask students to research Inuit artists' cooperatives: When, where, and why have they been formed? How do they function? What benefits do they offer to Inuit artists?

Handbook Cross-Reference
For additional information about Lucy Lewis, direct students to the Artist Profile, *Handbook* page **290**.

Cooperative Learning
This Studio Lesson has suggested using a school mascot as the subject. If your school has no mascot, let the class participate in suggesting two to three animals that might be used as models for the lesson. Kenojuak's work on page **204** shows several kinds of stylized animals interlinked in a harmonious design. Guide the discussion to include animals found in arctic regions, such as whales, penguins, and fishes.

ANSWERS TO "CHAPTER 13 REVIEW"

Building Vocabulary

1. coiled pot
2. petroglyphs
3. pueblos
4. totem pole
5. tepee
6. cradle board
7. Kachina doll
8. sand painting
9. polychrome
10. loom
11. warp
12. weft

Reviewing Art Facts

13. The Pueblo settled in what is known as The Four Corners section of the United States.
14. Northwest Coast Indians reached the area they settled in about 7000 B.C. The good climate convinced them to stay.
15. Six groups of Woodlands groups combined to form the Iroquois Nation.
16. The Northwest Coast tribe carved totem poles.
17. The Kachina are supernatural spirits who taught the Pueblo how to live in harmony with nature. The spirits are represented by Kachina dolls.
18. T.C. Cannon specialized in portrait and landscape painting.
19. The Inuit live in Canada and Alaska.

Thinking About Art

1. A critic who bases his/her aesthetic view on composition would say this sculpture was beautifully balanced and well done. The viewer's eye travels diagonally from the feet up the body to the warrior's eye looking at the arrow and back down the curved bow to the body.
2. The Inuit artists are isolated in a cold climate and use bone, ivory and stone because they are easy to obtain.

BUILDING VOCABULARY

Number a sheet of paper from 1 to 12. After each number, write the term from the box that best matches each description below.

coiled pot	pueblos
cradle board	sand painting
Kachina doll	tepee
loom	totem pole
petroglyphs	warp
polychrome	weft

1. A pot formed by coiling long ropes of clay in a spiral.
2. Rock carvings and paintings.
3. Stacked, many-family dwellings made of adobe.
4. An upright log carving picturing stories of different families or clans.
5. A portable house.
6. A harness worn on the shoulders and used to carry a small child.
7. A hand-carved statuette used to teach children about Pueblo rituals.
8. The pouring of different colors of powdered rock on a flat section of earth to create an image or design.
9. Having many colors.
10. A frame holding a set of crisscrossing threads.
11. Threads running vertically and attached to the loom's frame.
12. Threads passed horizontally over and under the warp.

REVIEWING ART FACTS

Number a sheet of paper from 13 to 19. Answer each question in a complete sentence.

13. In what areas did the early Pueblo settle?
14. When did the Northwest Coast Indians reach the region they settled? What convinced them to remain in this region?
15. Which group of Woodlands people became organized as one large nation?
16. Which group of Native Americans is famous for its totem poles?
17. What were the Kachina?
18. What Native American artist was famous for his portraits and landscapes?
19. Where do the Inuit live?

THINKING ABOUT ART

On a sheet of paper, answer each question in a sentence or two.

1. **Analyze**. One of the three aesthetic views holds that the most important feature of a work of art is its composition. Tell how an art critic accepting this view would react to the sculpture that opened this chapter (page **192**). Explain why you believe the critic would have this reaction.
2. **Extend**. Explain how the part of the world the Inuit live in is a factor in their artists' choice of media.

MAKING ART CONNECTIONS

1. **Science**. Find all the works in this chapter that make use of geometric patterns. Identify the number and kind of motifs that appear in each one. See if you can make any general statements about the use of patterns from nature used in Native American design.
2. **Social Studies**. In the encyclopedia or another library reference book, read about (a) the Seminole Native Americans of Florida, or (b) the Iroquois Native Americans of New York State. Find out when the people arrived in the region they settled. Learn about the customs and art of the group. Share your findings with the class in the form of an interesting audio-visual presentation.

CHAPTER 13 REVIEW

LOOKING AT THE DETAILS

The detail shown below is from Allan Houser's *Sacred Rain Arrow.* Study the detail and answer the following questions using complete sentences.

1. How has the artist depicted strength in this sculpture?
2. Look at the credit line. In what year was this sculpture created? Does this infor-mation give you more insight into the values of the artist and his culture?
3. How has Houser created the impression of anticipated movement?
4. Explain how the element of line is used to show contrast in this work.

Alan Houser. *Sacred Rain Arrow.* 1988. Bronze. (Detail.) 249 x 99 x 78.7 cm (98 x 39 x 31″). Glenn Green Galleries, Phoenix, Arizona.

Chapter Evaluation

The purpose of this chapter is to introduce students to the artists and art styles of Native Americans both past and pre-sent. Methods of evaluation include:

1. Find a pictorial representation of each vocabulary term presented in the chapter. Glue each picture onto a sepa-rate sheet of construction paper. Number each picture and rotate the pictures to the students. On a separate sheet of paper have students number their papers and identify the terms by the correct number.
2. Give students a blank map of the United States. Have them label the regions where the following Native Ameri-can groups settled: Inuit, Northwest Coast, Pueblo, Plains, and Woodlands.
3. Have students complete Chapter 13 Test, (TRB, Re-source 13-10).

European Art of the Early 1800s

Chapter Scan

TRB Resources

- 14-8 Chapter Test
- Color Transparency 27
- Color Transparency 28

TEACHING THE CHAPTER

Introducing the Art Work

Direct students' attention to Auguste Renoir's *Oarsmen at Chatou.* Inform them that Auguste Renoir was a French Impressionist painter of the late nineteenth and early twentieth centuries. Renoir was born in Paris and as a youth apprenticed to a porcelain decorator in Limoges, where he copied flower and other eighteenth-century motifs and developed his remarkable sense of color. He returned and settled in Paris becoming one of the founders of the Impressionist movement and one of its most popular masters. Renoir had an established reputation as a brilliant portrait painter, who was especially receptive to women and children. Like most of his fellow Impressionists, Renoir frequently painted out of doors. One of the hallmarks of his style is the sense of high spirits and well-being which radiates from his work.

▲ The artist once stated that his desire was to paint pictures that were happy and pretty. Do you suppose this is one of them? Explain your answer.

Auguste Renoir. *Oarsmen at Chatou.* 1879. Canvas. 81.3 x 100.3 cm (32 x 39½"). National Gallery of Art, Washington, D.C. Gift of Sam A. Lewisohn.

European Art of the Early 1800s

The 1600s, you have learned, was the age of Baroque art; the 1700s, of Rococo. The 1800s can be thought of as an age of change. No single art style dominated. One art style was hardly in place before it was challenged and re-placed by another.

The century began with artists looking to the past for ideas. By mid-century they were roaming the countryside, painting every-day scenes with dabs of paint. One work done in this manner is shown at the left. In this chapter you will learn about such works and the artists who created them.

OBJECTIVES

After completing this chapter, you will be able to:

- Describe the Neoclassic, Romantic, and Impressionist styles of art.
- Discuss the importance of the Salon to artists of the day.
- Create art work in the Neoclassic and Impressionist style.

WORDS YOU WILL LEARN

art movement   Neoclassic
Impressionism   Romanticism
landscape   Salon

ARTISTS YOU WILL MEET

Jacques Louis David   Auguste Renoir
Eugène Delacroix   Auguste Rodin
Claude Monet   Joseph M. W. Turner
Berthe Morisot

Examining the Art Work
Explain to students that this scene is from the banks of the Seine, where Renoir and his friends en-joyed swimming and boating. It is a scene from the real world depicting recognizable subjects and objects, yet it veers away from realism. Point out the way color is used, blurring objects together, such as in the face, shirt, hands and slacks of the man on the left. Point out the lack of detail in the faces, the inside of the canoe, the sailboat and boats in the distance. Explain that these objects are portrayed as impres-sions of the real thing, rather than detailed replicas. Also point out the visible brush strokes and the em-phasis on light. Suggest that Im-pressionist art works are most ef-fective when viewed from a distance rather than up close.

Discussing the Art Work
Ask students to think about how Renoir used light in this scene. Ex-plain that the way light reflects off of objects was the main concern of the Impressionists. Point out the way color is broken up by incorpo-rating light. Refer to the woman's skirt, the white jacket, and the water as prime examples of this.

Ask students if they think this technique affects the texture of the work. Suggest that the visible brush strokes and reflections of light tend to create more visual texture than would be seen in works using solid blocks of color or in works of real-ism.

Ask students what kind of mood they sense in this work. Point out the openness of the scene, the carefree posture of the figures, and the focus on light. Suggest that all of these things create a carefree, high spirited mood, but not particu-larly intense in any way.

Tell students that in this chapter they will learn about Neoclassic, Romantic and Impressionist styles of art, and create their own art works in two of these styles.

Building Self-Esteem
Tell students that in this chapter they will be seeing work by a number of artists who broke with tradition. Jacques Louis David, having been influenced by the archaeological discov-eries at Pompeii, introduced a new, very realistic and classi-cal style. Delacroix, responding to the French people's desire to escape depressing political unrest, founded the Romantic style of painting. Claude Monet, Auguste Renoir, and Berthe Morisot, whose paintings had not been selected to appear in the most important annual French art show, founded their own new art movement called Impressionism. In each case, indi-viduals who disagreed with the system found a constructive and creative way to succeed. Although some of the Impres-sionist art was ridiculed when it was first shown, today it hangs in museums and is highly valued. Help students to appreci-ate the strength of character it took for these individuals to break with the artistic traditions of their day.

LESSON 1

Neoclassic and Romantic Art

LESSON PLAN
(pages 210–213)

Objectives

After completing this lesson, students will be able to:
- Describe the Neoclassic and Romantic styles of art.
- Explain what a landscape is.
- Create watercolor paintings evoked by specific sounds.

Supplies

- Slides or photographs of Baroque buildings and of ancient Greek temples.
- Sheets of drawing paper, pencils, watercolors, brushes, water.
- Recording of music by Richard Wagner, sheets of drawing paper, watercolors, brushes, water, black markers.

TRB Resources

- 14-1 *Eugéne Delacroix,* (artist profile)
- 14-2 *Compare the Spirit,* (cooperative learning)
- 14-3 *Artists Expressing the Times,* (reproducible master)
- 14-4 *Writing About the Times,* (appreciating cultural diversity)

TEACHING THE LESSON

Getting Started

Motivator. Begin by showing students slides or photographs of Baroque buildings, focusing on Rococo details if possible. Let students identify and describe what they see. Then ask: What style of art and architecture that you have already studied seems most different from this Baroque style? Let several students respond, and encourage them to give specific reasons to support their ideas. Then show slides or photographs of ancient Greek temples, and have students describe the differences between these works and the Baroque works. Explain to students that they will learn about two art movements in this lesson; in one of these movements, artists reacted against the Baroque style and began working in a style intended to echo the works of ancient Greece and Rome.

210

Neoclassic and Romantic Art

The late 1700s and early 1800s were stormy times in France. Outraged by the shameless greed of the wealthy ruling class, the poor people rose up in revolt. This uprising, known as the French Revolution, began with a bloody reign of terror. Thousands lost their heads on the guillotine. The following 20 years, marked by war and struggle, were no less bitter. Finally, the troubled French government was turned over to a popular young general. His name was Napoléon Bonaparte (nuh-**pol**-yuhn **boh**-nuh-part).

▲ **Figure 14–1** Notice how the artist arranged the three groups of figures. Do the arches and columns help unify the groups?

Jacques Louis David. *The Oath of the Horatii.* 1786. Toledo Museum of Art, Toledo, Ohio.

Note

Help students understand the differences between Neoclassicism and Romanticism. Explain that Neoclassicism was the official style of the French Academy throughout the century, but particularly during the first half. This style made use of ancient Greek and Roman sculptures as models. It stressed the importance of balanced compositions, flowing contour lines, figures modeled in light and dark, subdued colors, and noble gestures and expressions.

Romanticism was the style that developed and flourished during the first half of the century. It favored the use of rich, dramatic color and a sense of movement rather than balance. Paintings done in this style did not begin with contour lines, but with patterns of color which were used to create shapes and figures.

NEOCLASSIC ART

Artists of the day believed these events were equal in importance to the rise and fall of ancient Greece and Rome. They even chose to show the events using an updated version of the styles of ancient Greece and Rome. As a result, their work became known as **Neoclassic** (nee-oh-**klas**-ik), meaning "new classic," *an art style that borrowed from the early classical period of ancient Greece and Rome.*

One of the most successful of the Neoclassic artists was Jacques Louis David (**zhahk** loo-**ee** dah-**veed**). Even though he later took part in the revolt against the French king, David was Louis XVI's painter. It was the king who asked David to paint what would become one of his most famous pictures. The painting, shown in Figure 14–1, shows two families living in neighboring ancient Roman cities. The families are related by marriage but divided by a war between their cities. A father and three sons of one family are shown pledging to fight to the death. All know their relatives will be among those they must battle. The women, helpless to prevent the tragedy, weep.

The picture is made up of three groups of figures. These are arranged across the canvas as though it were a stage. Notice David's skillful use of the background arches and columns to separate and frame these groups. The artist's careful painting of details — the swords, the helmets — adds to the picture's realism. His use of light adds drama to the picture.

ROMANTIC ART

As the 1800s wore on, people became weary of the political unrest and fighting. They looked for things that would take their minds off the upsetting events around them. Some artists shared this same desire. These artists were responsible for developing a new style of art called **Romanticism** (roh-**mant**-uh-siz-uhm). This is *a style of art that found its subjects in the world of the dramatic and exotic.*

France

To Romanticists, nothing stirred the imagination better than far-off places and colorful, action-filled adventures. The two are combined in the paintings of Eugène Delacroix (oo-**zhen** del-uh-**kwah**), a leader of the Romantic school. One of his paintings is pictured in Figure 14–2. In this work, Delacroix refused to allow his taste for action to interfere with his sense of design. He planned his painting so the viewer would miss none of its exciting details.

Study this work. Find the diagonal line beginning in the horse and rider at the lower left. This line leads your eye upward to the figures at the right. From there the gunsmoke pulls your gaze across the picture to the far-off figures and fortress.

England

Another artist who turned to his imagination for ideas was the English painter Joseph M. W. Turner. Unlike other Romanticists, however, Turner expected his viewers to use their imaginations as well. His glowing colors and blurred images free viewers to interpret his pictures in their own ways.

Turner spent his life painting landscapes. A **landscape** is *a drawing or painting focusing on mountains, trees, or other natural scenery*. He was fascinated in particular by sunlight and its shimmering reflection on water. This fascination can be seen in the painting in Figure 14–3. The work excites the viewer's curiosity with its dazzling sky and shimmering waters. There are ships in the center of the painting, and a church is visible on the right. With the use of light on the structures, the artist leads the viewer's eye down the canal and out to sea. As in all of Turner's best works, the real subjects are light and color.

Vocabulary. Help students consider the terms *Neoclassic* and *Romantic*. Encourage them to use dictionaries as they respond to these questions: To what culture does the word *classic* refer? What meaning does the prefix *neo-* add? What are some of the meanings of the adjective *romantic?* Which of those meanings relates to art? Does romantic art relate more directly to facts or to imagination?

Developing Concepts

Exploring Aesthetics. Let students discuss their responses to Joseph M. W. Turner's landscape, Figure 14-3 on page 213: What is the subject of this art work? What colors do you see in the work? What mood do those colors create? If you could *hear* this painting, what sounds would you describe?

Using Art Criticism. Help students discuss and compare Jacques Louis David's *The Oath of the Horatii*, Figure 14-1, and Eugene Delacroix's *Arabs Skirmishing in the Mountains*, Figure 14-2: How do these two paintings differ in subject, in composition, and in content? How do the two works reflect the interests and concerns of the Neoclassic art movement and the Romantic art movement?

Understanding Art History. The works of artists in France—and indeed throughout Europe—reflected the impact of the French Revolution. Ask students to research this period in French history: Who ruled France before the Revolution? What were the main objections to that ruler? How did the revolt against that ruler begin? How did it progress? Who ruled France after the Revolution? How did the Revolution change the lives of French citizens? Lead a class discussion in which students share what they have learned and discuss its effects on art works created during this time.

Also ask several volunteers to read about the life and works of Jacques Louis David. How did the French Revolution affect his life? How did it affect his works? Ask these volunteers to share their findings with the rest of the class.

Background Information

Joseph Mallord William Turner (England, 1775–1851) is generally considered an outstanding and highly original landscape artist. He had very little schooling, but he devoted himself early to art, and in 1790 he exhibited his first watercolor at the Royal Academy.

Turner made the first of his nearly annual sketching tours of the British Isles in 1792. He first traveled to Europe in 1802. He made several more trips, especially to Switzerland and Italy, with his sketchbook always at hand.

Turner's growing reputation and his financial success permitted him to develop independent ideas and an individualistic style. He revolutionized the concept of landscape paintings in watercolors. Using pure colors to enhance the changing moods of nature, Turner painted sunlight, clouds, breezes, and weather in his landscapes.

Turner was intensely interested in light and color, and his later paintings seem to anticipate the style of the Impressionists.

After students have completed the "Studio Experience" activity, remind them that music can influence or even inspire works of visual art. For example, the Romantic artist Gustave Dore reported that he painted one of his best-known works, *Ship Trapped by an Iceberg,* in response to a musical composition by Richard Wagner. Play a recording of music by Wagner; let students listen for a while and then use watercolors to record their responses to the music. Remind them that they can use either the wet-on-wet technique employed in the "Studio Experience" or the wet-on-dry technique, in which they do not brush their papers with water. Once the watercolors have dried, let students use black markers to draw in lines separating the colors and defining the shapes and figures. How do these lines affect the impact of the paintings?

Appreciating Cultural Diversity. Have students work in two groups. Ask one group to find reproductions of Romantic landscape paintings. Ask the other group to find reproductions of Japanese landscape prints and paintings. Then have the two groups share and discuss the art works they have chosen: How are they alike? What are the most important differences?

▲ Figure 14–2 **Delacroix often painted pictures that included action and adventure. Look at the figures in the foreground. Notice how they help to lead the viewer's eyes around the painting.**

Eugène Delacroix. *Arabs Skirmishing in the Mountains.* 1863. Canvas. 92.5 x 74.6 cm (36⅜ x 29⅜"). National Gallery of Art, Washington, D.C. Chester Dale Fund.

212 📖 Lesson 1 *Neoclassic and Romantic Art*

Background Information
Eugène Delacroix (France, 1798–1863) believed that art should electrify the viewer. He chose subjects filled with action, showing men and animals caught up in a conflict with nature or each other. The Romanticists were striving to show optical truth as well as things as they were in reality. Delacroix reflected the influence of David and Gericault. In addition, he chose to portray spectacular drama that would fire the imagination and appeal to a wide audience. He also realized that content was not the only concern. Of technique he said, "It is advisable not to fuse brush strokes, as they will [appear to] fuse naturally at [a]. . . distance". In this respect, he anticipated the Impressionists' experiments with light and color. His work might be said to be the precursor of the epic film.

✔CHECK YOUR UNDERSTANDING

1. Describe events in France in the late 1700s and early 1800s.
2. What is Neoclassic art? What led artists to begin creating art in this style?
3. What is Romantic art? What led artists to begin creating art in this style?

STUDIO EXPERIENCE

Using your imagination, sketch an image that goes with one of these sounds: a bird's song, the roar of the ocean, or breaking glass. Decide what mood or feeling the blending of sound and image communicates to you. Then brush water over your drawing and paint it with watercolors. Use colors that best express the mood your work calls to mind. Display your finished painting. What mood do the blurred images communicate to other students?

Following Up

Closure. Let students work in groups to compare and discuss their "Studio Experience" paintings. Ask group members to guess the sound that inspired each painting. How are paintings inspired by the same sound alike? How are they different?

Evaluation. 1. Review students' written responses to the "Check Your Understanding" questions. 2. Consider their contributions to the "Closure" group discussion.

Reteaching. Work with small groups of students to review the differences between Neoclassicism and Romanticism: To what other art movement was each a reaction? What political and social events helped shape Neoclassicism and Romanticism? How do the two art movements differ in subject and in style? Then have group members browse through art books or collections of art reproductions. Ask each group member to find and share with the class at least one Neoclassic art work and one Romantic art work.

Enrichment. Let students work together to plan and create their own work in either the Neoclassic or Romantic style. Have group members begin by selecting the style and then by deciding on a subject suitable to that style. Let students work together to select their media and support media, and to plan and execute their work. Encourage the members of each group to present their work to the rest of the class.

▲ **Figure 14–3** Earlier in his career the artist painted pictures with more realistic subjects. What do you like about the way he painted this one?

Joseph M. W. Turner. *The Grand Canal, Venice.* 1835. Canvas. 91.4 x 122.2 cm (36 x 48⅛"). The Metropolitan Museum of Art, New York, New York. Bequest of Cornelius Vanderbilt, 1899.

Lesson 1   *Neoclassic and Romantic Art*   📖   **213**

Answers to "Check Your Understanding"

1. Outraged by the shameless greed of the wealthy ruling class, the poor people rose up in a revolt called the French Revolution.
2. Neoclassical art is an art style borrowed from the early classical period of ancient Greece and Rome. Artists began using this style because they believed the events occurring during the French Revolution were equal in importance to the rise and fall of Greece and Rome.
3. Romanticism is a style of art that found its subjects in the world of the dramatic and exotic. People were weary of war and political unrest, and the artists began to develop works that would be uplifting.

Objectives
After completing this lesson, students will be able to:
- Design and build three-dimensional models for stage sets.
- Describe, analyze, interpret, and judge their own stage set models.

Supplies
- Pencils, sheets of sketch paper, mixing trays, tempera paint, wide-tipped brushes, fine-tipped brushes, shoe boxes, sheets of mat board, scissors, white glue.
- Clay, wire, and/or other sculpting media.

TRB Resource
- 14-5 *Step Back in Time,* (art history)

TEACHING THE LESSON

Getting Started

Motivator. Introduce this studio lesson by encouraging students to discuss their own experiences with theater productions—both in audiences and behind the scenes. Ask students to tell about plays or other live productions they have seen: Where was the play? What did the stage background look like? What furniture or other objects were on the stage? If any students have participated in or helped with school or community productions, ask them to describe the stage: How big was it? How much of it could the audience see? How was the stage prepared for the play? Which parts were painted? What furniture or other objects were used on the stage?

Vocabulary. Ask students to suggest several definitions of the noun *set.* Then ask: What is a stage set? How is this meaning of the noun *set* related to the noun *setting* (as in "the setting of the story")? Who works to create stage sets? How do you think you might create a model of a stage set?

Designing a Neoclassic Stage Set

Look at the painting in Figure 14–4. It is by Jacques Louis David. As in the other work by this foremost Neoclassicist you studied (Figure 14–1), the figures appear almost as actors. The setting is like a stage.

Imagine for a moment that the stone dungeon in this work *is* part of a stage set. Imagine that just beyond the rightmost figure in the painting are wings—the area in a theater leading backstage. Imagine that to the left of the shadowed archway the set continues. What lies beyond the left edge of this painting? In this lesson you will invent a continuation of this scene.

WHAT YOU WILL LEARN

Design and build a three-dimensional model for a stage set. Your model will extend the stage in Figure 14–4. Match as closely as possible the colors, textures, and patterns of the walls and floor. Make two pieces of furniture to place in your model. These will emphasize the real space in the model. Your stage set will have the same feeling or mood suggested by David's painting.

▲ **Figure 14–4** Socrates, a great Greek philosopher, is shown in prison. He has been placed here after falsely being accused of denying the existence of Greek gods. His punishment is to drink poison.

Jacques Louis David. *The Death of Socrates.* 1787. Oil on canvas. 129.5 x 196.2 cm (51 x 77¼"). The Metropolitan Museum of Art, New York, New York. Catherine Lorillard Wolfe Collection.

Background Information
Jacques Louis David (France, 1748–1825) was a leading painter of the Neoclassical movement. David spent five years studying in Rome, where he devoted most of his efforts to the study of ancient art.

The Oath of the Horatii was David's first masterpiece. His next major work, *Brutus and His Dead Son,* presented a clear anti-monarchy statement. David became a strong supporter of the Revolution. He was elected to the National Convention in 1792, and he voted for the death of King Louis XVI. He painted several paintings depicting the martyrs of the Revolution; the most familiar of these is *The Death of Marat.*

After David's Revolutionary hero, Robespierre, was put to death, David was sent to prison for a time. After his release, he became an ardent supporter of Napoleon. David soon became Napoleon's principal painter. Following Napoleon's exile, David left France. He spent the rest of his life in Belgium; during these final years he produced no major works.

WHAT YOU WILL NEED

- Pencil and sheets of sketch paper
- Mixing tray, tempera paint, and 2 brushes — one wide, one fine-tipped
- Shoe box and 2 sheets of mat board
- Scissors and white glue

WHAT YOU WILL DO

1. Brainstorm with your classmates for possible answers to the question "What lies beyond the left border of this painting?" Then working by yourself, sketch several ideas for extending the stage. Create windows, doorways, stairs, arches, and other design features you like. Let your imagination and David's painting guide you. Choose your best sketch and set it aside.

2. Mix hues of tempera paint to match the lighted portions of the walls and the floor in David's painting. Create darker values of the same hue to match the shaded portions. Using the thick brush, paint the back, sides, and bottom of the shoe box. Using the fine-tipped brush, add the thin lines between stone blocks.

3. With scissors, cut from mat board doors, arches, and other design features appearing in your sketch. Make sure all added features match the colors, patterns, and textures found in the painting. Glue these features in place in your model.

4. Make furniture, such as a table, bench, or bed, to complete your design.

EXAMINING YOUR WORK

- **Describe** Tell whether the walls, floor, and other features of your model look real. Point out the features that help viewers identify your model as an extension of David's painting.
- **Analyze** State whether the colors and textures in your work match those in David's painting. Point out similarities between the patterns on the walls and floor in your model and those in the painting. Show ways in which you used real space in your model.
- **Interpret** Tell whether your stage set has the same mood or feeling as the one David's painting communicates. Decide what words you would use to describe that mood or feeling.
- **Judge** Decide in what way your model most succeeds. Tell whether it succeeds because of its realistic appearance, its composition, or its content.

5. When dry, display your model. Compare it with the stage set in the painting and with other student models. Decide which were most successful in matching the look of David's painting.

OTHER STUDIO IDEAS

- Look through a magazine to find figures to cut out and use as actors for your stage. Glue cardboard backings to your figures so they will stand. Pose them in your model so they appear to be relating to one another.

- ●● Imagine the words each of your actors is speaking. Write these on pieces of white paper cut to look like the dialogue balloons in comic strips. Glue these to each actor so the words seem to be coming from his or her mouth.

LESSON PLAN
(pages 216–219)

Objectives

After completing this lesson, students will be able to:
- Describe the Impressionist style of art.
- Discuss the importance of the Salon to artists of the day.
- Identify and discuss the works of important Impressionist artists.
- Make Impressionist-style drawings of familiar objects.

Supplies

- Slides or reproductions of Romantic paintings and of Impressionist paintings.
- Pencils; sheets of drawing paper, 9 x 12 inches (23 x 30 cm); colored chalk or crayons.
- Sheets of white paper, pencils, tempera paint in black and white, brushes.

> **TRB Resource**
> - 14-6 *The Many Faces of Realism,* (aesthetics)

TEACHING THE LESSON

Getting Started

Motivator. To introduce this lesson, display slides or reproductions of two or three Romantic paintings (by artists such as Philipp Otto Runge, Caspar David Friedrich, Eugène Delacroix, John Constable, for example.) Encourage students to discuss what they see in each work and what reaction it evokes in them. Then display slides or reproductions of two or three Impressionist paintings. Again, encourage students to describe and react to each work. Then have students compare the two groups of paintings: What are the main differences in subject? How are the uses of color different? How do the moods and messages of the two groups differ? What other important differences can you identify? Explain to students that the paintings in the second group are examples of the Impressionist art movement, about which they will learn more in this lesson.

216

LESSON 3

European Art — Late 1800s

Each age has its customs and fashions. One custom common in Paris and London during the 1800s was a yearly art show. The **Salon** (suh-**lahn**), *an annual exhibition of art*, was a major social event. An artist's reputation often depended upon whether or not his or her work was selected for showing at the Salon.

In this lesson you will read how the Salon led to the formation of an **art movement**, *a trend formed when a group of artists band together to create works of a single style*.

▲ Figure 14–5   Cool colors — blues and greens — seem to move back in space. Warm colors — reds and yellows — seem to come forward. How has the artist used warm and cool colors in this work? Why do you think he made these choices?

Claude Monet. *Banks of the Seine, Vetheuil.* 1880. Canvas. 73.4 x 100.5 cm (28⅞ x 39⅝"). National Gallery of Art, Washington, D.C. Chester Dale Collection.

Cooperative Learning
Tell students that an art critic of the 1800s wrote the following description of Impressionism:

> The Impressionists take a canvas, some paint and brushes. . . [They] throw some tones [colors] onto the canvas and then sign it. This is the way in which the lost souls of Ville-Evard [a mental hospital] pick up pebbles from the roadway and believe they have found diamonds.

Working in pairs, have students restate this idea in their own words. Have them explain what they believe led the critic to react in this way.

IMPRESSIONIST PAINTING

In 1874 a group of discouraged young artists decided to hold an exhibition of their own. They found an empty studio in Paris. There they hung pictures that had been rejected by the Salon. The people who came to view the exhibition reacted in different ways. Some were confused. Others laughed. Still others were angry. On one point most viewers were agreed: the paintings looked more like quick sketches than like finished art works. One angry critic, after viewing a painting titled *Impression: Sunrise*, referred to all the paintings as "impressionistic." The name stuck and continued to be used to identify paintings done in this new style.

This style, **Impressionism**, is *a style that attempted to capture the rapidly changing effects of light on objects*. Members of the Impressionist movement left their studios to paint outdoors. They looked at life around them and found subjects everywhere they looked. They painted landscapes and street scenes; they even set up their easels in cafes.

Claude Monet

The painting that gave Impressionism its name was the work of one of the movement's founders, Claude Monet (**klohd** moh-**nay**). Imagine Monet as he prepares to paint the landscape in Figure 14–5. He notes how the sunlight flickers on the gently swaying flowers. He notices how it reflects on rippling waters and glows through gray clouds. He observes, too, how the strongest sunlight blurs forms and blots out details. Now, taking brush in hand, he applies small dabs and dashes of paint to his canvas. He works quickly, trying to capture the effect of sunlight on every object. Each stroke of paint is a little different from the next in hue, value, and intensity. Monet knows the yellows and blues he is using will play against each other in the viewer's eye. They will give the painting a sparkle and brilliance to match that of the sun. Where does the artist use different values of yellow in the work? Where does he use different values of blue?

Auguste Renoir

One of the most productive of the Impressionists was a man named Pierre Auguste Renoir (pee-**ehr** oh-**goost** ren-**wahr**). Another of the movement's founders, Renoir painted right up to the day he died.

An area of painting Renoir explored using the Impressionist style was portraits. He was especially attracted to the eyes of his subject and often made these the focus of attention. Look at the portrait in Figure 14–6. The eyes, you will notice, are painted in sharp focus. The rest of the figure, meanwhile, is blurred. Renoir knew that when we look at a person or object, not all parts appear in focus at once. Only the part where our eyes rest at a given moment is seen sharply. Everything else appears fuzzy and slightly out of focus.

▲ Figure 14–6   The eyes in this work look right out at you. Even when you glance at other parts of the painting, your attention is always attracted back to the eyes.

Auguste Renoir. *Madame Henriot.* c. 1876. Canvas. 65.9 x 49.8 cm (26 x 19⅝"). National Gallery of Art, Washington, D.C. Gift of Adele R. Levy Fund, Inc.

Lesson 3   *European Art — Late 1800s*   📖   **217**

Handbook Cross-Reference
For additional information about Claude Monet refer students to the Artist Profile, *Handbook* page **292**.
   Refer students to Artist Profile, *Handbook* page **293** for additional information about Berthe Morisot.

Vocabulary. Let students suggest several meanings for the noun *movement.* Then ask them to define such terms as *political movement* and *civil rights movement.* Keeping these definitions in mind, ask what students think the term *art movement* means.

Then help students consider the term *Impressionism:* What is an impression? What words have about the same meanings as *impression?* What words or phrases have about the opposite meaning? What do you think artists who espoused Impressionism tried to do in their art works?

Developing Concepts

Exploring Aesthetics. Help students examine and discuss Auguste Rodin's sculpture shown in Figure 14-8 on page **219**: Who is the subject of this work? What message or mood does the work communicate to you? Then present the following quotation from Rodin: "The main thing is to be moved, to love, to hope, to tremble, to live. . ." Ask: What does this quotation tell you about Rodin as an artist? How does it help you understand or appreciate this sculpture?

Using Art Criticism. Have students work in groups to examine and discuss the Impressionist paintings in Figures 4-5, 4-6, and 4-7. Let the members of each group begin by selecting one of the works (by Monet, Renoir, or Morisot). Then have the group members work together to describe, analyze, interpret, and judge the work. Finally, have the group members write a short interpretation of the painting, explaining the meaning or mood of the work.

Understanding Art History. Ask a group of volunteers to work together to research the Salon and its impact on the art works of France. Have the volunteers find answers to these questions: Who sponsored the first Salon? When did juries begin to accept and reject art works submitted for exhibitions in the Salon? What was the Salon des Refuses? When was it started and what was its purpose? Where did Impressionist artists exhibit their works? Why? When they have finished their research, let the volunteers share their findings with the rest of the class.

Remind students that, when the Impressionists were creating their startling new works of art, photographers were beginning to experiment with their new medium. In fact, the Impressionists' first exhibition was held in the studio of Nadar, a portrait photographer and caricaturist. Ask students to experiment with creating black-and-white paintings that might suggest the response of Impressionist artists to early black-and-white photographs. Have students use pencils to sketch scenes lightly onto drawing paper. Then have them imagine their scenes as black-and-white photographs: Which areas would be very dark? Which would be very light? Instruct them to dab black tempera paint onto their sketches for both the black and the gray areas. Then they should dab white tempera paint onto areas of light and over the black to create areas of gray. When the paint is dry, students may want to re-apply both black and white to their works. Remind them that the paint is to be applied in dabs—not mixed. Encourage students to compare and discuss their finished paintings.

Appreciating Cultural Diversity. Impressionism was basically an art movement of France. Artists in other countries, however, were influenced by the ideas and works of the Impressionists. Ask students to work in groups to study the life and works of one of these artists: James A. M. Whistler, Mary Cassatt, John Singer Sargent, Childe Hassam, Phillip Wilson Steer. To what extent could each artist be considered an Impressionist? How were the works of each influenced by the French Impressionists? After their research is complete, have the groups share and discuss what they have learned.

▶ Figure 14–7 The artist has painted her sister. How might it be harder to paint a portrait of someone you know? In what ways might it be easier?

Berthe Morisot. *The Artist's Sister at a Window.* 1869. Canvas. 54.8 x 46.3 cm (21⅝ x 18¼"). National Gallery of Art, Washington, D.C. Ailsa Mellon Bruce Collection.

Berthe Morisot

Another important member of the Impressionist movement, Berthe Morisot (**behrt** maw-ree-**zoh**), had strong family ties to art. Her great-grandfather, Jean Honoré Fragonard (**zhahnh** oh-nor-**ay** frah-goh-**nahrh**), was an important painter of the Rococo period. Her parents solidly supported her decision to follow a career as an artist. Like Renoir, Morisot chose portraits as a main avenue of expression for her work. One of these is pictured in Figure 14–7. Notice how the artist uses rapidly applied dabs of paint to capture her subject's expression. What mood does the artist communicate in this painting?

SCULPTURE

A sculptor working during the same time as the Impressionist movement was a man named Auguste Rodin (oh-**goost** roh-**dan**). Rodin used bits of wax or clay in his creations. Their rough, bumpy surfaces make his sculptures appear as though in a flickering light. Examine Rodin's work in Figure 14–8. Note how the sculpture looks as if it were created in an instant.

Background Information
Auguste Rodin (France, 1840–1917) is generally credited with revitalizing the art of sculpture and returning it to the concerns and attention of the public. Rodin was profoundly affected by the works of Michelangelo (Italy, 1475–1564). He created his first major work, *The Age of Bronze,* which depicts a naturalistic, lifelike figure. Viewers found the sculpture shockingly different from the works to which they were accustomed, and some accused Rodin of taking a cast from a live model.

Rodin was commissioned to create a huge bronze door for the Museum of Decorative Arts in Paris. The work was *The Gates of Hell,* inspired by Dante's *Inferno.* It fascinated Rodin for the rest of his life; though he did not complete it, the complex work with nearly 200 separate figures is a masterpiece. Rodin deliberately left some of his sculptures incomplete, so that the figure merges into the stone from which it is cut. His *Balzac* of 1897 is a most moving example of this kind of sculpture.

▲ Figure 14–8　This is a sculpture of a painter from the seventeenth century named Claude Lorrain. How has Rodin shown the artist at work here?

Auguste Rodin. *Claude Lorrain*. Musee Rodin. Paris, France.

▲ Figure 14–9　Student work. Object painted in Impressionist style.

✔CHECK YOUR UNDERSTANDING

1. What was the Salon? How was the Salon tied to the beginning of the Impressionist movement?
2. What are some of the ways people reacted at the first showing of Impressionist works in 1874?
3. What did the Impressionists try to capture in their pictures? Where did they go to find subjects for their work?
4. What sorts of paintings did Auguste Renoir and Berthe Morisot specialize in?
5. In what area of art did Auguste Rodin work? How did he give his works the look and feel of Impressionist paintings?

Lesson 3　*European Art — Late 1800s*　　**219**

Painting an Impressionist Landscape

Painting an Impressionist Landscape

Impressionist artists, you have learned, were interested in painting everyday scenes they saw around them. To Claude Monet, in particular, it made little difference whether he was painting a haystack, a few ordinary trees, or—as in Figure 14–10—a bridge. What mattered was how best to show the colors reflected from these subjects. Study the painting in Figure 14–10. Up close the picture appears to be little more than dabs of color.

WHAT YOU WILL LEARN

Use tempera to paint a summer landscape. You will use a variety of colors, values, and intensities, applying these as dots of paint.

Warm colors—yellows, reds, oranges—will be used to paint foreground objects. Cool colors—blues, purples, greens—will be used for background objects. Together these colors will be used to create an illusion of space. (See Figure 14–11.)

WHAT YOU WILL NEED

- Pencil and sheets of sketch paper
- Sheet of white paper, 9 x 12 inches (23 x 30 cm)
- Several brushes, tempera paint, and mixing tray

▶ Figure 14–10 Monet painted 16 separate views of this bridge. The scenes show the bridge at all different times of day. Some, moreover, show the bridge during rain or heavy fog. What reason might the artist have had for making so many paintings of the same scene?

Claude Monet. *Waterloo Bridge.* 1903. Oil on canvas. 65.4 x 92.9 cm (25⅝ x 36½"). Worcester Art Museum, Worcester, Massachusetts.

Sidebar (left column)

Painting an Impressionist Landscape

LESSON PLAN
(pages 220–221)

Objectives
After completing this lesson, students will be able to:
- Use tempera to paint summer landscapes in the Impressionist style.
- Describe, analyze, interpret, and judge their own landscapes.

Supplies
- Slides or reproductions of paintings and drawings by Edgar Degas (if available).
- Pencils; sheets of sketch paper; sheets of white paper, 9 x 12 inches (23 x 30 cm); brushes; tempera paint; mixing trays.

> **TRB Resource**
> - 14-7 *Experiment in the Styles of the 1800s and 1900s,* (studio)

TEACHING THE LESSON

Getting Started

Motivator. Write the following quotation from Edgar Degas on the chalkboard: "One sees as one wishes to see, and it is that falsity that constitutes art." (If you have slides or reproductions of some of Degas's paintings or drawings, display them with the quotation.) Let several volunteers restate the quotation in their own words. Then ask: What do these words tell you about the artist who said them? What do they tell you about Impressionism?

Vocabulary. Review with students the meaning of the terms *warm colors* and *cool colors:* What are examples of each? Why are some colors called warm and others cool? Also help students recall the definitions of *value* and *intensity:* What is the difference between the value of a hue and the intensity of that hue? What colors can you mix to change a hue's value? What colors can you mix to change a hue's intensity?

220

Background Information
When Claude Monet (France, 1840–1926) was still in his teens, he was persuaded to join Eugene Boudin (France, 1824–1898) in an outdoor painting expedition. Of this experience Monet later wrote, "It was as if a veil had suddenly been torn from my eyes. I understood. I grasped what painting was capable of being." At least in part as a result of this experience, Monet spent his artistic career painting from nature, nearly always out of doors. He even had a boat constructed as

a studio, so he could paint the water and the light's reflection as he observed them.

Monet and a group of his friends, including Paul Cézanne (France, 1839–1906), Edgar Degas (France, 1834–1917), Camille Pissarro (France, 1830–1903), Pierre Auguste Renoir (France, 1841–1914), and Alfred Sisley (French-born, 1839–1899) organized an independent exhibition in Paris in 1874. There Monet's painting *Impression: Sunrise* inspired the derisive comment that gave the art movement its name.

WHAT YOU WILL DO

1. On a sheet of paper, list the different items that might be found in a landscape painting, such as a tree, stream, and valley. Pick three items from this list. Combine them in simple pencil sketches of warm, sunlit landscapes. Use the space technique of size to place some of the objects near to the viewer. Place others farther back. Draw only very light outlines or indications of your shapes.

2. Choose the best of your sketches. Draw it on the sheet of white paper. Fill the whole sheet with your drawing.

3. Without mixing colors, load a medium-pointed brush with a cool color of paint. Use dots and dabs of the brush to apply the paint to a background object. Pick a second cool hue that, when seen from a distance, will blend with the first to create a new hue. For example, dots of green placed next to dots of blue would create blue-green. Dots of complementary colors can be added to lessen or increase the intensity of the colors.

4. Use warm colors for foreground objects, applying paint in the same fashion. Stand back from your work from time to time. This will help you make sure the colors selected are blending as you expect them to.

5. When the paint is dry, display your work. View all the works, first from a distance, then close up.

OTHER STUDIO IDEAS

- Using colored markers, create a winter landscape in the Impressionist style. Again, make a list of objects. This time, however, include those you might see on a winter's day. Think how you might go about showing the effects of sunlight on snow.

●● Using watercolors, paint a view of the bridge in Figure 14–10 as it might appear at night. Begin by sketching the lines of the bridge. Think about what might serve as a source of light in your painting. Be sure to apply your paint as dots and dashes of color.

EXAMINING YOUR WORK

- **Describe**   Identify the landscape objects you used.
- **Analyze**   Point out the variety of hues you used in your work. Show the different values and intensities of paint. Tell whether you used warm colors for the foreground and cool ones for the background. State whether your use of warm and cool colors helps create a sense of space in your work.
- **Interpret**   Point out the features that help viewers understand the scene is of a warm, sunny day.
- **Judge**   Explain in what ways your painting shares the look and feel of the Impressionist work in Figure 14–11. Tell whether any part of your work is more successful than the rest. Explain.

▲ **Figure 14–11   Student work. Impressionist landscape.**

Lesson 4   *Painting an Impressionist Landscape*   **221**

Developing Concepts

Exploring Aesthetics. Let students discuss their responses to Claude Monet's *Waterloo Bridge,* shown in Figure 14-11: What mood do you think this work was intended to create? How does this painting make you feel? What aspects of the work help you identify it as an Impressionist painting?

Understanding Art History. Ask volunteers to research pointillism: How was the development of pointillism related to Impressionism? How was pointillism different from Impressionism? Who were the best-known pointillists? Have the volunteers share their findings with the rest of the class.

Following Up

Closure. Let students present their landscape painting to the rest of the class, identifying the aspect of the work of which they are most proud. Display all the paintings in the classroom. Then have each student write a one-paragraph analysis of any landscape on display, following the "Analyze" instructions in "Examining Your Work."

Evaluation. Review students' landscapes, listen to their presentations of their own paintings, and read their analyses of other students' paintings.

Reteaching. Ask students to create second versions of their landscapes, this time using different media: colored markers, crayons, watercolors, or colored pencils. Let students compare and discuss their new works: How have the images and mood changed? Which of your two works most effectively suggests the style of Impressionist paintings?

Enrichment. Let students work in small groups to discuss written works that best accompany Impressionist paintings: Do poems, stories, autobiographical sketches, or essays seem most appropriate? Why? Then have each student write a short piece inspired by his or her own landscape painting.

Handbook Cross-Reference
In this lesson students will be asked to match the colors, textures, and patterns of the walls and floor. See *Handbook,* page **280,** for tips on how to make lighter and darker values of the same color. Remind students to add small amounts of the basic color to white for a light value. If they want a darker value, a small amount of black should be added to the basic color. Stress *small amounts.* More can always be added, but too much means starting over.

Developing Perceptual Skills
Have students select a site to observe how changing light affects the mood of a scene at different times. Allow enough time for them to schedule observations at various odd hours. Have them record when they made their observations, the quality and color of light present at each time, and how it altered the mood or character of the scene. Have them discuss their discoveries.

ANSWERS TO "CHAPTER 14 REVIEW"

Building Vocabulary

1. Neoclassic
2. Romanticism
3. landscape
4. Salon
5. art movement
6. Impressionism

Reviewing Art Facts

7. Artists began using a new style of art because they believed the events occurring during the French Revolution were equal in importance to the rise and fall of Greece and Rome. They called this the Neoclassical style.
8. Jacques-Louis David was an important painter of the Neoclassical school.
9. People were weary of war and political unrest, and the artists began to develop works that would be uplifting and portray life as it *might* be.
10. Two themes found in Delacroix's work are action-filled adventures and far-off places.
11. Turner felt that using blurred images and glowing colors would free viewers to interpret his pictures in their own ways.
12. Claude Monet and Pierre Auguste Renoir were turned down by the Salon. They developed Impressionism.
13. Berthe Morisot belonged to the Impressionist movement.
14. Auguste Rodin used a rough, bumpy surface to make his sculptures look as if a flickering light were playing over the surface.

Thinking About Art

1. Answers will vary. Students should mention Impressionism, Neoclassicism or Romanticism and demonstrate they know the characteristics of the style they name.
2. Answers will vary. Similarities include shimmering light and water with reflections. Differences include Turner's busy ship/dock scene vs. Monet's quiet nature setting.
3. Artists whose work had been rejected by the Salon decided to hold an exhibition of their own in 1874.
4. Perhaps she was rejected because the critics paid closer attention to the male artists. She was probably well regarded by her fellow Impressionists.

BUILDING VOCABULARY

Number a sheet of paper from 1 to 6. After each number, write the term from the box that best matches each description below.

art movement	Neoclassic
Impressionism	Romanticism
landscape	Salon

1. An art style that borrowed from the early classical period of ancient Greece and Rome.
2. A style of art that found its subjects in the world of the dramatic and exotic.
3. A drawing or painting focusing on mountains, trees, or other natural scenery.
4. An annual exhibition of art.
5. A trend formed when a group of artists band together to create works of a single style.
6. A style that attempted to capture the rapidly changing effects of light on objects.

REVIEWING ART FACTS

Number a sheet of paper from 7 to 14. Answer each question in a complete sentence.

7. How did the French Revolution help give rise to a new art style? What was the name of this style?
8. Name an important painter of the Neoclassic school.
9. What events helped bring about the Romantic movement?
10. What sorts of themes are found in the paintings of Eugène Delacroix?
11. Why did Joseph M. W. Turner use glowing colors and blurred images in his works?
12. Name two artists whose works were turned down by the Salon. Tell what movement they went on to develop.
13. To what school of art did Berthe Morisot belong?
14. What is Auguste Rodin's special contribution to art?

THINKING ABOUT ART

On a sheet of paper, answer each question in a sentence or two.

1. **Analyze.** Imagine you lived in France during the 1800s. Which of the three art styles you learned about in this chapter would best fit your view of life? Explain your answer using information from the chapter.
2. **Compare and Contrast.** Look at the landscape paintings by Joseph M. W. Turner (Figure 14–3) and Claude Monet (Figure 14–5). In what ways are the two works alike in subject matter, composition, and content? In what ways are they different in these three areas?
3. **Summarize.** What prompted the Impressionists to decide to hold their own art show in 1874?
4. **Extend.** Berthe Morisot's paintings were ignored by critics during her lifetime. Why do you think this was so? How did her fellow Impressionists regard her?

MAKING ART CONNECTIONS

1. **Social Studies.** You are looking at the painting by Eugène Delacroix (Figure 14–2) with two friends. One notes that some of the figures seem to be in awkward poses. The other remarks that the artist "probably had problems drawing these figures." How would you reply?
2. **History.** Another art movement that took shape in the 1800s is one called Realism. In an encyclopedia or other library resource, learn about this movement. Find the names of key artists and what they were trying to show in their works. Share your findings with the class.

LOOKING AT THE DETAILS

The detail shown below is from Auguste Renoir's *Oarsmen at Chatou*. Study the detail and answer the following questions using complete sentences.

1. What gives this painting the "impression" of realism? What defines it as a painting done in the Impressionist style?
2. Look at the credit line. In what year was it painted? How would you describe clothing styles of this period?
3. Compare this detail to the complete work on page **208**. Does this look like the type of everyday scenes that Impressionist painters preferred? Explain your answer.
4. What time of the day do you think is shown in the painting? How is this effect created?

Auguste Renoir. *Oarsmen at Chatou*. 1879. Canvas. (Detail.) 81.3 x 100.3 cm (32 x 39½"). National Gallery of Art, Washington, D.C. Gift of Sam A. Lewisohn.

ANSWERS TO "LOOKING AT THE DETAILS"

1. The use of realistic colors, shapes and forms, and the subject matter give this work the impression of reality. Also the quality of the light contributes to its realistic feeling. It is an Impressionist painting because of its lack of definitive detail both in the subjects and objects, its blurred colors between different objects, and the visible brush strokes.
2. It was painted in 1879. Students' responses will vary but may include: Their dress is tailored and formal.
3. It seems like a work that Impressionist painters preferred because it is outdoors and movement and light on the water is shown.
4. The time of the day is probably early afternoon. The use of light and shadows create this effect.

Chapter Evaluation

The purpose of this chapter is to introduce students to European art of the early 1800s. Methods of evaluation include:

1. Have students write a short paper comparing the works of art from early classical periods of Greece and Rome to the Neoclassic style.
2. Divide students into small groups and have them write a script for a play that could be performed on a Neoclassic stage set.
3. Have students complete Chapter 14 Test, (TRB, Resource 14-8).

Art of the Late Nineteenth Century

Chapter Scan

TRB Resources

- 15-9 Chapter Test
- Color Transparency 29
- Color Transparency 30

TEACHING THE CHAPTER

Introducing the Art Work

Direct students' attention to Edgar Degas's *Dancers Practicing at the Bar*. Inform them that Edgar Degas was a French painter in the nineteenth century. Degas's earliest works were influenced by the Renaissance masters. As his artistic skill matured, he learned to incorporate that influence into his own creative vision. Living in Paris, Degas absorbed different styles of various artists of his day, including Manet, Cézanne, and Renoir. Degas came to be known as the most unpredictable master of the Impressionist movement. Along with some of his fellow Impressionists, Degas felt the need to expand his work from placing sole emphasis on the importance of light, to the inclusion of both composition and the expression of mood. With this, Degas began painting in the Impressionist style, but moved into the Post-Impressionist style. Degas portrayed intimately human scenes, and many of his works reflect very private moments.

▲ How do you think composition and content affect the mood of this painting by Degas? Do you think that the artist has expressed a sense of realism in this work?

Edgar Degas. *Dancers Practicing at the Bar*. Date Unknown. Oil colors, mixed with turpentine, on canvas. 75.6 x 81.3 cm (29¾ x 32"). Metropolitan Museum of Art, New York, New York. H. O. Havemeyer Collection.

Art of the Late Nineteenth Century

To some artists working toward the end of the 1800s, Impressionism was the perfect means of self-expression. To others, the new style raised as many questions as it answered. These artists, who had been working as Impressionists, felt that something was missing from their pictures. Their own works struck them, for one reason or another, as "unfinished."

In time, this dissatisfaction led to still newer forms of expression. One is showcased in the work at the left. In this chapter you will learn about such efforts and the pioneers behind them.

OBJECTIVES

After completing this chapter, you will be able to:

- Identify the artists who became known as the Post-Impressionists.
- Describe different ways the Post-Impressionists tried to solve the problems of Impressionism.
- Name artists who affected the development of American art of the 1800s.
- Create art works in the style of the Post-Impressionists.

WORDS YOU WILL LEARN

arbitrary colors   Post-Impressionism
optical colors   Realism
Pointillism

ARTISTS YOU WILL MEET

Mary Cassatt   Vincent van Gogh
Paul Cézanne   Winslow Homer
Edgar Degas   Albert Pinkham Ryder
Thomas Eakins   Georges Seurat
Paul Gauguin   Henry O. Tanner

225

Examining the Art Work

Tell students that *Dancers Practicing at the Bar* is a Post-Impressionist work. Explain how Degas uses light, not only to give depth and radiance to the subjects and objects, but also to create a sense of feeling. Point out the subtle quality of the light and how it helps to create a quiet, contemplative mood. Explain that the composition builds on this mood by showing a large empty floor space, creating the feeling that these two figures are alone. The diagonal lines direct the viewer's eye across that space to the subjects. Point out how Degas doesn't blur the lines between objects, creating a smoother, gentler feeling and a more definitive composition than the Impressionist style.

Discussing the Art Work

Ask students to think about the type of balance displayed in this work. Ask: What is the point of emphasis? What provides balance for the yellow bow? Direct students' attention to the floor and wall space and explain that if the painting was folded in half, the dark area in the lower right takes up about as much space as the brighter area in the upper left. The larger darker watering can is on the same diagonal line as the brighter bow. The left dancer's standing leg could be considered the middle of the painting and her extended leg to the left balances her head and arms on the right. Explain that all of these things create asymmetrical balance and that the overall painting also displays informal balance.

Ask students to think about how differently this painting would look if Degas had placed the figures in the center of the canvas, rather than from the perspective of the left. Explain how Degas was influenced by photography and the unique perspectives it portrayed.

Tell the students that in this chapter they will learn about the development of Post-Impressionism and the artists who affected American art. They will also create their own art work in the Post-Impressionist style.

Building Self-Esteem

Tell students that in this chapter they will see works of art by painters who were called Realists. One of these Realists, Thomas Eakins, was criticized because he painted his subjects so accurately and honestly that many rejected his portraits and others destroyed them. It was his misfortune to live in a time when painting was sometimes valued more for social than artistic reasons. Walt Whitman, however, preferred the portrait Eakins painted of him above all others, saying, "I never knew of but one artist, and that's Tom Eakins, who could resist the temptation to see what they thought ought to be rather than what is." Eakins sacrificed popularity to paint realistically. Help students understand that perceiving accurately is one of the most important skills in communicating artistically.

Objectives

After completing this lesson, students will be able to:

- Identify the artists who became known as the Post-Impressionists.
- Describe different ways the artists tried to solve the problems of Impressionism.
- Distinguish between arbitrary colors and optical colors.
- Make paintings in the style of Paul Cézanne.

Supplies

- Sheets of sketch paper, colored pencils.
- One bottle (of dark glass, if possible), sheets of white paper, pencils, tempera paint, brushes.
- Art books that include reproductions of Impressionist and Post-Impressionist paintings.

TRB Resources

- 15-1 *Tracing Art Movements,* (reproducible master)
- 15-2 *Bring History Into the Arts,* (cooperative learning)
- 15-3 *Art Nouveau,* (aesthetics)
- 15-4 *Cézanne and Form,* (art criticism)

TEACHING THE LESSON

Getting Started

Motivator. Introduce this lesson by having students review the definitions of *composition* and *content.* Then ask: Can works of art be created without composition or content? How does a viewer who emphasizes composition approach a work of art? How does a viewer who emphasizes content approach a work of art? How does a primary interest in composition affect the work of a painter? How does a primary interest in content affect a painter's work?

Art of the Post-Impressionists

Have you ever created something that pleased you at first but didn't seem right later? This was the case with several artists working toward the close of the 1800s. These artists worked as Impressionists but came to feel that there were problems with this style. The more they studied their art, the more dissatisfied they became. Art, they believed, should do more than just show the changing effects of light on objects. **Post-Impressionism** is *the name given to an art movement that appeared after the Impressionist movement.* The word *post* means "after."

▲ Figure 15–1 **The artist repeated colors throughout this work to give it a sense of harmony. Can you find places where colors have been repeated?**

Paul Cézanne. *Mont Sainte-Victoire.* 1902–04. Oil on canvas. 69.8 x 89.5 cm (27½ x 35¼"). Philadelphia Museum of Art, Philadelphia, Pennsylvania. George W. Elkins Collection.

Background Information

The term *Post-Impressionism* was first used in 1910, when Roger Fry (England, 1866–1934) arranged a London exhibit entitled "Manet and the Post-Impressionists." Some of the artists represented, such as Paul Cézanne (France, 1839–1906), Paul Gauguin (France, 1848–1903), and Vincent van Gogh (Holland, 1853–1890), were by this time already dead and still unknown. The exhibition caused laughter among members of the public and anger among serious art critics. All the works in the exhibit seemed to attack traditional ideas of good art.

The impact of Post-Impressionism was decisive and diverse. Twentieth-century art movements such as Fauvism, Cubism, and the Nabis were strongly influenced by the works and ideas of the Post-Impressionists. Non-representational artists, such as Wassily Kandinsky (Russian-born, 1866–1944), and almost all modern graphic artists also developed largely from Post-Impressionism.

In this lesson you will learn about the key artists of the Post-Impressionist movement. You will also look at the important contributions they made to the history of art.

POST-IMPRESSIONIST ART

While the Post-Impressionists agreed that there were problems with Impressionism, their solutions to these problems differed. Some argued that art should be more carefully designed — that composition should not be forgotten. Others claimed feelings and emotions should be emphasized — that content deserved its rightful place. Still others championed design and mood — both composition *and* content — as important features.

Composition

One of the Post-Impressionists was also, interestingly, an original member of the Impressionist movement. This artist's name was Paul Cézanne (say-**zan**). Cézanne objected to the loss of composition arising from the Impressionist blurring of shapes. His solution was to use patches of color. These he joined together like pieces of a puzzle to create solid-looking forms.

The painting in Figure 15–1 illustrates Cézanne's technique. This mountain near the artist's home in southern France was one of his favorite subjects. He painted it more than 60 times and from nearly every angle.

◀ Figure 15–2 Besides their bright colors, van Gogh's paintings are known for their rich textures. He often squeezed his colors from the tubes right onto the canvas. He would then use his brush, fingers, or anything else at hand to spread the paint with swirling strokes.

Vincent van Gogh. *Hospital at Saint-Remy.* 1889. The Armand Hammer Collection, Los Angeles, California.

Lesson 1   *Art of the Post-Impressionists*   227

Then have students experiment with drawings that emphasize either composition or content. Have students choose a particular section of the room or a specific object in the room, and ask all students to sketch that section or object. Let each student choose as a primary objective either to show how he or she can use a principle of art (composition) or to show how he or she feels about the subject (content). Let students share and discuss their finished sketches: Which approach did each student use?

Vocabulary. Let students discuss the meanings of the words *arbitrary* and *optical,* using dictionaries if they like: What other words have about the same meaning as *arbitrary?* What sentences can you make up, using the word *arbitrary?* What does the word *optical* mean? What part of the body is associated with the word *optical?* Then encourage students to speculate about the meanings of the terms *arbitrary colors* and *optical colors;* let a volunteer check the suggested definitions against the definitions given in the Glossary.

Developing Concepts

Exploring Aesthetics. Guide students in examining and discussing the three paintings reproduced in this lesson. Direct students' attention to Paul Cézanne's *Mont Sainte-Victoire,* Figure 15-1, and ask: What is the subject of this painting? What message or mood do you think it communicates? What indicates that Cézanne's main interest is the composition of this painting? Which elements and principles of art can you identify in this work?

Next, direct attention to Vincent van Gogh's *Hospital at Saint-Remy,* Figure 15-2, and ask: What is the subject of this work? How have the principles of art been used to organize the visual elements? What indicates that van Gogh's main interest is the content of his work? What idea or feeling does this work communicate to you?

Finally, have students examine Paul Gauguin's *Ancestors of Tehamana,* Figure 15-3, and ask: What is the subject of this painting? How has Gauguin used the principles of art to organize the elements in his work? What idea or feeling does this painting communicate to you? In this particular painting, do you think Gauguin was more interested in composition or in content? Why?

Handbook Cross-Reference
For additional information about Paul Cézanne refer students to the Artist Profile, *Handbook* page **289**.

Note
Vincent van Gogh's career in art spanned just ten years. In that time he had one public showing, got one favorable review, and sold one painting.

228

Using Art Criticism. Help students compare the three paintings by Cézanne (Figure 15-1), van Gogh (Figure 15-2), and Gauguin (Figure 15-3). Ask students to consider the works in terms of all three aesthetic views: Does each painting succeed depicting its subject effectively? Why, or why not? Does each painting succeed in terms of its composition? Why, or why not? Does each painting succeed in communicating its message or mood? Why, or why not? Then ask: Which painting do you consider the most successful work of art? Why is there no "correct" answer to this question?

Understanding Art History. Have students work in groups to consider the development of Post-Impressionism from Impressionism. Ask the members of each group to select one of the paintings reproduced in this lesson and compare it to two of Claude Monet's Impressionist paintings, *Banks of the Seine* shown in Figure 14-5 on page **216** and *Waterloo Bridge* shown in Figure 14-10 on page **220**. What changes from Impressionism can you identify in the Post-Impressionist painting? Do you consider the Post-Impressionist painting an improvement over the Impressionist style—or simply a change? Why?

In addition, ask several volunteers to research these questions: Did any painters who worked in the Impressionist style go on to paint as Post-Impressionists? Who were they? What characterized their Post-Impressionist works? Ask these volunteers to share their finding with the rest of the class.

Developing Studio Skills. Ask students to review the drawings they made earlier, emphasizing either composition or content. (See "Motivator.") Now have students draw the same object again, this time trying to give equal emphasis to composition and to content. How does the new drawing differ from the first?

▲ **Figure 15–3** How many different objects draw attention to the figure on the left? How does the use of color help communicate the difference between the background and the main subject?

Paul Gauguin. *Ancestors of Tehamana*. 1893. Oil on canvas. 76.3 x 54.3 cm (30 x 21"). Art Institute of Chicago, Chicago, Illinois. Gift of Mr. and Mrs. Charles Deering McCormick.

Background Information

Paul Gauguin (France, 1848–1903) was a rebel. He took painting lessons and enjoyed painting as an amateur so much that he resigned from his successful brokerage business in 1883 to paint full time. His family suffered financially as a result, and his art never sold well enough in his lifetime to support them. His attitude about color was as adventuresome as his willingness to change careers mid-life. He said, "A meter of green is greener than a centimeter if you wish to express greenness. . . And that shadow, a little bluish? Don't be afraid. Paint it as blue as you can." He chose to spend the later years of his life in the South Seas, where he painted primitive life and used his imaginative sense of color to convey his love of the simple life lived there.

Cézanne's main interest, however, was not showing the mountain as it really looked. It was to demonstrate how color patches could be turned in different directions to create a solid form. Notice how the artist uses the same color patches to form buildings, trees, and other objects. All are combined to create a richly colored pattern of geometric forms.

Content

The most famous of the Post-Impressionists was Vincent van Gogh (**goh**). Van Gogh's goal was not, like the Impressionists', to reproduce what the eye saw. It was to capture his own deepest feelings about a subject. He expresses these feelings with twisted lines and forms, intense colors, and rich textures.

Near the end of his short life, van Gogh suffered from mental illness. Hoping for a cure, he entered a private hospital. It was there that van Gogh painted the work in Figure 15–2 on page 227. Take a moment to examine this picture. The artist treats the viewer to his private view of the world of the hospital. We see yellow walls and several small figures. But the twisting trees against a blue sky are the true focus of the painting. Through them, the artist communicates his mental agony and his sensitivity to the forces of nature. What principle of art is used to organize the curving lines of the trees?

Composition and Content

Paul Gauguin (goh-**ganh**) also used color and shapes in new and exciting ways. He also created art works that could be enjoyed for their decorative appearance.

The painting in Figure 15–3 shows a scene in the South Seas, where Gauguin spent part of his life. The artist has portrayed his wife against a decorated background. The painting has two parts, a portrait and a scene from the past. The composition hints at the relationship between past and present. Notice how the fan points to the small figure painted on the wall. Like most of Gauguin's other works, this one is filled with meaningful colors. **Arbitrary** (**ahr**-buh-trehr-ee)

colors are *colors chosen to communicate different feelings*. **Optical colors**, on the other hand, are *colors viewers actually see*. What feelings do you associate with each of the different colors in Gauguin's painting?

✔ CHECK YOUR UNDERSTANDING

1. Define *Post-Impressionism*. Name two leading Post-Impressionists.
2. What were three different solutions Post-Impressionists found to the problems of Impressionism?
3. What was Cézanne's goal? What was van Gogh's goal?
4. What is arbitrary color? Which two Post-Impressionists used arbitrary color in their works?
5. What is optical color?

LESSON PLAN
(pages 230–231)

Objectives
After completing this lesson, students will be able to:
- Create paintings in the style of one of the Post-Impressionists.
- Describe, analyze, interpret, and judge their own paintings.

Supplies
- Sheets of white paper, tempera paints, brushes.
- Pencils; sheets of white paper, 9 x 12 inches (23 x 30 cm); tempera paint; brushes; mixing trays.

> **TRB Resource**
> - 15-5 *Post-Impressionist Self Portrait,* (studio)

TEACHING THE LESSON

Getting Started

Motivator. Explain to students that they will be creating paintings in the style of various Post-Impressionists; they can begin by trying out all three painting techniques. Ask each student to work with only two colors of paint and to work on a single sheet of paper. On separate areas of the paper, have students try painting small dots, painting swirling and twisted lines, and painting flat, colorful shapes. Emphasize that students should experiment with the feel and effect of each style of painting. As they work, let them discuss each technique and their reactions to it: Which process do you most enjoy using? Why? Which effect do you find most interesting? Why?

Vocabulary. Write the word *pointillism* on the chalkboard. Ask students to identify the smaller word they see within this word. Then ask: Which of the painting techniques you just tried is most likely to be called Pointillism? Why?

Painting in the Style of Post-Impressionists

The painting in Figure 15–4 shows yet another Post-Impressionist solution to the problems posed by Impressionism. The work is by an artist named Georges Seurat (**zhorzh** suh-**rah**). Like Cézanne, Seurat felt the Impressionists' attempt to show the blurring effect of sunlight on forms was misguided. Seurat's solution was to use *a technique in which small, carefully placed dots of color are used to create forms*. This technique, called **Pointillism** (**poynt**-uh-liz-uhm), reached its height in Seurat's painting of a sunny summer day in a park. When seen from close up, the picture looks like a grouping of tiny dots. When the viewer stands back, however, the picture totally changes. The dots seem to blend together to create new colors and clear shapes.

WHAT YOU WILL LEARN

You will create a painting in the style of Seurat or one of the other Post-Impressionists. Use color, line, shape, or texture in the manner of the artist you choose. (See Figure 15–5).

WHAT YOU WILL NEED

- Pencil
- Sheet of white paper, 9 x 12 inches (23 x 30 cm)
- Tempera paint, several brushes, and mixing tray

SAFETY TIP
When an assignment calls for paints, use watercolors, liquid tempera, or school acrylics.

▶ **Figure 15–4** This large painting is the artist's best known work. Thousands of colored dots are arranged with great precision to create the simple forms you see. Why do you suppose the artist made the work as large as he did? What kind of mood does it communicate to you?

Georges Seurat. *Sunday Afternoon on the Island of La Grande Jatte.* 1884–86. Oil on canvas. 207.6 x 308 cm (81½ x 121¼"). Art Institute of Chicago, Chicago, Illinois. Helen Birch Bartlett Memorial Collection.

Background Information
The artistic career of Georges Seurat (France, 1859–1891) was brief but brilliant; he is regarded as having a pivotal role in the development of modern art. Seurat's first experiments were with light and color. He was interested in transferring the perfect combination of light and color, as seen in nature, to the canvas. To this end, Seurat studied not only the great art works of ancient and Renaissance times, but also the theory of color and the science of optics. He set himself the goal of developing what he called a "formula for optical painting."

In 1884 Seurat met Paul Signac (France, 1863–1935), who became his friend and his disciple. Together, the two refined the techniques of Pointillism; Signac explained the theories of painting with scientific precision in his 1899 work, *From Delacroix to Neo-Impressionism.*

WHAT YOU WILL DO

1. Look once again at the paintings in Figures 15–2, 15–3, and 15–4. With classmates, discuss the main features of each artist's style.
2. Look through the pages of a magazine or newspaper. Look for a black-and-white illustration that has an interesting design or communicates a mood.
3. Using pencil, lightly redo the illustration on the sheet of white paper. Make your drawing large enough to fill the whole sheet. Keep the shapes in your drawing simple. Do not include details.
4. Finish and paint your work using one of the following styles: (a) With a fine-tipped brush, cover your drawing with closely spaced tiny dots of paint. Use colors opposite each other on the color wheel to create new hues and intensities. In this way, your work will resemble the Pointillist style of Seurat. (b) With a medium brush, apply paint in a swirling motion, creating twisted lines and shapes. Use bright, arbitrary colors to express a certain mood or feeling. In this way, your work will look like that of van Gogh. (c) Paint your drawing as a pattern of flat, colorful shapes. Paint dark outlines around these shapes. This will give your painting the same decorative look as Gauguin's.
5. When the paint is dry, display your work alongside those of classmates. See whether you can identify the Post-Impressionist style in the works of your fellow students.

OTHER STUDIO IDEAS

- Make another painting in the Post-Impressionist style, this time in the style of Cézanne. Base your painting on a familiar scene in your community or town. Use two hues of paint. Make sure to turn your color patches in different directions.

- Complete a painting in which you combine Seurat's Pointillism style with van Gogh's concern for expressing emotions and feelings. When you are finished, tell whether you think the Pointillism style is an effective one to use when you are trying to express emotions. Explain why or why not.

EXAMINING YOUR WORK

- **Describe** Hold your painting next to the illustration on which it is based. Tell whether you can identify the objects in the illustration.
- **Analyze** Explain how you used color, line, shape, and texture. Tell which Post-Impressionist artist you used as a guide in using these elements. Point to places in your work where your use of elements was similar to that of your chosen artist.
- **Interpret** State what mood or feeling, if any, you were attempting to express. Note whether others are able to pinpoint this mood or feeling.
- **Judge** Compare your work with that of the artist who served as your guide. Tell whether your painting is similar in style to that work. Show in what ways, if any, your work is different.

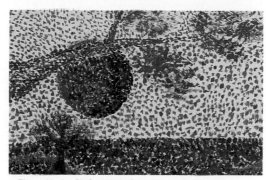

▲ Figure 15–5 Student work. Post-Impressionist painting.

Developing Concepts

Exploring Aesthetics. Let students examine Georges Seurat's *Sunday Afternoon on the Island of La Grand Jatte*, Figure 15-4, and discuss their responses: What do you notice first about this work? How do you feel when you look at it? How does the technique of Pointillism affect your response to the painting?

Understanding Art History. Ask students to research the development and the influence of Georges Seurat. With whom did he study? By what other artists was he most influenced? How did his works influence other artists? Let students share and discuss their findings.

Appreciating Cultural Diversity. Japanese woodblock prints had an important influence on the works of certain Post-Impressionist artists, including some by Seurat. Ask volunteers to find reproductions of several Japanese prints and to share them with the rest of the class: How might these works have affected the paintings of the Post-Impressionists?

Following Up

Closure. Have students work in groups to discuss their paintings in the style of Post-Impressionists. Can the other students identify the style chosen by each group member? Can they identify the mood or feeling each group member intended to express? What do group members like best about each painting?

Evaluation. Review students' paintings and consider their contributions to the "Closure" group discussions.

Reteaching. Have students work with partners to further explore the techniques of Post-Impressionist painting. Let each pair of students choose a subject and make three small paintings of it, each in a different Post-Impressionist technique.

Enrichment. Ask students: What was the primary intention of the painting you created in this lesson? Then have each student write a short story, poem, or essay that has the same intention.

Cooperative Learning

In this studio lesson students are given the choice of painting in one of three different styles; that of Seurat, van Gogh, or Gauguin. After the paintings have been completed, let the students who have selected the same style share their paintings. Let them discuss how their interpretations have differed. Let them compare the choice of colors they have used as well as their experiences using the particular style they chose. Did those using Pointillism finish later than the others? Were they able to convey a mood as easily as the other two groups? Encourage the sharing of ideas about how students felt when they were painting in the style of their choice.

American Painting in the Late 1800s

LESSON PLAN
(pages 232–235)

Objectives
After completing this lesson, students will be able to:
- Name artists who affected the development of American art in the 1800s.
- Describe the art movement known as Realism.
- Draw nighttime landscapes, emphasizing the element of texture.

Supplies
- Small objects, either manufactured or natural, brought in by the students; sheets of drawing paper; colored pencils or markers.
- Sheets of drawing paper; pencils; crayons; pieces of burlap; bits of dried grass and leaves; other materials with rough surfaces, such as scraps of sandpaper, bricks, and so on.
- Sheets of drawing paper, colored markers or pencils.

> **TRB Resources**
> - 15-6 *The American Landscape of the Nineteenth Century,* (art history)
> - 15-7 *Albert Pinkham Ryder,* (artist profile)
> - 15-8 *The Changing Goals of Art Education,* (appreciating cultural diversity)

TEACHING THE LESSON

Getting Started
Motivator. Let students begin by observing small objects (either natural or manufactured) they have brought to class and then making drawings of those objects. Ask students to draw exactly what they see when they look at their objects—nothing more and nothing less. When they have finished, let students work in groups to share their drawings and the objects depicted: How realistic is each drawing?

American Painting in the Late 1800s

The 1800s was a period of great change and growth in the United States. The country grew in size as pioneers and the railroad pushed westward. It grew in wealth as trade and industry boomed. By the end of the century, America had taken its place as a world power. It had also emerged as a force to be reckoned with in the world of art.

In this lesson you will read about the artists who helped put America on the map.

AMERICAN REALIST ART

During the 1800s many American artists journeyed to the art centers of Europe to study. Some were greatly influenced by the art styles they encountered. Others were mainly unaffected by European art movements. They came home to develop styles that were unmistakably American. One of these was an artist named Thomas Eakins (**ay**-kuhnz).

▲ **Figure 15–6   Everything in this picture is made to look real. The artist even included himself in the picture. He is the person in the center holding the oars.**

Thomas Eakins. *Max Schmitt in a Single Scull (The Champion Single Sculls).* 1871. Oil on canvas. 81.9 x 117.5 cm (32¼ x 46¼"). The Metropolitan Museum of Art, New York, New York. Alfred N. Punnett Endowment Fund and George D. Pratt Gift.

Background Information
Thomas Eakins (United States, 1844–1916) is generally regarded as the foremost American painter in the Realism style. From 1866 until 1869 he studied with Jean-Leon Gerome (France, 1866–1869) at the Ecole des Beaux-Arts in Paris, and he spent much of the following year in Spain, where he was deeply impressed by the works of Diego Velazquez (Spain, 1599–1660) and Jusepe de Ribera (Spain, 1591–1652). In spite of this background, Eakins' paintings are completely American.

Eakins was interested in anatomy, and he wished to be as scientific and as accurate as possible in his work. His paintings are sometimes as realistic as photographs; he did, in fact, devote some time and energy to photographic experiments. Although he received little acclaim or financial reward for his work, he is now regarded as one of the best portraitists in the United States. One of his most interesting works is a portrait of Walt Whitman, painted in 1888.

▲ **Figure 15–7** Paintings like this capture the look and mood of the sea. With a little imagination, you can hear the roaring surf crashing against a rocky shore.

Winslow Homer. *Northeaster.* 1895. Oil on canvas. 87.4 x 127.6 cm (34⅜ x 50¼"). The Metropolitan Museum of Art, New York, New York. Gift of George A. Hearn.

Eakins, who painted only what he saw, is held to be one of America's first Realists. Realism was a movement that had its start in France in the mid-1800s. **Realism** is *a style of art in which everyday scenes and events are painted as they actually look.* Eakins, for example, stubbornly refused to show his subjects in a flattering light. As a result, he was scorned throughout his lifetime. His painting of a man in a racing boat in Figure 15–6 reveals Eakins's devotion to realism. The picture tells no story; it holds no suspense. What it does is offer a carefully studied and designed record of a simple scene that the artist witnessed. Note the care the artist took in painting even the reflections in the water.

Another artist who, like Eakins, painted exactly what he saw, was Winslow Homer.

Unlike Eakins, Homer painted pictures that often told stories, usually of people in the midst of some outdoor activity, such as hunting, fishing, or sailing.

Late in the 1880s Homer set up a studio on a rocky stretch of the Maine coast. There he painted scenes of the sea. At first his pictures were of action-filled struggles between nature and seafaring people. As time went on, the people in his works shrank in importance. His paintings began to focus instead on the power of the sea in its many moods. The work pictured in Figure 15–7 is from this later period. How would you describe the mood of the sea in this painting? What elements and principles of art help communicate this mood?

Vocabulary. Let students discuss what kinds of works they would expect from an art style called Realism: What subjects would probably be depicted? How idealized would those subjects be? Then let students read the definition of Realism given in the Glossary at the back of the text.

Developing Concepts
Exploring Aesthetics. Ask students about Thomas Eakins's approach to painting: Why do you imagine Eakins refused to paint his subjects in a flattering light? What response do you believe he expected from his subjects? What response did he usually get? Did Eakins believe that a work had to be beautiful in order to be an art work? Do you believe that all art should be beautiful? Why, or why not? Encourage students to present and support varying points of view.

Using Art Criticism. Have students work with partners to examine and discuss one of the paintings reproduced in this lesson. Let each pair of students begin by choosing a specific work: *Max Schmitt in a Single Scull* by Thomas Eakins, Figure 15-6; *Northeaster* by Winslow Homer, Figure 15-7; *Moonlight Marine (Toilers of the Sea)* by Albert Pinkham Ryder, Figure 15-8; or *Sewing Woman* by Mary Cassatt, Figure 15-9. Then have the partners discuss their responses to these questions about the chosen work: What do you see in this painting? What is the size of the painting? What medium was used? What people and objects do you see, and what is happening in the painting? Which elements of art can you identify? How have the principles of art been used to organize the visual elements within the painting? What idea, mood, or feeling does the painting communicate? Is this a successful work in terms of subject, in terms of composition, and in terms of content? Why, or why not? After the discussion, have each student write a summary of the ideas exchanged.

Note
One of Eakins's most famous works shows doctors doing surgery. The blood in the picture so shocked viewers in Eakins's time the work was banned from showings. Eakins himself was called a "butcher."

Understanding Art History.
Have students work in groups to research the social and political developments during the lifetimes of Eakins, Homer, Ryder, and Cassatt. Group members should begin by checking the dates of birth and death for the four artists; then they should decide how to divide the research among all group members. After students have completed their research, let group members share what they have learned and discuss the probable impact of American events on the works of the four artists.

Developing Studio Skills.
Have students draw a familiar scene, such as the school lunch room during lunchtime. Ask them to make their drawings as realistic as possible and, at the same time, to tell stories in their drawings. Let students compare and discuss their completed drawings: Why is it difficult to use the style of realism in creating narrative works?

Appreciating Cultural Diversity. Ask several volunteers to learn about the style of realism practiced by artists in Russia during the twentieth century. Have the volunteers summarize their findings for the rest of the class, showing several reproductions if possible. Then guide the class in discussing the realism of painters in the United States and the realism of painters in the Soviet Union: How are the styles similar? What are the most important differences?

◄ **Figure 15–8   Light is important in the artist's paintings. He often showed the source of light in the form of the sun or, as here, the moon.**

Albert Pinkham Ryder. *Moonlight Marine (Toilers of the Sea).* c. 1885. Oil on wood panel. 28.9 x 30.5 cm (11⅜ x 12"). The Metropolitan Museum of Art, New York, New York.

► **Figure 15–9   Notice the looseness of the brush strokes. Does this take away from the impression of detail?**

Mary Cassatt. *Sewing Woman.* c. 1880–1882. Oil on canvas. 92 x 63 cm (36 x 25"). Musee d' Orsay, Paris.

Note
Ryder was rarely satisfied a picture was done. He spent as many as 20 years on some paintings, building up layer on layer of paint. In some cases the paint reached a thickness of one-quarter inch.

Portraying Realism

Two other artists who affected the development of American art in the 1800s were a colorful figure by the name of Albert Pinkham Ryder and Mary Cassatt.

A loner who paid little attention to the work of others, Ryder painted dreamlike images, often borrowed from literature. His style made use of large areas of color and thick layers of paint. The painting by him in Figure 15–8 shows the simple silhouette of a ship beneath a ghostly moon. The vessel seems to glide silently across the water, carrying its crew into a night filled with mystery and wonder.

Mary Cassatt, an American who studied at the Pennsylvania Academy of Fine Arts, went on to Paris for further training. There she met Degas and was influenced by his Impressionist paintings. She often chose women and children as her subjects, using the Impressionist play of light to enhance the gentle mood she created. Her work in Figure 15–9 shows why she is considered to be one of America's finest women painters.

✔ CHECK YOUR UNDERSTANDING

1. What is Realism?
2. Why were the works of Thomas Eakins shunned during his lifetime?
3. What were favorite subjects of Winslow Homer?
4. Name four artists who affected the development of American art in the 1800s.
5. What kinds of works did Albert Pinkham Ryder create? Where did he get the ideas for his works?

STUDIO EXPERIENCE

One element that helps viewers sense the mood of the work in Figure 15–8 is texture. Look again at the painting. Notice how the sky and sea both appear alive, although in different ways.

Working lightly in pencil, sketch a nighttime landscape. Include trees, a lake, and the moon. Make your drawing large enough to fill a large sheet of paper. Switching to crayon, trace over all the pencil lines, pressing hard. Place a sheet of burlap beneath your paper. Using the side of an unwrapped crayon, rub over the sky in your drawing. Replace the burlap with bits of dried grass and leaves. Rub the crayon over the lake in your work. Examine the results. Use other materials with rough surfaces as a base for rubbing the remaining forms in your work. (For further information on rubbings, see Technique Tip **25**, *Handbook* page **286**.)

Following Up

Closure. Let students share and discuss their "Studio Experience" drawings: How does the use of rubbings affect the drawing? How does texture help create a mood? Then display all the drawings, and encourage students to compare these drawings with the paintings of American artists reproduced in the lesson: What similarities can you identify?

Evaluation. 1. Review students' written responses to the "Check Your Understanding" questions. 2. Consider students' contributions to the "Closure" discussion.

Reteaching. Have students form four research groups, and assign each group one of the artists presented in the lesson: Thomas Eakins, Winslow Homer, Albert Pinkham Ryder, or Mary Cassatt. Have group members work together to find reproductions of other works by their assigned artist. Then ask each group to share its reproductions with the rest of the class.

Enrichment. Let students work in groups to research and discuss the purposes of portrait painting: When did artists begin painting portraits? Why did those early artists paint portraits? Have the purposes of portrait painters changed since those earliest works? If so, how? Does an artist who paints a flattering portrait fulfill the purpose of portrait painting? Does an artist such as Eakins, who refused to flatter his subjects, fulfill the purpose of portrait painting? Let group members conclude their discussion by drawing and discussing portraits of one another: What is the purpose of each of these portraits?

Lesson 3 *American Painting in the Late 1800s* **235**

Answers to "Check Your Understanding"

1. Realism is a style of art in which everyday scenes and events are painted as they actually look.
2. Eakins's work was shunned during his lifetime because he stubbornly refused to show his subjects in a flattering light.
3. Winslow Homer liked to paint pictures that told a story. At first he showed people engaged in outdoor activities; later he painted scenes showing the power of the sea.
4. Four artists who affected the development of American art in the 1800s were Thomas Eakins, Winslow Homer, Albert Pinkham Ryder, and Mary Cassatt.
5. Albert Pinkham Ryder created dreamlike images using large areas of color and thick layers of paint. He often got his ideas from literature.

LESSON PLAN
(pages 236–237)

Objectives
After completing this lesson, students will be able to:
- Use watercolor paints to create their own expressive scenes.
- Describe, analyze, interpret, and judge their own watercolor paintings.

Supplies
- Containers of water; sheets of white paper, 9 x 12 inches (23 x 30 cm); watercolor paints; brushes in several sizes; tempera paint in several hues; pen; India ink.
- Reproduction of one of Henry Tanner's paintings of a Bible scene (if available), sheets of drawing paper, pencils, wide-line and fine-tipped colored markers.

TEACHING THE LESSON

Getting Started
Motivator. Ask students to recall the work of Thomas Eakins: Why is Eakins called a Realist? What did Eakins paint? How important were story and mood in his paintings? Then explain to students that they will be considering a work by a painter who became Eakins's student—and friend—at the Pennsylvania Academy of Fine Arts. Though this painter, Henry Tanner, also worked in Realism, he usually created more expressive works than did Ryder, communicating a greater sense of mood and emotion. Let students speculate about how this slightly different approach might have affected the paintings Tanner created. Then have them look at Tanner's painting, *The Seine*, Figure 15-10.

Vocabulary. Review with students the definition of *intensity:* What are low-intensity hues? What are high-intensity hues? What effect do differences in intensity have?

Making an Expressive Watercolor Painting

Henry Tanner was a former student of Thomas Eakins and one of America's most talented black artists. Because his paintings did not sell in America, Tanner decided to move to Europe. Settling in Paris, he painted scenes from the Bible, which were well received. After one of his paintings was accepted in the Paris Salon, a highly respected French artist insisted that it be hung in a place of honor.

Although better known for his religious pictures, some of Tanner's best works were portraits and outdoor scenes. One of his scenes can be viewed in Figure 15–10. Notice the low-intensity hues, contrasting light and dark values, and fuzzy shapes in this painting. What kind of mood does Tanner create with these hues, values, and shapes?

WHAT YOU WILL LEARN
You will use watercolor paint to create your own expressive scene. Your scene will exhibit the same low-intensity hues, contrasting dark and light values, and fuzzy shapes found in Tanner's painting. Your painting will also express the same quiet stillness. (See Figure 15–11.)

▶ **Figure 15–10   The artist's interest in art was born when, as a child, he watched an artist at work in a park.**

Henry O. Tanner. *The Seine*. 1902. Canvas. 23 x 32.9 cm (9 x 13"). National Gallery of Art, Washington, D.C. Gift of the Avalon Foundation.

Background Information
Henry Tanner (United States, 1859–1937) was an American-born artist who studied briefly at the Pennsylvania Academy of Fine Arts, where Thomas Eakins (United States, 1844–1916) became both his teacher and his friend. Tanner went to Paris in the 1890s, at least in part to escape racial prejudice, and he remained a resident of France until his death. In the early years of his career, Tanner used African-American life as his subject. Later, he turned to religious subjects, for which he is most famous. He traveled twice to Palestine, where he did research for his paintings of Bible scenes. Tanner's personal faith gave him the desire to express his feelings through painting. While his religious paintings were well received in Europe, they were not the products of commissions.

Tanner chose the medium of watercolor over others because of its ability to capture light. He was especially concerned with the effects of light, particularly moonlight. Tanner used layers of glaze to capture the depth and intensity of light.

WHAT YOU WILL NEED

- Container of water
- Sheet of white paper, 9 x 12 inches (23 x 30 cm)
- Watercolor paint and several brushes
- Tempera paint in different hues
- Pen and India ink

WHAT YOU WILL DO

1. With water, completely wet the sheet of white paper.
2. Load a medium-pointed brush with a light color paint, and apply this carefully to the damp paper. The area painted might represent a lake or river. Add other areas of light colors to suggest sky and clouds.
3. Use the same technique to add dark shapes to your paper. These could suggest the shoreline, distant rooftops, boats, a bridge, or other objects. Do not worry about details. Concern yourself with creating areas of color with different dark values.
4. While your picture is drying, study it carefully. Use your imagination to identify the general outlines of the different objects.
5. When your painting is dry, use a pen and India ink to outline the objects. Add details.
6. Use white paint to create highlights and additional details.

EXAMINING YOUR WORK

- **Describe**   Identify the different objects in your scene. Name the hues you used.
- **Analyze**   Point out the low-intensity hues, contrasting light and dark values, and fuzzy shapes.
- **Interpret**   Explain how your work expresses a quiet, still mood.
- **Judge**   Compare your work with that of Tanner. Tell how your picture is similar in content and composition. Point out the differences.

▲ Figure 15–11   Student work. Expressive watercolor painting.

OTHER STUDIO IDEAS

- Make another watercolor painting of the same outdoor scene. This time use high-intensity hues instead of low-intensity ones. Compare this second painting with the first. How does the use of high-intensity hues change the mood of the picture?

- ●● With colored chalk, create a picture of a different outdoor scene. Add a sense of space to your picture by using low-intensity hues to color background objects and high-intensity hues to color foreground objects.

Lesson 4   *Making an Expressive Watercolor Painting*   **237**

Developing Concepts

Exploring Aesthetics. Let students share and discuss their responses to Tanner's painting shown in Figure 15-10: How does this work make you feel? What mood do you think the artist intended to communicate? How does his choice of medium contribute to that mood?

Developing Studio Skills. If possible, show students a reproduction of one of Tanner's paintings depicting scenes from the Bible. Then ask students to draw their own scenes from favorite books or stories. They should begin by sketching the scene in pencil; then they should use markers to add color. Ask students to try to make their drawings realistic, as Tanner's works are. Encourage students to share and discuss their completed drawings.

Following Up

Closure. Have students work in groups to discuss their watercolor paintings. Let each student describe, analyze, interpret, and judge his or her own painting for the rest of the group, following the steps in "Examining Your Work." Then have each student write a short interpretation of another group member's watercolor painting.

Evaluation. Review students' expressive watercolor paintings, consider their participation in the "Closure" group discussions, and read their interpretations of one another's paintings.

Reteaching. Guide students in discussing Tanner's use of watercolor. Explain that some critics say "real artists" don't use watercolors, because watercolors are a medium for amateurs: Do you agree? Why, or why not? How important is the choice of medium in creating a work of art? Then have students find and bring to class reproductions of other watercolor paintings. Help students compare and discuss the style of these works.

Enrichment. Ask students to identify important events in their own lives and to paint expressive scenes from those events. How can they depict their feelings and, in the same work, show what happened?

Note
In this lesson, students are working with a piece of paper that has been dampened. Show how watercolors can be made to run. Apply a brushful of a light color to the sky area using enough paint and water to flood the area. Gently pick up the paper by the top edges and let the paint flow down, feathering as it goes. Explain that this can be used for foliage by picking the page up by its lower edge. Ask students for suggestions of other ways this technique could be applied.

ANSWERS TO "CHAPTER 15 REVIEW"

Building Vocabulary
1. Post-Impressionism
2. optical colors
3. arbitrary colors
4. Pointillism
5. Realism

Reviewing Art Facts
6. Problems should include lack of composition and content. Solutions include making shapes more identifiable, conveying more emotion, and creating art that could be enjoyed purely for its decorative appearance.
7. Paul Cézanne was a former Impressionist.
8. Georges Seurat was also interested in making the forms in his painting clearer and more solid looking.
9. Van Gogh also used arbitrary color.
10. Seurat used tiny dots of color. He used this technique to create new colors and clear shapes.
11. Eakins refused to show his subjects in a flattering light.
12. Homer's early paintings showed people engaged in outdoor activities. Later works focused on the power of the sea and its many moods.
13. Homer and Albert Pinkham Ryder both painted pictures of the sea.
14. Eakins, Homer, Ryder, and Mary Cassatt affected development of American art in the 1800s.
15. Ryder used large areas of color and thick layers of paint.

Thinking About Art
1. Students should mention that Cézanne has painted his mountain, trees and buildings using patches of color to give his forms three dimensions, and that he has used the cone, sphere and cylinder shapes in this painting.
2. Cézanne painted his favorite subjects from every angle because he wanted to show how he could create solid-looking forms using color patches turned in different directions.
3. Students should discuss the content, describing Eakins's realism, lack of mystery, and photographic quality. They should see Ryder's heavy, mysterious mood, few details, simple composition. Similarity consists between subject matter: boats, sky, water, and a few people.

BUILDING VOCABULARY

Number a sheet of paper from 1 to 5. After each number, write the term from the box that best matches each description below.

arbitrary colors	Post-
optical colors	Impressionism
Pointillism	Realism

1. An art movement that appeared after the Impressionists.
2. Colors viewers actually see.
3. Colors chosen to communicate different feelings.
4. A technique in which small, carefully placed dots of color are used to create forms.
5. A style of art in which everyday scenes and events are painted as they actually look.

REVIEWING ART FACTS

Number a sheet of paper from 6 to 15. Answer each question in a complete sentence.

6. Name two problems and solutions some artists of the later 1800s found in the Impressionist style.
7. Which Post-Impressionist artist was a former Impressionist?
8. Which artist besides Cézanne was interested in making the forms in his paintings clearer and more solid-looking?
9. Which Post-Impressionist besides Gauguin used arbitrary colors in his works?
10. What painter filled his works with tiny dots of color? Why did he do this?
11. What was there about his works that made Eakins unpopular during his lifetime?
12. How did Homer's paintings change from his early to his later years in Maine?

13. Which two American artists of the late 1800s often painted pictures of the sea?
14. Name the artists who affected the development of American art in the 1800s.
15. Describe Ryder's painting techniques.

THINKING ABOUT ART

On a sheet of paper, answer each question in a sentence or two.

1. **Analyze.** Paul Cézanne claimed that all forms in nature are based on three forms: the sphere, the cone, and the cylinder. Examine his painting in Figure 15–1. Tell how his work supports this idea.
2. **Extend.** Like Claude Monet, Cézanne painted the same subject again and again. Explain his reasons for doing so.
3. **Compare and contrast.** Acting as a critic, interpret the works by Albert Pinkham Ryder (Figure 15–8) and Thomas Eakins (Figure 15–6). Tell how the two interpretations differ. Tell how they are alike.

MAKING ART CONNECTIONS

1. **Language Arts.** You are at a museum standing before the painting by Georges Seurat shown in Figure 15–4. As you are looking at the canvas, you overhear a viewer say, "Why, this painting is nothing but dots! Anyone can paint dots." What information could you give that would help the viewer better appreciate the work? What advice might you give?
2. **History.** Imagine you lived in America during the 1800s. Using history and literature books for reference, write a short report on what life would have been like for a teen growing up in this time. List some of the historical and social events that would shape your life.

CHAPTER 15 REVIEW

LOOKING AT THE DETAILS

The detail shown below is from Edgar Degas' *Dancers Practicing at the Bar*. Study the detail and answer the following questions using complete sentences.

1. What similarities to the Impressionist style do you see in this work? What differences do you see?
2. Where is the emphasis in this detail? Look at the entire work on page **224**. Has the emphasis changed? Explain your answer.

3. Look at the entire work on page **224**. Do you think Degas emphasized composition, content, or both? Explain your answer.
4. Both van Gogh and Degas are considered Post-Impressionist painters. Compare this work with Figure 15–2 on page **227**. What do the two works have in common? How are they different?

Edgar Degas. *Dancers Practicing at the Bar*. Date Unknown. Oil colors, mixed with turpentine, on canvas. (Detail.) 75.6 x 81.3 cm (29¾ x 32"). Metropolitan Museum of Art, New York, New York. H. O. Havemeyer Collection.

ANSWERS TO "LOOKING AT THE DETAILS"

1. Similarities to the Impressionist style include visible brush strokes, use of light reflecting off certain objects, and the emphasis of light instead of detail on the faces of the dancers. The differences include no blurring of shapes, unusual composition, and the use of more realistic detail.
2. The emphasis in the detail is on the yellow bow on the girl's dress. This is the point of emphasis in both views, because it is the brightest and most pure hue in the entire work.
3. Student responses may vary. Possible explanations include: Degas emphasized both composition and content. He doesn't blur the shapes, his design successfully achieves balance, and he uses line in a unique way to direct the viewers' eye to the subjects. He expresses a definite quiet, almost reflective mood in the work through his use of color and light.
4. Both works have visible brush strokes and use color to express mood. Degas has a more realistic style emphasizing both composition and content. Van Gogh stresses content over composition.

Chapter Evaluation

The purpose of this chapter is to introduce students to Post-Impressionism and to American painting. Methods of evaluation include:

1. Ask students to write a paragraph or two that describes the steps leading from the Impressionist painting style, the work of Post-Impressionists, and progressing to the development of Realism in art of this period.

2. List several colors on the board and have students discuss how each color could evoke a particular feeling and why.
3. Have students complete Chapter 15 Test, (TRB Resource 15-9).

Art of the Early Twentieth Century

Chapter Scan

TRB Resources

- 16-9 Chapter Test
- Color Transparency 31
- Color Transparency 32

TEACHING THE CHAPTER

Introducing the Art Work

Direct students' attention to Wassily Kandinsky's *Painting Number 200*. Inform them that Wassily Kandinsky was a Russian painter in the early twentieth century. Kandinsky was born in Moscow, studied law, and had a promising legal career. He was nearly thirty years old before he decided to become a painter. In 1896, he gave up his law practice and moved to Germany, where he felt that artistic training and opportunities were more promising than in Russia. From the beginning of his studies, Kandinsky found something lacking in the literal presentation of reality in painting. He experimented with Neo-Impressionism, Expressionism, and Fauvism, and was eventually inspired to create what many critics believe to be the first non-objective painting in 1910. Other artists were also heading in that direction, but Kandinsky pioneered it and was the first to break with the tradition of painting realistic objects.

▲ Wassily Kandinsky's work was characterized by a sense of color and pattern. He experimented freely with established methods until he developed a new and exciting style to express feeling in his works.

Wassily Kandinsky. *Painting Number 200*. 1914. Oil on canvas. 162.5 x 80 cm (64 x 31½″). Museum of Modern Art, New York, New York. Mrs. Simon Guggenheim Fund.

Art of the Early Twentieth Century

Art has the power to delight. Art has the power to teach. Art also has the power, as history has shown time and again, to shock. No style throughout art's long history shocked viewers more than the one highlighted in the painting at the left. This style, which developed early in the twentieth century, came about purely by accident. Do you know the name of this style? Can you identify its main features? In the pages that follow you will learn the answers to these and other questions.

OBJECTIVES

After completing this chapter, you will be able to:
- Identify the major art movements of the early twentieth century.
- Name the leaders of those movements.
- Describe art trends in the United States and Mexico in the early twentieth century.
- Use the elements and principles of art in the style of the Cubists.
- Create an art work showing rhythm and movement.

WORDS YOU WILL LEARN

Ashcan School   Fauvism
Cubism   muralist
The Eight   non-objective art
Expressionism   Regionalism

ARTISTS YOU WILL MEET

George Bellows   Käthe Kollwitz
Georges Braque   Jacques Lipchitz
John Steuart Curry   Henri Matisse
Wassily Kandinsky   Diego Rivera
Ernst Ludwig   John Sloan
    Kirchner   Alfred Stieglitz

Examining the Art Work

Tell students that this is an abstract or non-objective painting, representing an abstract image rather than a particular subject or realistic object. Explain to students that since the title provides no clues into the content of the image, and the image is abstract, the viewer must approach it from a compositional point of view in order to evaluate this work.

Explain to students how the elements of line, color, and shape direct the viewer's eye through the painting. Point out the dark purple crescent shape—the darkest, most prominent hue—and suggest that it leads the viewer's eye to the bright colors in the lower left, then the eye moves up the middle of the painting, through the red rocket shape toward the right to the most pure yellow hue.

Discussing the Art Work

Ask students to think about the elements of art that give this painting unity. Point out the way Kandinsky uses the same hues in various areas of the work.

Point out the artist's use of the black lines against the white background at the top of the painting. Ask students what images, if any, they see in the lines. Introduce possibilities using some examples such as a hat, a man in a coat, an odd structure on a hill. Explain to them that abstract works can be used to stretch the imagination and perceptive powers of the viewer.

Tell students that in this chapter they will learn about major art movements of the early twentieth century and its leaders. They will become familar with art trends in the United States and Mexico at this time, and will create a work of art showing rhythm and movement.

241

Building Self-Esteem

Tell students that in this chapter they will learn about a group of eight artists who painted in the early 1900s and chose subjects from everyday life in the big city. They called themselves The Eight, but when their work was first shown publicly, viewers laughed and said they might better be called the Ashcan School. The criticism of their choice of style and subject matter, realistic paintings of working-class America, was obvious from the word chosen to characterize it. However, these artists had all come from a background as newspaper cartoonists or magazine illustrators which required them to extract the essence of a scene and communicate it in easily-understandable form. A cartoon must capture an amusing contradiction; a magazine illustration, an essential moment of truth. These artists were accustomed to taking a basic approach to art. Stress the importance of isolating the subject. Let students ask themselves, "What is the most important thing I want to communicate?" and "How do I go about doing it?"

LESSON 1

Art of the Early Twentieth Century in Europe

LESSON PLAN
(pages 242–245)

Objectives

After completing this lesson, students will be able to:
- Identify the major European art movements of the early twentieth century.
- Name the leaders of those art movements.
- Create collages that capture the look and feel of twentieth-century American street scenes.

Supplies

- Sheets of drawing paper, colored markers.
- Old magazines with photographs and/or illustrations, scissors, white glue, sheets of white paper.
- Sheets of sketch paper; pencils; several objects with distinctive shapes, such as a basket, a vase, a small doll, a figurine.

TRB Resource
- 16-1 *Elements of Cubism,* (reproducible master)

TEACHING THE LESSON

Getting Started

Motivator. Explain to students that many works of modern art focus on expressing feelings. Ask students to try creating their own drawings that express feelings. Let students suggest several different feelings or emotions that might be depicted in art works—rage, joy, sorrow, disappointment, and so on. Then have each student choose one emotion and use colored markers to draw an expression of that emotion. Suggest that students may want to use colors, lines, and/or shapes to express the chosen emotion; remind them to depict the emotion itself, not a person causing or feeling that emotion. When students have finished their drawings, let them work in small groups to share their work. Can other group members identify the depicted emotion?

242

Art of the Early Twentieth Century in Europe

Every age, it has been said, learns from and builds on the one before it. The truth of these words is clear from developments in art in the early 1900s. Several new styles came along, each borrowing in a different way from Post-Impressionism. These styles, which stunned the art world, continue to affect art through the present day. In this lesson you will learn about the pioneers behind these innovative ways of making art.

FAUVISM

In 1905 a showing by a group of French artists started the art community buzzing. The most striking feature of the works in the show was their raw, sizzling colors. No effort had been made to paint realistic pictures. The artists' goal was to express their feelings through sharply contrasting colors and heavy outlines. One angry critic wrote that the paintings looked as though they had

▶ **Figure 16–1   Describe the lines in this painting. How have the elements been used to give the work a sense of oneness?**

Henri Matisse. *The Red Studio.* Issy-les-Moulineaux. 1911. Oil on canvas. 181 x 219.1 cm (71¼ x 86¼"). Museum of Modern Art, New York, New York. Mrs. Simon Guggenheim Fund.

Background Information

Paul Cézanne (France, 1839–1906) was considered an important Impressionist painter, but Impressionism was only one of the phases of his artistic creativity. In the late 1870s Cézanne broke away from Impressionism, remarking that he wanted to create "something solid and durable, like the art of the museums." He felt that the Impressionist painters depended too much on sensation.

Cézanne believed that structure was the most important component of art—certainly more important than the artist's subjective impressions. In Cézanne's view, every art work should try to achieve a structural order; shape and color were the most important elements within this structure. His analysis of structure led Cézanne to identify the sphere, the cone, and the cylinder as the three shapes that comprise all forms in nature.

Cézanne never created abstract art works, but his analysis of structure exerted a strong influence on Cubism and other modern painting styles.

been done by *fauves* (**fohvs**). This term, which is French for "wild beasts," gave the movement its name: Fauvism (**fohv**-iz-uhm). **Fauvism** is *an art movement in which artists used wild, intense color combinations in their paintings.*

The leader of the Fauves was a law student who chose to become an artist. His name was Henri Matisse (ahnh-**ree** mah-**tees**). For his paintings, Matisse chose colors that communicated a joyous or happy mood. He then combined them, as in the picture in Figure 16–1, to create rich, decorative patterns. To understand the importance of color in Matisse's works, try to imagine Figure 16–1 in black and white. In what way would the painting be different? How would its mood change?

EXPRESSIONISM

Matisse and the Fauves wanted to show feelings in their art. In Germany the same goal was shared by another group of artists, who developed a movement known as Expressionism (ek-**spresh**-uh-niz-uhm). Artists using **Expressionism** worked in *a style that emphasized the expression of innermost feelings.* They ignored the contemporary rules of art. They had the strength to experiment with, to exaggerate, and in other ways to change, the proportions of figures and objects.

Painting

An early leader of the Expressionist movement was an artist named Ernst Ludwig Kirchner (**ehrnst lood**-vig **keerk**-nuhr). Figure 16–2 shows Kirchner's inner view of a street scene. Note his use of brilliant, clashing colors and sharp, twisted shapes. The people in Kirchner's world are crammed together in a small space. Yet they manage not to notice one another. How might you sum up the artist's feelings toward these people and their world?

▲ **Figure 16–2** The artist has used twisted shapes to express his emotions. An earlier artist you read about did the same thing. Do you recall that artist's name?

Ernst Ludwig Kirchner. *Street, Berlin*. 1913. Oil on canvas. 120.6 x 91.1 cm (47½ x 35⅞"). Museum of Modern Art, New York, New York.

Printmaking

The power of Expressionism can also be seen in the prints and drawings of Käthe Kollwitz (**kay**-tuh **kohl**-wits). At a time when most artists were exploring color, Kollwitz created works mainly in black and white. Many, like the print in Figure 16–3, focus on the ills of working-class life. Can you identify the emotions on the faces of these people?

CUBISM

Paul Cézanne, you will remember, was interested in showing objects as solid-looking forms. A guiding idea behind Cubism was Cézanne's notion that all forms in nature are made up of three shapes. Those three are the sphere, cone, and cylinder. This idea led to the development of **Cubism**, *a style in which objects are shown from several different angles at once.*

Lesson 1   *Art of the Early Twentieth Century in Europe*   📖   **243**

Vocabulary. Help students discuss the meaning of the term *non-objective:* What is another word that has the same meaning as *object*? What does the prefix *non-* mean? What would you expect to see in a non-objective work of art?

You may also want to help students discuss the origins of the names *Fauvism* and *Cubism*. Explain that *fauves* is a French word meaning "wild beasts"; a critic used this word to describe the painters who had created works with wild, intense color combinations. Ask: If you had been one of those painters, how do you think that critic's remark would have made you feel? Would you have adopted the name *Fauvism* to identify your new art movement? Why, or why not? Then explain that another art critic made this disparaging comment about a painting by Georges Braque: It "reduces everything to little cubes." Again ask: If you had been the painter, how would you have felt about the critic's remark? Would you have adopted the name *Cubism* to identify your new art movement? Why, or why not?

Developing Concepts

Exploring Aesthetics. Guide students in discussing the non-objective painting by Kandinsky reproduced on page **240**. Ask: What do you see in this painting? How would you characterize the use of color, line, shape, space, and texture? Which principles of art have been used to organize the elements within the work? What message or feeling does the painting communicate to you? What makes this painting a work of art?

Continue by explaining that non-objective art has many detractors; some people feel that works without recognizable subjects are not art. Ask students for their opinions: Is non-objective art really art? Why, or why not? Do you think that creating non-objective paintings or sculptures requires as much talent as creating representational art works? Why, or why not?

Handbook Cross-Reference
Refer students to Artist Profile, *Handbook* page **289** for additional information about Paul Cézanne.

Understanding Art History. Twentieth-century art movements differed from earlier movements in several ways: one important difference was the new concept of the artist as an activist. Members of many modern art movements considered themselves concerned with the social/political community as well as the art community. Encourage students to discuss how an artist's political beliefs might influence his or her feelings about the meaning of art and the place of art in society.

After this discussion, ask students to read about the life and works of Käthe Kollwitz. Then let them work in groups to compare their findings and their responses to these questions: How did social and political events in Europe affect Kollwitz's work? What kinds of statements did she intend to make with her art? What message do you think Kollwitz intended to communicate with her print shown in Figure 16-3? How would her art works have been different if she had lived in a different time or if she had not concerned herself with contemporary social and political issues?

Developing Studio Skills. Remind students that Cubist works show objects from several different angles at once. Set out one or two objects with distinctive shapes—such as baskets, vases, figurines, and so on—at each of several work stations. Let students choose their own work stations and sketch the object or objects shown there from several different angles. Each student should make four or five different sketches of the same subject. Then have students draw new pictures of their chosen subjects, combining the perspectives used in several of their sketches. How does making this new drawing help them understand the objects?

▲ **Figure 16–3** This was from a series of prints showing an angry German peasant revolt in the 1500s. What might the artist's choice of subject tell us about events in her own time?

Käthe Kollwitz. *The Prisoners.* 1908. Etchings. Library of Congress, Washington, D.C.

Painting

The founder of Cubism was an artist you have met before in this book. Even if you had not met him here, his name is one you would instantly recognize. It is Pablo Picasso.

Picasso's early Cubist paintings were different arrangements of bits and pieces of his subject viewed from different angles. The subjects of these works are at times difficult to pick out. Later he began using brighter colors and larger shapes in his works. He also added texture and pattern, often by gluing found objects to his paintings. The picture in Figure 3–7 on page **42** is one of Picasso's later Cubist works. Are you able to identify the objects in this picture?

Sculpture

The Cubist style also found its way into sculpture of the early twentieth century. Jacques Lipchitz (**zhahk lip**-shuts), a Lithuanian-born sculptor who studied in Paris, used Cubism in his bronze castings. One of these works is pictured in Figure 16–4. Notice how the many fragments of a figure add up to a carefully designed three-dimensional whole. How has the artist used texture to give the work a sense of harmony?

Background Information
At the turn of the twentieth century, Jacques Lipchitz, (Lithuania, 1891–1973) was influenced by the new art movements in painting. Some of his early sculpture pieces were done in the Cubist style reflecting three-dimensional forms with the same kinds of geometric shapes found in paintings by Picasso and Braque. Flat surfaces of different shapes were placed at various angles to one another.

Later Lipchitz's sculptures became more emotional. He was affected by events such as the Great Depression and World War II that are reflected in his work. Like the Expressionist painters, he was no longer satisfied to work on solving design problems of form and space. He felt that art had to say something and to be more exciting and emotional.

▲ **Figure 16–4** What has the artist done to create different light and dark values? Can you point to places where a variety of lines and forms is used?

Jacques Lipchitz. *Bather.* 1923–25. Bronze. 198.5 x 79.1 x 70.5 cm (78⅛ x 31⅛ x 27¾"). Dallas Museum of Art, Dallas, Texas. Gift of Mr. & Mrs. Algur H. Meadows and the Meadows Foundation, Inc.

NON-OBJECTIVE ART

One evening in 1910 after painting outdoors all day, a weary artist returned to his studio. There he was greeted by a surprise that changed the course of art history. Perched on his easel was a painting unlike anything he had ever seen. Its brightly colored shapes and lines seemed to glow and shimmer in the dim light. Rushing to the canvas, the artist had his second surprise of the night. The work was his own; he had carelessly placed it upside down on the easel! The artist's name was Wassily Kandinsky (**vahs**-uh-lee kuhn-**din**-skee). His discovery led to the birth of a new style called **non-objective art**. These are *works in which no objects or subjects can be readily identified*.

In the experiments that followed, Kandinsky found he could express feelings using only colors, shapes, and lines. These elements could be arranged, just as the notes of a song are, to create a mood. Look at the painting that opens this chapter on page **240**. Imagine the colors, shapes, and lines to be musical notes. What kind of tune do these elements seem to play? Do they play a loud and brassy melody, or a soft and mellow one?

 CHECK YOUR UNDERSTANDING

1. What is Fauvism? Who was the leader of the Fauves?
2. What is Expressionism? In what way did the Expressionists ignore the rules of art?
3. To what movement did the artist Käthe Kollwitz belong? What media did she favor?
4. Define *Cubism*. Name the Post-Impressionist artist whose ideas influenced the Cubist movement.
5. Tell in what area of art Jacques Lipchitz worked. By what art movement was he influenced?
6. Tell how non-objective art got its start. Name the originator of the movement.

LESSON PLAN
(pages 246–247)

Objectives
After completing this lesson, students will be able to:
• Create still-life drawings in the later style of the Cubists.
• Describe, analyze, interpret, and judge their own drawings.

Supplies
• Potted plant, cut flowers in a vase, or another object; pencils; sheets of sketch paper.
• Pencils; sheets of sketch paper; sheets of white paper, 18 x 24 inches (46 x 60 cm); colored chalk; spray fixative; sheets of facial tissue.
• Several art books that include reproductions of Cubist works.

> **TRB Resource**
> • 16-2 *American Realism in Art,* (aesthetics)

TEACHING THE LESSON

Getting Started

Motivator. Place a potted plant, a small bouquet, or some other defined object in a central location, where all students can see it. Ask students to stay in their seats, look closely at the object, and then draw a quick sketch of it, concentrating on an interesting shape or detail. Then let students compare and discuss their sketches: How is each drawing different from the others? What accounts for these differences? How did differences in physical point of view affect your sketches? How did differences in your perceptions and your responses to the subject affect your sketches?

Vocabulary. Help students review the definition of *Cubism*. Ask students how their different sketches of the same object (from the "Motivator" activity above) relate to Cubism. Could several different sketches be combined to create a single Cubist drawing? If so, which sketches? What idea or mood would the resulting drawing communicate?

246

Making a Cubist Chalk Drawing

A co-founder of the Cubist movement was an artist named Georges Braque (**zhorzh brahk**). A favorite form of expression for Braque was the still life. Instead of fruits or flowers, he usually chose household objects as subjects. Figure 16–5 shows one of his still lifes. Notice how the table, other objects, and background are combined to make a flat, decorative design. All parts of the work are equally interesting to look at. The different colors, shapes, lines, and textures are organized into an interesting whole.

In this lesson you will use the elements and principles of art in the same way.

WHAT YOU WILL LEARN

You will create a still life with chalk in the later style of the Cubists. You will repeat colors, shapes, lines, and textures to make a flat, decorative pattern. Your pattern will fill the paper. A warm or cool color scheme will be used to add harmony and express a mood. (See Figure 16–6.)

WHAT YOU WILL NEED

• Pencil and sheets of sketch paper
• Sheet of white paper, 18 x 24 inches (46 x 60 cm)
• Colored chalk and spray fixative
• Sheets of facial tissue

▶ **Figure 16–5** How many different objects can you identify? What other objects could be used to make an interesting still life? Describe the different textures. How has the artist added unity to this design?

Georges Braque. *Still Life: Le Jour.* 1929. Canvas. 150 x 146.7 cm (45¼ x 57¾"). National Gallery of Art, Washington, D.C. Chester Dale Collection.

Background Information
The Cubist art movement is generally considered to have been founded by two artists: Pablo Picasso (Spain, 1881–1973) and Georges Braque (France, 1882–1963). Picasso created the first Cubist work, *Les Demoiselles d'Avignon,* in 1907. Braque was one of the few artists who apparently understood and appreciated the work; he stopped working in the Fauvist style and became a Cubist. The two worked together closely during the early years of the movement.

After several years Picasso and Braque developed a style called Analytic Cubism. Each work consisted of many carefully analyzed facets of the same subject, superimposed over one another. The colors used were generally muted.

The next Cubist style, Synthetic Cubism, emerged around 1912, and used brighter colors and more decorative devices. During the 1920s Picasso created works that echoed a Classical style, while Braque developed a more personal interpretation of Cubism.

WHAT YOU WILL DO

1. Bring to class an object with an interesting shape. Some possibilities are an old violin or guitar, an oddly shaped bottle, or a house plant. Working with three other students, arrange the objects on a tabletop. Each student should have a clear view of the objects.
2. Make several rough pencil sketches for a still life. You may exaggerate or in other ways change shapes and lines for added interest. Shapes should be shown as simple, flat planes. Repeat the lines of the objects in the background areas.
3. Working lightly in chalk, transfer your best sketch to the sheet of white paper. Fill the whole sheet with your design.
4. Choose four or five sticks of chalk to create either a warm or cool color scheme. As you choose, keep in mind the mood you want your work to communicate.
5. Color your still life. Color some shapes by blending two or more hues with facial tissue. Repeat colors throughout the picture to add harmony. Make some shapes stand out clearly by adding heavy contour lines. Use the chalk to create different textures in some shapes.
6. Spray your still life with fixative. Compare it with the one in Figure 16–5 and those by other students.

SAFETY TIP

Remember to use chalk in a place with plenty of ventilation. If you begin to have breathing problems, finish the lesson using crayon. Use spray fixative outdoors or in a space with plenty of ventilation.

OTHER STUDIO IDEAS

- Make another still life, this time using a different color scheme. Some possibilities are split complementary or analogous colors. (See the color wheel on page 2.)

EXAMINING YOUR WORK

- **Describe**   Point to and name the different objects in your picture. Explain how and why you changed the shapes and lines of those objects.
- **Analyze**   Point out places where you have repeated colors, shapes, and lines. Explain how these elements have been used to create a flat, decorative pattern. Tell whether your design fills the whole sheet of paper.
- **Interpret**   Tell how the warm or cool color scheme adds a mood to your work. Identify this mood.
- **Judge**   Tell whether you feel your work succeeds. Explain your answer.

▲ Figure 16–6   Student work. Cubist chalk drawing.

●● Make another still life, this time using India ink thinned with water. Using a pen, create different shades of gray. Leave some shapes white for contrast. Use different parts of the pen point to add texture and contour lines.

Lesson 2   *Making a Cubist Chalk Drawing*   **247**

Exploring Aesthetics. Guide students in discussing Georges Braque's *Still Life*, shown in Figure 16-5: What is the subject of this painting? Which principles of art have been used to organize the visual elements in the work? What idea or mood does the painting communicate to you? How is this painting similar to—and different from—other still life paintings you have seen?

Using Art Criticism. Present the following quote from Guillaume Apollinaire, a poet and critic during the early modern art era: "Cubism differs from the old school of painting in that it aims not at an art of imitation but at an art of conception." Ask: What do you think Apollinaire meant? Have students support their responses by pointing out specific examples in modern works reproduced in this chapter.

Following Up

Closure. Let students work with partners to compare and discuss their Cubist chalk drawings. Encourage each pair of students to respond to all the instructions in "Examining Your Work." Then have students write short descriptions of their partners' drawings.

Evaluation. Review students' chalk drawings and read their descriptions of one another's work.

Reteaching. Work with small groups of students, and ask group members to browse through art books. Let each student select and share reproductions of two Cubist paintings or sculptures. Ask: Why did you choose this work of art? What made you identify it as an example of Cubism? Which art element do you find most interesting in this work?

Enrichment. Ask each student to choose a favorite object and create two drawings or paintings of it: one as realistic as possible and the other in the style of later Cubism. Display the pairs of paintings or drawings, and encourage students to discuss and compare the two works in each pair.

Handbook Cross-Reference
After students have completed the Cubist chalk drawing, suggest that they mount their work. Refer them to Technique Tip 24, *Handbook* page **286** for instructions on how to mount a two-dimensional work.

LESSON PLAN
(pages 248–251)

Objectives

After completing this lesson, students will be able to:

• Describe art trends in the United States and Mexico in the early twentieth century.
• Name leading artists in those trends.
• Create abstract drawings with images that capture specific concepts.

Supplies

• Magazines (current or old).
• Wall map of the United States.
• Old magazines, pencils, tracing paper, pens, India ink.
• Sheets of drawing paper, colored pencils.
• Sheets of butcher paper, pencils, tempera paints, brushes.

TRB Resources

• 16-3 *WPA and American Art*, (art history)
• 16-4 *School Mural*, (cooperative learning)
• 16-5 *Alfred Stieglitz*, (artist profile)
• 16-6 *Comparing Murals*, (appreciating cultural diversity)
• 16-7 *Ashcan School View*, (studio)
• 16-8 *Cubist Collage*, (studio)

TEACHING THE LESSON

Getting Started

Motivator. Begin with a class discussion in which students select a topic of concern to them; examples include the environment, homeless people, poverty, and drug abuse. Guide students in discussing the problem and their feelings in response to it—fear, sadness, optimism, and so on. Then ask students to look in magazines

Art of the Early Twentieth Century in America

In the early twentieth century the pace of life quickened in the United States. The airplane, assembly line, and telephone were all part of a new fascination with speed. A search for new formulas in American art mirrored the restlessness of the age. In this lesson you will learn about the most important of the new art movements. You will also learn about developments in the art of Mexico.

THE ASHCAN SCHOOL

As the 1800s gave way to the 1900s, the important names in American art remained unchanged. Homer, Eakins, and Ryder continued on as the unchallenged leaders. In New York a group of lesser-known painters felt a change was overdue. Since there were eight members in all, they called themselves, simply, **The Eight**. This was a *group of artists who created art work that reflected the spirit of the times in which they lived, the early 1900s.*

The members of The Eight were all one-time newspaper cartoonists or magazine illustrators. These experiences influenced their choice of subjects for their paintings. Their works drew on images from everyday life in the big city. These pictures of crowded city streets, dark alleys, and gray slums were recorded in a no-nonsense, realistic style. When The Eight held their first public showing in 1908, viewers politely examined their works. Then they laughed. A more fitting name for these chroniclers of working-class American life, some decided, was the **Ashcan School**. This became *the popular name given to the group of artists who made realistic paintings of working-class America.*

Painting

One of the most talented members of the Ashcan School was John Sloan. His pictures capture the color, movement, and humor of big-city life. Look at the painting by Sloan in Figure 16–7. The hairdresser in the picture goes about her business with hardly a care. Below, meanwhile, passersby stop and stare as if witnessing an important event. Locate the girls at the bottom of the picture. One, you will notice, seems to be talking excitedly. What do you suppose she is saying?

▲ **Figure 16–7** What has the artist done to emphasize the figures in the second-story window? How has movement been introduced?

John Sloan. *Hairdresser's Window.* 1907. Oil on canvas. 81 x 66 cm (31⅞ x 26"). Wadsworth Atheneum, Hartford, Connecticut. Ella Gallup Sumner and Mary Catlin Sumner Collection.

Background Information

The influential poet and critic Guillaume Apollinaire (France, 1880–1918) made this remark: "Each god creates in his own image, and so does every painter. Only photographers manufacture precise duplicates of nature." His comment—especially as it relates to painters—rings true. Modern artists have attempted to revise and recreate notions of appropriate art images. But the second part of Apollinaire's remark—the contrast between painters and photographers—is not entirely true.

Photographers do not necessarily succeed in duplicating nature, nor do they always intend to.

Alfred Stieglitz (United States, 1864–1946) developed a method of photography that was related to Expressionism. Initially, Stieglitz used photography in a documentary manner, depicting everyday realism. Later, however, Stieglitz became a promoter of abstract art works and explored abstraction in his photography. Stieglitz wanted to show that photography could be non-objective.

◀ Figure 16–8 Do you think this painting would be more dramatic if the artist had added more detail or taken away some detail? What has the artist done to create a feeling of movement? What aesthetic view would you use when judging this work?

George Wesley Bellows. *Both Members of This Club.* 1909. Canvas. 115 x 160.5 cm (45¼ x 63⅛"). National Gallery of Art, Washington, D.C. Chester Dale Collection.

An artist who was closely tied to the Ashcan School, though not one of The Eight, was George Bellows. His painting in Figure 16–8 is of one of his favorite subjects, a prizefight. The work shows two boxers clashing furiously at center ring while onlookers cheer them on. Study the faces of the crowd. The quick, slashing brush strokes with which they are captured match the action in the ring.

Photography

The Ashcan painters were not alone in using city scenes as subjects for art. The same look and feel was achieved in the works of artist Alfred Stieglitz (**steeg**-luhts). Stieglitz played an important part in the early development of photography as a new art form. Examine his photograph in Figure 16–9. What details in the work reveal it to be of a bitterly cold winter day? What mood does the picture communicate?

◀ Figure 16–9 Find the curving and diagonal lines that help pull the viewer in. How does the variety of light and dark values add interest to the work?

Alfred Stieglitz. *The Terminal.* c. 1892. Photogravure. 25.4 x 33.7 cm (10 x 13¼"). The Art Institute of Chicago, Chicago, Illinois. The Alfred Stieglitz Collection.

Lesson 3   *Art of the Early Twentieth Century in America*   📖   **249**

Handbook Cross-Reference
Refer students to the Career Spotlight, *Handbook* page **302** for information about becoming a photojournalist. You may also want to use Studio Lesson 3, *Handbook* pages **308-309** as an extension for students who are particularly interested in photography. Following the directions of the studio lesson, students will create a photo essay which deals with a theme that focuses on some aspect of a human condition.

for visual works related to the selected topic. What messages do the photographs, paintings, and drawings communicate? What styles have the photographers and artists chosen? Are the works realistic or abstract? How have such visual elements as color, line, and shape been used? If you were not able to read the words that accompany each illustration, would you understand its subject and the message it conveys?

Vocabulary. Display a map of the United States. Ask volunteers to identify various regions of the country (such as the Midwest or the South) and to point them out on the map. Help students discuss how these regions differ from one another in climate, in history, in industry, in agriculture, and so on. What special interests and concerns might artists from each region have? Why would people from different regions have different concerns? After this discussion, introduce the term *Regionalism* and explain that it identifies a style of art. Let students speculate about the meaning of the term and then check the definition in the Glossary at the back of the text.

Developing Concepts

Exploring Aesthetics. Lead the class in a discussion of John Sloan's *Hairdresser's Window,* Figure 16-7: What is the subject of the painting? How is the subject depicted? What mood or idea does the painting communicate to you? Then remind students that the Ashcan School painters were laughed at for depicting working-class Americans in a realistic way; such city scenes were not considered suitable subjects for "real" art. Ask: Why do you think people had that kind of attitude toward works of art? What makes the works of Ashcan School artists different from those of more traditional realistic painters, such as Winslow Homer? How are the concerns of the artists different? How do you respond to the work of this Ashcan School painter?

Using Art Criticism. Have students work with partners to discuss the five different works of art reproduced in this lesson. Ask each pair of students to agree on a favorite work and then to write a short description and analysis of that painting or photograph.

249

▶ Figure 16–10 **How is the principle of emphasis used in this painting? Point to lines that lead to the figures of the preacher and the girl.**

John Steuart Curry. *Baptism in Kansas.* 1928. Oil on canvas. 101.6 x 127 cm (40 x 50"). Whitney Museum of American Art, New York, New York. Gift of Gertrude Vanderbilt Whitney.

REGIONALISM

After World War I a different brand of realistic art enjoyed brief popularity in the United States. Several artists used a style that became known as **Regionalism** (**reej**-uhn-uhl-iz-uhm) to record *local scenes and events from the artist's own region, or area, of the country.*

An example of the Regionalist style may be found in Figure 16–10. The artist of the work, John Steuart Curry (**stoo**-urt **ker**-ee), was a native of Kansas. In this painting he shows a preacher about to baptize, or spiritually cleanse, a young girl. The setting is a Kansas farm. Relatives and friends have gathered to witness this ritual of passage. They all look at the preacher and girl, automatically directing the viewer's eyes there. The legs of a windmill point to the scene as well as to the glowing clouds in the sky.

ART IN MEXICO

The early twentieth century was a time of unrest and revolution in Mexico. Hardworking peasants, treated like slaves by rich landlords, struggled to free themselves. Several artists witnessed the struggle. They used their art to lend their support to the people. One who did so was Mexico's foremost muralist (**myoor**-uh-luhst). A **muralist** is *an artist who paints large art works directly onto walls or ceilings.* His name was Diego Rivera (dee-**ay**-goh rih-**vehr**-uh). In the mural in Figure 16–11, the artist tells of the only true escape for the poor: death. Several soldiers of the common people kneel around one of their own who has fallen in battle. In the distance flames rise from the landlord's house; the peasant's death has already been avenged.

✔ CHECK YOUR UNDERSTANDING

1. Who were The Eight? What were their backgrounds as artists? What kinds of paintings did they create?
2. When did The Eight stage their first showing? How did the public react? What nickname were The Eight given?
3. What art form was the specialty of Alfred Stieglitz?
4. What style of art became popular after World War I? Name an artist who created works in this style.
5. What is a muralist? Who was Mexico's foremost muralist?
6. What theme appears in the work of Diego Rivera?

Following Up

Closure. Let students work in groups to discuss their ink drawings from the "Studio Experience" activity. Ask each group member to display his or her work, and have other members identify the theme word selected. Then have students identify and discuss the aspects of their own drawings that they consider most successful.

Evaluation. 1. Review students' written responses to the "Check Your Understanding" questions. 2. Consider students' contributions to the "Closure" group discussions.

Reteaching. Work with small groups of students to review the art trends of the early twentieth century in the United States and Mexico. Then let group members select one of the paintings reproduced in this lesson and compare it to the work of Thomas Eakins, Winslow Homer, or Albert Pinkham Ryder. (See Figures 15-6, 15-7, and 15-8 on pages 232-234.)

Enrichment. Have students work in groups to plan and paint murals that suggest the work of Diego Rivera. Group members should begin by selecting a story and a message that they want to depict in their mural. Then have them work together to plan, sketch in, and paint all the parts of the mural. Let group members display their completed murals, answering any questions other students may have about the story or the message.

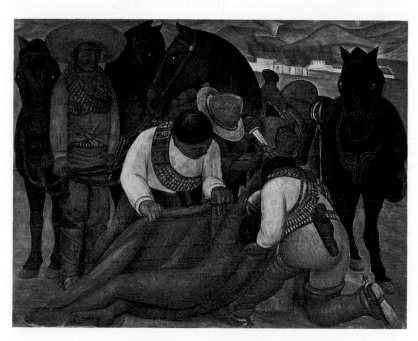

◄ **Figure 16–11** Describe the way in which these soldiers care for the dead. What feelings do you think this painting stirred up in Mexican viewers of the artist's day?

Diego Rivera. *Liberation of the Peon.* 1931. Fresco on plaster. 187.9 x 241.3 cm (74 x 95"). Philadelphia Museum of Art, Philadelphia, Pennsylvania. Gift of Mr. & Mrs. Herbert Cameron Morris.

Answers to "Check Your Understanding"

1. The Eight were a group of lesser-known painters. They were all one-time newspaper cartoonists or magazine illustrators who created art work that reflected the spirit of the times in which they lived, the early 1900s.
2. The Eight staged their first showing in 1908. The public reacted politely, then they laughed. The Eight were given the nickname, "The Ashcan School."
3. Photography was the specialty of Alfred Stieglitz.
4. A style of art called "Regionalism" became popular after World War I. John Steuart Curry created works in this style.
5. A muralist is an artist who paints large art works directly onto a wall or ceiling. Diego Rivera was Mexico's foremost muralist.
6. The theme appearing in the works of both Diego Rivera and Rufino Tamayo is the struggle for liberty.

Making a Print of a Figure in Action

Making a Print of a Figure in Action

LESSON PLAN
(pages 252–253)

Objectives
After completing this lesson, students will be able to:
• Make prints showing figures in action.
• Describe, analyze, interpret, and judge their own prints.

Supplies
• Pencils; sheets of sketch paper; paper towels; ballpoint pens; foam trays; brayers; scissors; water-based printing ink; shallow trays; scrap paper; sheets of drawing paper, 10 x 12 inches (25 x 30 cm).

TEACHING THE LESSON

Getting Started

Motivator. Let groups of students work together to draw and discuss lines that convey movement. Have members of each group experiment with different kinds of lines. Remind them to use both the tips and the sides of their pencils, and encourage them to experiment with thick lines and thin lines, straight lines and diagonal lines, curved lines, and jagged lines. What kinds of movement do the different lines convey?

Vocabulary. Review with students the definition of the term *print:* How is a print created? What steps are involved? How is a print different from a reproduction of an original painting?

Developing Concepts

Exploring Aesthetics. Encourage students to discuss their responses to the painting shown in Figure 16-12: How does this work make you feel?

Figure 16–12 shows another action scene by George Bellows. This is one of six paintings the artist made on the subject of prize-fights. He also made many prints and countless drawings. Here, as elsewhere, he uses slashing diagonal lines to show movement. In this lesson you will do the same.

WHAT YOU WILL LEARN
You will overlap a series of prints showing a figure in action. You will use diagonal lines to complete the figure. These lines will add to a feeling of rhythm or movement. (See Figure 16–13.)

WHAT YOU WILL NEED
• Pencil and sheets of sketch paper
• Ballpoint pen and paper towels
• Styrofoam meat tray
• Brayer
• Water-based printing ink and shallow tray
• Scissors
• Sheet of drawing paper, 10 x 12 inches (25 x 30 cm)

▶ **Figure 16–12 What has been done to emphasize the two figures? What kinds of lines have been used?**

George Wesley Bellows. *Stag at Sharkey's.* 1909. Oil on canvas. 93 x 122.5 cm (36¼ x 48¼"). The Cleveland Museum of Art, Cleveland, Ohio. Hinman B. Hurlbut Collection.

Classroom Management Tip
You may suggest that students make a masking tape handle that could be applied to the back of the figure for easy lifting.

WHAT YOU WILL DO

1. Take turns with your classmates in acting as models. Each model will strike an action pose, such as running, reaching, or pushing.
2. Make a series of gesture drawings of students in different poses. Quickly drawn diagonal lines will help you catch a sense of action. Avoid details. Focus on showing movement. (For more on gesture drawing, see Technique Tip 1, *Handbook* page 277.)
3. Select your best drawing. Place it on top of the styrofoam meat tray and transfer the figure to the tray by tracing over it firmly with a ballpoint pen. Cut your figure out of the tray with scissors. This is to be your printing plate.
4. Squeeze a small amount of water-based printing ink into the tray. Roll the brayer back and forth through the ink until the whole brayer is covered with ink.
5. Put the figure on a paper towel. Roll the brayer over the figure. Pick up the figure by the edges and place it ink-side down on your sheet of drawing paper. Press the back of the figure firmly all over to transfer ink.
6. Ink the plate again and make another print. This time overlap images on your paper until you are satisfied with your design. Arrange your images in a horizontal or vertical line to add a feeling of rhythm.
7. Title your work, sign it, and place it on display.

EXAMINING YOUR WORK

- **Describe** Identify the figure in your print. Point out different features of the figure.
- **Analyze** Explain how the diagonal lines in your print carry a sense of rhythm.
- **Interpret** Find out whether viewers can identify the action in your print. Reveal the action you were trying to show.
- **Judge** Tell whether you feel your work succeeds. Tell what you would do to improve your work on a second effort.

▲ Figure 16–13 Student work. Figure in action.

OTHER STUDIO IDEAS

- Print your image again, this time using complementary colors of paper and ink. Compare the result with your first print. Tell which gives more of a sense of movement.
- ● Have a model act out a series of poses showing one non-stop act. One possibility would be walking, stopping, and bending to pick up something. Make a printing plate for each pose. Print your images horizontally on a long sheet of paper. Make sure the different images overlap.

Lesson 4   *Making a Print of a Figure in Action*   **253**

Understanding Art History. Ask volunteers to explore the art works created by Futurists, such as Umberto Boccioni, Giocomo Balla, Gino Severini. What was the interest of these artists in movement? What techniques did they use to convey movement in their works? Let the volunteers share their findings with the rest of the class; encourage students to discuss how the Futurists' method of conveying movement differed from more traditional methods.

Developing Studio Skills. Let each student carve several styrofoam trays into printing plates that show basic shapes, either geometric or organic. Then have students use their plates to create several different printed designs, each demonstrating a different principle of organizing the shapes and colors. For example, ask students to create prints that convey balance, emphasis, or rhythm.

Following Up

Closure. Let groups of students work together to compare and discuss their prints, following the steps in "Examining Your Work." Be sure each student has an opportunity to get the responses of other group members (see "Interpret"). Then have students write answers to the "Judge" section of the activity.

Evaluation. Review students' prints, listen to their "Closure" group discussions, and read their judgments of their own work.

Reteaching. Work with small groups of students; help them review the principle of movement. Then have group members browse through the text or other books that include reproductions of art works; ask each student to select and share at least two works that convey a sense of movement. What techniques have the artists used?

Enrichment. Display all the prints. What stories do the prints suggest? Do some of the prints seem to work together to suggest a narrative? Have students write original stories inspired by one of several prints.

Background Information

In the United States, especially during the early modern period, Realism was the style most often taught and practiced in schools of art. Yet the ideas of speed and movement were so strong that they eventually led to an American form of Abstract Expressionism, which has become known as Action Painting. In this style of art, the process of painting is as important as the product of painting. The artist becomes part of the art work. Action Painting retains the dynamism found in art styles such as Futurism, but its works are non-objective.

Jackson Pollock (United States, 1912–1956) is the artist most often associated with Action Painting. For several years Pollock created his paintings by laying his canvases on the floor and pouring paint across them. Later Pollock painted large, swirling patterns of color and a series of works done entirely in black and white. Pollock used a variety of techniques and media, always emphasizing the action of the artist.

ANSWERS TO "CHAPTER 16 REVIEW"

Building Vocabulary

1. Fauvism
2. Expressionism
3. Cubism
4. non-objective art
5. The Eight
6. The Ashcan School
7. Regionalism
8. muralist

Reviewing Art Facts

9. One feature Fauvism and Expressionism had in common was the use of wild color.
10. Paul Cézanne's idea led to the formation of the Cubist movement.
11. Wassily Kandinsky was credited with developing the non-objective style.
12. Both Stieglitz and the Ashcan painters used city scenes as subjects.
13. The regionalist movement began after World War I. One member of the movement was John Steuart Curry.
14. Diego Rivera was a muralist.

Thinking About Art

1. Students could answer either yes or no. But the reason given should focus on the emotional power Kollwitz conveys by distorting proportion.
2. Students could say Expressionists *feel* their way through a painting.
3. Answers will vary. Students should justify choices by showing how the artist used emphasis to lead the viewers' eyes to the most important feature.

BUILDING VOCABULARY

Number a sheet of paper from 1 to 8. After each number, write the term from the box that best matches each description below.

Ashcan School	Fauvism
Cubism	muralist
The Eight	non-objective art
Expressionism	Regionalism

1. An art movement in which artists used wild, intense color combinations in their paintings.
2. A style that emphasized the expression of innermost feelings.
3. A style in which objects are shown from several different angles at once.
4. A style in which no objects or subjects can be readily identified.
5. A group of New York artists who created art work that reflected the spirit of the times in which they lived, the early 1900s.
6. The popular name given to the group of artists who made realistic paintings of working-class America.
7. A style that records local scenes and events from an artist's own region, or area, of the country.
8. An artist who paints large art works directly onto walls or ceilings.

REVIEWING ART FACTS

Number a sheet of paper from 9 to 14. Answer each question in a complete sentence.

9. What feature did Expressionism and Fauvism have in common?
10. Identify the artist whose idea led to the forming of the Cubist movement.
11. What artist is credited with developing the non-objective style?
12. In what way were the photographs of Alfred Stieglitz linked to the work of the Ashcan painters?
13. When did the Regionalist movement begin? Name a member of the movement.
14. Which artist that you read about in this chapter was a muralist?

THINKING ABOUT ART

On a sheet of paper, answer each question in a sentence or two.

1. **Extend.** Imagine that Käthe Kollwitz had chosen to do her print *The Prisoners* (Figure 16–3) in color. Do you think such a decision would have added to the power of the work? Explain your answer.
2. **Interpret.** Cubists, it has been noted, relied mostly on their minds to think their way through a painting. Think of a verb you might use in place of *think* to make this statement fit the work of the German Expressionists.
3. **Analyze.** The work by John Steuart Curry (Figure 16–10) offers an excellent example of an artist's use of emphasis. Find another work in this chapter that uses emphasis. Explain what the artist of that work does to lead the viewer's eye to the most important feature.

MAKING ART CONNECTIONS

1. **Language Arts.** Divide a sheet of paper into three columns. Label one column *Subject*, one *Composition*, and one *Content*. Then, going through the art works in this chapter one by one, decide in which column or columns each artist's name belongs. Compare your completed list with those of other students in your class.
2. **Language Arts.** What might you say to someone who claimed photography is not art? Would you agree or disagree? How might you use the work by Alfred Stieglitz (Figure 16–9) to support your argument?

LOOKING AT THE DETAILS

The detail shown below is from Wassily Kandinsky's *Painting Number 200*. Study the detail and answer the following questions using complete sentences.

1. What do you notice in this work that suggests that a drawing medium has been used. Explain your answer.
2. Which aesthetic view would you use in judging this work? Give reasons to support your answer.
3. Look at the entire work on page **240**. The viewer's eye tends to follow this image from the center of the canvas to the lower left, then upward through the middle. Which elements of art help to define this path?
4. Which principles of art unify this work?

Wassily Kandinsky. *Painting Number 200*. 1914. Oil on canvas. (Detail.) 162.5 x 80 cm (64 x 31½"). Museum of Modern Art, New York, New York. Mrs. Simon Guggenheim Fund.

Art of Today

Chapter Scan

TRB Resources

- 17-8 Chapter Test
- Color Transparency 33
- Color Transparency 34

TEACHING THE CHAPTER

Introducing the Art Work

Direct students' attention to Frank Stella's *Shards III*. Inform them that Frank Stella is a contemporary American artist. He studied art at the Philips Academy and Princeton University, after which he moved to and settled in New York City. Stella's earliest works were "minimalist" paintings, using simple geometrical patterns as images. In the 1970s Stella radically departed from his minimalist style and has remained a continually-developing artist, refusing to adhere to a fixed painting style. His current works borrow from the arts of sculpture and architecture, without leaving the domain of painting. His works require not only the inner commitment of an artist, but an enormous expenditure of physical energy as well. Stella's works remain in the painting domain because they are frontal—understood only when seen straight on.

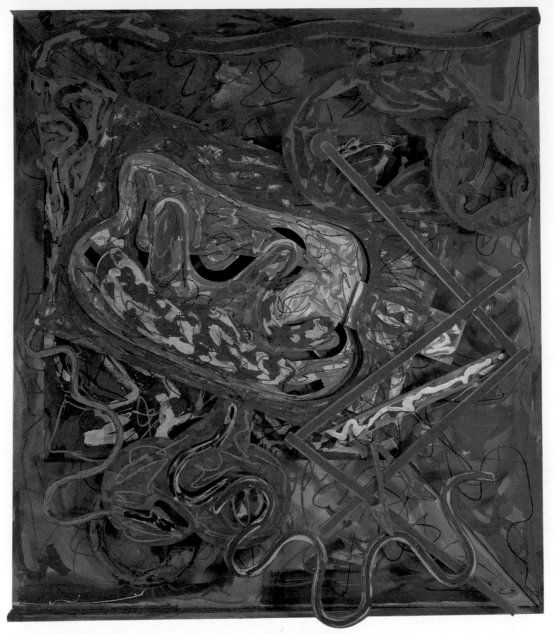

▲ Can you imagine Giotto, Rembrandt, or Monet creating a work like this? Like their paintings, this one was made using media, techniques, and ideas of its time.

Frank Stella. *Shards III*. 1983. Mixed media on aluminum. 346.7 x 304.2 x 62.2 cm (136½ x 119¾ x 24½"). Leo Castelli Gallery, New York, New York.

CHAPTER 17

Art of Today

The story of art is a story of change. With each passing age, the search for untried forms of expression is renewed. A style that shocks viewers of one generation becomes part of the mainstream in the next.

At no time in history has the search for new directions been more visible than now. The last 40 years have seen more changes in art styles and techniques than all the thousand years before. One recent style appears in the work at the left. How does this style differ from those developed earlier? In this chapter you will learn how this and other recent styles originated.

OBJECTIVES

After completing this chapter, you will be able to:

- Identify major art movements of the last 50 years.
- Identify the characteristics and leaders of those art movements.
- Create a painting in the Surrealist style.
- Create a work using contemporary styles and techniques.

WORDS YOU WILL LEARN

Abstract Expressionism
Dada
Hard-Edge painting
kinetic art
mobile
multi-media art
New Realism
Op Art
social protest painting
Surrealism

ARTISTS YOU WILL MEET

Alexander Calder
Giorgio de Chirico
Gene Davis
Arshile Gorky
Duane Hanson
Barbara Hepworth
Ellsworth Kelly
Paul Klee
Jacob Lawrence
René Magritte
Marino Marini
Joan Miró
Henry Moore
Louise Nevelson
Nam June Paik
Judy Pfaff
Sandy Skoglund
Frank Stella
Andrew Wyeth

257

Examining the Art Work
Explain to students that *Shards III* is a multi-media art work. It is only one of five in the Shards Series which are related to Stella's Circuit Series. The Circuit Series is named after automobile race tracks and the works are concerned with speed and change. Shards refers to fragments of former objects.

Point out the way the two shapes at the bottom of the work extend beyond the border. Explain that when viewing a photograph of this work, it is clearly identified as a multi-media piece. When seen in person, the viewer more clearly sees the assembled and interlocking shapes, the depth and dimension, and the negative space.

Explain to students that a sense of unity is created through color, shape, and form. Point out the serpentine or snake-like form as the most obvious unifying shape.

Discussing the Art Work
Ask students how Stella created depth in this work. Explain that he placed shapes on different physical planes, many of which extend far from the wall. Stella created a three-dimensional piece which in itself has depth, yet he does it only with the frontal view in mind. Explain that the artist also used negative space to create shadows and obvious elevations which create depth for the viewer.

Ask students what kind of mood this work evokes. Point out the variety of both bold and subtle colors and how the green hue provides a calming effect while the brighter colors provide a sense of staccato rhythms in the floating unusual shapes. Suggest that this work creates a mood that is whimsical and jazzy.

Tell students that in this chapter they will learn about the major art movements of the last fifty years and its leaders.They will also create their own contemporary art works.

Building Self-Esteem
Tell students that in this book they have seen art created over a period of thousands of years, from before history was recorded to the present day. They have seen everything from the most primitive animals scratched into cave walls and colored with ground earth pigments to the multi-media pieces shown in this chapter. They have learned how critics discuss and evaluate art, how historians keep track of it and judge it, and what principles are used to design a successful work of art. What should have become apparent is that human beings, from the earliest times, have expressed themselves creatively. Whether they use paint and brushes, clay and fire, or building blocks and concrete, artists have interpreted reality in their own very personal ways. Styles and tastes have changed over the centuries, but what the artist produces is ultimately a personal expression. Encourage students to continue experimenting with art materials and visual self-expression. Help them realize it can enrich their lives in many ways.

LESSON 1

European Art Today

LESSON PLAN
(pages 258–261)

Objectives
After completing this lesson, students will be able to:
- Describe the Dada and Surrealist art movements.
- Name three twentieth-century European artists whose art was based on the inner workings of the human mind.
- Describe some of the new explorations undertaken by twentieth-century sculptors.
- Name three twentieth-century sculptors.

Supplies
- Sheets of paper.
- Pencils.
- Crayons or colored chalk.
- Colored pencils or felt tip markers.
- Reproductions of Marino Marini's prints and paintings.
- Modeling clay.
- Clay modeling tools.

> **TRB Resource**
> - 17-1 *A Personal Aesthetic,* (aesthetics)

TEACHING THE LESSON

Getting Started
Motivator. Have students play the Surrealist game known as "Exquisite Corpse." Give each student a sheet of paper to fold crosswise into three equal sections. On the top third, students should draw a head and neck of any animal, person, or creature, making sure that the necklines extend slightly into the middle section. Students should fold the paper so that only the middle section shows and pass it to someone else. Students should then draw a body down to the waist, once again leaving starting lines. Pass the papers again and fill in the rest of the body. At each stage the papers should be folded under so that students cannot see the other parts of the drawing. Then students should open the drawings and view them. According to the Surrealists, games like this reveal subconscious truths that people generally ignore.

European Art Today

The Impressionists went outdoors to find ideas. The Expressionists looked to their own hearts. The second decade of the twentieth century found artists exploring still another source for art ideas. That was the inner workings of the mind.

FANTASY ART

Imagine yourself a visitor at a showing of new art. Suddenly your eye falls upon a work that is at once familiar and shocking. It is familiar because it is a photograph of the *Mona Lisa*. It is shocking because someone has drawn a mustache on Leonardo da Vinci's world-famous portrait.

It was this very experience that outraged members of Europe's art community in 1916. The artist behind the work was a one-time Cubist named Marcel Duchamp (mar-**sel** doo-**shahnh**). The movement he belonged to, **Dada** (**dahd**-ah) was *founded on the belief that Western culture had lost its meaning.* For Dadaists (**dahd**-uah-ists), the beauty of art was in the *mind*, not the eye, of the beholder. Art, in other words, did not have to be beautiful or express important ideas. Usually the point was driven home, as in Duchamp's photograph, by poking fun at art of the past.

SURREALISM

Although Dada lasted only six years, it paved the way for other art explorations of the mind. The most important of these was **Surrealism** (suh-**ree**-uh-liz-uhm). This movement *probed the unconscious world of dreams* for ideas, and was touched off by the works of a Greek-born Italian artist named Giorgio de Chirico (**jor**-joh duh **kir**-ih-koh). Like the artists who followed him, de Chirico created mysterious, nightmarish landscapes

▲ Figure 17–1   What gives this picture its dreamlike appearance? What kinds of feelings does it arouse in you?

Giorgio de Chirico. *The Nostalgia of the Infinite.* 1911. Oil on canvas. 135.2 x 64.8 cm (53¼ x 25½"). The Museum of Modern Art, New York, New York.

258   Lesson 1   *European Art Today*

Background Information
The Dada movement was rooted in disgust at bourgeois, middle-class life and sought to subvert it. The irrationality of the human condition had been made all too clear by the savagery of World War I. Cultivating a kind of artistic spontaneity that was meant to reveal the inadequacy and stupidity of conventional beliefs, Dadaists hoped to find what they termed an "unreasoned order." Dadaists valued the act of producing art more than the art work itself. Dada pioneer Marcel Duchamp eventually reduced the act of creation to one of mere selection, entirely eliminating the longstanding cult of craftsmanship and personal touch. Dadaists also denounced the practice of painting as escapist and ineffective. Cubist painting was singled out and accused of being devoid of passion and fantasy. Surrealism shared Dada's fascination with all that seemed irrational, but systematized it according to Freudian theory. Surrealists gathered a wild array of subject matter from the unconscious by various means and then played with it on a canvas.

where time had no meaning. One of these is shown in Figure 17–1. Notice the two small figures seen as silhouettes at the center of the work. Their importance seems to shrink before the huge tower looming behind them. In the stillness a sudden breeze begins whipping at some flags atop the tower. Who are these people? What is the meaning of the tower and the flags? Like a dream, the painting raises many unanswerable questions. Attempts to answer these questions only adds to the feeling that the viewers are experiencing a nightmare from which they cannot awaken.

By the end of the 1920s the Surrealist movement had spread to many countries. One artist who seemed comfortable with the movement was the Spanish painter Joan Miró (**zhoo**-ahn mee-**roh**). Miró created fantasy worlds that were free not only of rhyme and reason but also of realism. In the work in Figure 17–2 he brings the viewer face-to-face with a scene depicting strange, imaginary creatures. See how the subjects whirl and twist in a playful ballet.

◀ Figure 17–2 Why do you suppose the artist called this painting "Dutch Interior"? Are there any shapes that look like animals or musical instruments?

Joan Miró. *Dutch Interior*. 1928. Guggenheim Collection. Venice.

Lesson 1 *European Art Today* 259

Fantasy and humor are key ingredients also in the art of Swiss-born Paul Klee (**klay**). Though not a Surrealist, Klee based his work on images glimpsed through his mind's eye. Most, like his picture of a tightrope walker (Figure 17–3), are like simple, childlike creations. Notice how the walker makes his way boldly across a wire supported by a flimsy network of thin lines. These lines look as though they will collapse at any second. What statement might the artist be making about people who foolishly enter situations without weighing the consequences?

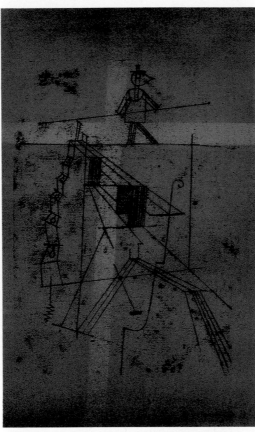

▲ Figure 17–3 What has the artist done to add a sense of harmony? Can you point to places where variety is used? What property of this work is most important — its realism, its design, or its meaning?

Paul Klee. *Tightrope Walker.* 1923. Color lithograph. 43.1 x 26.7 cm (17 x 10½"). McNay Art Museum, San Antonio, Texas.

SCULPTURE
Over the last 40 years sculptors have also explored new areas of self-expression. Some have continued to create recognizable images. Others have taken the path toward non-objective art.

The works of Marino Marini (muh-**reen**-oh muh-**reen**-ee), an Italian sculptor, draw on a single haunting image. That image — peasants fleeing their villages on horseback during bombing raids — was one the artist witnessed during World War II. Sculptures like the one in Figure 17–4 are attempts to capture the suffering of civilians during wartime.

▲ Figure 17–4 What kinds of real and imaginary lines help add a feeling of tension? What makes this work successful or unsuccessful?

Marino Marini. *Horse and Rider.* 1951. Bronze. 55.7 x 31.1 x 43.5 cm (21⅞ x 12¼ x 17⅛"). Hirshhorn Museum and Sculpture Garden, Smithsonian Institution, Washington, D.C. Gift of the Lily Harmon Foundation.

An artist best known for her non-objective creations was English sculptor Barbara Hepworth. A trademark of her work is the use of holes. As in the work in Figure 17–5, these create centers of interest within gently curving forms.

Background Information
Although the Swiss painter Paul Klee was never a Surrealist, fantasy was an important part of his painting. On scraps of burlap, paper, glass, and linen, he produced pictures based on his own imagination and wit. Often he worked on several paintings at the same time, sitting before his easels for hours. He was fascinated by a world that he said was filled with wonders and spent hours studying seashells, coral, butterfly wings, stained glass, and mosaics. His reactions to the world resulted in pictures that free viewers from their accustomed way of looking at things and often cause them delight and amusement. Klee himself agreed with those who found his art childlike. Hoping to regain the unspoiled imagination of the child, he purposely patterned his art on that of children.

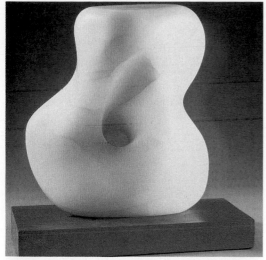

▲ Figure 17–5 Notice the smooth texture of the alabaster. Would you be tempted to run your hands over the surface of the work?

Barbara Hepworth. *Merryn*. 1962. Alabaster. 33 x 29 x 20 cm (13 x 11½ x 8"). National Museum of Women in the Arts. Washington, D.C., Gift of Wallace and Wilhelmina Holladay.

▲ Figure 17–6 Notice how the sculptor gave the family members a feeling of unity. How did he provide variety?

Henry Moore. *Family Group*. 1948–49. Cast 1950. Bronze. 150.5 x 118.1, base 114.3 x 75.9 cm (59¼ x 46½, base 45 x 29⅞"). Museum of Modern Art, New York, New York. A Conger Goodyear Fund.

STUDIO EXPERIENCE

Using your imagination, picture a scene you might expect to find in a nightmare. On a sheet of paper, list objects you imagine. Do not include people. Using pencil, draw the scene as a Surrealist might. Try to capture the feeling of fear the image stirs up in you. Use crayon or chalk to color your picture. Make sure you choose hues that help emphasize the fear you are trying to express.

Another sculptor, Henry Moore, created both non-objective works and works that were sometimes nearer to realism. The close relationship of family members is expressed in Figure 17–6. Moore stylized the figures and yet clearly defined them as mother, father, and child. The figures of the parents are linked by the child, the touching knees, and the husband's hand on his wife's shoulder, providing a unified whole.

✔ CHECK YOUR UNDERSTANDING

1. What did the Dadaists believe? How did they usually give expression to this belief?
2. What is Surrealism? What artist's works initiated the movement? Name another Surrealist.
3. For what kinds of works is Paul Klee best known?
4. What image turns up again and again in the works of Marino Marini?
5. What is the trademark of sculptor Barbara Hepworth?

Painting in the Surrealist Style

Objectives

After completing this lesson, students will be able to:
- Describe the characteristics of René Magritte's art.
- Create a painting in the Surrealist style.

Supplies

- Pencils.
- Sketch paper.
- Sheets of white drawing paper, 10 x 12 inches (25 x 30 cm).
- Tempera paints.
- Assorted brushes.
- Mixing trays.
- Prints by M. C. Escher.
- India ink.

> **TRB Resource**
> - 17-2 *Art—The Heartbeat of the World*, (art history)

TEACHING THE LESSON

Getting Started

Motivator. Invite students to share accounts of dreams in which there were peculiar juxtapositions of people, objects, or events. Write on the board the bizarre combinations or coincidences that occurred in the students' dreams. If they wish, students may offer interpretations of their dreams. Discuss whether very strange or seemingly senseless imagery in paintings and dreams should be considered meaningless.

Developing Concepts

Using Art Criticism. Have each student show Figure 17-7 to at least three people who are unfamiliar with Surrealist art and ask their interpretation. Students should write this information down. Discuss the various responses and categorize them by the three aesthetic theories. Then discuss whether people's opinions varied according to their age, gender, or personality.

262

Painting in the Surrealist Style

Another artist who painted in the Surrealist style was Belgian painter René Magritte (ren-**ay** muh-**greet**). Magritte was a painter of riddles. In his pictures, familiar objects turn up together in unusual relationships or strange settings. Look at the work in Figure 17–7. At first glance this appears to be little more than a realistic painting of an ordinary looking room with a fireplace suggesting stillness and peace. The clock on the mantle notes the slow, regular passing of time. But bursting out of the wall is a steaming locomotive! This is an image of speed, energy and noise that disturbs the peacefulness of the room. What does it mean? Perhaps the only purpose here is to create surprise. We are shocked to see ordinary objects put together in ways that make no sense at all.

WHAT YOU WILL LEARN

You will draw and paint a work in the Surrealist style. You will combine familiar objects in strange, surprising ways. Objects will be painted realistically with a variety of hues, values, and intensities. (See Figure 17–8.)

WHAT YOU WILL NEED

- Pencil and sheets of sketch paper
- Sheet of white drawing paper, 10 x 12 inches (25 x 30 cm)
- Tempera paint
- Assorted brushes
- Mixing tray

▲ Figure 17–7   How does Magritte's dream world differ from de Chirico's (see Figure 17–1)? Does the realistic painting style add to or take away from the idea the work communicates?

René Magritte. *Time Transfixed*. 1938. Oil on canvas. 147 x 98.7 cm (58 x 39″). The Art Institute of Chicago, Chicago, Illinois. Joseph Winterbotham Collection.

262   Lesson 2   *Painting in the Surrealist Style*

Background Information
The Belgian artist René Magritte began his loose association with the Surrealist group in 1930. His images are mysterious and derived from fantasy, but they are executed in a highly naturalistic style that is entirely opposed in spirit to the spontaneous, automatic handwriting that was cultivated by more central members of the Surrealist movement. Besides painting, Magritte also experimented with photography. Although he did not pursue this medium for very long, his influence on Surrealist photography was considerable. Photographers such as Herbert Bayer have translated Magritte's paradoxical pictures into photomontaged visual riddles that question everyday conceptions of reality.

WHAT YOU WILL DO

1. Pick a common object to be featured in your picture. Using your imagination, sketch this object in a setting that makes little or no sense. You might, for instance, feature a thumbtack as tall as a house. You might choose to draw a bed on which eggs are frying. Make your image as offbeat and surprising as you can.

2. Carefully transfer your best sketch to the sheet of drawing paper. Make your finished drawing as realistic as possible. Using tempera, paint your work. Add details. Mix and blend hues, values, and intensities of color to make your objects lifelike.

4. Give your work a title unrelated to the objects in it. Write this title on the back of the picture.

5. Exchange paintings with a classmate. Write a brief explanation of the painting you receive. Your explanation, like the painting itself, can be offbeat.

6. Display your work along with its explanation. Compare it with those done by other students. Which were most surprising? What qualities in them caused you to react this way?

OTHER STUDIO IDEAS

- Think about two animals that look nothing alike. On a sheet of paper, list the features of each. Make a drawing of an imaginary animal that has features from both lists. Color your animal with watercolors. Add a background scene. Title your work.

- • Walk around your school grounds searching for an object that people might normally overlook. Two possibilities are a door to a storage closet and a flag pole. Design a picture in which this object is the center of attention. Do not change the appearance of the object. Instead, use your imagination to place it in a new and unusual setting.

EXAMINING YOUR WORK

- **Describe** Identify the objects in your picture. Explain what steps you took to make these objects appear lifelike.
- **Analyze** Point to the variety of hues, values, and intensities in your work. Identify any other elements and principles you used to make objects more real-looking.
- **Interpret** Explain what steps you took to surprise and shock viewers.
- **Judge** Tell whether you feel your work succeeds. State what aesthetic view you feel would be best for judging your work.

▲ Figure 17–8   Student work. Surrealist painting.

Developing Studio Skills. Show students copies of M. C. Escher prints that contain Surrealist-inspired architecture, such as *Concave and Convex, High and Low, House of Stairs, Relativity,* and *Balcony.* Then ask students to use India ink to draw a building of their own that incorporates Surrealist features.

Following Up

Closure. Have students write a paragraph that states whether the strange juxtapositions in art by Magritte and other Surrealists are appealing. Do they find Surrealist art meaningless and confusing, or does it strike a chord in their own experience?

Evaluation. 1. Review students' Surrealist paintings. 2. Examine the Surrealist architecture drawings. 3. Assess student paragraphs on Surrealist art.

Reteaching. Have students carry out a writing exercise based on the Surrealist notion of arbitrary juxtaposition. Give each student three slips of paper on which they are to write a brief description of a person, a goal, and an obstacle. Put the slips into three paper bags and have students draw out one in each category. Then students should write a Surrealist short story based on the character, goal, and problem on their slips. Discuss the similarities between their stories and the style of Figure 17-7.

Enrichment. Have groups of students investigate a woman Surrealist artist such as Frida Kahlo, Kay Sage, Dorothea Tanning, Leonor Fini, Remedios Varo, Leonora Carrington, and Lee Miller. The groups should write a page that provides basic background information on their artist and discusses the themes of her art. Each group should also make a brief oral presentation that explains why the work of its subject is Surrealist.

Developing Perceptual Skills
Explain to students that one relatively simple way to make a relief print is to place paper over a section of low-relief sculpture and make a crayon rubbing. Ask students to look for interesting relief designs on buildings, walkways, manhole covers, gates, fences, cemetery markers, and other structures. Have students make rubbings of these designs, if possible. (Remind students that they should get permission before making rubbings from historic landmarks or from private property.)

American Art Today

LESSON 3

American Art Today

Objectives

After completing this lesson, students will be able to:
• Describe the style of Abstract Expressionism.
• Explain why some artists were dissatisfied with Abstract Expressionism.
• Name three styles of painting that emerged soon after Abstract Expressionism.
• Name two artists who created new forms of non-objective sculpture.

Supplies

• Laundry bleach.
• Cotton swabs.
• Sheets of dark-colored construction paper.
• Reproductions of works by Duane Hanson.
• Scissors.
• Colored paper.
• Sheets of plain paper.
• Medium-weight wire.
• Aluminum cans.
• Cutting pliers and tin snips or heavy duty scissors.
• Hammer and nails.
• Spray enamel paint.

TRB Resources

• 17-3 *Jacob Lawrence,* (artist profile)
• 17-4 *The American Art Image,* (reproducible master)

TEACHING THE LESSON

Getting Started

Motivator. Point out to students that each of the artists in this lesson was working at a time when other prominent artists were working in their own styles. Have students compare the experiences of these artists with that of Italian Renaissance artists, whose artistic styles were much more consistent. Is it harder for artists to develop a style of their own than to work in the same style as others?

Vocabulary. Have students look up the definition of *mobile* in a dictionary. Compare the usages of the term as a noun and as an adjective. Discuss how the two senses are related.

264

In the late 1800s the United States was recognized as a global power. It began slowly but surely to emerge as a world leader in art. By 1950 the change was complete. New York replaced Paris as the center of painting and sculpture.

Art since that time has been rocked by one new style after another. Countless new materials and techniques have been tried as artists attempt to solve an age-old problem. That problem is how best to speak to viewers through the language of art. In this lesson you will look at some solutions.

ABSTRACT EXPRESSIONISM

The first new form of expression was a bold style that was influenced by several past styles. Its name is **Abstract Expressionism**. In this art style, *paint was dribbled, spilled, or splashed onto huge canvases to express painting as an action*. Abstract Expressionist artists rejected the use of subject matter in their work. They dripped, spilled, and splashed rich colors on canvas to create their paintings. The *act* of painting was so tied to their work that the Abstract Expressionists became labeled "action painters."

One of the first members of the Abstract Expressionist movement was an Armenian-born artist named Arshile Gorky (**ar**-shuhl **gor**-kee). Gorky's early works show strong traces of Surrealism. By the mid-1940s, however, he was showing real objects as doodle-like lines and shapes in his paintings. Figure 17–9 shows a painting completed a year before his death. To appreciate such works demands that viewers open themselves to the artist's one-of-a-kind blending of colors, shapes, and lines.

▲ **Figure 17–9** Does a viewer need to see things in a painting to enjoy it? Can a painting be enjoyed for the beauty of the visual elements?

Arshile Gorky. *Golden Brown Painting.* 1947. Oil on canvas. 110.8 x 141.3 cm (43⅝ x 55⅝"). Washington University Gallery of Art, St. Louis, Missouri.

▲ **Figure 17–10** What is the positive shape in this work? What is the negative shape?

Ellsworth Kelly. *Red/White.* 1964. Oil on canvas. 95.3 x 91.4 cm (37½ x 36"). Courtesy Blum Helman Gallery, New York, New York.

Background Information

Ellsworth Kelly's paintings are perfect examples of the Hard Edge movement's love of smooth surfaces, hard edges, pure colors, and simple geometric shapes rendered with great precision. Art historians have attributed Kelly's keen awareness of color and shape to early experiences of bird watching with his grandmother and to his stint in a camouflage battalion during World War II, when he was responsible for designing educational posters on how to create camouflages. Kelly does not base his paintings on any mathematical formula. He simply arranges the forms according to his eye, although the design is often abstracted from his nature photographs. Best known for his bold canvases, Kelly also intermittently has made sculptures, some of which are composed of his familiar geometric forms painted with primary colors. He later forsook almost all color and created works that had polished metal surfaces. In both his paintings and his sculpture, Kelly betrays a fascination with edges and how they slice through space.

Equally dazzling in their use of color are the paintings of Helen Frankenthaler (**frank-uhn-tahl-uhr**), another Abstract Expressionist. Frankenthaler's action paintings often begin on the floor of her studio. Standing above a blank canvas, the artist pours on layer after layer of thinned color. With each new addition, the work grows. Study the painting by Frankenthaler in Figure 2–5 on page **20**. Like most works by the artist, edges of shapes are sometimes sharp, sometimes blurred. Find the flamelike shape at the center. Notice how it appears to be spreading outward to other parts of the canvas.

OTHER DIRECTIONS IN PAINTING

It was not long after Abstract Expressionism appeared on the scene that other artists began challenging it. The style, they argued, was too personal—too much in the mind of the artist. Among the solutions that arose were:

- **Hard-Edge painting**. This was *a style that emphasized clear, crisp-edged shapes*. The work shown in Figure 17–10 is by Hard-Edge painter Ellsworth Kelly. Notice how the square shape of the canvas shows off the simple positive and negative shapes. What would you see first if the colors were reversed?

- **Social protest painting**. Emerging in the 1930s, this was *an art style that attacked the ills of big-city life*. It remained alive through the 1960s in the works of Jacob Lawrence, a black artist. Study the painting by Lawrence in Figure 17–11. Like the artist's other works, this one tells a story. What words would you use to describe the story?

- **New Realism**. Not all artists of the past few decades have been content to use non-objective styles. Some formed a movement called **New Realism**, *an art movement that rediscovered the importance of realistic detail*. Figure 17–12 shows a work by Andrew Wyeth, who has been a realist throughout his long career. The painting, you will notice, offers more than just a photographic record of its subject. It gives a glimpse of the kind of person the man is. Notice that he is turned away from the viewer. In this way he cannot see the pity in our eyes. Alone in his empty room he stubbornly guards the possessions left to him—his pride and dignity.

◀ **Figure 17–11   This is an example of social protest painting. What symbols did the artist use to convey his ideas?**

Jacob Lawrence. *Toussaint L'Overture Series*. 1938. Tempera on paper. 46.4 x 61.6 cm (18¼ x 24¼"). Fisk University.

Lesson 3   *American Art Today*   📖   **265**

Developing Concepts

Exploring Aesthetics. Have students examine Figure 17-14 (page **267**). Discuss how Nevelson unified the sculpture by repeating shapes and painting it a single color. Ask students to identify a local building or public sculpture that is unified by the same aesthetic means. Visit these structures or have students sketch them on the board. Discuss which forms are repeated and how the use of a single color lends unity to the work.

Using Art Criticism. Have students select the art work that they like the least in this lesson and write a four-part art critical discussion about it. In this case, however, ask students to arrive at a *positive* judgment of the work. Invite students to read aloud their evaluations. Discuss the reasons why certain works are less appealing and whether it was difficult to see their positive elements.

Understanding Art History. Tell students that Jacob Lawrence, whose work is pictured in Figure 17-11, worked on the WPA Federal Arts Project for eighteen months. Have students research this program and write a short report that explains why the U.S. government developed it, which artists participated, and how it benefited the artists and the public. Many WPA works were sold for four cents a pound in 1943 as scrap canvas and used to insulate pipes, but if there are any local WPA works have the class visit them.

Understanding Art History. Show students pictures of other sculptures by Duane Hanson to familiarize them with the range of his subjects. Ask students if Hanson would want to make a sculpture that looks like them. Students who think they would make a good Duane Hanson sculpture should assume the pose and expression they would strike for Hanson. Discuss how the student sculptures would fit into Duane Hanson's profile of American culture.

Background Information
Jacob Lawrence's paintings communicate his feelings about black culture and consciousness, often in the form of visual stories. Born in New Jersey in 1917, Lawrence moved to Harlem in the 1920s during the tremendous upswing in black culture that has come to be known as the Harlem Renaissance. Although the Harlem Renaissance was beginning to fade by the time Lawrence arrived with his mother, sister, and brother, the seeds of his artistic career were sown there. The Work Projects Administration (WPA) Federal Arts Project under Franklin Delano Roosevelt's administration also played a role in Lawrence's artistic development. In the Harlem Community Art Center and Harlem Art Workshop, Lawrence gained valuable experience and encouragement. In 1939 he had his first one-man show. He found that he often needed more than one frame of a painting to tell a story. Many of his works, including Figure 17-11, are parts of multi-canvas series that speak of the experience of African-Americans.

▲ Figure 17–12   Notice how the man in the picture is turned away from the viewer. What reason might the artist have had for positioning him this way?

Andrew Wyeth. *That Gentleman.* 1960. Tempera on panel. 59.7 x 45.1 cm (23½ x 17¾"). Dallas Museum of Art, Dallas, Texas.

SCULPTURE

Painters have not been alone in the search for new methods of self-expression. Sculptors, too, have experimented with new styles. One of them, Alexander Calder, was able to number among his contributions the invention of a new term. That term, **mobile** (**moh**-beel), was used to describe a *sculpture made of carefully balanced shapes hung on wires*. Most of Calder's mobiles, like the one in Figure 17–13, are non-objective. Imagine this moving sculpture as it might appear as you stand near it. Try to picture the ever-changing patterns created by the bobbing and twisting of the shapes. What images do you think might come to mind?

A different approach to non-objective sculpture is found in the three-dimensional collages of Louise Nevelson (**nev**-uhl-suhn). Her works, one of which appears in Figure 17–14, were assembled from found objects and wood scraps. Viewers often experience these sculptures as at once familiar and foreign. The wood scraps in Figure 17–14 are easily identified. They are combined in such a way, however, that they create something

entirely new and different. Are they gates or doors? If so, what kind of fascinating world lies beyond?

Just as some painters of recent times have made realism their goal, so have some sculptors. One is artist Duane Hanson. Hanson's sculptures are so lifelike they are often mistaken for real people. Imagine yourself

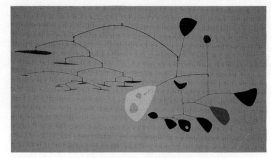

▲ Figure 17–13   What shape is emphasized in this mobile? How is this emphasis achieved? Is pattern an important principle? How is pattern shown?

Alexander Calder. *Zarabanda* (Un Disco Blanco). 1955. Painted sheet metal, metal rods and wire. 106.6 x 166.1 cm (42 x 65⅜"). Hirshhorn Museum and Sculpture Garden, Smithsonian Institution, Washington, D.C. Gift of Joseph H. Hirshhorn.

266   Lesson 3   *American Art Today*

▲ Figure 17–14   What would happen if this sculpture were painted in several different colors? Would it be as successful? Why or why not?

Louise Nevelson. *Mrs. N's Palace.* 1971. Painted wood, mirror. 355.6 x 607 x 457.2 cm (140 x 239 x 180"). The Metropolitan Museum of Art, New York, New York. Gift of the artist.

▲ Figure 17–15   The people in this work are types you might pass on the street or at a shopping mall. Why do you think the artist has chosen to freeze these types in time? What are we able to learn about them? What can we learn about ourselves?

Duane Hanson. *Tourists.* 1970. Polyester and fiberglass. Lifesize. OK Harris Works of Art, New York, New York.

STUDIO EXPERIENCE

Experiment with your own action painting using laundry bleach.

Dip a cotton swab into a small container of bleach. Rub the bleach over a sheet of dark-colored construction paper. You will notice faded, white areas beginning to form.

Use this technique to complete several works, each expressing a different feeling. Display your finished works along with those of classmates. Which are most successful? Why?

standing before Hanson's sculpture of tourists in Figure 17–15. Typical of his work, these people are average-looking and wear everyday clothing. What reaction do you suppose the artist wants viewers to have? What message about life in present-day America might he be sending?

✔CHECK YOUR UNDERSTANDING

1. What is Abstract Expressionism? Name two members of the movement.
2. Besides Abstract Expressionism, name three directions painting has taken in the last 40 years. Define each school.
3. What term did Alexander Calder invent? Describe the kinds of sculptures he created.
4. Which of the artists you learned about in this lesson created three-dimensional collages?

Following Up

Closure. Ask students to briefly state whether there is an artist discussed in this lesson whose style they would like to be able to imitate. Have students explain their responses and state which elements of their own art would need to change in order for it to resemble the chosen artist's style.

Evaluation. 1. Review students' written responses to the "Check Your Understanding" questions. 2. Assess critical writings on an art work in this lesson. 3. Evaluate reports on the use of two-dimensional design in other cultures.

Reteaching. Show prints or slides of as many clear examples of Abstract Expressionist, Hard Edge, New Realist, and social protest art works as possible. Have students try to categorize each work according to the four movements and give the reasons for their judgments. You need not discuss individual works in depth for this exercise, but concentrate on examples of the movements that confuse students the most.

Enrichment. Ask students to name all the black American artists they can and list them on the board. Discuss why the list, which may be limited to Jacob Lawrence, is so short. Then have students choose one aspect of black art to research. Students may interview a local black artist, explore the ways in which racism affects black artists, and investigate the history of the Studio Museum in Harlem, whose collection focuses on traditional African art and art by twentieth-century African-American artists and Caribbean artists.

Answers to "Check Your Understanding"

1. Abstract Expressionism is a style in which paint was dribbled, spilled, or splashed onto huge canvases to express a feeling. Two Abstract Expressionist painters are Arshile Gorky and Helen Frankenthaler.
2. There are three other directions painting took in the last forty years. *Hard-Edge* painting used clear, crisp edges around shapes; *social protest* painting attacked the ills of big-city life; *New Realism* rediscovered the importance of realistic detail.
3. Alexander Calder invented the term "mobile." He created sculptures of carefully balanced shapes hung on wires.
4. Louise Nevelson made three-dimensional collages.

LESSON PLAN
(pages 268–269)

Objectives
After completing this lesson, students will be able to:
- Explain how Op artists create optical illusions.
- Create an art work that combines elements of Op Art and Hard Edge painting.

Supplies
- Pencils.
- Sketch paper.
- Rulers.
- Pieces of illustration board, 12 x 12 inches (30 x 30 cm).
- India ink.
- Pen holders.
- Assorted pen points or nibs.
- Copies of works by Victor Vasarely and other Op artists.

TEACHING THE LESSON

Getting Started
Motivator. Have students discuss the following quote by Gene Davis: "Far from being narrow and confining, the stripe has an astonishing potential for breadth and complexity. . . . If I worked for fifty more years, I wouldn't exhaust the possibilities." Ask students whether they agree with Davis's attitude toward stripes. Are there other formal elements that an artist could spend a lifetime happily exploring?

Vocabulary. Explain to students that *Op Art* sought to create a sense of movement on the picture surface by means of optical illusion. Have students examine Figure 17-16 and show other examples of Op Art. Ask them how Op Art's optical illusionism differs from that of other art works in this text. Discuss whether or not all art relies on optical illusions. Have students refer to specific illustrations when they explain the different uses of optical illusion.

268

Making a Hard-Edge Op Art Work

The painting in Figure 17–16, by artist Gene Davis, is typical of another movement of the second half of the twentieth century. The movement's name is **Op Art**. Artists working in this style *made use of precise lines and shapes to create optical illusion*. Stare at Davis' painting for a moment. Notice how the vertical lines in the picture appear to vibrate with color.

Compare this work with the Hard-Edge painting on page **264**. Imagine the artists of the two had decided to combine their styles in a single painting. What would it look like?

WHAT YOU WILL LEARN

Using India ink, you will create a pattern of black and white values. You will create this design over another made up of simple positive and negative shapes. The finished work—a blend of Op Art and Hard-Edge styles—will give a feeling of dizzying movement. (See Figure 17–17.)

WHAT YOU WILL NEED

- Pencil, sheets of sketch paper, and ruler
- Piece of illustration board, 12 x 12 inches (30 x 30 cm)
- India ink
- Pen holder and assorted points, or nibs

▶ **Figure 17–16** How does the artist add variety to this composition? Where are the most intense colors found? When you stare at it, does this picture seem to vibrate?

Gene Davis. *Cool Buzz Saw.* 1964. Acrylic on canvas. 189.9 x 291.1 cm (113¾ x 115"). San Francisco Museum of Modern Art, San Francisco, California. Gift of the Women's Board.

Background Information
Stripe painter Gene Davis spent the first part of his professional life as a successful Washington, D. C. journalist who wrote detective stories and science fiction on the side. Captivated by the Klee paintings at the Phillips Collection in Washington, Davis began a serious study of modern art and soon afterward tried his hand at painting in 1949. His first effort was in a flat, Hard Edge style, but Davis's subsequent paintings were in the Abstract Expressionist style that was popular in the 1950s. By 1958, however, Davis had tired of the exaggerated brushwork and existential philosophy of Abstract Expressionism and painted his first edge-to-edge vertical stripe painting. This work was in pastel tones that he swiftly abandoned in favor of bright colors. By 1962 Davis had decided to use only vertical stripes. In his words, "Horizontal stripes are unthinkable, because they carry the illusion of landscape. I want my work to have no `literary' overtones."

WHAT YOU WILL DO

1. Look once again at the Hard-Edge painting by Kelly on page **264**. Draw several pencil sketches of a single Hard-Edge shape. The negative and positive shapes on your paper should be equally interesting.
2. Pick your best sketch. Using pencil and ruler, draw it on the piece of illustration board.
3. Study the Op Art painting by Gene Davis in Figure 17–16. Again working with ruler and pencil, cover the illustration board with closely spaced vertical lines. The spaces between the lines need not be exact. No two lines, however, should be more than a half inch apart.
4. With a pen and India ink, fill in the shape at the top left corner of your design. Be careful to stay within the lines. Working downward, leave the next shape white. Ink in every other shape until you reach the bottom of the illustration board. Repeat the process for the next vertical strip, this time leaving the topmost shape white. Continue in this fashion until all the strips have been completed.
5. Display your work alongside those of classmates. Which have the most interesting Hard-Edge designs? Which give the same kind of vibrating effect found in Figure 17–16?

EXAMINING YOUR WORK

- **Describe**   Point out the positive and negative shapes in your work.
- **Analyze**   Explain how the pattern of dark and light values causes the picture to seem to vibrate.
- **Interpret**   Tell whether your work gives a dizzying feeling.
- **Judge**   Tell whether you feel your work succeeds. State which aesthetic view you would use in explaining your judgment.

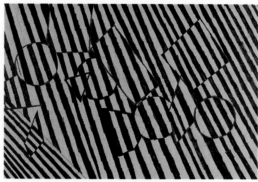

▲ Figure 17–17   Student work. Hard-Edge Op Art.

OTHER STUDIO IDEAS

- Do a second version of the work, this time using two complementary colors of tempera paint. Use horizontal lines in place of vertical ones if you like.

- ●● Create a simple landscape or still life. Use India ink or tempera and the Op Art technique detailed in the lesson.

Developing Concepts

Using Art Criticism. Have students examine Figure 17-16 and use the four steps of art criticism to arrive at a judgment. Then have students turn the picture so that the stripes run horizontally. Does this alter the effect and meaning of the work?

Understanding Art History. Tell students that Davis painted Abstract Expressionist paintings early in his career. Have students write a letter from Davis to his gallery dealer that speculates on why he made such a sudden and radical change in the style of his art.

Following Up

Closure. Have each student briefly state their opinion of Op Art. Do they find it fun, boring, exciting, mesmerizing, too mathematical, or painful to look at?

Evaluation. 1. Review students' studio projects. 2. Assess the letters from Davis.

Reteaching. Show students copies of Victor Vasarely paintings. Then have them create their own optically distorted and undulating checkerboards. Students should first use a pencil to draw a checkerboard with sections of curved lines modeled on Vasarely's work. Black markers should be used to fill in the squares after the overall design has been sketched on white paper.

Enrichment. Have students investigate the work of other artists who have focused on stripes for at least part of their career. These artists include Bridget Riley, Sean Scully, Frank Stella, Barnett Newman, and Kenneth Noland. Have students prepare a brief presentation on one of these artists. Then discuss how the various stripe painters differ.

Background Information

Op Art is concerned with the physical and psychological processes of vision. Developed in the United States after 1960, this non-objective art movement had parallels in several European countries including Germany and Italy. Op artists sought to create an impression of movement on the picture surface by means of optical illusion. In traditional paintings, the aim was to draw the viewer into the work. In contrast, Op pictures seem to vibrate and reach out to the spectator. Victor Vasarely is generally regarded as the founder of this movement. He used dazzling colors and precise geometric shapes to create surfaces that appear to move. They seem to project forward in some places and to recede in others. Numerous art movements, of course, have had optical illusion as one of their goals. What is unique about Op Art is that it extended illusionism into the realm of non-representational art.

270

Art of the Next Frontier

Artists have never been content to stay in one place for long. They are a restless breed, forever moving on, thirsting after new challenges. As we move swiftly toward the year 2000, questions arise: What challenges will open themselves to the artists of tomorrow? What will art be like in the twenty-first century?

Answering these questions would take a crystal ball. Still, possible glimpses of the art of tomorrow are afforded by innovative developments in the art of today. In this lesson you will look at some of these developments.

ART AND TECHNOLOGY

If there is one word most closely identified with art of today, it is *technology*. Technology is the use of science to make life better. Art of the past few years has drawn on such technological advances as the computer and laser. It has also redefined the boundaries between one branch of art and the next.

Staged Photography

In the late 1800s the new art of photography changed the way painters looked at their subjects. In more recent times another new art — filmmaking — has had the same effect on photographers. Some have begun staging pictures in much the way movie directors set up a scene.

Figure 17–18 shows a staged photograph by artist Sandy Skoglund (**skoh**-gluhnd). For this work the artist sculpted each of the goldfish individually from clay. She also painted the room and directed the location of the two people. What twentieth-century style of painting does this work call to mind? What message might the photographer be sending to viewers?

▲ **Figure 17–18** How would you describe the artist's use of color? Would this work have a different appearance if it had been shot in black and white?

Sandy Skoglund. *Revenge of the Goldfish*. 1981. Staged Photograph. Lorence Monk Gallery. New York, New York.

Multi-Media Art

The ancient Hindus, you may recall, believed temples to be as much sculpture as architecture. This idea has been carried forward in recent years by artists of multi-media works. **Multi-media art** is *a work that makes use of tools and techniques from two or more areas of art*.

A careful merging of architecture and sculpture is found in the expressions of sculptor Judy Pfaff (**faf**). Study the multi-media work by her in Figure 17–19. Parts of the work are the floor of the room, walls, and ceiling themselves. The viewer is able to move not only around this sculpture but also *within* it.

Kinetic Art

Examine the "sculpture" in Figure 17–20 by Nam June Paik. This work loosely belongs to a movement begun in the 1960s called **kinetic** (kuh-**net**-ik) **art**. This is *a style in which parts of works are set into motion*. The motion can be triggered by a form of energy or by

▲ Figure 17–19   In what ways has the artist created a "real" landscape? What other branches of art besides sculpture and architecture are brought into play in this multi-media work?

Judy Pfaff. *Kabuki (Formula Atlantic)*. 1981. Mixed media. Hirshhorn Museum and Sculpture Garden, Smithsonian Institution, Washington, D.C.

the viewer moving past the work. Some art gives the impression of movement without actually moving. The work in Figure 17–20 is made up in part of 300 television screens. The viewer experiences a number of different images and sounds all at the same time. What do you imagine this experience would be like? What statement might the artist be making about the age of television?

✔CHECK YOUR UNDERSTANDING

1. What is technology? What part has technology played in art of the present?
2. What is a staged photograph?
3. Define *multi-media art*.
4. To what two art movements does the painting in Figure 17–16 belong?

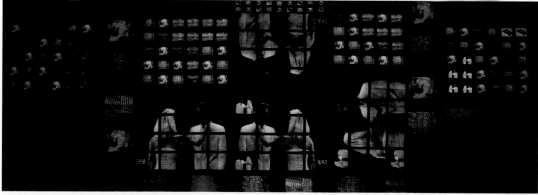

▲ Figure 17–20   A computer is used to "flip" and enlarge images on the different screens in this work. How many different images can you count?

Nam June Paik. *Fin de Siècle II*. 1989. Video installation: Approximately 300 television sets. Originally shown at the Whitney Museum of American Art, New York, New York.

Lesson 5   *Art of the Next Frontier*   📖   **271**

ANSWERS TO "CHAPTER 17 REVIEW"

Building Vocabulary

1. Dada
2. Surrealism
3. Abstract Expressionism
4. Hard-Edge painting
5. social protest painting
6. New Realism
7. mobile
8. Op Art
9. multi-media art
10. kinetic art

Reviewing Art Facts

11. Marcel Duchamp was a member of the Dada movement.
12. Paul Klee's works were simple and childlike, filled with fantasy and humor.
13. Marino Marini sculpted peasants fleeing a bombing raid.
14. Barbara Hepworth is known for non-objective sculpture.
15. Arshile Gorky was one of the first Abstract Expressionists.
16. Louise Nevelson created three-dimensional collages.
17. Sandy Skoglund uses staged photography.
18. Judy Pfaff is known for multi-media architecture/sculpture.

Thinking About Art

1. Answers can vary. Students should show they understand playful and experimental art can be well done.
2. Students should show they know the mobile is a free-floating, moving piece and the Miró is a painting. The common characteristics are the use of non-objective shapes. Answers will vary on the use of an aesthetic view.

BUILDING VOCABULARY

Number a sheet of paper from 1 to 10. After each number, write the term from the box that best matches each description below.

Abstract Expressionism	multi-media art
Dada	New Realism
Hard-Edge painting	Op Art
kinetic art	social protest painting
mobile	Surrealism

1. An art movement founded on the belief that Western culture had lost its meaning.
2. An art movement that probed the unconscious world of dreams.
3. An art style in which paint was dribbled, spilled, or splashed onto huge canvases to express painting as an action.
4. An art style that emphasized clear, crisp-edged shapes.
5. An art style that attacked the ills of big-city life.
6. An art movement that rediscovered the importance of realistic detail.
7. A sculpture made of carefully balanced shapes hung on wires.
8. An art style that made use of precise lines and shapes to create optical illusion.
9. A work that makes use of tools and techniques from two or more areas of art.
10. An art style in which parts of works are set into motion by a form of energy.

REVIEWING ART FACTS

Number a sheet of paper from 11 to 18. Answer each question in a complete sentence.

11. Name an artist of the Dada movement.
12. Describe the works of Paul Klee.
13. What sculptor did works of Italian peasants fleeing a bombing raid?
14. For which type of sculpture was Barbara Hepworth best known?
15. In what art movement was Arshile Gorky a pioneer?
16. What sculptor you learned about created three-dimensional collages?
17. Name an artist who works in the area of staged photography.
18. For what kinds of works is Judy Pfaff known?

THINKING ABOUT ART

On a sheet of paper, answer each question in a sentence or two.

1. **Analyze**. React to the opinion that art must be serious to be good. Find works from the chapter that support your position.
2. **Compare and contrast**. Compare the works in Figure 17–2 and Figure 17–13. Aside from the fact one is a painting and the other a sculpture, how do they differ? What do they have in common? Would you use the same aesthetic view in judging the two? Explain.

MAKING ART CONNECTIONS

1. **Language Arts**. Choose one of the non-objective works you learned about in this chapter. Make a list of points about this work you would bring up in a debate with someone who claimed a two-year-old could create the same "art."
2. **History**. In this chapter you learned of some art movements that appeared in the late twentieth century. The following are several others: Pop Art, Earth Art, and Concept Art. Using an encyclopedia or other library resource, find out the names of artists who worked in the movement, and identify their goals. Report your findings to the class.

LOOKING AT THE DETAILS

The detail shown below is from Frank Stella's *Shards III*. Study the detail and answer the following questions using complete sentences.

1. How would you know that this was a multi-media work if a credit line was not available?

2. Identify the two art media that Stella used to create this work.
3. How has the artist created depth?
4. Look at the entire work on page **256**. What shape has been used to unify the art work?

Frank Stella. *Shards III*. 1983. Mixed media on aluminum. (Detail.) 346.7 x 304.2 x 62.2 cm (136½ x 119¾ x 24½"). Leo Castelli Gallery, New York, New York.

Chapter 17 Review **273**

ANSWERS TO "LOOKING AT THE DETAILS"

1. The viewer can tell that this is a multi-media work by the way the curved green shape and the edge of the red line extend beyond the edge of the canvas.
2. Stella combined the media of aluminum and paint in this work.
3. Frank Stella creates depth by placing shapes on different planes, and cutting out shapes in the canvas itself, to create shadows and obvious elevations which emphasize the depth.
4. The most obvious unifying shape is the snake-like shape—a repetitively curved line.

Chapter Evaluation

The purpose of this chapter is to introduce students to contemporary styles and techniques used by artists in the last 50 years. Some possible methods of evaluation include:

1. Ask students to list the art movements included as vocabulary terms and to briefly compare the different styles.

2. Divide students into groups and have each group develop an argument supporting the style of one contemporary art movement and how it best communicates the artist's purpose.

3. Have students complete Chapter 17 Test (TRB, Resource 17-8).

Using the Handbook

PURPOSE OF THE HANDBOOK

The Handbook is a convenient reference section which offers students step-by-step procedures, additional career and artist profile information, and optional studio lessons. This material is designed to complement and enrich the narrative and studio lessons that appear earlier in the book.

The Handbook is divided into the following sections:

Part 1 Technique Tips
Part 2 Artist Profiles
Part 3 Career Spotlights
Part 4 Additional Studios

▲ Working on group murals is an excellent way to practice artistic skills, gain recognition, and at the same time, have fun.

HANDBOOK CONTENTS

• The **Technique Tips** section offers students step-by-step procedures of how to do specific skills related to the areas of drawing, printmaking, painting, and sculpting. General techniques in these areas are described and, when appropriate, illustrated with line drawings. Other general skills, such as making a mat or using glue, are included in this reference section.

• The **Artist Profiles** provide students with background information of fourteen artists whose works appear in the text. The information gives a short biographical sketch about the artist and gives the reader an account of world events which occurred during the artist's life. The material is written in a warm, personal tone and will motivate students to seek more in-depth outside information about the artist.

• The **Career Spotlights** introduce students to fourteen careers within the art-related fields. Students are presented with an overview of the type of work and personal qualifications required of a person working in the featured occupation. In the *Teacher's Wraparound Edition*, addresses are provided so that students can research and obtain further information about the careers that interest them.

• The **Additional Studios** section contains five studio lessons that provide an extension to various chapters. These lessons can be used as independent practice for gifted and talented students, as co-operative learning projects, or as projects to culminate the objectives of specific chapters. In contrast to the lessons which appear within the text, these lessons generally take an extended period of time to complete. Each studio lesson has been reviewed and given an approximate time allotment that should be allowed.

• Within the Handbook you will find the chapter and lesson reference. The Handbook can be used in conjunction with specific chapters and lessons, or you may wish to use each section of the Handbook for independent study. For example, if you want to cover careers or art history in two separate weeks, you can use the Artist Profiles for one week and Career Spotlights for the next week. Regardless of the way you integrate the material, the *Teacher's Wraparound Edition* offers additional information in the outside column to help you teach, apply, and reinforce these materials.

1. Making Gesture Drawings

Gesture drawing is a way of showing movement in a sketch. Gesture drawings have no outlines or details. You are not expected to draw the figure. Instead, you are expected to draw the movement, or what the figure is doing. Follow these guidelines:

• Use the side of the drawing tool. Do not hold the medium as you would if you were writing.

• Find the lines of movement that show the direction in which the figure is bending. Draw the main line showing this movement.

• Use quickly drawn lines to build up the shape of the person.

2. Making Contour Drawings

Contour drawing is a way of capturing the feel of a subject. When doing a contour drawing, remember the following pointers:

• If you accidentally pick up your pen or pencil, don't stop working. Place your pen or pencil back where you stopped. Begin again from that point.

• If you have trouble keeping your eyes off the paper, ask a friend to hold a piece of paper between your eyes and your drawing paper. Another trick is to place your drawing paper inside a large paper bag as you work.

• Tape your paper to the table so it will not slide around. With a finger of your free hand, trace the outline of the object. Record the movement with your drawing hand.

• Contour lines show ridges and wrinkles in addition to outlines. Adding these lines gives roundness to the object.

3. Drawing with Oil Pastels

Oil pastels are sticks of pigment held together with an oily binder. The colors are brighter than wax crayon colors. If you press heavily you will make a brilliant-colored line. If you press lightly you will create a fuzzy line. You can fill in shapes with the brilliant colors. You can blend a variety of color combinations. For example, you can fill a shape with a soft layer of a hue and then color over the hue with a heavy layer of white to create a unique tint of that hue.

If you use oil pastels on colored paper, you can put a layer of white under the layer of hue to block the color of the paper.

4. Drawing Thin Lines with a Brush

Drawing thin lines with a brush can be learned with a little practice. Just follow these steps:

1. Dip your brush in the ink or paint. Wipe the brush slowly against the side, twirling it between your fingers until the bristles form a point.

2. Hold the brush at the beginning of the metal band near the tip. Hold the brush straight up and down.

3. Imagine that the brush is a pencil with a very sharp point. Pretend that pressing too hard will break the point. Now touch the paper lightly with the tip of the brush and draw a line. The line should be quite thin.

   To make a thinner line still, lift up on the brush as you draw. After a while, you will be able to make lines in a variety of thicknesses.

5. Making a Grid for Enlarging

Sometimes the need arises to make a bigger version of a small drawing. An example is when you create a mural based on a small sketch. Follow these steps:

1. Using a ruler, draw evenly spaced lines across and up and down your original drawing (Figure T–1). Count

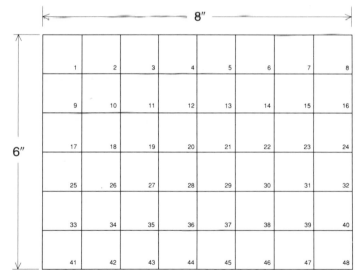

▲ Figure T–1

Using the Technique Tips

The technique tips listed on these and the following pages give students helpful hints for handling different media and tools. The technique tips offer students step-by-step procedures which they can use to assist with their art production skills. Each technique tip contains procedures that should be followed in sequential order for maximum success.

USING THE DRAWING TIPS

1. Making Gesture Drawings
   Use with:
   • Chapter 9, Lesson 1, page **133**, Personality Drawing. Studio Experience.
   • Chapter 16, Lesson 3, page **251**, Idea Drawing. Studio Experience.
   • Chapter 16, Lesson 4, page **253**, Making a Figure in Action.

2. Making Contour Drawings
   Use with:
   • Chapter 11, Lesson 2, page **167**, Drawing a Still Life.
   • Chapter 11, Lesson 4, page **172**, Designing a Visual Symbol.
   • Chapter 12, Lesson 2, page **182**, Drawing Expressive Hands.

3. Drawing with Oil Pastels
   Use with:
   • Chapter 10, Lesson 1, page **149**, Illumination. Studio Experience.
   • Chapter 11, Lesson 2, page **167**, Still Life.
   • Chapter 16, Lesson 2, page **247**, Cubist Chalk Drawing.
   • Handbook, Lesson 5, page **312**, Space Colony.

4. Drawing Thin Lines with a Brush
   Use with:
   • Chapter 5, Lesson 2, page **69**, Perceiving an Object. Studio Experience.
   • Chapter 7, Lesson 2, page **102**, Making a Painting for a Greek Vase.
   • Chapter 14, Lesson 2, page **214**, Designing a Neoclassic Stage Set.

5. Making a Grid for Enlarging
   Use with:
   • Chapter 3, Lesson 4, page **43**, Painting in the Cubist Style. Other Studio Ideas.
   • Chapter 6, Lesson 4, page **93**, Making a Stylized Motif.

Classroom Management

Try these suggestions to help stretch your school budget:

• Some drawings look better without a mat. A backing board with a lightweight acetate covering will do the trick. If the drawing is on tracing paper or vellum, however, there needs to be a piece of inexpensive white poster or tagboard between the corrugated board and the drawing. The corrugated board will discolor any drawing in a few years. Thin paper will show the corrugation ridges from the backing.

• Check with the local art club to see if it has a benevolence fund for aid to education. Check with the local art directors' club, designer's association, or society of illustrators (in cities larger than 300,000).

• Tracing vellum and some watercolor rendering papers can be bought less expensively in rolls or by the foot than by the sheet or pads. A 100% rag, twenty-pound vellum is pretty tough—and you can iron the back of it to smooth it after using liquid media.

6. Using Shading Techniques
Use with:
- Chapter 1, Lesson 2, page **6**, Using the Elements of Art.
- Chapter 11, Lesson 2, page **167**, Still Life.
- Chapter 12, Lesson 2, page **183**, Drawing Expressive Hands.

7. Using Sighting Techniques
Use with:
- Chapter 11, Lesson 4, page **172**, Designing a Visual Symbol.
- Chapter 12, Lesson 3, page **187**, Drawing Object. Studio Experience.

the number of squares you made from side to side. Count the number of squares running up and down.

2. Measure the width of the surface to which the drawing is to be transferred. Divide that figure by the number of side-to-side squares. The resulting number will be the horizontal measure of each square. You may work in inches or centimeters. Using a ruler or yardstick, mark off the squares. Draw in light rules.

3. Measure the height of the surface to which the drawing is to be transferred. Divide that figure by the number of up-and-down squares. The resulting number will be the vertical measure of each square. Mark off the squares. Draw in pencil lines.

4. Starting at the upper left, number each square on the original drawing. Give the

same number to each square on the large grid. Working a square at a time, transfer your image. (See Figure T–2.)

6. Using Shading Techniques

When using shading techniques, keep in mind the following:
- Lines or dots placed close together create dark values.
- Lines or dots placed far apart, on the other hand, create light values. To show a change from light to dark, start with lines or dots far apart and little by little bring them close together.
- Use care also to follow the shape of the object when adding lines. Straight lines are used to shade an object with a flat surface. Rounded lines are used to shade an object with a curved surface.

7. Using Sighting Techniques

Sighting is a technique that will help you draw objects in proportion.

1. Face the object you plan to draw. Hold a pencil straight up and down at arm's length. Your thumb should rest against the side of the pencil and be even with the tip.

2. Close one eye. With your other eye, focus on the object.

3. Slide your thumb down the pencil until the exposed part of the pencil matches the object's height. (See Figure T–3.)

▲ Figure T–3

4. Now, without moving your thumb or bending your arm, turn the pencil sideways.

5. Focus on the width of the object. If the height is greater, figure out how many "widths" will fit in one "height." If the width is greater, figure out how many "heights" will fit in one "width."

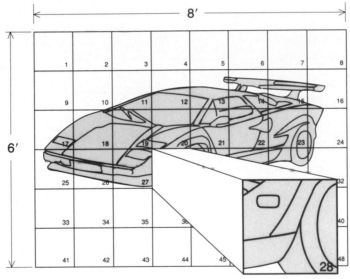

▲ Figure T–2

Cooperative Learning

Explain to students that thumbnail sketches are small sketches drawn quickly to record ideas and information for a finished drawing. Tell them that they are called thumbnail because they are almost small enough (5 x 5 inches, [13 x 13 cm]) to have been drawn on a thumbnail. Explain that they are usually done with pen and ink.

Have students think about situations in which the artist would prefer to use thumbnail sketches. For example, graphic artists and illustrators use them to record ideas and also to show ideas to other artists, art directors, and executives. Have students work in small groups and develop a series of thumbnail sketches that could be used to plan a series of paintings of animal totems, or symbols of ancestry. When students have completed their sketches, have them display their work.

8. Using a Viewing Frame

Much in the way a camera is used to focus on one area of a scene, you can better zero in on an object you plan to draw by using a viewing frame (Figure T–4). To make a viewing frame do the following:

1. Cut a rectangular hole in a piece of paper about 2 inches (3 to 5 cm) in from the paper's edges.
2. Hold the paper at arm's length and look through the hole at your subject. Imagine that the hole represents your drawing paper.
3. Decide how much of the subject you want to have in your drawing.
4. By moving the frame up, down, sideways, nearer, or farther, you can change the focus of your drawing.

9. Using a Ruler

There are times when you need to draw a crisp, straight line. By using the following techniques, you will be able to do so.

1. Hold the ruler with one hand and the pencil with the other.
2. Place the ruler where you wish to draw a straight line.
3. Hold the ruler with your thumb and first two fingers. Be careful that your fingers do not stick out beyond the edge of the ruler.
4. Press heavily on the ruler so it will not slide while you're drawing.
5. Hold the pencil lightly against the ruler.
6. Pull the pencil quickly and lightly along the edge of the ruler. The object is to keep the ruler from moving while the pencil moves along its edge.

▲ Figure T–4

PAINTING TIPS

10. Cleaning a Paint Brush

Cleaning a paint brush properly helps it last a long time. *Always*:
1. Rinse the thick paint out of the brush under running water. Do not use hot water.
2. Gently paint the brush over a cake of mild soap, or dip it in a mild liquid detergent (Figure T–5).

▲ Figure T–5

Technique Tips **279**

Developing Perceptual Skills

Tell students that seeing the item they are drawing as a whole rather than just a collection of parts results in more successful drawings. Explain the fact that we naturally see things as a whole was discovered in Germany in 1912 by a psychologist named Max Wertheimer. He founded a branch of psychology called Gestaltism. The German word gestalt means pattern or form. According to Gestalt psychology, we only recognize objects by seeing total patterns or forms, not by adding up the individual parts we see. Tell students that in making most drawings, they should do the large shapes first and add the details later. Encourage them to look at things from an overall point of view.

3. Gently scrub the brush against the palm of your hand to work the soap into the brush. This removes paint you may not have realized was still in the brush.

4. Rinse the brush under running water while you continue to scrub your palm against it (Figure T–6).

▲ Figure T–6

5. Repeat steps 2, 3, and 4 as needed.
When it is thoroughly rinsed and excess water has been squeezed from the brush, shape your brush into a point with your fingers (Figure T–7). Place the brush in a container with the bristles up so that it will keep its shape as it dries.

▲ Figure T–7

11. Making Natural Earth Pigments

Anywhere there is dirt, clay, or sand, there is natural pigment. To create your own pigments, gather as many different kinds of earth colors as you can. Grind these as finely as possible. (If you can, borrow a mortar and pestle.) (See Figure T–8.) Do not worry if the pigment is slightly gritty.

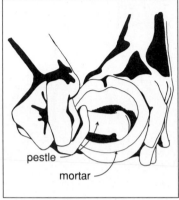

pestle

mortar

▲ Figure T–8

To make the binder, mix equal parts of white glue and water. Place a few spoonfuls of your powdered pigment into a small jar. Add a little of the binder. Experiment with different amounts of each.

When you work with natural pigments, remember always to wash the brushes before the paint in them has a chance to dry. The glue from the binder can ruin a brush. As you work, stir the paint every now and then. This will keep the grains of pigment from settling to the bottom of the jar.

Make a fresh batch each time you paint.

12. Mixing Paint to Change the Value of Color

You can better control the colors in your work when you mix your own paint. In mixing paints, treat opaque paints (for example, tempera) differently from transparent paints (for example, watercolors).

• *For light values of opaque paints.* Mix only a small amount of the hue to white. The color can always be made stronger by adding more of the hue.

• *For dark values of opaque paints.* Add a small amount of black to the hue. Never add the hue to black.

• *For light values of transparent paints.* Thin a shaded area with water (Figure T–9). This allows more of the white of the paper to show through.

• *For dark values of transparent paints.* Carefully add a small amount of black to the hue.

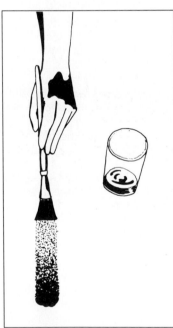

▲ Figure T–9

Classroom Management
Always supervise students carefully. Adequate supervision of students is required for both safety and liability reasons. Safety rules should be posted and explained at the start of each term—and these rules should be rigidly enforced. At no time should students be allowed to work in the classroom without direct supervision. Teachers should also make it a rule that students not bring to class and use their own art materials. It is possible that these art materials could contain unknown hazards.

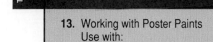
13. Working with Poster Paints (School Tempera)

When using poster paints (school tempera) remember the following:

- Poster paints run when wet. To keep this from happening, make sure one shape is dry before painting a wet color next to it.

14. Working with Watercolors

- If you apply wet paint to damp paper, you create lines and shapes with soft edges.
- If you apply wet paint to dry paper, you create lines and shapes with sharp, clear edges.
- If you dip a dry brush into damp paint and then brush across dry paper, you achieve a fuzzy effect.
- School watercolors come in semi-moist cakes. Before you use them, place a drop of water on each cake to let the paint soften. Watercolor paints are transparent. You can see the white paper through the paint. If you want a light value of a hue, dilute the paint with a large amount of water. If you want a bright hue, you must dissolve more pigment by swirling your brush around in the cake of paint until you have dissolved a great deal of paint. The paint you apply to the paper can be as bright as the paint in the cake.

PRINTMAKING TIP

15. Making a Stamp Printing

A stamp print is an easy way to make repetitive designs. The following are a few suggestions for making a stamp and printing with it. You may develop some other ideas after reading these hints. Remember, printing reverses your design, so if you use letters, be certain to cut or carve them backwards.

- Cut a simple design into the flat surface of an eraser with a knife that has a fine, precision blade.
- Cut a potato, carrot, or turnip in half. Use a paring knife to carve a design into the flat surface of the vegetable.
- Glue yarn to a bottle cap or a jar lid.
- Glue found objects to a piece of corrugated cardboard. Make a design with paperclips, washers, nuts, leaves, feathers, or anything else you can find. Whatever object you use should have a fairly flat surface. Make a handle for the block with masking tape.
- Cut shapes out of a piece of inner tube material. Glue the shapes to a piece of heavy cardboard.

There are several ways to apply ink or paint to a stamp:

- Roll water-based printing ink on the stamp with a soft brayer.
- Roll water-based printing ink on a plate and press the stamp into the ink.
- Apply tempera paint or school acrylic to the stamp with a bristle brush.

SCULPTING TIPS

16. Working with Clay

To make your work with clay go smoothly, always do the following:

1. Dip one or two fingers in water.
2. Spread the moisture from your fingers over your palms.

Never dip your hands in water. Too much moisture turns clay into mud.

17. Joining Clay

If you are creating a piece of sculpture that requires joining pieces, do the following:

1. Gather the materials you will need. These include clay, slip, (a creamy mixture of clay and water), a paint brush, a scoring tool, (perhaps a kitchen fork) and clay tools.
2. Rough up or scratch the two surfaces to be joined (Figure T–10).

▲ Figure T–10

Classroom Management

Remind students to always wipe any remaining ink from a block and brayer after they have finished printing. If they have used a water-based printing ink, they can use water for cleaning. If they have used oil-based ink, however, they should use a solvent such as turpentine. Remember that if they use a solvent, they should be careful not to get the solvent on their skin, or let it come in contact with their eyes.

Classroom Management

Place kilns in a separate room. If that is not possible, locate the kiln in an out-of-the-way part of the room where students are not likely to come into contact with it when it is in operation. In addition, all kilns should have local exhaust ventilation.

3. Apply slip to one of the two surfaces using a paint brush or your fingers (Figure T–11).

▲ **Figure T–11**

4. Gently press the two surfaces together so the slip oozes out of the joining seam (Figure T–12).

▲ **Figure T–12**

5. Using clay tools and/or your fingers, smooth away the slip that has oozed out of the seam (Figure T–13). You may wish to smooth out the seam as well, or you may wish to leave it for decorative purposes.

▲ **Figure T–13**

18. Making a Clay Mold for a Plaster Relief

One of the easiest ways to make a plaster relief is with a clay mold. When making a clay mold, remember the following:

- Plaster poured into the mold will come out with the opposite image. Design details cut into the mold will appear raised on the relief. Details built up within the mold will appear indented in the relief.
- Do not make impressions in your mold that have *undercuts* (Figure T–14). Undercuts trap plaster, which will break off when the relief is removed. When cutting impressions, keep the deepest parts the narrowest.
- In carving a raised area in the mold, take care not to create a reverse undercut (Figure T–15).

If you want to change the mold simply smooth the area with your fingers.

19. Mixing Plaster

Mixing plaster requires some technique and a certain amount of caution. It can also be a very simple matter when you are prepared. Always do the following:

- Use caution when working with dry plaster. Wear a dust mask or work in a well-ventilated room.
- Cover your work space to keep the dust from spreading.
- Always use a plastic bowl and a stick for mixing. Never use silverware you will later eat from.
- Always use plaster that is fine, like sifted flour. Plaster should never be grainy when dry.
- Always add the water to the bowl first. Sift in the plaster. Stir slowly.
- Never pour unused plaster down a drain. Allow it to dry in the bowl. To remove the dried plaster, twist the bowl. Crack the loose plaster into a lined trash can.

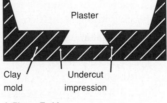

▲ **Figure T–14**

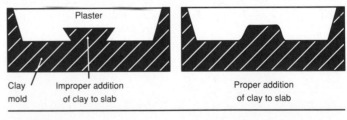

▲ **Figure T–15**

Background Information

Pottery is any object made from clay and hardened by fire. Pottery is also the name given to the craft of making such objects. Another word for both is *ceramics.* On its way to becoming finished pottery, clay takes six different forms. These are:

- *Plastic clay*—clay wet enough to be worked but dry enough to hold its shape.
- *Slip*—clay with enough water added to make it runny. Slip is used to glue together shaped pieces of damp clay.

- *Leather hard clay*—clay which is still damp but too hard to model. Pieces of leather hard clay can be joined with slip.
- *Greenware*—very dry clay that will break easily. An object at the greenware stage is ready to be fired.
- *Bisqueware*—fired pottery that is hard but not ready to use.
- *Glazeware*—pottery coated with powdered chemicals that melt during firing into a hard, glass-like finish.

Most ceramic objects are made hollow. This is so they will not explode or crack during firing.

20. Working with Papier-Mâché

Papier-mâché (**pay**-puhr muh-**shay**) is a French term meaning "chewed paper." It is also the name of several sculpting methods using newspaper and liquid paste. These methods can be used to model tiny pieces of jewelry. They can also be used to create life-size creatures.

In creating papier-mâché sculptures, the paper-and-paste mixture is molded over a support. You will learn more about supports shortly. The molded newspaper dries to a hard finish. The following are three methods for working with papier-mâché:

• **Pulp Method**. Shred newspaper, paper towels, or tissue paper into tiny pieces. (Do not use glossy magazine paper; it will not soften.) Soak your paper in water overnight. Press the paper in a kitchen strainer to remove as much moisture as possible. Mix the mashed paper with commercially prepared papier-mâché paste or white glue. The mixture should have the consistency of soft clay. Add a few drops of oil of cloves to keep the mixture from spoiling. A spoonful of linseed oil makes the mixture smoother. (If needed, the mixture can be stored at this point in a plastic bag in the refrigerator.) Use the mixture to model small shapes. When your creations dry, they can be sanded. You will also be able to drill holes in them.

• **Strip Method**. Tear newspaper into strips. Either dip the strips in papier-mâché paste or rub paste on them. Apply the strips to your support (Figure T–16). If you do not want the strips to stick to your

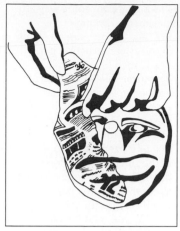

▲ Figure T–16

support, first cover it with plastic wrap. Use wide strips for large shapes. Use thin strips for smaller shapes. If you plan to remove your finished creation from the support, apply five or six layers. (Change directions with each layer so you can keep track of the number.) Otherwise, two or three layers should be enough. After applying the strips to your support, rub your fingers over the surface.

As a last layer, use torn paper towels. The brown paper towels that are found in schools produce an uncomplicated surface on which to paint. Make sure no rough edges are sticking up. Store any unused paste mixture in the refrigerator to keep it from spoiling.

• **Draping Method**. Spread papier-mâché paste on newspaper. Lay a second sheet on top of the first. Smooth the layers. Add another layer of paste and another sheet of paper. Repeat until you have four or five layers of paper. Use this method for making drapery on a figure. (See Figure T–17.) If you allow the lay-

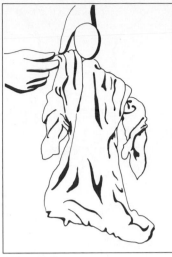

▲ Figure T–17

ers to dry for a day or two, they will become leathery. They can then be cut and molded as you like. Newspaper strips dipped in paste can be used to seal cracks.

Like papier-mâché, supports for papier-mâché creations can be made in several different ways. Dry newspaper may be wadded up and wrapped with string or tape (Figure T–18). Wire coat hangers may be padded with rags. For large figures, a wooden frame covered with chicken wire makes a good support.

▲ Figure T–18

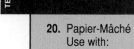
20. Papier-Mâché
Use with:
• Chapter 9, Lesson 4, page **140**, Making a Mood Mask Relief.
• Handbook, Studio Lesson 4, page **310**, False Face Mask.
• Material in the Teacher's Resource Binder.

Classroom Management

Most art teachers work with a variety of students who may have physical limitations. Here are some suggestions. At the beginning of each school year or new term, determine if any of your students are asthmatic, visually impaired or hearing impaired, or on prescribed medication. If asthmatic students are enrolled in the art class, they should not be exposed to dusts, fumes, or vapors because of breathing difficulties. Visually impaired students understandably operate very close to their art work, and as a consequence, are more likely to inhale dusts, vapors, and fumes. Students with hearing impairments should not be exposed to activities requiring loud hammering or noisy machinery. This could aggravate their condition. If students are found to be on medication, the teacher should seek a physician's advice regarding the potential harmful interaction between the prescribed medicine and art materials used in the class.

OTHER TIPS

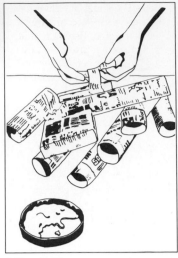

▲ Figure T–19

To create a base for your papier-mâché creations, tape together arrangements of found materials. Some materials you might combine are boxes, tubes, and bowls. (See Figure T–19.) Clay can also be modeled as a base. If clay is used, be sure there are no undercuts that would keep the papier-mâché from lifting off easily when dry. (For an explanation of undercuts, see Technique Tip **18**, *Handbook* page **276**.)

Always allow time for your papier-mâché creations to dry. The material needs extra drying time when thick layers are used or when the weather is damp. An electric fan blowing air on the material can shorten the drying time.

21. Making a Paper Sculpture

Another name for paper sculpture is origami. The process originated in Japan and means "folding paper." Paper sculpture begins with a flat piece of paper. The paper is then curved or bent to produce more than a flat surface. Here are some ways to experiment with paper.

- **Scoring.** Place a square sheet of heavy construction paper, 12 x 12 inch (30 x 30 cm), on a flat surface. Position the ruler on the paper so that it is close to the center and parallel to the sides. Holding the ruler in place, run the point of a knife or a pair of scissors along one of the ruler's edges. Press down firmly but take care not to cut through the paper. Gently crease the paper along the line you made. Hold your paper with the crease facing upward.
- **Pleating.** Take a piece of paper and fold it one inch from the edge. Then fold the paper in the other direction. Continue folding back and forth.
- **Curling.** Hold one end of a long strip of paper with the thumb and forefinger of one hand. At a point right below where you are holding the strip, grip it lightly between the side of a pencil and the thumb of your other hand. In a quick motion, run the pencil along the strip. This will cause the strip to curl back on itself. Don't apply too much pressure, or the strip will tear. (See Figure T–20.)

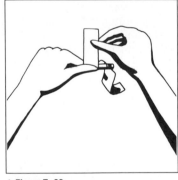

▲ Figure T–20

OTHER TIPS

22. Measuring Rectangles

Do you find it hard to create perfectly formed rectangles? Here is a way of getting the job done:

1. Make a light pencil dot near the long edge of a sheet of paper. With a ruler, measure the exact distance between the dot and the edge. Make three more dots the same distance in from the edge. (See Figure T–21.)

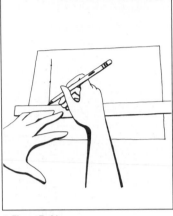

▲ Figure T–21

2. Line a ruler up along the dots. Make a light pencil line running the length of the paper.
3. Turn the paper so that a short side is facing you. Make four pencil dots equally distant from the short edge. Connect these with a light pencil rule. Stop when you reach the first line you drew. (See Figure T–22.)
4. Do the same for the remaining two sides. Erase any lines that may extend beyond the box you have made.
5. Trace over the lines with your ruler and pencil.

The box you have created will be a perfectly formed rectangle.

Classroom Management

The instructional strategy that is probably most familiar to art teachers is demonstration. This is an especially effective method of instruction when applied to studio activities. When preparing for a demonstration, always practice beforehand using the same materials students will be expected to use. Include continuous commentary with the demonstration explaining in detail what you are doing and why you are doing it this way. Detailed explanation increases the likelihood that the information will be better understood and assimilated by students.

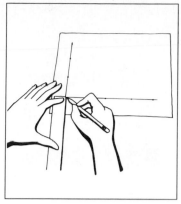

▲ Figure T–22

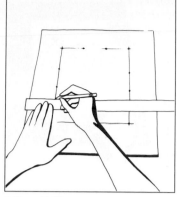

▲ Figure T–23

23. Making a Mat

You can add appeal to an art work by making a mat, using the following steps.

1. Gather the materials you will need. These include a metal rule, a pencil, mat board, cardboard backing, a sheet of heavy cardboard to protect your work surface, a mat knife with a sharp blade, and wide masking tape.

2. Wash your hands. Mat board should be kept very clean.

3. Measure the height and width of the work to be matted. Decide how large a border you want for your work. (A border of approximately 2½ inches on three sides with 3 inches on the bottom is aesthetically pleasing.) Your work will be behind the window you will cut.

4. Plan for the opening, or window, to be ¼ inch smaller on all sides than the size of your work. For example, if your work measures 9 by 12 inches, the mat window should measure 8½ inches (9 inches minus ¼ inch times two) by 11½ inches (12 inches minus ¼ inch times two). Using your metal rule and pencil, lightly draw your

window rectangle on the back of the board 2½ inches from the top and left edge of the mat. (See Figure T–23.) Add a 2½ inch border to the right of the window and a 3 inch border to the bottom, lightly drawing cutting guidelines.

Note: If you are working with metric measurements, the window should overlap your work by 0.5 cm (centimeters) on all sides. Therefore, if your work measures 24 by 30 cm, the mat window measures 23 cm (24 − [2 × 0.5]) by 29 cm (30 − [2 × 0.5]).

▲ Figure T–24

5. Place the sheet of heavy, protective cardboard on your work surface. Place the mat board, pencil marks up, over the cardboard. Holding the metal rule firmly in place, score the first line with your knife. Always place the metal rule so that your blade is away from the frame. (See Figure T–24.) In case you make an error you will cut into the window hole or the extra mat that is not used for the frame. Do not try to cut through the board with one stroke. By the third or fourth stroke, you should be able to cut through the board easily.

6. Working in the same fashion, score and cut through the board along all the window lines. Be careful not to go beyond the lines. Remove the window.

7. Cut a cardboard backing for your art work that is slightly smaller than the overall size of your mat. Using a piece of broad masking tape, hinge the back of the mat to the backing. (See Figure T–25.)

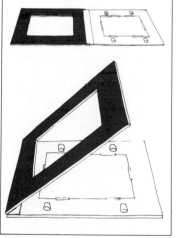

▲ Figure T–25

Technique Tips **285**

TECHNIQUE TIPS

Classroom Management

The need to direct time and effort to safeguarding the health of students in the art studio cannot be ignored. Art teachers, aware of this responsibility may feel that assistance is needed. Many instructors have turned to the Center for Occupational Hazards (COH) for this assistance. COH is a national clearinghouse for research and information on health hazards in the arts. It publishes a newsletter which covers a range of topics including new hazards, precautions, government regulations, lawsuits, and a calendar of events. Those interested teachers can write to the following address:

The Center for Occupational Hazards
5 Beekman Street
New York, New York 10038

Position your art work between the backing and the mat and attach it with tape. Anchor the frame to the cardboard with a few pieces of rolled tape.

24. Mounting a Two-Dimensional Work

Mounting pictures that you make gives them a professional look. To mount a work, do the following:

1. Gather the materials you will need. These include a yardstick, a pencil, poster board, a sheet of heavy cardboard, a knife with a very sharp blade, a sheet of newspaper, and rubber cement.
2. Measure the height and width of the work to be mounted. Decide how large a border you want around the work. Plan your mount size using the work's measurements. To end up with a 3-inch (8 cm) border, for example, make your mount 6 inches (15 cm) wider and higher than your work. Record the measurements for your mount.
3. Using your yardstick and pencil, lightly draw your mount rectangle on the back of the poster board. Measure from the edges of the poster board. If you have a large paper cutter available, you may use it to cut your mount.
4. Place the sheet of heavy cardboard on your work surface. Place the poster board, pencil marks up, over the cardboard. Holding the yardstick firmly in place along one line, score the line with your knife. Do not try to cut through the board with one stroke. By the third try, you should be able to cut through the board.

▲ Figure T–26

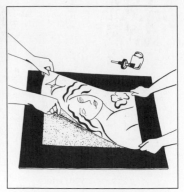

▲ Figure T–27

5. Place the art work on the mount. Using the yardstick, center the work. Mark each corner with a dot. (See Figure T–26.)
6. Place the art work, face down, on a sheet of newspaper. Coat the back of the work with rubber cement. (*Safety Note:* Always use rubber cement in a room with plenty of ventilation.) *If your mount is to be permanent, skip to Step 8.*
7. Line up the corners of your work with the dots on the mounting board. Smooth the work into place. *Skip to Step 9.*
8. After coating the back of your art work, coat the poster board with rubber cement. Be careful not to add cement to the border area. Have a partner hold your art work in the air by the two top corners. Once the two glued surfaces meet, you will not be able to change the position of the work. Grasp the lower two corners. Carefully lower the work to the mounting board. Line up the two corners with the bottom dots. Little by little, lower the work into place (Figure T–27). Press it smooth.

9. To remove any excess cement, create a small ball of nearly dry rubber cement. Use the ball of rubber cement to pick up excess cement.

25. Making Rubbings

Rubbings make interesting textures and designs. They may also be used with other media to create mixed-media art. To make a rubbing, place a sheet of thin paper on top of the surface to be rubbed. Hold the paper in place with one hand. With the other hand, rub the paper with the flat side of an unwrapped crayon. Always rub away from the hand holding the paper. Never rub back and forth, since this may cause the paper to slip.

26. Scoring Paper

The secret to creating neat, sharp folds in cardboard or paper is a technique called scoring. Here is how it is done:
1. Line up a ruler along the line you want to fold.
2. Lightly run a sharp knife or scissors along the fold line. Press down firmly enough to leave a light crease. Take care not to cut all the way through the paper (Figure T–28).

Classroom Management
Remind students to clean up thoroughly and often. They should make certain to clean up spills immediately to prevent accidents. If dust results, have them use a wet mop or vacuum rather than a broom. Sweeping stirs up dust that could prove harmful to some students, particularly those who are asthmatic.

▲ Figure T–28

3. Gently crease the paper along the line you made. To score curved lines, use the same technique. Make sure your curves are wide enough to ensure a clean fold. Too tight a curve will cause the paper to wrinkle (Figure T–29).

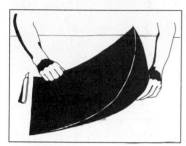

▲ Figure T–29

27. Making a Tissue Paper Collage

For your first experience with tissue, make a free design with the tissue colors. Start with the lightest colors of tissue first and save the darkest for last. It is difficult to change the color of dark tissue by overlapping it with other colors. If one area becomes too dark, you might cut out a piece of white paper, glue it over the dark area carefully, and apply new colors over the white area.

1. Apply a coat of adhesive to the area where you wish to place the tissue.
2. Place the tissue down carefully over the wet area (Figure T–30). Don't let your fingers get wet.
3. Then add another coat of adhesive over the tissue. If your brush picks up any color from the wet tissue, rinse your brush in water and let it dry before using it again.
4. Experiment by overlapping colors. Allow the tissue to wrinkle to create textures as you apply it. Be sure that all the loose edges of tissue are glued down.

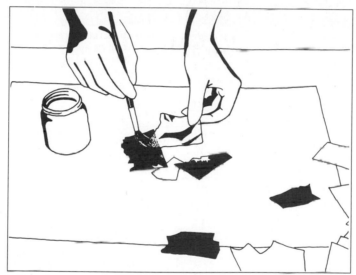

▲ Figure T–30

28. Working with Glue

When applying glue, always start at the center of the surface you are coating and work outward.

• When gluing papers together don't use a lot of glue, just a dot will do. Use dots in the corners and along the edges. Press the two surfaces together. Keep dots at least ½ inch (1.3 cm) in from the edge of your paper.
• Handle a glued surface carefully with only your fingertips. Make sure your hands are clean before pressing the glued surface into place.
• *Note:* The glue should be as thin as possible. Thick or beaded glue will create ridges on your work.

Classroom Management

To protect drawings you can spray them with fixative to protect them from smearing. Drawings in just about any medium will be damaged by rubbing against other surfaces if they aren't sprayed.

Spray fixative is sold both in aerosol cans and in small bottles with atomizers. Fixative in a bottle is applied by blowing through the atomizer. Test the spray first on a piece of scrap marked with the same drawing medium used in the drawing.

Avoid getting the spray device too close to the drawing. Hold the spray device 12 to 18 inches (30 to 46 cm) from it. Keep the sprayer moving. Several light coats are better than one heavy one. Fixative dries rapidly. Spray fixative labeled *workable* is best. This term means that after you spray an area of a drawing lightly, you can still draw on it.

When using spray fixative, always use it outside the studio in a well-ventilated area—outdoors, if possible. Breathing the fixative over a long period of time can be lethal.

Using the Artist Profiles

Role playing, games, and bulletin boards can be effective ways to involve students and to help them grasp information about the various artists, the time in which the artists lived, their particular art style and techniques, and their contributions to the world of art. On the following pages are teaching strategies designed to help you introduce, reinforce, and teach students about artists and their works.

▲ Artists, down through the ages, have helped us visualize what we learn about history. Art historians are responsible for much of what we know about the artists who have lived in the past.

Paul Cézanne

1839–1906
French Painter

The Card Player
page 19

Mont Sainte-Victoire
page 226

In 1839 the art of photography was born in France. Another French birth the same year—that of Paul Cézanne—would lead to equally important developments in the future of pictures.

Cézanne was born in the town of Aix (**ex**) in southern France. At the age of 22 he journeyed to Paris to study with the Romantics. He soon learned of other styles of painting that held even greater appeal for him.

By the end of the 1870s Cézanne began experimenting with an art style all his own. He returned to the south of France to perfect it. His goal, as he described it, was "to make of Impressionism something solid and permanent, like the art of the museums."

A loner, Cézanne struck the people of his little town as a strange figure. Who, they wondered, was this man who spent his days alone in the fields, making paintings no one bought? It was while out in the fields one rainy day during his sixty-seventh year that Cézanne developed a bad cough. A few days later he died of pneumonia.

Cézanne's one-of-a-kind use of color patches to create solid forms is showcased in *Mont Sainte-Victoire* (page 226). This is one of over 60 views of a favorite subject the artist painted.

The widespread availability in the early 1300s of a product called paper ushered in a new era in writing. A new era in painting came about during this same period. The person responsible for this second development was a gifted Italian artist named Giotto di Bondone (**jah**-toh dee-bahn-**dohn**-ee).

Giotto's lifelong calling as an artist was clear from the time he was 10. The son of a shepherd, he liked to pass the time drawing on flat stones in the fields. According to a popular story, one day a famous artist named Cimabue (chee-muh-**boo**-ay) came across young Giotto at work. Amazed at the boy's skill, Cimabue took him into his studio. Soon Giotto's skill as a painter was recognized throughout Italy.

In the early 1300s Giotto was asked to paint a series of frescoes on the walls of a church in Padua, Italy. One of these, *The Flight into Egypt*, is shown on page 154. Like other religious paintings of the day, Giotto's works focused on familiar stories from the Bible. Unlike anything ever done before, however, Giotto's paintings were peopled with flesh-and-blood figures. These figures moved about in what appeared to be real space. They also exhibited feelings and emotions with their facial expressions and gestures. Painting had taken a giant step forward.

So great was Giotto's contribution that when he died, a statue was created in his honor. On its base were the words "I am Giotto, that is all. The name alone is a victory poem."

Giotto (di Bondone)

1266–1337
Italian Painter

The Flight into Egypt
page 154

Visual Presentation. Divide the class into groups of two or three and assign different time periods to each group. Have each group research that period and report on it to the class. Encourage the students to use as many visual aids as they can, and to use the school media center and local library. Suggest that they use large prints of art works if they are available; the library is a good source of either prints or oversize art books. The media center might have equipment with which the students can make slides from books to use in the report. Slides ensure that everyone in the class can see the works being discussed. Dressing up in costumes, role playing, or presenting a dramatization can also make a report more enjoyable and meaningful for everyone.

Dramatization. A good choice for a dramatization is one event from the artist's life. Dramatizations make stronger impressions than straight reports. For example a debate on style between the Impressionists and Post-Impressionists would be interesting, especially if students took on the roles of real characters, such as Monet, Renoir, Cézanne, or van Gogh.

Artist Profiles **289**

Background Information

By creating multiple variations of a landscape instead of rendering a single perspective, Paul Cézanne asserts that nature—and all objects—may be seen from a number of views. Even within each individual image, such as his *Mont Sainte-Victoire*, Cézanne provokes his viewers into creating their own perspectives by providing details that suggest qualities rather than illustrate them. The rolling quality of the mountain is instilled by the same brush strokes that delineates houses and yields bushes. Cézanne forces the viewer to decide for him or herself exactly what each dab of paint represents.

Cézanne's philosophy is exemplified in his still life works. Notions such as depth and texture are all implied by the painter rather than depicted. For example, when Cézanne uses bright and unshaded colors to paint an apple, the viewer singles out the distant fruit regardless of its relative placement in the work's composition. By doing this, Cézanne reminds his audience that perspective is highly selective.

Francisco Goya

1746–1828
Spanish Painter

Cornered (From the Disasters of War)
page 187

The early 1800s found the world on the move. The invention of the steamboat was followed quickly by the building of the first railroad. The art world, too, was on the move — into a realm of self-expression where it has stayed to this day. The artist most identified with this move is a free spirit named Francisco Goya (fran-**sis**-koh **goy**-uh).

Goya was born in Saragossa (sar-uh-**goh**-suh), Spain. As a young man he traveled to Italy. He was not impressed by the Renaissance masterpieces and returned home. There he went to work as a portrait painter. His works flattered the members of the Spanish ruling class, who were his subjects. In 1786 he was named personal painter to King Charles IV.

An illness four years later left the artist deaf. Far from plunging him into despair, his handicap seemed to fuel his imagination. When war broke out in 1808, the artist created a series of prints unlike anything done before. Goya's view of war has no heroes or acts of glory. Like *Cornered* (page **187**), the prints in this series speak, rather, of senseless waste and brutality.

As Goya grew older, his view of the world grew grimmer still. His later works drew more and more on his own inner dreams and visions.

Puzzles. Turn some extra prints found in magazines into puzzles. Dry mount the print on a strong backing, such as poster board or mat board. If you are going to make more than one puzzle, put each on a different color backing so that if the pieces get mixed up they can be separated by color. Laminate the work, if possible, to protect the surface. Then, using a sharp cutting blade, cut the print into puzzle pieces. Try to keep the puzzle pieces large to help students become familiar with the art work. Use a separate storage container for each puzzle. Puzzles can help slower learners, or you can use them to hold a puzzle speed competition. Teams of students can compete to see which team can assemble a puzzle the fastest.

By the mid-1890s the United States had entered the age of communication. The newly invented telephone and wireless telegraph made it possible for people to communicate with one another over great distances. Not all people benefited from these inventions, however. To Native Americans tucked away in the New Mexico wilderness, time had stood still. It was in that quiet place at this not-so-quiet time that an artist named Lucy Lewis was born.

Lucy Lewis was raised in a pueblo in the town of Acoma (uh-**coh**-muh). She learned early of the importance of pottery to her people. As a child, Lewis watched her aunt make wide-mouthed pots called *ollas* (**oy**-uhs). She was taught where to dig for the best clay and how to mix the clay with water. As she grew, she began to experiment with different natural pigments. The pots she designed and crafted were unusually lightweight and handsome.

In time, people in the pueblo became aware that Lucy Lewis had a special gift. They encouraged her to enter craft fairs and shows. She followed their advice — and came away with many awards.

Today Lewis still lives in the Acoma area with her family. There she and her daughters teach others the fine craft of pottery.

Lucy Lewis

1897–
Native American Craftsperson

Polychrome Pots
page 201

Background Information
While Francisco Goya demonstrates his insightful mind and deft talent in paintings such as the compassionate *Third of May, 1808* and the sarcastic *The Family of Charles IV*, he created what might be his most unique works in etching. In his *Caprices*, finished in 1799, Goya provided a compilation of prints that made succinct points about the foolishness of humankind. Captions such as "The Sleep of Reason Produces Nightmares," "Eat That, You Dog," and "There Is a Lot to Suck" provided commentary on provocative ideas and images.

Inspired by experiences with corrupt politicians and war, the mature Goya later returned to the black and white medium to further criticize the stupidity of humankind in *The Disasters of War* and *The Proverbs*. Focusing on the vileness of warfare, Goya spares no one. He castigates soldiers in "Why?" and "That Is Wrong" but reveals the peasants—whom he celebrates in *Third of May, 1808*—to be as barbaric as warriors.

Judith Leyster
1609–1660
Dutch Painter

Self-Portrait
page 181

The late 1800s were a time of great discovery. In Germany a scientist named Roentgen (**rent**-guhn) discovered X-rays. In France a husband and wife named Curie (**kyu**-ree) discovered the element radium. Another discovery in France at the time had important consequences for the art world. It was the discovery of a signature on a painting long thought to be by the great Dutch artist Franz Hals. The surprising signature read "Judith Leyster" (**ly**-stuhr), not Franz Hals.

This "mystery" artist had been born some 250 years earlier in the Dutch city of Haarlem (**har**-luhm). At a time when women seeking art careers were often helped by artist fathers, Leyster—a brewer's daughter—had to rely on talent alone. Another difference between her and other female painters was her choice of subject matter. Instead of delicate still lifes, Leyster did robust genre paintings and portraits. One of these, her now-famous *Self-Portrait*, appears on page **181**. By 17 she had gained a reputation as an artist of great promise.

Leyster learned—and learned well—from other major painters of her day. Most notable among these are Hals, for his brush technique, and Caravaggio (see page **179**), for his use of light. Still, her works have a look that on careful inspection is unmistakably hers. Her portraits, especially, seem to invite the viewer in as if subject and viewer were close friends.

The voyages in the late 1400s of Christopher Columbus and Vasco da Gama broadened the world's horizons. So did the birth during that period of possibly the greatest artist the world has ever known. His name was Michelangelo Buonarroti (my-kuh-**lan**-juh-loh bwohn-uh-**rah**-tee).

Michelangelo was born in Florence to a poor family. At the age of six he was sent to live with the family of a stonecutter. There he came to love the feel of a sculptor's chisel and hammer in his hands. Art had found its way into his life.

Over the next 10 years Michelangelo's genius was given shape and direction through study with Florence's foremost artists. By the time he was 24, he had completed his first masterpiece, the *Pietà* (page **165**).

Despite his great talents, Michelangelo was hampered by some very human shortcomings. One was a hot temper, which made him hard to work with. Another was a need to see every project he took on in larger-than-life terms. Because of this second weakness, many of his works were never finished. One that was completed—and one of his most famous achievements—was his magnificent painting of the ceiling of the Sistine Chapel in Rome. The heroic job took four years to complete. During that time Michelangelo worked flat on his back on a platform he had built 68 feet (20 m) above the chapel floor!

Michelangelo (Buonarroti)
1475–1564
Italian Sculptor, Painter

Pietà
page 165

Card Games. Use prints in card games to help students become familiar with the names of artists and the titles of the works. To make a card game, mount medium-size prints on poster board, leaving a small margin around the print. Cut the print in fourths. Print the name of the artist and the title in the margin of each section of the print. Laminate the sections to make them last longer. Using about 10 prints (40 sections), create a deck of cards with which the students can play a variation of the card game, "Go Fish." The students must ask for the cards by artist and/or title. If you have many works by one artist, they must always use titles, but if you only have one print from each artist, they may use just artist. The students should request the work by saying, "Do you have any Picasso?" After a player has collected all four sections of a print, that print must be placed on the table for all to see. This exposes all players and observers to the print. The more times the students hear the names repeated, the more they learn. Use artists and works that you think are worth learning about.

Background Information
Although Plato himself distrusted artists—and poets—discrediting them as irrational and subversive to reason, the works of Michelangelo have been rightfully described as Platonic. Always concerning himself with "formal" and "ideal" notions, Michelangelo shared unlikely perspectives with the art-loathing philosopher. As Plato attempted to associate language, ideas, and forms, Michelangelo attempted to capture the ideal form of his subjects with sculpture. He viewed sculpting as a discovery process. Instead of trying to create a form by shaping stone, Michelangelo removed excess stone to reveal an existing essence that represented both truth and beauty.

The equation of form, truth, and beauty also characterized Michelangelo's architectural endeavors. Combining his aesthetic principles with functional necessities, Michelangelo designed and supervised the construction and renovation of several structures, including the Laurentian Library and the Capitoline Hill in Rome.

Joan Miró

1893–1983
Spanish Painter

Femme
  page 27

Dutch Interior
  page 259

The year was 1925. The world had scarcely recovered from "the war to end all wars" when it was shaken again. This time the explosion took place within the art world of Paris. It was caused by paintings like *Dutch Interior* (page **259**), created by a shy little Spanish artist named Joan Miró (zhoo-**ahn** meer-**roh**).

Miró was born in a town outside of Barcelona (bahr-suh-**loh**-nuh), Spain. As an art student, he was made to draw objects by "feeling" them rather than looking at them. For someone more fascinated by the world within than the one outside, the exercise was perfect training.

In 1919 Miró traveled to Paris, the capital of the art world. There he fell upon hard times. He was forced to get by on one meal a week. In between he ate dried figs to keep up his strength. It may have been the visions brought about by hunger that led to his first important Surrealist pictures.

After his first showing, Miró was hailed as a major new talent. He went to live on the island of Majorca (muh-**yor**-kuh), off the coast of Spain. There he painted in a room so small he had trouble moving around in it.

Later in his long career Miró broadened his interests to include sculpture. He also created huge weavings that, like *Femme* (page **27**), mirror the colorful designs of his paintings.

After the Brooklyn Bridge opened in the late 1800s, bridge building would never be the same. After a showing of paintings in Paris during this same period, art would never be the same. The showing was by a group of artists who had been turned down by the Salon. Their style, which became known as Impressionism, took its name from a work by one of the group's founders. His name was Claude Monet (**klohd** moh-**nay**).

Monet was born in Paris in 1840. His father, a grocer, moved the family to the port city of Le Havre (luh **hahv**-ruh) soon after his son's birth. Even as a child, Monet saw something magical in sunlight's effects on water. He studied with a noted landscape artist, who taught him the basics of Realist painting.

It was while a student that Monet met two other young artists, Auguste Renoir (oh-**guste** ren-**wahr**) and Alfred Sisley. The three soon became friends. They also began experimenting together, making paintings outdoors in natural sunlight. At first their works were laughed at by critics. Today the works of these three artists are among the most admired in the history of art.

It was during a stay in England that Monet painted *Waterloo Bridge, London* (page **220**). Like his other mature works, this work contains no solid lines or forms. Rather, these elements are hinted at through dabs and dots of color.

Claude Monet

1840–1926
French Painter

Banks of the Seine, Vetheuil
  page 216

Waterloo Bridge, London
  page 220

292   *Artist Profiles*

Time-Period Recognition Game. If you can find individual prints that are small enough, you might organize them into a time-period recognition game. For example, you might set up one deck with four Ancient Egyptian works, four Gothic, four Renaissance, four African-American, four Near East, and so forth. At the beginning of the year you can use stick-on labels that identify the periods. Later you can remove the labels. Be careful that each set of four in a deck is distinctly different from every other set in that deck.

Time-Style Recognition Game. For a more advanced game than the one above, organize the cards by style. In this deck you might include four Impressionist works, four Cubist works, four Surrealist works, and so forth. Again, be careful not to use two styles that might be confused, such as American Regionalist and English Landscape.

Background Information

As one of the first successful Surrealist painters, Miró has had a profound impact on the art community, lending his talents to painting, sculpting, and mural making. Miró transformed his subjects into organic shapes to create symbolic images. *Still Life with Old Shoe* suggests his disappointment with the Spanish fascist movement. He alludes to consumption, inebriation, waste, and death with distorted depictions of an apple portion, a gin bottle, an unmatched shoe, and a skull.

The meaning of Miró's *The Harlequin's Carnival* is more difficult to explicate, but while the actual objects in the composition are mostly unrecognizable, the mood is undeniably buoyant. The painting is divided into symbolic black and white halves. Still, the viewer's eye is lifted upward by unrestrained vertical movement. An open window and floating objects reinforce the sense of freedom, while various eyes, ears, and mouths add a sensuous element.

Berthe Morisot

1841–1895
French Painter

*The Artist's Sister at a
Window*
page 218

The last decade of the 1800s was a time of change. In 1896 Thomas
Edison burst on the scene with the invention of the motion picture.
A year earlier the art world mourned the passing of a maker of pictures of a different sort. Her name was Berthe Morisot (**behrt** maw-
ree-**zoh**).

Berthe Morisot was born into an art family. Her parents were art
lovers and her great-grandfather, Jean-Honoré Fragonard (**zhahnh**
oh-nor-**ay** frah-goh-**nahrh**), had been an important painter of the
1700s. From the time she was a young girl, she knew she would
become a painter. At 15 she met and became good friends with
Edouard Manet (ay-doo-**ahrh** mah-**nay**), a leading artist of the day.
Several years later she married Manet's brother.

Like Manet, Morisot focused on indoor scenes and portraits. Her
portrait titled *The Artist's Sister at a Window* (page **218**) is one of her
best-known works.

Although other artists praised her work, during her lifetime Morisot was ignored by critics. Many did so merely because she was a
woman. It was not until her death that her work began receiving the
respect it had always deserved.

In 1905 Albert Einstein published his theory of relativity. In so
doing, he challenged age-old beliefs about the meaning of time and
space. In that same year a young girl moved with her family from
Russia to America. She would grow up to create art that would challenge age-old beliefs about the meaning of sculpture. Her name was
Louise Nevelson (**nev**-uhl-suhn).

As a child in Maine, Nevelson spent long hours playing in her
father's lumberyard. She loved to carve and build using the scraps of
wood she found.

At the age of 20 Louise married and two years later gave birth to a
child. In time, she came to resent the responsibilities of marriage and
motherhood that took time away from her art. In 1931 she left her son
with her parents and headed to Europe to study art.

Nevelson's first showing came in 1941. The reviews, which were
favorable, spurred her on. In the decades that followed, she began
more and more to experiment with "found" media. It was not uncom-
mon to find her studio littered with wood scraps very much like the
ones she had played with in her father's lumberyard. Most of Nevelson's works from the 1960s on are, like *Mrs. N's Palace* (page **267**),
three-dimensional collages. Most invite viewers to use their imaginations as well as their eyes.

Louise Nevelson

1900–1988
American Sculptor

Mrs. N's Palace
page 267

Bulletin Boards. Divide the
class into groups and have each
group choose one of the artists from
the Artist Profiles, *Handbook* pages
289–295. Set aside one small bulletin board as an "Artist of the
Week" board and assign each
group the responsibility of featuring
their artist for one week. Set up
some guidelines for the student displays and share this with the class.
Some criteria for the display could
be:
• catchy title and neat lettering
• quantity and accuracy of information
• creativity, and aesthetic quality.
The minimum information would include artist's name, country, dates
of birth and death, style, and titles
of works displayed, example of
artist's works, information about the
artist, and portrayal of the artist's
style or of the time and place in
which the artist lived. Grade the display according to the guidelines established.

Artist Profiles **293**

Background Information

The roots of assemblage art were established during the first
decade of the twentieth century. Dadaists and Cubists had
profound effects on assemblage art fifty years later when it
was defined and recognized as its own genre. While it may at
first seem nonsensical, assemblage sculpture is a natural
medium for affecting an audience. Using common objects that
have not been designed for artistic purposes, the artist effectively bridges the gap between the viewer's world and the artistic world. When the viewer sees an everyday object in the context of art, he or she is forced to consider its place in the work
and in society.

Louise Nevelson is known for her use of household items
and pieces of old Victorian houses. Painting them and arranging them in boxes or other frames, Nevelson questions
notions about homes, tradition, and antiquity. She has complemented her works with the experimental use of such visual
components as aluminum and clear plastic.

Albert Pinkham Ryder

1847–1917
American Painter

Moonlight Marine (Toilers of the Sea)
page 234

The first two decades of the twentieth century were a politically stormy time. The winds of revolution swept through Russia and China. In 1914 the world went to war. To take their minds off gloomy events of the day, some people turned inward. One who did—and came back to the world with a rare gift of art—was Albert Pinkham Ryder.

Ryder was born in New Bedford, Massachusetts. When he was a young man, his family moved to New York City. There an older brother helped pay his way through art school. Showing little interest in the works of other artists, Ryder forged his own one-of-a-kind style. Among the features of his style were paint layers so thick that his pictures sometimes looked three-dimensional.

Always given to strange personal habits, Ryder developed still odder ways during his middle years. He gave up his Greenwich Village apartment and moved into a run-down rooming house. Burdened by poor eyesight, he spent his days indoors, his nights roaming the streets alone. After 1900 he became a hermit altogether.

It may have been during his silent night walks that Ryder dreamed up ideas for his pictures. Most, like *Moonlight Marine* (page 234), are glimpses of a dream world, which capture the viewer's imagination.

In 1921 a bitterly fought revolution in Mexico ended. Honest, hard-working people, long treated as slaves by rich landlords, were free at last. In that same year a talented Mexican artist returned from abroad. He began the first of many larger-than-life chronicles of the struggle for freedom. His name was Diego Rivera (dee-**ay**-goh rih-**vehr**-uh).

Rivera was born in the city of Guanajuato (gwahn-uh-**waht**-oh). As a young man, he journeyed to Paris, where he met Picasso and Matisse. While in Europe he also studied the art of the great Italian fresco painters. The size of the frescoes—some covered entire walls—appealed to him. Such an art form, he felt, would be a fitting tribute to those who had fought so bravely in the Mexican Revolution. It would also be a reminder to Mexico's rich of the power of the people.

Murals like *The Liberation of the Peon* (page 251) reveal Rivera's skill as a storyteller. They also reveal the influences of both Giotto and Rivera's pre-Columbian ancestors.

After making a name for himself, Rivera was asked to paint murals in the United States. He created works that, like those in Mexico, were filled with people and action. These illustrated the American fascination with speed and the machine. Unfortunately, many of these magnificent murals were destroyed.

Diego Rivera

1886–1957
Mexican Painter

The Liberation of the Peon
page 251

Alfred Stieglitz
1864–1946
American Photographer

The Terminal
page 249

Around 1900 the United States opened its doors to Americans-to-be from all nations. To young Abstract painters hoping to enter the art world of the day, the door was firmly shut. Abstract painting was misunderstood and unappreciated by the public and most art critics. One free thinker who provided an outlet for these brave new talents was himself an artist. He was photographer Alfred Stieglitz (**steeg-luhts**).

Stieglitz was born in Hoboken, New Jersey. His interest in photography began when he was young. Early in his career he began seeing photography's potential as an art medium. He spent long hours—sometimes in swirling snow—waiting for just the right shot.

In 1902 he formed Photo-Secession, an organization devoted to the art of photography. Three years later he opened a gallery at 291 Fifth Avenue in New York City. Known as 291, the gallery became a haven for struggling young artists from all areas of art. One artist whose work was displayed at 291 was a native of Wisconsin named Georgia O'Keeffe. Stieglitz and O'Keeffe developed a friendship that grew over time. Despite an age difference of 23 years, the two were married in 1924.

Stieglitz spent his life championing the world of other photographers. Still, his own photographs are among the most sensitive ever taken. Through instant human studies, like *The Terminal* (page **249**), he carried photography to new heights.

In 1875 Congress passed an act giving African Americans the right to serve on juries. Eight years later the Supreme Court declared the act unconstitutional. It was not long after that decision that artist Henry Tanner made a decision of his own. Tanner, an African American artist having little success selling paintings in America, decided to set sail for Europe.

Tanner had been born 32 years earlier in Philadelphia, Pennsylvania. His father was a minister, who later became a bishop. Tanner's interest in art began when he was only 12. Walking through a park with his father, he saw a landscape painter at work. Tanner watched in fascination. As his fascination grew, so did his desire to become a painter.

Tanner entered the Pennsylvania Academy of Fine Arts, where his teacher was Thomas Eakins. Eakins advised his student to turn from landscapes to genre scenes—which Tanner did. But Tanner found there was little market for paintings of any kind by an African American. Wanting, in any case, to focus on Biblical subjects, he headed for Paris. Within five years one of his Biblical pictures was hanging in a place of honor at the Paris Salon.

While Tanner painted mostly religious works, he still found time now and then to exhibit his skills at painting landscapes. *The Seine* (page **236**) is one of these works.

Henry O. Tanner
1859–1937
American Painter

The Seine
page 236

Artist Profiles **295**

Multi-Media. Slides, filmstrips, videos, and cassettes are excellent ways for students to learn more about artists and their works of art. Contact distributors for a catalog.

ART SLIDE, FILMSTRIP, AND CASSETTE DISTRIBUTORS

Boston Museum of Fine Arts
Department of Photographic Services
Slide Library
465 Huntington Avenue
Boston, MA 02115

Educational Dimensions Corporation
Stamford, CT 06904

Metropolitan Museum of Art
255 Gracie Station
New York, NY 10028

Wilton Art Appreciation Programs
P.O. Box 302
Wilton, CT 06897

COLOR REPRODUCTION SUPPLIERS

Harry N. Abrams
100 E. 59th Street
New York, NY 10022

Art Education, Inc.
28 E. Erie Street
Blauvelt, NY 10913

Art Extension Press
Box 389
Westport, CT 06881

Associated American Artists
663 Fifth Avenue
New York, NY 10022

Catalda Fine Arts
12 W. 27th Street
New York, NY 10001

Imaginus, Inc.
R. R. 1, Box 552
Lee, MA 01238

Metropolitan Museum of Art
Book and Art Shop
Fifth Avenue and 82nd Street
New York, NY 10028

Museum of Modern Art
11 W. 53rd Street
New York, NY 10019

National Gallery of Art
Department of Extension Programs
Washington, D.C. 20565

New York Graphic Society
140 Greenwich Avenue
Greenwich, CT 06830

Oestreicher's Prints
43 W. 46th Street
New York, NY 10036

Penn Prints
31 W. 46th Street
New York, NY 10036

Konrad Prothmann
2378 Soper Avenue
Baldwin, NY 11510

Shorewood Reproductions
Department S
475 10th Avenue
New York, NY 10018

UNESCO Catalogues
Columbia University Press
562 W. 113th Street
New York, NY 10025

University Prints
21 East Street
Winchester, MA 01890

Using the Career Spotlights

Try the following teaching strategies to introduce students to the many art-related job opportunities and careers. At the bottom of the pages are addresses of organizations that students can write to for additional career information.

▲ There are many career opportunities in art and art-related fields.

Art Director

Art Teacher

You may know that movies are the work of hundreds of people. You may also know there is one person in charge of all others, called the director. But did you know that advertisements, books, and magazines also have directors?

Many people with an interest in art and a desire to share their knowledge become art teachers.

Art directors are experienced artists whose job is to lead or supervise other artists. Like film directors, art directors are responsible for seeing that all other jobs in a project are done.

Art directors are hired by advertising agencies, book publishers, and television or radio stations. The specific tasks of the job may differ slightly from place to place. In general, the art director hires and oversees the work of illustrators, photographers, and graphic designers. Together, the art director and the people who report to him or her are called a team. The art director has the responsibility for signing off, or approving, all work done by team members.

A career in art teaching requires a college education. Part of that education is devoted to methods of teaching. Part is devoted to developing a broad background in the history of art and the use of art materials and techniques.

Good art teachers open their students to a wide variety of art experiences. They give students the chance to create their own art and to react to the art of others. They also make sure their students learn about such important areas as aesthetics, art criticism, and art history.

While most art teachers work in schools, some find employment opportunities in other areas. Some art teachers work in museums or hospitals. Some teachers work in retirement centers. Still others work in nursery schools and day-care centers.

Analyzing Advertisements.
Divide students into small groups and explain that art directors supervise advertising campaigns used to market and promote products. Have students select a variety of magazines from different interest areas, such as high fashion, mechanics, photography, architecture, teen life, current events, health, sports, science, science fiction, television, and so forth. Have each group compare such things as the types of advertisements and the types of advertising techniques used to capture the attention of the specific audience. Have them present their findings to the class.

Art Teacher. Invite a school counselor to speak to the class and explain the requirements (grade point averages and portfolio requirements) for attending art and design schools. Have the counselor explain the additional requirements for becoming an art teacher in your state.

Note
You may wish to have students write to the following for information about careers in advertising management.
American Advertising Federation
1400 K Street NW, Suite 1000
Washington, D.C. 20025

Note
Have students contact the following organizations to learn more about teachers' unions and education-related issues:
American Federation of Teachers
555 New Jersey Avenue, NW
Washington, D.C. 20001
National Education Association
1201 16th Street, NW
Washington, D.C. 20036

Computer Graphics Specialist

Editorial Cartoonist

What do computers have to do with art? To the person known as a computer graphics specialist, the answer is "everything!"

Computer graphics specialists are skilled professionals who use state-of-the-art electronic equipment to create designs. The work they do has brought the world of commercial art into the space age. A career in this field combines a strong background in design with a knowledge of computers.

The computer graphics specialist works with tools such as electric light pens on electronic tablets. With these tools, any image may be drawn and colored in. Such computer drawings may be stored permanently in the computer's memory. They can then be called up and reworked by the designer as needed.

Some computer graphics specialists work with systems that allow them to see their finished work in different sizes and colors. Computer-made designs can also be sent along telephone lines around the world.

Newspaper editorials are written accounts that invite readers to form an opinion about important news topics. Editorial cartoons do the same work in pictures.

Editorial cartoonists, the people who create such pictures, work for newspapers and magazines. Their creations usually appear as single drawings without titles or captions. Sometimes editorial cartoons go hand-in-hand with the main editorial, which is printed nearby. At other times they comment on other issues figuring in current events.

Many editorial cartoonists use a style of art called *caricature* (**kar**-ih-kuh-chur). This is the exaggerating of facial features or expressions to poke fun at well-known figures. Some editorial cartoonists use symbols to communicate their meanings. A bear, for instance, is often used by editorial cartoonists to symbolize the Soviet Union.

Exhibit and Display Designer

The next time you pass a display of clothing or other goods in a department store, look carefully. Somewhere within that display will be a hidden message: artist at work.

Exhibit and display designers work in a number of retail and non-profit settings. Some of these settings are trade shows, department stores, showrooms, art galleries, and museums. Such designers plan presentations of collections, exhibits, and traveling shows of all kinds. They are responsible for such matters as deciding what items should be grouped together. They also take into account how displays should be arranged and lighted.

The display designer is an important part of the sales team. Displays attract customers. They can affect a customer's decision to buy. The way the display designer does his or her job can make all the difference between whether or not a sale is made.

Graphic Designer

There are artists all around us. They are there behind every billboard, street sign, and soup can label. These artists are called graphic designers. They use pictures and words to inform or decorate.

Graphic designers work in a great many areas. Each area has its own special tasks and title. Technical illustrator is one of these titles. Sign maker is another.

The field of graphic design has its roots in the 1500s. It was in that century that the printing press was invented. People were needed to arrange words and pictures on the printed page. To this day that task, known as layout, is a job of graphic designers. Graphic designers also pick type faces, or styles of lettering, for printed material. They must also decide how drawings or photographs will be used as illustrations.

Display Designer. Divide students into small groups and assign them to create either a window display, point-of-purchase display, or exhibit display. Have them select a product of their choice and create a three-dimensional display. Set up criteria for evaluating the display such as: neatness, product identity, eye-catching, informative, and so forth. Set up a panel of students to judge the displays.

Resource People. Bring in resource people during the time that you are presenting careers to make the material more meaningful to students. Students will be interested in learning from people who work directly in the art-related field. You may also invite the guidance counselor to discuss art-related careers and to talk about the various schools and colleges that specialize in art-related careers.

If you live in an urban area it will not be difficult to find people who work at some of these careers. Even the smallest newspaper in a rural area needs a layout person. The local television station will also employ someone who fits one of the career categories mentioned in this section. Remember that artists are also hired by industry. Other employees to consider are florists or window display people who can demonstrate how the elements and principles of art are used in their jobs.

If you cannot find a commercial artist, a local art hobbyist or craftsperson may substitute, as well as a college art student who may be home on vacation. If there is a local artist in your area, a field trip to this person's studio can be exciting.

Note
For a list of accredited schools of art and design, contact:
National Association of Schools of Art and Design
11250 Roger Bacon Drive, Suite 21
Reston, Virginia 22090

Industrial Designer

What do toys, vacuum cleaners, and cars have in common? All are designed to work easily and have a pleasing look. These and countless other items you see and use each day are the work of industrial designers.

Industrial designers work for makers of products. These artists work closely with engineers who develop the products. Sometimes industrial designers are asked to work on things as simple as tamper-proof caps for medicines. At other times they are asked to work on projects as complicated as space vehicles. Before they begin work, industrial designers need to know how the product is to be used.

Because different brands of the same product are sold, industrial design sometimes crosses over into advertising. The appearance of a design becomes especially important in the case of very competitive products such as cars and entertainment systems, for example.

Interior Designer

Architects give us attractive, functional spaces in which to live, work, and play. Interior designers fill those spaces with attractive and useful furnishings and accessories.

The job of the interior designer is to plan the interior space. This includes choosing furniture, fabrics, floor coverings, lighting fixtures, and decorations. To do this job well, the designer must take into account the wants and needs of the users of the space. In planning a home, for example, the interior designer will learn as much as possible about the lifestyle of the family that lives there.

Interior designers help their clients envision their ideas through the use of floor plans, elevations, and sketches. Once a client has agreed to a plan, the designer makes arrangements for buying materials. He or she also oversees the work for builders, carpenters, painters, and other craftspeople.

300   *Career Spotlights*

Note

For a list of accredited schools of art and design, contact:
  National Association of Schools of Art and Design
  11250 Roger Bacon Drive, Suite 21
  Reston, Virginia 22090
For information about careers in interior design, contact:
American Society for Interior Designers
1430 Broadway
New York, New York 10018

A brochure that describes careers in industrial design and lists academic programs in the field is available from the Industrial Designers Society of America. For price and ordering information write:
  Industrial Designers Society of America
  1142-E Walker Road
  Great Falls, Virginia 22066

Magazine Designer

Magazine designers are graphic designers who work for publications called *periodicals*. These are booklets or pamphlets that come out on a regular basis in issues.

There are two parts to a magazine design—the fixed design and the variable design. The fixed design includes the features of the magazine that seldom change. These include the different type faces and decorative elements such as page borders. The magazine designer works mostly on the variable design. This includes making sure all the pages in an issue are a standard length. Another part of variable design is figuring out where illustrations should go and how large they should be.

At times a magazine designer is called upon to create special features for a periodical. These are used to highlight a theme running throughout the issue.

Medical Illustrator

Among Leonardo da Vinci's many achievements were his drawings of *anatomy* or human body parts. Ever since his time there has been a call for medical illustrators.

Medical illustrators work for medical schools, teaching hospitals, and publishers of medical journals and textbooks. All have a basic knowledge of medicine and an ability to work with many different art media. Among these are transparencies (trans-**pare**-uhn-sees), or illustrations that are placed on overhead projectors.

The work of medical illustrators falls into two main areas. One is the drawing of diagrams showing various details, such as the heart and limbs. The second is doing step-by-step illustrations of surgical and other medical procedures.

At times medical illustrators are called upon to work with such medical equipment as X-ray machines, microscopes, and scanners.

Field Trips. Field trips contribute greatly to a course. If class field trips are not possible, individual trips which one or more students may take after school or on weekends might be arranged.

All trips will be more successful if guidelines are set up to help students understand the objectives. Research done prior to the trip and a follow-up evaluation will add to the value of the experience. Students should know what to look for and what to expect to gain from the experience. It might be pointed out that the business people they visit may be possible employers and that appropriate conduct and dress on a trip may make a future interview more likely. Students should know what kind of follow-up will be expected. For example, a written evaluation, quiz, or participation in a class discussion might be required.

The instructor should make the necessary arrangements well in advance to ensure the students' welcome. A time schedule should be established and carefully followed. While museums, organizations, and industries are happy to conduct tours of their facilities, the staff members usually have other responsibilities, and group tours must be prearranged.

Field trip possibilities vary in each community. The suggested list includes trips which are possible in your area. It may also suggest others to you which are not on the list but which would be valuable. Suggestions for possible field trips: display rooms in furniture stores; model apartments in new apartment buildings; rug and carpet salesrooms; wallpaper stores; interior design studios; decorator showrooms; historic houses and museums; advertising agencies.

Career Spotlights **301**

Note
For information on careers in illustration have students contact:
  The Society of Illustrators
  128 East 63rd Street
  New York, New York 10021

Museum Curator

Like universities and libraries, museums have the job of preserving and passing on culture. The person in charge of seeing that the museum does its job is called the museum curator (**kyoor**-ayt-uhr).

Curators are part custodian, part scholar, and part historian. The tasks of the curator are many. They include securing, caring for, displaying, and studying works of art. The curator makes sure works are arranged so they teach, inform, and delight.

As holders of advanced college degrees, curators carry on research in their own areas of interest. They report their findings in books, lectures, and journals.

Photojournalist

Photography, as you have learned, was unheard of until the mid-1800s. No sooner had photography emerged on the scene, however, than the field of photojournalism was born. Photojournalism is the taking of pictures for newspapers and magazines.

One of the earliest photojournalists was a photographer named Mathew Brady. Brady lived in America during the Civil War. His early black-and-white snapshots offer dramatic glimpses of life on and off the battlefield.

Since Brady's time the field of photojournalism has grown and with it, the responsibilities of the photographer. Photojournalists are expected to seek out and record newsworthy scenes. They must also be able to take action pictures quickly and process them with equal speed.

Some photojournalists in recent decades have chosen specialties for themselves. Two of these areas are politics and sports.

Photojournalist. Have students look through local newspapers and notice the credit lines under the photographs. They should note that some have come in over the wires, and they carry labels such as "UPI." Others have been taken locally. Have students note the name of the photographer. Ask: Is there just one photographer working for the paper or can you find many different names on the credit lines? Does one person seem to specialize in one type of photography, such as sports or entertainment?

Note
For general information about careers as a curator and schools offering courses in curatorial science, contact:
   American Association of Museums
   1225 I Street NW, Suite 200
   Washington, D.C. 20005

Special Effects Designer

Are you the sort of person whose imagination works overtime? Then maybe the field of special effects design is for you.

Unlike people in other art careers, special effects designers may not attend special schools. The field is very new. The people who have created film and television magic to date have come up through the ranks. They may have started by building sets for plays or designing film backgrounds.

Special effects artists are one part painter, one part sculptor, and one part engineer. They have the ability to imagine, and then create, fantasy scenes or creatures. They are masters of make-believe.

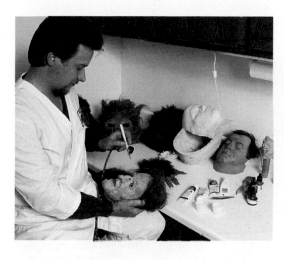

There is no limit to the tools used by special effects designers. Depending on the needs of a project, they might use papier-mâché, plaster, plastic molds, or paint. Makeup, trick photography, and computers are just a few of the other media they use.

Urban Planner

Have you ever wondered how big cities come to look the way they do? The two-word answer to this question is urban (or city) planners.

City planners are people whose job is to supervise the care and improvement of a city. Every large American city has a planner.

A main task of city planners is to enforce zoning laws. These are laws controlling what part of a city may be used for what purposes. Thanks to city planners, garbage dumps are not located in residential communities.

A second task of the city planner is to look after the growth and development of the urban areas. The planner works with the mayor and other city officials to create parks, harbors, and shopping malls.

City planners are trained as architects. Their knowledge of design helps them to plan a pleasing cityscape.

City Planner. Have students work in small groups and imagine that they have been hired as a city planning team to improve their town. If they live in a big city, have them limit the area to their own neighborhood. Ask them to prepare a survey to ask people what they like most and what they like least about the town or neighborhood. They should find out which building is considered the most important and which is considered the most attractive. Ask about traffic flow, stores, recreation, entertainment, health services, police protection, and water and sewerage. They can add other questions to the survey. Then they should carry out the survey. Have them talk to students at their school and adults who live in the area. Have them put all of their findings in graph or chart form. Compare adult and teen replies. Do the two groups agree or disagree on each item?

Career Spotlights **303**

Note
For additional information on careers in urban and regional planning, have students contact:
American Planning Association
1776 Massachusetts Avenue, NW
Washington, D.C. 20036

ADDITIONAL STUDIOS

LESSON 1

Computer-Type Drawing

- Arrange a group of objects or simple shapes, such as a book, a cardboard box, a piece of fruit. Students can choose to copy one of these objects, or can choose to draw a geometric shape not based on an object.
- This lesson can incorporate mathematical concepts. Review with students the skills required to enlarge or reduce a picture using graph paper.
- If you do not have computers in the classroom, but do have a computer lab in the building, arrange with your school administrators to have the class visit the lab for a demonstration. If computers are not available in your building, ask local computer stores if they would be willing to come in and demonstrate their computers; or arrange a trip to another school or store for the purpose of seeing a computer demonstration. Or, simply bring in illustrated computer books or magazines to show the students how pixels work.
- Remind students that cool colors are black, blues, and greens; and that warm colors are yellows, oranges, reds and browns. Discuss how these colors can be used to create shape and form.

Computer-Type Drawing

Look back at the painting in Figure 15–4 on page **230**. The work illustrates the Pointillist technique of Georges Seurat. When you look at this work, your eye connects the dots to make forms and colors. Taking an approach similar to Seurat's, computer artists in recent years have started creating pictures like the one shown in Figure S–1. The tiny squares of color, called pixels (**piks**-els), work exactly as the dots do in a Seurat painting. When seen from a distance they blend together into a recognizable three-dimensional image.

WHAT YOU WILL LEARN

You will plan and create a computer-type drawing emphasizing a single three-dimensional form. You will use colored pencils and graph paper to create pixels of color. Warm and cool colors will be combined to suggest a three-dimensional form. (See Figure S–2.)

WHAT YOU WILL NEED

- Pencil, eraser, and colored pencils
- Sheet of graph paper, 9 x 12 inches (23 x 30 cm)

► **Figure S–1** How does the use of warm and cool hues help to show form in this computer-generated work?

Background Information

Georges Pierre Seurat was one of the most famous Pointillists of the Post-Impressionist era. He was born in Paris in 1859 and died tragically at the age of 31. Seurat did not invent Pointillism, but he was the artist most often identified with the movement. While many critics felt that the art was mechanical and nonartistic, Seurat felt that he was reflecting the concerns of a society in which science and technology were paramount. Structure and precision were important to him.

During his brief career, he managed to create art of such impact that it played a crucial role in the development of modern art. His first important work was exhibited when he was 24, called *Une Baignade Asniere*. The following years showed that his genius was not a one-time affair; a very consistent series of works assured him a place in the history of art. While his works were not as critically acclaimed during his life as they are now, many modern artists took them as inspiration.

WHAT YOU WILL DO

1. Pick colors for your work ranging from very warm to very cool. Choose an equal number of each type, no fewer than eight.
2. Working lightly in pencil, draw the outline of a large, interesting shape on the graph paper. The shape may be either organic or geometric but should fill most of the page. Use the eraser to make adjustments. When you are pleased with the shape you have created, trace over it in a very cool hue.
3. Find the square that is roughly in the center of your shape. Color in this first square using the warmest, brightest hue. This could be a bright orange or yellow. Using the same hue, fill in the squares directly above, below, and to either side.
4. Continue to work outward from the center square. As you do, switch little by little to warm hues that are less bright. When you reach roughly the halfway point between the center and outermost squares, begin to use bright cool colors. The squares closest to the outline of the shape should be filled with color.
5. When you have finished, display your work along with those of your classmates. Stand back and look at the different drawings. Which of the shapes look most three-dimensional?

EXAMINING YOUR WORK

- **Describe** Name the colors used. Identify those that are warm colors and those that are cool colors. Explain how the warm and cool colors have been used to suggest a three-dimensional form.
- **Analyze** Explain how step-by-step changes in color are used to change a shape into a form. Tell how this form is emphasized in the drawing.
- **Interpret** State what image, if any, your shape calls to mind. Create a title for your work.
- **Judge** Tell whether you have succeeded in suggesting a three-dimensional form. If you have not, tell what you could do to improve your work.

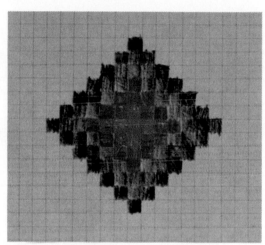

▲ Figure S–2 Student work. Computer-type drawing.

ADDITIONAL STUDIOS

- Bring in examples of Seurat's and other Impressionists' paintings. Compare them with the computer picture in Figure S-1 and with the students' computer-type drawings, pointing out how form is suggested by different artists, and how color is used in different ways.
- In this lesson, color is not being used to convey the "real" color of the object being drawn. It is being used for other purposes.
- Have the students discuss the different ways in which color can be used in painting and drawing.
- The Pointillists were accused of being too mechanical in their approach to art. Computer-aided art is also mechanical. Discuss this criticism with the students. Ask: Is the art created through the use of computers less valuable than the art created through use of media such as paints, pencils, and ink?
- Have the students experiment with using color to create form. Have them use only a few colors on a sketch; then have them use many colors. What are the differences between few and many colors? Is one more successful than the other? Can one have too few colors to create form? Can one have too many?

OTHER STUDIO IDEAS

- Repeat the assignment, this time using only lead pencil. Leave the squares closest to the center white. Press harder and harder as you move outward. The boxes at the outer edge should be as black as you can make them. Notice how gradual changes in value can also be used to suggest a three-dimensional form.

- ●● Repeat the assignment, this time using tempera paint in place of the colored pencils. Add a background of sky and clouds to your shape, painting freely. Identify what style of art the finished work most resembles.

Coil Pot

LESSON 2

Coil Pot

- Review the element of rhythm in art. Have the students describe the purpose of rhythm and explain how rhythm can be created in pottery.
- Many artists prefer to work clay by hand instead of using a wheel. Discuss with students the reasons why an artist might use a wheel, and also why an artist might prefer to use his or her hands to create a piece of pottery.
- Ask the students to define the difference between fine art and applied art. Have them decide which their coil pot is and why.
- Pottery is an old craft that is practiced in every part of the world, and was practiced by all cultures that had access to clay. Why might people find pottery so fascinating?

Look at the object in Figure S–3. This is an example of an early Native American coil clay pot. Scientific dating of artifacts like this helps experts estimate the earliest time ancient people may have arrived on this continent. Works like this also provide a window on the way of life of those people.

WHAT YOU WILL LEARN

You will create a clay pot in the style of prehistoric Native Americans. You will give the work a sense of rhythm by increasing and then decreasing the size of coils. Your finished pot should be both useful and decorative.

WHAT YOU WILL NEED

- 2 pounds of clay, and slip
- Canvas-covered clay board
- Large plastic bag and bowl of water
- Scrap piece of heavy cardboard

WHAT YOU WILL DO

1. Review Technique Tip **16**, *Handbook* page **281**. It will give you some general background information on working with clay.
2. Gently throw your clay against the clay board. Doing this will remove any air pockets that might cause your work to explode when fired.

▶ **Figure S–3   What do you suppose were some of the functional uses of a pot like this in the Pueblo culture?**

Pueblo. Ceramic Jar. Prehistoric. White slip with black painted decoration. 10.8 x 15.8 cm (4¼ x 6¼"). Indian Arts Research Center, Santa Fe, New Mexico.

Background Information

Native American pottery was not produced in any quantity in America until about 500 A.D. The first pottery was molded from slabs and set in the sun to dry. Most later pottery was made using the coil technique and variations on this technique were used throughout the centuries. Native Americans did not develop a wheel and most did not develop a high-firing clay.

After the coil technique was invented, the Native Americans experimented with different kinds of surface treatment. Sometimes the coils were smoothed over, and the piece was shaped and polished with a smooth stone. Sometimes the coils were left partially or completely unsmoothed. Applied decorations were at first simply black shapes over a white surface. These decorations appeared about 700–1100 A.D. By the 1500s, polychrome techniques were being used throughout America. Most of the decorations were highly symbolic. Everyday ware tended to be unadorned.

3. Pinch off a lump of clay about the size of a lemon. With the heel of your hand, flatten the lump into a circle about ½ inch (13 mm) thick. Set it aside. (See Figure S–4.)

4. Pinch off a second smaller lump, and roll it into a rope. The rope should be about ½ inch (13 mm) thick and 12 inches (30 cm) long. Form the rope into a ring, joining the two ends with slip. Seal the ring to the circle you made. This is to be the base of your pot.

5. Create four more ropes. All should be the same thickness as the first rope. Each, however, should be slightly longer than the one before it. Form the shortest rope into a ring, as you did earlier. Using slip, attach it to your base. Form the next longest rope into a ring. Attach it to the outer edges of the last coil. Continue to work in this fashion until your work is five coils high.

6. Roll out five more ropes, this time making each slightly shorter than the one before it. Form the longest into a ring. Attach it to the inner edges of the last coil on your pot. Continue working in this manner until you have used all your ropes. (*Hint:* If it takes longer than one class period to finish your pot, store it in the plastic bag. This will keep it moist until you are ready to work with it again.)

7. Allow your pot to dry to the greenware stage. Use the scrap of cardboard as a scraper to smooth out any bumps. Fire the pot in a kiln. Display your finished pot alongside those of classmates. Which pots succeed in showing a sense of rhythm?

OTHER STUDIO IDEAS

● Make a second pot similar to the first one. This time, use your fingernails or a pencil point to dent each coil every inch (3 cm) or so. This will add an interesting texture. Compare your pot with the coiled pot in Figure 13–2 on page **194**.

- **Describe** Tell whether all the coils in your pot have the same thickness. Describe the form of your pot. Explain what you did to obtain this form.
- **Analyze** Tell which principles were used to organize the elements in your work. State whether your pot has a sense of rhythm. Explain how this sense of rhythm is realized.
- **Interpret** Point out in what ways your pot is similar to a prehistoric Native American coil pot.
- **Judge** Tell whether you have succeeded in creating a work that is both useful and decorative. Tell what changes you would make if you were going to redo your pot.

▲ Figure S–4　Student work in progress.

●● Make a second pot similar to the first one. This time, use your cardboard scraper to smooth out the coils. Using a sharp clay tool, carve a geometric design in the surface of your pot. This design should be made so that it fits comfortably within the shape of your pot.

- Supply a variety of clay pots, or have students bring in samples. Compare the differences between the clay pieces. Do they have a sense of rhythm or texture? Is color used? Bring in pictures of various clay artifacts and discuss the principles of art and how they are used.
- Have students keep their clay in the plastic bag, and take out only as much as they need to shape one coil at a time. This way, the clay will not dry out while they are in the middle of the project.
- Emphasize to students the importance of eliminating air bubbles from the clay. Be sure they are using the proper technique for doing this thoroughly, and assist them as necessary.

Lesson 2　*Coil Pot*　**307**

Photo Essay

LESSON 3

Photo Essay

- Have students select a theme for their photo essay and make a list of possible illustrations for it. For instance, a student might choose the theme of hunger, and possible illustrations would be a food kitchen, a beggar, a malnourished child. The student can keep this in mind when he or she goes to take the actual pictures.
- Arrange to show a sound-sight presentation, if possible. If not, bring in several samples of photo essays and ask the students to identify the theme of the essay. Have them describe how the essay succeeds or fails, and why.
- Bring in different kinds of music—from classical to blues to rock to country and western. Have the students listen to short segments of each kind of music, and help them select possible kinds of music to use for their presentations.
- Have each student take a preliminary picture with your supervision so that each student knows how to operate the camera effectively.

Dorothea Lange (dahr-uh-**thee**-uh **lang**) was a portrait photographer of the 1920s and 1930s who grew tired of making "pretty" pictures. Looking for a more meaningful outlet for her talents, she turned to photo essays. These are collections of photographs that together make a statement about the human condition. The photo essay in Figure S–5 is one from an essay Lange shot during the Great Depression of the 1930s. This was a time when many people were out of work. Hunger and homelessness were widespread. Study the photograph. In it, Lange offers more than just a portrait of a starving mother and her children. She captures the hopelessness and despair of a bleak time.

▶ Figure S–5 **Can you identify any of the elements of art that work to capture feeling or mood in this photograph?**

Dorothea Lange. *Migrant Mother.* Nipomo, California. 1936. Library of Congress, Washington, D.C.

Background Information

Photography became a very popular form of art during the early modern art movement. Different schools of art have used photography for different reasons. For instance, the Dadaists used the camera to express their mechanical view of art. In America, Alfred Stieglitz was the father of modern photography. Stieglitz perfected a form of documentary photography which still expressed his feelings and philosophies. From this "documentary" photography he developed a form of "pure" photography which is expressionistic in aim, not realistic. He also tried to create non-objective photography—without subject or personality.

Later in the modern period, art attempted to imitate the photograph, so that art had a "Kodachrome" appearance. These Hyper-Realists took their inspiration from photography, as opposed to Pop artists, who took their inspiration from commercial graphics. A form of Conceptual Art, Documentation, relies on photographs to capture the activity of the artist.

WHAT YOU WILL LEARN

You will create a photo essay dealing with a theme that focuses on some aspect of the human condition today. You will contrast color and value to emphasize a center of interest in your photos. You will share your work with your class as part of a sound-sight presentation.

WHAT YOU WILL NEED

- Instant camera and color slide film
- Slide projector and screen
- Tape recorder or phonograph

WHAT YOU WILL DO

1. Pick a theme for your photo essay. The theme should deal with some aspect of the human condition today. Some possibilities are pollution, problems of the aging, overcrowding, or Americans' fascination with speed.
2. Carefully read the directions for using your camera and film. Think about the angle from which you will shoot your subjects. Decide whether shooting your subjects from above or below eye level might add to your statement. Decide whether close-ups or long shots will best serve your needs.
3. Explore your neighborhood or town looking for subjects for photos that fit your theme. Be creative in your search for ideas. An elderly person seated alone on a park bench might be used to support the theme of loneliness. A person looking impatiently at his or her watch might be used to illustrate the American "rat race."

EXAMINING YOUR WORK

- **Describe**   Identify the theme you chose. Tell why you chose it. Explain how you decided what pictures to shoot to illustrate this theme.
- **Analyze**   Tell whether your pictures were in focus. Tell from what angles you shot your pictures. Explain how your decisions affected your work. Point out the center of interest in your photos. Tell how you used color and value to emphasize this center of interest.
- **Interpret**   State the theme of your essay. Tell whether viewers understood your theme. Give your photo essay a title.
- **Judge**   Tell whether you were satisfied with your presentation. Explain what, if anything, you would do to improve it on a second try.

4. Photograph your subjects. Be sure to hold the camera still while shooting. When possible, rest the camera on a ledge or other stationary object. Consider contrasts of color and value to make your subject the center of interest.
5. Have your slides developed. While they are being developed, locate musical recordings that go along with your theme.
6. Present your work to the class. Do your classmates understand the theme? Do they get your message?

- Discuss possible places that students might find subjects for their presentations. Ask: Where are there big factories? Where are the local homeless shelters? (Adult supervision may be required.)
- Suggest that the students take several preliminary pictures, from different angles, in different lighting and have them developed. The students can look at these pictures and determine what adjustments they might need to make before shooting the pictures for their presentations.
- Discuss the elements of art in relation to photography. Color, harmony, unity—all of these are important to photography. Ask the students to be sure their pictures contain these elements.
- When the students have completed the picture-taking, and have developed the pictures, have them decide how to arrange the presentation. Do they want to tell a story with the pictures? Do they want to contrast different pictures? Help them arrange the slides to have the most impact.
- Set aside a time in class for the presentations to be shown. Or arrange to have them shown at a parent's night or an open house.

OTHER STUDIO IDEAS

- Repeat the activity, this time using photos clipped from magazines. Mount the photos on a sheet of poster board. Plan your arrangement so that it effectively expresses your theme. Include the title of your essay in your design.

●● Repeat the activity, this time using color or black-and-white print film. Mount the developed prints on a sheet of poster board. Plan your arrangement to express the theme. Include the title of your essay in your design.

Lesson 3   *Photo Essay*   **309**

Background Information
Dorothea Lange left the security of a portrait studio to cover the world of the poor, downtrodden masses during the years of the Great Depression. Often donning overalls, Lange pictorially recorded the elemental parts of life that included scenes of migrating Okies escaping the dust bowl as well as farmers in other parts of the country going about their daily lives. Working for the Farm Security Administration photo project, she captured for all time the seamed, poverty-lined faces of sharecroppers in which the hardness of their lives was often reflected. In doing this project, she filled a portfolio with images that have never faded.

ADDITIONAL STUDIOS

False Face Mask

LESSON 4

False Face Mask

- Have students wear old clothes. The paste can be messy, and the acrylic paints can stain clothing. Assist the students in mixing the papier-mâché paste, so that it is not too thick or too runny.
- If students elect to use plaster and cloth or gauze, be sure to show them how it is used before allowing them to start work.
- Discuss various ways the students can convey the "spirit" of the mask. For instance, the eye and breathing holes can be shaped in certain ways to express certain characteristics. The paints can be used in certain color combinations to convey a certain feeling. (If the acrylic is drying too fast, have the students blend retarder into the paint.)
- Have students collect found objects to decorate their masks. Such objects as bird feathers, interesting leaves and even empty gum wrappers might be used to express the spirit's personality.

Among the finest examples of early Native American art are the false face masks created by the Iroquois (**ir**-uh-kwoy). Carved from living trees, these masks were thought to be alive with spiritual powers. So completely did the Iroquois believe in the life force of these masks that they fed them!

Study the mask in Figure S–6. In what ways is this object similar to the African face mask in Figure 9–8 (page **136**)? In what ways are the two different?

WHAT YOU WILL LEARN

You will make a false face mask using papier-mâché or strips of cloth or gauze dipped in plaster. Your mask will stand for a particular guardian spirit and show that spirit's character. You will paint your mask using either an analogous or a complementary color scheme. You will use feathers, straw, or shredded paper for hair to add texture to your mask and increase its visual interest. (See Figure S–7.)

WHAT YOU WILL NEED

- Sketchbook and pencil
- Lifesize model of a human skull or Styrofoam wig support
- Plastic wrap, mixing bowl, and water
- Commercially prepared papier-mâché paste
- Strips of newspaper
- *Optional:* Plaster, strips of cloth or gauze instead of papier-mâché
- Sandpaper, scissors, and white glue
- Acrylic paint and several brushes
- Feathers, straw, or shredded paper
- String or ribbon

▶ **Figure S–6   Can you tell what the decoration on this mask is made from?**

Iroquoian. *Husk Face Mask.* National Museum of American History, Smithsonian Institution, Washington, D.C.

Background Information

The ceremonial masks of African tribes are an expression of visual art. They are symbolic and representative and not representational or even abstract. The typical African mask is one in which there are no facial expressions and are decorated with hairstyles, ornaments, and sacrificial patterns. The masks were usually made of wood, and with some typical African characteristics. For instance, African artists tend to depict the head as larger than it actually is. Thus, masks tend to be large, top-heavy and out of proportion to the body. In addition, the African tendency is to have complete balance and symmetry.

Masks were used for mostly religious purposes. They were used to honor the dead, ask for a fertile growing season, cure sickness, or recognize a god. In some cultures, they represented membership in a certain society—for example, an adult male would be initiated into the group of adult males. At the time of the initiation, he would be given a mask to symbolize his belonging.

WHAT YOU WILL DO

1. Decide what guardian spirit your mask will stand for. Some possibilities are the spirit of good luck and the spirit of fair weather. Once you have chosen a spirit, make pencil sketches of how you believe your spirit should look. Your sketches should also show the character of the spirit — friendly, fierce, or frightening. Choose your best sketch.

2. Cover the skull model with plastic wrap. In the mixing bowl, combine commercially prepared papier-mâché paste and water. Soak strips of newspaper in the mixture, and apply these to the model's face. (For more on the use of papier-mâché, see Technique Tip **20**, *Handbook* page **283**.)

3. When the mask is thick enough to hold its shape, set it on a support to dry.

4. Remove the dried mask from the support. Use sandpaper to rid the mask of any rough spots. With the point of the scissors, carefully make eye and breathing holes. Cut a pinhole at eye level close to the edge on either side.

5. Using two or more hues of acrylic, paint your mask. Refer back to your pencil sketch. Use either an analogous or a complementary color scheme.

6. When the paint has dried, add hair in the form of feathers, straw, or shredded paper. Try to create a variety of textures. Attach the hair with white glue. Lace a piece of string or ribbon through the pinholes at the side. (Leave enough slack in the string so that the mask may be worn.)

7. Display your mask. Can classmates guess the guardian spirit living in your mask?

OTHER STUDIO IDEAS

- Using white glue, add feathers, beads, and other items to your mask in a decorative pattern. Use acrylic or tempera to paint shapes and lines that add to this decorative pattern. Tell whether this adds to or takes away from the mask's appeal.

EXAMINING YOUR WORK

- **Describe**   Identify the guardian spirit your mask stands for. Point out and describe the different textures you used. Tell what colors you used to paint your mask.
- **Analyze**   Explain what kind of color scheme you used. Show where texture variety adds visual interest to your mask.
- **Interpret**   Explain how your choice of color scheme helped identify the character of the guardian spirit it represents. Create a legend to go with your mask.
- **Judge**   Tell whether your work succeeds. Explain your answer.

▲ **Figure S–7   Student work. False face mask.**

•• Create another mask in which you use a color scheme that emphasizes the gentle or fierce character of the spirit. Colors and color combinations should be as expressive as possible. Determine if viewers can identify the character of your spirit.

- Using their language arts skills, the students can write a brief history or legend of the "spirit" of the mask and display the history/legend with the mask. This would be an opportunity for the students to work on their storytelling skills.
- Have the students compare their pencil sketches with the final mask. Does the mask succeed or fail? Is it better than the sketch? If not, why not? If so, how? How did the preliminary drawing help in planning the mask?
- Ask the students to compare the different masks. Can they tell what kind of spirit lives in the mask? Which masks best convey character? How do these masks convey the character of the spirit? How would the students change their masks if they could?

Lesson 4   *False Face Mask*   **311**

Space Colony

LESSON 5

Space Colony

- One of the rules of architecture is that "form follows function." Have the students consider the needs of the Space Colony community. Have them decide how to show such necessities as shipping and transportation, agriculture, defense, health care. What would a futuristic hospital look like? Have the students think about how their buildings will be used before they create them.
- Suggest that students read descriptions of other planets as we know them. For instance, there are interesting craters on the moon, and no gravity. Other planets are very close to the sun. Using this knowledge, they can come up with imaginative ideas about a planet that has just been discovered.
- Have students take a tour of the town. Tell them to look at the buildings and how they fit into the environment. Which buildings fit? Which do not? Which buildings seem comfortable? Do some buildings seem unwelcoming? Have them select their favorite buildings and describe why. Have each student explain how the buildings fit or do not fit into their surroundings. What would the students do differently if they were planning the town?

The technological advances of each age give artists new subject ideas. In the 1800s artists could, if they chose, base a work on the locomotive. In the early twentieth century the car became an option as the basis for a painting or drawing. More recently artists have found still other frontiers to explore. One such frontier is illustrated in the painting in Figure S–8. What do you suppose an artist of today might find as a next subject?

WHAT YOU WILL LEARN

You will design a space colony that will provide housing on another planet for humans of the future. The colony should be both practical and pleasant to live in. The forms of buildings and other structures should vary in size and shape. They should also harmonize with the natural forms of the planet. You will use shading techniques to give your forms depth.

WHAT YOU WILL NEED

- Pencil and sketch paper
- Sheet of black construction paper, 12 x 18 inches (30 x 46 cm)
- Oil pastels

▲ **Figure S–8   This art work appears at a national science museum. What kind of statement does this make about the role of art in our modern culture?**

Robert McCall. *Space Station #1*. Poster created for the MGM film "2001: A Space Odyssey." National Air and Space Museum, Washington, D.C.

Background Information
Science and technology are part of the modern world. If the lights go out or the furnace quits, we realize how dependent we are on science and technology. The importance of these things has increased dramatically in the past century, and art has reflected that importance. For many of the modern art movements and much of the art today, science and technology have had a great impact.

For the contemporary world of art, science and technology has suggested "science-fiction" as a basis for art. That is, many artists paint and draw their ideas of what life on other planets is like, or what our life would look like on other planets, and what life will be like in the next century.

Part of the fascination artists have with science and technology is the way these discoveries and inventions change us and challenge our humanity. The mechanization of the world has lead to increased alienation and isolation of the individual, and this has had an impact on the world of art.

WHAT YOU WILL DO

1. Make pencil sketches of rock formations and other natural land features you might find on a strange, newly discovered planet. Be as imaginative as you can. Choose your best sketch. Make a second set of sketches that show the main features of your colony. Include buildings of different types and sizes. The building forms should appear to grow out of the landscape on the planet and should not look like buildings on our own planet Earth. Again, choose your most imaginative sketch.

2. Turn the sheet of construction paper so it is lengthwise. Using a white oil pastel crayon, fill in the lower third of the sheet. This is to serve as a foundation for other colors in your work. Fill the upper two-thirds of the sheet with white dots. These are to appear as stars in a night sky. You might wish to show far-off moons and other planets as well. (For more on the use of oil pastels, see Technique Tip **3**, *Handbook* page **277**.

3. Switching to a black crayon, lightly transfer features from the two sketches you chose. Blend the two into a harmonious whole by making the buildings appear to grow out of the landscape. Fill in the building forms with hues of pastel that add to the overall harmony. Use different shading techniques to give your forms depth. (For information on shading techniques, see Technique Tip **6**, *Handbook* page **278**.)

EXAMINING YOUR WORK

- **Describe**   Describe the land features of the new planet. Describe the forms of the buildings and other structures in your colony. Tell what colors you used for your colony.
- **Analyze**   Identify the variety of building forms in your drawing. Tell whether the natural forms of the planet harmonize with the humanmade forms of your colony. Point to the shading techniques you used to give depth to the forms in your picture.
- **Interpret**   Identify the different purposes for which the buildings in your colony might be built. Tell whether the space colony would be a practical and comfortable place to live.
- **Judge**   Tell whether your work succeeds. Explain your answer.

4. Display your works beside those of classmates. Decide which show the most imagination. Which seem most believable?

OTHER STUDIO IDEAS

- Make a map of the area in which your space colony is located. Create a color-coded legend for your map showing height of objects. Create a scale of miles (kilometers).

- •• Create a three-dimensional relief of your space colony. Create buildings and other structures out of heavy-duty cardboard. Paint the relief using the same colors you did in your oil pastel version.

ADDITIONAL STUDIOS

- Arrange a visit to a local planetarium, if possible. Or have a local college or high school science teacher talk about astronomy. Have the students find out about "astrobiology."
- Remind students that even though the space colony is alien, they should remember to use the principles of art in their chalk drawing, including harmony.
- Have the students describe the colors they used in their drawings and how they can convey harmony and unity. Are they also used to convey the alien character of the space colony? What other principles of art could be used to convey the alien environment?

Lesson 5   *Space Colony*   **313**

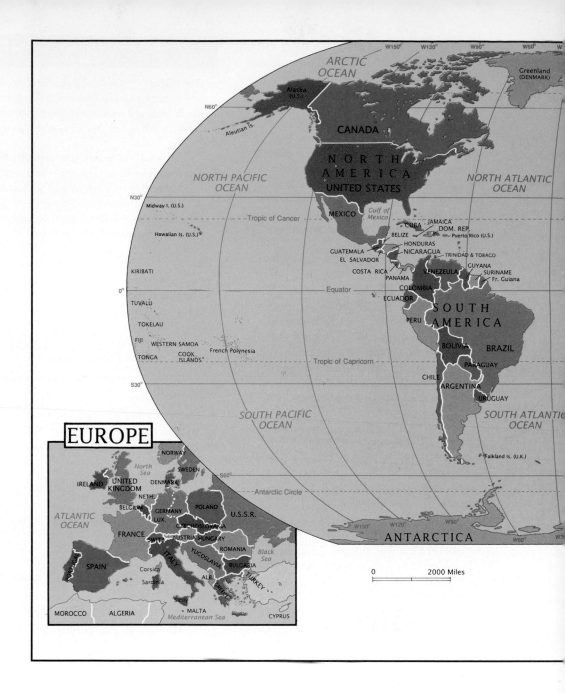

ARCTIC OCEAN

Greenland (DENMARK)

Alaska (U.S.)

N60°

CANADA

Aleutian Is.

NORTH PACIFIC OCEAN

N O R T H A M E R I C A

NORTH ATLANTIC OCEAN

N30°

UNITED STATES

Midway I. (U.S.)

MEXICO

Gulf of Mexico

Tropic of Cancer

CUBA JAMAICA
DOM. REP.
BELIZE Puerto Rico (U.S.)
HONDURAS
GUATEMALA NICARAGUA
EL SALVADOR TRINIDAD & TOBAGO
COSTA RICA GUYANA
PANAMA VENEZUELA SURINAME
COLOMBIA Fr. Guiana

Hawaiian Is. (U.S.)

KIRIBATI

0°

Equator

ECUADOR

TUVALU

PERU

S O U T H A M E R I C A

TOKELAU

FIJI

WESTERN SAMOA

French Polynesia

BOLIVIA

BRAZIL

TONGA

COOK ISLANDS

Tropic of Capricorn

PARAGUAY

CHILE

S30°

ARGENTINA

URUGUAY

SOUTH PACIFIC OCEAN

SOUTH ATLANTIC OCEAN

Falkland Is. (U.K.)

S60°

Antarctic Circle

EUROPE

NORWAY

North Sea

SWEDEN

IRELAND UNITED KINGDOM DENMARK

NETH.

ATLANTIC OCEAN

BELGIUM

GERMANY POLAND

LUX.

U.S.S.R.

CZECHOSLOVAKIA

FRANCE SWITZ. AUSTRIA HUNGARY

ROMANIA

Black Sea

ITALY YUGOSLAVIA

BULGARIA

PORTUGAL

SPAIN

Corsica

ALB. TURKEY

GREECE

Sardinia

Sicily

MALTA

MOROCCO ALGERIA Mediterranean Sea CYPRUS

ANTARCTICA

W150° W120° W90° W60°

0   2000 Miles

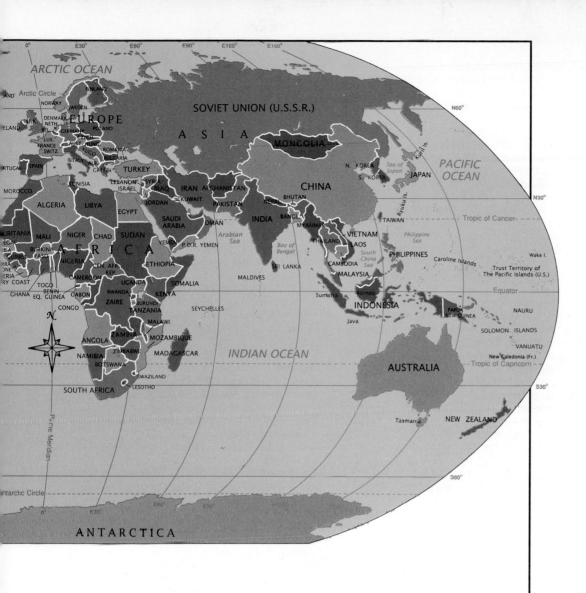

THE CONTEMPORARY WORLD

Artists and Their Works

Glossary

Abstract Expressionism An art style in which paint was dribbled, spilled, or splashed onto huge canvases to express a feeling. (Ch. 17-3)

Abstract work A work in which the artist uses a recognizable subject but portrays it in an unrealistic manner. (Ch. 9-1)

Adobe (uh-**doh**-bee) Sun-dried clay. (Ch. 6-3)

Aesthetic view (ess-**thet**-ik) An idea, or school of thought, on what is important in a work of art. (Ch. 3-1)

Amphora (**am**-fuh-ruh) A twin-handled vase. (Ch. 7-1)

Aqueduct (**ak**-wuh-duhkt) A network of channels meant to carry water to a town or city. (Ch. 7-3)

Arabesques (ar-uh-**besks**) Swirling geometric patterns of plant life used as decoration. (Ch. 8-3)

Arbitrary colors (**Ahr**-buh-trehr-ee) Colors chosen to communicate different feelings. (Ch. 15-1)

Architecture The planning and creating of buildings. (Ch. 2-3)

Art criticism Studying, understanding, and judging works of art. (Ch. 3-1)

Art history The study of art from past to present. (Ch. 3-3)

Artifacts Simple handmade tools or objects. (Ch. 6-1)

Art movement A trend formed when a group of artists band together to create works of a single style. (Ch. 14-3)

Ashcan School The popular name given to the group of artists who made realistic paintings of working-class America. (Ch. 16-3)

Balance A principle of art concerned with arranging the elements so that no one part of a work overpowers, or seems heavier than, any other part. (Ch. 1-3)

Baroque (buh-**rohk**) An art style emphasizing movement, contrast, and variety. (Ch. 12-1)

Batik (buh-**teek**) A method of designing on fabric using wax and dyes. (Ch. 8-2)

Binder A liquid that holds together the grains of pigment in paint. (Ch. 2-1)

Buttress A brace or support placed on the outside of a building. (Ch. 10-3)

Calligraphy (kuh-**ligg**-ruh-fee) A method of beautiful handwriting sometimes using a brush. (Ch. 8-3)

Castles Fortlike dwellings with high walls and towers. (Ch. 10-1)

Cathedral A large, complex church created as a seat of office for a bishop. (Ch. 10-3)

Coiled pot A pot formed by coiling long ropes of clay in a spiral. (Ch. 13-1)

Collage (kuh-**lahzh**) An art work made up of bits and pieces of two-dimensional materials pasted to a surface. (Ch. 8-4)

Color An element of art that refers to what the eyes see when light is reflected off an object. (Ch. 1-1)

Composition The way the art principles are used to organize the art elements of color, line, shape, form, space, and texture. (Ch. 3-1)

Concrete A finely ground mixture of small stones and powdered minerals used in building. (Ch. 7-3)

Content The idea, feeling, mood, or message expressed by an art work. (Ch. 3-1)

Contour drawing (**kahn**-toor) Drawing an object as though your drawing tool is touching the edges of the form. (Ch. 11-2)

Cradle board A harness worn on the shoulders and used to carry a small child. (Ch. 13-1)

Crafts The different areas of applied art in which craftspeople work. (Ch. 2-3)

Cubism An art style in which objects are shown from several different angles at once. (Ch. 10-1)

Culture The ideas, beliefs, and living customs of a people. (Ch. 4-1)

Dada (**dahd**-ah) An art movement founded on the belief that Western culture had lost its meaning. (Ch. 17-1)

Edition A series of identical prints made from a single plate. (Ch. 2-1)

Effigy (**eff**-uh-jee) An image that stands for ideas or beliefs. (Ch. 6-1)

The Eight A group of New York artists who created art work that reflected the spirit of the times in which they lived, the early 1900s. (Ch. 16-3)

Emphasis A principle of art concerned with making an element or object in a work stand out. (Ch. 1-3)

Etching An intaglio print made by scratching an image onto a specially treated copper plate. (Ch. 12-3)

Expressionism (ek-**spresh**-uh-niz-uhm) A style that emphasized the expression of innermost feelings. (Ch. 16-1)

Facade (fuh-**sahd**) The outside front of a building. (Ch. 12-1)

Face mask A mask worn to hide the identity of the wearer. (Ch. 9-3)

Fauvism (**fohv**-iz-uhm) An art movement in which artists use wild, intense color combinations in their paintings. (Ch. 16-1)

Form An element of art that refers to an object with three dimensions. (Ch. 1-1)

Freestanding sculpture Sculpture surrounded on all sides by space. (Ch. 2-3)

Fresco (**fres**-koh) A painting created when pigment is applied to a section of wall spread with fresh plaster. (Ch. 10-3)

Frieze (freez) A decorative band running across the upper part of a wall. (Ch. 7-1)

Funerary urns (**fyoo**-nuh-rehr-ee)   Decorative vases or vessels found at burial sites. (Ch. 6-2)

Gargoyle   A projecting ornament on a building carved in the shape of a fantastic animal or grotesque creature. (Ch. 10-4)

Genre pieces (**zhahn**-ruh)   Art works that focus on a subject or scene from everyday life. (Ch. 6-1)

Glaze   Glass-like finish on pottery. (Ch. 5-1)

Hard-Edge painting   An art style that emphasized clear, crisp-edged shapes. (Ch. 17-3)

Harmony   A principle of art concerned with blending elements to create a more calm, restful appearance. (Ch. 1-3)

Headpieces   Masks carved of wood and worn on the head like a cap. (Ch. 9-3)

Hieroglyphic (hy-ruh-**glif**-ik)   An early form of picture writing. (Ch. 4-3)

Illuminations   Hand-painted book illustrations. (Ch. 10-1)

Impressionism   An art style that attempted to capture the rapidly changing effects of light on objects. (Ch. 14-2)

Intaglio (in-**tal**-yoh)   A printmaking method in which the image to be printed is cut or scratched into a surface. (Ch. 9-2)

Kachina doll   A hand-carved statuette used to teach children about Pueblo rituals. (Ch. 13-1)

Kinetic art (kuh-**net**-ik)   An art style in which parts of works are set into motion by a form of energy. (Ch. 17-5)

Landscape   A drawing or painting focusing on mountains, trees, or other natural scenery. (Ch. 14-1)

Line   An element of art that refers to the path of a moving point through space. (Ch. 1-1)

Linear perspective (puhr-**spek**-tiv)   The use of slanted lines to make objects appear to extend back into space. (Ch. 11-1)

Loom   A frame holding a set of crisscrossing threads. (Ch. 13-2)

Madonna   A work showing the Virgin Mary with the Christ Child. (Ch. 11-1)

Media   The plural of *medium*. (Ch. 2-1)

Medium of art   A material used to create a work of art. (Ch. 2-1)

Megaliths   Large stone monuments, such as Stonehenge in England. (Ch. 4-1)

Mihrab (**meer**-ahb)   A highly decorated nook found in a mosque. (Ch. 8-3)

Minaret (min-uh-**ret**)   A slender tower from which Muslims are called to prayer. (Ch. 8-3)

Mixed media   The use of more than one medium in a work of art. (Ch. 3-1)

Mobile (**moh**-beel)   A sculpture made of carefully balanced shapes hung on wires. (Ch. 17-3)

Monolith (**mahn**-uh-lith)   A structure created from a single stone slab. (Ch. 6-3)

Mosque   A Muslim house of worship. (Ch. 8-3)

Motif (moh-**teef**)   Part of a design that is repeated over and over in a pattern or visual rhythm. (Ch. 6-2)

Movement   A principle of art used to create the look and feeling of action and to guide a viewer's eye throughout the work. (Ch. 1-3)

Multi-media art   A work that makes use of tools and techniques from two or more areas of art. (Ch. 17-5)

Muralist   An artist who paints large art works directly onto walls or ceilings. (Ch. 16-3)

Neoclassic (nee-oh-**klas**-ik)   An art style that borrowed from the early classical period of ancient Greece and Rome. (Ch. 14-1)

New Realism   An art movement that rediscovered the importance of realistic detail. (Ch. 17-3)

Non-objective   Having no recognizable subject matter. (Ch. 2-1)

Non-objective art (nahn-uhb-**jek**-tiv)   Art works in which no objects or subjects can be readily identified. (Ch. 1-2), (Ch. 16-1)

Oil paint   A mixture of pigment, linseed oil, and turpentine. (Ch. 11-3)

Op art   An art style that made use of precise lines and shapes to create optical illusion. (Ch. 17-4)

Optical colors   Colors viewers actually see. (Ch. 15-1)

Pagoda (puh-**gohd**-uh)   A tower several stories high with roofs curving slightly upward at the edges. (Ch. 5-3)

Papier-mâché (pap-yah-muh-**shay**)   A sculpting technique using newspaper and liquid paste. (Ch. 9-4)

Perceive   Look deeply at a subject. (Ch. 5-1)

Perceiving   Looking at and thinking deeply about what you see.

Petroglyphs (**peh**-truh-glifs)   Rock carvings and paintings. (Ch. 13-1)

Pietà (pee-ay-**tah**)   A work showing Mary mourning over the body of Christ. (Ch. 11-1)

Pigment   A finely ground powder that gives every paint its colors. (Ch. 2-1)

Pointed arch   A curved arrangement of stones reaching up to a central point. (Ch. 10-3)

Pointillism (**poynt**-uh-liz-uhm)   A technique in which small, carefully placed dots of color are used to create forms. (Ch. 15-2)

Polychrome (**pahl**-ee-krohm)   Having many colors. (Ch. 13-3)

Porcelain (**pore**-suh-luhn)   A fine-grained, high-quality form of pottery. (Ch. 5-1)

Portrait   A painting of a person. (Ch. 12-1)

Post and lintel system (**lint**-uhl)   An approach to building in which a crossbeam is placed above two uprights. (Ch. 4-3)

Post-Impressionism   An art movement that appeared after the Impressionists. (Ch. 15-1)

Printing plate A surface onto or into which the image is placed. (Ch. 2-1)

Printmaking A technique in which an inked image from a prepared surface is transferred onto another surface. (Ch. 2-1)

Proportion A principle of art concerned with the relationship of one part to another and to the whole. (Ch. 1-3)

Pueblos Stacked, many-family dwellings made of adobe. (Ch. 13-1)

Realism A style of art in which everyday scenes and events are painted as they actually look. (Ch. 15-3)

Regionalism (**reej**-uhn-uhl-iz-uhm) An art style that records local scenes and events from an artist's own region, or area, of the country. (Ch. 16-3)

Relief sculpture Sculpture partly enclosed by space. (Ch. 2-3)

Renaissance (ren-uh-**sahns**) A period of great awakening. (Ch. 11-1)

Rhythm A principle of art concerned with repeating an element to make a work seem active or to suggest vibration. (Ch. 1-3)

Rococo (ruh-**koh**-koh) An art style stressing free, graceful movement; a playful use of line; and bright colors. (Ch. 12-3)

Romanticism (roh-**mant**-uh-siz-uhm) A style of art that found its subjects in the world of the dramatic and exotic. (Ch. 14-1)

Round arch A curved arrangement of stones over an open space. (Ch. 7-3)

Salon (suh-**lahn**) An annual exhibition of art. (Ch. 14-3)

Sand painting The pouring of different colors of powdered rock on a flat section of earth to create an image or design. (Ch. 13-3)

Screen A partition used as a wall to divide a room. (Ch. 5-3)

Scroll A long roll of illustrated parchment or silk. (Ch. 5-1)

Shape An element of art that refers to an area clearly set off by one or more of the other elements of art. (Ch. 1-1)

Shoulder masks Large, carved masks made to rest on the shoulders of the wearer. (Ch. 9-3)

Social protest painting An art style that attacked the ills of big-city life. (Ch. 17-3)

Solvent A material used to thin a paint's binder. (Ch. 2-1)

Space An element of art that refers to the distance between, around, above, below, and within things. (Ch. 1-1)

Stained glass Colored glass pieces held in place with lead strips. (Ch. 10-3)

Stele (**stee**-lee) A carved upright stone slab used as a monument. (Ch. 4-3)

Stupas (**stoop**-uhs) Beehive-shaped domed places of worship. (Ch. 8-1)

Style An artist's personal way of using the elements and principles of art and expressing feelings and ideas in art. (Ch. 3-3)

Stylized Simplified or exaggerated to fit the rules of a specific type of design. (Ch. 6-3)

Subject The image viewers can easily identify in an art work. (Ch. 3-1)

Surrealism (suh-**ree**-uh-liz-uhm) An art movement that probed the unconscious world of dreams. (Ch. 17-1)

Symbolism The use of an image to stand for a quality or an idea. (Ch. 11-3)

Tempera (**tem**-puh-ruh) A painting medium in which pigment mixed with egg yolk and water is applied with tiny brush strokes. (Ch. 10-1)

Tepee (**tee**-pee) A portable house. (Ch. 13-1)

Texture An element of art that refers to the way a thing feels, or looks as though it might feel, if touched. (Ch. 1-1)

Totem pole An upright log carving picturing stories of different families or clans. (Ch. 13-1)

Triumphal arch (try-**uhm**-fuhl) A monument built to celebrate great army victories. (Ch. 7-3)

Ukiyo-e (oo-**kee**-yoh-ay) An art style meaning "pictures of the floating world." (Ch. 5-3)

Unity The arrangement of elements and principles with media to create a feeling of completeness or wholeness. (Ch. 1-3)

Urban planning Arranging the construction and services of a city to best meet its people's needs. (Ch. 4-4)

Variety A principle of art concerned with combining one or more elements to create interest by adding slight changes. (Ch. 1-3)

Warp Threads running vertically and attached to the loom's frame. (Ch. 13-2)

Weaving A craft in which fiber strands are interlocked to make cloth or objects. (Ch. 13-1)

Weft Threads passed horizontally over and under the warp. (Ch. 13-2)

Woodblock printing Making prints by carving images in blocks of wood. (Ch. 5-3)

Yamato-e (yah-**mah**-toh-ay) An art style meaning "pictures in the Japanese manner." (Ch. 5-3)

Ziggurat (**zig**-uh-raht) A stepped mountain made of brick-covered earth. (Ch. 4-4)

Index

Acknowledgements: The art work executed and submitted by the following students was exemplary. Because of book design constraints, all of the student work could not be included. The authors feel, however, that each student who contributed should be recognized.

Jennifer Alexander, Taylor Road Middle School; Dina Anderson, Colonial Junior High; Amy Antonini, Taylor Road Middle School; Andrea Armstrong, Highlands Junior High School; Chris Bayliss, Standon College Preparatory School; Jennifer Beaver, Taylor Road Middle School; Daniel Bense, Taylor Road Middle School; Angelia Black, Taylor Road Middle School; Ryan Bray, Marvin Pittman Laboratory School; Erin Brock, Stanton College Preparatory School; Natalie Brown, North Augusta High School; Bertina Brunson, North Augusta High School; Shawn Burke, Telfare County High School; Christine Camplone, Taylor Road Middle School; Robbee Coates, Taylor Road Middle School; Pat Cone, Marvin Pittman Laboratory School; Krisha Craven, Marvin Pittman Laboratory School; Dee Dee Crawford, Stanton College Preparatory; Kris DeMasse, Taylor Road Middle School; Elizabeth Dewey, Marvin Pittman Laboratory School; Chris Drago, Taylor Road Middle School; Maria Carolina Dugue, Savannah County Day School; Liza Dupont, North Augusta High School; Jason Easley, Taylor Road Middle School; Eric Elliot, Marvin Pittman Laboratory School; Shari Erwin, Taylor Road Middle School; Steve Eubanks, North Augusta High School; Rachel Ferrara, Savannah County Day School; Danny Fredt, Taylor Road Middle School; Robert Freemantle, Taylor Road Middle School; Heather Gatlin, Telfare County High School; Rachel Goossen, Taylor Road Middle School; Brandy Hartman, Hillside School; Sierra Hartman, Mountain View School; Jason Hebert, Tecumseh Middle School; Jennifer Herron, Stanton College Preparatory School; Wendy Hester, Telfare County High School; Matt Hickman, Marvin Pittman Laboratory School; Charlotte Hollingsworth, Fletcher Junior High School; Chris Holsapple, Fletcher Junior High School; Chad Hope, Taylor Road Middle School; Jennifer Howard, Taylor Road Middle School; Ashley Hoynowski, Taylor Road Middle School; Raymond Hubbard, Bradwell Institute High School; Kyle Ivey, Marvin Pittman Laboratory School; Kim Jones, Marvin Pittman Laboratory School; Rick Jones, Taylor Road Middle School; Ryan Kight, North Augusta High School; Cornelius Lewis, Marvin Pittman Laboratory School; Cindy Sang-Ching Li, Stanton College Preparatory School; Myron Linder, Marvin Pittman Laboratory School; Joshua A. Lipps, Ridgeway Junior/Senior High School; Alice Long, Tecumseh Middle School; Mahrien Louis, Colonial Junior High School; Todd Lowe, North Augusta High School; Tara Martin, Telfare County High School; Jimmy McCrory, Taylor Road Middle School; Mark McGlen, Taylor Road Middle School; Jenifer Meeks, Ridgeway Junior/Senior High School; Kelvin Mercer, Marvin Pittman Laboratory School; Mazi Merritt, Marvin Pittman Laboratory School; Kouthy Mom, Colonial Junior High; Brian Monaco, Taylor Road Middle School; Paola Morrongiello, Stanton College Preparatory School; Douglass Myers III, Stanton College Preparatory School; Artis Nails, Highlands Junior High School; Danielle Nelson, Highlands Junior High School; Jason Nelson, Fletcher Junior High School; Wichelle Norton, Marvin Pittman Laboratory School; Dana Odom, Marvin Pittman Laboratory School; Marina Patrick, Taylor Road Middle School; Melanie Pearson, Mabry Middle School; Shanti Persad, Savannah County Day School; Eloy Powell, North Augusta High School; David Reed, John Sevier Middle School; J. R. Rees, Tecumseh Middle School; Sindye Reich, Taylor Road Middle School; Sharon Reinertsen, Stanton College Preparatory School; Sharon Muse Renfrow, Savannah County Day School; Matthew Richmond, Douglas Anderson School of the Arts; Rebecca Ritter, Mabry Middle School; Loretta Rosenfeld, Taylor Road Middle School; Kristen Rudi, Taylor Road Middle School; Shani Russeau, Stanton College Preparatory; P. J. Samara, Taylor Road Middle School; Katie Schnellman, Savannah County Day School; Fred Shackelford, Ridgeway Junior/Senior High School; Garrett Shook, Stanton College Preparatory School; Jason Slider, Taylor Road Middle School; Alexia Strauch, North Augusta High School; Kelli Sumerau, North Augusta High School; Tiffany-Claire Teague, Mabry Middle School; Anna Thomas, Savannah County Day School; Marilyn Touchstone, Colonial Junior High; James Vaughan, Taylor Road Middle School; Amy Wallace, Marvin Pittman Laboratory School; Matthew Werner, Tecumseh Middle School; Deborah Wilcox, Telfare County High School; Latoya Wiley, Marvin Pittman Laboratory School; Andre Wilkey, Marvin Pittman Laboratory School; Matt Williams, Telfare County High School; Donna Wilson, Telfare County High School; Heather Wilson, North Augusta High School; Coretta Wintz, Bradwell Institute High School; Monica Woodruff, Taylor Road Middle School; Chad Yonell, North Augusta High School.